THE UNIVERSITY OF WINCHESTER

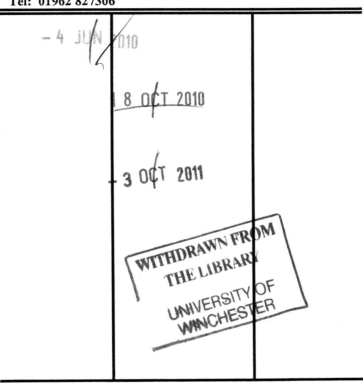

Georgi Plekhanov

Selected Philosophical Works

IN FIVE VOLUMES

Volume III

University Press of the Pacific
Honolulu, Hawaii

Selected Philosophical Works:
Volume Three

by
Georgi Plekhanov

ISBN: 1-4102-1386-2

Reprinted from the 1960 edition

University Press of the Pacific
Honolulu, Hawaii
http://www.universitypressofthepacific.com

CONTENTS

6 CONTENTS

G. V. PLEKHANOV'S CRITICISM OF IDEALISM AND DEFENCE OF MARXIST PHILOSOPHICAL IDEAS IN HIS WRITINGS OF 1904-13

Volume III of G. V. Plekhanov's *Selected Philosophical Works* contains material written by him mainly between 1904 and 1913. Most of the articles published in this volume are directed against idealism and especially Machism and god-building, against what Plekhanov called "the theoretical bourgeois reaction". Plekhanov criticises and exposes the untenability and reactionary essence of idealist theories with great polemical skill. This volume contains: *Fundamental Problems of Marxism* (1908), in which Plekhanov expounds the philosophical principles of Marxism—dialectical and historical materialism; *Materialismus Militans* (1908-10), a criticism of Machian philosophy and a defence of Marxist materialism; *On the So-Called Religious Seekings in Russia* (1909), directed against the religious world-outlook of god-builders and god-seekers; the articles "Cowardly Idealism", "Henri Bergson", "On H. Rickert's Book", which criticise fashionable bourgeois-idealist trends in philosophy and sociology; a number of works on the history of West European philosophy, socialist teachings, the history of Marxist philosophy, and several other works.

These were published by Plekhanov during the Menshevik period of his activities, which began at the end of 1903. At the beginning of the twentieth century, when the centre of the world revolutionary movement shifted to Russia and the first revolution under the conditions of imperialism took place there in 1905, Plekhanov proved unequal to the role of ideologist of the revolution. He disagreed with Lenin on fundamental issues of revolutionary theory and tactics. Plekhanov consigned the Marxist idea of the hegemony of the proletariat in the revolution to oblivion; he did not understand the significance of the alliance of the working class and the peasantry, incorrectly assessed the role of the Russian bourgeoisie and failed to reveal its counter-revolutionary essence; he came out against the preparation and execution of the 1905 armed uprising, and declared after the December 1905 armed uprising in Moscow that the people should not have taken to arms. True, during the years of reaction Plekhanov fought the enemies of the revolution, the liquidators of the workers' party. It was during this period that Lenin and the Bolsheviks considered it possible to form and, in fact, did form, a bloc on principle with the group of "pro-Party Mensheviks" headed by Plekhanov. However, Plekhanov changed his position and, in 1914, went over entirely to opportunism and social-chauvinism, opposing the socialist revolution in Russia. Plekhanov's political dissidence and his transformation from a revolutionary and ideologist of the socialist revolution into a Menshevik and opponent of revolutionary Marxism may be explained primarily by his misunderstanding of the nature and peculiarities of the new historical epoch—the epoch of imperialism and proletarian revolutions. In assessing new developments in the revolutionary struggle under the conditions of imperialism when the socialist revolution was on the order of the day, Plekhanov often drew analogies with the old bourgeois revolutions. He was unable to analyse creatively theoretical and tactical questions of the proletarian revolution in keeping with the new conditions of the imperialist stage of capitalism, when the proletariat and its Party, confronted by monopoly capitalism, required new forms and methods of struggle, great revolutionary organisation and creative initiative on the part of the masses, and a strengthening of the organising and leading role of the Party.

However, while sharing many of the defects and narrow political views held by the leaders of the Second International, Plekhanov at the same time differed from them in his critical attitude to the philosophical principles of bourgeois ideology. He waged a relentless war against all kind of bourgeois-idealist trends. Following the Russian revolution of 1905, when the counter-revolution was attacking on all fronts, including ideology, Plekhanov fought resolutely against the various manifestations of bourgeois ideology in philosophy, sociology, art, literature, and in other spheres of the cultural life of society. As Lenin said, Plekhanov combined in himself radicalism in theory and opportunism in practice. As sometimes happens, a change of his political views did not bring about an immediate, automatic, fundamental change of his philosophical world-outlook. Plekhanov, in going over to opportunism in the tactical field and having become a Menshevik, renounced revolutionary theory on such issues of scientific socialism as the dictatorship of the proletariat, the nature of the driving forces of the socialist revolution, the alliance of the working class and the peasantry, etc. But the political opportunism of Plekhanov the Menshevik could not but have an effect on his philosophical standpoint and led him to make a number of deviations from Marxist philosophy. Even then, however, Plekhanov remained a distinguished propagandist of Marxist philosophy, a fighter for the materialist world-outlook, and even during this period he continued, although not always consistently, to defend the principles of Marxist philosophy and made a profound analysis of the basic issues of historical materialism.

During the period 1904-13, he came out against the numerous enemies of dialectical and historical materialism, against the various trends of idealism, in order to protect the workers' Social-Democratic movement from the reactionary influence of the Machians, the god-builders, the god-seekers, and other representatives of idealism.

Lenin valued Plekhanov's struggle against revisionism and bourgeois-idealist philosophy highly, and attached great importance to his philosophical works in defence of dialectical and historical materialism.

In the article "Marxism and Revisionism" (1908), Lenin wrote: "...the only Marxist in the international Social-Democratic movement to criticise the incredible platitudes of the revisionists from the standpoint of consistent dialectical materialism was Plekhanov. This must be stressed all the more emphatically since profoundly mistaken attempts are being made at the present time to smuggle in old and reactionary philosophical rubbish disguised as a criticism of Plekhanov's tactical opportunism." * It was not by chance that Lenin on a number of occasions recommended the study of Plekhanov's philosophical works.

Despite his opportunism in tactics, Plekhanov contributed much to the criticism of Machism, a variation of the idealist world-outlook, and made particularly fierce attacks on the Russian leaders of Machism—Bogdanov, Lunacharsky, and others. In his third letter to Bogdanov in *Materialismus Militans*, Plekhanov wrote: "Those abroad who hold the same views as ourselves are very much mistaken in thinking, like my friend Kautsky, that there is no need to cross swords over that 'philosophy' which is disseminated in Russia by you and similar theoretical revisionists. Kautsky does not know the relationships existing in Russia. He disregards the fact that the theoretical bourgeois reaction which is now causing real havoc in the ranks of our advanced intellectuals is being accomplished in our country under the banner of philosophical idealism, and that, consequently, we are threatened with exceptional harm from such philosophical doctrines, which, while being idealist to the core, pose as the last word in natural science, a science foreign to every metaphysical premise. The struggle against such doctrines is not only not superfluous, it is obligatory, just as obligatory as it is to protest against

* V. I. Lenin, *Collected Works*, Vol. 15, pp. 33-34.

the *reactionary* 'revaluation of values' which the prolonged efforts
of Russian *advanced* thought have produced."* However, Plekhanov's fight against Machism was somewhat influenced by Menshevik factional interests. As a Menshevik, Plekhanov tried to
link the Bolsheviks with Machism. Lenin was fully justified in
writing: "Plekhanov in his criticism of Machism was less concerned with refuting Mach than with dealing a factional blow at
Bolshevism."** But it would be a mistake to think—as Lenin
often repeated—that Plekhanov, while being a Menshevik, did
not wage war on Machism and god-building, in defence of Marxist
philosophy.

It is interesting to note that Plekhanov, in a letter to F. I. Dan,
on November 26, 1908, criticising the Machism of the Mensheviks Valentinov, Yushkevich, and others, wrote: "I did not at
any time presume that ... we could go arm in arm in the legal
press with Valentinov, Yushkevich, and other semi-Marxist scoun-
drels (don't blame me for not expressing myself so sharply about
them earlier—this has always been my opinion of them).... Write
where you like, but make sure *in advance that you give a wide berth
to those who are bringing elements of heresy into Marxism.* It is now
time to cut adrift from the *semi-Marxists* Valentinov, Potresov,
etc.... I do not think we should be more severe with Bogdanov
than with Yushkevich on the grounds that the first is a Bolshevik
and the second a Menshevik.... *To me, heterodoxy from the Bolshevik camp is no whit worse than heterodoxy from the Menshevik
camp....* I shun both."

Plekhanov's struggle against Machism, god-building, and other
varieties of idealism was significant in the history of Marxist
philosophy, and the allegation that, in combating Machism, Plekhanov simply wrote a few insignificant articles, is wrong. Plekhanov did not shun this struggle, but wrote a number of valuable
works against Machian philosophy, in which he made a thorough
criticism of the idealist views of the Russian Machians and their
foreign mentors—Mach and Avenarius.

Subsequently, in May 1914, Lenin wrote an article entitled:
"Plekhanov, Who Knows Not What He Wants",in which he said:
"Among intellectualist *anti-Marxist* circles, among the flotsam
of bourgeois democracy—this is where poor Plekhanov has accidentally landed. This is where you will find chaos, disintegration
and tiny factions, which are opposing the unity achieved in the
course of two years by thousands of workers' groups of the Pravdist
trend.

---

* See pp. 282-83 of this volume.
** V. I. Lenin, "Empirio-Criticism and Historical Materialism", *Collected
Works*, Moscow, Vol. 14, p. 355, footnote.

"We are sorry for Plekhanov. Considering the struggle he waged against the opportunists, Narodniks, Machists and liquidators, he deserves a better fate."*

Plekhanov came somewhat late to the fight against Machism, but his action was nevertheless of the greatest importance. At that time, Bogdanov, Lunacharsky, Yushkevich, Bazarov, and other Russian Machians were trying to conceal the open idealism of their views with all kinds of terminological devices and "new" words, such as "elements of the world", etc. At the same time, they were hypocritically declaring themselves Marxists, who were "deepening" and "supplementing" the philosophy of Marxism with new principles. Actually, Machian idealist philosophy was the direct antithesis of Marxist philosophy. Plekhanov wittily ridiculed Bogdanov and his Machian philosophy which he was presenting as Marxist philosophy. "While not a Marxist yourself," he wrote in his first letter to Bogdanov in *Materialismus Militans*, "you would like nothing better than that we Marxists should accept you as our *comrade*. You remind me of the mother in one of Gleb Uspensky's stories. She wrote to her son, saying that since he lived a long way off and was in no hurry to see her, she would complain to the police and demand that the authorities send her son 'under escort' for her to 'embrace' him. Uspensky's philistine, to whom this maternal threat was addressed, burst into tears whenever he remembered it. We Russian Marxists will not weep for such reasons. But this will not stop us from telling you quite bluntly that we wish to take full advantage of our right to dissociate ourselves and that neither you nor any one else ⟨no matter who it may be⟩ will succeed in 'embracing' us 'under escort'."** In the same letter to Bogdanov, Plekhanov wrote: "...*You and I represent two directly opposed world-outlooks.* And as the question for me is the defence of my outlook, you are, in relation to me, not a comrade, but the most resolute and irreconcilable opponent."***

The Russian idealists—the Machians, following in the footsteps of their mentors Mach and Avenarius, considered that material bodies do not exist in the real world, objectively, independently of human consciousness, but only in human sensations and consciousness. Bogdanov, as Plekhanov pointed out, reiterated Mach's proposition that it is not bodies that cause sensations, but complexes of sensations that form bodies. This old, hackneyed thesis had been formulated long since by Bishop Berkeley. Truly scientific, materialist philosophy, said Plekhanov, holds to other principles. "We call material objects (bodies) those objects that

---

* V. I. Lenin, *Collected Works*, Vol. 20, p. 312.
** See p. 194 of this volume.
*** See p. 189 of this volume.

exist independently of our consciousness and, acting on our senses, arouse in us certain *sensations* which, in turn, underlie our notions of the external world, that is, of those same material objects as well as of their relationships."*

The Machian interpretation of this question, i.e., of the comprehension of material phenomena as a complex of sensations, is the idealist standpoint and contradicts the basic conclusions of natural science. Bogdanov only "supplemented" Mach a little, and said of objective phenomena that these exist not in the individual human consciousness, but in the collective consciousness of people, whose opinions and ideas are socially-coordinated, and this is what underlies their experience. In Bogdanov's opinion, the objectivity of the physical world is its universal significance, expressed by people's identical opinions and ideas, by coordination among people. Proceeding from this, Bogdanov saw truth as the socially-organised and socially-coordinated ideological experience of men. None of this changes the essence of Bogdanov's idealist views, because such a standpoint leaves untouched the main tenet of idealism, that material bodies and phenomena are sensations and not objective reality existing independently of the consciousness of people, of their experience. Plekhanov used the data and conclusions of natural science in subjecting this proposition of Bogdanov's to annihilating criticism. "...We are aware," he wrote, "that at one time there were no people on our planet. And if there were no *people*, neither was there their *experience*. Yet the earth was there. And this means that it (also a thing-in-itself!) existed *outside* human experience.... The object does not cease to exist even when there is as yet no subject, or when its existence has already ceased. And anybody to whom the conclusions of modern natural science are not an empty phrase must necessarily agree with this."**

Plekhanov also sharply criticised the inconsistency of a number of idealists of the positivist trend, such as J. Petzoldt, who, assuming the existence of a world of things-in-themselves, independent of people, at the same time said that the world existed only for us. Nevertheless, J. Petzoldt finally came to the conclusion that the existence of an object independently of our minds is only its existence in the minds of other people. "Therefore," Plekhanov wrote, "Petzoldt himself must be placed among the idealists. But his idealism does not acknowledge its own existence and is afraid of its own essence. This is unconscious and cowardly idealism."*** We have many such idealists among the positivists of today.

* See p. 214 of this volume.
** See pp. 219, 220 of this volume.
*** See p. 433 of this volume.

Plekhanov also severely castigated idealism and its variant, Machism, for its anti-scientific interpretation of space and time. "If space and time," he wrote, "are only forms of contemplation (Anschauung) that I myself possess, it is clear that when I did not exist these forms did not exist either, that is to say, there was no time and no space, so that, when I assert, for instance, that Pericles lived long before me, I am talking arrant nonsense."* Plekhanov argues that contemporary science has nothing in common with such views.

In his struggle against Machism, Plekhanov dismissed the idealist theory of cognition advocated by Mach and his Russian disciples as untenable, and countered it with the scientific view on questions of epistemology. Moreover, Plekhanov proceeded from the materialist recognition of the objectively existing world. Man's sensations and consciousness allow him to know real phenomena and objects, as a result of which "things-in-themselves" become "things-for-us". Plekhanov wrote: *"There is not and cannot be any other knowledge of the object than that obtained by means of the impressions it makes on us.* Therefore, if I recognise that matter is known to us only through the sensations which it arouses in us, this in no way implies that I regard matter as something 'unknown' and unknowable. On the contrary, it means, first, that matter is knowable and, secondly, that it has become known to man in the measure that he has succeeded in getting to know its properties through impressions...."**

But on this important issue Plekhanov deviated somewhat from the Marxist theory of cognition, towards agnosticism. In the theory of cognition Plekhanov committed an error along the lines of Helmholtz's "theory of hieroglyphs", when he maintained that impressions and sensations were conventional signs and not reflections or copies of things. This error was criticised by Lenin in *Materialism and Empirio-Criticism.* Yet, on the whole, Plekhanov held to the Marxist position on the theory of cognition, and made repeated sharp attacks on agnosticism. He later renounced the "theory of hieroglyphs". In 1908, in *Materialismus Militans,* Plekhanov wrote: "In the new edition of my translation of *Ludwig Feuerbach* published abroad in 1905 and in Russia in 1906, I declared that while I continued to share Sechenov's *view* on this question, his *terminology*" (impressions—conventional signs of things—*A. M.*) "seemed somehow ambiguous to me." "In 1905, I said I was against the *Sechenov terminology.*"*** Plekhanov was wrong in this reference to Sechenov, who had never been an agnostic. At the same time Plekhanov very competently exposed the

---

  * See p. 464 of this volume.
 ** See p. 221 of this volume.
*** See pp. 226, 227 of this volume.

hollowness of the Machians' agnosticism, shared by Bogdanov, who camouflaged his agnosticism with talk of experience and social coordination of men's views as the criteria for the verisimilitude of human knowledge. Socially-coordinated experience cannot be regarded as truth, since not all people's opinions and ideas which are both universally significant and identical, that is to say, socially-coordinated, are true and correct. Everybody knows, for example, that religious feelings and views are common to an enormous number of people even to the present day, but this does not make them correct and authentic. Plekhanov justifiably demonstrated that, from the point of view of the Machian Bogdanov, even hobgoblins and sprites exist and perceptions of them are authentic. "No, Mr. Bogdanov," he wrote, "no matter how you twist and turn you will never shake off the hobgoblins and sprites, as they say, neither by the cross nor by the pestle. Only a correct doctrine of experience can 'relieve' you of them, but your 'philosophy' is as far removed from such a doctrine as we are from the stars of heaven."*

While defending and expounding the principles of the Marxist theory of cognition, Plekhanov frequently made inaccurate statements. In a number of cases, he linked up Marxist materialism with pre-Marxist materialism, not realising that the Marxist epistemology differed from that of the pre-Marxist materialists in being based on the dialectical method, which includes practice as the basis and criterion for cognition. So one cannot, for instance, agree with Plekhanov's assertion that "Marx's epistemology stems directly from that of Feuerbach, or, if you will, it is, properly speaking, the epistemology of Feuerbach, only rendered more profound by the masterly correction brought into it by Marx".**

Plekhanov was also mistaken in his contention that "Marx was wrong when he reproached Feuerbach for not comprehending 'practical-critical activity'. Feuerbach did understand it."*** Here, Plekhanov did not take account of the contemplative and incomplete nature of Feuerbach's materialism, for Feuerbach could not provide a materialist explanation of history and without this, there can be no really scientific understanding of the practical, material activity of people as the criterion for the authenticity of knowledge.

We should also stress that Plekhanov, while combating the idealism of Machian philosophy, was unable to expose its connection with the crisis in natural science. True, he did criticise individual naturalists for their idealism and their vain attempts to

---

* See   p. 255 of this volume.
** See p. 129 of this volume.
*** See p. 639 of this volume.

"overcome" materialism. "The German chemist Ostwald, a well-known exponent of energetics," Plekhanov wrote, "has for long been applying himself to 'the overcoming of scientific materialism'.... But this is a mere misunderstanding. The good chemist Ostwald hopes to 'overcome' materialism by means of energetics only because he is too *poorly versed in philosophy*."* But Plekhanov's criticism of the idealism of individual naturalists was no profound analysis of the crisis in natural science and the relation of Machism to this crisis. Lenin wrote in *Materialism and Empirio-Criticism*: "To analyse Machism and at the same time to ignore this connection—as Plekhanov does—is to scoff at the spirit of dialectical materialism, i.e., to sacrifice the method of Engels to the letter of Engels."**

In spite of a number of shortcomings, Plekhanov's works criticising Machian philosophy occupy an important place in Marxist philosophy. They helped to combat idealism in philosophy, and armed the revolutionary movement in the struggle against bourgeois ideology and its philosophical foundations. However, Plekhanov remained at the nineteenth century level, and was incapable of creatively developing Marxist philosophy in conformity with the new historical conditions, of raising it to a new stage, of exposing the crisis in natural science and indicating how it might be solved by the study and application of dialectical materialism to analysis of problems in natural science. This task was fulfilled by Lenin in his masterly work *Materialism and Empirio-Criticism*, which, together with his other philosophical works, represents a new and higher stage in the development of Marxist philosophy.

* * *

G. V. Plekhanov, while criticising bourgeois idealist trends in philosophy, simultaneously did significant positive work in scientifically analysing many important philosophical questions. In his *Fundamental Problems of Marxism, Materialismus Militans*, "Translator's Preface to the Second Edition of F. Engels' *Ludwig Feuerbach...*", and other works published in this volume of the present edition, Plekhanov devotes much attention to ascertaining the essence of Marxist philosophy, the dialectical method, the theory of cognition and fundamental questions of historical materialism.

The philosophy of Marxism, as Plekhanov demonstrates, is an entire world-outlook, contemporary materialism, which is, at

---

* See p. 598 of this volume.
** V. I. Lenin, *Collected Works*, Vol. 14. p. 32.

present, the highest stage of development of materialist philosophy. The philosophy of Marx and Engels rests upon the achievements
of pre-Marxist thought, in particular, upon those of classical German philosophy—the dialectics of Hegel and the materialism of
Feuerbach.

At the same time, Plekhanov emphasised the qualitatively new
nature of Marxist philosophy, calling the emergence of Marx's
materialist philosophy a genuine revolution, the greatest revolution ever in the history of human thought.

While correctly remarking that Marx had critically fathomed
and refashioned Feuerbach's materialism, Plekhanov made certain wrong formulations, making it appear as though Marx and
Engels at one stage in their philosophical development were Feuerbachians and only later became dialectical materialists. Plekhanov's portrayal of the evolution of Marx and Engels does not
correspond to reality, since Marx and Engels, while to some extent
influenced by Feuerbach, did not proceed, as he did, from the principles of abstract man, but from recognition of the decisive role
played in history by the masses. From the very beginning of their
activities, Marx and Engels were revolutionaries and thinkers.
While they were influenced by Feuerbach and shared his views on
a number of important issues, they were not and did not become
"pure" ("orthodox") followers of Feuerbach. Moreover: they were
always dialecticians. Even in the early period of their activities
Marx and Engels understood Feuerbach's philosophy as dialecticians, as revolutionary democrats who were beginning to comprehend the role played by the revolutionary activity of the masses,
their role as the remakers of history, which was never a feature
of Feuerbach's philosophy.

Plekhanov's elaboration of materialist dialectics, its interrelation with formal logic, is of considerable importance. He distinguishes the peculiarities of dialectical materialism from the metaphysical, and considers materialist dialectics as the teaching on
the development and motion of all reality. The philosophy of
Marxism is not simply materialism, but *dialectical* materialism.
Its basic principle is that it recognises development and motion.
If metaphysics, formal logic, says Plekhanov, adheres to the
principle: "yea—yea and nay—nay", then dialectics says: "yea—
nay and nay—yea."

"Every definite question," he wrote, "as to whether a particular
property is part of a particular object must be answered *either yea
or nay*. That is indisputable. But how should one reply where the
object *is changing*, when it *is already shedding* the particular
property or *is still only acquiring it*? Needless to say, a definite
answer is demanded here too; but the point is that it will be
definite only if it is based on the formula: *"yea—nay* and

nay—yea."* Thus, formal logic fixes the existence of the object and its properties abstracted from their changes, while dialectics indicates processes, the development of objects, phenomena. At the same time, it is extremely important to emphasise, as Plekhanov did, that dialectical logic is the reflection in the minds of people, in their conceptions, of the contradictions and development inherent in reality itself and in its phenomena. Plekhanov wrote: "Materialism puts dialectics 'the right way up' and thereby removes the mystical veil in which Hegel had it wrapped. By the very fact of this, it brings to light the *revolutionary character* of dialectics."** Dialectical logic is the logic of objective reality and is its reflection in human thought. "The rights of *dialectical thinking*," said Plekhanov, "are confirmed by the *dialectical properties of being*," as being itself determines thinking. However, Plekhanov was inexact in the formulations on the interrelationship of dialectical and formal logic. He said that "*just as rest is a particular case of motion, so thought, according to the rules of formal logic (conforming to the 'basic laws' of thought) is a particular case of dialectical thought*". This is inaccurate and incorrect, since formal logic does not and cannot enter into dialectical logic, for dialectical logic, having as its own object motion and development, cannot embrace the laws of formal logic which do not deal with change and development but consider objects outside of change. When dealing with dialectics, Plekhanov emphasised its revolutionary character and, citing Herzen, referred to it as the algebra of the revolution, quoting Marx's famous words that dialectics regards every historically developing social form as in fluid movement, and therefore takes into account its transient nature no less than its momentary existence, because it lets nothing impose on it, and it is in its essence critical and revolutionary.

Throughout his work in philosophy, Plekhanov paid constant attention to questions of historical materialism. He showed that dialectical materialism extended to society is historical materialism, the theory of the materialist conception of the historical process. In the works which make up the present volume, Plekhanov examines many problems of the theory of historical materialism: social being and social consciousness, forms of social consciousness and their role in history, the laws of development of productive forces and relations of production, the part played by the geographical environment in the life of society, the role of the basis and superstructure in the development of society, the place of the masses and the individual in history, and

---

* See p. 76 of this volume.
** See p. 79 of this volume.

other issues. In propagating the fundamentals of historical materialism, Plekhanov underlined its methodological importance for the different social sciences, for the study of various aspects and areas of social life. "I am referring," he wrote in his *Fundamental Problems of Marxism*, "not to the *arithmetic* of social development, but to its *algebra*; *not to the causes of individual phenomena, but to how the discovery of those causes should be approached.* And that means that the materialist explanation of history was primarily of a *methodological significance.*"*

Historical materialism establishes that the mode of production, which includes the productive forces and relations of production, is at the root of social life, of historical development. But what gives rise to and determines the development of productive forces and relations of production? In *Fundamental Problems of Marxism*, Plekhanov replies to this question as follows: "The properties of the geographical environment determine the development of the productive forces, which, in its turn, determines the development of the economic relations, and therefore of all other social relations."** This reply is not quite accurate. Here Plekhanov overestimates the role of the geographical environment. Plekhanov's formulation transforms the geographical environment from one of the conditions accelerating or retarding social development into a factor determining the development of the productive forces of society, the basis on which the life of society is built. In many of his other works, however, Plekhanov gave a correct reply to this question.

In examining the relationship of the economic basis to the superstructure, Plekhanov set out a five-point formula: 1) the state of the productive forces; 2) the economic relations determined by them; 3) the socio-political structure erected on the given economic base; 4) mentality of social man, determined partly by the direct influence of the economy and partly by the socio-political system which has grown upon it; 5) ideology, reflecting the properties of the mentality. As a scheme, the "five-point" formula has serious shortcomings. Productive forces and relations of production, which are known to be two aspects of the mode of production, are isolated from each other in this formula. The mentality of social man is made the fourth stage of Plekhanov's scheme; this, he mistakenly believes, finds reflection later (at the fifth stage) in various forms of ideology. But ideology as a system of views, conceptions, ideas of one or other class, is the reflection of social being, the expression of the interests of a particular class;

---

* See p. 137 of this volume.
** See pp. 143-44 of this volume.

it is rooted in the economic relationships of people, in the struggle of classes, and not in the psyche.

It would be wrong to consider, for example, that political ideology or belles-lettres reflect the psyche, for the simple reason that both these forms of ideology, of social consciousness, reflect social beings, the conditions of the material life of society, the class struggle, expressing the interests of different classes in society either in the form of ideas and conceptions or in the form of artistic images. Plekhanov was well aware of this and, in many of his writings, he adduced splendid reasons to prove the principles of the materialist conception of history in its application to the history of ideology, explaining the objective sources of social ideology.

But in the present instance—in his *Fundamental Problems of Marxism*—he is inaccurate in saying that ideology is the reflection of the mentality, as it were, the condensed mentality. It follows from this that the content of ideological forms is the mentality, but this does not correspond to the truth. Lenin pointed out, for example, that politics is the concentrated expression of economics, and not the mentality, as Plekhanov would have it.

While sometimes inaccurate or erroneous in his views, Plekhanov, on the whole—in his analysis of the basic questions of the theory of historical materialism—held a correct Marxist position. For instance, he convincingly elaborated one of the fundamental theses of historical materialism—on the progressive development of society, on the change of socio-economic structures in the history of society. He repeated Marx's statement that no socio-economic structure will disappear before all the productive forces for which it has room have developed, and that the new, advanced relations of production will never replace the old before the material conditions for their existence have matured within the old society. This is why mankind always undertakes those tasks which are feasible, that is to say, those tasks which are ripe for solution, springing from the prevailing conditions of the material life of society. In this, we have one of the manifestations of the objective natural-historical character of the development of the human society. Such a conception differs intrinsically from the dogmatic view of the Second International about the level of development of the productive forces, that the socialist revolution would begin only in that capitalist country in which the productive forces had developed most. However, while giving a correct reply to this question from a general theoretical standpoint, Plekhanov in his analysis of the revolution in Russia relapsed into an opportunist position, leaning to the views of the Second International. For example, in his Notes to the 1910 German edition of *Fundamental Problems of Marxism* he stated that in the autumn of 1905 "certain Marxists ... considered a *socialist* revolution possible in Russia, since, they claimed, the country's productive forces were sufficiently developed for such a revolution". Plekhanov did not comprehend the new historical epoch—the epoch of imperialism and proletarian revolutions, its peculiarities, and so he sometimes approached questions of the theory of the revolution dogmatically, not realising the necessity for the bourgeois-democratic revolution to develop into the socialist revolution.

The credit for creatively developing Marxism in the new historical epoch belongs to Lenin. He proved brilliantly that under the conditions of imperialism the proletarian revolution would first be accomplished in that country where the contradictions of imperialist capitalism were most acute. Of course, a definite level in the development of the productive forces of capitalism was essential in order to bring about the social revolution. There could be no question of a proletarian revolution without the necessary material prerequisites and conditions. But this was quite different from the contention of the leaders of the Second International, including Plekhanov, that the socialist revolution was possible only in the country with the highest level of development of the productive forces of capitalism, and in which the proletariat comprised the majority of the population.

Plekhanov justifiably and profoundly criticised the conception of "automatism" in historical development. The neo-Kantian Stammler, misunderstanding the Marxist proposition on causal necessity in social development, contended that if social development were accomplished exclusively by virtue of *"causal necessity,* it would be patently senseless to consciously try to further it.... Who would attempt to assist the necessary, i.e., inevitable, rising of the sun?" he asked.* The revisionist Bernstein considered the historical teachings of Marx and Engels to consist in a recognition of the automatic operation of the economic situation in history. Plekhanov exposed this wrong conception of Marxism as a fatalist doctrine, and argued that the history of people has nothing in common with Nature and its phenomena, that the history of society has its own peculiarities and is made by man. But man makes history in a definite direction, not arbitrarily. At different stages of historical development, men's actions have different tasks and aims which are determined by historical necessity and by the conditions of the given epoch. Consequently, "once this necessity is given," wrote Plekhanov, *"then given too, as its effect, are those human aspirations which are an inevitable factor of social development. Men's aspirations do not exclude neces-*

---

* See p. 180 of this volume.

sity, but are themselves determined by it."* Pre-Marxist materialism, while stating correctly that people are the product of circumstances and education, failed to note that circumstances are
changed by people and that the tutor himself must be taught.
Hence it follows that Marxist philosophy places enormous importance on the activities of people, of the masses, in the historical
development of society, and views history as the deeds and
struggle of the masses. "*With the thoroughness of the historical
action*," Plekhanov recalls the words of Marx, "*the size of the mass
whose action it is will therefore increase.*"**

Thus, the logical course of development of society includes the
activities of the people. The proposition that society develops
according to definite laws and by necessity in no way precludes
recognition of the tremendous role played by people, the popular
masses, in history. On this basis, Plekhanov rejected the revisionist Bernstein's conception denying the activity and struggle of
the masses.

Defending and explaining the Marxist view that society develops
in accordance with laws, Plekhanov waged a struggle against the
Rickertian variety of neo-Kantianism which negates the objective
nature of historical laws. Rickert maintained that laws were only
effective in nature and its phenomena which are studied by natural science. In the history of society, all phenomena are so individual
and unique that there can be no question of history conforming to
laws. Rickert counterposed the "sciences" of culture to those of
Nature. This conception met with a sharp rebuff from Plekhanov.
Upholding the Marxist thesis on the laws of historical development, he wrote: "History becomes a science only in so far as it
succeeds in explaining from the point of view of sociology the processes it portrays.... Rickert's attempt to *oppose* the sciences of
culture to the sciences of nature has no serious basis."***

Plekhanov devoted considerable attention in his writings of
that time to the inverse influence of the superstructure, social
consciousness, on the development of existence, of economics.
When the superstructure has developed on a specific economic basis to which it corresponds, the former, as Plekhanov rightly
indicated, in turn exerts a powerful influence on the course of
economic development. "Political relations," he remarked, "indubitably influence the economic movement, but it is also indisputable that *before they influence that movement they are created by it....*
The *Manifesto* gives convincing proof that its authors were well
aware of the importance of the ideological 'factor'."****

---

* See p. 180 of this volume.
** See p. 183 of this volume.
*** See p. 486 of this volume.
**** See p. 156 of this volume.

Plekhanov was basically correct in his observations concerning the inverse influence of the superstructure, social consciousness, on the development of society, but he failed to elucidate the role of socialist consciousness in application to the labour movement. Moreover, he somewhat underestimated the role of the Party in introducing socialist consciousness into the working-class movement and the subjective factor and its place in the revolution.

Despite individual errors and serious shortcomings in Plekhanov's philosophical works, those contained in this volume reveal an enormous interest in the philosophy of Marxism and the writer's efforts to preserve the Marxist philosophy in all purity and make it the property of the working class.

Plekhanov wanted Marxist philosophy to be studied by advanced workers.

Once, after receiving a letter about the study of philosophy by workers, Plekhanov wrote a special article on the subject in *Dnevnik sotsial-demokrata* [Diary of a Social-Democrat] (No. 12, June 1910). He believed the study of philosophy essential, but maintained it was important for the studies to be well organised and, even more so, for the philosophy to be sound, that is to say, for it to be Marxist philosophy. "We make it extremely difficult for ourselves to acquire sound philosophical conceptions," he wrote. "How do our comrades study philosophy? They read, or I will say for politeness' sake, they 'study' the now fashionable philosophical writers. But these philosophical writers who are now in fashion are thoroughly saturated with idealism."* Plekhanov explained that study of fashionable idealist trends could bring nothing but harm. Only the study of Marxist philosophy would give a correct world-outlook, but study of the predecessors of Marxist philosophy was also essential. "Neither Mach nor Avenarius," he wrote, "neither Windelband nor Wundt, nor even Kant must lead us to the sanctuary of philosophical truth, but only Engels, Marx, Feuerbach, and Hegel. Only from these teachers can we learn what we need to know."** However, these views did not cause Plekhanov to conclude that reading the works of bourgeois philosophers was not worthwhile. On the contrary, he advised that they be read, studied, and criticised from the standpoint of Marxist philosophy.

*   *   *

The present volume contains a number of Plekhanov's works criticising religion and the religious seekings in Russia: "On the So-called Religious Seekings in Russia"; "On Boutroux's Book";

---

* See p. 457 of this volume.
** See pp. 457-58 of this volume.

"On Fr. Lütgenau's Book"; "On A. Pannekoek's Pamphlet" and others. In these works he explains the origin and essence of religion and examines the reactionary role of the religious seekings and their links with idealist philosophy. In accordance with the principles of historical materialism, and utilising vast historical and ethnographical data, Plekhanov made a materialist analysis of the problems of religion and atheism.

Plekhanov considered religion to be a system of notions and sentiments fantastically distorting reality. He was basically correct in tracing the origin of religion to the socio-economic conditions of primitive society, when the productive forces were at a very low level of development, when man's power over nature was negligible and he was helpless before natural phenomena, and did not understand them; it was precisely under these conditions that man began to endow phenomena with a personality and to worship them. Animism was one of the first religious notions of primitive man. Plekhanov wrote: "Primitive man believes in the existence of numerous spirits, but worships only some of them. Religion arises from the combination of the *animistic ideas* with certain *religious acts*."* Under the conditions of primitive society, there also arose totemism, signifying belief in the kinship of one or another clan of people and one or other animal, and subsequently the deification of animals, plants, etc. "The Greek philosopher Xenophanes," Plekhanov noted wittily, "was mistaken when he said that man always creates his god in his own image and likeness. No, at the beginning he creates his god in the image and likeness of an animal. Man-like gods appeared only later, as a consequence of man's new successes in developing his productive forces. But even for a long time afterwards, deep traces of zoomorphism are preserved in man's religious ideas. It is enough to recall the worship of animals in ancient Egypt and the fact that statues portraying Egyptian gods very often had the heads of beasts."**

Plekhanov used many examples to trace back and prove convincingly that religious ideas and conceptions depend on socio-economic conditions, on social being. He noted that the social relations on Mount Olympus were reminiscent of the structure of Greek society during the Heroic period. In the new period, when the transition of society from feudalism to capitalism was being accomplished, deism became widespread. This was connected with the desire of the bourgeoisie in that period to restrict the royal power. "Alongside the efforts to limit the powers of kings," wrote Plekhanov, "came the trend towards 'natural religion' and to deism, that is, to a system of ideas wherein the power of God is

---

* See p. 312 of this volume.
** See p. 328 of this volume.

restricted on all sides by the *laws of Nature*. Deism is celestial parliamentarism."* But under all conditions, religion retains the mythological element, a fantastic conception of the world, the worship of divine power. Changes in religious ideas and the religious cult are really the adaptation of religion to new historical conditions and the needs of the exploiting classes, as their ideology, as their means of keeping the working masses in subjection.

Plekhanov made a great contribution to the struggle against the god-builders, against those who *"seek a road to heaven"*, as he put it, *"for the simple reason that they have lost their way on earth"*. The "religion of socialism", created by Lunacharsky and his associates, fully corresponded to the idealism of Machian philosophy, and the declaration of the god-builders to the effect that they were materialists was, to say the least, absurd. Plekhanov wrote: "Only as a consequence of his complete ignorance of materialism could our prophet of the 'fifth religion'" (A. Lunacharsky.—*A. M.*) "call himself a materialist."**

Plekhanov exposed the anti-scientific and harmful nature of the Russian Machian god-builders' attempt to create their religion without god, a religion purporting to be a "belief in socialism", the idolisation of the "potential of mankind". He demonstrated that their talk of a proletarian religion had nothing in common with Marxism, with the working class and its socialist ideology.

God-building is the "padded-jacket of modern despondency", said Plekhanov, and not an ideology of struggle. In combating god-building Plekhanov also criticised the errors made by Gorky at that time, saying that Gorky's *Confession* preached the new religion. But simultaneously with his criticism of Gorky's ideological mistakes, Plekhanov fought for Gorky the artist; although he did not always correctly assess Gorky's works (*Mother*), he was well aware that Gorky was a great realist writer who paid only temporary homage to the propagation of the new religion.

Plekhanov's writings against the religious world-outlook retain their vital force even today. Basically they give a correct scientific idea of religion, its social essense and purpose, and help to resolve the question of the attitude of the proletariat and its Party to religion, and to wage the struggle against religious prejudices.

* * *

In this volume there are a number of Plekhanov's works containing many profound statements and comments on the history of philosophy.

---

* See p. 341 of this volume.
** See p. 358 of this volume.

Plekhanov was one of the few Marxists in the Second International to make an important contribution to the Marxist history of
philosophy and to create valuable works on the history of philosophical thought. He was not only an eminent propagandist of
Marxist philosophy, but also a notable historian in this field.
He contended both with the idealist historians of philosophy, who
explained the development of philosophical thought by the development of the absolute idea, and with the vulgarisers of Marxism,
such as Shulyatikov, who did not understand the relative independence of ideology, including philosophy.

In several of his works, Plekhanov gives a clear elucidation of
the basic principle of historical materialism—that social existence
determines social consciousness, including philosophical thought.
He wrote: "Marx's materialism shows in what way the *history of
thinking* is determined by the *history of being*,"* just as the content of philosophy is determined by economics. But at the same
time, Plekhanov considered that one or other of these philosophical ideas and theories spring from economics, not directly, but
indirectly, while being influenced by a number of other factors
and phenomena. In his opinion, the content of ideological phenomena may be explained and determined by the economic development of society only in the very last analysis.

In class society, ideology, including philosophy, has a class
character and reflects the interests and aspirations of one or other
of the classes. Plekhanov gives some remarkable examples of
materialist analysis of different philosophical systems and ideas:
of French materialism, classical German philosophy, the philosophy of Russian revolutionary thinkers, and others. He was able
to do all this because, having mastered the Marxist method, the
principles of historical materialism, he utilised them in his historico-philosophical studies.

Criticising the efforts of Shulyatikov and other vulgarisers to
derive the content of philosophical concepts directly from production, Plekhanov, in an article written specially against Shulyatikov, exposed the untenability and vulgar simplification of his
historico-philosophical "researches" which appeared in his book
*Justification of Capitalism in West European Philosophy (from
Descartes to Mach)*. Using Shulyatikov's examination of Kantian
philosophy as an example, Plekhanov made devastating criticism
of his vulgar views on the history of philosophy. Shulyatikov
claimed that the philosophical views of any bourgeois thinker
represented a picture of capitalist production drawn with the aid
of conventional signs. All philosophical terms and formulas, concepts, ideas, opinions, impressions, "things-in-themselves", "phe-

---

* See p. 168 of this volume.

nomena", "substances", "modi", etc., etc., served, in Shulyatikov's view, to designate classes and their interests.

"After all," wrote Plekhanov, "to assert that 'all philosophical terms without exception' serve to designate social classes, groups, nuclei, and their relationships, is to reduce an extremely important question to a simplicity that can only be characterised by the epithet: 'Suzdalian'. This word denotes neither a 'social class' nor a 'group', nor a 'nucleus', but simply a vast woodenheadedness."* That is why Shulyatikov and his ilk, using such "methodology", gave a distorted, crude, and vulgarly simplified analysis of philosophical theories, particularly the philosophy of Kant. Plekhanov scoffed bitterly at Shulyatikov: "According to him, when Kant wrote about noumena and phenomena, he not only had in mind various social classes, but also, to use the expression of the old wife of one of Uspensky's bureaucrats, he 'aimed at the pocket' of one of these classes, namely, the bourgeoisie." **

These words of Plekhanov's, castigating those who vulgarly simplified philosophical history, have not lost their significance even today. Those historians of literature, art, philosophy, and other forms of ideology, who analyse historico-philosophical phenomena, if not completely, then approximately in the spirit of such vulgarism and "woodenheadedness", are not yet extinct.

Plekhanov devoted a great deal of attention to elucidating the historico-philosophical and ideological roots of contemporary trends in idealism. Thus, for instance, he illustrated how the ideological and philosophical sources of Machism are rooted in the views of Berkeley. Whereas Berkeley pronounced matter to be a "collection of ideas", a combination of sensations, that is to say, resolved the question of matter in the spirit of subjective idealism, Mach and his supporters maintained that physical phenomena, material bodies, are essentially complexes of sensations. So Plekhanov was fully justified in writing: "Mach ... *adheres firmly on this question to the point of view of the eighteenth-century idealist Berkeley.*"***

In the writings contained in the present volume, Plekhanov also touches on many historico-philosophical and sociological questions connected with the preparation, formation, and development of Marxist philosophy and scientific socialism. In such works as *Fundamental Problems of Marxism*; "From Idealism to Materialism"; "Utopian Socialism of the Nineteenth Century", and others, he gives a detailed, though not always accurate, analysis of the philosophies of Hegel, Feuerbach, the French materialists, and the views of the Western utopian socialists.

---

* See p. 302 of this volume.
** See pp. 302, 305 of this volume
*** See p. 214 of this volume.

His analysis shows the importance of the philosophical ideas of Hegel, Feuerbach, and the teachings of the utopian socialists in the origination of Marxism.

Plekhanov's merit lies particularly in the fact that he became one of the first and most prominent historians of socialist ideas, who made a profound Marxist analysis of their role and importance in the preparation of scientific socialism. In the articles "French Utopian Socialism of the Nineteenth Century" and "Utopian Socialism of the Nineteenth Century", he gives a convincing portrayal of the progressive nature of the utopian socialists' ideas, their critique of capitalism, and simultaneously sheds light on the inherent narrowness of their views, their inability to indicate the way out of capitalist slavery, since they could not discover the laws of social development or understand the class struggle of the proletariat against the bourgeoisie. Plekhanov was right in saying that "like Fourier, Saint-Simon was horrified at the very thought of the class struggle and sometimes liked to intimidate his readers with 'the propertyless class', the 'people'".*

Noting the negative attitude of the utopian socialists to the class revolutionary struggle, Plekhanov quoted the words of Cabet, which are pertinent in this respect: "*If I had the revolution in my grasp, I would not open my hand even if I had to die in exile for it.*"**

Following in the Marx's footsteps, Plekhanov indicated the connection between socialist teachings and the materialist world-outlook. "If man," Plekhanov wrote, "draws all his knowledge, sensations, etc., from the world of the senses and the experience gained from it, as was taught by the eighteenth-century materialists, then the empirical world must be arranged so that in it man experiences and gets used to what is really human and that he becomes aware of himself as man."***

Despite the errors and deviations from Marxist philosophy, the works of G. V. Plekhanov contained in this volume, today, too, serve the cause of defending Marxist philosophy, and the struggle against bourgeois ideology, idealist philosophy, and all kind of revisionism.

A. MASLIN

---

* See p. 499 of this volume.
** See p. 506 of this volume.
*** See p. 493 of this volume.

SELECTED
PHILOSOPHICAL
WORKS

VOLUME
III

[PREFACE TO THE THIRD EDITION OF ENGELS' *SOCIALISM: UTOPIAN AND SCIENTIFIC*]

The Russian translation of Engels' brochure, *Socialism: Utopian and Scientific* is now appearing in its third edition. The second edition was published in 1892. [1] At that time, opinion that socialist theory in general could not be described as *scientific* did not yet find expression in international socialist literature. Today such opinions are being proclaimed very loudly and are not remaining without influence among some readers. Therefore, we consider it timely to examine the question: *what is scientific socialism and in what does it differ from utopian socialism?*

But to begin with, let us listen to one of the "critics".

In a paper read on May 17, 1901 to the Berlin Student Union for the Study of Social Science (Sozialwissenschaftlicher Studentenverein zu Berlin), Mr. Bernstein posed the selfsame question, although he formulated it differently: "How is scientific socialism possible?" (Wie ist wissenschaftlicher Sozialismus möglich?). His investigations brought him to a negative reply. To use his own words, no "*ism*" can "*be scientific*": "'ism' designates system of outlooks, tendencies, systems of ideas or demands, but not science. The basis of every true science is experience. Science builds its edifice on accumulated knowledge. Socialism, however, is the teaching on a future social system and for that reason its most characteristic feature cannot be established scientifically."*

Is that right? We shall see.

First of all, let us discuss the relationship between "*isms*" and *science*. If Mr. Bernstein were right in saying that no "ism" can be a science, then it is clear, for instance, that Darwin*ism* too is not a "science". Let us accept that for the moment. But what is Darwin*ism*? If we are to go on accepting Mr. Bernstein's theory as correct we must include Darwinism in the "*systems of ideas*". But cannot a system of ideas be a science, or is not a science a system of ideas? Mr. Bernstein evidently thinks *not* but he is

---

* Ed. Bernstein, *Wie ist wissenschaftlicher Sozialismus möglich?* Berlin, 1901, p. 35.

labouring under a misapprehension and all because there is an astonishing and dreadful confusion in his own "system of ideas".

Every intelligent schoolchild now knows that science builds upon the basis of experience. But that is not the question. The question is: *what exactly does science build on the basis of experience?* And there is only one answer to this question: science builds on the basis of experience certain *generalisations* ("systems of ideas") which, in turn, underlie certain *previsions* of phenomena. But this refers to *the future*. Therefore, not every consideration regarding the future is devoid of scientific basis.

⟨What kind of conclusion is it that says socialism is a world-outlook and is therefore unscientific? Evidently Mr. Bernstein seems to think this is indisputable. But before it could indeed be indisputable, it would be necessary to prove from the beginning that *no and nobody's world-outlook can be scientific*. Mr. Bernstein has not done and will never do so; therefore, we take exception to him and say: parlez pour vous, cher monsieur!

Further. A *trend* is not a *science*. *But science can discover and daily does discover trends* peculiar to phenomena under investigation. *Scientific* socialism, in particular, establishes a certain *trend* (the trend to social revolution) *prevailing in the present capitalist society*; socialism was a teaching on the *future social order* even before it emerged from the *utopian* stage.

One would have to be a Bernstein in order to imagine that science is not a "system of ideas". It is a truly monstrous suggestion. Science is precisely knowledge worked up into a system. Bernstein, as usual, confuses matters. He heard about the appearance in contemporary natural science of a "trend" to free science completely from *hypotheses*, and decided that science had nothing in common with any "systems of ideas". In fact, this same scientific "trend" which led Mr. Bernstein to his monstrous thesis, is groundless. Haeckel was quite right when, in criticising this mistaken "trend", he said: "ohne Hypothese ist Erkenntnis nicht möglich" (*Die Lebenswunder*, Stuttgart, 1904, S. 97).⟩

If the proposition is true that the present is pregnant with the future, a scientific study of the present must give us the opportunity of foreseeing some phenomena—in this case, socialisation of the means of production—of the future, not on the basis of some kind of mysterious prophecies or arbitrary and abstract reasoning, but precisely on the basis of "experience", on the basis of knowledge accumulated by science.

If Mr. Bernstein wished seriously to ponder over the question he himself posed about the possibility of scientific socialism, he should first of all have decided whether the proposition we have indicated above was true or untrue in application to *social phenomena*. Even a moment's thought would have shown him that in this case it was no less true than in all others. Being then sure of this, he ought to have considered whether contemporary social science possessed such a store of information about present-day social relations as, when put to use, would enable science to foresee an impending replacement of these social relations by others — the capitalist mode of production by the socialist. If he had observed that there was not and never could be such a store of information, the question of the possibility of scientific socialism would have solved itself *negatively*. But if he had been convinced that this information already existed, or could be accumulated with time, he would then have come inevitably to a *positive* decision on the question. But no matter how he resolved this question, one thing would have become perfectly clear to him, that which — because of his erroneous method of investigation — still remains for him wrapped in the mist of an ill-balanced and ill-considered "system of ideas". He would have seen that the impossibility of the existence of scientific socialism could be proved only if it became obvious that prevision of social phenomena was impossible, in other words, that before resolving the question of the possibility of scientific socialism it was essential to resolve the question of the *possibility of any social science at all*. If Mr. Bernstein had perceived all this, he might perhaps have observed also that the subject he had selected for his paper was "of enormous dimensions",[2] and that he who has no other means of analysis than the muddleheaded contrasting of science and "isms", of experience and a "system of ideas" can do very little to elucidate such a subject.

Incidentally, we are being unjust to our author. The means of analysis at his disposal were not really restricted to such contrasts. Here, for instance, on pages 33-34 of his paper we also come across the idea that science has no other aim than knowledge, whereas "political and social doctrines" strive to resolve certain practical tasks. During the discussion which followed the reading of Mr. Bernstein's paper, a member of the audience pointed out to him in connection with this idea that medicine had the practical aim of *healing*, and yet it must be regarded as a science. But our lecturer replied to this by saying that healing was the task of medical *art*, which, in any case, presupposed a basic knowledge of medical *science*; but that medical science itself aims not at healing, but at the study of the means and conditions of healing. To this Mr. Bernstein added: "If we take this distinguishing of conceptions as a typical example (als typisches Muster), we shall have no trouble in defining, in the most complex cases, where science ends and where art or doctrine begins."*

---

* Ibid., p. 34. Note.

We take as our "example" the "distinguishing of conceptions" recommended by Mr. Bernstein and argue thus: in socialism, as in medicine, we have to distinguish two sides: the *science* and the *art*. Socialism as a *science* studies the means and conditions of the socialist revolution, while socialism as a *"doctrine"*, or as a *political art*, tries to bring about this revolution with the help of acquired knowledge. And we add that if Mr. Bernstein takes as a *"typical example"* the distinction we have made in accordance with his own example, he will readily understand exactly where in the socialist system science ends and doctrine or art begins.

Robert Owen, addressing the "British public" in one of his appeals serving as a preface to his book, *A New View of Society, or Essays on the Principle of the Formation of the Human Character*, wrote:

"Friends and Countrymen,

"I address myself to you, because your primary and most essential interests are deeply involved in the subjects treated in the following Essays.

"You will find existing evils described and remedies proposed.... Beneficial changes can only take place by well-digested and well-arranged plans....

"It is however an important step gained when the cause of evil is ascertained. The next step is to devise a remedy.... To discover that remedy, and try its efficacy in practice, have been the employments of my life; and having found a remedy which experience proves to be safe in its application, and certain in its effects, I am now anxious that you should all partake of its benefits.

"But be satisfied, fully and completely satisfied, that the principles on which the New View of Society is founded are true; that no specious error lurks within them, and that no sinister motive gives rise to their publicity."*

We are now in a position to follow this great British socialist's train of thought from the angle of Mr. Bernstein's "distinguishing of conceptions"; it is clear that Robert Owen began with a study of the prevailing evils and the revelation of their causes. This part of his work corresponds to what is known in medicine as *aetiology*. Then he went on to study the means and conditions of the treatment of the social diseases in which he was interested. Having found the remedy, which seemed to him to be quite effec-

---

* Not having the English original at hand I quote from the German edition, translated by Professor Oswald Kollmann and published in Leipzig in 1900, entitled: *Eine neue Auffassung der Gesellschaft. Vier Aufsätze über die Bildung des menschlichen Charakters, als Einleitung zu der Entwicklung eines Planes, die Lage der Menschheit allmählich zu verbessern.* The extract cited is on page 6. [We are quoting from the original. London, 1817, pp. 11-12.]

tive, he proceeded to put it to a practical test. We might call this his *therapeutics*. Only after his experiments had given entirely satisfactory results did he decide to offer his treatment to the "British public", in other words to begin *medical practice*. Previously he had been engaged in medical *science*, now he had to begin practising medical *art*. Here is a complete parallel: once Mr. Bernstein admits that it is possible to have a *science of medicine*, it is obvious he must admit that it is possible to have a *science of socialism*, if he wishes to be true to his own "distinguishing of conceptions". Those same lines of investigation which we discerned in Robert Owen according to his own words may be just as easily noted among the French socialists, his contemporaries. As an example, we shall take Fourier. He said that he had brought to the people the *art of being rich and happy*. This part of his teaching corresponds to *medical art*. On what did he base this practical part of his teaching? *On the laws of moral attraction*, which he said had remained unknown until he finally discovered them after long and intensive research. Here we are no longer dealing with *art*, but with *theory*, with "knowledge worked up into a system", that is to say, with *science*. And Fourier insistently repeated that his *art* was based on his *scientific discoveries*.* It goes without saying that Mr. Bernstein is in no way bound to attach to these discoveries the same great significance that Fourier and his school did. This, however, does not affect the point at issue. Of course, Mr. Bernstein did not consider himself obliged to believe in the infallibility of all the medical theories of our time. But that did not prevent him from coming to the conviction that medical art is one thing and medical science is another, and that the existence of medical art, far from precluding the existence of medical science, presumes it as a necessary condition of its own existence. Why, then, is such a correlation between art and science not possible also in socialism? Why should the existence of socialism as a socio-political "doctrine" preclude the existence of socialism as a science?

Mr. Bernstein does not reply to these questions. Until he does his proposed "distinguishing of conceptions" will not corroborate but refute his contention that scientific socialism is impossible. And he cannot reply to these questions for the very simple reason that he has nothing to answer. Of course, there can and must be doubts about the theoretical justification of comparing medical art to socialism. But precisely on this matter our author had no

---

* See, for example, *Manuscrits de Fourier*, Paris, 1851, p. 4, where he compares himself with Kepler and Newton. Cf. also any of the expositions of his teaching made by his followers. In each of them, the practical plans of social reconstruction are founded on Fourier's *theoretical discoveries*.

doubts, and could not have had any, since *his* point of view on social life in no way precludes such comparisons.

Thus, Mr. Bernstein's "distinguishing of conceptions" not only leaves us unconvinced about the impossibility of scientific socialism, but, on the contrary, encourages us to believe that even the socialism of Robert Owen, Fourier and other *utopians* was, at least partly, *scientific socialism*. As a consequence of this, we have begun to see less clearly that "distinguishing of conceptions", in virtue of which, until now, we had considered that the socialist theory of Marx and Engels had marked an epoch in the history of socialism. Indeed, this "distinguishing" is unclear not to us alone. With Mr. Bernstein it also turns out that, although the teaching of Marx and Engels has a *great deal more* of the scientific element than the teachings of Fourier, Owen and Saint-Simon, yet, like these, though to a lesser degree, it contains elements of utopianism alongside elements of science and therefore the difference between them has more of a *quantitative* than a *qualitative* character.*

This opinion fitted naturally in the context of Mr. Bernstein's paper: if *scientific* socialism generally is impossible, *Marxism* is obviously one of the unscientific "isms" that contain some admixture of utopianism. Mr. Bernstein's belief in the impossibility of scientific socialism is based on premises which, when correctly interpreted, lead to diametrically opposite conclusions, that is to say, oblige us to acknowledge that scientific socialism, like scientific medicine, is *fully possible*. Since this is the case and as we have no desire to entangle ourselves forever in Mr. "Critic's" logical contradictions, we shall break the thread of this argument and instead ask ourselves the question: how, ultimately, is *scientific* socialism distinguished from *utopian* socialism?

In order to answer this question, we shall have to define the distinguishing features of both types of socialism.

On page 14 of the pamphlet in question, Engels says: "The Utopians' mode of thought has for a long time governed the socialist ideas of the nineteenth century, and still governs some of them. Until very recently all French and English socialists did homage to it. The earlier German communism, including that of Weitling, was of the same school. To all these socialism is the expression of absolute truth, reason and justice, and has only to be discovered to conquer all the world by virtue of its own power. And as absolute truth is independent of time, space, and of the historical development of man, it is a mere accident when and where it is discovered."[3]

Mr. Bernstein reproaches Engels with having exaggerated in this passage. He says: "I cannot agree with him when he says that they

---

* On this point read especially pages 21, 22, 28, 29 and 30.

the utopian socialists) regarded as a matter of chance, independent of historical development, in terms of place and time, the truths revealed by them to the world. This generalisation misrepresents their views on history."*

If Mr. Bernstein had only taken the trouble to get better acquainted with the literature of utopian socialism and to ponder more deeply over the fundamental historical views of the utopian socialists, he would have seen that there is not the least shade of exaggeration in Engels' statement.

Fourier was firmly convinced that he had succeeded in discovering the laws of moral attraction, but he was never able at any time to see his theory as *the fruit of France's social development*. He had often wondered why hundreds, even thousands of years ago people had not made the discoveries which he had finally made. And he could answer this only by referring to man's lack of vision as well as the *force of chance*. He even wrote a very characteristic dissertation on the *"tyranny of chance"*, in which he argued "that this colossal and despicable force presides almost alone all discoveries".** He said that he paid it tribute in his "discovery of the calculus of attraction" (dans la découverte du calcul de l'attraction). As with Newton, the idea was suggested to him by an apple. "A fellow traveller who dined with me in Février's restaurant in Paris paid 14 sous for this famous apple. I had just come in from a part of the country where apples equal or even superior in quality were selling at half a liard each, or less than 14 sous per hundred. I was so struck by the difference in the price of apples in two places with the same climate that I began to suspect a basic defect in the industrial mechanism; out of this came those investigations which after four years led me to discover the theory of series of industrial groups and then the laws of general movement which Newton had missed.... Since then I found that one could count four famous apples, two of them noted for the trouble they caused (Adam's apple and the apple of Paris) and two for the services they rendered to science. Do not these four apples deserve a special page in history?"***

This would seem to be sufficiently expressive; but it is not yet all. In Fourier's theory, chance plays a much greater role than might appear from his ingenuous reflections on the four apples. In this theory, the whole historical development of man's views, the whole destiny of human prejudice are determined by chance. "If people have persisted so long in their admiration for civilisation," said Fourier, "this was because none of them took Bacon's

---

* Ibid., p. 30, Note.
** *Les manuscrits de Fourier*, p. 14. Cf. also *Œuvres complètes*, t. 4, Paris, 1841, pp. 3, 4, 5.
*** Ibid., p. 17.

advice and made a critical analysis of the flaws and shortcomings of each profession."* Why did no one take Bacon's advice? Very simply, because the chance that might have inspired them to follow his advice did not occur. The present order of things, which itself is only an exception to the general rule, only a digression from the true destiny of mankind, proved to be more prolonged than it need have been, thanks to "the thoughtlessness of the sophists, who forgot that they ought to enquire into the universal aims of Providence (oublièrent de spéculer sur l'universalité de la Providence) and discover that code of laws which it had to compile for human relations".**

Now the reader may judge for himself whether there is even the slightest exaggeration in Engels' statement which we quoted above.

Faith in the historical omnipotence of chance was not so clearly expressed and was perhaps not so great among other eminent utopians as it was with Fourier. But to what extent it affected even the most sober of them, Robert Owen, may be seen from the simple fact that he addressed his socialist appeals to the *potentates of the earth*, to those who had a substantial interest in maintaining the exploitation of man by man. Such appeals were sadly out of tune with all Robert Owen's teaching on the formation of the human character. In the literal and clear meaning of this teaching, the potentates of the earth were wholly incapable of initiating the elimination of that same social order which influenced the formation of their own views and the existence of which was so closely connected with their own vital interests. Nevertheless, Robert Owen,*** tirelessly and solicitously, with the help of detailed calculations, exact plans, and excellent drawings, explained to the monarchs of Europe what constituted a *"rational"* social system. In this respect Owen, like all the other utopian socialists, was closely akin to the great French Enlighteners from whom (mainly Helvétius) he borrowed almost all of his teaching on the formation of the human character, and who, like him, and with a persistence fully deserving a better fate, explained to the crowned "legislators" how and in what manner human happiness could be assured. They fulminated eloquently against the "despots" and just as tenaciously placed their hopes in *enlightened despotism*. This was an obvious contradiction and, of course, it could not escape their own notice. They all realised it, some more clearly than others, but all of them consoled themselves *precisely with*

---

* *Œuvres complètes*, t. 4, p. 121.
** *Manuscrits de Fourier*, p. 78.
*** See, for example, his work, *A Development of the Principles and Plans on which to Establish Self-Supporting Home-Colonies, etc.*, London, 1841, and especially the introduction to his autobiography, *The Life of Robert Owen Written by Himself*, Vol. I, London, 1857.

a trust in chance. Suppose you have a large urn in which there are very many black balls and two or three white ones and that you take one ball after the other. It need hardly be said that in each separate instance you have less chance of removing a white ball than a black one. But if you continue taking out the balls you will inevitably pull out a white one at last. The same applies to crowned "legislators". In each separate instance there is a much greater chance of finding a *bad* "legislator" on the throne than a *good* one. But a good one will eventually appear. He will do everything prescribed by "*philosophy*" and then reason will triumph.

This was how the French Enlighteners saw matters and this essentially deeply pessimistic view, *tantamount to the admission of the utter helplessness of their "philosophy"*, had a close causal connection with their general historical outlook. It is known that even those of the eighteenth-century French Enlighteners who were convinced *materialists* held *idealist views on history*. They believed that the development of knowledge, and man's mental development generally, was the basic cause of historical progress. In this regard, the utopian socialists were completely at one with them. Thus, for example, Robert Owen said that "these false notions have ever produced evil and misery in the world, and that they still disseminate them in every direction. That the soled cause of their existence hitherto has been *man's ignorance of human nature*".* In accordance with this, the elimination of social evil, too, was to be expected solely from the dissemination among the people of a correct understanding of their own nature. Robert Owen was firmly convinced that such understanding would spread inevitably among the people. Only a few months before his death he wrote that man was "created to acquire knowledge by experience, and happiness by obeying the laws of his nature".** But experience is knowledge. What determines its more or less rapid accumulation? Why is it that in the course of one historical epoch mankind acquires an enormous treasure-house of knowledge, and during another, often incomparably longer period, adds only completely insignificant crumbs of knowledge to its previous stores and sometimes loses even the stores themselves? Owen did not and could not answer this question, an extremely important one

---

* See *Neue Auffassung, etc.* S. 65-66. Incidentally, this thought is repeated in all his works. [We are quoting from Robert Owen, op. cit., pp. 114-15.]

* See his extremely interesting article, headed: "On the absolute necessity, in the nature of things, for the attainment of Happiness, that the system of Falsehood and Evil should precede the system of Truth and Good", in the appendix to the first volume of his autobiography, issued as a separate book; pp. XXX-XXXIII.

for a scientific explanation of historical phenomena. *In general people who hold idealist views on history do not and cannot answer this question.* And that is understandable. To be able to answer it, they would have to explain what it is that determines man's mental development, that is to say, they would have to perceive this development *not as the basic cause of the historical process, but as the outcome of another, more deep-seated cause.* And this would be tantamount to *acknowledging the bankruptcy of the idealist conception* of history. He who does not yet acknowledge this, must inevitably give chance a very large place in his interpretation of historical events and in his consideration of the future. *Chance* furnishes him with an explanation of all that he cannot explain by the *conscious activity* of historical persons. *Reference to chance is the first unconscious and involuntary step towards recognising that the development of man's consciousness is conditioned by causes that are independent of him.* That is why the Enligheners of the eighteenth century and the utopian socialists alluded so often to the element of chance. Fourier's "*four apples*" are as absurd now as the French Enligheners' "urn" full of balls. But both the "urn" and the "apples" had their adequate basis in the deep-seated qualities of the idealist conception of history; and the political and social reformers and revolutionaries who held such views had to appeal, more often than other philistines, to the "urn", the "apples" and much more of the unexpected. Indeed, if the historical process of *accumulation* of knowledge is determined in the last analysis by a series of chance phenomena which have no necessary connection with the course of social life and the development of social relations, then each individual contribution to the general treasure-house of knowledge, every discovery made by this or that thinker, including the author of this or that plan of social reconstruction, must inevitably be a gift of chance. And if the *discovery* of truth is dependent upon chance, then the *dissemination* of this truth and its embodiment, more or less rapidly, in social life, must also be subordinated to that same "colossal and despicable force". Hence that coquetting of the French Enligheners and the utopian socialists with the potentates of the earth which excites so much wonder today. With them, *practice* corresponded to *theory*, "art" to "science".

True, at times there was a marked *dissatisfaction* among the utopian socialists *with the theory they had inherited from the Enligheners,* an endeavour to escape from the narrow circle of *idealism* and stand on more *real ground. They were striving to create a social science.* Hence all their "*discoveries*". Some of these were remarkable, in the full sense of the word. They threw a vivid light on many paramount aspects of the historical process, for instance, the role of the class struggle in the modern history of West European societies,* and thus prepared the way for the scientific explanation of social phenomena. But they only *prepared the way* for it. Historical *idealism*, which was the standpoint of all socialists in the first half of the nineteenth century, made much more difficult the final elaboration of a scientific view of social life. Only phenomena which *conform to objective laws* can be subjected to scientific explanation. This conformity to laws presupposes the *subordination of phenomena* to the law of *necessity*, whereas historical idealism considers historical progress almost exclusively as the product of the *conscious* and consequently the *free* activity of men. So long as this contradiction existed, a scientific explanation of social life was impossible. Not only were the socialists of that time unable to resolve this contradiction; they could not even formulate it with the necessary precision, although it had already been clearly grasped and precisely formulated by German philosophy in the person of Schelling.

Schelling demonstrated that the *freedom* of human activity not only *did not preclude necessity*, but, on the contrary, *presupposed* necessity as its own condition.** Schelling's profound thought was developed fundamentally and in detail by Hegel. To put it into everyday language, it means that man's activity may be considered *from two sides*. First, man appears before us as the *cause* of some or other social phenomena. In so far as man realises that he himself is such a cause, he believes that the question of whether these social phenomena should or should not be produced *depends on him*. And to that extent he believes that his activity is *conscious and free*. But the man who acts as the cause of a given social phenomenon can and must also be seen as the *effect* of those social phenomena which fashioned his personality and the trend of his volition. When considered *as an effect*, social man cannot be regarded as a *free* agent, since *the circumstances that determine the trend of his volition are independent of him*. Thus, his activity appears to us as *subject to the law of necessity*, that is to say, as activity *conforming to law*. We may conclude from this that *freedom* does not in any way preclude *necessity*. It is very important to know this truth because it—and it alone—opens the way to a *scientific explanation* of social life. We already know that only those phenomena which are subject to the law of necessity are open to scientific explanation. If we knew social man only as the *cause* of social phenomena, we would understand his activity only from the point of view of *freedom*, and therefore it would always be inaccessible to scientific explanation. The Enlighteners of the

---

* See my Preface to [the Russian edition of] the *Manifesto of the Communist Party*.[4]

** *System des Transcendentalen Idealismus*, Tübingen, 1800, S. 422.[5] Cf. N. Beltov's *The Development of the Monist View of History*, pp. 105 et seq.

eighteenth century, and the utopian socialists of the nineteenth century, in their judgements on history, saw social man only as the *cause* of social phenomena. This was because of their idealist view of history: whoever considers mental development to be the most basic cause of historical progress will take account only of the *conscious* activity of men, and *conscious* activity is precisely that activity which we call free.*

Necessity does not preclude freedom. Moreover, the conscious and, in this sense, the free activity of men is possible only because their actions are necessary. This may seem paradoxical, but it is an irrefutable truth. If men's actions were not *necessary*, it would be impossible to *foresee* them, and where that is impossible, there is no place for free activity in the sense of conscious influence on surrounding life.** Thus, *necessity* proves to be the *guarantee of freedom*.

This was all very well elucidated already by the German idealists, and in so far as they held to this standpoint in their opinions of social life, they were on the firm ground of *science*. But just because they were *idealists*, they could not put their own brilliant ideas to proper use. True, their philosophical idealism was not necessarily connected *with the idealist view of history*. Hegel remarks in his *Lectures on the Philosophy of History* that although, of course. reason governs the world, it does so in the same sense as it governs the motion of the celestial bodies, i.e., *in the sense of conformity to law*. The motion of the celestial bodies conforms to definite laws, but their motion is *unconscious* motion. According to Hegel, the historical progress of mankind is accomplished in the same way; human progress is subject to certain laws, but men are not conscious of these laws and one may say, therefore, that historical progress is *unconscious*. Men err when they think that their ideas are the principal factors in historical progress. The ideas of any given epoch are themselves determined by the character of that epoch. Moreover, the owl of Minerva flies out only at night.

---

* "Necessity in opposition to freedom, is nothing else than the unconscious," Schelling rightly observes (op. cit., p. 424).

** "I might hope to foresee them (the acts of my fellow-citizens) only on the condition that I could examine them as I examine all other phenomena of the world surrounding me, i.e., as the *necessary* consequences of *definite causes* which are already known, or may become known, to me. In other words, my freedom would not be an empty phrase only if *consciousness* of it could be accompanied by *understanding the reasons* which give rise to the *free* acts of my neighbours, i.e., if I could examine them from the aspect of their *necessity*. Exactly the same can my neighbours say about *my own* acts. But what does this mean? This means that the *possibility of the free (conscious) historical activity of any particular person is reduced to zero, if at the very foundation of free human actions there does not lie necessity which is accessible to the understanding of the doer*" (N. Beltov, *The Development of the Monist View of History*, p. 106).[6]

When men begin to study their own social relations, it may be said with certainty that these relations have outlived their day and are preparing to yield place to a new social order, the true character of which will again become clear to mankind only when its turn, too, has come to leave the historical scene.*

These arguments of Hegel's are very far removed from the naive notion, representing the essence of the idealist explanation of history, that historical progress is determined, in the final analysis, by the development of ideas, or, as the French Enlighteners sometimes expressed it, that "*opinion*" governs the world. Hegel did, at least, point out correctly *how historical progress cannot be explained*. But his arguments likewise contain nothing to indicate the true cause. And it could not be otherwise. If Hegel was far from the naive historical idealism of the French Enlighteners and the utopian socialists, this did not in the least disturb the idealist foundation of his own system, but this foundation could not but hinder the elaboration of an entirely scientific explanation of the social and historical process. According to Hegel, the basis of all world development is the development of the *Absolute Idea*. With him it is the development of this idea which, in the final analysis, explains all human history. But what is this Absolute Idea? It is—as Feuerbach** explained very well—only the *personification of the process of thinking*. Thus, world development generally and historical development in particular are to be explained by the laws of human thought, or, in other words, *history* is explained by *logic*. Just how unsatisfactory this explanation is may be seen from many of Hegel's own works. With him historical progress is comprehensible only when it is interpreted not by logic but by the development of social—and predominantly economic—relations. When he says, for instance, that Lacedaemon fell mainly as a consequence of *economic inequality*, this is quite understandable in itself and is fully in accord with the conclusions of modern historical science. But the Absolute Idea has definitely nothing to do with this, and when Hegel turns to it for a final elucidation of the fate of Greece and Lacedaemon, he has literally nothing to add to what he has already explained by referring to economics.*

Hegel was fond of repeating that *idealism reveals itself as the truth of materialism*. But his *Philosophy of History* proves the exact opposite. It makes clear that in application to history *materialism must be acknowledged as the truth of idealism*. In order

---

* See N. Beltov, op. cit., p. 101.[7]
** See his *Grundsätze der Philosophie der Zukunft*, § 23.
*** For more detail see my article "Zu Hegel's sechzigstem Todestag" in *Neue Zeit*, November 1891.[8]

finally to find the straight and true road to a scientific explanation
of the social-historical process, investigators had to lay aside all
varieties of idealism and adopt the materialist standpoint. This
was done by Marx and Engels. Their materialist conception of history is characterised as follows in the present pamphlet:

"The materialist conception of history starts from the proposition that the production of the means to support human life and,
next to production, the exchange of things produced, is the
basis of all social structure; that in every society that has appeared in history, the manner in which wealth is distributed and
society divided into classes or orders is dependent upon what is
produced, how it is produced, and how the products are exchanged.
From this point of view the final causes of all social changes and
political revolutions are to be sought, not in men's brains, not in
men's better insight into eternal truth and justice, but in changes
in the modes of production and exchange. They are to be sought
not in the *philosophy*, but in the *economics* of each particular epoch.
The growing perception that existing social institutions are
unreasonable and unjust, that reason has become unreason and
right wrong (Vernunft Unsinn, Wohlthat Plage geworden), is
only proof that in the modes of production and exchange changes
have silently taken place with which the social order, adapted to
earlier economic conditions, is no longer in keeping. From this it
also follows that the means of getting rid of the incongruities that
have been brought to light must also be present, in a more or less
developed condition, within the changed modes of production
themselves. These means are not to be invented by deduction
from fundamental principle, but are to be discovered in the
stubborn facts of the existing system of production."[9]

If the growing perception that existing social institutions are
unreasonable and unjust is itself a consequence of socio-economic
development it is clear that a certain *conformity to law* may also
be found in the conscious activity of men, which is conditioned
by their conceptions of reason and justice. Since this activity is
determined, in the last analysis, by the development of economic
relations, now, having ascertained the trend of the economic
development of society, we thereby acquire the possibility to
foresee in which direction the conscious activity of its members
must proceed. Thus, here as with Schelling, *freedom* flows from
necessity and necessity is transformed into freedom. But whereas
Schelling, because of the idealist nature of his philosophy, could
not get beyond general—though extremely profound—considerations in this respect, the materialist conception of history allows
us to use these general considerations for the investigation of
"living" life, for the scientific explanation of all the activity of
social man.

In providing the possibility to observe the *conscious* activity of social man from the point of view of its *necessity*, the materialist conception of history thus paves the way for socialism on a scientific basis. In the passage we quoted from Engels, he says that the means of getting rid of the social incongruities cannot be invented, that is to say, *devised* by some brilliant thinker, but must be *discovered* in the changed economic relations of the particular epoch. *And to the extent that such discoveries are possible, so also is scientific socialism possible.* We now have, therefore, a very definite answer to the question raised by Mr. Bernstein regarding the possibility of scientific socialism. True, it looks as though Mr. Bernstein himself does not suspect that such an answer exists. But that only goes to show that he has understood nothing at all of the basic teaching of the people he has professed to follow for the last twenty years.

One may *devise* something that is completely non-existent; a *discovery* applies only to that which *already exists in reality*. What is, therefore, to *discover* in economic reality the means of getting rid of social incongruities? *It is to demonstrate that the very development of this reality has already created and continues to create the economic basis of the future social order.*

Utopian socialism proceeded from *abstract principles*; scientific socialism takes as its starting point the objective course of economic development of bourgeois society.

⟨*Utopian* socialism readily worked out plans for the future social structure. *Scientific* socialism, notwithstanding Mr. Bernstein's assertion quoted earlier, occupies itself not with the future society, but with defining that tendency which is peculiar to the present social order. It *does not paint the future in glowing colours*: it studies the *present*. A vivid example: on the one side, Fourier's image of the *future* life of mankind in the Phalansteries; on the other side, Marx's analysis of the present capitalist mode of production.⟩

If the means of getting rid of the present social incongruities cannot be *devised* on the basis of general considerations about human nature, but must be discovered in the economic conditions of our time, it is patent that their discovery likewise cannot be a *matter of chance*, independent of these conditions. No, the discovery itself is a *process conforming to law and accessible to scientific study*.

The basic principle of the materialist explanation of history is that men's *thinking* is conditioned by their *being*, or that in the historical process, the course of the development of *ideas* is determined, in the final analysis, by the course of development of *economic relations*. If this is the case, it is plain that the formation of new economic relations must necessarily bring with it the

appearance of new ideas corresponding to the changed conditions
of life. And should a new socio-political idea enter the head of
some brilliant man and should he *realise*, for example, that the
old social order cannot last, but must be replaced by a *new* one,
then this happens not "*by chance*", as the utopian socialists believed, but by the force of quite comprehensible historical necessity.
Similarly, the *dissemination* of this new socio-political idea, its
assimilation by the brilliant man's supporters, cannot be attributed to chance; it gains ground precisely because it corresponds to
the new economic conditions, and pervades precisely that class or
strata of the population which more than any other feels the
disadvantages of the obsolete social system. The process of the
dissemination of the new idea also turns out to be in conformity
to law. And since the *dissemination* of the idea corresponding
to the new economic relations must sooner or later be followed by
its *realisation*, that is to say, the elimination of the old
and the triumph of the new social order, it follows that the whole
course of social development, all social *evolution*—with its various aspects and the *revolutionary* features peculiar to it—is now
perceived from the *point of view of necessity*. Here, then, we have in
full view the main feature which distinguishes *scientific* socialism
from *utopian*. The scientific socialist envisages the realisation of
his ideal as a matter of historical *necessity*, whereas the utopian
socialist pins his hopes on *chance*. This brings a corresponding
change in methods of propaganda for socialism. The utopians
worked *at random*, today addressing themselves to enlightened monarchs, tomorrow to enterprising and profit-hungry
capitalists and on the following day to disinterested friends of
humanity and so on.* The scientific socialists, on the other hand,
have a well-balanced and consistent programme based on the
materialist understanding of history. They do not expect all classes of society to sympathise with socialism, being aware that the
ability of a given class to be amenable to a given revolutionary
idea is determined by the economic position of that class, and

---

* Le seul baume à notre servitude, c'est, de temps en temps, un prince
vertueux et éclairé; alors les malheureux oublient pour un moment leurs
calamités. [The sole consolation in our servitude is the appearance from time
to time of a virtuous and enlightened sovereign; then the unfortunate forget
their misfortunes for a moment.] So said the well-known Grimm in the
eighteenth century (quoted from L. Ducros, *Les Encyclopédistes*, Paris,
1900, p. 160). It is plain to anyone that the hopes of Grimm and his followers were really adjusted to chance. We know by now that the utopian
socialists differed very little in this respect from the Enlighteners of the
eighteenth century. True, the Enlighteners put their trust only in *monarchs*,
while the utopian socialists also expected miracles from the goodwill of
simple mortals among the propertied classes. This difference is to be explained by changed social relations, but it does not erase the fundamental
resemblance resulting from identical views on history.

that of all classes in contemporary society only the proletariat finds itself in an economic position inevitably pushing it into revolutionary struggle against the prevailing social order. Here, too, as everywhere, the scientific socialists are not content to view the activity of social man as the *cause* of social phenomena; they look more deeply and perceive this cause itself as the *consequence* of economic development. Here as everywhere they examine the *conscious* activity of men from the point of view of its *necessity*.

"If for the impending overthrow of the present mode of distribution of the products of labour, with its crying contrasts of want and luxury, starvation and surfeit, we had no better guarantee than the consciousness that this mode of distribution is unjust, and that justice must eventually triumph, we should be in a pretty bad way, and we might have a long time to wait. The mystics of the Middle Ages who dreamed of the coming millennium were already conscious of the injustice of class antagonisms. On the threshold of modern history, three hundred and fifty years ago, Thomas Münzer proclaimed it to the world. In the English and French bourgeois revolutions the same call resounded—and died away. And if today the same call for the abolition of class antagonisms and class distinctions, which up to 1830 had left the working and suffering classes cold, if today this call is re-echoed a millionfold, if it takes hold of one country after another in the same order and in the same degree of intensity that modern industry develops in each country, if in one generation it has gained a strength that enables it to defy all the forces combined against it and to be confident of victory in the near future—what is the reason for this? The reason is that modern large-scale industry has called into being on the one hand a proletariat, a class which for the first time in history can demand the abolition, not of this or that particular class organisation, or of this or that particular class privilege, but of classes themselves, and which is in such a position that it must carry through this demand on pain of sinking to the level of the Chinese coolie. On the other hand this same large-scale industry has brought into being, in the bourgeoisie, a class which has the monopoly of all the instruments of production and means of subsistence, but which in each speculative boom period and in each crash that follows it proves that it has become incapable of any longer controlling the productive forces, which have grown beyond its power; a class under whose leadership society is racing to ruin like a locomotive whose jammed safety-valve the driver is too weak to open. In other words, the reason is that both the productive forces created by the modern capitalist mode of production and the system of distribution of goods established by it have come into crying contradiction with that mode of production itself, and in fact to such a degree that, if the whole of modern society is not to perish, a revolution in the mode of production and distribution must take place, a revolution which will put an end to all class distinctions. On this tangible, material fact, which is impressing itself in a more or less clear form, but with insuperable necessity, on the minds of the exploited proletarians—on this fact, and not on the conceptions of justice and injustice held by any armchair philosopher, is modern socialism's confidence in victory founded."*[10]

That is what Engels said in his dispute with Dühring, and his words portray in full clarity the distinguishing features of scientific socialism with which we are now familiar: the view that the emancipation movement of the proletariat is a law-regulated social process; the conviction that only *necessity* can ensure the triumph of *freedom*.**

Taine says somewhere that perfect science reproduces with great accuracy *in ideas* the nature and consistency of *phenomena*. *Such* a science can make accurate forecasts about each separate phenomenon. And there is nothing easier than to show that social science does not and cannot have *such* accuracy. But neither has scientific socialism ever claimed such accuracy. When its opponents object that *sociological prediction is impossible*, they confuse two quite distinct concepts; the concept of the direction and general outcome of a particular social process, and the concept of separate phenomena (events) out of which the process is composed. Sociological prediction is distinguished, and always will be distinguished, by its having very little accuracy in everything that concerns the forecast of separate events, whereas it possesses quite considerable accuracy where it has to define the general character and trend of social processes. Let us take an example. Statistics prove that the mortality rate fluctuates according to the time of the year. Knowing how it fluctuates in a particular country or locality, it is easy to forecast to what extent the number of deaths will go up or down from one period of the year to another. Here we are speaking about the general character and trend of a particular social process, so it is possible to make a very exact

---

* *Herrn Eugen Dührings Umwälzung der Wissenschaft*, dritte Auflage, S. 161-62.
** When our Belinsky—on his being first attracted to Hegel—resolutely abandoned for a time his aspirations to freedom, he gave a striking and incontestable proof of the depth of his theoretical understanding. His renunciation of freedom-loving aspirations was inspired precisely by the consciousness that the triumph of freedom could be assured only by objective necessity. But since he saw nothing in Russian reality to indicate the objective necessity of such a triumph he gave up all hope of it as being *theoretically unsound*. Later he said of himself that he had been unable to "*develop the idea of negation*". This concept, in its application to bourgeois society, was developed by the founders of scientific socialism.

forecast. But if we should wish to know the particular phenomena in which will be expressed, say, the increase in mortality with the coming of autumn, or if we should wish to ask ourselves *which particular* persons will not survive the autumn and *what will be the concrete circumstances* which will bring about their demise, we should not expect an answer from social science; and if we still hoped to get one we should have to resort to the services of a magician or a fortune-teller. Another example. Suppose that in the parliament of a given country there are representatives of the big landowners whose income is being seriously reduced by competition from neighbouring countries; of the industrial employers who market their products in the same neighbouring countries; and lastly of the proletarians who exist solely by selling their labour power. A Bill to impose a high tariff on grain imports has been brought before this parliament. What do you think? Will the sociologist be able to *foretell* how the parliamentary representatives of the various social classes will react to this Bill? We think that in this case the sociologist (and not only the sociologist, the man of science, but any one who has any political experience and common sense) has every possibility to make an *accurate forecast*. "The representatives of the landowners," he will say, "will support the proposal with all their energy; the representatives of the proletariat will just as energetically reject it, and in this respect the employers' representatives will not lag behind them in opposition, unless the landowners' representatives have bought their agreement not to oppose the Bill by making some kind of really important economic concession to them in some other field." This forecast will be made on the basis of analysing the economic interests of the different social classes and it will have the definiteness and accuracy of a mathematical deduction, at least as far as the landowners and the proletariat are concerned. Further, knowing the voting strength of the representatives of each of these classes in parliament, our sociologist will be able easily and accurately to forecast the fate of the Bill. Here again his forecast can have a very large measure of accuracy and reliability. But since you may not be satisfied with having a general forecast of the nature and trend of this particular social process—the process of struggle over the Bill—and wish to know in advance who exactly will speak on the Bill, and exactly what kind of scenes their speeches will give rise to in the parliament, the sociologist will reply to such questions, not by *scientific prediction*, but with more or less witty conjectures; and if you are still dissatisfied, your only remaining hope is again the fortune-teller. A third example: if you take the works of the great French Enlighteners of the eighteenth century—say, for instance, Holbach—you will find in them *the whole social programme of the Great French Revolution*. But

what you will not find in them is one single forecast about the
historical events which later constituted the process by which
the demands advanced by the French Enlighteners on behalf of
the entire third estate were put into effect. Whence this difference?
It is clear where it comes from. The nature and trend of a given
social process is one thing; the separate events which go to make
up the whole process are quite another matter. If I understand
the nature and trend of the process, I can foretell its *outcome*.
But no matter how profound my comprehension of this process
may be, it will not enable me to foretell separate events and their
particular features. When people say that sociological prediction
is impossible, or, at least, extremely difficult, they almost always
have in mind the impossibility of foretelling particular events,
completely forgetting that this is not the business of sociology.
Sociological prediction has as its object, not isolated events, *but
the general results of that social process which*—as, for example, the
process of development of bourgeois society—*is already being
accomplished at the given time.* That these general results can be
determined beforehand is well illustrated by the above-mentioned
example of the French Revolution, the entire social programme of
which was formulated, as we have said, by the advanced literary
representatives of the bourgeoisie.*

Scientific socialism says, *first of all*, that the victory of socialist
ideals presupposes *as its essential condition*, a certain course of
economic development of bourgeois society, taking place independently of the will of the socialists; *secondly*, that this essential
condition *is already at hand*, determined by the nature and development of the relations of production peculiar to that society;
thirdly, that the very dissemination of socialist ideals among the
working class of the contemporary capitalist countries is caused
by the economic structure and development of these countries.
Such is the general idea of scientific socialism. And this general
idea is not invalidated in any way by the completely correct proposition that sociology will never be a perfect science in the sense
meant by *Taine*. Well, and what of it? Although sociology is
not a perfect science, the general conception of scientific socialism is nonetheless indisputable, rendering all doubts of the
possibility of such socialism groundless.

---

* In his recently published book, *Les classes sociales, analyse de la vie sociale*,
the Paris Professor Bauer expresses a similar view regarding sociological
prediction. His book is interesting in many respects. It is a pity that the
learned Professor is very badly informed on the history of the views he is
developing. Evidently it does not enter his head that among his "predecessors" he should have included the philosophers Schelling and Hegel, and
the socialists Marx and Engels.

The bourgeois theoreticians and the "critics" of Marx often advance also the following argument in discussions on the possibility of scientific socialism: "If scientific *socialism* is possible," they say, "then *bourgeois* social science is also possible, which is self-contradictory nonsense, since science can be neither socialist nor bourgeois. Science is integral. *Bourgeois* political economy is as unthinkable as socialist mathematics."

This argument, too, is based on a confusion of ideas. Mathematics can be neither socialist nor bourgeois—that is true. But what is true in application to mathematics is untrue when applied to social science.

What is the sum of the squares of the shorter sides of a right-angled triangle equal to? To the square of the hypotenuse. Is that right? It is. Is it always right? Always. The relation of the square of the hypotenuse to the sum of the squares of the other two sides *cannot vary, since the properties of mathematical figures are invariable.* And what do we find in sociology? Does the subject of *its* investigation remain invariable? It does not. The subject of sociological investigation is *society* and society *develops* and, consequently, *changes.* It is just this *change,* this *development,* that provides the possibility of *bourgeois* social science and, in like manner, of scientific *socialism.* In its development, society passes through *certain phases to which the phases of development of social science correspond;* for example, that which we call *bourgeois* economics is one phase in the development of economic science, and that which we call *socialist* economics is another phase, following directly after the first. What is surprising about this? Where is the self-contradictory nonsense here?

It would be wrong to think that bourgeois economics consists of errors alone. Nothing of the kind. In so far as bourgeois economics *corresponds* to a definite phase of social development it will contain irrefutable *scientific truth.** But this truth is *relative* precisely because it corresponds *only to a certain phase of social development.* However, the bourgeois theoreticians, who imagine that society must always remain at the bourgeois phase, attribute *absolute significance* to their relative truths. This is their basic error, one that is being set right by scientific socialism which has come into being owing to the fact that the bourgeois epoch of social development is drawing to a close. Scientific socialism may by likened to the same Minerva's owl which Hegel spoke about and which, he said, flies out only when the sun of the prevailing social order—in this case, the capitalist—is setting. Once again:

---

* This is why the class bourgeois point of view *in its time* not only did not impede the progress of science, *but was its essential condition.* In my preface to the *Manifesto of the Communist Party* I have shown this by the example of the French bourgeois historians at the time of the Restoration.

where is the contradiction here? Where is the nonsense? Here there is neither contradiction nor nonsense; here, on the contrary, we have the opportunity *to glance at the very process of the development of science as a process conforming to law.*

Be that as it may, the main distinguishing feature of scientific socialism is now quite clear to us. Its adherents are not satisfied with the *hope* that socialist ideals, because of their lofty nature, will attract general sympathy and will therefore triumph. No, they require the *assurance* that this very attraction of general sympathy to socialist ideals is a *necessary social process*, and they derive this assurance from the analysis of contemporary economic relations and the course of their development.* The apologists of the existing social order feel well enough, although they do not always clearly realise it, that this main distinguishing feature is just what constitutes the main strength of socialist theory. Therefore, their "criticism" is directed at this point. They usually begin with the argument that economics cannot be regarded as the mainspring of social development, since man is not fashioned of stomach alone, but has also a soul, a heart, and other imperishable treasures. However, these sentimental arguments, which are evidence of the utter inability of present-day bourgeois theoreticians to understand what is the most important, fundamental task of social science, play only a secondary role with them. The main force of their arguments is concentrated on the question of the trend of contemporary economic development. Here they try to refute, one by one, every tenet of scientific socialism.** Even though their attempts come to nothing, they constantly renew them and cannot help doing so since the question at issue is the very existence of a social order so dear to their hearts. They realise that if economic development actually proceeds along the lines indicated by the scientific socialists, the social revolution is *inevitable.* And this *is equivalent to admitting that scientific socialism is possible.*

We have indicated one distinguishing feature of scientific socialism; Engels indicates another in his controversy with

---

* Some writers, for example Stammler, contend that if the triumph of socialism is a historical necessity, the practical activity of Social-Democracy is *completely superfluous.* Why promote the occurrence of something which is certain to happen? That is, of course, a pitiful and ridiculous sophism. Social-Democracy, in analysing historical development from the point of view of necessity, looks on its own activity as an *essential link* in the chain of those *necessary conditions,* the totality of which makes the victory of socialism inevitable. An *essential* link cannot be *superfluous*: its elimination would break the whole chain of events. The logical weakness of this sophism is clear to anybody who understands what we have said above about freedom and necessity.

** See my article "A Critique of Our Critics", published in the second and third issues of *Zarya.*[11]

Dühring when he says that this socialism dates only from the discovery of the nature and origin of *surplus value*, and that all of it has been "*built up*" around this discovery. ⟨The reader will understand in what sense this is said.⟩ As the aim of the socialist movement is the abolition of exploitation of one social class by another—the proletariat by the bourgeoisie—*scientific* socialism became possible only from the time when science succeeded in defining the nature of class exploitation generally and, in particular, that form which it assumes in present-day society. Prior to this, socialism could not go beyond more or less vague strivings, and in its criticism of the prevailing system lacked the most important ingredient: an understanding of where lay the economic kernel of this system. The discovery of surplus value gave it this understanding. How great is the importance of this discovery is evidenced by the mere fact that the defenders of the existing order of things try with all their might to disprove its truth. The theory of marginal utility[12] is now meeting with a very cordial welcome from the bourgeois economists precisely because it envelops in a dense cloud the question of the exploitation of the worker by the capitalist and even throws doubt upon the very fact of this exploitation.* ⟨Therein lies the whole "scientific" meaning of this theory, the uselessness of which is far from marginal.⟩

But no matter how important the discovery of surplus value was in the history of socialism, scientific socialism would, nevertheless, have remained impossible if the abolition of the bourgeois relations of production and, consequently, the abolition of the exploitation of the proletariat by the bourgeoisie, had not been conceived as a historical necessity, conditioned by the whole process of contemporary economic development.

A few words more. Three chapters of the celebrated book, *Herrn Eugen Dührings Umwälzung der Wissenschaft [Anti-Dühring]*, devoted to a criticism of the Dühring "force theory" are, as in pre-

---

* When the English translation of Böhm-Bawerk's *Positive Theorie des Kapitals* was issued, the biggest of the British bourgeois newspapers, *The Times*, welcomed it as "the best antidote to the exploitation theories of the Marxist school". The bourgeois social system is in a state of decay. Parallel with this there is a decline in bourgeois science. In defending bourgeois social relations, the bourgeois theoreticians degrade themselves to the level of lower-grade sophists. ⟨We may note the following in passing: when Engels said that Marx *discovered* surplus value he did not mean that, in his opinion, no economist *before Marx* had had any idea on the subject. Not at all. Marx himself remarked in his *Zur Kritik der Politischen Ökonomie* that even the physiocrats[13] had tried to determine in which particular sphere of production surplus value was created. Marx collected much extremely valuable material for a history of the theories of surplus value. Part of this material has only just been published by Kautsky in a special book.[14] Marx *discovered* surplus value *in the sense that the long history of the theories of this value was finally completed in his economic theory*, freed from all unclarity and contradictions.⟩

vious editions of this book, published as an appendix to the present edition. These chapters contain, by the way, an outline of history of the art of war in the civilised states of modern times as well as an analysis of the causal connection of the development of this art with the economic development of society. These chapters may appear "one-sided" to people inclined to eclecticism. Such people will retort: "Not everything can be explained by economy." We consider it useful, therefore, to draw their attention to one book which owes its origin to *experts in military affairs*. It is entitled: *Les maîtres de la guerre. Frédéric II—Napoléon—Moltke. Essai critique d'après des travaux inédits de M. le général Bonnal par le Lt.-Colonel Rousset, professeur à l'Ecole supérieure de Guerre.* This interesting book deals with the same subject as that examined by Engels in the chapters mentioned above and it draws almost exactly the same conclusions. "The social conditions obtaining in each epoch of history," we read on page four, "exert a preponderant influence, not only on the military organisation of a nation but also on the character, the abilities, and the trends of the military men. Generals of the ordinary stamp make use of the familiar and accepted methods, and march on towards successes or reverses according to whether attendant circumstances are more or less favourable to them.... As for the great captains, these subordinate to their genius the means and procedures of warfare, or, to be more exact, guided by a kind of divinatory instinct, they transform the means and procedures in accordance with the parallel laws of a social evolution, whose decisive effect (and repercussion) on the technique of their art they alone understand in their day." This is by no means far from the materialist explanation of history, although the author has probably not got the slightest notion what that is. Surely if the development of the art of war is determined by social development and social development by economic development, it must follow that military technique, and not technique alone, but also the "character, the abilities, and the aspirations of military men" are determined, in the last analysis, by economic development. This conclusion, which has astonished so many, many "intellectuals" of every nationality by its "one-sidedness", would scarcely have frightened our military author, who, recognising that the development of military technique is determined by social development, also recognises at the same time that this development, in turn, is conditioned by "the progress of science, arts, and industry" (page 2). If he is not lacking in the ability to think consistently, and evidently he is not, it would be easy for him to understand the historical theory according to which *social* development is accomplished on the basis of *economic* development and economic development is determined *by the course of development of the productive forces.*

The historical essay on the art of war written by the same author from the unpublished materials of General Bonnal is extremely reminiscent of the essay on the same subject which Engels wrote in *Anti-Dühring*. Here and there the resemblance is so great, indeed, that one could presume that it had been borrowed, were this not precluded by the simple chronological fact that Engels' *Anti-Dühring* was published twenty-three years before Lt.-Colonel Rousset's book. It is just as unthinkable to imagine that Rousset (or General Bonnal) had borrowed from Engels. We may be sure that the works of the great German socialist were completely unknown to these learned French officers. The matter is very simply explained by the fact that Engels was an expert on military matters and a consistent thinker, able to apply the fundamental principles of his historical theory to the study of the most varied aspects of social life. Guided by these fundamental principles, he discerned that which, to quote Rousset, was discerned only by the greatest generals: the decisive impact of social evolution on the technique of war. This particular case proves convincingly that the materialist explanation of history, when correctly understood, does not lead to "*one-sidedness*", but broadens and sharpens the investigator's vision as nothing else could.

We should have liked to say something, too, about *dialectics and its relation to formal logic*. But lack of space compels us to put this off to another, more favourable, occasion. (That it would be useful to carry out this intention may be seen from those extremely vague conceptions of dialectics with which far too often even orthodox Marxists are satisfied. It must be admitted that in the polemics aroused by the "critical" efforts of Mr. Bernstein and Co., the majority of the orthodox Marxists proved to be weakest precisely in the defence of *dialectics*. This weakness must be eliminated; we are in duty bound to repulse decisively all the attacks of our enemies on our logical stronghold.)

SYNOPSIS OF LECTURE

"SCIENTIFIC SOCIALISM AND RELIGION"

1st Hour

The theme. It may appear to be somewhat abstract. It does not touch on even one of the urgent issues around which there is so much heated argument, so many swords are being broken and so much ink is flowing in the disputes between the various revolutionary parties, and within these, between the various shades of one and the same trend: neither the question of the proletariat and the peasantry, nor the attitude of the "Bund"[15] to the Party, nor the organisational question.

But I thought it worthwhile sometimes to dwell on abstract questions. Each of us will find it useful to pay attention to them; this will help each of us to become a *whole man* (Heine). Heine (Romantische Schule) says that Lessing was a whole man (*ein ganzer Mann*). Like another German writer, he compared him to those pious Jews who, while building the second temple of Jerusalem, repulsed their enemies with one hand and continued erecting the temple with the other. As far as we can, we must act in the same way; with one hand fight incessantly and tirelessly against our numerous enemies, beginning with those who arrest and imprison us, exile and shoot us (Yakutsk[16]) and ending with those who *more or less intentionally, more or less consciously, more or less systematically, distort our ideas*—and with the other hand we must try to bring together at least a few stones for the construction of our *theoretical* edifice. He who cannot extend it, must at least keep it in order. "Wissen ist Macht, Macht ist Wissen." This thought has encouraged me not to fear the abstract character of the theme. Besides, the question is not without practical significance.

In the year 1902, the editors of the journal *Mouvement socialiste* produced a whole enquête on the question of the attitude of the socialist parties of the various countries to *clericalism*.[17] This question is now becoming an important *practical* one for international socialism. And this *practical* question has an obvious and close connection with that *theoretical* question which you and I will examine this evening. This practical question is not yet on the order of the day for us in Russia; we still cannot influence legislation directly; but we have another practical question—the dissenters and sectarians. Religion means very much to them.

Terms: *Scientific Socialism, Religion*.

1. *Scientific socialism* I define as that socialism whose adherents are convinced of the future triumph of their ideal, not because it seems great and beautiful to them, but because the realisation of this ideal—which they undoubtedly consider both great and beautiful and react to with the greatest enthusiasm, as is recognised even by their enemies—because they are of the opinion that its realisation is being determined and prepared by the whole course of the internal development of contemporary, that is to say, *capitalist* society. Examples: a) ⟨communism,⟩ b) *international peace*. ⟨Stammler. Eclipse of the moon.⟩[18]

In explaining the course of social development, the adherents of scientific socialism adopt the standpoint of the *materialist explanation of history*. The *materialist explanation of history is its essential foundation*. What must we bear in mind of the principles of the materialist explanation of history? Not consciousness determines being, but being consciousness. The *mode of thought is determined by the mode of life*. The mode of life—by the economy.

All ideologies are, in the last analysis, the fruits of *economic development*. So too is *religion*. Example from the history of art: *bourgeois drama* in Britain and France. Religion. We shall see shortly how to understand this in its application to religion. Marx: *Der Mensch macht die Religion, nicht die Religion den Menschen*.[19]

2. *What is religion?* Derivation. *Religio—bond*. Some contest this derivation. In my opinion, it is very probable. Historically, religion can be considered as *having arisen* only when a bond between social man and certain powers is established: with *spirits* whose existence he acknowledges and who, in his opinion, can influence his destiny. Religion distinguishes man from animal. Yes, as the ability *to make mistakes*.

Animism. At the first stage of his development man ⟨imagined that the whole of nature was peopled by spirits⟩. He *personified* individual *phenomena* and *forces* of nature. Why? Because he judged these phenomena and forces *by analogy with himself*; the world appeared to him to be *animated*; he conceived *phenomena* to be the result of the activity of living creatures like himself, i.e., endowed with consciousness, will, needs, desires and passions. These living creatures are spirits. What is a spirit? Where did this conception come from? Dreams; fainting fits; death.

The world as perceived by primitive man is a realm of spirits. Spiritualism—primitive philosophy, *the savage's conception of the world*. Evaluation of the spirits: equal to him, lower, higher. He is afraid of the latter. He tries to win their favour by *bribes, gifts of sacrifice.*

Lucretius: *Primus in orbe deos fecit timor.* This is indisputable. although *not every frightening spirit is a god; the devil is terrifying* to the Russian peasant (the devil was terrifying even to Luther), *but the devil is not a god. What then is a god? A god is the spirit with whom the savage has established relations of moral dependence* (religio), I would say goodwill relations. The savage reveres the god; the god bestows patronage on the savage (The Old Testament —Abraham's Covenant with Jehovah). When such a covenant has been established, then there is a god. But—you ask—what has the *economy* to do with it? Well, listen. The fact is that every stage of *economic* development has its own distinct conception of the role of the god. Example: Jupiter. Primitive communist society—mutual guarantee; individualistic society—punishment after death. The conception of immortality as understood by contemporary Christians is the outcome of prolonged historical development. Another example: Jupiter (Zeus), *daylight, clear skies*; with the development of cattle-breeding and agriculture his god is the giver of fertility and abundance (*Liber*) ⟨in his honour, feasts of the gathering of the grapes⟩, the patron of agriculture; with the development of intercourse, protector of covenants—*Deus Fidius.* He becomes the guardian of frontiers, property (Juppiter Terminus) and so forth.

In the measure that social relations develop, these relations and the abstract concepts arising from them are deified: Fides, Concordia, Virtus and so on.

Now we know that there are two elements in religion: 1) a conception of the world, 2) social morality. This conception of the world is the conception of the ignoramus. It is founded upon ignorance. But the boundaries of the *unknown* shrink with the broadening out of *experience, with the increase of man's power over nature*; when man *is able to influence nature without player*, by *technical influence*, he *ceases to pray.* Auguste Comte's remark about the god of gravity. *Put your trust in God, but keep your powder dry.* Here are two elements: God and Self. *The Australian Bishop* refusing to pray for rain: no trust in God here, only keep your powder dry. But does the Bishop also believe? Of course: 1) there is much in nature he still does not know; 2) the social relations themselves are mysterious and obscure to him.

When will the need for religion disappear? *When man feels himself master of nature and his own social relations.*

Conclusions from the *Ramayana.* A holy and wise anchorite— one of those who inhabit the deserts of India in great numbers— once prayed to the god Indra. But the capricious god would not listen to him; the prayer, ascending to heaven from the pure heart of the pious man, returned without having achieved the desired results. The holy man then became angry with Indra and rebelled against him. He brought to bear all the holiness he had "accumulated by his innumerable sacrifices and prolonged self-tortures", and felt himself stronger than Indra. He in turn began to command the heavens. At his command, new stars were born. He himself became a *creator*. He wished even to create new and *better* gods. Indra took fright, granted the will of the holy man and peace was restored. The history of mankind is partly similar to this from the religious aspect. But only partly. First of all, it is *not holiness* that men have accumulated, but now *knowledge, power over nature* and—with time—over their own social relations. And the time will come when this knowledge will be sufficient for there to be no need of Indra. Mankind will manage without God. But no matter how much God takes fright, man will not conclude peace with him; *poor Indra will be irrevocably doomed to die*. There are no better gods, they are all bad, there are only some less bad than others ⟨Schopenhauer⟩, Engels.[20]

"We want to sweep away everything that claims to be supernatural and superhuman.... For that reason we have once and for all declared war on religion and religious ideas...."[21]

BUT MORALITY?

"We have no need, in order ... to recognise the development of the human species through history, its irresistible progress, its ever-certain victory over the unreason of the individual, ... its hard but successful struggle against nature until the final achievement of free, human self-consciousness, the discernment of the unity of man and nature, and the independent creation—voluntarily and by its own effort—of a new world based on purely human and moral social relationships—in order to recognise all that in its greatness, we have no need first to summon up the abstraction of a 'God' and to attribute to it everything beautiful, great, sublime and truly human; we do not need to follow this roundabout path, we do not need first to imprint the stamp of the 'divine' on what is truly human, in order to be sure of its greatness and splendour. On the contrary, the 'more divine', in other words, the more inhuman, something is, the less we shall be able to admire it.... The more 'godly' they are, the more inhuman...."[22]

2nd Hour

The primitive religious notion has two elements: 1) a philosophical element, a *conception of the world*, 2) a *social-moral* element. There is no doubt that *experience* ousts the first element of religion. As an explanation of *phenomema*, reference to *God* is untenable. But some people, believing in religion, or desiring to live at peace with it, have allotted the other sphere to it. Spencer, Kant, our neo-Kantians.

1. *The unknowable.* We do not know that which is inaccessible to our senses. There will always be *an unknown.* But why shall we *deify* it? It will be a subject of hypotheses but not of religious *worship.* Spencer calls *religious thought* that which studies what is inaccessible to our *senses.* But this is partly *science,* or, if you will, philosophy. The moon, etc.

Man, says Spencer, will always feel himself to be in the presence of *infinite and eternal energy,* the source of all being. Of course, but why must man *endow* this infinite energy, this source of all being, *with personality?* On what basis will he isolate it from nature and place it above nature? But only on this condition can it become an object of religious worship.

Kant. Religion—die Erkenntnis aller unserer Pflichten als göttlicher Gebote. Die Moral in Beziehung auf Gott als Gesetzgeber (K. d. Urth. § 89). But morality is not identical with *religion.* Historical reference: Morality *united* with religion; it will also separate from religion. Lastly, morality is a question of *social estates, of classes, of mankind,* but not of the *world.* It is a question of *humanity* rather than of the *universe.* Bulgakov[23] and Smerdyakov[24]. To Bulgakov: you feel the need for God because your ghosts are inordinately strong, as the witch Wittichen says in Hauptmann's play.[25] This is *lack of moral development.* *"Marxism will not prove that I must serve the working class".* No. And it is not necessary. *Feeling does not require proof.* Sonate, que me veux tu?[26] *Ni dieu, ni maître.*[27]

PSYCHOLOGY OF RELIGION

Here Feuerbach's analysis remains true to the present day. Religion *deprives* man and nature of their best properties and attributes these to God.

ENGELS

"Religion by its very essence drains man and nature of substance, and transfers this substance to the phantom of the other-worldly God, who in turn then graciously permits man and nature to receive some of his superfluity."[28]

Once we have understood *the secret of this draining* we cannot conscientiously abandon ourselves to it.

QUELCH

"The Church is one of the pillars of capitalism and the true function of the clergy is to chloroform the workers to make them docile wage-slaves, patient and contented with their lot in this world while expecting a glorious reward in the next. As long as the Church holds the minds of the workers in its grip, there will be little hope of freeing their bodies from capitalist domination."

The way out: Rückkehr, nicht zu Gott, sondern zu sich selbst.[29]

Marx—the abolition of religion as the illusory happiness of the people is required for their real happiness. See quotations.[30]

MARX [I]

"The criticism of religion is ... in embryo the criticism of the vale of tears, the halo of which is religion.

"Criticism has torn up the imaginary flowers from the chain not so that man shall wear the unadorned, bleak chain but so that he will shake off the chain and pluck the living flower."

MARX [II]

"The criticism of religion disillusions man to make him think and act and shape his reality like a man who has been disillusioned and has come to reason, so that he will revolve round himself and therefore round his true sun."

"*Religion is a private affair.*" There can be no peace with religion, as there can be no peace with error. Schopenhauer. Our attitude to the dissenters: religion is a private matter. But we retain the right to struggle against the *religious* idea and supplant it with the *scientific*.

Social-Democracy must, to use a well-known expression, snatch from *tyrants* their *sceptres* and from *heaven* its *fire*.

NOTES DURING THE DISCUSSION
OF THE REPORT

KHARAZOV

Formulation of the question.

1) G. Kharazov's bewilderment. *My definition.* If we are to agree with him, we must admit that the question of religion is finished. The existence of God cannot be proved. He considers my ideas common to all people. Very glad!

The religious question is not reduced to the existence of a deity. The concept of god had its own evolution. Many people use the word god while not sharing the superstitious idea of god as a personality.

Remark. The origin of religion. Allegedly I began from the etymological definition of the word religion. That again is *Cicero*. False. I said and *proved* that it is *right*. I pointed to the development of religious conceptions. Then I indicated Spencer, Kant, for whom religion is a moral world system. Deity is not God. And what is it? A pity *you did not say*. Historical remarks. *Mutual guarantee* before God. My idea is original but not proved. The story of Alcibiades. Allegedly I said that Alcibiades, etc. Where did I get it from, etc.

History of Egypt. Personal responsibility there. Yes, but what of that? Probably it can be explained by theocratic organisation.

Abraham and Sarah—head of tribe.

Kant. He is surprised at comparing of Kant and Berdayev. Not Berdayev, but Bulgakov. Kant: the idea of God is a regulative idea. With Kant, God is not a personality but an idea. I am supposed to have distorted Kant's argument. No, I indicated his two *Critiques*,[31] quoting almost his own words. I am supposed to have said that the Westphalian miners are Kantians. Never said anything of the kind. How does that follow?

VOLSKY[32]

Social-Democracy will not be able to combat concealed religious aspirations. But the examination of religion in concealed form is beyond the scope of scientific socialism. Religious people penetrate the ranks of Social-Democracy. I said too little about religion being founded on the conservative aspirations of the ruling classes. Good; I shall repeat: Social-Democracy cannot protect the proletariat from the intrigues of the ruling classes. For scientific socialism itself is not rid of religious conceptions. Proof. *First of May*. The workers' assembly on May First is a religious event. Why? We think of the time when there will be neither rich nor poor. No, it is not so. There is no religion here.

Bourgeois property cannot be attacked today. Only our descendants can do this. And you? Why don't you attack? The business of socialism is to propagate the future system and not to attack the present one. If we follow up, etc., at first the time of the socialist revolution seems very near, but later it has to be postponed further and further. The "real acquisition" of scientific socialism—the masses convinced of the triumph of socialism. The working class already *values* bourgeois progress. Changes in the matter of attacking bourgeois property and religion appear with special clarity in Russia. There the working class is accomplishing the bourgeois revolution. This means that it is strengthening and not demolishing the house of bondage. We see the same in Poland. The question arises: where is there even a trace of a religious basis in scientific socialism? The religious basis is found in scientific socialism itself.

What is the basis of religious sentiments? The fact that in the contemporary system of human bondage, mankind will unite and strive towards a common goal. The same in the bourgeoisie. It is absolutely essential to unite the bourgeoisie and the proletariat for the attack on the autocracy. No, we are not uniting. Apparently, Mr. Volsky calls anything that does not please him religion. But that is too sweeping.

First work of creating religious fiction—point to the economy. We conceive society as a united whole. No, *we speak of the struggle of classes*.

Collaboration and slavery. What is our attitude to this? Providence, creating slavery as a step towards socialism.

In place of scientific socialism? Social-Democracy did nothing but refashion the revolutionary movement of the working class into collaboration with other classes. Antagonism of the working masses to scientific socialism *will manifest itself*. I make so bold as to pronounce this a *religious prophecy*. Religious prediction which is based on no one knows what.

Not enough to attack only the class of capitalists but all society. Rupture with the intelligentsia. Expropriation of all bourgeois society. Family right, according to which some are born with property and others propertyless.

AKIMOV

My position. Akimov differs from me on the formulation of the question. Social-Democracy for me is something unitary. I spoke not about Social-Democracy but about *Marxism*, about *scientific socialism*. According to Akimov, Marx and Engels do not exhaust the whole of scientific socialism. Let's assume that. But show me what exactly. Opinions of Vandervelde as a representative of scientific socialism. Is Vandervelde a Marxist? He has said so himself more than once.

Typical feature of my views. I did not give a solution for the problems facing us. That is exactly what Bulgakov said. I do not give one either. But why did you not name the problems that apparently face us?

Windelband, and not only primitive man, takes his stand on religion.

What motive compels us to act thus and not otherwise? This....

TRANSLATOR'S PREFACE TO THE SECOND EDITION OF F. ENGELS'
LUDWIG FEUERBACH AND THE END OF CLASSICAL GERMAN PHILOSOPHY

Much water has flowed under the bridges since the first Russian edition of this pamphlet appeared. In the Preface to that edition, I said that the triumphant reactionaries in our country were donning philosophical robes and that for the struggle against this reaction the Russian socialists would inevitably have to study philosophy. My premonition was entirely confirmed by subsequent events. The Russian socialists—and I had and have in mind the Social-Democrats—had indeed to take up philosophy. But as they took it up very late and, to use a popular expression, were not exactly *pulling together*, the results have not been particularly gratifying. At times one almost regretted that books on philosophy had ever fallen into the hands of our Comrades, because they were unable to take a critical attitude to the authors they were studying and finished by themselves falling under the influence of these authors. Since contemporary philosophy, not only in Russia but in the West too, bears the imprint of reaction, its reactionary content found its way into the heads of revolutionaries giving rise to the utmost confusion which sometimes received the bombastic title of *criticism of Marx* and sometimes bore the more modest name of *combination of Marxism* with the philosophical views of one or other of the bourgeois ideologists (neo-Kantians, Mach, Avenarius, and others). There is not the slightest doubt that *Marxism* can be combined with anything, even with *spiritualism*; the whole question is *how* this may be done. Even the least intelligent person cannot answer this otherwise than by pointing to *eclecticism*. With the aid of eclecticism one may "combine" anything with everything that comes into one's head. But eclecticism never produced anything good either in theory or in practice. Fichte said: "To philosophise means not to act; to act means not to philosophise", and this is quite true. However, it is no less true to say that only a consistently thinking person is capable of being consistent in his activity. And for us who claim the honour to represent the most revolutionary class that has at any time appeared on the historical scene, consistency is obligatory under pain of treachery to our cause.

What is behind the desire to combine Marxism now with one, now with another of the bourgeois ideologies?

First of all *fashion*.

Nekrasov says about one of his heroes:

> *What the latest book tells him*
> *Lies upmost in his heart.*

Such heroes can always be found; they make their way into every camp. Unfortunately, we meet them in ours too.

We had a crop of them in the second half of the nineties, when for many and many of our "intellectuals" the "latest book" lying "upmost in the heart" was Marxism itself. It seemed as though such "intellectuals" had been deliberately created by history in order to promote the "combination" of Marxism with other "latest books".[33] We have no regrets for them; they were empty-headed people anyway.

But it is a pity that more serious Comrades, too, often feel the urge to "combine". The explanation here is not the craze for fashion. Here we have something which, though very harmful and regrettable in itself, reveals the presence of good intentions.

Imagine that a particular Comrade feels the need to work out for himself an orderly world-outlook; this Comrade has mastered— more or less well—the philosophical-*historical* aspect of Marx's teaching, but the strictly *philosophical* aspect of this teaching is still obscure and inaccessible to him. In the circumstances, he decides that this aspect of Marx's teaching has still *not* been "*worked out*", and he sets about "*working it out*" himself. When he is engaged on this—not very easy—task, some representative of bourgeois "criticism" turns up and appears to bring at least a little semblance of order where nothing but chaos had hitherto seemed to prevail. Our inquisitive Comrade, who is inadequately prepared and insufficiently independent in his search for philosophical truth, easily succumbs to the influence of this bourgeois "critic". And lo, we have a ready-made "combiner". His intentions were good, but they turned out badly.

No, whatever our opponents may say, one thing is indisputable: the efforts to "combine" the theory of Marx with other theories which, to use a German expression, are a slap in the face for that theory, reveal a striving to achieve an orderly world-outlook, but at the same time they expose a *weakness of thought, an inability strictly and consistently to adhere to one fundamental principle*. In other words, an inability to comprehend Marx.

How can one help this sad state of affairs? I do not see any other way than to disseminate the correct view of the philosophy of

Marx and Engels. And in this respect, I think the present pamphlet can do very much.

More than once I myself have heard the question: why cannot historical materialism be combined with the transcendental idealism of Kant, the empirio-criticism of Avenarius, the philosophy of Mach, and so on? I have always replied to this in almost the same terms I shall use now. As regards Kant, my comments (see page 95) show how it is utterly impossible to "combine" the philosophical doctrine of Kant with the theory of development.[34] The views of Mach and Avenarius, which are the latest variety of Hume's philosophy, are no more capable of being combined with the theory of development than is Kant's philosophy. To hold consistently those views is to arrive at *solipsism*, that is to say, to a denial of the existence of all people apart from oneself. Don't think we are joking, reader. Although Mach protests energetically against the identification of his philosophy with Berkeley's* subjective idealism, he thereby demonstrates only his own inconsistency. If bodies or things are only mental symbols of our sensations (more exactly, of groups, complexes of sensations) and if they do not exist outside our consciousness—and such is Mach's theory—subjective idealism and solipsism can be rejected only by means of a howling inconsistency. It is not for nothing that one of Mach's pupils, G. Cornelius, in his book *Einleitung in die Philosophie*, München, 1903, comes close to solipsism. He states (page 322) that science cannot, either affirmatively or negatively, resolve for man the question: is there any kind of psychical life apart from one's own? This is incontestable from the point of view of Machism; but if I still have doubts about the existence of psychical life alien to myself, if, as we have seen, bodies generally are only the symbols of sensations, all that remains is to become reconciled to solipsism, which, however, Cornelius does not venture to do.

It should be said that Mach does not consider Cornelius to be a pupil of his, but of Avenarius. This is not surprising, since there is very much in common between the views of Mach on one hand and Avenarius on the other, as Mach himself admits.** The question which Fichte described as the *plurality of individuals* is the major difficulty both for the philosophy of Avenarius and the philosophy of Mach and one which neither can cope with otherwise than by admitting the truth of materialism or landing in the impasse of solipsism. This must be obvious to every thinking person who takes the trouble to read, for instance, Avena-

* *Die Analyse der Empfindungen*, vierte Ausgabe, S. 282-83.
** See, in the above-mentioned book, the chapter headed "Mein Verhältnis zu R. Avenarius und anderen Forschern", p. 38.

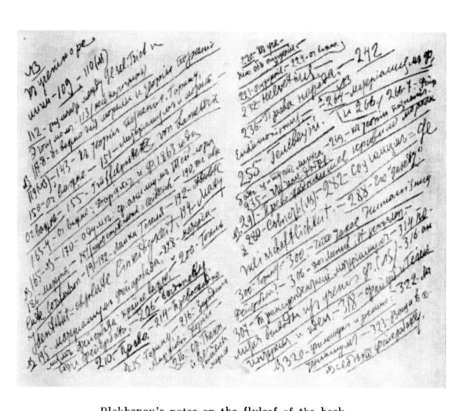

Plekhanov's notes on the flyleaf of the book,
Ludwig Feuerbach's Collected Works, new edition, Vol. X

rius' *The Human Concept of the World** of which a Russian translation has been published.

It is self-evident that only a follower of Poprishchin[35] could
"combine" solipsism with any other (not only the materialist)
view of history.

The contemporary theory of development, of which our own
explanation of history is a part, finds firm ground for itself *only*
in materialism; and it is no wonder, therefore, that the founders
of scientific socialism *took materialism seriously*, as Engels expressed it, applying it consistently in all the branches of
knowledge which had hitherto been the strongholds of idealism.

And please note that it is not only *scientific* socialism which
is closely linked with materialism. *Utopian* socialism, which liked
to flirt with idealism and even with religion, must also be recognised as a legitimate offspring of materialism, as is clear from the
first appendix to this pamphlet (*Karl Marx on French Materialism
of the 18th Century*).[36]

"Just as *Cartesian* materialism passes into *natural science proper*,
the other trend of French materialism leads directly to *socialism*
and *communism*.

"There is no need for any great penetration to see from the
teaching of materialism on the original goodness and equal intellectual endowment of men, the omnipotence of experience, habit
and education, and the influence of environment on man, the great
significance of industry, the justification of enjoyment, etc., how
necessarily materialism is connected with communism and socialism. If man draws all his knowledge, sensation, etc., from the
world of the senses and the experience gained in it, then what has
to be done is to arrange the empirical world in such a way that
man experiences and becomes accustomed to what is truly human
in it and that he becomes aware of himself as man. If correctly
understood interest is the principle of all morality, man's private
interest must be made to coincide with the interest of humanity.
If man is unfree in the materialistic sense, i.e., is free not through
the negative power to avoid this or that, but through the positive
power to assert his true individuality, crime must not be punished
in the individual, but the anti-social sources of crime must be
destroyed, and each man must be given social scope for the vital
manifestation of his being. If man is shaped by environment,
his environment must be made human. If man is social by nature,
he will develop his true nature only in society, and the power

---

* One German writer remarks that for empirio-criticism *experience* is
only an object of investigation and not a means of knowledge. If this
is right, there is no point in opposing empirio-criticism to materialism, and
to argue whether it is destined to replace materialism is a sheer waste
of time.

of his nature must be measured not by the power of the separate individual but by the power of society.

"These and similar propositions are to be found almost literally even in the oldest French materialists."[37]

Marx then goes on to reveal the kinship of the various utopian schools of France and Britain with materialism.

However, those who are endeavouring to "combine" Marxism with this or that variety of more or less consistent idealism pay not the slightest attention to all this. And it is unfortunate, the more so indeed that "there is no need for any great penetration" to grasp the thorough inconsistency of all these attempts at combination.

But how should one understand *materialism*? Right to the present day people are still arguing a lot about it. Engels says: "Thus the question of the relation of thinking to being—the paramount question of the whole of philosophy—has, no less than all religion, its roots in the narrow-minded and ignorant notions of savagery. But this question could for the first time be put forward in its whole acuteness, could achieve its full significance, only after humanity in Europe had awakened from the long hibernation of the Christian Middle Ages. The question of the position of thinking in relation to being, a question which, by the way, had played a great part also in the scholasticism of the Middle Ages, the question: which is primary, spirit or nature—that question, in relation to the church, was sharpened into this: Did God create the world or has the world been in existence eternally?

"The answers which the philosophers gave to this question split them into two great camps. Those who asserted the primacy of spirit to nature and, therefore, in the last instance, assumed world creation in some form or other—and among the philosophers, Hegel, for example, this creation often becomes still more intricate and impossible than in Christianity—comprised the camp of idealism. The others, who regarded nature as primary, belong to the various schools of materialism.

"These two expressions, idealism and materialism, originally signify nothing else but this; and here too they are not used in any other sense. What confusion arises when some other meaning is put into them will be seen below."[38]

Thus the most important distinguishing feature of materialism is that it does away with the *dualism of spirit and matter, god and nature*, and deems nature to be the basis of all those phenomena which the primitive hunting tribes could not explain without reference to the activity of *souls, spirits*. To the opponents of materialism, who for the most part have only the most absurd notions of it, it seems that Engels wrongly defined the essence of materialism and that, in fact, materialism *reduces psychic phe-*

nomena to material phenomena. This is why they were greatly surprised when, in my dispute with Mr. Bernstein, I listed *Spinoza* among the materialists. But for proof of the correctness of Engels' definition of materialism, suffice it to quote some extracts from the writings of the eighteenth-century materialists.

"Let us not go beyond the confines of nature (demeurons dans la nature) when we wish to apprehend natural phenomena," says the author of the celebrated work *Le bon sens puisé dans la nature* (Holbach), "and let us ignore causes that are too subtle to act upon our senses;* let us be convinced that by going beyond the confines of nature we shall never solve the problems nature places before us."**

Holbach expresses himself in exactly the same way in another, better known work, *Système de la nature*, which I shall not quote precisely because it is better known. I shall be content to indicate that the passage dealing with the question we are interested in will be found in Chapter 6 of Volume II of this work (page 146 of the London 1781 edition).

Helvétius held the same point of view. "Man," he said, "is the work of nature; he is in nature; he is governed by its laws; he cannot free himself from it; he cannot go outside it even in thought.... For a being formed by nature, nothing exists outside the great whole of which he himself is a part.... Beings supposed to be above nature and distinct from it are chimeras," and so forth.***

True, there have been materialists who acknowledged the existence of God and regarded nature as his creation. One of these was Joseph Priestley.**** But the celebrated naturalist's faith was a simple theological appendage to his materialist teaching, the basic principle of which was the conception that man is the creation of nature and that "the corporeal and mental faculties inherent in the same substance, grow, ripen, and decay together".***** This substance is *matter*, as Priestley repeats more than once in this and others of his works.*)

Feuerbach justly remarks that the substance which Spinoza refers to theologically as God, on closer examination (bei Lichte besehen), proves to be nature.**) This is just as true as another

---

* Note that Holbach calls everything that acts on our senses matter.
** I am quoting from the Paris edition of "the first year of the Republic".
*** "Le vrai sens du système de la nature", Chapter I of *De la Nature*.
**** See his *Disquisitions Relating to Matter and Spirit*, in Vol. I of the Birmingham edition, 1782. There God is declared to be "our Maker" (p. 139), the "All in all" (p. 143), and so on.
***** Ibid., p. 69.
*) "Matter being capable of the property of sensation or thought" (*The History of the Philosophical Doctrine Concerning the Origin of the Soul...*— in the first volume of the same edition of his *Works*, p. 400).
**) *Werke*, IV. Band, S. 380.

of Feuerbach's remarks: "The secret, the true meaning of Spinoza's philosophy is Nature."* This is precisely why Spinoza, in spite of the theological covering to his fundamental philosophical conception, must be considered a materialist. This was appreciated by Diderot who, as may be seen from his article "Spinosiste", in Volume 15 of the *Encyclopédie*, counted himself and those who held similar views as modern Spinozists (spinosistes modernes). When "Marx's critics" uttered their unanimous gasp of surprise at the declaration I made in the course of my debate with Mr. Bernstein that the materialism of Marx and Engels was a kind of Spinozism (eine Art Spinosismus), they were simply betraying their own amazing ignorance.** To be able to grasp this thought more easily, one should, first, remember that Marx and Engels passed through Feuerbach's philosophy and, secondly, try to elucidate what exactly it is that distinguishes Feuerbach's philosophy from Spinoza's. Anyone who can understand the above will soon see that in his basic view on the relation of being to thinking, Feuerbach is Spinoza who has ceased to call nature god and has been through Hegel's school.

Let us go on. If, as we have seen, Priestley taught that matter is capable of *sensation* and *thought*, it is clear from this that *materialism in no way tries to reduce all psychical phenomena to the motion of matter*, as its adversaries contend.*** To the materialist, sensation and thought, consciousness, are the internal state of matter in motion. But none of the materialists who have left their mark on the history of philosophical thought has ever "*reduced*" consciousness to *motion*, or *explained* one by the other. When the materialists maintained that there is no need to devise a special substance—the soul—to explain psychical phenomena, and that matter is capable of "sensation and thought", this property of matter seemed to them just as basic and therefore inexplicable as motion. Thus, for example, La Mettrie, whose teaching is usually described as the most crude variety of materialism, stated categorically that he considered motion to be the same "mystery of nature" as consciousness.**** Besides, different materialists had different views of matter's ability to possess consciousness. Some of them, for example, Priestley and, apparently, Holbach (who did not, however, express himself quite definitely) believed that consciousness arises in moving matter only in those cases where

---

* Ibid., p. 391.
** I was asked by objection: what does *a kind of* Spinozism mean. This is easy to answer: In Marx and Engels as well as in Diderot, Spinozism was freed of its theological exterior. That is all.
*** See, for example, Lasswitz, *Die Lehre Kant's von der Idealität des Raumes und der Zeit*, Berlin, 1883, S. 9.
**** *Oeuvres philosophiques de Monsieur de La-Mettrie*, Amsterdam, MDCCLXIV, tome premier, pp. 69 et 73.

it is organised in a certain fashion. Others—Spinoza, La Mettrie, Diderot—thought that matter always possesses consciousness, although it only reaches a significant degree of intensity when organised in a certain way. The celebrated Haeckel is now known to hold this view. As to the general question of whether matter has the ability to "think", hardly any conscientious naturalist would place himself in difficulty by answering it negatively. The "agnostic" Huxley wrote in his book on Hume: "Surely no one who is cognisant of the facts of the case, nowadays, doubts that the roots of psychology lie in the physiology of the nervous system."* This is exactly what the materialists say and Engels is perfectly correct in this pamphlet when he calls agnosticism simply shamefaced materialism. Contemporary psycho-physiology is thoroughly saturated with the spirit of materialism. True, some psycho-physiologists evade having to draw materialist conclusions by relying on the doctrine of *concomitance* of psychical and physical phenomena. But in this case, the stating of concomitance is but a means of discovering the causal connection of phenomena, as was expounded already by Alexander Bain.**

Now let us consider another aspect of the matter. The philosophy of Marx and Engels is not just a *materialist* philosophy. It is *dialectical materialism*. It is objected to this teaching, firstly, that dialectics will not stand criticism and, secondly, that materialism is incompatible with dialectics. Let us consider these objections.

The reader will no doubt remember that Mr. Bernstein attributed what he called the errors of Marx and Engels to the harmful influence of dialectics. There is a formula in common logic: "yea— yea and nay—nay". Dialectics transforms this into its direct opposite: "yea—nay and nay—yea". Mr. Bernstein did not like this latter "formula" and declared that it could lead one into the most dangerous logical temptations and errors. And probably the great majority of so-called educated readers agreed with him, since the formula: "yea—nay and nay—yea" evidently contradicts sharply the basic, fixed laws of thought. We shall have to examine this aspect of the matter here.

There are said to be three "basic laws of thought": 1) the law of identity; 2) the law of contradiction; 3) the law of excluded middle.

The law of identity (principium identitatis) runs: A is A (omne subjectum est predicatum sui) or, otherwise, A equals A.

The law of contradiction—A is not non-A —is only the negative form of the first law.

---

* See p. 181 of the French translation of this book [*Thomas Hume*, by T. H. Huxley, London, 1879, p. 80].

** *Mind and Body*, Russian translation of the 6th English edition, Kiev, 1884, pp. 24-25.

According to the law of excluded middle (principium exclusi tertii) two contradictory propositions excluding one another cannot both be wrong. Indeed, A is either B or non-B; the truth of one of the propositions unerringly signifies the falsity of the other and vice versa. There is not and cannot be a middle here.

Überweg remarks that the law of contradiction and the law of excluded middle can be combined in the following rule of logic: *each fully defined question—always understood in the same fully defined sense—of whether a particular predicate belongs to a particular subject must be answered either yea or nay and cannot be answered both yea and nay.** It is difficult to raise any objection to the truth of this rule. But if it is true, then the formula *"yea—nay* and *nay—yea"* seems altogether unsound; we can only ridicule it like Mr. Bernstein, and throw up our hands in dismay as to why such undoubtedly profound thinkers as Heraclitus, Hegel, and Marx could find it more satisfactory than the formula *"yea—yea* and *nay—nay"* which has a firm basis in the above-mentioned basic laws of thought.

This conclusion, a fatal one for dialectics, is apparently irrefutable. But before we accept it, let us consider another aspect of the matter.

The basis of all natural phenomena is matter in motion.** But what is motion? It is an obvious contradiction. If you were asked: is a body in motion in a given place at a given time, even with the best intentions in the world you would not be able to reply according to Überweg's rule, i.e., the formula *"yea—yea* and *nay—nay"*. A body in motion *is* in a given place and *at the same time is not in it.**** It can be judged only by the formula *"yea—nay* and *nay—yea."* It is therefore an irrefutable witness in favour of the *"logic of contradiction,"* and he who refuses to be reconciled

---

* *System der Logik*, Bonn, 1874, S. 219.

** I am speaking of the *objective* side of phenomena. "Une volition est, pour le cerveau, un mouvement d'un certain système de fibres. Dans l'âme c'est ce qu'elle éprouve en conséquence du mouvement des fibres..." (Robinet, *De la Nature*, t. I, ch. XXIII, partie IV). [For the brain, volition is the movement of a certain system of fibres; in the soul it is what it feels as a result of the movement of the fibres.] Cf. Feuerbach's: "Was für mich oder subjectiv ein rein geistiger ... Akt, ist *an sich* oder objectiv ein materieller, sinnlicher" (*Werke*, II, 350). [What for me or subjectively is a purely spiritual act..., is in itself or objectively a material sentient act.]

*** Even the most decided opponents of the dialectical method were compelled to recognise this. "Die Bewegung," says A. Trendelenburg, "die vermöge ihres Begriffs an demselben Punkte zugleich ist und nicht ist." (*Logische Untersuchungen*, Leipzig, 1870, 1, 189). [Motion, which by virtue of its own concept is and is not simultaneously at one and the same point.] It is almost superfluous to remark here, as Überweg has already done, that Trendelenburg should have said *"matter in motion"* rather than *"motion"*.

to this logic must declare along with the ancient Zeno that motion is no more than an illusion of the senses. This is evidently not understood by our compatriot Mr. N. G., who is also a very firm opponent of dialectics but, unfortunately, not a very serious one. He says that if a body in motion, with *all* its parts, "is in one place, its simultaneous presence in another place is a manifest appearance out of nothing, for whence could it get to another place? From the first place? But the body has still not left the first place." But, he continues, if we assume that the body *with not all* its parts is in a given place at a given time, do not the different parts of a body which is at rest also occupy different places in space?*

Very good, though very old. However, what do Mr. N. G.'s arguments prove? *They prove that motion is impossible.* Splendid; here, too, we shall not argue, but we remind Mr. N. G. of Aristotle's remark which is daily and invariably justified by natural science, that by negating motion we make all study of nature impossible.** Was that what Mr. N. G. wanted? Was that the wish of the "literary monthly" which printed his profound work? If neither one nor the other wished to negate motion, they should have understood that by warming up the "aporia" of Zeno they left themselves with no alternative but to recognise that motion is contradiction in action, that is to say, to admit precisely what Mr. N. G. wanted to refute. Well, some "critics"!

However, we ask all those who do not deny motion: what should we think of that *"basic law" of thought* which contradicts the *basic fact of being?* Should we not approach it ... with some circumspection?

It looks as if we are now faced with an unexpected choice: *either* to acknowledge the "basic laws" of formal logic and negate motion, *or*, on the contrary, to acknowledge motion and negate those laws. It is a rather unpleasant choice. Is there no way round it?

Matter in motion lies at the basis of all natural phenomena. Motion is contradiction. It must be judged dialectically, that is to say, as Mr. Bernstein would put it, by the formula: *"yea—nay* and *nay—yea".* Therefore we must admit that so long as we are speaking about this basis of all phenomena, we are in the domain of *"the logic of contradiction".* But the molecules of matter in motion, joining one with the other, form certain *combinations,* things, objects. Such combinations are distinguished by the greater or lesser degree of their stability, exist for a more or less prolonged period, and then pass away, with others taking their place: only the motion of matter is eternal, while matter itself is the indestructible substance. But once a certain temporary combination of

---

* "Materialism and Dialectical Logic", *Russkoye Bogatstvo,*[39] July 1898, pp. 94 and 96.
** *Metaphysics,* I, VII, 59.

matter has taken place as the result of its eternal motion, and as
long as that combination has not yet passed away in consequence
of this motion, we have to resolve the question of its existence
in the affirmative. So that if someone points at the planet Venus
and asks if it exists, we shall say without hesitation: *yes*. And if
we are then asked: do witches exist, we should just as resolutely
reply: *no*. What does this mean? It means that when we are speaking about individual objects we are obliged to judge them according to Überweg's above-mentioned rule and generally be guided
by the "basic laws" of thought. *This* domain is governed by Mr.
Bernstein's favourite formula: "*yea—yea* and *nay—nay*."*

Nonetheless, even here the powers of that worthy formula are
not unlimited. A definite answer must be given to the question of
the existence of an object *already in being*. But if this object is
as yet only coming into being, one might sometimes be justified
in hesitating to answer. When half of a man's hair has fallen
out we may say he is bald. But just try to determine exactly at
what point falling hair becomes baldness.

Every definite question as to whether a particular property is
part of a particular object must be answered *either yea or nay*.
That is indisputable. But how should one reply where the object
is changing, when it *is already shedding* the particular property
or *is still only acquiring it*? Needless to say, a definite
answer is demanded here too; but the point is that it will
be definite only if it is based on the formula "*yea—nay* and *nay—
yea*". It is impossible to answer the question according to the
Überweg formula: "*either yea or nay*".

Of course, it may be objected that the property *being shed* has
not *yet* ceased to exist, and the property *being acquired already*
exists, and therefore it is possible and obligatory to give a definite answer according to the formula "*either yea or nay*", even when
the object is in a *state of change*. However, this is wrong. The young
man on whose chin "down" has appeared is certainly beginning
to grow a beard, but this still does not give us the right to call
him bearded. Down on the chin is not yet a beard, although it is
changing into a beard. To become *qualitative* a change must reach

---

* *Historical judgments* of the kind, as indicated by Überweg (in *Logik*, 196):
was Plato born in the year 429, or 428, or 427 B.C. must also be answered
according to this formula. This reminds me of the amusing reply made by
a young Russian revolutionary who arrived in Geneva, if I am not mistaken,
in 1882. He had to give the police some information about himself. "Where
were you born?" asked the friend who was arranging the matter, the late
N. 1. Zhukovsky. "In various gubernias," replied the overcautious "conspirator" evasively. Zhukovsky flared up and exclaimed: "Nobody will believe
that, my friend!" And here even the most zealous advocate of the dialectical
method would agree with him.

a certain *quantitative limit*. Whoever forgets this loses precisely the power to express *definite* judgments on the properties of objects.

"Everything is fluid, everything changes," said the ancient Ephesian thinker. The combinations we call objects are in a state of constant—more or less rapid—*change*. In so far as the combinations concerned remain *particular combinations*, we must judge them by the formula "*yea—yea* and *nay—nay*". But in so far as they *change* and *cease to exist* as such we must turn to the *logic of contradiction*; we must declare, while risking the disapproval of Messrs Bernstein, N. G., and others of their metaphysical brethren: "*Both yea and nay; they exist and they do not exist*."

Just as rest is a particular case of motion, so thought, according to the rules of formal logic (conforming to the "basic laws" of thought) is a particular case of dialectical thought.

It was said of Cratylus, one of Plato's teachers, that he did not agree even with Heraclitus who had declared: "We cannot enter the same stream twice." Cratylus asserted that we cannot do so even once; while we enter the stream it is already changing, becoming *another stream*. In such judgments, it is as though the element of *determinate being* is being replaced by the element of *becoming*.* This is a misuse of dialectics, not a correct application of the dialectical method. Hegel remarked: "Das Etwas ist die erste Negation der Negation" (The Something is the first negation of the negation).**

Those of our critics who have not completely lost touch with philosophical literature, like to cite Trendelenburg who is supposed to have shattered completely all the arguments in favour of dialectics. But these gentlemen have evidently read Trendelenburg badly, if they have read him at all. They have forgotten— if it was ever known to them, which I strongly doubt—the following trifle. Trendelenburg acknowledges that the principium contradictionis is *applicable not to motion but only to those objects that are created by motion*.*** He is right. But motion does not only *create* objects. As we have said, it *constantly changes them*. That is why the *logic of motion* ("the logic of contradiction") never loses its sovereignty over the objects created by motion, so that while paying due tribute to the "basic laws" of formal logic we must remember that their significance is limited to the extent that they do not hinder us from also giving proper recognition to dialectics. This is how the matter actually stood with Trendelenburg, although he did not draw the appropriate logical con-

---

* I retain here the terms used by N. Lossky in his translation of the book on Hegel by Cuno Fischer: Dasein—*determinate being*; Werden—*becoming*.
** *Werke*, III, S. 114.
*** *Logische Untersuchungen*, dritte Auflage, Leipzig, 1870, Bd. II, S. 175.

clusions from the principle that he himself stated—*an extremely important one for the scientific theory of cognition.*

In passing, we shall add here that there are very many useful remarks scattered throughout Trendelenburg's *Logische Untersuchungen* which speak not against us but in our favour. This may seem strange, but it can be very simply explained by the very simple circumstance that Trendelenburg, strictly speaking, was combating *idealist* dialectics. For instance, he diagnosed the weakness of dialectics as that it "asserts the spontaneous motion of pure thought which is at the same time the self-generation of being" (behauptet ... eine Selbstbewegung des reinen Gedankens, die zugleich die Selbsterzeugung des Seins ist).*

This is indeed a very great mistake. But who can fail to realise that this weakness is peculiar only to idealist dialectics? Who does not know that when Marx wanted to place dialectics "the right way up" he began by correcting this fundamental error which had grown from its old idealist roots? Another example. Trendelenburg says that to Hegel motion is indeed the basis of that logic which apparently does not require any presuppositions to justify it.** This again is perfectly true; but once again it is an argument in favour of *materialist* dialectics. A third and the most interesting example. According to Trendelenburg, it is wrong to think that to Hegel nature was only applied logic. Just the contrary. Hegel's logic is by no means the result of pure thought; it was created by preliminary abstraction from nature (eine antizipierte Abstraktion der Natur). In Hegel's dialectics almost everything is drawn from experience, and if experience could take from dialectics all that dialectics has borrowed from experience, dialectics would indeed be left with a beggar's staff.*** That is so, exactly so! But then that is just what Hegel's pupils said when they rebelled against his idealism and went over to the camp of *materialism.*

I could adduce many more similar examples but that would only distract me from my subject. I simply wished to show our critics that it would probably have been better for them not to have cited Trendelenburg at all in their fight with us.

To proceed. I said that motion is contradiction in action and that therefore the "basic laws" of formal logic are inapplicable to it. In order that this proposition should not give rise to misunderstandings, a qualification is needed. When we are confronted with the question of the transition from one type of motion to another—say, from mechanical motion to heat—we also have to reason in accordance with Überweg's basic rule. This type of motion is *either* heat *or* mechanical motion *or*, etc. That is clear.

---

* Ibid., I, 36.
** Ibid., I, 42.
*** Ibid., I, 78 and 79.

But if this is so, the basic laws of formal logic are *applicable* within certain limits *also to motion*. It follows once more that dialectics does not abrogate formal logic, but simply deprives its laws of the *absolute significance* attached to them by the metaphysicians.

If the reader has followed attentively what has been said above, he should have no difficulty in understanding how little "value" there is in the now oft-repeated idea that *dialectics is irreconcilable with materialism.** On the contrary, *the foundation of our dialectics is the materialist conception* of nature. Our dialectics is based on materialism and would collapse were materialism to collapse. And vice versa: the *materialist theory of cognition* would be incomplete, one-sided—more than that, it would be *impossible* without dialectics.

With Hegel, *dialectics* coincides *with metaphysics*; with us *dialectics* rests upon the *study of nature*.

With Hegel, the demiurgos of the real world, to use one of Marx's expressions, is the *Absolute Idea*. For us, the absolute idea is only an *abstraction from motion* which gives rise to all *combinations and conditions of matter*.

With Hegel, thought moves forward as a consequence of the revelation and solution of the *contradictions* within *conceptions*. According to our—*materialist*—teaching, the contradictions within conceptions are only the reflections, *translated into the language of thought*, of the contradictions within *phenomena* due to the contradictory nature of their common basis, that is to say, *motion*.

With Hegel, the course of things is determined by the course of ideas. With us the course of *ideas* is explained by the course of *things, the course of thought by the course of life*.

Materialism puts dialectics "the right way up" and thereby removes the mystical veil in which Hegel had it wrapped. By the very fact of this it brings to light the *revolutionary character* of dialectics.

Marx wrote: "In its mystified form, dialectic became the fashion in Germany, because it seemed to transfigure and to glorify the existing state of things. In its rational form it is a scandal and abomination to bourgeoisdom and its doctrinaire professors, because it includes in its comprehension and affirmative recognition of the existing state of things, at the same time also, the recognition of the negation of that state, of its inevitable breaking up; because it regards every historically developed" (to be exact: which has emerged, become—gewordene—*G. P.*) "social form as in fluid movement, and therefore takes into account its transient

---

* "It seems to us that materialism and dialectical logic are elements which may be considered incompatible philosophically," said the profound Mr. N. G. (*Russkoye Bogatstvo*, June, p. 59).

nature not less than its momentary existence; because it lets nothing impose upon it, and is in its essence critical and revolutionary."*

That materialist dialectics is an abomination to the through and through reactionary bourgeoisie is in the nature of things; but that even people who sincerely simpathise with revolutionary socialism sometimes turn their backs on dialectics is both ridiculous and extremely sad; it is the height of nonsense.

After all I have said, it seems to me that I can afford to shrug my shoulders at the astonishing invention of Mr. N. G. who attributes to us the principle of a *"dual organisation* of mind", a principle which, according to him, is the "premise" which can alone make our "dialectical logic the least bit plausible".** Well, well! Our implausible critic has indeed found a mare's nest!

Now we must turn our attention to something else. We know already that Überweg was right—and to what extent he was right—in demanding that logically thinking people give definite answers to definite questions as to whether a particular property belongs to a particular object. But suppose we are dealing, not with a *simple* object, but with a *complex* one which unites in itself *directly opposing phenomena* possessing directly opposing properties. Is Überweg's rule applicable to such an object? No, Überweg himself, who is just as decided an opponent of Hegel's dialectics as Trendelenburg, finds that this has to be considered in accordance with another rule, namely, the *combination of opposites* (principium coincidentiae oppositorum). But the vast majority of the phenomena that are the concern of natural science and social science belong to the list of "objects" of exactly this type: the most directly opposed phenomena are combined in the most simple clot of protoplasm, in the life of the most undeveloped society. Consequently, the dialectical method must occupy an important place in natural science and social science. From the moment such a place was allocated to the dialectical method in these sciences they have made enormous advances.

Would you like to know, reader, how dialectics won its spurs in biology? Recall the disputes about what constituted *species* which were aroused by the appearance of the theory of transformism. Darwin and his supporters were of the opinion that the various species of one and the same genus of animals or plants

---

* See Preface to the Second German edition of *Capital*.[40]
** [*Russkoye Bogatstvo*,] June, p. 64. Parmenides in his polemic with Heraclitus' pupils called them *two-headed philosophers* to whom many things appear in dual form: as existing and as *non*-existing. Mr. N. G. now advances as a philosophical principle that which for Parmenides was a display of polemical guile. What progress we are making, "God help us", in the "first questions" of philosophy!

were none other than the variously developed descendants of one and the same original form. Besides this, in accordance with the theory of development, all genera of one and the same succession also stem from one common form and the same must be said of all successions of one and the same class. Darwin's opponents, on the other hand, took the contrary view that all animal and vegetable species are completely independent of one another and that only individuals belonging to one and the same species come from a common form. The same conception of species had already been expressed by Linnaeus who said: "There are as many species as were originally created by the Supreme Being." This is a purely metaphysical view, since metaphysics perceives that things and ideas "are isolated, are to be considered one after the other and apart from each other, are objects of investigation fixed, rigid, given once for all" (Engels). Dialectics, on the other hand, comprehends things and ideas, in Engels' own words, "in their essential connection, concatenation, motion, origin, and ending".[41] This conception has been an integral part of biology since Darwin's time and will always remain so no matter what corrections are introduced into the theory of transformism by the further development of science.

To comprehend the great significance of dialectics in *sociology*, it is sufficient to recall how *socialism* was transformed from a *utopia* to a *science*.

The utopian socialists held the abstract point of view of human nature and judged social phenomena by the formula "yea—yea and nay—nay". Property *either* conforms *or does not* conform to human nature; a monogamic family *either* conforms *or does not* conform to human nature, and so on and so forth. Since human nature was supposed to be *unchangeable*, socialists had the right to expect that among all the *possible* social systems there would be one which corresponded to human nature *more than all the others*. Hence arose the endeavours to find this *best system*, that is to say, *one* that conformed most to human nature. Each founder of a school *thought he had discovered such a system*; each proposed *his own utopia*. Marx introduced the dialectical method into socialism and thus converted it into a *science*, dealing a mortal blow at *utopianism*. Marx does not appeal to human nature; he knows of no social institutions that *either* conform *or do not* conform to human nature. In his *Poverty of Philosophy* we find the following remarkable and characteristic rebuke to Proudhon: "M. Proudhon does not know that all history is nothing but a continuous transformation of human nature."* In *Capital*, Marx says: "By thus acting on the external world and changing it, he [man] at

---

* *Misère de la Philosophie*, nouvelle édition, Paris, 1896, p. 204.[42]

the same time changes his own nature."* This is the dialectical point of view, shedding quite new light on questions of social life. Take the issue of private property. The utopians wrote and argued much among themselves and with the economists about whether private property must exist, that is to say, whether it conforms to human nature. Marx put the question on a concrete basis. He stated that *the forms of property and property relations are conditioned by the development of the productive forces.* To one stage of the development of these forces corresponds one form; to another stage another form—but there is not and cannot be an *absolute decision* since everything is fluid, everything changes; "wisdom becomes madness, bliss—torment".[44]

Hegel said: "Contradiction leads forward." Science finds splendid confirmation of this dialectical view in the *class struggle,* without consideration of which nothing can be understood of the development of the social and spiritual life of *class* society.

Why then is the "logic of contradiction" which, as we have seen, is the reflection of the eternal process of motion in the human mind, called *dialectics*? To avoid a protracted discussion on the matter, I shall quote from Cuno Fischer.

"Human life may be compared with dialogue in this respect, that with age and experience our views of people and things are gradually transformed, like the opinions of the disputants in the course of a debate which is fruitful and rich in ideas. It is this spontaneous and necessary transformation of our views of life and the world which actually constitutes experience.... That is why Hegel, in comparing the course of development of consciousness with the course of philosophical debate, called it by the name *dialectic*, or dialectical motion. This expression had already been adopted by Plato, Aristotle, and Kant in a sense important and distinctive to each of them, but in no system did it receive such a comprehensive significance as in Hegel's."**

There are many, too, who do not understand either why views such as those of Linnaeus on animal and vegetable species, for example, are described as *metaphysical.* Apparently these words—*metaphysics, metaphysical*—mean something quite different. We shall try to explain this as well.

What is *metaphysics*? What is its subject?

Its subject is the so-called *unconditional* (the absolute). And what is the main distinctive feature of the *unconditional*? *Immutability.* This is not surprising, since the *unconditional* is not dependent on changing circumstances (*conditions*) of time and place, which alter the ultimate objects accessible to us. That is

---

* *Das Capital,* III, Auflage, S. 155-56.[43]
** *Hegel, His Life and Works,* Half Volume I, translated by N. O. Lossky, St. Petersburg, p. 308.

why it does not change. What then is the most distinctive feature of those concepts which have been and are used by the people described in the language of dialectics as metaphysicians? This also is their *immutability*, as we noted in the example of Linnaeus' teaching on species. In their own way, these concepts are *unconditional*, too. So their nature is identical with that of the *unconditional*, the subject matter of metaphysics. *That is why* Hegel described as *metaphysical* all those concepts which are elaborated (to use his own words) *by reason*, that is to say, which are accepted as immutable and are isolated from one another by an impassable gulf. The late Nik. Mikhailovsky thought that Engels was the *first writer* to use the terms *"metaphysical"* and *"dialectical"* in the sense we now know. But this is wrong. These terms were originally used by Hegel.*

I shall probably be told that Hegel had his own metaphysics. I do not deny this: he had. But *his metaphysics* merged with *dialectics*, and in dialectics there is nothing immutable, everything is in motion, everything changes.

When I sat down to write this preface, I had intended to say something about Mr. Berdayev's review in the journal *Voprosy Zhizni*[46] of Engels' *Anti-Dühring*, a Russian translation of which has recently been published. Now I realise I cannot carry out this intention for want of space. I cannot say that I am very sorry about it; Mr. Berdayev's review will convince only those readers who are already convinced and whom, therefore, there was no need to convince. Mr. Berdayev's own opinions, however, *do not* deserve attention. Spinoza said of Bacon that he *did not prove* his opinions; he only *described them*. The same might be said of Berdayev, if his method of presenting his thoughts would not be better described by the word *decree*. But when such a thinker as Bacon describes, or, for that matter, decrees, his views, much exceptionally valuable material will be found in his descriptions and decrees. And when such a muddlehead as Mr. Berdayev takes to issuing decrees, absolutely nothing instructive will come of them.

But wait.... It is clear from Mr. Berdayev's decrees where, according to his practical reason, the main weakness of Engels' world-outlook lies. It lies in this, that it impedes the transformation of *social* democracy into *bourgeois* democracy. And that is very interesting; so we shall put it on record.

Chexbres s./Vevey, July 4, 1905.

---

* See § 81 of the First Volume of his *Great Encyclopaedia*.[45]

6*

PATRIOTISM AND SOCIALISM

In launching the first issue of my *Diary*, I informed the readers that in it I should be examining, among other things, questions and events of interest not only to ourselves, the Russian Social-Democrats, but also to the Social-Democrats of the whole world. One question of this kind is undoubtedly that of the relationship of patriotism to socialism, which has now been sharply raised in the notorious and somewhat paradoxical announcement of the French Socialist Hervé.[47] On this subject, the editorial board of the journal *La vie socialiste* undertook a full "enquiry", i.e., it appealed to Socialists of the various countries to write in their opinions on this subject. I, too, received one of these invitations. My reply is contained in the following letter to the editors of the journal concerned.

Dear Comrades,

I have only now found time to reply to your questions. I am a bit late, but better late than never. Your questions are as follows:

"1) What is your view of the statement in the *Communist Manifesto* that the workers have no fatherland?

"2) What actions and what forms of propaganda does internationalism demand from Socialists, in view of militarism, 'colonialism',' and their causes and consequences?

"3) What part must Socialists play in international relations (tariffs, international labour legislation, etc.)?

"4) What is the duty of Socialists in the event of war?"

I begin, as is proper, at the beginning.

Some people think that the lines you quote from the *Communist Manifesto* are more an expression of the indignation of Marx and Engels at the distressed condition of the working class in capitalist society than their true opinion on the relationship of patriotism to socialism. Thus, for example, Jaurès, in his dispute with Hervé, described them as a pessimistic flight of rhetoric, partly explained—mark you, Comrades, only partly—by the circumstances at the time when the *Communist Manifesto* was written, when the economic crisis had reached its highest point and the

workers were deprived of elementary human rights. E. Bernstein
holds nearly the same view. According to him, the "thesis" with
which we are concerned might be "justified" by the fact that when
Marx and Engels wrote their famous *Manifesto* "the workers everywhere had not the right to vote, that is to say, the right to
participate in the administration"![48]

I cannot agree either with Jaurès or with Bernstein.

If they were right, it would mean restricting the limits of socialist internationalism now in favour of patriotism, since the proletarians of the advanced capitalist countries already possess
the greater part of the political rights they lacked on the eve of
the revolutionary movement of 1848, and since even the Russian
proletariat is within reach of acquiring civil rights. And this
would mean that *internationalism must retreat to the extent of the
successes won by the international labour movement.* It seems to me
to be just the reverse, that internationalism has penetrated more
deeply into the hearts of the proletarians and that its influence
among them is stronger now than it was at the time of the *Communist Manifesto.* I should think that the "thesis" of Marx and Engels
needs not "*justification*" but only *correct interpretation.*

The words: "The working men have no country" were written
in reply to the bourgeois ideologists who were accusing the Communists of desiring to "abolish the fatherland". Clearly, therefore,
the authors of the *Manifesto* were speaking about the "*fatherland*"
in a quite definite sense, namely, the sense bestowed on this conception by the bourgeois ideologists. The *Manifesto* declared that
the workers had no *such* fatherland. This was true at the time;
it is still true now when the proletariat of the advanced countries
enjoy certain, more or less extensive, more or less lasting, political rights; it will remain true in the future, no matter how
great are the political gains which are still to be won by the working class.

Indeed, Comrades, you will not have forgotten, I trust, how
Jaurès, in the Salle Elysée-Montmartre, depicted the patriotism
of that happy future when communism becomes the predominant
mode of production. Then, "fatherlands" will exist only as representing the innate spiritual characteristics peculiar to "individual
peoples". "Just as individuals with their own characteristics and
their own diversity will not dissolve in socialist organisation,
but retain and consolidate in greater harmony the originality
of their natures, so also will historical individualities called
fatherlands—the British fatherland, the German fatherland, the
French fatherland, the Italian fatherland, the Russian fatherland,
the Chinese fatherland (when the yellow race is emancipated from
the oppressive tutelage of the white race)—all these fatherlands,
each with its own moral individuality created by history, each

with its own language and literature, its own conception of life,
its memories, the special form of its hopes, the particular quality
of its passion, mind, and genius—all these individualities will
comprise the great communist humanity of tomorrow." This
declamation is not irreproachable from the standpoint of logic:
*the individual is a biological category; nationality is a historical
category*, therefore these two concepts are incommensurable. But that
by the way. The main point for me is that the "fatherlands" of the
future, as portrayed for us by Jaurès, are *totally unlike* the "fatherland" which the bourgeois journalists had in mind when attacking
the Communists and which Marx and Engels spoke about when
refuting them. The numerous and multi-coloured "fatherlands"
of the future in Jaurès' vivid description are nothing but *nationalities*. If the authors of the *Manifesto* had declared that the workers
had no nationality this would not have been a pessimistic flight
of rhetoric, but ridiculous nonsense. They wrote, however, not
about nationalities, but about the "fatherland" and, what is
more, not of that fatherland which *will prevail*, according to Jaurès, in the happy reign of communism, but of that which prevails
now under the oppressive rule of the capitalist mode of production.
This fatherland, as I said, has features which make it very unlike
the future "fatherlands" described by Jaurès with his characteristic
eloquence. What are these features? Jaurès himself indicated
them.

To use his own words: after "the definitive and complete social
revolution" (la révolution sociale complète et définitive), fatherlands will *cease to exist* "as forces of distrust, exclusiveness, and
mutual oppression". Thus, at the present time, under the rule of
capitalism, "the fatherland" serves not only as the expression of
the spiritual peculiarities of different peoples, but also—and
most of all—as *the expression of national exclusiveness, mutual
distrust between peoples, and the oppression of one people by another*.
What must be the attitude of the class-conscious proletarians
to this, bourgeois, fatherland?

The *Communist Manifesto* said that the working men had no
such country. Now were its authors not right?

Their reply was neither a "pessimistic flight of rhetoric", nor is
it in need of "justification". It must be made the foundation of the
whole international policy of the socialist proletariat.

Marx said, as we know, that the German proletariat is the heir
to German classical philosophy. Jaurès exclaims: "No. Kant
with his autonomy, Fichte with his pride of absolute consciousness, Hegel with his revolutionary dialectics, could be understood and represented only by such a working class, they could
be embodied only in that revolutionary class of proletarians
which aims to emancipate all wills, leave nature only in the

power of the moral law of consciousness and open to eternal dialectics new horizons of the unending human revolution."

I have no idea what is meant by leaving nature only in the power of the moral law, and I am afraid that the revolutionary proletariat will never succeed in resolving this brain-racking problem. Nevertheless, I am still ready to applaud the eloquence of Comrade Jaurès. But I do not understand in what sense this eloquent part of his speech calls in question the idea of Marx and Engels that the working men have no country.

Jaurès continues: "This is the reply to those who tell the working class that they need not interest themselves in matters concerning the fatherland, in all national traditions." Again I am surprised. Marx and Engels never at any time said that the working class "could not have interest in matters concerning their country". To be interested in these "matters" does not mean that one has to be a *patriot*. Political power, class dictatorship, is without doubt a "matter" which is very closely related to "fatherland", yet the authors of the *Manifesto* always explained to the workers the need to conquer power. Jaurès is mistaken in thinking that a negative attitude to the idea of "fatherland" is the same as indifference to the cultural acquisitions of the people. It is precisely successes in culture which lead people to understand the narrowness of this idea.

Jaurès reproached Hervé with sophistry. In this instance, Hervé would have been justified in returning the reproach and saying that Jaurès' argument recalled that sophism to which the bourgeois economists resort when they assert that the *abolition of capital* is tantamount to the *abolition of the means of production*. Capital is one thing; the means of production is quite another. In exactly the same way, the cultural achievements of a particular people, their civilisation, are one thing; the "fatherland" is another. An essential condition for the existence of capitalism is the absence of means of production among the enormous majority of the population. Similarly, that lack of respect for the rights of *foreign fatherland*, which Jaurès himself called the *spirit of exclusiveness*, is an essential psychological condition for love of *one's own country*. And if the revolutionary proletariat has indeed to "emancipate all wills", it must on this score alone *rise above the idea of fatherland*.

Jaurès pointed to the celebrated journalist of the Restoration, Armand Carrel, who had the courage to oppose his own country when it began an unjust war against Spain.[49] To this may be added that during the Polish revolution of 1863 some Russian officers, not wishing to be the executioners of a neighbouring people fighting for its freedom, joined the ranks of the Polish "insurgents". I look upon these as heroic feats which do honour to the French and Russian peoples. But considered *from the standpoint of patriotism, they are most shameful crimes: high treason.*

For all Jaurès' eloquence, he succeeded in making his "thesis" partially acceptable only by the expedient of not separating one idea from the other—the idea of *fatherland as it is now* is confused with the idea of the *fatherland as, in his view, it must and will be.* By this method you may prove absolutely anything you like. But such confusion of ideas does nothing to elucidate the problem.

I repeat: fatherland is a historical category, i.e., essentially a passing phase. Just as the idea of *tribe* gave way to the idea of *fatherland,* at first restricted to the boundaries of the *town community,* later extending to the present-day *national* frontiers, so the idea of *fatherland* must give way before the incomparably greater idea of *humanity.* This is vouched for by that same force which generated and modified the patriotic idea: *the force of economic development.*

The idea of fatherland ties the people of one country in close bonds of solidarity in all that concerns the interests of that country in opposition to the interests of other countries. The hero of one of Turgenev's novels,[50] the Bulgarian Insarov, says: "The last peasant, the last beggar, in Bulgaria wants the same thing as I do. We all have the same aim," viz.: to achieve the independence of Bulgaria. Such an aim, of course, deserves every sympathy from the class which is striving to "emancipate all wills". But it has to be remembered that the Turkish patriots, in turn, had no less unanimously, forgetting all class distinctions, to strive for the opposite aim: *the maintenance of Turkish rule in Bulgaria.* During the uprising of 1897 in the island of Crete,[51] the Young Turks[52] who were publishing the journal *Osmanlis* in Geneva, wrote that Crete belonged to Turkey by right of conquest. This was a patriotic claim in its pure, unsophisticated form.

But this pure patriotism is possible only on two conditions. It presupposes, firstly, that the class struggle is at a low stage of development and, secondly, that there is no great, conspicuous similarity in the position of the oppressed classes of two, or several, "fatherlands". Where the class struggle has assumed a sharp, revolutionary character, shattering all the old conceptions inherited from former generations, and where, in addition, the oppressed class can easily convince itself that its interests are very similar to the interests of the oppressed class of foreign countries, and are opposed to the interests of the ruling class in its own country, in such a case, *the idea of fatherland* loses a great deal of its former attraction. This was demonstrated to us already by the example of ancient Greece, where the lower classes of citizens felt a greater sense of solidarity with the lower classes of other states than with the upper classes of their own city-state.

The Peloponnesian war, that war between democracy and aristocracy which embraced a large part of the then Greek world, is a
clear confirmation of this. In modern times, we see something
similar, though on a smaller scale, in some of the international
conflicts generated by the great French Revolution at the end of
the eighteenth century. Anyone who wishes seriously to clear up
for himself the historical significance of the idea of patriotism
must consider these events. But no matter how important these
events were, they pale into insignificance in comparison with
what we are observing in the emancipation movement of the proletariat today.

Capitalism, which by its very nature, must strive to break
through the frontiers of any particular "fatherland" and penetrate
every country involved in international exchange, is a mighty
economic factor in shattering and disintegrating the same idea
of fatherland which—*in its up-to-date form*—was once created by
capitalism itself. The relations between exploiters and exploited,
despite numerous and often important local distinctions, are
essentially the same in all capitalist countries. Consequently,
every class-conscious *worker* in each particular capitalist country
feels himself pre-eminently closer to the worker in every other
capitalist country than to his own compatriot—the *capitalist*.
And just as in the conditions of contemporary world economy the
socialist revolution, which will put an end to the rule of capital,
must be *international*,[53] so the idea of *fatherland*, uniting in one
solid and "unique" whole all classes of society, must necessarily
give way in the minds of the class-conscious workers to the infinitely wider conception of the solidarity of revolutionary humanity,
viz.: *"working men of all countries"*. And the more widely flows the
mighty stream of the modern labour movement, the more the
psychology of *patriotism* will yield to the psychology of *internationalism*.

Until the class struggle in Greece had shattered the patriotism
of the town communities, an Athenian citizen looked upon the
citizens of Sparta as foreigners who were there to be exploited
either through trade or temporary political unions and whose
interests could be neither dear nor near to him. Today, the native
of Athens, with the *modern* conception of patriotism, thinks
of Lacedaemon as part of his own country, whose interests are
equally dear to him *throughout its length and breadth*. This means
that the present-day Greek patriot has none of the "exclusiveness" that marked the patriotism of the town communities. But
this does not imply that he is hostile or at least indifferent to the
"matters" of his own native town. No, his patriotism is wholly
compatible with the most fervent and tireless service to the "matters" of his home town. There is one thing his patriotism will not

stand, however—the exploitation of other parts of his fatherland to the advantage of his home town. To such a person salus patriae—suprema lex. Similarly, modern socialist internationalism is also fully compatible with the most ardent and indefatigable work for the good of one's own country, but it is completely incompatible with readiness to support one's own country where its *interests come into conflict with the interests of revolutionary humanity, that is to say, the modern international proletarian movement, that is to say: progress.* The interests of this movement represent that higher point of view from which the modern socialist who does not wish to betray his principles must assess the international relations, both where they touch upon questions of *war and peace,* and where it is a question of *commercial policy in general and "colonialism" in particular.* To such a socialist salus revolutiae—suprema lex.

I am quite well aware that what I have said contains only a general formula and not a ready-made reply to each particular case. But, to use Marx's splendid phrase, our theory is not a passepartout that will save us from the need for attentively studying particular social phenomena. Contemporary socialist theory is the *algebra of the revolution* capable of furnishing us only with *algebraic* formulas. To be guided by these formulas in practice we must be able to replace the *algebraic* symbols in them by *arithmetical* quantities and to do this we have to take into account all the particular conditions in each particular case. Only when used in this way will these formulas preserve their living dialectical nature and not become dead metaphysical dogmas....

It is in the nature of dead dogma to assert, for instance, that socialists must be against *every* war. Our Chernyshevsky once wrote that such absolute verdicts were unsound, and contended that the battle of Marathon was a beneficial event in the history of mankind. It is no less dogmatic to argue that we socialists can support only *defensive* wars. That would be correct only from the angle of the conservative suum cuique, but the international proletariat, holding consistently to its own point of view, must give sympathetic consideration to every war—whether defensive or offensive—which promises to remove some important obstacle from the path of the social revolution.

It is, however, unquestionable that at the present time wars between civilised peoples do very great harm in many ways to the emancipation movement of the working class. That is why class-conscious workers are the most determined and reliable supporters of peace.*

---

* There is no doubt also that the colonial practice of the bourgeois "fatherlands" has already furnished the international proletariat with sufficient material for the decisive condemnation of this practice. One need only look at the decisions of the recent international congresses.[54]

Nevertheless, it is also impossible to give one unalterable, ready-made reply to the question of how the proletarians of countries at war with one another must conduct themselves. It is known that this question came up at the Zurich International Congress in 1893. Domela Niewenhuis advanced the same proposal now being made by Hervé; he stated that the answer to a declaration of war must be a *strike against military service*. As the reporter of the Commission on Militarism at the Congress, I came out strongly against the proposal and was supported energetically by the Marxists of all countries, to the great indignation of the semi-anarchists and semi-bourgeois elements who were present at the Congress in great numbers. I still think that the idea of a strike against military service is a very poor one. Imagine that a war has started between two countries in one of which there is an influential working-class party, while in the other, a very backward country, the workers' movement has scarcely begun. What will happen if the socialists call upon the proletarians to organise a strike against military service and the proletarians accept this call? That is easy to foresee. The advanced country will be defeated; the backward country will triumph. Will that be a gain for the international socialist movement? No, it will be very harmful. Therefore, in this case, a strike against military service will not benefit the movement.

But Hervé evidently thinks that such a strike would be opportune only in the case of a war between two countries in each of which there is a well-developed labour movement. In that case, of course, the drawback I have referred to would not exist; but there is another objection.

Hervé himself admits that a strike of this type makes sense only when it is a first step of the workers' revolution. That is correct. But surely the revolutionary proletariat must always strive for revolution, even apart from wars? Why does it not do this now, at this moment? Obviously because it is not yet strong enough. If this is true, the question in dispute is consequently reduced to another question: would a declaration of war give the proletariat the strength necessary for a revolution? Of course this question cannot be answered by using a stereotyped formula valid for all countries and for every given period. It is clear from this alone that the international proletariat cannot adopt the strike against military service as a kind of general tactical remedy; but then the international proletariat would never prescribe such a remedy for itself.

If the organised working-class party of any given country found at the moment of declaration of war that the hour of social revolution had arrived it could resort to the strike against military service *among other means of achieving its great aim*. However, the "thesis" of such a strike would then be the subject of all-round discussion, taking into account all conditions of time and place. It would be risky, to say the least, to adopt such a policy in advance.

In summarising my views on the subject, I shall say that the decisions of the 1891 Brussels International Congress still retain all their profound meaning.[55] The best means of struggle against militarism is not this or that possible—or assumed as possible— action of the working class, *but the whole range of successes of the proletarian emancipation movement.* Our struggle against militarism generally cannot be adjusted to isolated actions. It is a whole process.

On the question of labour legislation, I think I can reply very briefly. None of us international socialists doubt that this legislation must be *international.* Doubt may arise only when speaking of competition in the sale of labour power between the less exacting proletarians of the backward countries and the more exacting proletarians of the advanced countries. In this connection, some of our comrades have adopted the idea of *prohibitive legislation.* I find this idea at variance with the principles of international socialism. It is my firm conviction that we have to keep to another method of fighting this competition. *The revolutionary proletariat of the advanced countries must try to awaken class-consciousness in the minds of their competitors in the backward countries, and organise them for joint struggle against capitalism, not protect themselves with the help of frontier guards.*

That, Comrades, is what I can say in reply to your questions. Forgive me if I have taken up too much of your time.

Yours sincerely,
G. Plekhanov.

ON A. PANNEKOEK'S PAMPHLET

Anton Pannekoek, *Socialism and Religion.*
Translated from the German by A. Ratner. Edited by P. Rumyantsev.
Cheap Library of the Znaniye Society, No. 121.
Price 5 kopeks. 1906

Mr. P. Rumyantsev, who edited the Russian translation of this pamphlet, wrote a brief foreword to it. Here it is in full. "This pamphlet represents a lecture delivered in Bremen by Dr. Anton Pannekoek of Leiden, Holland, on September 14, 1905, to a very large meeting of workers and sponsored by the Education Committee of the Bremen Trades Cartel and the Social-Democratic Union. The consistency of the author's views on historical materialism, the lucidity and popular style of his presentation, prompt us to recommend the pamphlet to Russian readers, especially since such a large gap is felt in our literature on the relationship of socialism to religion."

There is indeed a large gap in literature—and not only Russian literature—on the question of the relationship of socialism to religion. Therefore, it can be said with certainty that this pamphlet will be read by very many people; that is why I think it my duty to devote special attention to it here.

I shall begin by saying that Anton Pannekoek is not pronounced Panne*kek* but Panne*kuk*, since the Dutch "oe" is like our Russian "u". So now we may pronounce his name properly.

Pannekoek's pamphlet does not bridge any gaps for the simple reason that it contains too many gaps itself. You cannot plug a hole with a hole, as some wiseacre remarked. And if Mr. Rumyantsev deems it necessary to recommend Pannekoek's pamphlet to Russian readers he is simply confirming the presence of numerous gaps in his own world-outlook.

Anton Pannekoek undoubtedly possesses a sufficiently remarkable ability as well as good intentions. He belongs to the left— *Marxist*—wing of Dutch Social-Democracy. But *even though* he is a "Dr." or, more truly, *because* he is one, he did not graduate from a strict Marxist school. This was already noticeable from the philosophical articles with which he transgressed in the columns of *Neue Zeit*[56] two years ago; the articles were very poor. And this pamphlet on socialism and religion is conclusive evidence that our young Dutch Marxist has mastered little of his teacher's method.

He says: "There are two scientific systems for which we are indebted to Karl Marx and which, taken together, provide the foundation of our ultimate aim. They are political economy and historical materialism" (p. 29). But that is not at all so. There is *one* "*system*", *the system of dialectical materialism*, which includes both political economy and the scientific explanation of the historical process and much else besides. Anyone who has studied *Capital* understands that this outstanding work is nothing but *the materialist explanation of economic relations in bourgeois society*, which itself is of a transient, i.e., *historical nature*. Many people describe *Capital* as a *historical* work, but by far not all of these comprehend the whole profound meaning of this description. Anton Pannekoek is obviously among those who are completely blind to the fact that Marx's fundamental economic views are permeated throughout with the materialist conception of history. For a Marxist, this is an unpardonable failing.

Further, in speaking of "bourgeois materialism", A. Pannekoek launches on talk about the bourgeois Enlighteners who "hoped by disseminating knowledge to tear the masses away from the priests and the feudal lords". Perhaps you think he means the famous French materialists—Holbach, Diderot, and Helvétius? You are wrong. He has in mind "the now rather outmoded popular writings of L. Büchner" (p. 22). It is simply ridiculous. He asserts that "there was no trace of sociology" in "bourgeois materialism". That is untrue as regards Helvétius, in whose works one can find extremely interesting and remarkable rudiments of the materialist conception of history. But A. Pannekoek went through a poor school and therefore has not the slightest notion about French materialism. He attributes to the materialists the "establishment" of the truth that "ideas are born in the brain-matter" (p. 29). The classical materialists expressed themselves otherwise.

Let us go on to religion. On page 8 of Pannekoek's pamphlet there is the following remark: "In the question we are now discussing, we understand by religion that which has always been its essential feature: the belief in *a supernatural being* who is supposed to govern the world and to direct the destinies of men."

That, too, is wrong and in two respects. Firstly, the majority of religions ascribed the governing of the world not to *one* but to *many* supernatural beings (polytheism). And secondly, belief in the existence of such beings still *does not constitute the main distinctive feature of religion*. Our author has a poor conception of the process which one English researcher called "the making of religion".*

---

* [The words: "The making of religion" are written by Plekhanov in English.]

Religion begins only when a tribe starts to believe that between the tribe and the particular supernatural being or beings there is a certain relationship which is binding not only on the people but even on those beings. The main distinctive feature of religion is *belief in a god or gods*. Pannekoek is very much mistaken if he imagines that god means the same thing as a supernatural being. Of course, every god is a supernatural being; but not every supernatural being by far is considered a god. *To become a god, such a being must go through an entire evolution.*

Note the grounds upon which Pannekoek makes his hapless reference to the distinctive feature of religion. There are people who say that because the contemporary proletariat displays much selflessness and devotion to a lofty ideal, it cannot be said, as Pannekoek does by the way, that this class is becoming less and less religious. These people cannot even conceive of *non-religious* morality. Pannekoek's reply to them is that morality and religion are two distinct things and that the essential feature of religion is belief in supernatural beings. Then he goes on: "Hitherto, all of man's lofty and moral impulses were closely connected with this belief and were displayed in the garb of religion. This can be readily understood when one considers that the whole world-outlook was embodied in religion, so that everything beyond the pale of everyday life sought refuge in religion; for everything the origin of which was unknown, a supernatural explanation was sought and believed to be found in religion. The fact that the virtues and moral urges which are recognised by all men occupy first place in religious teaching does not, however, constitute the essential and particular feature of religion; its essence is rather the justification which it provides for them, the way in which it explains them as emanations of God's will. *We* know a *natural* cause of the higher moral urges of the proletariat; we know they stem from its special class position."

So, "we" explain the higher moral "urges" of the *proletariat* by a *natural* cause. Commendable, indeed. And how do "we" explain the moral "urges" of the *other classes in society*? By *supernatural* causes? Probably and even certainly not. But if not, then we should speak, not of the proletariat, but in general of the *man* whom Marx called *social man*. Marxists do, in fact, consider that the development of the morality of social man is conditioned by the development of the social relations, which in turn is conditioned by the development of the social forces of production. And precisely because Marxists are convinced of this, Pannekoek's assertion that "virtues" are explained "as emanations of God's will", sounds highly strange to them. Surely it would follow from this that virtues arise on a *completely idealist* basis. I am willing to concede that this is not confusion of thought, but simply an un-

fortunate expression (perhaps even an unfortunate translation:
I do not have the original at hand); but no matter how the muddle
has arisen it is there and will only mislead the reader. Then,
what is "this religion" Pannekoek talks about? The one whose
distinctive feature is belief in supernatural beings? But did he
himself not say that this essential feature belongs to *all religions*?
Why then "this" religion? Again an extremely unfortunate expression, which confuses the author's meaning. Finally—*and this,
of course, is the most important point*—it is again clear from our
last extract that Pannekoek is completely unfamiliar with the
historical process of the formation of religion. He thinks that
"hitherto" morality was always "closely connected with this
religion", i.e., with belief in supernatural beings. But that is
wrong. *In the first stages of social development, morality existed
quite independently of belief in supernatural beings.* Confirmation
of this may be found in the Russian translation of Tylor's *Primitive
Culture.* If Pannekoek knew this fact, he had only to cite it in
order to refute those who unreasonably affirm that there cannot be
morality without religion. But he did not know this, although he
ought to have known it, so he had to launch into perplexing arguments that demonstrated only too plainly that he himself, to
use a German expression, was not sitting firmly in the saddle.

On page 23 of his pamphlet, Pannekoek says: "This exposition
will suffice to show that the old bourgeois materialism and the
new bourgeois religiosity* are both directly opposed to the proletarian world-outlook." In regard to *religiosity*, this is correct,
but in relation to *bourgeois materialism* it is totally incorrect.

According to Pannekoek, there is no trace of sociology in "bourgeois materialism". I said earlier that this was not quite so, now I
shall take it for granted and shall ask: does this prove that "bourgeois materialism" *is opposed* to the world-outlook of the proletariat? No, it does not. It proves only that "bourgeois materialism" was *one-sided* in comparison with present-day dialectical
materialism. We cannot speak of *opposition*. "Bourgeois materialism", or to be more exact, the classical materialism of the seventeenth and eighteenth centuries, did not "die away", as Pannekoek
assures us, but was reborn in the "system" of Marx.

Pannekoek's final conclusion is that there will be no place
under socialism for belief in supernatural forces. This is right,
but it has been known since Marx's time. Pannekoek confined
himself to advancing several incorrect postulates as proof of
this correct idea and revealed his utter ignorance of the subject.
That is not enough.

---

* Prior to this he had said correctly that religiosity is spreading among
the contemporary bourgeoisie.

I have far from exhausted all Pannekoek's errors. But those I have dealt with do indicate the need to approach this pamphlet sceptically. In offering it to their Russian readers, the publishers of the Cheap Library indeed presented them with an article that is truly too "cheap".

The reader will see that there is nothing to thank Mr. Rumyantsev for either. We have very many people around just now editing and "recommending" works on subjects about which they themselves have not the faintest idea. These people, zealously disseminating their self-opinionated ignorance among the public, are the curse of our popular—mostly translated—literature.

7—01230

REPLY TO QUESTIONNAIRE FROM THE JOURNAL *MERCURE DE FRANCE* ON THE FUTURE OF RELIGION

You ask: are we witnessing the decay or the evolution of the religious idea and religious feeling?

Allow me to reformulate the question from a social-evolutionary point of view: is not the decay of the religious idea the natural end of its evolution?

To be able to answer this question, let us take into account what the evolution of the religious idea has been up to the present.

But, first of all, what is religion? If we use what Edward B. Tylor called "a minimum definition of the term religion", we shall say that religion is belief in spiritual beings existing alongside bodies and the natural processes.*

This belief, which constitutes the necessary element of every religion, serves also to explain all natural phenomena. But at a higher stage of social evolution a new element, namely, morality, joins this original one.

The link between these two elements grows more and more close. Then we come to what I might call "a maximum definition of the term religion": belief in spiritual beings associated with morality and serving as its sanction. This is why the essence of religion for many people is morality.

But we are a long way yet from the end of this evolution.

The seemingly indissoluble link between morality and religion is doomed to disappear as a consequence of the progress of human reason.

The scientific explanation of phenomena can only be materialist. The intervention of spiritual beings may explain phenomena to the mind of a savage, but it explains nothing to the mind of a Berthelot; the significance of such an explanation diminishes for every civilised person in proportion as he assimilates the results of scientific work.

---

* True, a spiritual being is not yet a god. To become a god, the spiritual being must complete a certain evolution. God is a spiritual being linked by mutual services with a given tribe or nationality. But every god is a spiritual being. In the present case that is all we need to know.

If many people still believe in spirits and supernatural beings, this is because, for various reasons, they have been unable to overcome the obstacles preventing them from adopting the scientific point of view.

When these obstacles have been removed—and there is every reason to believe that social evolution will accomplish this—every trace of supernatural conception will disappear and morality will come into its own. Religion, in the maximum sense of the word, will cease to exist. As regards religious feeling, this too will evidently disappear with the decay of the religious idea. But, of course, there is more conservatism in feelings than in ideas. There may and will be, in all probability, survivals which will produce mongrel, semi-materialist, semi-spiritualist conceptions of the world.

But these survivals too are in their turn doomed to pass away, especially with the passing of some social institutions seemingly sanctioned by religion.

Human progress sounds the death-knell both for the religious idea and for religious feeling. Timid people, or those with a stake in religion, express fears for the future of morality. But, I repeat, morality can have an independent existence.

Belief in spiritual beings even at the present time is very far from being a buttress of morality. On the contrary, the religious beliefs of civilised peoples in our day, in the majority of cases, are lagging behind the moral development of these peoples.

W. K. Clifford justly remarked: "If people were no better than their religions, the world would be a hell."

JOSEPH DIETZGEN

Ernest Unterman, *Antonio Labriola and Joseph Dietzgen, A Comparison of Historical Materialism and Monistic Materialism.* Translated from the German by I. Naumov. Edited by P. Dauge. St. Petersburg, 1907, published by P. Dauge.

Joseph Dietzgen, *The Positive Outcome of Philosophy; Letters on Logic, Especially Democratic Proletarian Logic.* Translated from the German by P. Dauge and A. Orlov, with a Preface to the Russian Edition by Eugene Dietzgen, and a Portrait of the Author. St. Petersburg, 1906

A section of the reading public in Germany, Holland, and Russia is now very much interested in Joseph Dietzgen. His philosophical works, which until recently were known only to a few, have begun to exert an influence on the development of philosophical thought among the enlightened European proletariat. That is why we consider it useful to discuss the books mentioned above.

The first of these is from the pen of the American Socialist Ernest Unterman in the form of a postscript to the English translation of the famous work by Antonio Labriola, *Discorrendo di socialismo e di filosofia* (the translation was published in Chicago in 1906).

Mr. Dauge thought it would be worthwhile to publish Unterman's work in the Russian translation by I. Naumov. But he was wrong. This book will not and cannot bring anything of value to Russian readers. The author knows too little of the subject which his book, or more correctly, his pamphlet, professes to explain. Anyone who does understand it—true, there are few now in Russia, and abroad too, unfortunately—may assure himself of this by reading the following—*in its own way* valuable—passage from Unterman's pamphlet.

"The founders of scientific socialism inverted Hegelian dialectics and transformed it into a practical method of historical research. They had, indeed, squared their own accounts with German classical philosophy and eighteenth and nineteenth century bourgeois materialism. But they limited themselves from the outset to the practical social implications of their new theory. They had to specialise in order to accomplish something great, and they selected with keen insight those specialties which bore most directly upon the practical problems of their time. To what extent they had penetrated independently into the problem of cognition before they made this choice, no one can know but those comrades who have charge of the unpublished joint manuscript of Marx and Engels written in 1845-46.[57] But it is safe to say that this manuscript would have been published by this time, if it contained such a contribution to historical materialism as that supplied by Joseph Dietzgen. This assumption is further strengthened by the fact that Marx and Engels acknowledged Dietzgen's merit and called him 'the philosopher of the proletariat'. And it is further borne out by the fact that even the latest writings of Engels, such as *Anti-Dühring* and *Feuerbach*, in the passages dealing directly with the problems of cognition, free will, moral consciousness, do not contain anything which materially modifies the original conception of human consciousness formulated by Marx" (p. 9).

What then was this "original conception of human consciousness formulated by Marx"? Mr. Unterman admits frankly that he does not know. But on the other hand he knows very well that the founders of scientific socialism inverted dialectics, placing it on its feet. But what is meant by placing dialectics on its feet? Mr. Unterman says nothing about that, so let us turn to the original. Marx says: "To Hegel, the life-process of the human brain, i.e., the process of thinking, which, under the name of 'the Idea', he even transforms into an independent subject, is the demiurgos of the real world, and the real world is only the external, phenomenal form of 'the Idea'. With me, on the contrary, the ideal is nothing else than the material world reflected by the human mind, and translated into forms of thought."[58]

What is that? It is a *theory of cognition* and, besides, a theory of a definite type, *a materialist theory of cognition*. Consequently, Mr. Unterman had every opportunity to form some idea of the "conception of human consciousness formulated by Marx" without waiting for the publication of the philosophical work of Marx and Engels, which has not been published to this day. But, evidently, he did not even realise that this opportunity was there for him to take. Like others before him, he repeated that "Marx and Engels inverted dialectics", but it seems to have escaped his notice that it would have been impossible for them to have done so without the aid of a definite theory of cognition. A most penetrating writer is Mr. Unterman! True, it looks as though he can plead an extenuating circumstance; the Marxist theory of cognition is still unelaborated. But he could have helped in this misfortune by exercising his own powers ... if he had had any. In the lines quoted from Marx that to Hegel the process of thinking is transformed into a subject, there is an idea taken wholly from *Feuerbach*. This should have reminded even Mr. Unterman of the generally known fact that Marx's theory emerged *by way of criticism* from Feuerbach's philosophy, just as Feuerbach's philosophy emerged *by the same way* from Hegel's philosophy. If Mr. Unterman had taken the trouble to acquaint himself with Feuerbach's philosophy he would have had plenty of data at hi disposal on which to judge Marx's theory of cognition. Unfortunately, he did not take that trouble. Further. Marx's well-known—*long since published*—theses on Feuerbach's philosophy would have revealed to our learned author precisely in what respects Marx considered Feuerbach's philosophy *unsatisfactory.*

This would have furnished him with new facts upon which to judge Marx's gnosiology. And if he had only put all these facts to use, he would not have found the perusal of Engels' *Anti-Dühring* and *Feuerbach* so fruitless, and would have understood in the end that it is out of the question to use Dietzgen to "supplement" Marx.

But Mr. Unterman has a very superficial knowledge of Marx's theory and knows nothing at all of its philosophical origin. Finally, and almost the most important point, E. Unterman is not even a dilettante in philosophy, but simply an ... ignorant philistine.

We are not surprised that he finds it necessary to *"supplement"* Marx. It is a well established custom nowadays that as soon as some self-professed Marxist finds rents and gaps in his own world-outlook he at once says to himself anxiously: "Marx's theory needs correcting and supplementing."

Mr. Unterman tells us also that Marx and Engels "squared accounts" with classical German philosophy and French bourgeois materialism. Good. But *how* did they do that? By utilising what had been acquired by both German philosophy and materialism. German philosophy, while keeping to the dialectical method, was saturated with idealism; "bourgeois" materialism,* on the other hand, ignored dialectics almost completely. *In making materialism dialectical*, Marx and Engels *rejected idealism for all time.* But this does not mean that by *making materialism dialectical* they rejected materialism, just as to place dialectics on its feet is not to finish with dialectics. Of course, the dialectical materialism of Engels and Marx differs in many respects from, say, eighteenth-century French materialism. But this difference is the simple and inevitable *result* of the historical development of materialism.

After all eighteenth-century French materialism in its turn differed not only from the materialism of Democritus and Epicurus but even from the materialism of Hobbes and Gassendi. It is plain from one of Engels' articles in the newspaper *Volksstaat*, in which he recommended the French socialists to popularise "the splendid materialist literature of the eighteenth century"[59]

---

* Evidently Mr. Unterman thinks that the materialism of the eighteenth and nineteenth centuries was "bourgeois" in character, but the idealism of the same period was not. Why he should think so is something he himself cannot explain.

among the French working class, that the founders of scientific socialism were not by any means as scornful of this "bourgeois" materialism as is the erudite Mr. Unterman.

But Mr. Unterman knows nothing at all of all this and very proudly considers himself, thanks to J. Dietzgen, as being farther advanced in comparison with Marx and Engels.

However that may be, our author is firmly convinced that Marx's original (and to him, Unterman, quite unknown, as may be seen even more clearly from his pamphlet than from his own admission) understanding of human consciousness has been considerably supplemented by J. Dietzgen.

What arguments did he use to substantiate this conviction in lecturing the "narrow Marxists"? Some excerpts from J. Dietzgen's works which prove unquestionably that this highly gifted German workman—J. Dietzgen was actually a manual worker—had great philosophical talent, but which do not contain *a single theoretical principle that could be acknowledged as new in comparison with those enunciated in the works of Marx, Engels, and Feuerbach.*

Mr. Unterman is naive enough to believe that his excerpts throw new light on the "problem of cognition". Comparing them with some quotations from the works of the late Antonio Labriola, he takes great satisfaction in pointing out to us that this comparison "reveals at a glance their characteristic theoretical difference. Historical materialism takes its departure from human society", proletarian monism from the "natural universe (Weltall)" (p. 24). This strange man, who has read both *Ludwig Feuerbach* and *Anti-Dühring*, has nevertheless not understood that historical materialism was only the application to sociology of the method of materialist dialectics, whose starting point is precisely the "Weltall". It would seem as if he had not really read that part of Engels' preface to *Anti-Dühring* where the author says that Marx and he *applied materialism to history.*[60] What is the point of *"departure"* of the materialism which *explains* social development? Society. The earth rests on whales, the whales rest on water, water on the earth.* Clear?

All this does not stop Mr. Dauge from thinking of Mr. Unterman as a serious writer and warmly recommending him to Russian readers. But Mr. Dauge appears even more naive than the quite naive Mr. Unterman. He says: "Joseph Dietzgen discovered dialectical materialism simultaneously with Marx and Engels and—as the latter openly acknowledged—independently and apart from them" (p. IV). One might conclude from this that J. Dietz-

---

* [In Russian folklore there is a saying that the earth rests on three whales.]

gen was a dialectical materialist. But further on in the same work
of Dauge's we read: "We indeed find many points of similarity between Bogdanov and Dietzgen and we are certain that
the former, by developing and extending the philosophical work
he has begun, will arrive finally and by the logic of things—
'independently' of Dietzgen, as Dietzgen did 'independently'
of Marx—at *proletarian natur-monism*, to which, perhaps, he may
give another name, but which will have the same philosophical
content" (p. VIII). So Mr. Bogdanov's "philosophical" thinking
is developing naturally in the direction of dialectical materialism.... You have no fear of God, Mr. Dauge! Conclusion: the
reader will lose exactly nothing even if Mr. Unterman's pamphlet
never came into his hands. Productions like these are instructive
only in one sense. The very fact that they can appear at all shows
to what a low level philosophical education in the international socialist movement of our day has sunk. But there is little need to
emphasise anew this most distressing truth. Suffice it to recall
that in "the land of thinkers" Mr. Bernstein's "critical" remarks
on materialism and dialectics did not get their deserts by being
laughed out of court by the Social-Democrats.[61]

Now to Joseph Dietzgen. His son, Eugene Dietzgen, in a preface
to the Russian translation, also describes his father's philosophical teaching as an important supplement to Marxism (p. IV). He
says: "If the founders of historical materialism, and their followers, in a whole series of convincing historical investigations,
proved the connection between economic and spiritual development, and the dependence of the latter, in the final analysis, on
economic relations, nevertheless they did not prove that this
dependence of the spirit is rooted in its nature and in the nature
of the universe. Marx and Engels thought that they had ousted
the last spectres of idealism from the understanding of history.
This was a mistake, for the metaphysical spectres found a niche
for themselves in the unexplained essence of the human spirit
and in the universal whole which is closely associated with the
latter. Only a scientifically verified criticism of cognition could
eject idealism from here" (same page).

Despite all our respect for the noble memory of the German
worker-philosopher, and despite our personal sympathy for his
son, we find ourselves compelled to protest resolutely against the
main idea of the preface from which we have just quoted. In it,
the relationship of J. Dietzgen to Marx and Engels is quite wrongly stated. If Engels wrote that historical materialism had driven
idealism from its last refuge, that is to say, from the science of
human society, he believed that the triumph of materialism over
idealism, as regards both "the nature of the universe" and the
human spirit, was an incontestable fact. Engels was a convinced

materialist. Of course, one may dispute his materialism, but he ought not to have reproaches hurled at him which he does not at all deserve. Evidently, Eugene Dietzgen thinks that materialism does not have its own "criticism of cognition". But that too is an error that could only have been committed by someone ill-informed on the history of materialism. Marx's words about materialist dialectics which I referred to earlier contain the basic foundation of historical materialism and at the same time, *even in the first place*, a very definite "criticism of cognition". It could be argued that this "criticism" is expounded there much too briefly, but even if that is the case, we are still confronted with the question of how this—perhaps indeed too briefly expounded—"criticism of cognition" stands in relation to the "criticism" set forth by the author of *The Positive Outcome of Philosophy*. If these two "criticisms" *contradict* each other, we have to *choose between them, not supplement one by the other*. If, on the other hand, J. Dietzgen's "criticism of cognition" *does not contradict* the criticism elaborated much earlier by the founders of scientific socialism, but is simply a more detailed and more or less successful exposition of it, then, surely, it is at least strange to talk of J. Dietzgen *supplementing* Marx, and supplementing in the sense meant by Eugene Dietzgen, viz., of giving a new philosophical *substantiation* of historical materialism. We must add that the *"criticism of cognition"* contained in Marx's characterisation of materialist dialectics is set out in much greater detail in Engels' works, especially in Part I of *Anti-Dühring* (Philosophy).*

True, it is expounded there in a polemical rather than a systematic form. However, *if* this is a shortcoming, then it is a purely *formal* one, in no way affecting the *content* of the philosophical ideas enunciated by Engels in his controversy with Dühring. Moreover the polemical form might, perhaps, make it difficult for some *novice in philosophy* to understand Engels correctly. But for people who venture to talk about the extent to which Marx's theory requires to be supplemented, such a formal difficulty should not be an obstacle to understanding the philosophical section of *Anti-Dühring*. But Eugene Dietzgen does not even mention these philosophical views of Marx and Engels. It is as if he had not even heard of them, which is very strange! After this, what value can be placed on his indication that Marx's theory is *"incomplete"*? Eugene Dietzgen says: "In our opinion, four main phases of dialectics can be distinguished in the nineteenth century: Hegelian, or purely reflective; Darwinian, or biological; Marxist, or histor-

---

* [Note from the collection *From Defence to Attack*.] Feuerbach's criticism of Hegel's speculative philosophy served as the basis for this very criticism. (See my pamphlet *Fundamental Problems of Marxism*.)[62]

ico-economic; and Dietzgenian, or universal natur-monistic"
(p. VI).

In view of what we have said, it is clear that to describe *materialist* dialectics as *historico-economic* dialectics is to commit a
serious blunder. And this blunder clearly proves by its very existence that Eugene Dietzgen completely fails to understand the
place of Marx's theory in the history of philosophy and its relation to the philosophy of Feuerbach, whose views were also,
without any doubt, "*natur-monistic*".

Since he fails to master this highly important fact it would
have been better if Eugene Dietzgen had refrained from trying
to show just what is "lacking" in Marx's theory.

It will be useful to note here one more point, that Eugene Dietzgen describes Hegel's dialectics as *purely reflective*.

We need only ponder the following lines written by the same
Eugene Dietzgen to understand just how naive this is.

According to him, his father's dialectics furnishes us with the
cognitive-critical key to:

"1) The solution of all riddles" (sic!) "by the consistent application of the dialectical-productive method of investigation which,
proceeding consciously from sensuous or concrete reality, and basing itself on the organic unity of being, is able to reconcile all
contradictions and at the same time sharply distinguish tempo-
rally or spatially limited, relative opposites.

"2) The more fundamental understanding of historical materialism and the Marxist analysis of the capitalist mode of production, clearly showing to the proletariat the means and aim of its
economic emancipation in socialism.

"3) Solving the problem of beginning and end, the relationship
between form and content, appearance and essence, might and
right, the individual in contrast to society and nature, the subject
and the object, freedom and dependence, equality and distinction, the temporary and the eternal, the relative and the absolute, the particular and the general.

"4) The knowledge of the essence of things and phenomena, or
the criterion of relative truth.

"5) Abolishing the opposition between materialism and idealism" (same page).

As regards a more thorough understanding of historical materialism and analysis of capitalism, we shall wait till these are
disclosed in the collected works of Eugene Dietzgen himself, or
those of Pannekoek or any of the other writers who prefer Joseph
Dietzgen's "*key*" to Karl Marx's *method*. In regard to the solution
of "all riddles" concerning the questions of beginning and end,
relation of form to content, etc., etc., we would ask Eugene Dietzgen: Is that not just "*purely reflective dialectics*", and did Hegel's

philosophy not deal with all that? He will tell us, perhaps, that Hegel resolved those reflective questions (*that is to say, questions concerning the mutual relations of concepts*) in an idealist sense, whereas the author of *The Positive Outcome of Philosophy* gives them a "natur-monistic" solution. But this can only mean that Hegel's dialectics has an *idealist* basis, while J. Dietzgen's dialectics has its basis in a "*natur-monistic*" world-outlook. From this it inevitably follows that Hegel's dialectics has as its main distinguishing feature its idealist basis. Why then does Eugene Dietzgen not call it idealist, instead of conjuring up a new, very inexact and very clumsy title for it? Inexact philosophical terminology leads to unclarity of philosophical concepts and sometimes, incidentally, the latter gives rise to the former and is evidence of it. But Eugene Dietzgen is reluctant to use the terms "*idealism*" and "*materialism*". They remind him of "one-sided" conceptions, the opposition between which was "abolished" by his father's monism. Let us see exactly how J. Dietzgen "abolishes" the opposition between idealism and materialism.

To abolish the opposition between two given concepts, it is essential to have at least an accurate idea of the one and the other. What idea did Joseph Dietzgen have, say, of materialism?

On pages 62-63 of the book we are analysing, *The Positive Outcome of Philosophy*, we read: "In order to explain the process of thought, we must elucidate it as a part of the universal process. It is not the cause which created the world, either in the theological or in the idealist sense, nor is it a mere act of the brain substance, as the materialists of the last century present it. The process of thought and its cognition are a particularity in the general cosmos."

Thus the materialists of the last, that is to say, the eighteenth century, did not understand that the process of thought is a particularity in the general cosmos. They thought it was "a mere act of the brain substance". However, we can distinguish three or even four shades in the materialism of the eighteenth century: the materialism of La Mettrie and Diderot; the materialism of Helvétius; the materialism of Holbach; and the materialism of the Englishmen Hartley and Priestley. Which of these shades of materialism has J. Dietzgen in mind? No one knows. And what is meant by *not a mere act* of the brain substance"? Again, nobody knows. But to proceed. Maybe the matter will be cleared up in the following exposition.

On page 97, in the *Letters on Logic*, J. Dietzgen says: "The human skull performs the function of thinking as involuntarily as the chest does that of breathing. However, we can, by our will, stop breathing for a while.... In the same way, the will can control the thoughts." We shall not dwell here on the question of the extent to which thought can be controlled by will, but shall ask our reader to pay attention to the words: "The human skull performs the function of thinking ... as the chest does that of breathing." That, according to our author, is exactly what the eighteenth-century materialists said. Why then does J. Dietzgen declare them to be one-sided? And what, *in his opinion*, is the difference between *function* and *action*? This, too, remains unknown.

On page 72 of the same book, it says: "The old logic could not lay down any valid laws of thought, because it had too high an idea of thinking itself. For it thought was not only an attribute, a mode, a particle of true nature, but the nature of truth was spiritualised by it into a mystical substance. Instead of forming the concept of spirit out of flesh and blood, it tries to resolve" (explain) "flesh and blood by means of the concept."

There is something very wrong said here about the "old logic".* It is quite true that not *"flesh"* must be explained by *concept* but *concept* by *"flesh"*. However, this is precisely what the eighteenth-century materialists said and what Feuerbach repeated after them in the nineteenth century, when he rebelled against Hegel. Why then does J. Dietzgen declare that materialism is one-sided? This also remains his secret.

On the following page, J. Dietzgen reproaches the "old logic" that "it elevates the spirit to the first place and" (but?—*G.P.*) "relegates flesh and blood to the last". Here, too, is a clumsy expression, probably the work of Messrs the Translators (traduttori traditori!) but the clumsily expressed idea is quite correct, and again it proves to be a completely *materialist* one. Once more: Why does J. Dietzgen declare that materialism is one-sided?

To put the matter bluntly, J. Dietzgen had only a vague idea of materialism. He says of himself (p. 169): "As a rule, I acquaint myself with philosophical works of the second and third order merely by glancing over the preface, the introduction and perhaps the first chapter. Then I am approximately informed as to what I may expect further on." It is our view that J. Dietzgen, because of the extremely widespread contempt for French materialism which prevailed in Germany, *"acquainted himself"* in just that way with the works of the French materialists too, and, having acquainted himself with them in such a superficial and totally unsatisfactory manner, he concluded that materialism

---

* It is possible, though, that the incorrectness is the fault of the translators. They did not translate J. Dietzgen into Russian literary language, but into some kind of special one of their own, which is more worthy of the title *barbarian*. I am sorry not to have at hand the original works of J. Dietzgen, which were so kindly sent to me by his son, with whom I now have to cross philosophical swords.

was really one-sided, as all the German pastors kept on repeating, and undertook to "abolish" its one-sidedness, to "reconcile" it with idealism. Such a method of "abolishing opposites" was, of course, doomed to utter failure from the start. And we must add that though J. Dietzgen had a much more correct conception of idealism than he had of materialism, he was not fully correct even in that. For instance, what he had to say about Kant was often far from true, although it did conform, we agree, to the widespread current opinions on that philosopher. Even Hegel's philosophy he obviously knew only in *general outline*. We get this impression because J. Dietzgen often seems to be knocking at an open door and solving with incredible effort contradictions that were long ago resolved incomparably better, more fully and deeply, in Hegel's *Logik*. Why should he have knocked at an open door if he knew that the door was already open? But that was just the trouble—he didn't know.

Marx and Engels, who were thoroughly familiar with both *idealism* and *materialism*, did not "abolish" the opposition between these two concepts, but firmly declared themselves to be materialists. Dietzgen son will probably tell us that this is what constitutes their one-sidedness.

But we take a different view of the matter, and to substantiate this we invite the reader to examine with us J. Dietzgen's key "to the solution of all (excusez du peu!) riddles".

The philosophical significance of this remarkable "key" could be characterised by a very brief sentence from J. Dietzgen himself: "Nature comprises all" (p. 12). But that is comprehensible only to people well-versed in the history of philosophy, and there are few such people. Consequently a more detailed exposition is needed.

"The red thread winding through all these letters," J. Dietzgen says in his Thirteenth Letter on Logic (p. 154), "refers to the following point: the thinking apparatus is a thing like all other things, a part or attribute of the universe. It belongs in the first place to the most general category of being, and is an apparatus which produces a detailed picture of human experience by classification or distinction into categories. In order to use this apparatus correctly, one must clearly recognise that world unity is multiform and that all multiformity is a monist whole."

The same thought is expressed in different words in the Fifth Letter:

"The zoologists have always known that all species of animals belong to the animal kingdom; but this order was, with them, more of a mechanical affair.... The grouping of all animals, from the minutest to the biggest, in one kingdom, appeared before the time of Darwin to be an order which had been accomplished

by thought alone, as an order of thought, while since Darwin it
has been known as an order of nature.

"What the zoologist did to the animal kingdom, must be done
by the logician to being in general, to the infinite cosmos. He must
show that the whole world, all forms of its being, including the
spirit, are logically connected, related and welded together.

"A certain narrow materialism asserts that everything is done
when it has pointed out the interconnection between thought and
brain. A good many things may still be discovered with the help
of the dissecting knife, microscope and experiment; but this does
not make the function of logic superfluous.

"True, thought and brain are connected just as intimately as the
brain and the blood, the blood and oxygen, etc.; but thought in
general is connected quite as intimately with all being as is the
whole of physics.

"That the apple is not dependent only on the stem which attaches it to the tree, but also on the sunshine and rain, that these
things are not one-sidedly but universally connected, this is
what logic shall especially teach you in regard to the spirit, to
thought" (p. 110).

We shall not stop here to prove what was well known to all,
even to the "narrowest" of materialists of all times: that "thought"
is connected not only with the "brain", but also with all being in
general.

Here again Joseph Dietzgen is knocking at an open door. and
again he need not have done so had he known better the subject
he undertook to expound. He would have found many pages
in Holbach's *Système de la Nature* explaining the connection between "thought" and "being".

The fallaciousness of J. Dietzgen's charge against materialism
is at once plain to anyone familiar with eighteenth-century materialism.* We shall not enlarge on the point that it is awkward to
oppose the classification *by "thought"* to classification *by "nature"*,
since the latter is certainly at one and the same time *reflective*. We
have already said something about this. Now we are not *arguing*
with J. Dietzgen, but trying to *understand* him. To do this we must
pay the greatest attention to that part of the extract quoted where
it says that the whole world, all forms of being, are logically
connected, related and welded together.

---

* It is interesting to note, by the way, that Feuerbach also advanced the
same fallacious charge against materialism. And this, too, is explained by the
fact that Feuerbach, in keeping with the good old German custom, had only
a very vague idea of the history of materialism. He shunned "La Mettrie's
truffle-pie" in the self-same work where he (Feuerbach) fully agreed with the
views of the author of *L'Homme-machine*.

This idea is the basis of all J. Dietzgen's logic, or—since his logic embraces his theory of cognition,*—*his gnosiology*. And this idea, in the most varied ways—with endless, wearisome, inessential, and often lumbering repetition—is set forth both in his *The Positive Outcome of Philosophy* and *Letters on Logic*. And it is, of course, a correct but badly expounded idea, which was developed by Heraclitus in ancient times (and he had nothing in common either with the proletariat or with a "proletarian logic" of some special kind) and in the nineteenth century by Hegel and the Hegelians, including the materialists Feuerbach, Marx, and Engels.** *In "Anti-Dühring" and "Ludwig Feuerbach" and in the extract from "Anti-Dühring" published as a pamphlet entitled "Socialism: Utopian and Scientific", this idea is a great deal better expounded, is more simply and lucidly explained than in J. Dietzgen's "Letters on Logic" and "The Positive Outcome of Philosophy". This idea is the basis of all dialectics.* And since it is the basis of *all* dialectics, it alone is insufficient to characterise a *particular* dialectical method. We know of the *idealist* dialectics of Hegel and the *materialist* dialectics of Marx. What was J. Dietzgen's dialectics? We know that his son calls it "natur-monist". What variety of dialectics is this? Well, listen.

On page 45 of the book we are analysing, *The Positive Outcome of Philosophy*, J. Dietzgen says: "I have thus explained that logic has as yet not been conscious that the knowledge it produces with its basic principles does not offer us truth itself, but only a more or less accurate picture of it.*** I have, furthermore asserted that the positive outcome of philosophy has substantially added to the clearness of the portrait of the human mind. Logic seeks to be 'the science of the forms and laws of thought'. Dialectics, the legacy of philosophy, aims to be the same, and its first paragraph runs: not thinking produces being, but being produces thinking, of which (being) thinking is the part which is engaged in *portraying* truth. From this follows a fact which can easily obscure the meaning of the theory, viz., that the philosophy which has bequeathed to us logical" (?) "dialectics or dialectic logic, must explain not only thinking, but also, at the same time, the original, of which thinking furnishes copies."

---

* "Our logic," says J. Dietzgen, "is a theory of cognition."

** Feuerbach was most undoubtedly a materialist, although he liked to attack the "limited" materialists, so great was the strength of this much honoured custom in Germany, from whose influence many, many German Social-Democrats, including the most "radical", have still not freed themselves.

*** J. Dietzgen is not responsible for the style: we have already mentioned that Messrs Dauge and Orlov have translated his book not into Russian but into a ponderous, barbarous language of their own which Herzen would have called "bird language".

Without stopping to consider some *awkward and inaccurate expressions*, we shall observe that the *principal idea* in this passage is *purely materialistic*. Even Engels' words are used, although according to Engels it is not that being *produces* thinking, but that it *determines* thinking. This is a substantial difference, but we shall not dwell on it since it is obviously a *slip of the pen* on J. Dietzgen's part. It is sufficient for us to know that our author is here a *materialist*, one who is convinced that thought is "engaged"* *in portraying truth*, i.e., *being*.

So the "first paragraph" of J. Dietzgen's "natur-monist" dialectics "proclaims" what had been proclaimed much earlier by Marx's materialist dialectics: "The ideal is nothing else than the material world reflected by the human mind, and translated into terms of thought." Where is the difference? There is none. How then did J. Dietzgen "supplement" Marx? In no way! True, the "first paragraph" of dialectics is set out in the book of J. Dietzgen— *whose main works were published much later than the main works of Marx and Engels*—much more wordily than in Marx and Engels. But although more lengthy, J. Dietzgen's exposition is so very haphazard, in places so ineffectual and so frequently befogged by the imperfect lucidity of the author's philosophical thinking, that sometimes it not only does not explain the meaning of the "first paragraph" but rather obscures it. What then is the matter? Why then did he undertake to "supplement" Karl Marx with Joseph Dietzgen? It is precisely because—and only because— Dietzgen's philosophical thinking is not distinguished by complete lucidity. This seems to be paradoxical, but, infortunately, it is true.

In the passage we have just quoted, there is one strange proposition: Being "produces" thought, which however is part of being. If the words "being produces thought" mean the same as Marx's "the ideal is nothing else than the material world reflected by the human mind, and translated into terms of thought", then the words "thought is ... a part of ... being" compel us to doubt whether J. Dietzgen's philosophy is identical to Marx's. And it is just this possible doubt which attracts to J. Dietzgen people who are influenced by contemporary idealism and wish at any cost to place an *idealist* head on historical *materialism*.

In his exposition, J. Dietzgen is partly loyal to materialism, and then he reiterates that metaphysical logic "has overlooked the fact that knowledge which is produced with its own rules, is not the truth, not the real world, but only an ideal, i.e., more or less apt picture of it" (p. 44).

---

* Again, an unfortunate expression, but we do not intend to waste time on expressions.

Here, the *ideal* world is only the *reflection* of the material world. But sometimes J. Dietzgen gets himself entangled in his own addition: "thinking is part of being", i.e., the ideal world is part of the material world. Then he writes in all seriousness: "Is not the air, or the scent an ethereal body?" (p. 22). And on page 122 we read: "being or the universe, spirit and matter, embraces all forces, including heaven and hell" (sic!) "in a single circle, a monistic whole". It is such a great muddle, so ambiguous, that here, indeed, J. Dietzgen's philosophy does begin to resemble the very "original" philosophy of Mr. Bogdanov. It is known that anything distinquished by muddled thinking is at home in this philosophy. Here, Mr. P. Dauge, *in his own way*, is right but he is mistaken when he takes this for *dialectical materialism*.*

Space does not permit us to follow up all the regrettable logical consequences of the muddle that has crept into J. Dietzgen's understanding of the "first paragraph" of materialist dialectics; his completely erroneous views of the criterion of truth, and so on. We shall restrict ourselves, therefore, to the remark that, in spite of his son's opinion, J. Dietzgen was *unable to solve the problem of the relation of the subject to the object*, and that it was this that brought about his logical downfall. We shall add that J. Dietzgen's error arose, apparently, from a highly praiseworthy endeavour to pull the theoretical ground from under the feet of speculative philosophy, which placed spirit—in one or other of its conceptions—*outside* and *above* the world. In opposition to this philosophy, J. Dietzgen put the proposition that "being is everything; it is the essential content of everything, outside it there is nothing and can be nothing, because it is the cosmos. i.e., the infinite" (p. 26). It goes without saying that as an argument against speculative philosophy, this has absolutely no value, since to repudiate the existence of extra-universal spirit by a simple recital of the proposition that the world contains in itself *all being*, is to base oneself on a *tautology*, fully identical with that which Eugene Dühring once placed as the cornerstone of *his* philosophy and which Engels ridiculed so scathingly in the first part of *Anti-Dühring*: "All-embracing being is one."** But J. Dietzgen thought

---

* At best—any resemblance with Mr. Bogdanov could, of course, only be at the worst possible—this confusion of thought includes an obscure allusion to Spinozism. But even with the aid of the most clear Spinozism, one cannot "*excel*" materialism. The materialists La Mettrie, Diderot, Feuerbach, Marx and Engels were Spinozists who had merely ceased to identify God with Nature (see *A Critique of Our Critics*, pp. 154-66[63]). Feuerbach has already explained Spinoza's relation to materialism.

** "'All-embracing being is one.' If tautology, the simple repetition in the predicate of what is already expressed in the subject—if that makes an axiom, then we have here one of the purest water. Herr Dühring tells us in the subject that being embraces everything, and in the predicate he intrepidly

this tautological expression was almost the most important "out-come" of philosophy. With its aid, he attempted to solve all con-tradictions. Thus on pages 127-28, in the Eighth Letter on Logic, addressed, as all these Letters were, to his son, he says: "The most vivid, and. perhaps, the most instructive illustration of the cor-rect meaning of contradictions, is given by the contrast between truth and untruth. These two poles are ... more widely separated than the North Pole and the South Pole, and yet they are as inti-mately connected as these two. Generally accepted logic will hardly listen to the demonstration of such a senseless unity as that of truth and untruth. Therefore you will pardon me, if I illus-trate this example by other opposites, if you like, by the con-trast between day and night. Let us assume that the day lasts twelve hours and the night likewise. Here day and night are opposites; where it is day it cannot be night, and yet day and night constitute one single day of twenty-four hours, in which they both dwell harmoniously. It is exactly the same with truth and untruth. The world is the truth, and error, the appearance and lies, embodied in it, are parts of the true world, just as night is part of day, without violation of logic.

"We may honestly speak of appearance *real* and *true* lies, with-out any contradiction. Just as unreason contains reason, so also untruth lives constantly and inevitably in truth, because the latter is all-embracing, it is the universe."

But in what way is day here reconciled with night? *Firstly*, it is assumed that a day is equal to *twelve* hours, *and then* it is postulated that a day stretches out to *twenty-four* hours, that is to say, *there is now no place for night*, the duration of which was formerly twelve hours. When there is no place for *night*, it is clear that *there can be no place either for opposition* between night and day. By means of such naive methods, based on the fact that *one and the same* expression is used in *different* senses, one may indeed with the greatest ease reconcile anything, solve all "riddles", and "abolish" all the oppositions in the world. But ... is that really an answer?

J. Dietzgen had to choose between Hegel's idealist dialectics and Marx's materialist dialectics, and he was strongly inclined towards the latter. But since he had not studied the question ade-quately, and was even insufficiently acquainted with it, he got himself *mixed up* in his own arguments against speculative philos-ophy and imagined that he had succeeded in *"reconciling"* the

---

declares that in that case there is nothing outside it. What colossal, 'system-creating thought'!" (Frederick Engels, *Philosophy. Political Economy. Social-ism (Anti-Dühring)*, Translated from the German, Fourth Edition, St. Petersburg, 1907, p. 30).[64]

opposition between idealism and materialism. To say nothing of the fact that this inability to cope with his own philosophical thinking was not a sign of strength but of *weakness* on J. Dietzgen's part. To Dietzgen himself, however, and just because he was unable to contend with his own philosophical thinking, this manifestation of *weakness* seemed, on the contrary, to be a manifestation of his *superiority* over "one-sided" materialism.

And those who are now trying to "supplement" Karl Marx and Frederick Engels with Joseph Dietzgen view this weakness of Dietzgen's in the same way as he did. We well understand what the Germans mean when they talk of *piety* in the relationship of children to parents. So that it does not enter our head to ridicule the undoubtedly exaggerated opinion which Eugene Dietzgen has of his father's philosophy. But Eugene Dietzgen must also, for his part, understand piety in the relationship of pupil to teacher. Therefore he must not complain because we have firmly rejected his attempt to "supplement" Marx. As for the Untermans, Dauges, Orlovs, etc., *their* inclination to "supplement" in the way mentioned appears to us the simple product of ignorance, weakness of philosophical thinking, and downright literary carelessness. These people have no other extenuating circumstances while those we have just enumerated hardly attenuate anything.

In No. 2 of *Rus*[65] for the present year (1907) there is a feature by G. V. Kolomiitsev, entitled "Music of Today (Richard Wagner and the Search for New Gods)". We were interested in the following passage:

"Here I should like to dwell on one phenomenon which seems to me very typical of our harassing and impetuous times. I refer to the strongly developed fear of being found 'backward' in questions of musical art, a fear aroused by falsely acquired snatches of the past. In connection with the search for something new at any cost, this fear prompts us to find 'novelty' and 'genius' far too often where at most there is something a good deal less 'significant', and above all, in its essence, anything but 'new'."

Such a fear is also noticeable in our Marxist literature. It explains—*in the first instance*—very much, including the constant efforts to "supplement" Marx: now with Kant, now with Mach, and now, finally, with J. Dietzgen.

In conclusion, we beg our readers not to think that we attach no importance to the philosophical works of the author of *Letters on Logic*. No, no, and no again! That is not at all our attitude to them. In our view, they merely have no significance *as supplementing Marx*, but in themselves they are sufficiently interesting and in places instructive; although J. Dietzgen's *Letters on Logic* are strikingly, awfully poor in comparison with Hegel's *Science of Logic (Wissenschaft der Logik)*.

J. Dietzgen's too fervent admirers do him the most harm; when they contrast him with giants like Hegel and Marx, they make him appear a lot smaller than he really was.

We advise *reading J. Dietzgen only after the most careful study of Marx's philosophy*. It will then be easier to see how he *approximates* in his teaching to the founders of scientific socialism, and where he has to *yield ground* to them, *lags behind* them. Otherwise, reading J. Dietzgen will give the reader, together with not unimportant and not uninteresting, *but in no way new*, details, much and harmful confusion.

Looking at the matter from another angle, it would be a great deal less awkward to study J. Dietzgen if someone at last took pity on Russian readers and retranslated the most important works of the German worker-philosopher from the barbarian language of Dauge and Orlov into literary Russian. That would be a great boon. indeed!

FUNDAMENTAL PROBLEMS OF MARXISM

Marxism is an integral world-outlook. Expressed in a nutshell, it is *contemporary materialism*, at present the highest stage in the development of that *view upon the world* whose foundations were laid down in ancient Greece by Democritus, and in part by the Ionian thinkers who preceded that philosopher. What was known as *hylozoism* was nothing but a naive *materialism*. It is to Karl Marx and his friend Frederick Engels that the main credit for the development of present-day materialism must no doubt go. The historical and economic aspects of this world-outlook, i.e., what is known as *historical materialism* and the closely related sum of views on the *tasks, method, and categories of political economy, and on the economic development of society, especially capitalist society*, are in their fundamentals almost entirely the work of Marx and Engels. That which was introduced into these fields by their *precursors* should be regarded merely as the preparatory work of amassing material, often copious and valuable, but not as yet systematised or illuminated by a single fundamental idea, and therefore not appraised or utilised in its real significance. What Marx and Engels' *followers* in Europe and America have done in these fields is merely a more or less successful elaboration of specific problems, sometimes, it is true, of the utmost importance. That is why the term "Marxism" is often used to signify only these two aspects of the present-day materialist world-outlook not only among the "general public", who have not yet achieved a deep understanding of philosophical theories, but even among people, both in Russia and the entire civilised world, who consider themselves faithful followers of Marx and Engels. In such cases these two aspects are looked upon as something independent of "philosophical materialism", and at times as something almost opposed to it.* And since these two aspects cannot but

---

* [Note to the German edition of 1910.] My friend Viktor Adler was perfectly right when, in an article he published on the day of Engels' funeral, he observed that socialism, as understood by Marx and Engels, is not only an economic but a universal doctrine (I am quoting from the Italian edition):

hang in mid-air when they are torn out of the general context of cognate views constituting their theoretical foundation, those who perform that tearing-out operation naturally feel an urge to "substantiate Marxism" anew by joining it—again quite arbitrarily and most frequently under the influence of philosophical moods prevalent at the time among *ideologists of the bourgeoisie*—with some philosopher or another: with Kant, Mach, Avenarius, or Ostwald, and of late with Joseph Dietzgen. True, the philosophical views of J. Dietzgen have arisen quite independently of bourgeois influences and are in considerable measure related to the philosophical views of Marx and Engels. The latter views, however, possess an incomparably more consistent and rich content. and for that reason alone cannot be *supplemented* by Dietzgen's teachings but can only be *popularised* by them. No attempts have yet been made to "supplement Marx" with Thomas Aquinas. It is however quite feasible that, despite the Pope's recent encyclical against the Modernists, the Catholic world will at some time produce from its midst a thinker capable of performing this feat in the sphere of theory.

Attempts to show that Marxism must be "supplemented" by one philosopher or another are usually backed up with reference to the fact that Marx and Engels did not anywhere set forth their philosophical views. This reasoning is hardly convincing, however, apart from the consideration that, even if these views were indeed not set forth anywhere, that could provide no logical reason to have them replaced by the views of any random thinker who, in the main, holds an entirely different point of view. It should be remembered that we have sufficient literary material at our dis-

Frederico Engels, *L'Economia politica. Primi lineamenti di una critica dell' economia politica. Con introduzione e notizia bio-bibliografiche di Filippo Turati, Vittorio Adler e Carlo Kautsky e con appendice. Prima edizione italiana, publicata in occasione della morte dell'autore (5 agosto 1895)*, pp. 12-17, Milano, 1895. However, the truer this appraisal of socialism "as understood by Marx and Engels", the stranger the impression produced when Adler conceives it possible to replace the *materialist* foundation of this "universal doctrine" by a *Kantian* foundation. What is one to think of a universal doctrine whose philosophical foundation is in no way connected with its entire structure? Engels wrote: "Marx and I were pretty well the only people to rescue conscious dialectics from German idealistic philosophy and apply it in the materialist conception of nature and history" (see the preface to the third edition of *Anti-Dühring*, p. xiv). Thus, despite the assertions of certain of their present-day followers, the founders of scientific socialism were *conscious materialists*, not only in the field of history, but in natural science as well.

posal to form a correct idea of the philosophical views of Marx and Engels.*

In their *final* shape, these views were *fairly fully* set forth. although in a polemical form, in the first part of Engels' book *Herrn Eugen Dühring's Umwälzung der Wissenschaft* (of which there are several Russian translations). Then there is a splendid booklet by the same author *Ludwig Feuerbach und der Ausgang der klassischen deutschen Philosophie* (which I have translated into Russian and supplied with a preface and explanatory notes; it has been published by Mr. Lvovich), in which the views constituting the philosophical foundation of Marxism are expounded in a positive form. A brief but vivid account of the same views, related to *agnosticism*, was given by Engels in his preface to the English translation of the pamphlet *The Development of Scientific Socialism* (translated into German, and published under the title of *Ueber den historischen Materialismus* in *Neue Zeit*, Nos. 1 and 2, 1892-93). As for Marx, I will mention as important for an understanding of the *philosophical aspect* of his teachings, in the first place, the characterisation of *materialist dialectic*—as distinct from Hegel's *idealist* dialectic—given in the afterword to the Second German edition of Volume I of *Capital*, and, secondly, the numerous remarks made *en passant* in the same volume. Also significant in certain respects are some of the pages in *La Misère de la philosophie* (which has been translated into Russian). Finally, *the process of the development* of Marx and Engels' philosophical views is revealed with sufficient clarity in their early writings, republished by F. Mehring under the title of *Aus dem literarischen Nachlass von Karl Marx*, etc., Stuttgart, 1902.

In his dissertation *Differenz der demokritischen und epikureischen Naturphilosophie*, as well as in several articles republished by Mehring in Volume I of the publication just mentioned, the young Marx appears before us as an idealist *pur sang* of the Hegelian school. However, in the articles which have now been included in the same volume and which first appeared in the *Deutschfranzösische Jahrbücher*,[67] Marx—like Engels, who also collaborated in the *Jahrbücher*—was a firm adherent of Feuerbachian *"humanism"*.** *Die heilige Familie, order Kritik der kritischen Kri-*

---

* The philosophy of Marx and Engels is the subject of W. Weryho's book *Marx als Philosoph*, Bern und Leipzig, 1894. It would, however, be difficult to imagine a less satisfactory work.

** [Note to the German edition of 1910.] Of considerable importance for a characterisation of the evolution of Marx's philosophical views is his letter of October 20, 1843, to Feuerbach. Inviting Feuerbach to come out against Schelling, Marx wrote the following: "You are just the man for this because you are *Schelling in reverse*. The *sincere thought*—we may believe the best of our opponent—of the *young* Schelling for the realisation of which however he did not possess the necessary qualities except imagination, he had no energy

tik, which appeared in 1845 and has been republished in Volume
II of the Mehring publication, shows us our two authors, i.e.,
both Marx and Engels, as having made several important steps
in the *further development* of Feuerbach's philosophy. The direction
they gave to this elaboration can be seen from the eleven *theses on
Feuerbach* written by Marx in the spring of 1845, and published
by Engels as an appendix to the aforementioned pamphlet *Ludwig
Feuerbach*. In short, there is no lack of material here; the only
thing needed is the ability to make use of it, i.e., the need to have
the proper training for its understanding. Present-day readers,
however, do not have the training required for that understanding, and consequently do not know how to make use of it.

Why is that so? For a variety of reasons. One of the principal
reasons is that nowadays there is, in the first place, little *knowledge
of Hegelian philosophy*, without which it is difficult to learn Marx's
method, and, in the second place, little *knowledge of the history
of materialism*, the absence of which does not permit present-day
readers to form a clear idea of the doctrine of Feuerbach, who was
Marx's immediate precursor in the field of philosophy, and in
considerable measure worked out the philosophical foundation of
what can be called the world-outlook of Marx and Engels.

Nowadays Feuerbach's "humanism" is usually described as
something very vague and indefinite. F. A. Lange, who has done
so much to spread, both among the "general public" and in the
learned world, an absolutely false view of the essence of materialism and of its history, refused to recognise Feuerbach's "humanism"
as a materialist teaching. F. A. Lange's example is being followed,
in this respect, by almost all who have written on Feuerbach in
Russia and other countries. P. A. Berlin too seems to have been
affected by this influence, since he depicts Feuerbach's "humanism"

---

but vanity, no driving force but opium, no organ but the irritability of
a feminine perceptivity, this sincere thought of his youth, which in his case
remained a fantastic youthful dream, has become truth, reality, manly
seriousness in your case. Schelling is therefore an *anticipated caricature* of
you, and as soon as reality confronts the caricature, the latter must dissolve
into thin air. I therefore regard you as the necessary, natural—that is, nomi-
nated by Their Majesties Nature and History—opponent of Schelling. Your
struggle with him is the struggle of the imagination of philosophy with
philosophy itself." K. Grün, *Ludwig Feuerbach in seinem Briefwechsel und
Nachlass*, I. Band, S. 361, Leipzig und Heidelberg, 1874.[68] This seems to
show that Marx understood Schelling's youthful thought in the meaning of
a materialist monism. Feuerbach, however, did not share this opinion of
Marx's, as will be seen from his reply to the latter. He considered that
already in his first works Schelling "merely converts the idealism of *thought*
into the idealism of the *imagination*, and attributes just as little reality to
things as to the 'Ich', with the only difference that it had a different appearance, and that he replaced the determinate 'Ich' by the non-determinate
Absolute, and gave idealism a pantheistic colouring" (ibid., p. 402).

First page of the variant of G. Plekhanov's
Fundamental Problems of Marxism

as a kind of materialism that is not quite "pure".* I must admit
that I do not know for certain how this question is regarded by
Franz Mehring, whose knowledge of philosophy is the best, and
probably unique, among German Social-Democrats. But it is
perfectly clear to me that it was the materialist that Marx and
Engels saw in Feuerbach. True, Engels speaks of Feuerbach's
inconsistency, but that does not in the least prevent him from
recognising the *fundamental propositions* of his philosophy as
*purely materialist.*** But then these propositions cannot be viewed
otherwise by anybody who has gone to the trouble of making a
study of them.

II

I am well aware that in saying all this I risk surprising very
many of my readers. I am not afraid to do so; the ancient thinker
was right in saying that astonishment is the mother of philosophy.
For the reader not to remain at the stage, so to say, of astonishment, I shall first of all recommend that he ask himself what
Feuerbach meant when, while giving a terse but vivid outline
of his philosophical *curriculum vitae*, he wrote, "God was my
first thought, Reason the second, and Man the third and last
thought". I contend that this question is conclusively answered
in the following meaningful words of Feuerbach himself, "In
the controversy between materialism and spiritualism ... the
human head is under discussion ... once we have learnt what kind
of matter the brain is made up of, we shall soon arrive at a clear
view upon all other matter as well, matter in general."*** Elsewhere
he says that his *"anthropology"*, i.e., his "humanism", merely
means that man takes for God that which is his own essence, his
own spirit.**** He goes on to say that Descartes did not eschew

* See his interesting book *Germany on the Eve of the Revolution of 1848*,
St. Petersburg, 1906, pp. 228-29.
** [Note to the German edition of 1910.] Engels wrote: "The course of
evolution of Feuerbach is that of a Hegelian—a never quite orthodox Hegelian,
it is true—into a materialist: an evolution which at a definite stage necessi-
tates a complete rupture with the idealist system of his predecessor. With
irresistible force Feuerbach is finally driven to the realisation that the Hegelian premundane existence of the 'absolute idea', the 'pre-existence of the
logical categories' efore the world existed, is nothing more than the fantastic
survival of the belief in the existence of an extramundane creator; that the
material, sensuously perceptible world to which we ourselves belong is the
only reality; and that our consciousness and thinking, however suprasen-
suous they may seem, are the product of a material, bodily organ, the brain.
Matter is not a product of mind, but mind itself is merely the highest product
of matter. This is, of course, pure materialism." *Ludwig Feuerbach*, Stuttgart,
1907, S. 17-18.[69]
*** "Über Spiritualismus und Materialismus", *Werle*, X, 129.
**** *Werke*. IV, 249.

this "anthropological" point of view.* How is all this to be understood? It means that Feuerbach made "Man" the point of departure of his philosophical reasoning *only because* it was from that point of departure that he hoped the sooner to achieve his aim—to bring forth a correct view upon matter in general and its relation to the "spirit". Consequently what we have here is a *methodological device*, whose value was conditioned by circumstances of time and place, i.e., by the thinking habits of the learned, or simply educated, Germans of the time,** *and not by any specificity of world-outlook.****

The above quotation from Feuerbach regarding the "human head" shows that when he wrote these words the problem of "the kind of matter the brain is made up of" was solved by him in a "purely" materialistic sense. This solution was also accepted by Marx and Engels. It provided the foundation of their own philosophy, as can be seen with the utmost clarity from Engels' works, so often quoted here—*Ludwig Feuerbach* and *Anti-Dühring*. That is why we must make a closer study of this solution; in doing so, we shall at the same time be studying the *philosophical aspect of Marxism.*

---

* *Werke*, IV, 249.
** Feuerbach himself has very well said that the *beginnings* of any philosophy are determined by the prior state of philosophical thought (*Werke*, II, 193).
*** [Note to the German edition of 1910.] F. Lange states: "A genuine materialist will always be prone to turn his glance to the totality of external Nature and consider Man merely as a wavelet in the ocean of the eternal movement of matter. To the materialist Man's nature is merely a particular instance of general physiology, just as thinking is a special instance in the chain of physical processes of life." *Geschichte des Materialismus*, 2. Band, S. 74, Leipzig, 1902. But Théodore Dézamy, too, in his *Code de la Communauté* (Paris, 1843) proceeds from the nature of Man (the human organism), yet no one will doubt that he shares the views of French eighteenth-century materialism. Incidentally, Lange makes no mention of Dézamy, whilst Marx counts him among the French Communists whose communism was more scientific than that of Cabet, for instance. "Like Owen ... *Dézamy, Gay* and others, developed the teaching of *materialism* as the teaching of *real humanism* and the *logical* basis of *communism*." Aus dem *literarischen Nachlass von Karl Marx, Friedrich Engels und Ferdinand Lassalle*, 2. Band, S. 240.[70] At the time Marx and Engels were writing the work just quoted (*The Holy Family*), they as yet differed in their appraisal of Feuerbach's philosophy. Marx called it "materialism coinciding with humanism": "But just as *Feuerbach* is the representative of *materialism* coinciding with *humanism* in the *theoretical* domain, French and English *socialism* and *communism* represent *materialism* coinciding with *humanism* in the *practical* domain." In general Marx regarded materialism as the necessary theoretical foundation of communism and socialism. Engels, on the contrary, held the view that Feuerbach had once and for all put an end to the old contraposing of spiritualism and materialism (ibid., pp. 232 and 196).[71] As we have already seen, he, too, later took note of the evolution, in Feuerbach's development, from idealism to materialism.

In an article entitled "Vorläufige Thesen zur Reform der Philosophie", which came out in 1842 and, judging by the facts, had a strong influence on Marx, Feuerbach said that "the real relation of thinking to being is only as follows: being is the *subject*; thinking, the *predicate*. Thinking is conditioned by being, and not being by thinking. Being is conditioned by itself ... has its foundation in itself."*

This view on the relation of being to thinking, which Marx and Engels made the foundation of the *materialistic explanation of history*, is a most important outcome of the criticism of Hegel's idealism already completed in its main features by Feuerbach, a criticism whose conclusions can be set forth in a few words.

Feuerbach considered that Hegel's philosophy had removed the contradiction between being and thinking, a contradiction that had expressed itself in particular relief in Kant. However, as Feuerbach thought, it removed that contradiction, *while continuing to remain within the latter*, i.e., within *one of its elements*, namely, *thinking*. With Hegel, *thinking is being*: "Thinking is the subject; being, the predicate."** It follows that Hegel, and idealism in general, eliminated the contradiction only *by removing one of its component elements, i.e., being, matter, nature.* However, removing one of the component elements in a contradiction does not at all mean doing away with that contradiction. "Hegel's doctrine that reality is '*postulated*' by the Idea is merely a translation into rationalistic terms of the theological doctrine that Nature was created by God,—and reality, matter, by an abstract, non-material being."*** This does not apply only to Hegel's absolute idealism. Kant's transcendental idealism, according to which the external world receives its laws from Reason instead of Reason receiving them from the external world, is closely akin to the theological concept that the world's laws were dictated to it by divine Reason.**** *Idealism does not establish the unity of being and thinking*, nor can it do so; *it tears that unity asunder.* Idealistic philosophy's point of departure—the "*I*" as the fundamental philosophical principle—is totally erroneous. It is not the "*I*" that must be the starting-point of genuine philosophy, but the "*I*" and the "*you*". It is such a point of departure that makes it possible to arrive at a proper understanding of the relation between thinking and being, between the subject and the object. I am "*I*" to myself, and at the same time I am "*you*" to others. The "*I*" is the *subject*, and at the same time the *object*. It must at the same time be noted that I am not the abstract being idealistic philos-

---

* *Werke*, II, 263.
** Ibid., 261.
*** Ibid., 262.
**** Ibid.. 295.

ophy operates with. I am an *actual* being; my *body* belongs to my *essence*; moreover, my body, as a whole, is my *I*, my genuine essence. It is not an abstract being that thinks, but that actual being, that body. Thus, contrary to what the idealists assert, an actual and material being proves to be the subject, and thinking—the predicate. Herein lies the only possible solution of the contradiction between being and thinking, a contradiction that idealism sought so vainly to resolve. None of the elements in the contradiction is *removed*; both are *preserved*, revealing their real *unity*. "That which to me, or subjectively, is a purely spiritual, non-material and non-sensuous act is in itself an objective, material and sensuous act."*

Note that in saying this, *Feuerbach stands close to Spinoza*, whose philosophy he was already setting forth with great sympathy at the time his own breakaway from idealism was taking shape, i.e., when he was writing his history of modern philosophy.** In 1843 he made the subtle observation, in his *Grundsätze*, that *pantheism is a theological materialism*, a negation of theology but as yet on a theological standpoint. This confusion of *materialism and theology* constituted Spinoza's inconsistency, which, however, did not prevent him from providing a "correct—at least for his time—philosophical expression for the materialist trend of modern times". That was why Feuerbach called Spinoza "the Moses of the modern free-thinkers and materialists".*** In 1847 Feuerbach asked: "What then, under careful examination, is that which Spinoza calls *Substance*, in terms of logics or metaphysics, and *God* in terms of theology? To this question he replied categorically, "Nothing else but Nature". He saw Spinozism's main shortcoming in the fact that "in it the sensible, anti-theological essence of Nature assumes the aspect of an abstract, metaphysical being". Spinoza eliminated the dualism of God and Nature, since he declared that the acts of Nature were those of God. However, it was just because he regarded the acts of Nature to be those of God, that the latter remained, with Spinoza, a being distinct from Nature, but forming its foundation. He regarded God as the subject and Nature as the predicate. A philosophy that has completely liberated itself from theological traditions must remove this

---

* *Werke,* II 350.
** [Note to the German edition of 1910.] By that time Feuerbach had already written the following noteworthy lines: "Despite all the oppositeness of practical realism in the so-called sensualism and materialism of the English and the French—a realism that denies any speculation—and the spirit of *all* of Spinoza, they nevertheless have their *ultimate* foundation in the viewpoint on *matter* expressed by Spinoza, as a metaphysician, in the celebrated proposition: 'Matter is an Attribute of God'." (K. Grün, *L. Feuerbach*, I, S. 324-25.)
*** *Werke.* II. 291.

important shortcoming in Spinoza's philosophy, which in its essence is sound. "Away with this contradiction!" Feuerbach exclaimed. "Not *Deus sive Natura* but *aut Deus aut Natura* is the watchword of Truth."*

Thus, Feuerbach's "humanism" proved to be nothing else but Spinozism disencumbered of its theological pendant. And it was the standpoint of this kind of Spinozism, which Feuerbach had freed of its theological pendant, that Marx and Engels adopted when they broke with idealism.

However, disencumbering Spinozism of its theological appendage meant revealing its true and *materialist* content. Consequently, *the Spinozism of Marx and Engels was indeed materialism brought up to date.***

Further. Thinking is not the *cause* of being, but its *effect*, or rather its *property*. Feuerbach says: *Folge und Eigenschaft. I* feel and think, not as a subject contraposed to an object, but as a *subject-object*, as an actual and material being. "For us the object is not merely the thing sensed, but also the basis, the indispensable condition of my sensation." The objective world is not only without me but also within me, inside my own skin.*** Man is only a part of Nature, a part of being; there is therefore no room for any contradiction between his thinking and his being. Space and time do not exist only as forms of thinking. They are also forms of being, forms of my contemplation. They are such, solely because I myself am a creature that lives in time and space, and because I sense and feel as such a creature. In general, the laws of being are at the same time laws of thinking.

That is what Feuerbach said.**** And the same thing, though in a different wording, was said by Engels in his polemic with Dühring.*****This already shows what an important part of Feuer-

---

* Ibid., 392.

** [Note to the German edition of 1910.] In *Die heilige Familie* (2. Band des Nachlasses) Marx remarks: "Hegel's *Geschichte der Philosophie* presents French materialism as the *realisation* of the Substance or Spinoza" (S. 240).[72]

*** [Note to the German edition of 1910.] "How do we cognise the external world? How do we cognise the *inner* world? For ourselves we have no other means than we have for others! Do I know anything about myself without the medium of my senses? Do I exist if I do not exist outside myself, i.e., outside my *Vorstellung*? But how do I know that I exist? How do I know that I exist, not in my *Vorstellung*, but in my sensations, in actual fact, unless I perceive myself through my senses?" (Feuerbach's *Nachgelassene Aphorismen* in Grün's book, II, S. 311.)

**** *Werke*, II, 334 and X, 186-87.

***** [Note to the German edition of 1910.] I particularly recommend to the reader's attention the thought expressed by Engels in *Anti-Dühring*, that the laws of external Nature and the laws governing man's bodily and mental existence are "two classes of laws which we can separate from each other at most only in thought but not in reality" (S. 157).[73] This is the self-same *doctrine of the unity of being and thinking, of object and subject*. Regarding

bach's philosophy became an integral part of the philosophy of
Marx and Engels.

If Marx began to elaborate his materialist explanation of history
by criticising *Hegel's philosophy of law*, he could do so *only because*
Feuerbach had completed his criticism of *Hegel's speculative
philosophy*.

Even when *criticising* Feuerbach in his Theses, Marx often develops and augments the former's ideas. Here is an instance from the
sphere of "epistemology". Before *thinking* of an object, man,
according to Feuerbach, *experiences* its action *on himself*, con-
templates and *senses it*.

It was this thought that Marx had in mind when he wrote:
"The chief defect of all previous materialism (that of Feuerbach
included) is that thing [Gegenstand], reality, sensuousness are
conceived only in the form of the *object* [Objekt], or of *contemplation*
[Anschauung], but not as *sensuous human activity, practice*, not
subjectively."[74] This shortcoming in materialism, Marx goes on
to say, accounts for the circumstance that, in his *Essence of Christianity*, Feuerbach regards theoretical activity as the only genuine
human activity. Expressed in other words, this means that, according to Feuerbach, our *I* cognises the *object by coming under
its action*.* Marx, however, objects by saying: our *I* cognises the
object, *while at the same time acting upon that object*. Marx's thought
is a perfectly correct one: as *Faust already said*, "*Am Anfang war
die Tat*". It may of course be objected, in defence of Feuerbach, that,
in the process of *our acting* upon objects, we cognise their properties only in the measure in which they, for their part, act upon
us. In both cases *sensation* precedes *thinking*; in both cases we
first *sense* their properties, and only then *think* of them. But that
is something that Marx did not deny. For him the gist of the
matter was not the indisputable fact that sensation precedes thinking, but the fact that man is induced to think chiefly by the
sensations he experiences in the process of his acting upon the
outer world. Since this action on the outer world is prescribed to
man by the struggle for existence, the theory of knowledge is
closely linked up by Marx with his materialist view of the history
of human civilisation. It was not for nothing that the thinker
who directed against Feuerbach the thesis we are here discussing
wrote in Volume I of his *Capital*: "By thus acting on the external
world and changing it, he at the same time changes his own na-

---

space and time, see Chapter 5 of Part I of the work just mentioned. This chapter shows that to Engels, just as to Feuerbach, space and time are not only
forms of contemplation, but also forms of being (S. 41-42).

* "Dem Denken," he says, "geht das Sein voran; ehe du die Qualität
denkst, *fühlst* du die Qualität" (*Werke*, II, 253). [Being comes before thinking, before you think about quality you feel it.]

ture."[75] This proposition fully reveals its profound meaning only in the light of Marx's theory of knowledge. We shall see how well this theory is confirmed by the history of cultural development and, incidentally, even by the science of language. It must, however, be admitted that Marx's epistemology stems directly from that of Feuerbach, or, if you will, it is, properly speaking, the epistemology of Feuerbach, only rendered more profound by the masterly correction brought into it by Marx.

I shall add, in passing, that this masterly correction was prompted by the "spirit of the times". The striving to examine the interaction between object and subject precisely from the point of view in which the subject appears in an *active* role, derived from the public mood of the period in which the world-outlook of Marx and Engels was taking shape.* The revolution of 1848 was in the offing....

III

The doctrine of the unity of subject and object, thinking and being, which was shared in equal measure by Feuerbach, and by Marx and Engels, was also held by the most outstanding materialists of the seventeenth and eighteenth centuries.

Elsewhere** I have shown that La Mettrie and Diderot—each after his own fashion—arrived at a world-outlook that was a "brand of Spinozism", i.e., a Spinozism without the theological appendage that distorted its true content. It would also be easy to show that, inasmuch as we are speaking of the unity of subject and object, Hobbes too stood very close to Spinoza. That, however, would be taking us too far afield, and, besides, there is no immediate need to do that. Probably of greater interest to the reader is the fact that today any naturalist who has delved even a little into the problem of the relation of thinking to being arrives at that doctrine of their unity which we have met in Feuerbach.

When Huxley wrote the following words: "Surely no one who is cognisant of the facts of the case, nowadays, doubts that the roots of psychology lie in the physiology of the nervous system", and went on to say that the operations of the mind "are functions of

---

* [Note to the German edition of 1910.] Feuerbach said of his philosophy: "My philosophy cannot be dealt with exhaustively by the pen; it finds no room on paper." This statement, however, was only of theoretical significance to him. He went on to say: "Since for it (i.e., his philosophy) the truth is not that which has been thought, but that which has been not only thought, but seen, heard and felt" (*Nachgelassene Aphorismen* in Grün's book, II, S. 306).

** See my article "Bernstein and Materialism" in the symposium *A Critique of Our Critics*.[76]

the brain",* he was expressing just what Feuerbach had said, only with these words he connected concepts that were far less clear. It was precisely because the concepts connected with these words were far less clear than with Feuerbach that he attempted to link up the view just quoted with Hume's philosophical scepticism.**

In just the same way, Haeckel's "monism", which created such a stir, is nothing else but a purely materialist doctrine—in essence close to that of Feuerbach—of the unity of subject and object. Haeckel, however, is poorly versed in the history of materialism, which is why he considers it necessary to struggle against its "one-sidedness"; he should have gone to the trouble of making a study of its theory of knowledge in the form it took with Feuerbach and Marx, something that would have preserved him from the many lapses and one-sided assumptions that have made it easier for his opponents to wage a struggle against him on philosophical grounds.

A very close approach to the most modern materialism—that of Feuerbach, Marx and Engels—has been made by August Forel in various of his writings, for instance in the paper, *Gehirn und Seele*, which he read to the 66th Congress of German Naturalists and Physicians held in Vienna (September 26, 1894).*** In places Forel not only expresses ideas resembling Feuerbach's but—and this is amazing—marshals his arguments just as Feuerbach did his. According to Forel, each new day brings us convincing proofs that the psychology and the physiology of the brain are merely two ways of looking at "one and the same thing". The reader will not have forgotten Feuerbach's identical view, which I have quoted above and which pertains to the same problem. This view can be supplemented here with the following statement: "I am the psychological object to myself," Feuerbach says, "but a physiological object to others."**** In the final analysis, Forel's main idea boils down to the proposition that consciousness is the "inner reflex of cerebral activity".***** This view is already materialist.

Objecting to the materialists, the idealists and Kantians of all kinds and varieties claim that what we apprehend is only the *mental* aspect of the phenomena that Forel and Feuerbach deal with. This objection was excellently formulated by Schelling, who said that "the Spirit will always be an island which one cannot

---

* [Plekhanov is quoting from the French translation of Huxley's *Hume, His Life and Philosophy*, i.e.,] *Hume, sa vie, sa philosophie*, p. 108. [We are quoting from the original, p. 80.]

** *Ibid.*, p. 110 [p. 82].

*** Cf. also *Chapter Three* in his book *L'âme et le système nerveux. Hygiène et pathologie*, Paris, 1906.

**** *Werke*, II, 348-49.

***** *Die psychischen Fähigkeiten der Ameisen*, etc., München, 1901, S. 7.

reach from the sphere of matter, otherwise than by a leap". Forel is well aware of this, but he provides convincing proof that science would be an impossibility if we made up our minds in earnest not to leave the bounds of that island. "Every man," he says, "would have only the psychology of his own subjectivism (*hätte nur die Psychologie seines Subjectivismus*) ... and would positively be obliged to doubt the existence of the external world and of other people."* Such doubt is absurd, however.** "Conclusions arrived at by analogy, natural-scientific induction, a comparison of the evidence provided by our five senses, prove to us the existence of the external world, of other people, and the psychology of the latter. Likewise they prove to us that comparative psychology, animal psychology and finally, our own psychology would be incomprehensible and full of contradictions if we considered it apart from the activities of our brain; first and foremost, it would seem a contradiction of the law of the conservation of energy."***

Feuerbach not only reveals the contradictions that inevitably beset those who reject the materialist standpoint, but also shows how the idealists reach their "island". "I am *I* to myself," he says, "and *you* to another. But I am such an *I* only as a sensible [i.e., material—*G.P.*] being. The abstract intellect isolates this being-for-oneself as Substance, the atom, ego, God; that is why, to it, the connection between being-for-oneself and being-for-another is arbitrary. That which I think of as extra-sensuous (*ohne Sinnlichkeit*), I think of as without and outside any connection."**** This most significant consideration is accompanied by an analysis of that process of abstraction which led to the appearance of Hegelian logic as an *ontological* doctrine.*****

---

* Ibid., S. 7-8.
** [Note to the German edition of 1910.] Moreover, on his return from exile, Chernyshevsky published an article "The Character of Human Knowledge", in which he proves, very wittily, that a person who doubts the existence of the external world should also doubt the fact of his own existence. Chernyshevsky was always a faithful adherent of Feuerbach. The fundamental idea of his article can be expressed in the following words of Feuerbach. "I am not different from things and creatures without me because I distinguish myself from them; I distinguish myself because I am different from them physically, organically, and in fact. Consciousness presupposes being, is merely conscious being, that-which-is as realised and presented in the mind" (*Nachgelassene Aphorismen* in Grün's book, II, S. 306).
*** *Die psychischen Fähigkeiten*, same page.
**** *Werke*, II, 322. I highly recommend these words of Feuerbach's to the attention of Mr. Bogdanov. Cf. also p. 249.
***** "Der absolute Geist Hegel's ist nichts Anderes als der abstrakte, von sich selbst abgesonderte sogenannte *endliche* Geist, wie das unendliche Wesen der Theologie nichts Anderes ist, als das abstrakte endliche Wesen." *Werke*, II, 263. [The Hegelian Absolute Spirit is nothing other than the abstract, distinct from itself, so-called, finite Spirit in the same way as the infinite essence of theology is nothing other than the abstract finite essence.]

9*

Had Feuerbach possessed the information provided by present-day ethnology, he would have been able to add that *philosophical idealism* descends, in the historical sense, from the *animism* of primitive peoples. This was already pointed out by Edward Tylor,* and certain historians of philosophy are beginning to take it, in part, into consideration, though for the time being more as a curiosity than a fact from the history of culture, and of tremendous theoretical and cognitive significance.**

These ideas and arguments of Feuerbach's were not only well known to Marx and Engels and given careful thought by them, but indubitably and in considerable measure helped in the evolution of their world-outlook. If Engels later had the greatest contempt for post-Feuerbachian German philosophy, it was because that philosophy, in his opinion, merely resuscitated the old philosophical errors already revealed by Feuerbach. That, indeed, was the case. Not one of the latest critics of materialism has brought forward a single argument that was not refuted either by Feuerbach himself or, before him, by the French materialists***; but to the "critics of Marx"—to E. Bernstein, C. Schmidt, B. Croce and the like—"the pauper's broth of eclecticism"[77] of the most up-to-date German so-called philosophy seems a perfectly new dish; they have fed on it, and, seeing that Engels did not see fit to address himself to it, they imagined that he was *"evading"* any analysis of an argumentation he had long ago considered and found absolutely worthless. That is an old story, but one that is always new. Rats will never stop thinking that the cat is far *stronger* than the lion.

In recognising the striking similarity—and, in part, also the identity—in the views of Feuerbach and A. Forel, we shall, however, note that while the latter is far better informed in natural science, Feuerbach had the advantage of a thorough knowledge of

---

* *La civilisation primitive*, Paris, 1876, tome II, p. 143. It should, however, be observed that Feuerbach made a truly masterly surmise in this matter. He said: "Der Begriff des Objects ist ursprünglich gar nichts Anderes als der Begriff *eines andern* Ich,—so fasst der Mensch in der Kindheit alle Dinge als freithätige, willkürliche Wesen auf, daher ist der Begriff des Objects überhaupt vermittelt durch den Begriff des Du des gegenständlichen Ich." II, 321-22. [The concept of the Object is originally nothing but the concept of another "Ego"—so man in his childhood apprehends all things as free-acting self-willed essences. Therefore the concept of the object is generally mediated through the concept of the Tu of the objective "Ego".]

** [Note to the German edition of 1910.] See Théodore Gomperz, *Les penseurs de la Grèce*, Trad. par Aug. Reymond, Lausanne, 1905, tome II, pp. 414-15.

*** [Note to the German edition of 1910.] Feuerbach called "cudchewers" (Wiederkäuer) those thinkers who tried to revive an obsolete philosophy. Unfortunately, such people are particularly numerous today, and have created an extensive literature in Germany, and partly in France. They are now beginning to multiply in Russia as well.

philosophy. That is why Forel makes mistakes we do not find in Feuerbach. Forel calls his theory the *psycho-physiological theory of identity*.* To this no objection of any significance can be raised, because all terminology is conventional. However, since the theory of identity once formed the foundation of an absolutely definite *idealist* philosophy, Forel would have done well to have straightforwardly, boldly and simply declared his theory to be *materialist*. He seems to have preserved certain prejudices against materialism, and therefore chose another name. That is why I think it necessary to note that *identity in the Forelian sense* has nothing in common with *identity in the idealist sense*.

The "critics of Marx" do not know even this. In his polemic with me, C. Schmidt ascribed to the materialists precisely the idealist doctrine of identity. In actual fact, materialism recognises the *unity* of subject and object, not their identity. This was well shown by the selfsame Feuerbach.

According to Feuerbach, the unity of subject and object, of thinking and being, makes sense only when man is taken as the basis of that unity. This has a special kind of "humanist" sound to it, and most students of Feuerbach have not found it necessary to give deeper thought to *how* man serves as the basis of the unity of the opposites just mentioned. In actual fact, this is how Feuerbach understood the matter: "It is only when thinking is not a *subject for itself*, but the predicate of a real [i.e., material—*G.P.*] being that thought is not something separated from being."** The question now is: where, in which philosophical systems, is thinking a "subject for itself", that is to say, something independent of the bodily existence of a thinking individual? The answer is clear: in systems that are *idealist*. The idealists first convert thinking into a self-contained essence, independent of man ("the subcjet for itself"), and then assert that it is in that essence that the contradiction between being and thinking is resolved, for the very reason that separate and independent being is a property of that independent-of-matter essence.*** Indeed, the contradiction is resolved in that essence. In that case, what is that essence? It is *thinking*, and this thinking exists—*is*—independently of any-

---

* See his article "Die psychophysiologische Identitätstheorie als wissen-schaftliches Postulat", in the symposium *Festschrift I. Rosenthal*, Leipzig, 1906, erster Teil, S. 119-32.

** *Werke*, II, 339.

*** [Note to the German edition of 1910.] Ernst Mach and his followers act in exactly the same way. First they transform *sensation* into an independent essence, non-contingent upon the sensing *body*—an essence which they call an element. Then they declare that this essence contains the resolution of the contradiction between being and thinking, subject and object. This reveals the grossness of the error committed by those who assert that Mach is close to Marx.

thing else. Such a resolution of the contradiction is a purely formal one, which, as we have already pointed out, is achieved only by eliminating one of its elements, namely, being, as something independent of thinking. Being proves to be a simple property of thinking, so that when we say that a given object exists, we mean that it exists only in our thinking. That is how the matter was understood by Schelling, for example. To him, thinking was the absolute principle from which the real world, i.e., Nature and the "finite" spirit, followed of necessity. But *how* did it follow? What was meant by the existence of the real world? Nothing but existence in thinking. To Schelling, *the Universe was merely the self-contemplation of the Absolute Spirit*. We see the same thing in Hegel. Feuerbach however, was not satisfied with such a purely formal resolving of the contradiction between thinking and being. He pointed out that there is no—there can be no—*thinking independent of man*, i.e., of an actual and material creature. Thinking is activity of the brain. To quote Feuerbach: "But the brain is the organ of thinking only as long as it is connected with the human head and body."*

We now see in what sense Feuerbach considers man the basis of the unity of being and thinking. Man is that basis in the sense that he is nothing but a material being that possesses the ability to think. If he is such a being, then it is clear that none of the elements of the contradiction is eliminated—neither being nor thinking, "matter" or "spirit", subject or object. They are all combined in him as the *subject-object*. "I exist, and I think ... only as a subject-object," Feuerbach says.

To be does not mean to exist in thought. In this respect, Feuerbach's philosophy is far clearer than that of J. Dietzgen. As Feuerbach put it: "To prove that something exists means to prove that it is not something that exists only in thought."** This is perfectly true but it means that *the unity of thinking and being does not and cannot in any way mean their identity.*

This is one of the most important features distinguishing materialism from ide-lism.

IV

When people say that, for a certain period, Marx and Engels were followers of Feuerbach, it is often inferred that, when that period ended, Marx and Engels' world-outlook changed considerably, and became quite different from Feuerbach's. That is how the matter is viewed by Karl Diehl, who finds that Feuerbach's influence on Marx is usually highly exaggerated.*** This is a gross

---

   * *Werke*, II, 362-63.
  ** *Werke*, X, 308.
 *** *Handwörterbuch der Staatswissenschaften*, V, S. 708.

mistake. When they ceased from being followers of Feuerbach, Marx and Engels did not at all cease from sharing a very considerable part of his philosophical views. The best proof of this is the Theses which Marx wrote in criticism of Feuerbach. The Theses in no way eliminate the fundamental propositions in Feuerbach's philosophy, but only correct them, and—what is most important— call for an application more consistent (than Feuerbach's) in explaining the reality that surrounds man, and in particular his own activity. It is not thinking that determines being, but being that determines thinking. That is the fundamental thought in all of Feuerbach's philosophy. Marx and Engels made that thought the foundation of the materialist explanation of history. The materialism of Marx and Engels is a far more developed doctrine than Feuerbach's. The materialist views of Marx and Engels, however, developed in the direction indicated by the inner logic of Feuerbach's philosophy. That is why these views will not always be fully clear—especially in their philosophical aspect—to those who will not go to the trouble of finding out just which part of the Feuerbachian philosophy became incorporated in the world-outlook of the founders of scientific socialism. And if the reader meets anyone who is much taken up with the problem of finding "philosophical substantiation" for historical materialism, he may well be sure that this wise mortal is very much deficient in the respect I have just mentioned.

But let us return to the subject. Already in his Third Thesis on Feuerbach, Marx tackled the most difficult of all the problems he was to resolve in the sphere of social man's historical "practice", with the aid of the correct concept of the unity of subject and object, which Feuerbach had developed. The Thesis reads: "The materialist doctrine concerning the changing of circumstances and upbringing forgets that circumstances are changed by men, and that the educator must himself be educated."[78] Once this problem is solved, the "secret" of the materialist explanation of history has been uncovered. But Feuerbach was unable to solve it. In history, he—like the French eighteenth-century materialists he had so much in common with—remained an *idealist*.* Here Marx and Engels had to start from scratch, making use of the theoretical material that had been accumulated by social science, chiefly

---

* [Note to the German edition of 1910.] This accounts for the reservations always made by Feuerbach when speaking of materialism. For instance: "When I go backward from this point, I am in complete agreement with the materialists; when I go forward, I differ from them" (*Nachgelassene Aphorismen* in K. Grün's book, II, S, 308). The meaning of this statement will be seen from the following words, "I, too, recognise the Idea, but only in the sphere of mankind, politics, morals, and philosophy" (Grün, II, S. 307). But whence Idea in politics and morals? This question is not answered by our "recognising" the Idea.

by the French historians of the Restoration period. But even here,
Feuerbach's philosophy provided them with some valuable pointers. "Art, religion, philosophy, and science", Feuerbach says,
"are but the manifestation or revelation of genuine human essence."* Hence it follows that the "human essence" contains the
explanation of all ideologies, i.e., that the development of the
latter is conditioned by the development of the "human essence".
What is that essence? "Man's essence," Feuerbach replies, "is
only in community, in Man's unity with Man."** This is very
vague, and here we see a border line that Feuerbach did not cross.***
However, it is beyond that border line that the region of the
materialist explanation of history, a region discovered by Marx
and Engels, begins; that explanation indicates the causes which
in the course of history determine the "community, Man's unity
with Man", i.e., the mutual relations that men enter into. This
border line not only *separates* Marx from Feuerbach, but testifies
to his *closeness* to the latter.

The sixth Thesis on Feuerbach says that *human essence is the
ensemble of the social relations*. This is far more definite than what
Feuerbach himself said, and the close genetic link between Marx's
world-outlook and Feuerbach's philosophy is here revealed with
probably greater clarity than anywhere else.

When Marx wrote this Thesis he already knew, not only the
direction in which the solution of the problem should be sought,
but the solution itself. In his *Critique of Hegel's Philosophy of
Law* he showed that no mutual relations of people in society,

---

* *Werke,* II, 343.
** *Werke,* II. 344.
*** [Note to the German edition of 1910.] Incidentally, Feuerbach too
thinks that the "human being" is created by history. Thus he says: "I think
only as a subject educated by history, generalised, united with the whole,
with the genus, the spirit of world history. My thoughts do not have their
beginning and basis directly in my particular subjectivity, but are the
outcome; their beginning and their basis are those of world history itself"
(K. Grün, II, S. 309). Thus we see in Feuerbach the embryo of a materialist
understanding of history. In this respect, however, he does not go further
than Hegel (see my article "For the Sixtieth Anniversary of Hegel's Death",
Neue Zeit, 1890),[79] and even lags behind him. Together with Hegel, he stresses
the significance of what the great German idealist called the geographic
basis of world history. "The course of the history of mankind," he says, "is
certainly prescribed to it, since man follows the course of Nature, the course
taken by streams. Men go wherever they find room, and the kind of
place that suits them best. Men settle in a particular locality, and
are conditioned by the place they live in. The essence of India is the essence
of the Hindu. What he is, what he had become, is merely the product of the
East-Indian sun, the East-Indian air, the East-Indian water, the East-Indian
animals and plants. How could man originally appear if not out of Nature?
Men, who become acclimatised to any kind of nature, have sprung from
Nature, which tolerates no extremes" (*Nachgelassene Aphorismen*, K. Grün,
II. S. 330).

"neither legal relations nor political forms could be comprehended whether by themselves or on the basis of a so-called general development of the human mind, but that on the contrary they originate in the material conditions of life, the totality of which Hegel, following the example of English and French thinkers of the eighteenth century, embraces within the term 'civil society'; that the anatomy of this civil society, however, has to be sought in political economy."[80]

It now remained only to explain the origin and development of the *economy* to obtain a full solution of a problem that materialism had been unable to cope with for centuries on end. That explanation was provided by Marx and Engels.

It stands to reason that, when I speak of the *full solution* of that great problem, I am referring only to its general or *algebraic solution*, which materialism could not find in the course of centuries. It stands to reason that, when I speak of a *full* solution, I am referring, not to the *arithmetic* of social development, but to its *algebra*; *not to the causes of individual phenomena, but to how the discovery of those causes should be approached.* And that means that the materialist explanation of history was primarily of a *methodological significance.* Engels was fully aware of this when he wrote: "It is not the bare conclusions of which we are in such need, but rather study [das Studium]; the conclusions are nothing without the reasoning that has led up to them."* This, however, is sometimes not understood either by "critics" of Marx, whom, as they say, may God forgive, or by some of his "followers", which is much worse. Michelangelo once said of himself, "My knowledge will engender a multitude of ignoramuses." These words have regrettably proved prophetic. Today *Marx's knowledge* is engendering ignoramuses. The fault lies, not with Marx, but with those who talk rubbish while invoking his name. For such rubbish to be avoided, an understanding of the *methodological significance of historical materialism* is necessary.

V

In general, one of the greatest services rendered to materialism by Marx and Engels lies in their elaboration of a *correct method.* Feuerbach, who concentrated his efforts on the struggle against the *speculative* element in Hegel's philosophy, had little appreciation of its *dialectical* element, and made little use of it. "True dialectic," he said, "is no more monologue by a solitary thinker with himself; it is a dialogue between the *ego* and the *tu*."** In

---

* *Nachlass...*, I, 477.[81]
** *Werke.* II. 345.

the first place, however, Hegel's dialectic did not signify a "monologue by a solitary thinker with himself"; and, secondly, Feuerbach's remark gives a correct definition of the *starting-point of philosophy, but not of its method.* This gap was filled by Marx and Engels, who understood that it would be mistaken, in waging a struggle against Hegel's speculative philosophy, to ignore his dialectic. Some critics have declared that, during the years immediately following his break with idealism, Marx was highly indifferent to dialectic too. Though this opinion may seem to have some semblance of plausibility, it is controverted by the aforementioned fact that, in the *Deutsch-französische Jahrbücher,* Engels was already speaking of the method as the soul of the new system of views.*

In any case, the second part of *La Misère de la philosophie* leaves no room for doubt that, at the time of his polemic with Proudhon, Marx was very well aware of the significance of the dialectical method and knew how to make good use of it. Marx's victory in this controversy was one by a man able to think dialectically, over one who had never been able to understand the nature of dialectic, but was trying to apply its method to an analysis of capitalist society. This same second part of *La Misère de la philosophie* shows that dialectic, which with Hegel was of a purely idealist nature and had remained so with Proudhon (so far as he had assimilated it), was placed on a *materialist foundation* by Marx.**

"To Hegel," Marx wrote subsequently, describing his own *materialist* dialectic, "the life-process of the human brain, *i.e.,* the process of thinking, which, under the name of 'the Idea', he even transforms into an independent subject, is the demiurgos of the real world, and the real world is only the external, phenomenal form of 'the Idea'. With me, on the contrary, the ideal is nothing else than the material world reflected by the human mind, and translated into forms of thought."[83] This description implies full agreement with Feuerbach, firstly in the attitude towards Hegel's

---

* Engels was not referring to himself but to all who shared his views. "Wir bedürfen:...," he said; there can be no doubt that Marx was one of those who shared his views.

** See Part II of *La Misère de la philosophie,* Observations, First and Second,[82] [Addendum to the German edition of 1910.] It should however be noted that Feuerbach too criticised Hegelian dialectic from the materialist viewpoint. "What kind of dialectic is it," he asked, "that contradicts natural origin and development? How do matters stand with its 'necessity'? Where is the 'objectivity' of a psychology, of a philosophy in general, which abstract itself from the only categorical and imperative, fundamental and solid objectivity, that of physical Nature, a philosophy which considers that its ultimate aim, absolute truth and fulfilment of the spirit lie in a full departure from that Nature, and in an absolute subjectiveness, unrestricted by any Fichtean non-ego, or Kantian thing-in-itself" (K. Grün, I, S. 399).

"Idea", and, secondly, in the relation of thinking to being. The Hegelian dialectic could be "turned right side up" *only* by one who was convinced of the soundness of the basic principle of Feuerbach's philosophy, viz., that it is not thinking that determines being, but being that determines thinking.

Many people confuse dialectic with the doctrine of development; dialectic is, in fact, such a doctrine. However, it differs substantially from the vulgar "theory of evolution", which is completely based on the principle that *neither Nature nor history proceeds in leaps and that all changes in the world take place by degrees.* Hegel had already shown that, understood in such a way, the doctrine of development was untenable and ridiculous.

"When people want to understand the *rise* or *disappearance* of anything," he says in Volume I of his *Wissenschaft der Logik*, "they usually imagine that they achieve comprehension through the medium of a conception of the *gradual character* of that rise or disappearance. However, changes in being take place, not only by a transition of one quantity into another, but also by a transition of qualitative differences into quantitative, and, on the contrary, by a transition that *interrupts gradualness*, and substitutes one phenomenon for another."* And every time *gradualness is interrupted, a leap* takes place. Hegel goes on to show by a number of examples how often *leaps take place both in Nature and in history*, and he exposes the ridiculous logical error underlying the vulgar "theory of evolution". "Underlying the doctrine of gradualness," he remarks, "is the conception that what is arising already exists in reality, and remains unobserved only because of its small dimensions. In like manner, people, when they speak of gradual disappearance, imagine that the non-existence of the phenomenon in question, or the phenomenon that is to take its place, is an accomplished fact, although it is as yet imperceptible.... But this can only suppress any notion of arising and destruction.... To explain appearance or disappearance by the gradualness of the change means reducing the whole matter to absurd tautology and to imagining in an already complete state [i.e., as already arisen or already gone.—*G.P.*] that which is in the course of appearing or disappearing."**

This dialectical view of Hegel's as to the *inevitability of leaps in the process of development* was adopted in full by Marx and Engels. It was developed in detail by Engels in his polemic with Dühring, and here he "turned it right side up", that is to say, on a *materialist foundation.*

---

* *Wissenschaft der Logik*, erster Band, Nürnberg, 1812, S. 313-14.
** Regarding the matter of "leaps" see my pamphlet *Mr. Tikhomirov's Grief*, St. Petersburg, M. Malykh's Publishing House, pp. 6-14.[84]

Thus he indicated that the transition from one form of energy to another cannot take place otherwise than by means of a *leap*.* Thus he sought, in modern chemistry, a confirmation of the dialectical theorem of the transformation of quantity into quality. Generally speaking, he found that the rights of *dialectical thinking* are confirmed by the *dialectical properties of being*. Here, too, being conditions thinking.

Without undertaking a more detailed characterisation of materialist dialectic (its relation to what, by a parallel with elementary mathematics, may be called elementary logic—see my preface to my translation of *Ludwig Feuerbach*), I shall remind the reader that, during the last two decades, the theory that sees only gradual changes in the process of development has begun to lose ground even in *biology*, where it used to be recognised almost universally. In this respect, the work of Armand Gautier and that of Hugo de Vries seem to show promise of epoch-making importance. Suffice it to say that de Vries' *theory of mutations* is a *doctrine that the development of species takes place by leaps* (see his two-volume *Die Mutations-Theorie*, Leipzig, 1901-03, his paper *Die Mutationen und die Mutations-Perioden bei der Entstehung der Arten*, Leipzig, 1901, and the lectures he delivered at the University of California, which appeared in the German translation under the title of *Arten und Varietäten und ihre Entstehung durch die Mutation*, Berlin, 1906).

In the opinion of this outstanding naturalist, *the weak point in Darwin's theory of the origin of species is that this origin can be explained by gradual changes*.** Also of interest, and most apt, is de Vries' remark that the dominance of the theory of gradual changes in the doctrine of the origin of species has had an unfavourable influence on the *experimental* study of relevant problems.***

I may add that, in present-day natural science and especially among the *neo-Lamarckians*, there has been a fairly rapid spread of the theory of the so-called *animism of matter*, i.e., that matter

---

* "Bei der Allmählichkeit bleibt der Übergang von einer Bewegungsform zur anderen immer ein Sprung, eine entscheidende Wendung. So der Übergang von der Mechanik der Weltkörper zu der kleineren Massen auf einem einzelnen Weltkörper; ebenso von der Mechanik der Massen zu der Mechanik der Moleküle—die Bewegungen umfassend, die wir in der eigentlich sogenannten Physik untersuchen", etc., *Anti-Dühring*, S. 57. [In spite of all gradualness, the transition from one form of motion to another always remains a leap, a decisive change. This is true of the transition from the mechanics of celestial bodies to that of smaller masses on a particular celestial body; it is equally true of the transition from the mechanics of masses to the mechanics of molecules—including the forms of motion investigated in physics proper....][65]

** *Die Mutationen*, S. 7-8.

*** *Arten*, etc., S. 421.

in general, and especially any *organised matter*, possesses a certain degree of *sensibility*. This theory, which many regard as being diametrically opposed to materialism (see, for instance, *Der heutige Stand der Darwinschen Fragen*, by R. H. Francé, Leipzig, 1907), is in fact, when properly understood, only a translation, into the language of present-day natural science, of Feuerbach's materialist doctrine of the unity of being and thinking, of object and subject.* It may be confidently stated that Marx and Engels, who had assimilated this doctrine, would have been keenly interested in this trend in natural science, true, *far too little elaborated as yet.*

Herzen was right in saying that Hegel's philosophy, which many considered conservative in the main, was a genuine algebra of revolution.** With Hegel, however, this algebra remained wholly unapplied to the burning problems of practical life. Of necessity, the speculative element brought *a spirit of conservatism* into the philosophy of this great absolute idealist. It is quite different with Marx's materialist philosophy, in which revolutionary "algebra" manifests itself with all the irresistible force of its dialectical method. "In its mystified form," Marx says, "dialectic became the fashion in Germany, because it seemed to transfigure and to glorify the existing state of things. In its rational form it is a scandal and abomination to bourgeoisdom and its doctrinaire professors, because it includes in its comprehension and affirmative recognition of the existing state of things, at the same time also, the recognition of the negation of that state, of its inevitable breaking up; because it regards every historically developed social form as in fluid movement, and therefore takes into account its transient nature not less than its momentary existence; because it lets nothing impose upon it, and is in its essence critical and revolutionary."[87]

If we regard materialist dialectic from the viewpoint of the history of Russian literature, we may say that this dialectic was the first to supply a method necessary and competent to solve the problem of *the rationality of all that exists*, a problem that so greatly troubled our brilliant thinker Belinsky.*** It was only Marx's dialectical method, as applied to the study of Russian life, that has shown us how much *reality* and how much *semblance* of reality *there was* in it.

---

* To say nothing of Spinoza, it should not be forgotten that many French eighteenth-century materialists were favourably inclined towards the theory of the "animism of matter".

** [Note to the German edition of 1910.] See Engels, *Ludwig Feuerbach*, pp. 1-5.[86]

*** See my article "Belinsky and Rational Reality" in the symposium *Twenty Years*.

VI

When we set out to explain *history* from the materialist stand-point, our first difficulty is, as we have seen, the question of the actual causes of the development of social relations. We already know that the "anatomy of civil society" is determined by its economy. But what is the latter itself determined by?

Marx's answer is as follows: "In the social production of their existence, men inevitably enter into definite relations, which are independent of their will, namely, relations of production appropriate to a given stage in the development of their material forces of production. The totality of these relations of production constitutes the economic structure of society, the real foundation, on which arises a legal and political superstructure...."*

Marx's reply thus reduces the whole question of the development of the economy to that of the causes determining the development of the productive forces at the disposal of society. In this, its final form, it is solved *first and foremost by the reference to the nature of the geographic environment.*

In his philosophy of history Hegel already speaks of the important role of *"the geographic foundation of world history".* But since, in his view, the *Idea* is the ultimate cause of all development, and since it was only *en passant* and in instances of secondary importance, against his will as it were, that he had recourse to *a materialist explanation of phenomena*, the thoroughly sound view he expressed regarding the historic significance of geographic environment could not lead him to all the fruitful conclusions that follow therefrom. It was only by the materialist Marx that these conclusions were drawn in their fullness.**

The properties of the geographic environment determine the character both of the natural products that serve to satisfy man's wants, and of those objects *he himself produces* with the same purpose. Where there were no metals, aboriginal tribes could not, unaided, emerge from what we call the *Stone Age*. In exactly the same way, for *primitive fishers and hunters* to go over *to cattle-breeding and agriculture*, the appropriate conditions of geographic environment were needed, i.e., in this instance, suitable fauna and flora. Lewis Henry Morgan has shown that the absence, in the New World, of animals capable of being domesticated, and the specific differences between the flora of the two hemispheres brought about the considerable difference in the course of their

---

* See the introduction to *Zur Kritik der politischen Oekonomie.*[88]
** [Note to the German edition of 1910.] In this case, Feuerbach, as I have already said, did not go further than Hegel.

inhabitants' social development.* Of the redskins of North America Waitz says: "... they have no domesticated animals. This is highly important, for in this circumstance lies the principal reason that forced them to remain at a low stage of development."** Schweinfurth reports that in Africa, when a given locality is overpopulated, part of the inhabitants emigrate and thereupon change their mode of life *in accordance with the new geographic environment*. "Tribes hitherto agricultural become hunters, while tribes that have lived from their flocks will turn to agriculture."*** He also points out that the inhabitants of an area rich in iron, which seems to occupy a considerable part of Central Africa, "naturally began to smelt iron".****

Nor is that all. Already at the lower stages of development, tribes enter into mutual intercourse and exchange some of their products. This expands the boundaries of the geographic invironment, influencing the development of the productive forces of each of these tribes and accelerating the *course* of that development. It is clear, however, that the greater or lesser ease with which such intercourse arises and is maintained also depends on the properties of the geographic environment. Hegel said that seas and rivers bring men closer together, whereas mountains keep them apart. Incidentally, seas bring men closer together when the development of the productive forces has reached a relatively high level; at lower levels, as Ratzel rightly points out, the sea is a great *hindrance* to intercourse between the tribes it separates.***** However that may be, it is certain that the more varied the properties of the geographic environment, the more they favour the development of the productive forces. Marx writes: "It is not the mere fertility of the soil, but the differentiation of the soil, the variety of its natural products, the changes of the seasons, which form the physical basis for the social division of labour, and which, by changes in the natural surroundings, spur man on to the multiplication of his wants, his capabilities, his means and modes of labour".*) Using almost the same terms as Marx, Ratzel says: "The main thing is not that there is the greatest ease in procuring food, but that certain inclinations, habits and finally wants are aroused in man."**)

---

* *Die Urgesellschaft*, Stuttgart, 1891, S. 20-21.
** *Die Indianer Nordamerikas*, Leipzig, 1865, S. 91.
*** *Au coeur de l'Afrique*, Paris, 1875, I, p. 199.
**** Ibid., t. II, p. 94. Concerning the influence of climate on *agriculture*, see also Ratzel, *Die Erde und das Leben*, Leipzig und Wien, 1902, II. Band. S. 540-41.
***** *Anthropogeographie*, Stuttgart, 1882, S. 92.
*) *Das Kapital*, I. Band, III. Auflage, S. 524-26.[89]
**) *Völkerkunde*, I. Band, Leipzig, 1887, S. 56.

Thus, the properties of the geographical environment determine the development of the productive forces, which, in its turn, determines the development of the economic relations, and therefore of all other social relations. Marx explains this in the following words: "These social relations into which the producers enter with one another, the conditions under which they exchange their activities and participate in the whole act of production, will naturally vary according to the character of the means of production. With the invention of a new instrument of warfare, firearms, the whole internal organisation of the army necessarily changed; the relationships within which individuals can constitute an army and act as an army were transformed and the relations of different armies to one another also changed."[*][90]

To make this explanation still more graphic, I shall cite an instance. The *Masai* of East Africa give their captives no quarter, the reason being, as Ratzel points out, that this pastoral people have no *technical possibility* of making use of slave labour. But the neighbouring *Wakamba*, who are *agriculturists*, are able to make use of that labour, and therefore spare their captives' lives and *turn them into slaves*. The appearance of slavery therefore presupposes the achievement of a definite degree in the development of the social forces, a degree that permits the *exploitation* of slave labour.[**] But slavery is *a production relation* whose appearance indicates the beginning of a division into *classes* in a society which has hitherto known no other divisions but those of *sex and age*. When slavery reaches full development, it puts its stamp on the entire economy of society, and, through the economy, on all other social relations, in the first place of the *political structure*. However much the states of antiquity differed in political structure, their chief distinctive feature was that every one of them was a political organisation expressing and protecting the interests of freemen alone.

---

* Napoleon I said: "La nature des armes décide de la composition des armées, des places de campagne, des marches, des positions, des ordres de bataille, du tracé et des profils des places fortes: ce que met une opposition constante entre le système de guerre des anciens et celui des modernes". *Précis des guerres de César*, Paris, 1836, pp. 87-88. [The nature of arms decide the composition of the armies, the theatres of war, the marches, the positions, the battle array, the plan and profile of fortresses. This makes constant opposition between the old system of war and the modern one.]

** *Völkerkunde*, I, 83. It must be noted that at the early stages of development the enslavement of captives is sometimes nothing more than their *forcible incorporation in the conquerors' social organisation, with equal rights being granted. Here there is no use of the surplus labour* of the captive, but only the common advantage derived *from collaboration with him*. However, even this form of slavery presupposes the existence of definite productive forces and a definite organisation of production.

VII

We now know that the development of the productive forces, which in the final analysis determines the development of all social relations, is determined by the *properties of the geographic environment*. But as soon as they have arisen, the social relations *themselves exercise a marked influence on the development of the productive forces*. Thus *that which is initially an effect becomes in its turn a cause*; between the development of the productive forces and the social structure there arises an *interaction* which assumes the most varied forms in various epochs.

It should also be remembered that while the *internal relations* existing in a given society are determined by a given state of the productive forces, it is on the latter that, in the final analysis, that society's *external relations depend*. To every stage in the development of the productive forces there corresponds a definite character of *armaments, the art of war*, and, finally, of *international* law, or, to be more precise, of *inter-social*, i.e., inter alia, *of inter-tribal* law. *Hunting tribes* cannot form large political organisations precisely because the low level of their productive forces *compels them to scatter* in small social groups, in search of means of subsistence. But the more these social groups are scattered, the more inevitable it is that even such disputes that, in a civilised society, could easily be settled in a magistrate's court, are settled by means of more or less sanguinary combats. Eyre says that when several Australian tribes join forces for certain purposes in a particular place such contacts are never lengthy; even before a shortage of food or the need to hunt game has obliged the Australians to part company, hostile clashes flare up among them, which very soon lead, as is well known, to pitched battles.*

It is obvious that such clashes may arise from a wide variety of causes. It is, however, noteworthy that most travellers ascribe them to *economic causes*. When Stanley asked several natives of Equatorial Africa how their wars against neighbouring tribes arose, the answer was: "Some of our young men go into the woods to hunt game and they are surprised by our neighbours; then we go to them, and they come to fight us until one party is tired, or one is beaten."** In much the same way Burton says, "All African wars ... are for one of two objects, cattle-lifting or kidnapping."***

---

* Ed. J. Eyre, *Manners and Customs of the Aborigines of Australia,* London, 1847, p. 243.

** [Plekhanov is quoting from the French translation of H. Stanley's *In Darkest Africa*, i.e., *Dans les ténèbres de l'Afrique*, Paris, 1890, tome II, p. 91. We are quoting from the original, 1890, Vol. II, p. 92.]

*** [Plekhanov is quoting from the French translation of R. Burton's *The Lake Regions of Central Africa*, i.e., *Voyage aux grands lacs de l'Afrique orientale*, Paris, 1862, p. 666. We are quoting from the original, London, 1860, Vol. II, p. 368.]

Ratzel considers it probable that in New Zealand wars among the natives were frequently caused simply by the desire to enjoy human flesh.* The natives' inclination towards cannibalism *is* itself *to be explained* by the paucity of the New Zealand fauna.

All know to what great extent the outcome of a war depends on the weapons used by each of the belligerents. But those weapons are determined by the state of their productive forces, by their economy, and by their social relations, which have arisen on the basis of that economy.** To say that certain peoples or tribes have been *subjugated* by other peoples does not yet mean explaining why the social consequences of that subjugation have been exactly what they are, and no other. The social consequences of the Roman conquest of Gaul were not at all the same as those of the conquest of that country by the Germans. The social consequences of the Norman conquest of England were very different from those that resulted from the Mongol conquest of Russia. In all these cases, the difference depended ultimately on the difference between the *economic structure* of the subjugated society on the one hand, and that of the conquering society on the other. The more the productive forces of a given tribe or people are developed, the greater are at least its *opportunities* to arm itself better to carry on the struggle for existence.

There may, however, be many noteworthy exceptions to this general rule. At lower levels of the development of the productive forces, the difference in the weapons of tribes that are at very different stages of economic development—for instance, nomadic

---

* *Völkerkunde*, I, S. 93.

** This is admirably explained by Engels in the chapters of his *Anti-Dühring* that deal with an analysis of the "force theory". See also the book *Les maîtres de la guerre* by Lieutenant-Colonel Rousset, professor at the École supérieure de guerre, Paris, 1901. Setting forth the views of General Bonnal, the author of this book writes: "The social conditions obtaining in each epoch of history exert a preponderant influence, not only on the military organisation of a nation but also on the character, the abilities, and the trends of its military men. Generals of the ordinary stamp make use of the familiar and accepted methods, and march on towards successes or reverses according to whether attendant circumstances are more or less favourable to them.... As for the great captains, these subordinate to their genius the means and procedures of warfare" (p. 20). How do they do it? That is the most interesting part of the matter. It appears that, "guided by a kind of divinatory instinct, they transform the means and procedures in accordance with the parallel laws of a social evolution whose decisive effect (and repercussion) on the technique of their art they alone understand in their day" (ibid.). Consequently, it remains for us to discover the causal link between "social evolution" and society's economic development for a materialist explanation to be given to the most unexpected successes in warfare. Rousset is himself very close to giving such an explanation. His historical outline of the latest in the military art, based on General Bonnal's unpublished papers, closely resembles what we find set forth by Engels in the analysis mentioned above. At places the resemblance approaches complete identity.

shepherds and settled agriculturists—cannot be so great as it subsequently becomes. Besides, an advance in economic development, which exerts a considerable influence on the character of a given people, sometimes reduces its warlikeness to such a degree that it proves incapable of resisting an enemy economically more backward but more accustomed to warfare. That is why *peaceable tribes of agriculturists* are not infrequently conquered by *warrior peoples*. Ratzel remarks that the most solid state organisations are formed by "semi-civilised peoples" as a result of the unifying— by means of conquest—of both elements, the agricultural and the pastoral.* However correct this remark may be on the whole, it should, however, be remembered that even in such cases (*China* is a good example) economically backward *conquerors* gradually find themselves completely subjected to the influence of a *conquered* but economically more advanced people.

The geographic environment exerts a considerable influence, not only on primitive tribes, but also on so-called *civilised peoples*. As Marx wrote: "It is the necessity of bringing a natural force under the control of society, of economising, of appropriating or subduing it on a large scale by the work of man's hand, that first plays the decisive part in the history of industry. Examples are the irrigation works in Egypt, Lombardy, Holland, or in India and Persia where irrigation by means of artificial canals, not only supplies the soil with the water indispensable to it, but also carries down to it, in the shape of sediment from the hills, mineral fertilisers. The secret of the flourishing state of industry in Spain and Sicily under the dominion of the Arabs lay in their irrigation works."**

The doctrine of the influence of the geographic environment on mankind's historical development has often been reduced to a recognition of the *direct* influence of "climate" on social man: it has been supposed that under the influence of "climate" one "race" becomes freedom-loving, another becomes inclined to submit patiently to the rule of a more or less despotic monarch, and yet another race becomes superstitious and therefore dependent upon a clergy, etc. This view already predominated, for instance, with Buckle.*** According to Marx, the geographic environment

---

* *Völkerkunde*, S. 19.
** *Das Kapital*, S. 524-26.[91]
*** See his *History of Civilisation in England*, Vol. I, Leipzig, 1865, pp. 36-37. According to Buckle, one of the four causes influencing the character of a people, viz., *the general aspect of Nature*, acts chiefly on the imagination, a highly-developed imagination engendering superstitions, which, in their turn, retard the development of knowledge. By acting on the imagination of the natives, the frequent earthquakes in Peru exercised an influence on the political structure. If Spaniards and Italians are superstitious, that too is the result of earthquakes and volcanic eruptions (ibid.,

affects man *through the medium of relations of production, which arise in a given area on the basis of definite productive forces, whose primary condition of development lies in the properties of that environment.* Modern ethnology is more and more going over to this point of view, and consequently attributes ever less importance to "race" in the history of civilisation. "Race has nothing to do with cultural achievement," says Ratzel.*

But as soon as a certain "cultural" level has been reached, it indubitably influences the bodily and mental qualities of the "race".**

The influence of geographic environment on social man is a *variable magnitude.* Conditioned by the properties of that environment, the development of the productive forces increases man's power over Nature, *and thereby places him in a new relation towards the geographic environment that surrounds him*; thus, the English of today react to that environment in a manner which is not quite the same as that in which the tribes that inhabited England in Julius Caesar's day reacted to it. This finally removes the objection that the character of the inhabitants of a given area can be substantially modified, although the geographic characteristics of that area remain unchanged.

VIII

The legal and political relations*** engendered by a given economic structure exert a decisive influence on social man's entire mentality. "Upon the different forms of property, upon the social

pp. 112-13). This *direct* psychological influence is particularly strong at the early stages of the development of civilisation. Modern science, however, has, on the contrary, shown the striking similarity of the religious beliefs of primitive tribes standing at the same level of economic development. Buckle's view, borrowed by him from eighteenth-century writers, dates back to Hippocrates. (See *Des airs, des eaux et des lieux* traduction de Coray, Paris, 1800, para. 76, 85, 86, 88, etc.)

* *Völkerkunde*, I, S. 10. John Stuart Mill, repeating the words of "one of the greatest thinkers of our time", said, "Of all vulgar modes of escaping from the consideration of the effect of social and moral influences on the human mind, the most vulgar is that of attributing the diversities of conduct and character to inherent natural differences." *Principles of Political Economy*, Vol. I. p. 396.

** Regarding race, see J. Finot's interesting work *Le préjugé des races*, Paris, 1905. [Addendum to the German edition of 1910.] Waitz writes: "Certain Negro tribes are striking examples of the link between the main occupation and the national character." *Anthropologie der Naturvölker*, II, S. 107.

*** Regarding the influence of the economy on the nature of the social relations, see Engels, *Der Ursprung der Familie, des Privateigenthums und des Staats*, 8. Auflage, Stuttgart, 1900; also R. Hildebrand, *Recht und Sitte auf den verschiedenen (wirtschaftlichen) Kulturstufen*, I. Teil, Jena, 1896. Unfortunately, Hildebrand makes poor use of his economic data. *Rechtsent-*

conditions of existence," says Marx, "rises an entire superstructure of distinct and peculiarly formed sentiments, illusions, modes of thought and views of life."[92] *Being* determines *thinking*. It may be said that each new step made by science in explaining the process of historical development is a fresh argument in favour of this fundamental thesis of contemporary materialism.

Already in 1877, Ludwig Noiré wrote: "It was joint activity directed towards the achievement of a common aim, it was the primordial labour of our ancestors, that produced language and the reasoning."* Developing this notable thought, L. Noiré pointed out that language originally indicated the things of the objective world, not as *possessing* a certain form, but as *having received that form* (nicht als *"Gestalten"*, sondern als *"gestaltete"*); not as *active and exerting* a definite *action* but as passive and *subjected to that action*.** He went on to explain this with the sound remark that "all things enter man's field of vision, i.e., become *things* to him, solely in the measure in which they are *subjected* to his action, and it is in conformity with this that they get their designations, i.e., names."*** In short, it is *human activity* that, in Noiré's opinion, gives meaning to the initial roots of language.**** It is noteworthy that Noiré found the first embryo of his theory in Feuerbach's idea that man's essence lies in the community, in man's unity with man. He apparently knew nothing of Marx, for otherwise he would have seen that his view on the role of *activity* in the formation of language was closer to Marx, who, in his epistemology, laid stress on human activity, unlike Feuerbach, who spoke mostly of "contemplation".

In this connection, it is hardly necessary to remind the reader, with reference to Noiré's theory, that the nature of man's activities in the process of production is determined by the state of the productive forces. That is obvious. It will be more useful to note that the decisive influence of *being* upon *thinking* is seen with particular clarity in primitive tribes, whose social and intellectual life is incomparably simpler than that of civilised peoples. Karl von den Steinen writes of the natives of Central Brazil that

---

stehung und Rechtsgeschichte, an interesting pamphlet by T. Achelis (Leipzig, 1904), considers law as a product of the development of social life, without going deeply into the question of what the latter's development is conditioned by. In M. A. Vaccaro's book, *Les bases sociologiques du droit et de l'état*, Paris, 1898, many individual remarks are scattered which throw light on certain aspects of the subject; on the whole, however, Vaccaro himself does not seem fully at home with the problem. See also Teresa Labriola's *Revisione critica delle più recenti teoriche sulle origini del diritto*, Rome, 1901.

    * *Der Ursprung der Sprache*, Mainz, 1877, S. 331.
   ** Ibid., S. 341.
 *** Ibid., S. 347.
**** Ibid.. S. 369.

we shall understand them only when we consider them as the outcome (Erzeugnis) of their *life as hunters*. "Animals have been the chief source of their experience," he goes on to say, "and it is mainly with the aid of that experience that they have interpreted Nature and formed their world-outlook."* The condition of their life as hunters have determined not only the world-outlook of these tribes but also their moral concepts, their sentiments, and even, the writer goes on to say, their aesthetic tastes. We see exactly the same thing in *pastoral* tribes. Among those whom Ratzel terms *exclusively herdsmen* "the subject of at least 99 per cent of all conversations is cattle, their origin, habits, merits and defects".** For instance, the unfortunate *Hereros*, whom the "civilised" Germans recently "pacified" with such brutality, were such "exclusively herdsmen".***

If *beasts* are the primitive hunter's foremost source of experience, and if his whole world-outlook was based on that experience, then it is not surprising that the *mythology* of hunting tribes, which at that stage takes the place of philosophy, theology and science, draws all its content from the same source. "The peculiarity of Bushman mythology," Andrew Lang writes, "is the almost absolute predominance of animals. Except 'an old woman' who appears now and then in these incoherent legends, their myths have scarcely one human figure to show."**** According to Brough Smith, the Australian aborigines—like the Bushmen, who have not yet emerged from the *hunting stage*—have as their gods mostly birds and beasts.*****

---

* *Unter den Naturvölkern Zentral-Brasiliens,* Berlin, 1894, S. 201.
** Ibid., S. 205-06.
*** Regarding such "exclusively herdsmen" see Gustav Fritsch's book *Die Eingeborenen Süd-Afrikas,* Breslau, 1872. "The Kaffir's ideal," Fritsch says, "the object of his dreams, and that which he loves to sing of, is his cattle, the most valuable of his property. Songs lauding cattle alternate with songs in honour of tribal chiefs, in which the latter's cattle again play an important part" (I, 50). With the Kaffirs, cattle-tending is the most honourable of occupations (I, 85), and even war pleases the Kaffir chiefly because it holds the promise of booty in the shape of cattle (I, 79). "Law-suits among the Kaffirs are the result of conflicts over cattle" (I, 322). Fritsch gives a highly interesting description of the life of Bushman *hunters* (I, 424, et seq.).
**** [Plekhanov is quoting from the French translation of Lang's *Myth, Ritual, and Religion,* i.e., *Mythes, cultes et religion.* trad. par L. Mirillier, Paris, 1896, p. 332. We are quoting from the original, London, 1887, Vol. II, p. 15.]
***** Worth recalling in this connection is R. Andrée's remark that man originally imagined his gods in the shape of animals. "When man later anthropomorphised animals, there arose the mythical transformation of men into animals." (*Ethnographische Parallelen und Vergleiche,* neue Folge, Leipzig. 1889, S. 116.) The anthropomorphisation of animals presupposes a relatively high level of the development of the productive forces. Cf. also Leo Frobenius, *Die Weltanschauung der Naturvölker,* Weimar, 1898, S. 24.

The religion of primitive tribes has not yet been adequately studied. However, what we already know fully confirms the correctness of the brief thesis of Feuerbach and Marx that "it is not religion that makes man, but man who makes religion". As Ed. Tylor says, "Among nation after nation it is still clear how, man being the type of deity, human society and government became the model on which divine society and government were shaped."* This is unquestionably a materialist view on religion: it is known that Saint-Simon held the opposite view, explaining the social and political system of the ancient Greeks through their religious beliefs. It is, however, far more important that science has already begun to discover the causal link between the technical level of primitive peoples and their world-outlook.** In this respect valuable discoveries evidently await science.***

In the sphere of the *ideology* of primitive society, *art* has been studied better than any other branch: an abundance of material has been collected, testifying in the most unambiguous and convincing manner to the soundness and, one might say, the *inevitability* of the materialist explanation of history. So copious is this material that I can here enumerate only the most important of the works dealing with the subject: Schweinfurth, *Artes Africanae*, Leipzig, 1875; R. Andrée, *Ethnographische Parallelen*, the article entitled "Das Zeichnen bei den Naturvölkern"; Von den Steinen, *Unter den Naturvölkern Zentral-Brasiliens*, Berlin, 1894; G. Mallery, *Picture Writing of the American Indians*, X Annual Report of the Bureau of Ethnology, Washington, 1893 (reports for other years contain valuable material on the influence of the mechanical arts, especially weaving, on ornamental design); Hörnes, *Urgeschichte der bildenden Kunst in Europa*, Wien, 1898; Ernst Grosse, *Die Anfänge der Kunst*, also *Kunstwissenschaftliche Studien*, Tübingen, 1900; Yrjö Hirn, *Der Ursprung der Kunst*, Leipzig, 1904; Karl Bücher, *Arbeit und Rhythmus*, 3. Auflage, 1902; Gabriel et Adrien de Mortillet, *Le préhistorique*, Paris, 1900, pp. 217-30; Hörnes, *Der diluviale Mensch in Europa*, Braunschweig, 1903; Sophus Müller, *L'Europe préhistorique*, trad. du danois par E. Philippot, Paris, 1907; Rich. Wallaschek, *Anfänge der Tonkunst*, Leipzig, 1903.

---

* *La civilisation primitive*, Paris, 1876, tome II, p. 322.
** Cf. H. Schurtz, *Vorgeschichte der Kultur*, Leipzig und Wien, 1900, S. 559-64. I shall return to this matter later, apropos of another question.
*** [Note to the German edition of 1910.] I shall permit myself to refer the reader to my article in the journal *Sovremenny Mir* entitled "On the So-called Religious Seekings in Russia" (1909, September). In it, I also discussed the significance of the mechanical arts for the development of religious concepts.

The conclusions arrived at by modern science as regards the question of the beginnings of art will be shown by the following quotations from the authors enumerated above.

"Decorative design," says Hörnes,* "can develop only from industrial activity, which is its material precondition.... Peoples without any industry ... have no ornamental design either."

Von den Steinen thinks that *drawing* (Zeichnen) developed from *designation of the object* (Zeichen), *used with the practical aim.*

Bücher has formed the conclusion that "at the primitive stage of their development, work, music and poetry were a fused whole, work being the chief element in this trinity, and music and poetry of secondary importance". In his opinion, "the origin of poetry is to be sought in labour", and he goes on to remark that no language arranges in a rhythmical pattern words making up a sentence. It is therefore improbable that men arrived at measured poetical speech through the use of their everyday language—the inner logic of that language operates against that. How, then, is one to explain the origin of measured, poetical speech? Bücher is of the opinion that the measured and rhythmical movements of the body transmitted the laws of their co-ordination to figurative, poetical speech. This is all the more probable if one recalls that, at the lower stages of development, rhythmical *movements* of the body are usually accompanied by *singing*. But what is the explanation of the co-ordination of bodily movements? It lies *in the nature of the processes of production.* Thus, *"the origin of poetry is to be sought in productive activities".***

R. Wallaschek formulates his view on the origin of *dramatic performances* among primitive tribes in the following way:*** "The subjects of these dramatic performances were:

"1. The chase, war, paddling (among hunters—the life and habits of animals; animal pantomimes; masks****).

"2. The life and habits of cattle (among pastoral peoples).

"3. Work (among agriculturists: sowing, threshing, vine-dressing).

"The entire tribe took part in the performance, all of them singing (in chorus). The words sung were meaningless, the content being provided by the performance itself (pantomime). Only actions of everyday life were represented, such as were absolutely essential in the struggle for existence." Wallaschek says that in many primitive tribes, during such performances, the chorus split into two opposite parts. "Such," he adds, "was the origin of Greek

---

* *Urgeschichte*, etc., S. 38.
** *Arbeit u. Rhythmus*, S. 342.
*** *Anfänge der Tonkunst*, S. 257.
**** Usually depicting animals too.—*G. P.*

drama, which was also an animal pantomime at the outset. The goat was the animal that played the most important part in the economy of the Greeks, which accounts for the word 'tragedy' being derived from 'tragos', the Greek for 'goat'."

It would be difficult to give a more striking illustration of the proposition that it is not being that is determined by thinking, but thinking that is determined by being.

IX

But economic life develops under the influence of a growth in the productive forces. Therefore the mutual relations of people engaged in the process of production undergo changes, and, together with them, changes take place in human mentality. As Marx puts it: "At a certain stage of development, the material productive forces of society come into conflict with the existing relations of production or—this merely expresses the same thing in legal terms—with the property relations within the framework of which they have operated hitherto. From forms of development of the productive forces these relations turn into their fetters. Then begins an era of social revolution. The changes in the economic foundation lead sooner or later to the transformation of the whole immense superstructure.... No social order is ever destroyed before all the productive forces for which it is sufficient have been developed, and new superior relations of production never replace older ones before the material conditions for their existence have matured within the framework of the old society.* Mankind thus inevitably sets itself only such tasks as it is able to solve, since closer examination will always show that the problem itself arises only when the material conditions for its solution are already present or at least in the course of formation."[94]

Here we have before us a genuine "algebra"—and *purely materialist* at that—of social development. This algebra has room both for *"leaps"* (of the epoch of social revolutions) and for *gradual changes*. Gradual quantitative changes in the properties of a given order of things lead ultimately to a *change in quality*, i.e., to the downfall of *the old mode of production*—or, as Marx expresses it here, of the old social order—and to its replacement by a new mode. As Marx remarks, in broad outline, the Asiatic, ancient, feudal, and modern bourgeois modes of production may be designated as successive epochs ("marking progress") in the economic development of society.[95] There is however reason to believe that

---

* [Note to the German edition of 1910.] Certain Marxists in our country are known to have thought otherwise in the autumn of 1905. They considered a *socialist* revolution possible in Russia, since, they claimed, the country's productive forces were sufficiently developed for such a revolution.[93]

later, when he had read Morgan's book on primitive society, he modified his view as to the relation of the mode of production in *antiquity* to that of the *East*. Indeed, the logic of the economic development of the *feudal* mode of production led to a social revolution that marked the triumph of *capitalism*. But the logic of the economic development of *China* or *ancient Egypt*, for example, did not at all lead to the appearance of the *antique* mode of production. In the former instance we are speaking of two phases of development, *one* of which *follows the other, and is engendered by it*. The second instance, on the other hand, represents rather *two coexisting types* of economic development. The *society of antiquity* took the place of the *clan social organisation*, the latter also preceding the appearance of the oriental *social system*. Each of these two types of economic structure was the outcome of the growth in the productive forces within the clan organisation, a process that inevitably led to the latter's ultimate disintegration. If these two types differed considerably from each other, their chief distinctive features were evolved *under the influence of the geographic environment*, which *in one case* prescribed *one kind* of aggregate production relations to a society that had achieved a certain degree of growth in the productive forces, and in the other case, *another kind*, greatly differing from the first.

The discovery of the *clan type* of social organisation is evidently destined to play the same part in social science as was played in biology by the discovery of the *cell*. While Marx and Engels were unfamiliar with this type of organisation, there could not but be considerable gaps in their theory of social development, as Engels himself subsequently acknowledged.

But the discovery of the clan type of organisation, which for the first time provided a key to an understanding of the lower stages of social development, was but a new and powerful argument *in favour* of the materialist explanation of history, *not against that concept*. It provided a closer insight into the way in which the first phases of social being take shape, and social being then determines social thinking. The discovery thereby gave amazing clarity to the truth that social thinking is determined by social being.

I mention all this only in passing. The main thing deserving of attention is Marx's remark that the property relations existing when the productive forces reach a certain level *encourage the further growth of those forces* for a time, and then begin to *hamper that growth*.* This is a reminder of the fact that, though a certain

---

* Let us take slavery as an instance. At a certain level of development it *fosters the growth* of the productive forces, and then begins to *hamper that growth*. Its *disappearance* among the civilised peoples of the West was due to their *economic development*. (Concerning slavery in the ancient world,

state of the productive forces *is the cause* of the given production relations, and in particular of the property relations, the latter (once they have arisen *as a consequence of the aforementioned cause*) begin themselves to influence that cause. Thus there arises an *interaction* between the productive forces and the social economy. Since a whole superstructure of social relations, sentiments and concepts grows on the economic basis, that superstructure first fostering and then hindering the economic development, there arises between the superstructure and the basis an *interaction* which provides the key to an understanding of all those phenomena which *at first glance* seem to contradict the fundamental thesis of historical materialism.

Everything hitherto said by "critics" of Marx concerning the supposed one-sidedness of Marxism and its alleged disregard of all other "factors" of social development but the economic, has been prompted by a failure to understand the role assigned by Marx and Engels to the *interaction between "basis" and "super-structure"*. To realise, for instance, how little Marx and Engels ignored the significance of the political factor, it is sufficient to read those pages of the *Communist Manifesto* which make reference to the liberation movement of the bourgeoisie. There we are told:

"An oppressed class under the sway of the feudal nobility, an armed and self-governing association in the medieval commune; here independent urban republic (as in Italy and Germany), there taxable 'third estate' of the monarchy (as in France), after-wards, in the period of manufacture proper, serving either the semi-feudal or the absolute monarchy as a counterpoise against the nobility, and, in fact, cornerstone of the great monarchies in general, the bourgeoisie has at last, since the establishment of Modern Industry and of the world market, conquered for itself, in the modern representative State, exclusive political sway. The executive of the modern State is but a committee for managing the common affairs of the whole bourgeoisie."[96]

The importance of the political "factor" is so clearly revealed here that some "critics" consider it even unduly stressed. But the origin and the force of this "factor", as well as the mode of its operation in each given period of the bourgeoisie's development, are themselves explained in the *Manifesto* by the course of economic

see Professor Et. Ciccotti's interesting work *Il tramonto della schiavitù*, Turin, 1899.) In his book *Journal of the Discovery of the Sources of the Nile*, 1865, J. H. Speke says that, among the Negroes, *slaves* consider it dishonest and disgraceful to run away from a master who has paid money for them. To this it might be added that these same *slaves* consider their condition more honourable than that of the *hired* labourer. Such an outlook corresponds to the phase "when slavery is still a *progressive* phenomenon".

development, in consequence of which the *variety of "factors"* in no way disturbs the *unity of the fundamental cause.*

Political relations indubitably influence the economic movement, but it is also indisputable that *before they influence that movement they are created by it.*

The same must be said of the *mentality* of man as a social being, of that which Stammler has somewhat one-sidedly called *social concepts.* The *Manifesto* gives convincing proof that its authors were well aware of the importance of the ideological "factor". However, in the same *Manifesto* we see that, even if the ideological "factor" plays an important part in the development of society, *it is itself previously created by that development.*

"When the ancient world was in its last throes, the ancient religions were overcome by Christianity. When Christian ideas succumbed in the eighteenth century to rationalist ideas, feudal society fought its death battle with the then revolutionary bourgeoisie."[97] In this connection, however, the concluding chapter of the *Manifesto* is even more convincing. Its authors tell us that the Communists never cease to instil into the minds of the workers the clearest possible recognition of the hostile antagonism between the interests of the bourgeoisie and of the proletariat. It is easy to understand that one who attaches no importance to the ideological "factor" has no logical ground for trying to instil any such recognition whatsoever into the minds of any social group.

X

I have quoted from the *Manifesto*, in preference to other works by Marx and Engels, because it belongs to the early period of their activities when—as some of their critics assure us—they were especially "one-sided" in their understanding of the relation between the "factors" of social development. We see clearly, however, that in that period too they were distinguished, not by any *"one-sidedness"*, but only by a striving towards monism, an aversion for the *eclecticism* so manifest in the remarks of their "critics".

Reference is not infrequently made to two of Engels' letters, both published in *Sozialistischer Akademiker.* One was written in 1890, the other in 1894. There was a time when Herr Bernstein made much of these letters which, he thought, contained plain testimony of the evolution that had taken place in the course of time in the views of Marx's friend and collaborator. He made two extracts from them, which he thought most convincing in this respect, and which I consider necessary to reproduce here, inasmuch as they prove the reverse of what Herr Bernstein was out to prove.

Here is the first of these extracts: "Thus there are innumerable intersecting forces, an infinite series of parallelograms of forces which give rise to one resultant—the historical event. This may in its turn again be regarded as the product of a power which operates as a whole *unconsciously* and without volition. For what each individual wills is obstructed by everyone else, and what emerges is something that no one intended."[98] (Letter of 1890.)

Here is the second extract: "Political, legal, philosophical, religious, literary, artistic, etc., development is based on economic development. But all these react upon one another and also upon the economic basis."[99] (Letter of 1894.) Herr Bernstein finds that "this sounds somewhat different" than the preface to *Zur Kritik der politischen Oekonomie*, which speaks of the links between the economic "basis" and the "superstructure" that rises above it. But in what way does it sound different? Precisely what is said in the preface, is repeated, viz., political and all other kinds of development rest on economic development. Herr Bernstein seems to have been misled by the following words, "but all these react upon one another and also on the economic basis". Herr Bernstein himself seems to have understood the preface to *Zur Kritik* differently, i.e., in the sense that the social and ideological "superstructure" that grows on the economic "basis" exerts no influence, in its turn, on that "basis". We already know, however, that nothing can be more mistaken than such an understanding of Marx's thought. Those who have observed Herr Bernstein's "critical" exercises can only shrug their shoulders when they see a man who once undertook to popularise Marxism failing to go to the trouble—or, to be more accurate, proving incapable—of first getting an understanding of that doctrine.

The second of the letters quoted by Herr Bernstein contains passages that are probably of greater importance for an understanding of the causal significance of the historical theory of Marx and Engels, than the lines I have quoted, which have been so poorly understood by Herr Bernstein. One of these passages reads as follows: "The economic situation therefore does not produce an automatic effect as people try here and there conveniently to imagine, but men make their history themselves, they do so however in a given environment, which conditions them, and on the basis of actual, already existing relations, among which the economic relations—however much they may be influenced by other, political and ideological, relations—are still ultimately the decisive ones, forming the keynote which alone leads to understanding."[100]

As we see, Herr Bernstein himself, in the days of his "orthodox" mood, was among the people "here and there", who interpret the historical doctrine of Marx and Engels in the sense that in history "the economic situation produces an automatic effect". These also include very many "critics" of Marx who have switched into reverse "*from Marxism to idealism*". These profound thinkers reveal great self-satisfaction when they confront and reproach the "one-sided" Marx and Engels with the formula that history is made by men and not by the automatic movement of the economy. They offer Marx what he himself gave, and in their boundless simplicity of mind, do not even realise that *the "Marx" they are "criticising"* has nothing except the name in common with the real Marx, since he is the creation of their own and really many-sided non-understanding of the subject. It is natural that "critics" of such calibre are utterly incapable of "supplementing" or "amending" anything in historical materialism. Consequently, I shall not deal with them any longer, and shall go over to the "founders" of that theory.

It is of the utmost importance to note that when Engels, shortly before his death, denied the "automatic" understanding of the historical operation of the economy, *he was only repeating* (almost in the same words) *and explaining what Marx had written as far back as 1845, in the third Thesis on Feuerbach, quoted above*. There Marx reproached the earlier materialists with having forgotten that if 'men are products of circumstances ... it is men who change circumstances'.[101] Consequently, the task of materialism in the sphere of history lay, as Marx understood it, precisely in explaining *in what manner "circumstances" can be changed by those who are themselves created by them*. This problem was solved by the reference to the relations of production that develop under the influence of conditions independent of the human will. Production relations are the *relations among human beings* in the social process of production. Saying that *production relations have changed* means saying that *the mutual relations have changed among people* engaged in that process. A change in these relations cannot take place "automatically", i.e., *independently of human activity*, because they are *relations established among men in the process of their activities*.

But these relations may undergo changes—and indeed often do undergo changes—in a direction far from that in which people *would like* them to change. The character of the "economic structure" and the direction in which that character changes depend, not upon human will but on the state of the productive forces and on the specific changes in production relations which take place and become necessary to society as a result of the further development of those forces. Engels explains this in the following words: "Men make their history themselves, but not as yet with a collective will according to a collective plan or even in a clearly defined given society. Their aspirations clash, and for that very

reason all such societies are governed by *necessity*, whose complement and manifestation is *accident*."[102] Here human activity is
itself defined as being not free, but *necessary*, i.e., as being *in
conformity with a law*, and therefore *capable of becoming an object
of scientific study*. Thus, while always pointing out that circumstances are changed by men, historical materialism at the same
time enables us, for the first time, *to examine the process of this
change from the standpoint of science*. That is why we have every
right to say that the materialist explanation of history provides
the necessary *prolegomena to any doctrine on human society claiming
to be a science*.

This is so true that at present the study of any aspect of social
life acquires *scientific significance* only in the measure in which it
draws closer to a *materialist* explanation of that life. Despite the
so vaunted "revival of idealism" in the social sciences, that explanation is becoming more and more common wherever researchers
refrain from indulging in edifying meditation and verbiage on
the "ideal", but set themselves the scientific task of discovering
the causal links between phenomena. Today even people who not
only do not adhere to the materialist view on history, but have
not the slightest idea of it, are proving materialists in their
historical researches. It is here that their ignorance of this view,
or their prejudice against it, which hinders an understanding of
all its aspects, does indeed lead to one-sidedness and narrowness
of concepts.

XI

Here is a good illustration. Ten years ago Alfred Espinas, the
French scholar (and incidentally a bitter enemy of the present-day
socialists), published a highly interesting—at least in conception—
"sociological study" entitled *Les origines de la technologie*. In
this book, the author, proceeding from the purely materialist
proposition that *practice* always precedes *theory* in the history of
mankind, examines the influence of *technology* on the development
of *ideology*, or to be more precise, on the development of religion
and philosophy in ancient Greece. He arrives at the conclusion that,
in each period of that development, the ancient Greeks' world-
outlook was determined by the state of their productive forces.
This is, of course, a highly interesting and important conclusion,
but anyone accustomed consciously to applying materialism to
an explanation of historical events may, on reading Espinas'
"study", find that the view expressed therein is one-sided. That
is so for the simple reason that the French scholar has paid practically no attention to other "factors" in the development of
ideology, such as, for example, the *class struggle*. Yet the latter
"factor" is of really exceptional importance.

In primitive society, which knows no division into classes, man's productive activities exert a *direct* influence on his world-outlook and his aesthetic tastes. Decorative design draws its motifs from technology, and dancing—probably the most important of the arts in such a society—often merely imitates the process of production. That is particularly to be seen in *hunting* tribes, which stand at the lowest known level of economic development.*
That is why I referred chiefly to them when I was discussing the dependence of primitive man's *mentality* on his *activities in the economy* he conducts. However, in a society that is divided into classes the *direct* impact of those activities on ideology becomes far less discernible. That is understandable. If, for instance, one of the Australian aboriginal women's dances reproduces the *work of root-gathering*, it goes without saying that none of the graceful dances with which, for instance, the fine ladies of eighteenth-century France amused themselves could depict those ladies' productive work, since they did not engage in such work, preferring in the main to devote themselves to the "science of tender passion". To understand the Australian native women's dance it is sufficient to know the part played in the life of the Australian tribe by the gathering of wild roots by the womenfolk. But to understand the minuet, for instance, it is absolutely insufficient to have a knowledge of the economy of eighteenth-century France. Here we have to do with a dance expressive of *the psychology of a non-productive class*. A psychology of *this kind* accounts for the vast majority of the "customs and conventions" of so-called good society. Consequently, in this case the *economic* "factor" is second to the *psychological*. It should, however, not be forgotten that the appearance of non-productive classes in a society is a product of the latter's economic development. Hence, the economic "factor" preserves its predominant significance even when it is second to others. Moreover, it is then that this significance makes itself felt, for it is then that it determines the *possibility and the limits of the influence of other "factors"*.**

* The hunters were preceded by the *gatherers* or Sammelvölker, as German scholars now term them. But all the savage tribes we know have already passed that stage.
[Note to the German edition of 1910.] In his work on the origin of the family, Engels says that purely hunting peoples exist only in the imagination of scholars. Hunting tribes are "gatherers" at the same time. However, as we have seen, hunting has a most profound influence on the development of the views and tastes of such peoples.
** Here is an example from another field. The "population factor", as it is called by A. Coste (see his *Les facteurs de population dans l'évolution sociale*, Paris, 1901), undoubtedly has a very big influence on social development. But Marx is absolutely right in saying that the abstract laws of propagation exist only for animals and plants. In human society the increase (or decline) of population depends on that society's organisation, which is determined

Nor is that all. Even when it participates in the productive process in the capacity of leader, the upper class looks upon the lower class with a disdain they do not trouble to conceal. This, too, is reflected in the ideologies of the two classes. The French medieval fabliaux, and particularly the chansons de gestes depict the peasant of the time in a most unattractive way. If we are to believe them, then:

> *Li vilains sont de laide forme*
> *Ainc si très laide ne vit home;*
> *Chaucuns a XV piez de granz;*
> *En auques ressemblent jâianz,*
> *Mais trop sont de laide manière*
> *Boçu sont devant et derrière...**

The peasants, of course, saw themselves in a different light. Indignant at the arrogance of the feudal seigneurs, they sang:

> *Nous sommes des hommes, tous comme eux,*
> *Et capable de souffrir, tout autant qu'eux.***

And they asked:

> *When Adam delved and Eve span,*
> *Who was then the gentleman?*

In a word, each of these two classes looked upon things from its own point of view, which was determined by its position in society. The psychology of the contending sides was coloured by the class struggle. Such, of course, was the case, not only in the Middle Ages and not only in France. The more acute the class struggle grew in a given country and at a given time, the stronger was its influence on the psychology of the conflicting classes. He who would study the history of ideologies in a society divided into classes must give close consideration to this influence; otherwise

---

by its economic structure. No abstract "law of propagation" will explain anything in the fact that the population of present-day France hardly grows at all. Those sociologists and economists who see in the growth of population the *primary* cause of social development are profoundly mistaken (see A. Loria, *La legge di populazione ed il sistema sociale*, Siena, 1882).

* [The villeins are ugly in shape
No man has seen uglier.
Each of them is 15 feet in stature,
Some resemble giants,
But much too ugly,
With humps both in front and behind.]

Cf. *Les classes rurales et le régime domanial en France au moyen âge, par Henri Sée*, Paris, 1901, p. 554. Cf. also Fr. Meyer, *Die Stände, ihr Leben und Treiben*, S. 8, Marburg, 1882.

** [We are men, just as they are,
And capable of suffering, just like they.]

he will be all at sea. Try to give a *bluntly economic* explanation
of the fact of the appearance of the David school of painting in
eighteenth-century France: nothing will come of your attempt
except ridiculous and dull nonsense. But if you regard that school
as an ideological reflection of the class struggle in French society
on the eve of the Great Revolution, the matter will at once assume an entirely different aspect: even such qualities in David's
art which, it would seem, were so far removed from the social
economy that they can in no way be linked up with it, will become
fully comprehensible.

The same has also to be said of the history of ideologies in
ancient Greece, a history that most profoundly experienced the
impact of the class struggle. That impact was insufficiently shown
in Espinas' interesting study, in consequence of which his important conclusions were marked by a certain bias. Such instances
might be quoted today in no small number, and they would all
show that the influence of Marx's materialism on many present-day
experts would be of the utmost value in the sense that *it would
teach them also to take into account "factors" other than the technical
and the economic*. That sounds paradoxical, yet it is an undeniable
truth, which will no longer surprise us if we remember that, though
he explains any social movement as the outcome of the economic
development of society, Marx very often thus explains that movement only as the *ultimate outcome*, i.e., he takes it for granted that
a number of various other "factors" will operate in the interim.

XII

Another trend, diametrically opposed to that which we have
just seen in Espinas, is beginning to reveal itself in present-day
science—a tendency to explain the history of ideas exclusively
by the influence of the class struggle. This perfectly new and as
yet inconspicuous trend has arisen under the direct influence of
Marxist historical materialism. We see it in the writings of the
Greek author A. Eleutheropoulos, whose principal work *Wirtschaft und Philosophie. I. Die Philosophie und die Lebensauffassung
des Griechentums auf Grund der gesellschaftlichen Zustände*; and II.
*Die Philosophie und die Lebensauffassung der germanisch-romanischen
Völker* was published in Berlin in 1900. Eleutheropoulos is convinced that the philosophy of any given period expresses the
latter's specific "world-outlook and views on life" (Lebens- und
Weltanschauung). Properly speaking, there is nothing new about
this. Hegel already said that every philosophy is merely the
ideological expression of its time. With Hegel, however, the
features of the various epochs, and, consequently, of the corresponding phases in the development of philosophy, were determined

by the movement of Absolute Idea, whereas with Eleutheropoulos any given epoch is characterised primarily by its economic con- dition. The economy of any particular people determines its "life- and world-understanding", which is expressed, among other things, in its philosophy. With a change in the economic basis of society, the ideological superstructure changes too. Inasmuch as economic development leads to the division of society into classes, and to a struggle between the latter, the "life- and world- understanding" peculiar to a particular period is not uniform in character. It varies in the different classes and undergoes modifi- cation in accordance with their position, their needs and aspira- tions, and the course of their mutual struggle.

Such is the viewpoint from which Eleutheropoulos regards the entire history of philosophy. It is self-evident that this point of view deserves the closest attention and the utmost approval. For quite a considerable period there has been discernible in philo- sophical literature a dissatisfaction with the usual view on the history of philosophy as merely a filiation of philosophical sys- tems. In a pamphlet published in the late eighties and dealing with ways of studying the history of philosophy, the well-known French writer Picavet declared that, taken by itself, filiation of this kind can explain very little.* The appearance of Eleuthero- poulos' work might have been welcomed as a new step in the study of the history of philosophy, and as a victory of historical material- ism in its application to an ideology far removed from economics. Alas, Eleutheropoulos has not displayed much skill in making use of the dialectical method of that materialism. He has over- simplified the problems confronting him, and for that reason alone has failed to bring forward any solutions other than the very one- sided and therefore most unsatisfactory. Let us cite his appraisal of Xenophanes. According to Eleutheropoulos, Xenophanes expressed, in the realm of philosophy, the aspirations of the Greek proletariat. He was the Rousseau of his time.** He wanted social reform in the meaning of the equality and unity of all citizens, and his doctrine of the *unity of being* was merely the theoretical foundation of his plans for reform.*** It was from this theoretical foundation of Xenophanes' reformational aspirations that all the details of his philosophy developed, beginning with his view on God, and ending with his doctrine of the illusoriness of representations received through our senses.****

The philosophy of Heraclitus, the "Dark Philosopher", was

---

* *L'histoire de la philosophie, ce qu'elle a été, ce qu'elle peut être.* Paris, 1888.
** *Wirtschaft und Philosophie...*, I, S. 98.
*** Ibid., S. 99.
**** Ibid., S. 99-101.

11*

engendered by the reaction of the aristocracy against the revolutionary aspirations of the Greek proletariat. According to that philosophy, universal equality is impossible, for Nature herself has made men unequal. Each man should be content with his lot. It is not the overthrow of the existing order that should be aspired towards in the State, but the elimination of the arbitrary use of power, which is possible both under the rule of a *few* and under the rule of the *masses*. Power should belong to *Law*, which is an expression of *divine law*. *Unity* is not precluded by divine law but unity that is in accord with the latter is a *unity of opposites*. The implementation of Xenophanes' plans would be a breach of the divine law. Developing and substantiating this idea, Heraclitus created his dialectical doctrine of Becoming (Werden).*

That is what Eleutheropoulos says. Lack of space prevents me from quoting more samples of his analysis of the causes determining the development of philosophy. There is hardly any need to do so. The reader, I hope, will see for himself that this analysis must be found unsatisfactory. The process of the development of ideologies is, in general, incomparably more complex than Eleutheropoulos imagines.** When you read his oversimplified notions on the influence of the class struggle on the history of philosophy, you begin to regret that he seems quite ignorant of the aforementioned book by Espinas: the one-sidedness inherent in the latter work, if superimposed on his own one-sidedness, might perhaps have corrected a good deal in his analysis.

Nevertheless, Eleutheropoulos' unsuccessful attempt testifies anew to the proposition—unexpected to many—that a more thorough assimilation of Marx's historical materialism would be useful to many contemporary investigators, precisely because *it will save them from one-sidedness*. Eleutheropoulos is acquainted with that materialism, but *poorly* so. That is borne out by the *"correction"* he has thought fit to introduce into it.

He remarks that the economic relations of a given people determine only *"the necessity of its development"*. The latter itself is a matter of individuality, so that this people's "life- and world-understanding" is determined in its content, first, by its character and the character of the country it inhabits; secondly, by its needs; and thirdly, by the personal qualities of those who come forward from its midst as reformers. It is only in this sense, according to Eleutheropoulos, that we can speak of the relation of philosophy towards the economy. Philosophy fulfils the demands

---

* Ibid., S. 103-07.
** To say nothing of the fact that, in his references to the economy of ancient Greece, Eleutheropoulos gives no concrete presentation of it, confining himself to general statements which here, as everywhere else, explain nothing.

of its time, and does so in conformity with the personality of the philosopher.*

Eleutheropoulos probably thinks that this view on the relation of philosophy to the economy differs from the materialist view of Marx and Engels. He deems it necessary to give a new name to his interpretation of history, calling it *the Greek theory of Becoming* (*griechische Theorie des Werdens***). This is simply ridiculous, and all one can say in this connection is that "the Greek theory of Becoming", which in fact is nothing but rather poorly digested and clumsily expounded historical materialism, nevertheless *promises* far more than is actually *given* by Eleutheropoulos when he proceeds from describing his method to applying it, for then he departs completely from Marx.

As for the "personality of the philosopher" and, in general, of any person who leaves an impress on the history of mankind, those who imagine that the theory of Marx and Engels has no room for it are in gross error. It has left room for that, but at the same time it has been able to avoid the impermissible *contraposing of the activities of any "personality" to the course of events, which is determined by economic necessity*. Anybody who resorts to such contraposing thereby proves that he has understood very little of the materialist explanation of history. The fundamental thesis of historical materialism, as I have repeated more than once, is that *history is made by men*. That being so, it is manifest that it is made also by "great men". It only remains to establish what the activities of such men are determined by. Here is what Engels writes in this connection, in one of the two letters quoted above:

"That such and such a man and precisely that man arises at a particular time in a particular country is, of course, pure chance. But if one eliminates him there is a demand for a substitute, and this substitute will be found, good or bad, but in the long run he will be found. That Napoleon, just that particular Corsican, should have been the military dictator whom the French Republic, exhausted by its own warfare, had rendered necessary, was chance; but that, if Napoleon had been lacking, another would have filled the place, is proved by the fact that a man was always found as soon as he became necessary: Caesar, Augustus, Cromwell, etc. While Marx discovered the materialist conception of history, Thierry, Mignet, Guizot and all the English historians up to 1850 are evidence that it was being striven for, and the discovery of the same conception by Morgan proves that the time was ripe for it and that it simply *had* to be discovered.

---

* Ibid., I. S. 16-17.
** Ibid.. I. S. 17.

So with all the other contingencies, and apparent contingencies, of history. The further the particular sphere which we are investigating is removed from the economic sphere and approaches that of pure abstract ideology, the more shall we find it exhibiting accidents in its development, the more will its curve run zigzag. But if you plot the average axis of the curve, you will find that this axis will run more and more nearly parallel to the axis of economic development the longer the period considered and the wider the field dealt with."*

The "personality" of anyone who has won distinction in the spiritual or social sphere is among those instances of *accident* whose appearance does not prevent the "average" axis of mankind's *intellectual* development running parallel to that of its *economic* development.** Eleutheropoulos would have understood that better had he given more careful thought to Marx's historical theory and been less concerned with producing his *own* "Greek theory".***

It need hardly be added that we are still far from being always capable of discovering the causal link between the appearance of a given philosophical view and the economic situation of the period in question. The reason is that we are only beginning to work in this direction; were we in a position already to answer all the questions—or at least most of the questions—that arise in this connection, that would mean that our work was already completed, or approaching completion. What is of decisive significance in this case is not the fact that *we cannot yet cope with all* the difficulties facing us in this field; there is not, neither can there be, such a method that can remove at one stroke all the difficulties appearing in a science. The important thing is that it is incomparably easier for the materialist explanation of history to cope with them than it is for the idealist or the eclectic explanations. That is borne out by the fact that scientific thought in the sphere of history has been most strongly attracted towards the materialist explanation of events, has, so to say, been persistently seeking for it, since the Restoration period.**** To this day, it has not ceased from gravitating towards it and seeking it, despite the fine indignation that comes over any self-respecting ideologist of the bourgeoisie whenever he hears the word *materialism.*

---

* *Der sozialistische Akademiker*, Berlin, 1895, No. 20, S. 374.[103]
** See my article "On the Role of Personality in History" in my book *Twenty Years*.[104]
*** He called it *Greek* because, as he put it, "its fundamental theses had been expressed by the Greek Thales, and later further developed by another Greek" (op. cit., p. 17), i.e., by Eleutheropoulos.
**** See my preface to the second edition of my Russian translation of the *Communist Manifesto*.[105]

A third illustration of the present *inevitability of attempts to find a materialist explanation of all aspects of human culture* is provided by Franz Feuerherd's book *Die Entstehung der Stile aus der politischen Oekonomie*, Part 1, Brunswick and Leipzig, 1902. "In conformity with the dominant mode of production and the form of State thereby conditioned," says Feuerherd, "the human intelligence moves in certain directions, and is excluded from others. Therefore the existence of any style [in art—*G.P.*] presupposes the existence of people who live in quite definite political conditions, are engaged in production under quite definite production relations, and have quite definite ideals. Given these conditions, men create the appropriate style with the same natural necessity and inevitability as the way linen bleaches, as bromide of silver turns black, and a rainbow appears in the clouds as soon as the sun, as the cause, brings about all these effects."* All this is true, of course, and the circumstance that this is acknowledged by a *historian of art* is of particular interest. When, however, Feuerherd goes on to ascribe the origins of the various Greek styles to economic conditions in ancient Greece, what he produces is something that is too schematic. I do not know whether the second part of his book has come out; I have not been interested in the matter, because it is clear to me how poorly he has learnt the modern materialist method. In their schematism, his arguments are reminiscent of those of our native-bred but second-rate Friche and Rozhkovs, who, like Feuerherd, may be well advised, first and foremost, to *make a study of modern materialism*. Only *Marxism* can save all of them from falling into *schematism*.

XIII

In a controversy with me, the late Nikolai Mikhailovsky once declared that Marx's historical theory would never gain much acceptance in the scholarly world. We have just seen, and will again see from what follows below, that this statement is not quite correct. But first we must remove certain other misconceptions which prevent a proper understanding of historical materialism.

If we wanted to express in a nutshell the view held by Marx and Engels with regard to the relation between the now celebrated "*basis*" and the no less celebrated "*superstructure*", we would get something like the following:

1) *the state of the productive forces*;
2) the *economic relations* these forces condition;

---

* Pp. 19-20.

3) the socio-*political system* that has developed on the given economic "basis";

4) the *mentality of social man*, which is determined in part directly by the economic conditions obtaining, and in part by the entire socio-political system that has arisen on that foundation;

5) the *various ideologies* that reflect the properties of that mentality.

This formula is comprehensive enough to provide proper room for all "forms" of historical development, and at the same time it contains absolutely nothing of the eclecticism that is incapable of going beyond the *interaction* between the various social forces, and does not even suspect that *the fact* that these forces *do interact* has provided no solution of *the problem of their origin*. This formula is a *monist* one, and this *monist* formula is thoroughly imbued with *materialism*. In his *Philosophy of the Spirit*, Hegel said that the Spirit is history's only motive principle. It is impossible to think otherwise, if one accepts the viewpoint of the *idealism* which claims that *being* is determined by *thinking*. Marx's materialism shows in what way the *history of thinking* is determined by the *history of being*. Hegel's idealism, however, did not prevent him from recognising *economic factors* as a cause "conditioned by the development of the Spirit". In exactly the same way, materialism did not prevent Marx from recognising the action, in history, of the "Spirit" as a force whose direction is determined at any given time and in the final analysis by the course of *economic* development.

That all ideologies have one common root—*the psychology of the epoch in question*—is not hard to understand; anyone who makes even the slightest study of the facts will realise that. As an example, we might make reference to French romanticism. Victor Hugo, Eugène Delacroix, and Hector Berlioz worked in three entirely different spheres of art. All three differed greatly from one another. Hugo, at least, did not like music, while Delacroix had little regard for romanticist musicians. Yet it is with good reason that these three outstanding men have been called *the trinity of romanticism*; their works are a reflection of one and the same psychology. It can be said that Delacroix's painting "Dante and Vergil" expresses the same temper as that which dictated his *Hernani* to Victor Hugo, and his *Symphonie fantastique* to Berlioz. This was sensed by their contemporaries, i.e., by those of them who in general were not indifferent to literature and art. A classicist in his tastes, Ingres called Berlioz "the abominable musician, monster, bandit, and antichrist".* This is reminiscent

* See *Souvenirs d'un hugolâtre* by Augustin Challamel, Paris, 1885, p. 259. In this case, Ingres revealed more consistency than Delacroix, who, while he was a romanticist in painting, retained a predilection for classical music.

of the flattering opinions voiced by the classicists regarding Delacroix whose brush they compared to a *drunken* besom. Like Hugo, Berlioz was the object of fierce attacks.* It is common knowledge, too, that he achieved victory with incomparably more effort and far later than Hugo did. Why was that so, despite the fact that his music expressed the same psychology as did romanticist poetry and drama? To answer this question, it would be necessary to understand many details in the comparative history of French music and literature,** details which may remain uninterpreted for long, *if not for always*. What is beyond doubt, however, is that the psychology of French romanticism will be understood by us only if we come to regard it as the psychology of a definite class that lives in definite social and historical conditions.*** "The movement of the thirties in literature and art," Jean-Baptiste Tiersot says, "was far from having the character of a people's revolution."**** That is perfectly true. The movement referred to was *bourgeois* in its essence. But that is not all. The movement did not enjoy universal sympathy among the bourgeoisie itself. In Tiersot's opinion, it expressed the strivings of a small "élite" sufficiently far-sighted to be able to discern genius wherever it lay in hiding.***** These words are a superficial, i.e., idealist, expression of the fact that the French bourgeoisie of the time did not understand much of what its own ideologists then aspired towards and felt in the sphere of literature and art. Such dissonance between ideologists and the class whose aspirations and tastes they express is by no means rare in history, and explains the highly numerous specific features in the intellectual and artistic

---

* Cf. Challamel, op. cit., p. 258.

** And especially *in the history of the part* each of them played therein, in expressing the temper of the times. As we know, various ideologies and various branches of ideology come to the fore at various times. For instance, in the Middle Ages theology played far more important a part than at present; in primitive society dancing is the most important art, whilst it is far from that nowadays, and so on.

*** E. Chesneau's book *Les chefs d'école*, Paris, 1883, pp. 378-79, contains the following subtle observation regarding the romanticists' psychology. The author points out that romanticism made its appearance *after the Revolution and the Empire*. "In literature and in art, there was a crisis similar to that which occurred in morals after the Terror—a veritable orgy of the senses. People had been living in fear, and that fear had gone. They gave themselves up to the pleasures of life. Their attention was taken up exclusively with external appearances and forms. Blue skies, brilliant lights, the beauty of women, sumptuous velvet, iridescent silk, the sheen of gold, and the sparkle of diamonds filled them with delight. People lived only with the eyes ... they had ceased from thinking." This has much in common with the psychology of the times we are living through in Russia. In both cases, however, the course of events leading up to this state of mind was itself the outcome of the course of economic development.

**** *Hector Berlioz et la société de son temps*, Paris, 1904, p. 190.
***** Ibid.

development of mankind. In the case we are discussing, this dissonance was the cause, among other things, of the contemptuous attitude of the "refined" élite towards the "obtuse bourgeois"—an attitude which still misleads naive people, and wholly prevents them from realising the arch-bourgeois character of romanticism.* But here, as everywhere, the origin and the character of this dissonance can be ultimately explained only by the economic position, the economic role, of the social class in whose midst it has appeared. Here, as everywhere, only *being* sheds light on the "secrets" of thinking. And that is why here—again as everywhere—it is only materialism that is capable of giving a *scientific* explanation of the "course of ideas".

XIV

In their efforts to explain that course, the idealists have never proved able to watch from the standpoint of the "*course of things*". Thus, Taine thinks that it is the properties of the artist's environment that account for a work of art. But what properties is he referring to? To the *psychological*, that is to say, the general psychology of the period in question, whose properties themselves require explanation.** When it explains the psychology of a particular society or a particular class, materialism addresses itself to the social structure created by the economic development, and so on. But Taine, who was an idealist, attempted to explain the origin of a *social system* through the medium of *social psychology*, thereby getting himself entangled in irresolvable contradictions. Idealists in all lands show little liking for Taine nowadays. The reason is obvious: by *environment* he understood the general *psychology of the masses*, the *psychology of the "man in the street"* at a particular time and in a particular class. To him, this psychology was the court of last instance to which the researcher could appeal. Consequently, he thought that a "*great*" man always thinks and feels at the behest of the "*man in the street*", at dictation from "mediocrities". Now this is wrong in point of fact, and, besides, offends bourgeois "intellectuals", who are always prone, at least in some small measure, to count themselves in the category of great men. Taine was a man who, after saying "A", was unable to carry on and say "B", thus ruining his own case. The only

---

* Here we have the same qui pro quo as that which makes the adherents of the arch-bourgeois Nietzsche look truly ridiculous when they attack the bourgeoisie.
** "L'œuvre d'art," he writes, "est déterminée par un ensemble qui est l'état général de l'esprit et des mœurs environnantes." [The work of art is determined by the ensemble which is the general state of mind and the surrounding morals.]

escape from the contradictions he got entangled in is through
historical materialism, which finds the right place for both the
"individual" and the "environment", for both *the man in the
street*" and "the man of destiny".

It is noteworthy that, in France, where, from the Middle Ages
right down to 1871, the socio-political development and the
struggle between social classes assumed a form most typical of
Western Europe, it is easier than anywhere else to discover the
causal nexus between that development and that struggle, on the
one hand, and the history of ideologies on the other.

Speaking of the reason why, during the Restoration in France,
the ideas of the theocratic school of philosophy of history were so
widespread, Robert Flint has had the following to say: "The
success of such a theory, indeed, would have been inexplicable,
had not the way for it been prepared by the sensationalism of
Condillac, and had it not been so obviously fitted to serve the
interests of a party which represented the opinions of large classes
of French society before and after the Restoration."* This is true,
of course, and it is easy to realise which class it was whose interests
found ideological expression in the theocratic school. Let us,
however, delve further into French history and ask ourselves: is
it not also possible to discover the social causes of the success
achieved by sensationalism in *pre-revolutionary France*? Was not
the intellectual movement that produced the theoreticians of
sensationalism in its turn an expression of the aspirations of a
particular social class? It is known that this was the case: this
movement expressed the emancipatory aspirations of the French
tiers état.** Were we to proceed in the same direction we would see
that, for instance, the philosophy of Descartes gave a clear reflection of the requirements of the economic development and the
alignment of social forces of his time.*** Finally, if we went back
as far as the fourteenth century and turned our attention, for
instance, to the romances of chivalry, which enjoyed such popular-
ity at the French court and among the French aristocracy of the

---

* *The Philosophy of History in France and Germany*, Edinburgh and London, 1874, p. 149.

** [Note to the German edition of 1910.] In his polemic against the Bauer
brothers, Marx wrote: "The French Enlightenment of the eighteenth century,
and in particular *French materialism*, was not only a struggle against the
existing political institutions and the existing religion and theology; it was
just as much an *open, clearly expressed* struggle against the *metaphysics of the
seventeenth century*, and against *all metaphysics*, in particular that of *Descartes, Malebranche, Spinoza* and *Leibnitz*" (*Nachlass*, 2. Band, S. 232).[106]
This is now common knowledge.

*** See G. Lanson's *Histoire de la littérature française*, Paris, 1896,
pp. 394-97, which gives a lucid explanation of the links between certain
aspects of the Cartesian philosophy and the psychology of the ruling class
in France during the first half of the seventeenth century.

period, we would have no difficulty in discovering that these romances mirrored the life and the tastes of the état referred to.* In a word, the curve of the intellectual movement in this remarkable country, which but recently had every right to claim that it "marched at the head of the nations", runs parallel to the curve of economic development, and that of the socio-political development conditioned by the latter. In view of this, the history of ideology in France is of particular interest to sociology.

This is something that those who have "criticised" Marx in various tones and keys have not had the least idea of. They have never understood that, though criticism is of course a splendid thing, a certain prerequisite is needed when you undertake to criticise, i.e., *an understanding of what you are criticising.* Criticising a given method of scientific investigation means determining in what measure it can help discover the causal links existing between phenomena. That is something that can be ascertained only through experience, i.e., through the application of that method. Criticising historical materialism means making a trial of the method of Marx and Engels in a study of the historical movement of mankind. Only then can the strong and the weak points of the method be ascertained. "The proof of the pudding is in the eating," as Engels said when explaining his theory of cognition.[107] This applies in full to historical materialism as well. To *criticise* this dish, you must first have a taste of it. To taste the method of Marx and Engels, you must first be able to use it. To use it properly presupposes a far higher degree of scientific grounding and far more sustained intellectual effort than are revealed in pseudo-critical verbiage on the theme of the "one-sidedness" of Marxism.[1]

The "critics" of Marx declare, some with regret, some in reproach, and some with malice, that to this day no *book* has appeared, containing a theoretical substantiation of historical materialism. By a "book" they usually understand something like a brief manual on world history written from the materialist viewpoint. At present, however, no such guide can be written either by an individual scholar, however extensive his knowledge, or by a whole group of scholars. A sufficiency of material for that does not yet exist, nor will it exist for a long time. Such material can be accumulated only by means of a lengthy series of investigations carried out in the respective fields of science, with the aid of the Marxist method. In other words, those "critics" who demand a "book" would like to have matters *started from the end,* i.e., *they want a preliminary explanation,* from the materialist viewpoint,

---

* Sismondi (*Histoire des Français,* t. X, p. 59) has voiced an interesting opinion of the significance of these romances, an opinion that provides material for a *sociological study of imitation.*

of that very historical process which is to be explained. In actual
fact, a "book" in defence of historical materialism is being written
in the measure in which contemporary scholars—mostly, as I
have said, without realising that they are doing so—are forced
by the present-day state of social science to furnish a materialist
explanation of the phenomena they are studying. That such scholars are not so few in number is shown convincingly enough by
the examples I have quoted above.

It has been said by Laplace that about fifty years elapsed before
Newton's great discovery was supplemented in any significant
degree. So long a period was required for this great truth to be
generally understood and for those obstacles to be overcome which
were placed in its way by the vortex theory and also perhaps by
the wounded pride of mathematicians of Newton's times.*

The obstacles met by present-day materialism as a harmonious
and consistent theory are incomparably greater than those that
Newton's theory came up against on its appearance. Against it
are directly and decisively ranged the interests of the class now
in power, to whose influence most scholars subordinate themselves
of necessity. Materialist dialectic which "regards every historically
developed social form as in fluid movement, and ... lets nothing
impose upon it",[108] cannot have the sympathy of the *conservative
class* that the Western bourgeoisie today is. It stands in such
contradiction to that class's frame of mind that ideologists of that
class naturally tend to look upon it as something impermissible,
improper, and unworthy of the attention both of "respectable"
people in general, and of "esteemed" men of learning in particular.**
It is not surprising that each of these pundits considers himself
morally obliged to avert from himself any suspicion of sympathy
with materialism. Often enough such pundits denounce materialism the more emphatically, the more insistently they adhere to
a materialist viewpoint in their *special* research.*** The re-

_____

* *Exposition du système du monde*, Paris, L'an IV, t. II, pp. 291-92.
** Regarding this, see, inter alia, Engels' above-mentioned article
"Über den historischen Materialismus".
*** The reader will remember how vehemently Lamprecht justified himself when he was accused of materialism, and also how Ratzel defended himself against the same accusation, in his *Die Erde und das Leben*, II, S. 631.
Nevertheless, he wrote the following words, "The sum total of the cultural
acquirements of each people at every stage of its development is made up of
material and spiritual elements.... They are acquired, not with identical
means, or with equal facility, or simultaneously.... Spiritual acquirements
are based on the material. Spiritual activity appears as a luxury only after
material needs have been satisfied. Therefore all questions of the origin of
culture boil down to the question of what it is that promotes the development
of the material foundations of culture" (*Völkerkunde*, I. Band, I. Auflage.
S. 17). This is unmitigated historical materialism, only far less considered,
and therefore not of such sterling quality as the materialism of Marx and
Engels.

sult is a kind of semi-subconscious "conventional lie", which, of course, can have only a most injurious effect on theoretical thinking.

XV

The "conventional lie" of a society divided into classes becomes ever more enhanced, the more the existing order of things is shaken by the impact of the economic development and the class struggle caused thereby. Marx very truly said that the greater the development of the contradiction between the growing productive forces and the existing social order, the more does the ideology of the master class become imbued with hypocrisy. The more the falseness of this ideology is revealed by life, the more elevated and virtuous does the *language* of that class become (*Sankt Max. Dokumente des Sozialismus*, August 1904, S. 370-71).[109] The truth of this remark is being brought home with particular force today, when, for instance, the spread of loose morals in Germany, as revealed by the Harden-Moltke trial, goes hand in hand with a "renascence of idealism" in social science. In our country, even among "theorists of the proletariat", people are to be found who do not understand the social cause of this "renascence", and have themselves succumbed to its influence, such as the Bogdanovs, the Bazarovs, and their like....

Incidentally, so immensely great are the advantages any researcher is provided with by the Marxist method that even those who have willingly submitted to the "conventional lie" of our time are beginning to publicly recognise them. Among such people, for instance, is the American Edwin Seligman, author of a book published in 1902 under the title of *The Economic Interpretation of History*. Seligman frankly admits that scholars have shied away from the theory of historical materialism because of the socialist conclusions drawn from it by Marx. However, he thinks that you can eat your cake and yet have it: "one can be an economic materialist" and yet remain hostile to socialism. As he puts it, "The fact that Marx's economics may be defective has no bearing on the truth or falsity of his philosophy of history."* In actual fact, Marx's economic views were intimately bound up with his historical views. A proper understanding of *Capital* absolutely implies the *necessity* of previous and careful thought on the celebrated preface to *Zur Kritik der politischen Oekonomie*. However, we are unable here either to set forth Marx's economic views or to demonstrate the incontrovertible fact that they form *merely* an indispensable component of the *doctrine* known as historical material-

---

* *The Economic Interpretation of History*, pp. 24 and 109.

ism.* I shall add only that Seligman is sufficiently a "pundit" also to be scared of *materialism*. This economic "materialist" thinks it is going to intolerable extremes "to make religion itself depend on economic forces" or to "seek the explanation of Christianity itself in economic facts alone".** All this goes to show clearly how deep are the roots of those prejudices—and consequently of the obstacles—that Marxist theory has to fight against. Yet the very fact of the appearance of Seligman's book and even the very nature of the reservations he makes give some reason to hope that historical materialism—even in a truncated or "purified" form—will in the end achieve recognition by those ideologists of the bourgeoisie who have not given up the idea of bringing order into their historical views.***

But the struggle against socialism, materialism, and other unpleasant extremes presupposes possession of a "spiritual weapon". What is known as subjective political economy, and more or less adroitly falsified statistics at present constitute the spiritual weapon mainly used in the struggle against socialism. All possible brands of Kantianism form the main bulwark in the struggle against materialism. In the field of social science, Kantianism is utilised for this purpose as a *dualist* doctrine which *tears asunder the tie between being and thinking*. Since consideration of *economic* questions does not come within the province of this book, I shall confine myself to an appraisal of the *philosophical* spiritual weapon employed by bourgeois reaction in the ideological sphere.

Concluding his booklet, *Socialism: Utopian and Scientific*,

---

* A few incidental words in explanation of what has been said. According to Marx, "economic categories are only the theoretical expressions, the abstractions of the social relations of production" (*The Poverty of Philosophy*, Chapter II, Second Observation).[110] This means that Marx regards the categories of *political economy* likewise from the viewpoint of the mutual relations among men in the social process of production, relations whose development provides him with the basic explanation of mankind's *historical* movement.

** *The Economic Interpretation of History*, p. 137. [Note to the German edition of 1910.] Kautsky's *Origin of Christianity*, as an "extremist" book, is of course reprehensible from Seligman's point of view.

*** The following parallel is highly instructive. *Marx* says that materialist dialectic, while explaining that which exists, at the same time explains its *inevitable destruction*. In this he saw its value, its progressive significance. But here is what Seligman says: "Socialism is a theory of what ought to be; historical materialism is a theory of what has been" (ibid., p. 108). For that reason alone, he considers it possible for himself to defend historical materialism. This means, in other words, that this materialism may be ignored when it comes to explaining the inevitable destruction of *that which is* and may be used to explain *that which has been in the past*. This is one of the numerous instances of the use of a double standard in the field of ideology, a phenomenon also *engendered by economic causes*.

Engels remarks that when the mighty means of production created by the capitalist epoch have become the property of society, and when production is organised in conformity with social needs, men will at last become masters of their social relations, and hence lords over nature, and their own masters. Only then will they begin *consciously* to make their own history; only then will the social causes they bring into play produce, in ever greater measure, effects that are desirable to them. "It is the ascent of man from the kingdom of necessity to the kingdom of freedom."[111]

These words of Engels' have evoked objections from those who, unable in general to stomach the idea of "leaps", have been either unable or unwilling to understand any such "leap" from the kingdom of necessity into the kingdom of freedom. Such a "leap" seemed to them to contradict that view on freedom which Engels himself voiced in the first part of his *Anti-Dühring*. Therefore, if we would see our way through the confusion in the minds of such people, we must recall exactly what Engels said in the book mentioned above.

And here is what he said. Explaining Hegel's words that "necessity is *blind* only *in so far as it is not understood*", Engels stated that freedom consists in exercising "control over ourselves and over external nature, a control founded on knowledge of natural necessity".* This idea is set forth by Engels with a clarity quite sufficient for people familiar with the Hegelian doctrine referred to. The trouble is that present-day Kantians only "criticise" Hegel, but do not study him. Since they have no knowledge of Hegel, they have been unable to understand Engels. To the author of *Anti-Dühring* they have made the objection that where there is submission to necessity, there is no freedom. This is quite consistent on the part of people whose philosophical views are imbued with a *dualism* that is incapable of uniting thinking with being. From the viewpoint of this dualism, the "leap" from necessity to freedom remains absolutely incomprehensible. But Marx's philosophy, like that of Feuerbach, proclaims the unity of being and thinking. Although, as we have already seen above, in the section on Feuerbach, Marxist philosophy understands that unity quite differently from the sense in which it is understood by absolute idealism, it [Marxist philosophy] does not at all disagree with Hegelian doctrine in the question we are concerned with, viz., the relation of freedom to necessity.

The gist of the whole matter is: precisely what should be understood by *necessity*. Aristotle** already pointed out that the con-

---

* *Herrn Eugen Dührings Umwälzung der Wissenschaft*, 5. Auflage, S. 113.[112]
** *Metaphysics*, Book V, Chapter 5,

cept of necessity contains many shades of meaning: medicine is necessary for a cure to be effected; breathing is necessary for life; a trip to Aegina is necessary for a debt to be collected. All these are, so to say, *conditional* necessities; we *must* breathe *if* we want to live; we *must* take medicine *if* we want to get rid of an illness, and so on. In the process of acting on the world about him, man has constantly to do with necessity of this kind: he must *of necessity* sow *if* he would reap, shoot an arrow *if* he would kill game, stock fuel *if* he would get a steam-engine operating, and so on. From the viewpoint of the neo-Kantian "criticism of Marx", it has to be admitted that there is an element of *submission* in this conditional necessity. Man would be *freer* if he were able to satisfy his wants without expending any labour at all. He always *submits* to nature, even *when he forces her to serve him*. This submission, however, is a condition of his becoming free: by submitting to nature, he thereby increases *his power over her*, i.e., *his freedom*. It would be the same under the planned organisation of social production. By *submitting* to certain demands of technical and economic necessity, men would put an end to that preposterous order of things under which they are dominated by the products of their own activities, that is to say, they would increase their *freedom* to a tremendous degree. Here, too, their submission would become a source of liberation to them.

Nor is that all. "Critics" of Marx, who have become used to considering that a gulf separates thinking and being, know of only one shade of necessity; to use Aristotle's wording, they imagine necessity only as a force that *prevents* us from acting *according* to our desires, and *compels* us to do that which *is contrary* to them. Necessity of *this* kind is indeed the opposite of freedom, and cannot but be irksome in greater or lesser degree. But we must not forget that a force seen by man as external coercion which is in conflict with his wishes may, in other circumstances, be seen by him in an entirely different light. As an illustration, let us take the agrarian question in Russia today. To the intelligent *landowner* who is a Constitutional-Democrat, the "forcible alienation of the land"[113] may seem more or less sad historical necessity—sad, that is to say, in reverse proportion to the size of the "fair compensation" given. But to the *peasant* who yearns for land, the reverse is true: the "fair compensation" will present itself as a more or less sad necessity, while "forcible alienation" is bound to be seen as an expression of his own unfettered will, and the most precious security of his freedom.

In saying this, I am touching upon what is perhaps the most important point in the doctrine of freedom—a point not mentioned by Engels only, of course, for its being self-evident to one who has gone through the Hegelian school.

In his philosophy of religion Hegel says, "*Die Freiheit ist dies: nichts zu wollen als sich*",* i.e., "Freedom lies in willing nothing but oneself".** This observation sheds a strong light on the entire question of freedom, insofar as that question bears upon social psychology. The peasant who demands that the landowner's land should be transferred to him wants "nothing but himself"; the Constitutional-Democratic landowner who agrees to give him land no longer wants "himself" but that which history *compels* him to want. The former is *free*, while the latter wisely *submits to necessity*.

It would be the same, as with the peasant, for the proletariat, which converts the means of production into social property and organises social production on a new foundation. It would wish nothing "but itself", and would feel *quite free*. As for the capitalists, they would, of course, at best feel that they were in the position of the landowner who has accepted the Constitutional-Democratic agrarian programme; they could not but think that *freedom* is one thing, and *historical necessity*, another.

As it seems to me, those "critics" who have objected to Engels' stand have failed to understand him also, incidentally, for the reason of their being able to imagine themselves in the position of the capitalist, but being totally unable to imagine themselves in the proletarian's shoes. I hold the opinion that this, too, has its *social*—and ultimately *economic*—cause.

XVI

Dualism, to which ideologists of the bourgeoisie are now so prone, has another charge to make against historical materialism. Through Stammler, it imputes that historical materialism fails to take *social teleology* into account. This second imputation, which incidentally is highly akin to the first, is equally groundless.

Marx says, "In the social production of their existence, men inevitably enter into definite relations."[114] Stammler makes reference to this formula as proof that, despite his theory, Marx was unable to avoid teleological considerations; Marx's words, in Stammler's opinion, mean that men *consciously* enter into the

---

* Hegel's *Werke*, 12. Band, S. 98.
** [Note to the German edition of 1910.] Spinoza already said (*Ethics*, Part III, Proposition 2, *Scholium*) that many people think they act freely because they know their actions but not the causes of those actions. "Thus an infant thinks that it freely desires milk, an angry child thinks that it freely desires vengeance, or a timid child thinks it freely chooses flight." The same idea was expressed by Diderot, whose materialist doctrine was. on the whole, Spinozism liberated from its theological setting.

mutual relations without which production is impossible. Consequently these relations are the outcome of *expedient action.**

It is easy to see in which part of this argument Stammler makes a logical error which leaves its impress on all his further critical remarks.

Let us take an example. Savages who live by hunting are pur suing a quarry, an elephant, let us say. For this they gather together and organise their forces in a definite way. What is the *aim* of this, and the *means?* The aim is obviously to catch or to kill the elephant, and the means is to join forces to pursue the animal. *By what* is the aim prompted? By the *wants* of the human *organism*. Now *by what* are the means determined? *By the conditions of the chase.* Do the wants of the human body depend on man's will? No, they do not; in general, that is the department of *physiology*, not of *sociology*. What then can we at present demand of sociology, in this connection? We can demand an explanation of the reason *why* men, in seeking to satisfy their wants—for instance, the need for food—sometimes enter into certain kinds of mutual relations, and sometimes into quite other kinds. *Sociology*—in the person of Marx—*explains this circumstance as the outcome of the state of their productive forces.* Now the question is: does the state of these forces depend on human will, or on the *aims* pursued by men? To this, sociology, again in the person of Marx, replies that it does not. If there is no such dependence, then that signifies that these forces are brought into being by virtue of a definite necessity, one that is determined by given conditions external to man.

What is the inference to be made? It is that if hunting is an *expedient activity* on the part of the savage, then this fact in no way detracts from the significance of Marx's observation *that the production relations arising among savages who are hunters* come into being by virtue of conditions *that do not fully depend on that expedient activity.* In other words, if the primitive hunter *consciously* strives to kill as much game as possible, it does not follow therefrom that the communism characteristic of that hunter's everyday life has evolved as *the expedient outcome of his activities.* No, this communism has arisen, or rather has been *preserved* of itself—seeing that it came into being long ago—as the *unconscious*, i.e., *necessary*, result of an organisation of labour in a way quite independent of the will of men.** It is this that the Kantian Stammler has failed to grasp; it is here that he has

---

* *Wirtschaft und Recht*, zweite Auflage, S. 421.
** "Necessity, in its contraposition to liberty, is nothing else but the unconscious," Schelling, *System des transzendentalen Idealismus*, 1800, S. 424.

ost his bearings, and led astray our Struves, Bulgakovs and other *emporary* Marxists, whose names are known to the Lord alone.*

Continuing his critical observations, Stammler says, that if social development were to take place exclusively in virtue of *causal necessity*, it would be patently senseless to consciously try to further it. The following is the alternative, in his opinion: either I consider a given phenomenon a *necessity*, i.e., inevitable, in which case there is no need for me to help further it, *or else* my activity is essential for that phenomenon *to take place*, in which case it cannot be termed a necessity. Who would attempt to assist the necessary, i.e., inevitable, rising of the sun?**

This is an amazingly vivid revelation of dualism characteristic of people steeped in Kantianism: *with them, thinking is always divorced from being.*

The rising of the sun is in no way connected with men's social relations, either as cause or as effect. As a natural phenomenon, it can therefore be contraposed to men's conscious aspirations, which, too, have no causal tie with it. But it is quite different when we have to deal with *social* phenomena, with history. We already know that history is made by men; therefore, human aspirations cannot but be a factor of the movement of history. But men make history in one way and not in another, in consequence of a particular necessity which we have already dealt with above. Once this necessity is given, *then given too, as its effect, are those human aspirations which are an inevitable factor of social development. Men's aspirations do not exclude necessity, but are themselves determined by it.* It is therefore a grave logical error to contrapose them to necessity.

When a social revolution is brought about by a class striving for its liberation, that class acts in a way that is more or less expedient in achieving the aim desired; in any case its activities are the *cause* of that revolution. However, together with all the aspirations that have brought them about, these activities are themselves a *consequence* of a definite course of the economic development, and are therefore themselves determined by *necessity*.

Sociology becomes a science only in the measure in which it succeeds in understanding the appearance of aims in social man (social "teleology"), as a necessary consequence of a social process ultimately determined by the course of economic development.

Highly characteristic is the circumstance that consistent antagonists of the materialist explanation of history see themselves

---

* This aspect of the matter is discussed in fairly great detail in various parts of my book on *historical monism*.[115]

** *Wirtschaft und Recht*, S. 421 et seq. Cf. also Stammler's article entitled "Materialistische Geschichtsauffassung" in *Handwörterbuch der Staatswissenschaften*, 2. Auflage, V. Band, S. 735-37.

forced to prove the *impossibility* of sociology *as a science*. This means that the "*critical approach*" *is now becoming* an obstacle *to the further scientific development of our times.* In this connection, an interesting problem arises for those who are trying to find a scientific explanation of the history of philosophical theories. That problem is: to determine in what way this role of the "critical approach" is linked up with the struggle of the classes in present-day society.

If I endeavour to participate in a movement whose triumph I consider a historical necessity, then that means that I look upon my own activities as an indispensable link in the chain of conditions whose sum will necessarily ensure the triumph of a movement that I hold dear. It means nothing more nor less than that. A dualist will fail to understand, but all this will be perfectly clear to anybody who has assimilated the theory of *the unity of subject and object*, and has understood how that unity reveals itself in social phenomena.

Highly noteworthy is the fact that theoreticians of Protestantism in the United States of America seem unable to understand the contraposition of freedom and necessity that has been exercising the minds of so many ideologists of the European bourgeoisie. H. Bargy says that "in America the most positive instructors in the field of energy (professeurs d'énergie) are little prone to recognise freedom of the will".* He ascribes this to their preference, as men of action, for "fatalist solutions". He is wrong, however, since fatalism has nothing to do with the matter. This is to be seen in his own remark about the moralist Jonathan Edwards: "Edwards' point of view ... is that of any man of action. To anyone who has had an aim once in his lifetime freedom is the faculty of putting all his soul in the service of that aim."** This is well put, and closely resembles Hegel's "willing nothing but oneself". But when a man "wills nothing but himself", he is in no way a fatalist: it is then that he is precisely a *man of action*.

Kantianism is not a philosophy of struggle, or a philosophy of men of action. It is a philosophy of half-hearted people, a philosophy of compromise.

The means of removing the existing social evil, Engels says, must be *discovered* in the existing material conditions of production, not *invented* by one social reformer or another.[116] Stammler is in agreement with this, but accuses Engels of unclear thinking, since in Stammler's opinion the gist of the matter lies in ascertaining "*the method with the aid of which* this discovery must be

---

* H. Bargy, *La religion dans la société aux États-Unis*, Paris, 1902, pp. 88-89.
  ** Ibid., pp. 97-98.

made".* This objection, which merely reveals Stammler's vague thinking, is eliminated by simply mentioning the fact that though the nature of the "method" is in such cases determined by a great variety of "factors", the latter can all be ultimately referred to the course of the economic development. The very fact of the appearance of *Marx's theory* was determined by the development of the capitalist mode of production, whereas the predominance of utopianism in pre-Marxist socialism is quite understandable in a society suffering not only from the development of the aforementioned mode of production, but also (and in greater degree) from the *insufficiency of that development.*

It would be superfluous to dilate on the matter. The reader will perhaps not complain if, in concluding this article, I will draw his attention to the measure in which *the tactical "method"* of Marx and Engels is intimately bound up with the fundamental theses of their historical theory.

This theory tells us, as we already know, that mankind always sets itself only such tasks that it can solve, for "the problem itself arises only when the material conditions for its solution are already present or at least in the course of formation".[117] Where these conditions *already exist*, the state of things is not quite the same as it is where they are still "*in the course of formation*". In the former instance the time for a "leap" *has already arrived*; in the latter instance the "*leap*" *is*, for the time being, a *matter* of the more or less distant *future*, "an ultimate aim" whose approach *is prepared by a series of* "*gradual* changes" in the mutual relations between social classes. What role should be played by innovators during the period in which a "leap" is *still impossible*? It evidently remains for them to contribute to the "gradual changes", i.e., they must, in other words, try to bring about *reforms*. In this way, both the "*ultimate aim*" and *reforms* find their place, and the very contraposition of reform and "ultimate aim" loses all meaning, is relegated to the sphere of utopian legends. Those who would make such a contraposition—whether they are German "revisionists" like Eduard Bernstein, or Italian "revolutionary syndicalists"[118] like those who took part in the latest syndicalist congress in Ferrara—will show themselves equally incapable of understanding the spirit and the method of modern scientific socialism. This is a good thing to remember at present, when reformism and syndicalism permit themselves to speak for Marx.

And what healthy optimism breathes in the words that mankind always sets itself only such tasks that it can solve. They do not, of course, mean that any solution of mankind's great problems, as suggested by the first utopian one meets, is a good one.

---

* *Handwörterbuch.* V. Band. S. 736.

A utopian is one thing; mankind, or, more precisely, a social class representative of mankind's highest interests in a given period, is something else. As Marx has very well said, "*With the thoroughness of the historical action, the size of the mass* whose action it is *will therefore increase.*"[119] This is conclusive condemnation of a utopian attitude towards great historical problems. If Marx nevertheless thought that mankind never sets itself unachievable tasks, then his words are, from the viewpoint of theory, only a new way of expressing the idea of the unity of subject and object in its application to the process of historical development; from the viewpoint of practice they express that calm and courageous faith in the achievement of the "ultimate aim" which once prompted our unforgettable N. G. Chernyshevsky to exclaim fervently, "Come what may, we shall win."

TWENTY-FIFTH ANNIVERSARY
OF THE DEATH OF KARL MARX

The class-conscious proletariat of all lands could best honour the memory of the great founder of the International by endeavouring to understand the immense significance Marx's theory has for our times.

This theory is known to have been the object of numerous assaults by the so-called *critics* of Marx. Unfortunately, these assaults were not lacking in effect. In the ranks of the militant proletariat of the whole civilised world there are not a few people who firmly believe that Marxism as a theory has already outlived its time and must now give way to new views, the motley combination of which is known as *critical socialism*. But their belief has as little foundation as had the "criticism of Marx" itself.

Marxism is not just an *economic* teaching (dealing with the course of development of capitalist society); nor is it just a *historical theory* ("historical materialism"); nor can it be described as economic teaching *plus* historical theory. Marx's economic teaching is not something standing *alongside* his historical theory. It is *thoroughly permeated with the historical theory*, or more truly, it is the outcome of the study of economic development during the present epoch from the standpoint of that historical theory, aided by the mighty method of historical materialism. That is why those who say that *Capital* is not only an *economic* but also a *historical* work are right.

However, even that is not all. The significance of Marx's achievements in theory is not limited to his remarkable works in the field of political economy, and, as it used to be called, *the philosophy of history*. "Historical materialism" is *only a part of Marx's materialist world-outlook*, as will be easily appreciated by anyone who undertakes the pleasant task of reading Engels' famous polemical work directed against Mr. Eugen Dühring. The first part of this work, written, so to speak, under the eyes of Marx and indeed partly with his assistance, is devoted to *philosophy* in the proper meaning of the term.

The philosophical side of Marxism is, however, almost completely ignored even by many of those who would like to remain loyal to Marxism. This is the sole reason why such ridiculous attempts have been made to combine Marxism either with the philosophy of Kant, or with the philosophy of Mach, or with some other philosophical systems having absolutely nothing in common with the world-outlook of the author of *Capital*. But to wish to combine Marxism with philosophies which have nothing in common with it is to reveal a total lack of comprehension of the fact that all aspects of Marx's world-outlook are closely linked with one another, and that, consequently, one cannot arbitrarily remove one of them and replace it by a combination of views no less arbitrarily selected from quite another world-outlook. And in fact we find that all those who have attempted to carry out this preposterous operation on Marxism have always turned out to be very bad Marxists. What they wrote about Marx's *philosophy*, and especially about his *dialectics*, was not only wrong, but simply ludicrous. And if their "critical" exercises of this kind were not met with homeric laughter by those who knew this subject, it was only because, as I said before, the number of people well versed in Marxism is very small.*

Quite recently, one respected Italian reformist, in the first chapters of his book on new roads to socialism, revealed the most complete, the most improbable, and the most childish lack of understanding of dialectics in general and the materialist dialectics of Marx in particular[120]—without evoking any ridicule.

But if the ideologists of the *proletariat* often display this total incomprehension of Marx's philosophy, they are the real losers, while the philosophy itself suffers but little. Their views lose all semblance of system, and enter into abnormal association with views elaborated by ideologists of the *modern bourgeoisie*, that is to say, of a class moving to its decline. It may be said without any exaggeration that a disapproving attitude to the philosophy of Marx is a variety of *philosophical decadence*.

---

* ⟨Marxism is an integral theoretical system, as may be judged by a reading of Dührings Umwältz[ung]. Every aspect of this system is closely linked with all other aspects, each one shedding light on all the others, thus aiding in their comprehension. One cannot select one aspect and limit oneself to its acknowledgement, while eliminating or ignoring the remainder. That would be mutilating Marxism, it would be plucking out its heart, transforming this living theory into a mummy, and not content even with that, concentrating all attention only on one part or another of the mummy. In this lies the grandeur of Marxism, and in this, too, lies the reason why so many of those who are honestly trying to understand it, do so wrongly. To understand Marxism correctly it is essential to have a very wide education, and none of the writers who have undertaken to criticise Marxism has that.⟩

Moreover, things are no better with regard to the "criticism" of *other aspects* of Marx's doctrine. Criticism is obviously an excellent thing. But it has this quality only when the person engaged in criticism does in fact take a critical attitude to his subject. It is anything but splendid when under the pretext of criticism, the "critic" only repeats ideas of others which he has adopted without any criticism. Such criticism is the direct opposite of what criticism *should be*. But it is just this type of alleged criticism of Marx with which the so-called *revisionists and syndicalists** have been busying themselves during the last ten years. This criticism was only *an uncritical repetition of what had been said with the more or less clearly acknowledged aim of apologetics by the present-day ideologists of the bourgeoisie*. If this criticism did signalise some kind of *movement*, it was a *regressive* and by no means progressive *movement*. And exactly because this type of criticism was a *movement* backwards and not forward, the most critical minds were in reality not those who abandoned themselves to its attractions, but those who displayed the most *critical* (I do not simply say: *negative*) attitude towards it.

The "critics" of Marx have said, and still repeat, that the course of economic development of capitalist society during the past quarter of a century has refuted Marx's expectations and predictions. But when they are called upon to state which specific expectations and predictions they mean, they point not to the ideas *expressed* by Marx, but to those *attributed to him* by people who were either unwilling or unable to understand him. I shall take as an example the notorious *"theory of impoverishment"*. Marx was said to have held the view that the position of the proletariat worsens in capitalist society, not only *relatively*, but also *absolutely*. It will suffice to read the following passage from *The Poverty of Philosophy*, to realise how wrong that is:

"As for the working classes, it still remains a very debatable question whether their condition has improved as a result of the increase in so-called public wealth. If the economists, in support of their optimism, cite the example of the English workers employed in the cotton industry, they see the condition of the latter only in the rare moments of trade prosperity. These moments of prosperity are to the periods of crisis and stagnation in the "correct proportion" of 3 to 10. But perhaps also, in speaking of improvement, the economists were thinking of the millions of

---

* Those who believe that the teaching of the self-styled revolutionary syndicalists is a *return to Marxism* are very much mistaken. As a matter of fact, under the banner of this doctrine a regressive movement to the views of Proudhon and Bakunin is taking place. In Italy, this regressive movement is occurring under the most powerful influence of modern "Manchesterism"— the bourgeois school of "pure economics".

workers who had to perish in the East Indies so as to procure for the million and a half workers employed in the same industry in England three years' prosperity out of ten.'*[121]

As you see, there is still a vast difference between this "very debatable question" and the theory of the absolute impoverishment of the proletariat which is usually ascribed to Marx by his "critics". And the theory of the *relative* worsening of the position of the proletariat[122] is actually developed in *Capital*.

Or perhaps I shall be told that in this respect there is no room for doubt: that in reality there is a very significant improvement in its position that can be achieved by the working class of today? In that case, I shall cite the situation of the British working class, who thanks to certain exceptional circumstances, have wrested much larger concessions from their employers than the proletariat of the European continent have been able to. Does the reader know why it is so important for the British working class to win *old age pensions*? Because, as Charles Booth has pointed out, one-third of the old people in Britain *die in workhouses*, i.e., fall into *pauperism*. It is not hard to guess to which class these aged people belong, who have to undergo this wretched experience. But in view of this, it is very difficult to deny that capitalism, while developing the productive forces of society to an enormous degree, allows the proletariat only insignificant access to the fruits of this development. That is precisely Marx's theory of impoverishment.

The so-called criticism of Marx has exposed, not the flaws that were peculiar to Marxism, but the failure to understand Marxism which was peculiar to its critics.

There is only one course for the real critic of Marxism to adopt: correctly to master the materialist method and apply it to the study of those aspects of historical development —for example, the *history of ideology*—on which Marx and his friend and collaborator, Engels, spent little or no time. *Only in this way* is it possible to uncover the weak points of any scientific method—if there are any. Of course, *such* a criticism demands a great deal more serious intellectual labour than that required to master the theories which now find such a ready market among both the erudite and the merely educated bourgeoisie: Kantianism, immanent philosophy, Brentanoism, "pure economics", and so on and so forth. Let us hope that the *second quarter of a century since the death of Marx* which is now beginning will witness, at last, the flowering of *such* a criticism, which will at the same time constitute the greatest *theoretical triumph of Marxism*.

---

* Compare *Wage Labour* and *Capital* where the theory of relative impoverishment is presented.

MATERIALISMUS MILITANS

REPLY TO MR. BOGDANOV

FIRST LETTER

"Tu l'as voulu, Georges Dandin!"*[123]

Dear Sir,

No. 7 of *Vestnik Zhizni*[124] for 1907 contains your "Open Letter to Comrade Plekhanov". This letter makes it clear that you are dissatisfied with me for many reasons. The most important of these, if I am not mistaken, is that for the past three years I have been, as you put it, polemising with empiriomonism "on credit", without adducing serious arguments against it and, again as you yourself put it, these "tactics" of mine seem to have had some success. Next, you reproach me for "constantly addressing" you as *Mr.* Bogdanov. Besides this, you are dissatisfied with my review of Dietzgen's *Das Akquisit der Philosophie* and *Briefe über Logik*. You say that I warn readers against being too credulous and unwary in their approach to Dietzgen's philosophy, on the grounds that it sometimes takes on a resemblance to yours. I will mention still another reason for your dissatisfaction with me. You assert that some of those who share my views are making what amounts to almost a "criminal" charge against you, and you claim that I am partly to blame for their "demoralisation". I could prolong the list of reproaches you level against me, but there is no need for this; the points I have mentioned are quite enough for us to begin an explanation which will not be without general interest.

Getting down to this, I shall begin with what seems to me to be a question of second-, if not third-rate, importance, but which is apparently of no small weight in your eyes, namely the question of your "title".

You consider yourself insulted when I address you as "Mr." and say that I have no right to insult you. I hasten to assure you on this point, dear Sir, that it was never my intention to insult you. But when you mention *rights*, it gives me reason to think that, in your opinion, one of my Social-Democratic *obligations* is to call you comrade. But, God and our Central Committee be my judges, I do not recognise any such obligation. And this for a very

---

* [You asked for it, Georges Dandin!]

simple and obvious reason—*that you are no comrade of mine.* And you are no comrade of mine because *you and I represent two directly opposed world-outlooks.* And as the question for me is the defence of my outlook, you are, in relation to me, not a comrade, but the most resolute and irreconcilable opponent. Why should I be hypocritical, then? Why should I put an utterly false meaning into words?

Boileau once gave the advice—"call a spade a spade...."* I take this sensible advice: I call a spade a spade, and you an empirio-monist. I call *comrades* only those who hold the same views as myself and serve the same cause I took up long before the Bern-steinians, Machists, and other "critics of Marx" made their appearance in our country. Think, Mr. Bogdanov, try to be unbiassed, and tell me—have I really *"no right"* to act in this way? Am I really *obliged* to act otherwise?

Further. You are terribly mistaken, dear Sir, if you imagine that I am throwing out more or less obvious hints to the effect that you should be, if not hanged, at least "banished" from the confines of Marxism at the earliest possible moment. If any one intended to treat you in this way, he would first of all have come up against the utter *impossibility of fulfilling* his harsh design. Even Dumbadze, with all his miraculous power, would not have been able to banish from his domains a person who did not dwell in them. Similarly, no ideological Pompadour[125] could possibly "banish" from the confines of a particular teaching a "thinker" who was already *outside them.* And that you are outside the confines of Marxism is clear for all those who know that the whole edifice of this teaching rests upon *dialectical materialism*, and who realise that you, as a convinced Machist, do not and cannot hold the materialist viewpoint. And for the benefit of those who do not know and do not realise this, I reproduce the following passage, which came from your own pen:

In characterising the attitude of various philosophers to the "thing-in-itself", you deign to remark:

"A golden mean has been adopted by materialists of a more critical shade who have rejected the *absolute* unknowability of the 'thing-in-itself', but at the same time regard it as being *fundamentally* different from the 'phenomenon', and, therefore, always only 'vaguely knowable' in the phenomenon, outside of experience as far as its content is concerned (that is, presumably, as far as the 'elements' are concerned, which are not the same as elements of experience), but yet lying within the bounds of what is called the forms of experience, i.e., time, space and causality. Such is approximately the standpoint of the French materialists of the

---

* [Literally: "call a cat a cat".]

HOTEL-PENSION MIRABEAU
CLARENS-MONTREUX

5. April 5(3)
ct. 1908,

Дорогіе товарищи Павелъ
и Алекс. Самойловичъ! Я
не знаю, сколько именно
буквъ въ моей статьѣ,
но я знаю, что сократить
ея нельзя. Т.е. собственно
можно, но нельзя на
несколько буквъ, чтобъ
и статья: некрологъ
сокращена на 10 буквъ. Но
по больше не могу
сократить. Коллиги не

Plekhanov's letter to the editors of the *Golos Sotsial-Demokrata*, October 5, 1908, with his protest against shortening of his article against Bogdanov (on two pages)

eighteenth century and among the modern philosophers—Engels and his Russian follower, Beltov."*

This passage (rather clumsy in its "content") will explain matters even to those people who, generally speaking, do not care about philosophy. It must now be plain even to them that you reject Engels' point of view. And those who know that Engels was completely at one with the author of *Capital* also in the domain of philosophy will easily understand that when you reject Engels' viewpoint you *thereby* reject Marx's viewpoint, and join *his* "critics".

I beg you, dear Sir, not to be afraid; don't regard me as some kind of philosophising Pompadour, and don't imagine that I establish your adherence to Marx's opponents for the purpose of your "banishment". I repeat: it is impossible to banish from the confines of any teaching a man who is already outside them. And so far as Marx's critics are concerned, everyone, even if he did not study in a seminary, now knows that these gentlemen have departed from the confines of Marxism and are scarcely likely ever to return.

"Sentence of death" is a measure incomparably more severe than "banishment". And if I were ever capable of hinting at the necessity of you, my dear Sir, being "hanged" (though only in quotation marks), I could. of course, on a suitable occasion, also be disposed to the idea of your "banishment". But in this, too, you either give way to quite unwarranted fear, or are indulging in perfectly groundless irony.

I tell you once and for all that I have never had any desire to "hang" anyone. I should be an extremely poor Social-Democrat if I did not acknowledge the complete freedom of theoretical research. But I should be an equally poor Social-Democrat if I did not understand that *freedom of research* must be accompanied and supplemented by *freedom for people to group according to their views*.

I am convinced—who could not be?—that people who differ fundamentally in theory have every right to differ in practice too, that is, to group themselves in different camps. I am convinced even that "situations" do arise when *it is their duty to do so*. Do we not know already from Pushkin's time:

> *It is not meet to harness*
> *Horse with trembling doe.*[126]

In the name of this unquestionable and incontestable *freedom of grouping*, I have repeatedly invited the Russian Marxists to

---

* А. Богданов, «Эмпириомонизм», кн. II, стр. 39, Москва, 1905. [A. Bogdanov, *Empiriomonism*, Book II, Moscow, 1905, p. 39.] ["Beltov" was Plekhanovs' pen name.]

form a special group for the propagation of their ideas, and to dissociate themselves from other groups which do not share Marxist ideas on some issues. Repeatedly, and with quite understandable passion, I have expressed the opinion that any unclarity in ideology brings great harm. I think that ideological unclarity is especially harmful for us now, when idealism of all varieties and shades, under the impact of reaction and the pretext of revising theoretical values, is holding veritable orgies in our literature, and when some idealists, probably for the sake of spreading their own ideas, proclaim their views to be Marxism of the very latest model. It is my deep conviction, and one which I am not in the least backward in expressing, that theoretical dissociation from these idealists is more essential now than ever. I understand that sometimes this might not be to the liking of one or other of the idealists (especially from among those who would like to have their theoretical merchandise passed under the flag of Marxism) but, nevertheless, I resolutely assert that those who reproach me on these grounds with attempting on somebody's *freedom* (by "banishment") or even on his *life* (by "hanging") reveal a much too narrow understanding of that freedom in whose name they indict me.

When I invite those who share my views to dissociate themselves from people who cannot be their comrades in ideology, I am using the inalienable right of every "man and citizen". And when you, Mr. Bogdanov, raise such a ridiculous clamour over this and suspect me of threatening your person, you simply demonstrate that you have badly assimilated the notion of that inalienable right.

While not a Marxist yourself, you would like nothing better than that we Marxists should accept you as our *comrade*. You remind me of the mother in one of Gleb Uspensky's stories. She wrote to her son, saying that since he lived a long way off and was in no hurry to see her, she would complain to the police and demand that the authorities send her son "under escort" for her to "embrace" him. Uspensky's philistine, to whom this maternal threat was addressed, burst into tears whenever he remembered it. We Russian Marxists will not weep for such reasons. But this will not stop us from telling you quite bluntly that we wish to take full advantage of our right to dissociate ourselves and that neither you nor any one else (no matter who it may be) will succeed in "embracing" us "under escort".

I shall add the following. If I at all resembled some inquisitor or other, and if I at all believed that there could be people deserving of capital punishment (even in quotation marks) for their convictions, I should, nevertheless, not count you, Mr. Bogdanov, among them. I should then say to myself: *"The right to be executed* is conferred by talent and there is no trace of talent in our theoretician of empiriomonism. He is unworthy of execution!"

You, dear Sir, challenge me insistently to be frank. So do not be offended if I am.

To me, you are not unlike Vasili Tredyakovsky of blessed memory—a man of considerable diligence, but, alas, very little talent. To busy oneself with people of the calibre of the late professor of eloquence and poetical subtleties one must be endowed with an enormous power of resistance to boredom. I do not possess much of this power. That is why I have not replied to you before now, in spite of your direct challenges.

I said to myself: J'ai d'autres chats à fouetter.* And that I was sincere and not merely seeking an excuse to avoid doing polemical battle with you is proved by my deeds; actually, since you began to challenge me I have in fact been under the regrettable necessity to "whip" quite a few "cats". Of course, you interpreted my silence differently. Obviously you thought that I lacked the courage to launch a frontal attack on your philosophical stronghold, preferring to direct empty threats at you, to criticise you "on credit". I do not deny you the right to self-flattery, but I, too, have the right to say that you were flattering yourself. To tell the truth, I simply did not think it necessary to argue with you, believing that the class-conscious representatives of the Russian proletariat would themselves be able to assess your *philosophical subtleties*. Besides, as I already said, j'avais d'autres chats à fouetter. Thus, as far back as late 1907, that is to say, immediately after the appearance of your open letter to me in *Vestnik Zhizni*, some of my comrades advised me to deal with you. But I replied that it would be more useful to deal with Mr. Arturo Labriola, whose views were being peddled in Russia by your fellow thinker Mr. Anatoly Lunacharsky under the guise of a weapon "sharpened for the orthodox Marxists". Supplied with an afterword by Mr. Lunacharsky, Labriola's book prepared the way for syndicalism[127] in Russia, and I preferred to work on that, and to postpone meanwhile my reply to your open letter. To tell you the truth, I am afraid of being bored, and would not have decided to answer you now, Mr. Bogdanov, if it had not been for the same Mr. Anatoly Lunacharsky. While you were elaborating your empiriomonism after the manner of Tredyakovsky, Lunacharsky (the rogue has a finger in every pie) began to preach a new religion,[128] and this preaching can have a much greater practical significance than the propagation of your alleged philosophical ideas. It is true that, like Engels, I consider that at the present time "all the possibilities of religion are exhausted" (alle Möglichkeiten der Reli-

---

* [I have plenty to do without that; literally: I have other cats to whip.]

gion sind erschöpft).* But I do not lose sight of the fact that. strictly speaking, these possibilities are exhausted only for *class-conscious proletarians*. Besides the class-conscious proletarians, there are those who are only partly conscious of their class position and those who are completely unconscious of it. In the course of development of *these* sections of the working class, religious preaching can have a strong negative effect. Finally, apart from the proletarians who are partly conscious or completely unconscious of their class position, we have a great multitude of "intellectuals", who naturally imagine themselves to be fully *conscious* of their position, but in fact are *unconsciously* infatuated with every fashionable trend and at the "present time" (Goethe said that all reactionary epochs are subjective)—are very much disposed to all varieties of mysticism. Inventions such as the new religion of your fellow thinker, dear Sir, are a real godsend to these people. They rush at them like flies at honey. And as quite a number of these gentlemen, grasping avidly at everything they have read about in the latest book, have unfortunately not completely severed their connection with the proletariat,** they may infect them too with these mystical infatuations. In view of this, I decided that we Marxists must give a resolute rebuff not only to the new gospel of Anatoly, but also to anything but new philosophy of Ernst (Mach), which has been more or less adapted by you, Mr. Bogdanov, for our use here in Russia. And for this reason alone, I undertook the task of replying to you.

I am aware that many comrades were surprised that I did not find it necessary to polemise with you before now. But this is an old story that remains eternally new. Even at the time when Mr. Struve published his well-known *Critical Notes*,[130] some of my fellow thinkers (then very few in number) quite rightly judged these *Notes* to be the work of a man who had not worked out a consistent manner of thinking and advised me to come out against him. This kind of advice became still more persistent after the same Mr. Struve published his article "On Freedom and Necessity" in *Voprosy filosofii i psikhologii*. I remember that, when I met Lenin in the summer of 1900, he asked me why I had done nothing about Struve's article. My reply was quite simple: the ideas expressed by Mr. Struve in his article "On Freedom and Necessity"

---

* See Engels' article: Die Lage Englands, which was first published in *Deutsch-Französische Jahrbücher* and reprinted in *Nachlass*, etc., Vol. I, p. 484.[129]

** They will soon do so. Our intellectuals' infatuation with every fashionable anti-materialist "ism" is a symptom of the adaptation of their "world-outlook" to the "complex" of ideas peculiar to the modern bourgeoisie. But as yet, many of the intellectuals who oppose materialism still imagine themselves to be spokesmen of the proletariat, whom they try to influence, sometimes not without success.

had been refuted in advance by me in my book: *The Development of the Monist View of History*. The new error made by the author of *Critical Notes* must have been clear to any one who had read and understood my book; I had no time to discuss the matter with those who had not read my book, or did not understand it. I did not consider myself in any way obliged in respect of our Marxist intelligentsia to play the part of Shchedrin's owl, relentlessly pursuing the eagle to instruct it by the phonetical method: "Your Majesty, say—A, B, C...". In Shchedrin's story the eagle became so completely fed up with the owl that at first it shouted at it: "Leave me alone, damn you", and then finally killed it. I do not know whether the part of tutor-owl to the Russian intelligentsia of a more or less Marxist turn of thought presented any dangers for me. But I had neither the inclination nor the opportunity to be cast in such a thankless role, since I had other practical and—above all—theoretical tasks. Would I be far advanced in theory if I "reacted" to everything to which I was (and am) expected to "react"? Suffice it to say that some readers would have liked me to express my opinion on our contemporary eroticism (i.e., on Mr. Artsybashev and his brethren) and others asked me what I thought about Madame Isadora Duncan's dancing. Woe to the writer who took it into his head to "react" to all the spiritual whims of that capricious and nervous lady, the ⟨Russian⟩ intelligentsia! Take any one of the philosophical fancies of this "lady". Is it so long since she was harping on Kant? Is it long since she was demanding that we reply to the Kantian "critique" of Marx? Not long at all! In fact it was so recently that this frivolous "lady" has not yet worn out the shoes in which she went running after neo-Kantianism. And after Kant came Avenarius and Mach; and after these two Ajaxes of empirio-criticism came Joseph Dietzgen. And now right behind Dietzgen we have Poincaré and Bergson. "Cleopatra had many lovers!" But let those who will take up the cudgels against them. I am all the less inclined to do so because I lay not the slightest claim to please our modern intelligentsia, who is not the heroine of my romance....

But because I do not think myself obliged to do battle with the numerous lovers of our Russian Cleopatra it does not follow that I have not the right to make some reference to them in passing, such being also one of the inalienable rights of man and citizen. For instance, I have never engaged in criticism of the Christian dogmatic theology, and probably I never shall. But this does not deprive me of the right to express my opinion about any of the Christian dogmas, should the occasion arise. What would you think, Mr. Bogdanov, of an orthodox theologian who seized upon some passing remarks of mine concerning Christian dogmas— and such remarks are likely to be found in my writings—and began to accuse me of criticising Christianity "on credit"? I think you would have enough common sense to shrug your shoulders at such a charge. So do not be surprised, dear Sir, if I have no less common sense, i.e., if I shrug my shoulders when I hear how you use my passing remarks about Machism to accuse me of what you call criticism—"on credit".

Earlier in this letter, to be on the safe side, I quoted your opinion on Engels' philosophical standpoint, an opinion which should not leave the slightest doubt of any kind in the minds of even the most slow-witted as to where you stand in relation to Marxist philosophy. But now I recall that, when at a recent meeting of Russians in Geneva, I drew your attention in my speech to those lines of yours, you were pleased to rise from your seat and shout: "That's what I used to think; now I see I was mistaken." That was an extremely important statement, and I, and with me every reader interested in our philosophical dispute, am bound to accept it, both as information and for guidance ... if only it contains sufficient logical sense for one to be guided by it.

Formerly it pleased you to think that Engels' philosophical standpoint was that of the golden mean and you rejected it as unsound. Now it does not please you to think so. What does this mean? Does it mean that you now recognise Engels' view as satisfactory? I should be very glad to hear this from you, even if it were only for one thing—I should not then have to overcome the boredom of having a philosophical dispute with you. But so far I have had to deny myself this pleasure, since nowhere have you declared that you have changed from Saul to Paul, that is to say, that you have abandoned Machism and become a dialectical materialist. Quite the contrary. In the third book of your *Empiriomonism*, you express exactly the same philosophical views you expounded in the second book, from which I took the quotation illustrating your complete disagreement with Engels. What has changed, then, Mr. Bogdanov?

I shall tell you exactly what (has changed). When the second book of your *Empiriomonism* was published—and that was not in the days of yore, but no further back than 1905—you still had the courage to criticise Engels and Marx with whom you disagreed and continue to disagree as much as an idealist can possibly disagree with a materialist. This courage was, of course, to your credit. If one who is afraid to look truth in the face is a poor thinker, still worse is the one who looks truth in the face and is then afraid to tell the world what he has seen there. And the worst of all is he who conceals his philosophical convictions in consideration of some practical benefits. *Such* a thinker obviously belongs to the species of Molchalins.[131] Let me repeat, Mr. Bogdanov, that the boldness you displayed as recently as 1905 was a credit to you. It is just a pity that you lost it so quickly.

You have seen that my "tactics", as you call them—in fact they could be reduced to a simple statement of what is ⟨for all⟩ an obvious fact, namely, that you are one of Marx's "critics"— have had, as you yourself have been pleased to say, some success, that is to say, our orthodox Marxists have ceased to regard you as their comrade. This has scared you, so you have thought up your own "tactics" against me. You decided that you would be in a more favourable position to contend with me if you declared that you sided with the founders of scientific socialism, and that I was a sort of critic of theirs. In other words, you decided to apply the "tactics" which are known as putting the blame on somebody else. Having taken this decision, you wrote that critical analysis of my theory of cognition which you published in the third book of *Empiriomonism* and in which—despite what you said in the second book—I am no longer counted among the followers of Marx and Engels. Your courage failed you, Mr. Bogdanov, and I am sorry for you. But we must be just even to people who are lacking in courage. Therefore, I must say that, unlike your usual self, on this occasion you displayed no little cleverness. In this perhaps you surpassed even the ⟨famous⟩ monk Gorenflot.

The French know of this monk. But he is probably not so well known to Russians, so I shall say a few words about him.

Once, I don't remember which particular fast day it was, the monk Gorenflot had an intense desire to eat chicken. But that would be a sin. What should he do to have his chicken and at the same time avoid committing a sin? The monk Gorenflot found a simple way out. He caught the tempting chicken and performed the ritual of christening it, bestowing on it the name of carp or of some other kind of fish. Fish is known to be a Lenten dish, not forbidden on fast days. So our monk ate his chicken on the pretext that it had been christened a fish.

You, Mr. Bogdanov, acted in exactly the same way as this ⟨cunning⟩ monk. You feasted and continue to feast on the idealist philosophy of "empiriomonism". But my "tactics" made you feel that this was a theoretical sin in the eyes of orthodox Marxists. So, after thinking the matter over briefly, you performed the holy ritual of christening on your "empiriomonism" and renamed it the philosophical teaching of Marx and Engels. Well, no orthodox Marxists will ever forbid such spiritual nourishment. So you manage to have it both ways: you continue to enjoy "empirio-monism" and at the same time you consider yourself a member of family of orthodox Marxists. And not only do you consider yourself one of that family, but you are offended (or pretend to be) at those who do not wish to recognise you "as one of them". Just like

the monk Gorenflot. But the monk was crafty in small things, while
you, Mr. Bogdanov, display craft in big things. That's why I
say you are much smarter than the famous monk ever was.

But, alas, even the sharpest wit is helpless *in the face of facts*.
The monk could christen his chicken by the name of fish, but it
went on being a chicken. Similarly, Mr. Bogdanov, you may call
your idealism Marxism, but this will not make you a dialectical
materialist. And the more zealously you apply your new "tactics",
the more noticeable it will be that your philosophical views are
wholly incompatible with the dialectical materialism of Marx
and Engels; moreover—and this is even worse—it will become
the more obvious that you are simply unable to understand what
is the chief distinguishing feature of this materialism.

In the interests of impartiality, however, it should be said that
materialism in general remains a closed book for you. Herein
lies the explanation of the innumerable blunders in your criticism of my theory of cognition.

Here is one of these blunders. Whereas in 1905 you described
me as a follower of Engels, now you certify that I am a disciple
of Holbach. On what grounds? Only on the grounds that your
new "tactics" direct you not to recognise me as a Marxist. You
have no other reason. And just because you have no other reason
for calling me a disciple of Holbach, apart from your need to
employ the "tactical" wisdom of the monk Gorenflot, you immediately reveal your weak side, your complete impotence in questions of materialist theory. Indeed, if you had even a nodding
acquaintance with the history of materialism, you would realise
that there are no grounds for describing me as a Holbachian—
holbachien, as Rousseau once expressed it. Since you describe me
as a Holbachian in connection with the theory of cognition I defend, I don't think it would be useless for me to inform you that
this theory has a much greater resemblance to Priestley's*
teaching than to Holbach's. In other respects, the philosophical
outlook I uphold is further removed from Holbach's teaching
than, for example, from that of Helvétius,** or even from that of
La Mettrie, as any one acquainted with the works of the last-named
will easily appreciate. But the trouble is that you know nothing about the works either of La Mettrie, or Helvétius, or Priestley, or, for that matter, Holbach himself, among whose disciples
you have enrolled me, after expelling me from the school of Marx

---

* See his *Disquisitions Relating to Matter and Spirit,* and his controversy
with Price.
** See his remarkable attempts at a materialist explanation of history,
which I mentioned in the second of my *Beiträge zur Geschichte des Materialismus.*

and Engels—probably because of my poor progress in understanding dialectical materialism. Yes, that is just the trouble: you know nothing at all of materialism, either its history or as it is today. And this is not only your trouble, Mr. Bogdanov; it is the old trouble of all opponents of materialism. It is an old story that even those who knew absolutely nothing about materialism claimed the right to speak against it. It is self-evident that this worthy habit could be so firmly established solely because it was fully in keeping with the prejudices of the ruling classes. But we shall speak of this later.

You send me to school to the author of *Système de la nature*, on the ground that, to quote your own words, I expound materialism in the name of Marx with the aid of quotations from Holbach.* But, first, Holbach is not the only author I quote in my philosophical articles. And secondly—and this is the main point—you do not understand at all *why* I had to quote so often from Holbach and other representatives of the eighteenth-century materialism. I did this by no means with the aim of setting forth Marx's views, as you would have everyone believe, but with the aim of defending materialism from those absurd reproaches which were advanced *against it* by its opponents in general, and the neo-Kantians in particular.

For example, when Lange says in his notorious but essentially quite superficial *History of Materialism* that "materialism obstinately takes the world of sensuous appearance for the world of real things", I consider it my duty to show that Lange is distorting historical truth. And since he states this opinion precisely in the chapter on Holbach, in order to expose him I had to quote Holbach, that is to say, the very author whose views Lange distorts. For approximately the same reason, I had to cite the author of *Système de la nature* in my controversy with Messrs. Bernstein and C. Schmidt. These gentlemen, too, talked a lot of nonsense about materialism, and I had to demonstrate to them just how badly they comprehended the subject they had undertaken to pass judgement on. Besides, in my arguments with them I had perforce to cite not only Holbach, but also La Mettrie, Helvétius, and especially Diderot. True, all these writers are representatives of the eighteenth-century materialism, and so anyone unfamiliar with the subject might, perhaps, ask himself: why is Plekhanov quoting particularly the eighteenth-century materialists? I have a very simple reply to this: I do so because the opponents of materialism, for example that same Lange, considered the eighteenth century to be the epoch of the greatest flowering of that teaching.

---

* *Empiriomonism*, Book III, preface, pp. X-XI.

⟨Lange directly refers to the eighteenth-century materialism as classical materialism.⟩

As you see, Mr. Bogdanov, the nut is quite easy to crack. But, being well versed in the sly "tactics" of the monk Gorenflot, you want not to *crack the nut*, but to *keep it whole*, since it is not in your interests to crack it. But do you know what? When one is endeavouring to becloud simple explanations, it is difficult to get along without sophisms, and the sophist requires at least some *skill in dealing with ideas*, as Hegel described it. As far as you are concerned, however much you imitate the crafty Gorenflot, you are very far from possessing such skill. That is why your sophisms are exceedingly awkward and clumsy. This is very inconvenient for you. So, every time you are in need of sophisms, I would advise you to turn to Mr. Lunacharsky, since his sophisms come far more easily and elegantly. This makes things all the more convenient for criticism. I don't know how it is with everybody else, but I find it much more pleasant to expose the elegant sophistry of Mr. Lunacharsky than to deal with your clumsy sophistical efforts, Mr. Bogdanov.

I cannot say if you will accept my well-intended advice, although as you see, it is not proffered quite disinterestedly; but for the time being it is with your clumsy sophistical concoctions that I have to deal. So, once more rallying my powers of resistance to boredom, I shall continue to expose them.

By listing me among Holbach's disciples, you wanted to discredit me in the eyes of your readers. In your preface to the Russian translation of Mach's *Analysis of Sensations*, you say that, as a counterweight to Mach's philosophy, my comrades and I advance "the philosophy of eighteenth-century natural science as formulated by Baron Holbach, a purely bourgeois ideologist, very far removed also from the moderate socialist sympathies of Ernst Mach". Here we find revealed, in all its ugly nakedness, your incredible ignorance of the subject and your extraordinarily comic awkwardness in "dealing with ideas".

Baron Holbach is indeed very far removed from the moderate socialist sympathies of Mach. And why shouldn't he be? He is removed from them by approximately one hundred and fifty years! In truth, one would really have to be a worthy descendant of Tredyakovsky to put the blame for this on Holbach or any of his eighteenth-century fellow thinkers. Surely it was not of his own will that Holbach *lagged behind* Mach in point of time. If we are to argue in this fashion we might as well blame Cleisthenes, for example, for being "far removed" even from the opportunist socialism of Mr. Bernstein. To every vegetable its own time, Mr. Bogdanov! But in class society, at any given time there are not a few varieties of philosophical vegetables on God's earth,

and men select one or other of them according to taste. Fichte was
right when he said that to know a man is to know his philosophy.
It seems to me therefore that Mr. Bogdanov's undoubted and
even immoderate sympathy for the "*moderate* socialist sympathies
of Ernst Mach" is very strange.

Hitherto I had supposed that Mr. Bogdanov was not only incapable of sympathising with any kind of "*moderate* socialist
sympathies", but that, as a man of an "*extreme*" mode of thought,
he would be inclined to brand them as opportunism unworthy of
our times. Now I see that I was mistaken. And on reflection, I
now understand why exactly I was mistaken. For a moment I
had forgotten that Mr. Bogdanov is one of the "critics" of Marx.
Not for nothing is it said: bind the cock's claws and lose the fight.
Mr. Bogdanov began by repulsing dialectical materialism and
ended with obvious and even immoderate sympathy for the "moderate socialist sympathies" of Mach. That is quite natural. "Wer
a sagt, muss auch *b* sagen."*

That Holbach was a baron is an incontestable historical truth;
but why did you, Mr. Bogdanov, remind your readers of the baronial status of Holbach? We must suppose that you did this,
not out of love for titles, but simply because you wanted to taunt
us, the defenders of dialectical materialism, with being the
alleged disciples of a *baron*. Well, you are entitled to do so. But
in trying to taunt us, don't forget. most honoured Sir, that you
cannot get two skins from one bull. It is you yourself who say
that Baron Holbach was the *purest ideologist of the bourgeoisie*. It is
clear, therefore, that his baronial title has no significance at all
in determining the sociological equivalent of his philosophy. The
whole question is: what role did this philosophy play in its time?
That in its time it played a supremely revolutionary role you
may learn from many commonly available sources, including,
by the way, Engels, who, in characterising the French philosophical revolution of the eighteenth century, said: "The French were
in open combat against all official science, against the church and
often also against the state; their writings were printed across
the frontier, in Holland or England, while they themselves were
often in jeopardy of imprisonment in the Bastille."** You may
believe me, dear Sir, when I tell you that among such revolutionary writers was Holbach, as well as other materialists of that
period. Moreover, the following must be noted.

Holbach, and in general the French materialists of that time,
were the ideologists not so much of the bourgeoisie as of the third
estate, in that historical period when this estate was thoroughly

---

* [Whoever says *A*, must say *B*.]
** *Ludwig Feuerbach*, St. Petersburg. 1906, p. 30.[132]

imbued with revolutionary spirit. The materialists made up the left wing of the ideological army of the third estate. And when the third estate in turn split up, when on the one hand the bourgeoisie and on the other the proletariat emerged from it, the proletarian ideologists based themselves on the teaching of the materialists precisely because it was the extreme revolutionary philosophical doctrine of its time. Materialism became the basis of socialism and communism. Marx pointed this out in his book: *Die heilige Familie.* He wrote therein:

"There is no need for any great penetration to see from the teaching of materialism on the original goodness and equal intellectual endowment of men, the omnipotence of experience, habit and education, and the influence of environment on man, the great significance of industry, the justification of enjoyment, etc., how necessarily materialism is connected with communism and socialism."*

Marx then goes on to remark that "the apologia of vices by *Mandeville,* one of Locke's early English followers, is typical of the socialist tendencies of materialism. He proves that in *modern* society vice is *indispensable* and *useful.* This was by no means an apologia for modern society."**

Marx is right. One does not have to be exceptionally intelligent to understand the necessary connection between materialism and socialism. However, it does demand some intelligence. That is why those ("critics") who completely lack intelligence do not see the connection pointed out by Marx and think they can support, and even find new principles as a "basis" for socialism, while opposing materialism. Moreover, those supporters of socialism who posses *no* intelligence whatever are ready to embrace any philosophy, except materialist philosophy. This explains why, when they begin to pass judgement on materialism, they utter the most inexcusable nonsense about it.

You too, dear Sir, did not notice the necessary connection between materialism and socialism. Why? I shall leave this for the reader to answer, and will confine myself to reminding you of how you even reproach us Marxists with spreading the ideas of French materialism—an action, which, according to you, does not conform to the tasks of modern socialist propaganda. Here, too, in your usual fashion, you are completely at variance with the founders of scientific socialism.

In the article—Programm der blankistischen Kommune-Flüchtlinge—published originally in No. 73 of the paper *Volksstaat* for 1874 and reproduced later in the collection *Internationales aus dem*

---

* Supplement I to Engels' *Ludwig Feuerbach*, St. Petersburg, 1906, p. 87. [133]
** Ibid., p. 88.[134]

"*Volksstaat*", Engels notes with satisfaction that the German Social-Democratic workers sind mit Gott einfach fertig (are simply
through with God) and that they live and think as materialists,*
and remarks on page 44 of the above-mentioned collection that
in all probability this holds true also for France. "If not," he
stipulates, "there could be nothing simpler than to organise the
mass distribution among workers of the splendid French materialistic literature of the last century" (i.e., the eighteenth century,
Mr. Bogdanov.—*G.P.*) "of the literature in which the French spirit has attained its sublime expression both as regards form and
content, and which, considering the then existing level of science,
even today stands exceedingly high as regards content" (dem
Inhalt nach auch heute noch unendlich hoch steht), and "still
unexcelled as regards form."[136]

As you see, Mr. Bogdanov, Engels was not afraid to spread
among the proletariat that "philosophy of natural science" which
you are pleased to call the philosophy of the "purest ideologists
of the bourgeoisie"; on the contrary, he directly recommended wide
dissemination of its ideas among the French workers who had
not yet become materialists. We, the Russian followers of Marx
and Engels, consider it worth while to propagate these ideas,
among others, in the ranks of the Russian proletarians, whose
class-conscious representatives, unfortunately, have not all by
any means accepted the materialist point of view. Considering
this task useful, about two years ago I planned the publication in
Russian of a library of materialistic literature in which first
place would have been given to translations of works of the eighteenth-century French materialists—works that are in fact in-
comparable in form and even now extremely instructive in content. However, nothing ever came of this. In Russia it is very
much easier to find a market for the works of those numerous
schools of contemporary philosophy which Engels designated by
the general contemptuous title of "the pauper's broth of eclecticism"[137] than for literature in any way devoted to materialism.
A clear example of this is the very poor sales of Engels' *Ludwig
Feuerbach*, which I translated into Russian and which is a splendid book in every way. Our reading public nowadays is indifferent
to materialism. But don't rejoice too soon, Mr. Bogdanov. The
indifference of our reading public to materialism is a bad sign,
since it means they are continuing to wear their long conservative
pigtails even in such periods when they themselves are full of
what would seem to be the most fearless and "advanced" theoretical "searchings". It is the historical misfortune of poor Russian

---

* Avis [advice] for you, Mr. Bogdanov, but especially for your colleague,
the Blessed Anatoly,[138] founder of the new religion.

thinking that, even in the moments of its greatest revolutionary
upsurge, it very seldom manages to shake off the influence of
Western bourgeois thinking, which can be nothing but conservative in view of the social relationships now prevailing in the
West.

The well-known renegade from the eighteenth-century French
liberation movement, La Harpe, said in his book *Réfutation du
livre "De l'Esprit"*, that when he first advanced his refutation of
Helvétius, his criticism found scarcely any response among
Frenchmen. Subsequently, he said, they began to take a totally
different attitude to it. La Harpe himself accounts for this by
the fact that his first effort was made in the pre-revolutionary
epoch, when the French public did not have as yet the opportunity to see in practice the dangerous consequences arising from
the dissemination of materialist views. In this case, the renegade
was right. The history of French philosophy *after* the Great Revolution could not show more clearly that its characteristic anti-
materialist trends were rooted in the instincts of self-preservation
of the bourgeoisie, who had somehow coped with the old regime
and therefore abandoned their former revolutionary infatuation
and turned conservative. And this to a greater or lesser degree is
applicable to other countries besides France. One would have to
be very naive indeed not to see how much cowardly hypocrisy
there is in the supposedly supercilious contempt with which
contemporary bourgeois ideologists everywhere regard materialism. The bourgeoisie fear materialism as a revolutionary doctrine,
well adapted to tear from the eyes of the proletariat the theological blinkers by means of which they wish to benight it and
impede its spiritual growth. Engels himself, better than anyone
else, demonstrated the truth of this in the article "Über historischen Materialismus", published in Nos. 1 and 2 of *Neue Zeit*,
1892-93, which had appeared originally in the form of an introduction to the English edition of the famous pamphlet: *Socialism:
Utopian and Scientific*. Engels, addressing the British reader,
furnishes a materialist explanation of the fact that the British
bourgeois ideologists do not like materialism.

Engels points out that materialism, which was an aristocratic
doctrine first in England and then in France, soon became a revolutionary doctrine in the latter country, "so much so that, when
the Great Revolution broke out, the doctrine hatched by English
Royalists gave a theoretical flag to French Republicans and Ter-
rorists, and furnished the text for the Declaration of the Rights
of Man". This alone would have been enough to intimidate the
"respectable" philistines of foggy Albion. "Thus, if materialism
became the creed of the French Revolution," continues Engels,
"the God-fearing English bourgeois held all the faster to his reli-

gion. Had not the reign of terror in Paris proved what was the upshot, if the religious instincts of the masses were lost? The more materialism spread from France to neighbouring countries, and was reinforced by similar doctrinal currents, notably by German philosophy, the more, in fact, materialism and free thought generally became on the Continent the necessary qualifications of a cultivated man, the more stubbornly the English middle class stuck to its manifold religious creeds. These creeds might differ from one another, but they were, all of them, distinctly religious, Christian creeds."[138]

The subsequent internal history of Europe with its struggle of classes and proletarian armed uprisings convinced the British bourgeoisie more than ever of the need to preserve religion as a curb on the people. Now this conviction began to be shared by all the Continental bourgeoisie. "The *puer robustus*, here," said Engels, "turned from day to day more *malitiosus*.* Nothing remained to the French and German bourgeoisie as a last resource but to silently drop their free thought, ... one by one, the scoffers turned pious ... spoke with respect of the Church, its dogmas and rites, and even conformed with the latter as far as could not be helped. French bourgeois dined *maigre* on Fridays, and German ones sat out long Protestant sermons in their pews on Sundays. They had

---

* [Note from the collection *From Defence to Attack*.] Allusion to Hobbes' reference to the people: *puer robustus et malitiosus* (a strong and malicious child). I should say, by the way, that even in Hobbes' system, materialism was far from being completely deprived of revolutionary spirit. The ideologists of the monarchy even at that time understood that monarchy by the grace of God was one thing, whereas monarchy according to Hobbes was quite another. Lange rightly said: "Dass jede Revolution, welche Macht hat, auch berechtigt ist, sobald es ihr gelingt, irgend eine neue Staatsgewalt herzustellen, folgt aus diesem System von selbst; der Spruch 'Macht geht vor Recht' ist als Trost der Tyrannen unnöthig, da Macht und Recht geradezu identisch sind; Hobbes verweilt nicht gern bei diesen Konsequenzen seines Systems und malt die Vortheile' eines absolutistischen Erbkönigtums mit Vorliebe aus; allein die Theorie wird dadurch nicht geändert" (F. A. Lange, *Geschichte des Materialismus*, Erstes Buch, Leipzig, 1902, S. 244). [That every revolution which is strong enough is also justified, as soon as it succeeds, in establishing a new form of state power follows of itself from this system: tyrants need not comfort themselves with the proverb: 'Might comes before Right' since might and right are actually identical. Hobbes is reluctant to dwell on the consequences of his system, and prefers to paint the advantages of an absolute hereditary monarchy; but that does not modify the theory.] The revolutionary role of materialism in the world of antiquity was mentioned by Lucretius, writing eloquently à propos of Epicurus: "When human life lay foully on the earth, before all eyes, 'neath Superstition crushed, who from the heavenly quarters showed her head and with appalling aspect lowered on men; Then did a Greek first lift eyes to hers—first brave her face to face. Him neither myth of gods, nor thunderbolts, nor sky with roar and threat could quell...". Even Lange, who, in general, is not well disposed to materialism, recognised that idealism had a protective role to play in Athenian society.

come to grief with materialism. 'Die Religion muss dem Volk erhalten werden',—religion must be kept alive for the people— that was the only and the last means to save society from utter ruin."[139]

Then began—for my own part I shall add—together with the "return to Kant", that reaction against materialism which still characterises the trend of European thought generally and philosophy in particular. The repentant bourgeois, more or less hypocritically, points to this reaction as the best proof of the success of philosophical "criticism". But we Marxists, who know that the course of development of thought is determined by the course of development of life, are not easily dislodged by such more or less hypocritical assertions. We are capable of defining the sociological equivalent of this reaction; we know that it was caused by the appearance of the revolutionary proletariat on the scene of world history. Since we have no reason to fear the revolutionary proletariat, since, on the contrary, we consider it an honour to be its ideologists, we do not renounce materialism. Indeed, we defend it against the cowardly and biassed "criticism" of the bourgeois wiseacres.

There is yet another reason why the bourgeoisie turned away from materialism, one which, incidentally, also has its roots in the psychology of the bourgeoisie as the ruling class in modern capitalist society. Every class which has attained power is naturally disposed to *complacency*. And the bourgeoisie, ruling in a society based upon bitter mutual competition among the commodity producers, is naturally inclined to a complacency in which there is no trace of altruism. The precious "ego" of every worthy representative of the bourgeoisie completely occupies his every aspiration and design. In Act II, Scene I of Sudermann's *Das Blumenboot*, Baroness Erfflingen impresses on her youngest daughter: "People of our rank exist in order to make all things in the world into a sort of merry panorama that passes or, rather, *seems* to pass before us." In other words, people such as the dazzling Baroness who, by the way, came of a most bourgeois family, must train themselves to regard everything which happens in the world exclusively from the viewpoint of their own more or less agreeable personal experiences.* *Moral solipsism*—these are

---

* [Note from the collection *From Defence to Attack*.] "Notre morale, notre religion, notre sentiment de nationalité," says Maurice Barrès, "sont choses écroulées, constatais-je, auxquelles nous ne pouvons emprunter des règles de vie, et en attendant que nos maîtres nous aient refait des certitudes, il convient que nous nous en tenions à la seule réalité, au Moi. C'est la conclusion du premier chapitre (assez insuffisant, d'ailleurs) de *Sous l'œil des Barbares*." (Maurice Barrès, *Le Culte du Moi. Examen de trois idéologies*, Paris, 1892.) [Our morality, our religion, our national sentiment have already suffered collapse, Inoted. We cannot draw rules of life from them, and until our

the two words which best of all describe the sentiments of the most typical representatives of the present-day bourgeoisie. It is not surprising that from such sentiments spring systems which recognise nothing except subjective "experiences", and which would inevitably come to theoretical solipsism if they were not saved from this by their founders' lack of logic.

In my next letter, I shall show you, dear Sir, by what monstrous feats of illogicality your dear Mach and Avenarius save themselves from solipsism. There, too, I shall demonstrate that for you yourself, who find it useful to keep aloof from them in some matters, there is also no safeguard from solipsism, other than lapsing into the most howling absurdities. But for the moment I must finish dealing with my attitude to eighteenth-century French materialism.

No less than Engels, I am enthralled with this teaching, which is so rich and varied in content and brilliant in form,* but also like Engels I understand that natural science has advanced considerably since the time when this doctrine flourished, and that now we can no longer share the views of that time—say, Holbach's—on physics, chemistry, or biology. I not only subscribe to the critical remarks made by Engels in *Ludwig Feuerbach* in regard to French materialism, but also, as you are aware, I have for my part augmented and reinforced these critical remarks by references to the sources. Knowing this, the unbiassed reader will only laugh to hear you say that, in defending materialism, I am defending the eighteenth-century philosophy of natural science as distinct from the same philosophy of the twentieth century (your preface to the Russian translation of *Analysis of Sensations*). He will laugh even more heartily when he recollects that Haeckel is also a materialist. Or perhaps you will tell us that Haeckel, too, does not rank with the natural scientists of our time? It is obvious that, in this regard, the only light of your eyes is Mach with, of course, those who think like him.

teachers have restored our confidence in these matters, it is fitting that we should cling to our only reality, our ego. This is the conclusion of the first chapter of the (not very adequate, by the way) book: *From the Barbarian Point of View.*] It is very clear that such sentiments must predispose those who hold them to idealism, and to its weakest variety at that—subjective idealism. People whose whole outlook is closed to everything except their precious ego, cannot have any sympathy for materialism. Yet there are people who consider materialism to be an *immoral* doctrine! It is not necessary to remind those who have even the slightest acquaintance with contemporary French literature, where Barrès, with his *cult of the ego*, finally landed.

* I say "varied", because in eighteenth-century French materialism there were several distinct trends, although all were akin to one another.

It is true that among the twentieth-century naturalists you will not find many who, like Haeckel, hold the materialist point of view. This, however, is not an argument against Haeckel, but rather in his favour, since it demonstrates that he has been able to withstand the influence of anti-materialist reaction, the sociological equivalent of which I defined above with the help of Engels. Natural science has nothing to do here, dear Sir, it is *not the gist of the matter*.*

No matter how things stand with natural science, it is as clear as daylight that you, as a defender of Machist philosophy, must definitely not claim to be a follower of Marx and Engels. Indeed, Mach himself, in the preface to the Russian translation of his *Analysis of Sensations*, and on page 292 of the Russian text, admits that his philosophy is akin to Hume's. And do you remember what Engels says about Hume?

He says that if the German neo-Kantians are attempting to resurrect Kant's views, and the English agnostics those of Hume, *"this is ... scientifically a regression"*.** This, it would seem, is quite unambiguous, and can hardly please you who would have us believe that one can and must *advance under the banner* of Hume and Mach.

Generally speaking, Mr. Bogdanov, it was not a happy day for you when you took it into your head to expel me from the school of Marx and Engels and enrol me among Holbach's pupils. In doing so, you not only sinned against truth, but revealed an astonishing lack of skill in controversy.

Now admire your own handiwork. You are pleased to write: "The basis and essence of materialism, according to Comrade Beltov, is the notion of the primacy of 'nature' over 'spirit'. This definition is very wide and, in this case, has its disadvantages."***

We shall let the disadvantages alone, meantime, and recall that you wrote these lines directly after you had stated that I was expounding materialism "in the name of Marx and with the aid

---

* [Note from the collection *From Defence to Attack*.] Confirmation of this may be found in a speech by the famous naturalist, J. Reinke on May 10, 1907 in the Prussian Upper Chamber about the League of Monists founded by Haeckel. This Kiel botanist tries in every possible way to convince himself and his audience that the "fanatic" Haeckel causes his displeasure by the scientific groundlessness of the "materialist monism" he preaches. (That is how Reinke, quite correctly, describes Haeckel's teaching.) However, any one who takes the trouble to read Reinke's speech carefully will find that he is defending, not science, but what he calls "the light of the old world-outlook" (Licht der alten Weltanschauung). There is no need to enlarge upon the social relations in which there arose this "light", so pleasing to Reinke and scientists such as he. (Reinke's speech was reproduced in a pamphlet: *Haeckels Monismus und seine Freunde*, von J. Reinke, Leipzing, 1907.)

** *Ludwig Feuerbach*, St. Petersburg, 1906, p. 43. My italics.—*G.P.*[140]
*** *Empiriomonism*, Book III, p. 11.

of quotations from Holbach". Consequently, one might think that my definition of the "basis and essence" of materialism was borrowed from Holbach and contradicted what in fact I would have the right to expound in the name of Marx. But how did the founders of scientific socialism define materialism?

Engels writes that on the question of the relation of being to thinking, the philosophers split into two great camps. "Those who asserted the primacy of spirit to nature and, therefore, in the last instance, assumed world creation in some form or other ... comprised the camp of idealism. The others, who regarded nature as primary, belong to the various schools of materialism."*

Isn't this exactly what I said about the "basis and essence of materialism"? So, at least in this case, I had every right to expound materialism in the name of Marx and Engels, without requiring any assistance from Holbach.

Did you not think, dear Sir, what situation you put yourself in by attacking the definition of materialism which I accepted? You wished to attack me, but, as it turned out, you attacked Marx and Engels. You wished to expel me from the school of these thinkers, but, as it happened, you have come out as a *"critic"* of Marx. This, of course, is not a crime, but it is a fact, and in the present instance, a very instructive one. (This again is evidence of your lack of courage. You want to criticise Engels, but are afraid to oppose him openly, so you attribute his ideas to Holbach and Plekhanov. Nothing could be more characteristic of you.) For me, it is not at all a question of *persecuting* you, but rather of *defining* you, that is to say, of explaining to my readers to which particular category of wiseacres you belong.

I trust that this has now become sufficiently clear to them. However, I must warn them: so far we have seen in you only the blossoms; we shall eat the berries in the next letter, in which we shall take a walk in the orchard of your criticism of my theory of cognition. There we shall find many juicy and tasty berries!

But now I must finish. Till we meet again, dear Sir, and may the pleasant god of Mr. Lunacharsky protect you!

G. V. Plekhanov

SECOND LETTER

"Tu l'as voulu, Georges Dandin!"

Dear Sir,

This letter of mine to you falls naturally into two parts. First, I consider myself *obliged* to reply to the "critical" objections raised by you against "my" materialism. Secondly, I wish to utilise

---

* *Ludwig Feuerbach*, p. 41.[141]

my *right* to go over to the offensive and examine the basis of that "philosophy" in whose name you attack me, and with the aid of which you would like to "supplement" Marx,—that is to say, the philosophy of Mach. I know that the first part will be pretty much of a bore to many readers. However, I am compelled to follow you, and if there is little that is amusing in our joint walk through your "critical" orchard, the blame is not mine, but his who planned and planted the orchard.

I

You criticise "my" definition of matter which you take out of the following passage from my book: *A Critique of Our Critics.*

"In contrast to 'spirit', we call 'matter' that which *acts on our sense-organs and arouses in us various sensations.* What is it exactly that acts on our sense-organs? To this question I answer with Kant: *things-in-themselves.* Thus, matter is nothing else than the totality of things-in-themselves, in so far as these things constitute the source of our sensations."

This passage seems to have provoked your mirth.

"Thus," you write smilingly, "'matter' (or 'nature' in its antithesis to 'spirit') is defined through 'things-in-themselves' and through their capacity to 'arouse sensations by acting on our sense-organs'. But what are these 'things-in-themselves'? 'That which acts on our sense-organs and arouses in us various sensations.' That is all. You will find that Comrade Beltov has no other definition, if you leave out of account the probably implied negative characteristics: *non*-'sensation', *non*-'phenomenon', *non*-'experience'."*

Wait, dear Sir, don't forget that rira bien, qui rira le dernier.**

I don't define matter "*through*" things-in-themselves at all. I assert only that *all* things-in-themselves are material. By the materiality of things, I understand—and here you are right—their ability one way or another, directly or indirectly, to act on our senses and thus arouse in us sensations of one kind or another. In my dispute with the Kantians, I thought I was entitled to confine myself to indicating simply that things had this ability. I did so because this ability was not only not questioned but was explicitly acknowledged by Kant on the very first page of his *Critique of Pure Reason.* But Kant was inconsistent. On the first page of the above-mentioned work he acknowledged things-in-themselves to be the source of our sensations, but at the same time he was by no means averse to recognising these things as

---

* *Empiriomonism*, Book III, St. Petersburg, 1906, p. XIII.
** [He laughs best who laughs last.]

something immaterial, that is to say, inaccessible to our senses. This inclination of his, which led him to contradict himself is especially clearly revealed in his *Critique of Practical Reason*. In view of this inclination of his it was quite natural for me to insist, in arguing with Kant's followers, that things-in-themselves are, on his own admission, the source of our sensations, i.e., they possess all the signs of being material. While insisting on this, I exposed Kant's inconsistency, indicating to his followers the logical necessity for them to declare for one or the other of the two irreconcilable elements of this contradiction, a way out of which their mentor, Kant, could not find. I said that they could not be content with Kant's dualism; they had to accept *either* subjective idealism *or* materialism.* Once our dispute took this turn, I found it worth while to note the main feature distinguishing subjective idealism from materialism, namely, that subjective idealism negates the material nature of things, whereas this is recognised by materialism. This may be known even to you, Mr. Bogdanov, who knows absolutely nothing of the history of philosophy.**

That is how matters stood. But you, not in the least grasping what was involved (and evidently not able to grasp it) at once seized on words the meaning of which remained quite "unknowable" to you, and pounced on me with your cheap irony. Haste makes waste, Mr. Bogdanov.

To proceed. In this dispute with you I shall have to refer, even more often than in arguing with the Kantians, to the main feature distinguishing materialism from subjective idealism. I shall therefore try to explain this feature for you, with the help of, I hope, some fairly convincing extracts.

In his work *Of the Principles of Human Knowledge*, the celebrated subjective idealist (and Anglican bishop) George Berkeley writes:

"It is indeed an opinion strangely prevailing amongst men, that houses, mountains, rivers, and in a word all sensible objects, have an existence, natural or real, distinct from their being perceived by the understanding."*** But this opinion may involve a manifest contradiction. "For, what are the forementioned objects but the

---

* [Note from the collection *From Defence to Attack*.] On this matter, see the articles: "Conrad Schmidt Versus Karl Marx and Frederick Engels", and "Materialism or Kantianism?" in my work *A Critique of Our Critics*, St. Petersburg, 1906, pp. 167-202.[142]

** Of course, absolute idealism, too, does not share the materialist view on matter; but its teaching on matter as the "other-Being" of spirit does not interest us here, just as it was of no interest to me in my dispute with the neo-Kantians.

*** The *Works* of George Berkeley D. D., formerly bishop of Cloyne, Oxford, MDCCCLXXI, Vol. I, pp. 157-58.

things we perceive by sense? And what do we perceive besides
our own ideas or sensations?"* Berkeley continues: colour, figure,
motion, extension are quite known to us as our sensations. But
we would entangle ourselves in contradictions if we considered
them as signs or images of things existing outside thinking.**

In contrast to the subjective idealists, Feuerbach, the materialist, says: to prove that something *is*, means to prove that something exists not only in thought (nicht nur gedachtes ist).***

Engels states exactly the same thing in his controversy with
Dühring, when opposing his view to the idealist view of *the world
as an idea*, he declares that the real unity of the world consists in
its materiality (besteht in ihrer Materialität).****

After this, is it necessary to explain further what exactly we
materialists understand by the materiality of objects? To be on
the safe side, I shall explain it.

We call material objects (bodies) those objects that exist independently of our consciousness and, acting on our senses, arouse
in us certain *sensations* which in turn underlie our notions of the
external world, that is, of those same material objects as well as
of their relationships.

That, I think, is enough. I shall only add this: Mach, whose
"philosophy" you, dear Sir, believe to be the "philosophy" of the
twentieth-century natural science, *adheres firmly on this question
to the point of view of the eighteenth-century idealist Berkeley*. He
even uses almost the same expressions as the worthy bishop. He
says: "It is not bodies that produce sensations, *but complexes of
elements* (complexes of sensations) that form bodies. If bodies
seem to a physicist to be something lasting and real, and *elements*
their fleeting, transient reflection, he does not notice that all
'bodies' are only the logical symbols for *complexes of elements*
(complexes of sensations)."*****

You are well aware, of course, Mr. Bogdanov, what precisely
your teacher says on this subject. But it is obvious that you do
not know at all what Berkeley said about it. You are like Molière's
Jourdain, who for a very long time did not realise that he was
speaking in prose. You have mastered Mach's view on matter,
but in your simplicity you had no idea that *this was a purely
idealistic view*. That is the reason for your astonishment at my

---

* Ibid.
** Ibid., p. 200.
*** Feuerbach's *Werke*, Bd. II, S. 308. I may be asked: does that *not
exist* which exists only in thought? It exists, I reply slightly changing Hegel's
expression, subsisting as the *reflection of real existence*.
**** *Herrn Eugen Dührings Umwälzung der Wissenschaft*, V. Auflage,
S. 31.[143]
***** *Analysis of Sensations*, translated by G. Kotlyar, published by
Skirmunt, p. 33.

Plekhanov's notes made during the discussion of Bogadnov's report in Geneva

definition of matter; the reason for your failure to guess why it was necessary for me to insist, when arguing with the neo-Kantians, on the materiality of things-in-themselves. Ridiculous Monsieur Jourdain! Poor Mr. Bogdanov!

If you had known at least a little of the history of philosophy, you would have been well aware that the definition of matter which has caused you so much hilarity is not my private property, but the common property of very many thinkers of the materialist, and even of the idealist camp. It was held, for example, in the eighteenth century by the materialists Holbach and Joseph Priestley.* And only the other day, we could say, the idealist (only not subjective idealist) E. Naville, in a paper he read in the French Academy answered the question: "What is matter?" saying: "C'est ce qui se révéle à nos sens" ("that which is revealed to our senses").** You can see from this, dear Sir, how widespread is "my" definition of matter.*** However, do not imagine that by referring to this I am trying to divert your "critical" blows from myself to others. Nothing of the kind. I can manage

---

* According to Priestley, matter is the object of any of our senses. [The last six words are in English in the original.] (*Disquisitions....* 1777, p. 142.)

** *La Matière, Mémoire présenté à l'Institute de France*, p. 5. The paper was read in April this year.

*** [Note from the collection *From Defence to Attack*.] When characterising Plato's theory of knowledge, Windelband said: "If notions include knowledge which, although formed by perceptions, does not develop from them and remains essentially distinct from them, then ideas, which are the objects of notions must possess, together with the objects of perceptions, an independent and higher reality. But the objects of perceptions in all cases are bodies and their movements, or as Plato put it in plain Greek, the *visible* world; consequently, ideas, as the object of cognition expressed in notions, must represent an independent, separate reality, the *invisible* and incorporeal world" (*Plato* p. 84). This will suffice for any one to understand why, in contrasting materialism to idealism, I defined matter as the source of our sensations. In doing so I was emphasising the main feature which distinguishes the materialist theory of knowledge from the idealist. Mr. Bogdanov did not understand this, and burst out laughing when he should have thought the matter over. My opponent says that all one can make out of my definition of matter is that it is not spirit. This again proves that he is not familiar with the history of philosophy. The concept "spirit" developed by way of abstraction from the properties of material objects. It is a mistake to speak of matter as non-spirit. We have to say: spirit (i.e., of course, the notion of spirit) is non-matter. Windelband asserts (p. 85) that the peculiarity of Plato's theory of knowledge "consists of the demand that the higher world must be an invisible or immaterial world". This demand could arise, obviously, only a very long time after man, on the basis of experience, had formed a notion of the world as "*visible*" and material. The "peculiarity" of the materialist criticism of idealism consisted in the revelation that it was inconsistent to demand the existence of a higher "world"—"invisible" and "immaterial". The materialists affirmed that there exists only the material world which we—in one way or another, directly or indirectly—perceive with the aid of our senses, and that there is and can be no other knowledge apart from experience.

to ward them off myself, and for that I need no great audacity or agility, since your blows are indeed very weak and clumsy, and, therefore, not to be feared in the least.

If I define matter as the source of our sensations, you believe, quite unjustifiably, that I am "probably" characterising matter in "a negative way", that is to say, as *non*-experience. It is even strange to me how you could be so grossly mistaken; indeed, many pages of the same book from which you quote, *A Critique of Our Critics*, should have made clear to you my conception of experience. Moreover, my conception of experience could have clarified for you the notes to Engels' *Ludwig Feuerbach*, which you also quote. In one of those notes I say, in polemising with the neo-Kantians: "Every experiment and every productive activity of man represents an *active* relation on his part to the external world, a deliberate calling forth of definite phenomena. And as a phenomenon is the fruit of the action of a thing in itself upon me (Kant says the *affecting* of me by that thing), in carrying out an experiment or engaging in production of this or that product, I force the thing in itself to 'affect' my 'ego' in a definite manner determined beforehand by me. Consequently, I know at least some of its properties, namely those through whose intermediary I force it to act."* The direct meaning of this is that experience presupposes interaction between the subject and the object *outside it*. It is clear from this that I would have got involved in an unpardonable contradiction with myself had I tried negatively to define the object by the words "*non*-experience". Good gracious, it is precisely "experience". More correctly: *one of the two essential conditions of experience*.

On the following page of your book (XIV), Mr. Bogdanov, you formulate somewhat differently the strange idea which you attributed to me. There you would have me say that "things-in-themselves", in the first place, do exist, and, moreover, outside our experience; secondly, they are subject to the law of causality. This again is most strange.

If things-in-themselves are "subject to the law of causality", it is plain that they do not exist outside experience. How did you fail to see that when you attributed to me two propositions sharply contradicting each other? And if you really thought I was contradicting myself here, you should have immediately drawn your readers' attention to my unforgivable lack of logic, since that disclosure alone would have sufficed to nullify "my" whole theory of knowledge. You are a bad polemicist, Mr. Bogdanov! Or, perhaps, you refrained from disclosing my contradiction only out of a vague realisation that it existed only in your imagination!

---

* *Ludwig Feuerbach*, St. Petersburg, 1906, p. 118.[144]

If so, you should have pondered this "experience" of yours in order to make it clear instead of vague. By doing so and coming to the conviction that my contradiction was but the fruit of your own imagination, you would not have put it down to me, and at the same time would have saved yourself from making a most ridiculous blunder. So here again it must be said: you are a bad and clumsy polemicist, Mr. Bogdanov.

Let's go on further, and first of all note that the expression: "things-in-themselves exist outside our experience" is not a very happy one. It could mean that things in general are inaccessible to our experience. This is how Kant understood it, and, as I remarked earlier, contradicted himself as a result.* Nearly all the neo-Kantians understand it in this way, too, and in this case, Mach is in agreement with them. To him, the words "thing-in-itself" are always linked with the notion of some kind of x which lies outside the bounds of our experience. By virtue of such a notion of what is called the thing-in-itself, Mach was quite logical in declaring the thing-in-itself to be an absolutely unnecessary metaphysical appendage to the conceptions we derive from experience. You, Mr. Bogdanov, are looking at this question through the eyes of your teacher and you evidently cannot even for a moment admit that there may be people who employ the term "thing-in-itself" in a quite different sense from the Kantians and Machists. This is the reason why you are completely unable to understand me, who is neither a neo-Kantian nor a Machist.

Yet the question is fairly simple. Even if I had decided to use the unfortunate expression: "things-in-themselves exist outside of experience", it would by no means have meant that things-in-themselves are *inaccessible* to our experience but only that they exist even when our experience does not extend to them, for one reason or another.

In saying: "*our experience*", I have in mind human experience. But we are aware that at one time there were no people on our planet. And if there were no *people*, neither was there their *experience*. Yet the earth was there. And this means that it (also a thing-in-itself!) existed *outside* human experience. *Why* did it exist outside experience? Was it because it could not in general be the object of experience? No, it existed outside experience *only* because the organisms, which by their structure are capable of having experience, had not yet appeared.** In other words, "existed outside experience", means "existed prior to experi-

---

* About this contradiction of Kant's see my *A Critique of Our Critics*, p. 167.[145]

** In fact, animals are also capable of experience, but there is no need to deal with this here, since what I have said about human experience suffices to make my point clear.

ence". That and nothing more. So that when experience began, it
(the earth) existed, not only outside experience, but also in
experience, constituting an essential condition of experience. All
this may be expressed briefly in these words: experience is the
result of the interaction of subject and object; but the object does
not cease to exist even when there is no interaction between it
and the subject, that is to say, when there is no experience. The
well-known proposition: "there is no object without subject" is
basically incorrect.* The object does not cease to exist even when
there is as yet no subject, or when its existence has already ceased.
And anybody to whom the conclusions of modern natural science
are not an empty phrase must necessarily agree with this. We
have seen that in accordance with the contemporary theory of evolution, the subject appears only after the object has reached a
certain stage of development.

Those who contend that there can be no object without a subject are simply confusing two quite distinct concepts: the existence
of the object "in itself", and its existence in the *conception of
the subject*. We have no right to identify these two forms of existence. Thus, for example, you, Mr. Bogdanov, exist first "in
yourself", and, secondly, in the conception, say, of Mr. Lunacharsky, who takes you for a most profound thinker. The confusing of the object "in itself" with the object as it exists for the
subject is the very source of the confusion by means of which the
idealists of all colours and shades "overthrow" materialism.

The objections you, dear Sir, raise against me are based on the
same confusion. In point of fact, you are dissatisfied with "my"
definition of matter as the source of sensations. Let us then examine more closely what precisely causes your dissatisfaction.

You liken "my" definition of matter to the proposition which
runs: "a soporific power is what induces sleep" (p. XIII). You
borrowed this expression from one of Molière's characters, but, as
usual, you have reproduced it badly. Molière's character says:
"opium induces sleep *because* it has soporific power". The funny
thing here is that a person accepts as explanation of a fact that
which in reality is only another way of stating the fact. If Molière's character had been content simply to state the fact, to say:
"opium induces sleep", there would have been absolutely nothing
to laugh at. Now recollect what I say: "Matter arouses in us certain sensations." Does this resemble the explanation given by
Molière's character? Not in the least. I am not explaining, but
simply stating what I believe to be an incontestable fact. All
other materialists act in exactly the same way. Those who know

---

* [Note from the collection *From Defence to Attack*.] "Kein Objekt ohne
Subjekt," said Schuppe, whose "immanent philosophy" in its basis is identical
with the teaching of Mach and Avenarius.

the history of materialism are aware that none of the representatives of this teaching ever asked themselves *why* the objects of the external world have the capacity to arouse sensations in us. True, some English materialists sometimes maintained that this took place by divine will. However, when they voiced this pious thought, they were abandoning the viewpoint of materialism. Once again it turns out, dear Sir, that you laughed at me for no good reason. And when a man laughs at another for no good reason, he simply makes himself look ridiculous.

Rira bien, qui rira le dernier.

You think that the definition: "Matter is what serves as the source of our sensations" is an utterly empty phrase. The sole reason why you think so is that you are chock-full of prejudices founded upon the idealist theory of knowledge.

In pestering me with the question, what is it precisely that arouses sensations in us, you really want me to tell you what exactly we know about matter apart from its action on us. And when I reply: apart from its action on us, it is completely unknown to us, you exclaim triumphantly: "That means we know nothing about it!" Now what grounds have you for triumph? The grounds of your idealist conviction that to know things only through the impressions they make upon us is not to know them at all. This conviction came to you from Mach, who borrowed it from Kant, who in turn had inherited it from Plato.* But no matter how respectable this conviction may be by its age, it is nevertheless quite incorrect.

There is not and cannot be any other knowledge of the object than that obtained by means of the impressions it makes on us. Therefore, if I recognise that matter is known to us only through the sensations which it arouses in us, this in no way implies that I regard matter as something "unknown" and unknowable. On the contrary, it means, first, that matter is knowable and, secondly, that it has become known to man in the measure that he has succeeded in getting to know its properties through impressions received from it during the lengthy process of his zoological and historical existence.

If this is so, if we can know the object only through the impressions which it produces on us, then it must be clear to any one capable of thought that if we *disregard* these impressions, we shall be quite unable to say anything about the object other than

---

* [Note from the collection *From Defence to Attack*.] "Therefore the kernel of Plato's philosophy is *dualism*, established in this philosophy between two types of cognition—thinking and perception—and similarly between their two objects—the immaterial and the material world" (W. Windelband, *Plato*, pp. 85-86).

that it exists.* Therefore whoever demands that we define the
object while disregarding these impressions, is demanding something absolutely absurd. In its logical sense, or, to be more precise, in its logical nonsense, this demand is tantamount to asking
in what relationship the object stands to the subject at a time
when there is no relationship at all between the two. And you,
dear Sir, ask me precisely this absurd question, demanding that I
should tell you what matter is when it does not arouse any sensations in us, that is to tell you the colour of a rose when no one
looks at it, what it smells like when no one smells it, and so
forth. The absurdity of your question is that the very manner of
its presentation precludes all possibility of giving a reasonable
reply to it.**

Following in the footsteps of Mach, who *in this instance* is the
true pupil of Berkeley (there it is, the "natural science of the
twentieth century"!), you, Mr. Bogdanov, will say: if the object
can be known to us only through the sensations, and, consequently, the notions, which it produces in us when the object is in
some form of contact with us, there is no logical need for us to
acknowledge that the object has existence independently of these
sensations and notions. Earlier, in the same passage where you
obtained "my" definition of matter***I replied to this objection,
which seems to my now fairly numerous idealist adversaries to be
irrefutable. But either you cannot or do not want to understand
that reply, so I shall repeat it in the second part of this letter
when examining Mach's "philosophy": since I am firmly resolved
"to force understanding", to use an expression of Fichte's, if not
on you—I have poor hopes of you—then at least on those of the
readers who have no interest in defending idealist prejudices.
However, before proceeding to repeat my reply, I shall analyse
and assess for what it is worth, the most important of the "critical
arguments" you advance in your polemic with me.

You "formulate carefully" in my "original expressions" the following idea: "To their [things-in-themselves—*G. P.*] forms and relationships there correspond forms and relationships of phenomena—
as hieroglyphics correspond to the things which they designate."
About this idea you enter upon the following lengthy discourse:

---

* "Das Ding an sich hat Farbe erst an das Auge gebracht, Geruch an die
Nase, u.s.w.," Hegel says. (Hegel, *Wissenschaft der Logik*, Erster Band,
Zweites Buch, Nürnberg, 1813). [The Thing in itself has colour only in
relation to the eye, smell in relation to the nose, and so forth.]

** [Note from the collection *From Defence to Attack*.] But this is precisely
why Messers the empiriomonists and "empirio-symbolists" try to answer it.
I examine the attempt made by J. Petzoldt and P. Yushkevich to answer
this, in the article *Cowardly Idealism* to be found in this work.

*** *A Critique of Our Critics*, pp. 193-94.[146]

"Here there is a talk of the 'form' and the 'relationships' of things-in-themselves. This means they are presumed to possess both one and the other. Splendid. And do they have 'appearance'? A silly question, the reader will say. How can they have *form* without having any *appearance*? But these two words express one and the same thing. I think so too. But here is what we read in Comrade Plekhanov's notes to the Russian translation of Engels' *Ludwig Feuerbach*:

"'But "appearance" is precisely the result of the action on us of things-in-themselves. *Apart from this action they have no appearance.* Therefore, to contrast their "appearance" as it exists in our consciousness to the "appearance" they allegedly have in reality, is to fail to realise what concept is connected with the word "appearance".... Thus, things-in-themselves can have no appearance of any kind. Their "appearance" exists only in the consciousness of those subjects on which they act...' (p. 112, 1906 edition, the year in which the collection referred to, *A Critique of Our Critics*, was published).

"Replace everywhere the word 'appearance' in the above quotation by the word 'form', its synonym, which in the present case fully conforms to it in meaning, and Comrade Plekhanov brilliantly refutes Comrade Beltov."

Isn't that fine! Plekhanov brilliantly refutes Beltov, that is to say, himself! Very spitefully said! But hold on, dear Sir, rira bien, qui rira le dernier. Remember the circumstances in which I expressed the idea which you are criticising and what was its *true* "appearance".

It was expressed in my controversy with Mr. Conrad Schmidt, who attributed to materialism the doctrine of the *identity* of being and thinking, and said, addressing me, that if I was "serious" in recognising the action of things-in-themselves upon me, I must also acknowledge that space and time exist objectively, and not just as forms of contemplation peculiar to the subject. I replied to this as follows: "That space and time are forms of consciousness, and that, therefore, *subjectivity* is their primary distinctive feature,[147] was already known to Thomas Hobbes, and would not be denied by any present-day materialist. The whole question is whether certain forms or relations of *things* correspond to these forms of consciousness. It goes without saying that materialists can give only an affirmative answer to this question, which, of course, does not mean that they recognise the false (or rather, absurd) identity, which the Kantians, including Herr Schmidt, would impose upon them with obliging naivety.* No, the forms

---

* On the question of the identity of being and thinking I may now refer to my work: *Fundamental Problems of Marxism*, St. Petersburg, 1908, pp. 9 et seq.[148]

and relations of things-in-themselves cannot be what they *seem*
to us, i.e., as they appear to us as 'translated' in our minds. Our
representations of the forms and relations of things are no more
than *hieroglyphics*; the latter designate exactly these forms and
relations, and this is enough for us to be able to study how things-
in-themselves affect us, and, in our turn, to exert an influence on
them."*

What is this passage all about? About the same thing as I discussed with you above, Mr. Bogdanov: that the *object in itself*
is one thing, and the object in the conception of the subject is
quite another thing. Now the question is: am I logically entitled
to replace here the word "form" by the word "appearance", which,
according to you, is its synonym? Let us try it and see what happens. "That space and time are appearances of consciousness, and
that, therefore, *subjectivity* is their primary distinctive feature,
was already known to Thomas Hobbes, and would not be denied
by any materialist...." Wait a moment, how can that be? What
is this subjective "appearance" of consciousness? I employ the
word "appearance" in the sense of that visual perception of an
object which exists in the subject's consciousness. The question
is one of the "sensuous contemplation" of the object, so that in
the passage we are discussing the expression "appearance of consciousness" must signify—if the word "appearance" is, in fact,
synonymous with the word "form"—nothing else than the visual
perception of the consciousness of consciousness. Leaving aside
for the moment the question as to whether a visual perception of
this kind is possible, I direct your enlightened attention, dear
Sir, to the circumstance that here the visual perception of the
consciousness of consciousness would prove to be space and time;
but this is utter rubbish, stuff and nonsense. And this, naturally
was unknown to Thomas Hobbes, and of course not a single materialist would acknowledge it. What brought us to this nonsensical
pass? An unfounded belief in your capacity to analyse philosophical concepts. We believed you when you said that the word "appearance" is a synonym of the word "form"; we substituted "appearance" for "form" and got a mishmash that is even difficult to put
into words. So "appearance" is not synonymous with "form"? It is
not; the concept "appearance" does not by a long chalk cover the
concept "form". As Hegel in his *Science of Logic* demonstrated very
well, the "form" of the object is identical with its "appearance"
only in a certain and, moreover, *superficial* sense, in the sense of
external form. A more profound analysis will lead us to conceive
form as a "law" of the object, or, more correctly, as its *structure*.

---

* *A Critique of Our Critics*, pp. 233-34.[149]

This important contribution of Hegel's* to the logical doctrine of form was already known in Russia in the 1820s to people who dealt with philosophy. To convince you of this I invite you to read the following excerpt from a letter written by D. Venevitinov to Countess "N.N." "You see now," he wrote, after defining the concept of science, "that the word *form* expresses not the external appearance of science, but the general law which science must follow" (Venevitinov, *Collected Works*, St. Petersburg, 1855, p. 125). It is indeed a very great pity, Mr. Bogdanov, that you are not aware of that which, thanks to Venevitinov, was known at least to some Russian ladies of society as long as eighty years ago!

Now, one more question: In what sense did I employ the expression "forms of consciousness" when arguing with Conrad Schmidt? In the sense of the external *appearance* of consciousness, as Venevitinov would say? Of course, not. I used the word "form" in the sense of the "law" of consciousness, its "structure". So that in no respect was the word "form" for me a synonym for "appearance"; and one would have to understand absolutely nothing about philosophy to propose that substitution of one word for the other, which you proposed in order to hold me up to ridicule.

Rira bien, qui rira le dernier.

Sometimes people become involved in lengthy arguments simply because they are using words in different senses. Such arguments are boring and futile. But far more boring and far more futile are the arguments in which one contestant attaches a definite concept to particular words, while his adversary, using the same words, attaches no definite concept at all to them, and, consequently, is able to play with them as he thinks fit. To my regret, I am now compelled to conduct such an argument with you. When I used the word "form", *I knew* what exactly should be understood by it, whereas *you did not know*, because of your astonishing ignorance of the history of philosophy; it did not even occur to you that it was something requiring study and thought. You permitted yourself to play with words, as only a person could do who did not even suspect how dissimilar were the two concepts connected with these words. The result was only what was to be expected. In exposing the utter emptiness of your "philology", not only was I bored myself, but I was also compelled to bore my readers; and you, dear Sir, made yourself a laughingstock just because your "philology" was so totally lacking in content. What did you need to do that for?

---

* [Note from the collection *From Defence to Attack*.] In mentioning this contribution of Hegel's, I am not saying that he was the first to *notice* this distinction in the concepts of *"appearance"* and *"form"*; I am only stating that he *defined this distinction* better than other great idealists.

Your "philology", amazing in its emptiness, is also remarkable in another respect, which I leave to the reader to characterise, if he or she is not already too bored trying to follow my argument with you.

I have in mind those "hieroglyphics" which are mentioned in the same part of my article quoted by you in which I deal also with the question of forms of consciousness.

This article ("Materialism Yet Again") dates to the beginning of 1899. I took the word "hieroglyphics" from Sechenov, who, at the beginning of the nineties had already written in the article "Objective Thought and Reality": "No matter what objects may be in themselves, independent of our consciousness—let our impressions of them be but conventional signs—in any case, the similarity and distinction of the signs we perceive correspond to the similarity and distinction of reality. In other words, the similarities and distinctions which man finds among the objects he perceives are real similarities and distinctions." Take note, dear Sir, that the thought expressed by me in "Materialism Yet Again", and which provided you with a pretext for a truly scandalous play on words, is completely identical with the idea expounded by Sechenov in the above passage. Nor did I in the least hide the similarity of my views to those of Sechenov; on the contrary, I stressed this in one of my notes to the first edition of my translation of Engels' *Ludwig Feuerbach* (issued in 1892).[150] Therefore, dear Sir, you had every opportunity to know that in matters of this kind I adhered to the point of view of contemporary materialist physiologists and not to that of eighteenth-century natural science. But that by the way. The main point here is: in the new edition of my translation of *Ludwig Feuerbach* published abroad in 1905 and in Russia in 1906, I declared that while I continued to share Sechenov's *view* on this question, his *terminology* seemed somehow ambiguous to me.

"When he admits," I said, "that our impressions may be only conventional signs of things in themselves, he seems to acknowledge that things in themselves have some kind of 'appearance' that we do not know of and which is inaccessible to our consciousness. But '*appearance*' is precisely only the result of the action upon us of the things in themselves; *outside this action they have no 'appearance' whatsoever*. Hence, to oppose their 'appearance' as it exists in our consciousness to that 'appearance' of theirs which they supposedly have in reality means not to realise which concept is connected with the word 'appearance'. Such an imprecision of expression underlies, as we said above, all the 'gnosiologal' scholasticism of Kantianism. I know that Mr. Sechenov is not inclined to such scholasticism; I have already said that his theory of knowledge is perfectly correct, but we must not make to our opponents in philosophy concessions in terminology which prevent us from expressing our own thoughts with complete precision."*

Strictly speaking, this remark of mine could be reduced to this: if the thing-in-itself has colour only when it is being looked at, and smell only when it is being smelled, and so on, then in calling our conceptions of it conventional signs, we give grounds for thinking that, in our view, to its colour, smell, etc., as these exist in our sensations, correspond some kind of colour-in-itself, some kind of smell-in-itself, and so forth—to put it briefly, some kind of *sensations-in-themselves* that cannot become objects of *our sensations.* That would have been a distortion of *Sechenov's views* which I share, and therefore in 1905 I said I was against the *Sechenov terminology.*** But since I myself had formerly used the same somewhat ambiguous terminology, I made haste to point this out. "Another reason why I make this reservation," I added, "is because in the notes to the first edition of my translation of this pamphlet by Engels I also failed to express myself quite exactly and only subsequently felt all the awkwardness of that inexactness."*** After this reservation it would seem that any misunderstanding would be impossible. But for you, dear Sir, even the impossible is possible. You gave the "appearance" of not noticing this reservation, and once again launched upon your wretched play on words, basing this on the identification of the terminology which I use *now* and that which I *formerly* used, and which I myself rejected as somewhat ambiguous. The "beauty" of such "criticism" is obvious to any unbiassed person, and there is no need for me to characterise it. Many of my opponents in the idealist camp are now following your example, "criticising" my philosophical views by cavilling at the weakness of the terminology which I myself declared to be unsatisfactory before they took up their "critical" pens. It is very likely that it was from me

---

* Pages 102-03 of the foreign edition; 111-12 of the Petersburg edition.[151]

** I became convinced of the unsatisfactory nature of this terminology when I reread *Critique of Pure Reason*, where I noticed the following passage in the first edition: "In order that the noumen signify a real object which is not to be confused with all phenomena, it is not sufficient for me to free my thought of all conditions of sensuous contemplation. Besides, I must have some grounds for recognising another form of contemplation apart from sensuous, in which a similar object could be given, otherwise my thought would be empty although free from contradictions" (*Critique of Pure Reason,* translation by N. M. Sokolov, p. 218, Note). I wished to emphasise that no other form of contemplation apart from the sensuous is possible, but this does not prevent us from knowing things through the impressions they produce on us. But you of course did not understand this, Mr. Bogdanov. What a lot of trouble you give me! Now you see what it means to begin studying philosophy straight from Mach!

*** *Ludwig Feuerbach*, St. Petersburg edition, p. 112.[152]

15*

that some of these gentlemen heard for the first time why in fact this terminology was unsatisfactory.* They should not therefore be surprised if I do not reply to their more or less voluminous works. By no means every "criticism" is worthy of counter-criticism.

To get back to you, Mr. Bogdanov. You point maliciously to the fact that the second edition of my translation of *Ludwig Feuerbach* was published in the same year (1906) as my collection *A Critique of Our Critics*. Why do you refer to this? This is why. You yourself were aware that it was ridiculous and absurd to seize on expressions which I myself had declared to be unsatisfactory before it had occurred to any of my adversaries to criticise them. So you decided to assure your readers that in 1906 I "brilliantly refuted" myself by simultaneously employing two different terminologies. You did not think it necessary to ask yourself to which period of time the polemical article included in the collection printed in 1906 belonged. I have said already that it dated back to the beginning of 1899. I did not find it possible to correct the terminology of this polemical article for the reasons I already indicated in the preface to the second edition of my *Monist View of History*. There I wrote: "I have here corrected only *slips* and *misprints* which had crept into the first edition. I did not consider it right to make any changes in my *arguments*, for the simple reason that this is a *polemical* work. Making alterations in the substance of a *polemical* work is like appearing before your adversary with a new weapon while compelling him to fight with his old weapon. This is impermissible...."

You have again got yourself into a stupid mess, Mr. Bogdanov, but this time it was because you ignored the voice of your literary conscience, warning you that you were acting wrongly in cavilling at terms which I had already abandoned. The moral of this story is: the twinges of literary conscience represent "experience" which it is sometimes very unwise to ignore. You should remember that, Mr. Bogdanov.

---

* [Note from the collection *From Defence to Attack*.] In saying this, I do not mean that my critics would be right if I continued to hold to the old terminology. No, even in this case, their views would remain completely unfounded, as are all the objections made by the idealists against the materialists. Here the difference may be one of degree only, but it must be recognised that my honourable opponents have revealed an extreme degree of weakness. Nevertheless, I have no doubt that my rejection of a term I once employed was responsible for drawing these gentlemen's attention for the first time to something which they began to portray as the weakest side of "my" materialism. I am very happy to have given them an opportunity to distinguish themselves. But I regret very much that even an opponent of idealism such as Vl. Ilyin thought it necessary to have a go at my hieroglyphics in his book: *Materialism* etc.; why should he have placed himself on this occasion in the same bracket with people who had given the most undeniable and obvious proof that they had not invented gunpowder![153]

Thus, we see that "Comrade Plekhanov" does not at all refute "Comrade Beltov". But you were not content to lay only one contradiction at my door. You had a broader plan. After ascribing to "Comrade Plekhanov" contradictions with "Comrade Beltov", you go on: "But a minute later Comrade Plekhanov cruelly avenges himself for Comrade Beltov" (p. XV). What, spiteful again? Well, good luck to you! But ... rira bien, qui rira le dernier.

You quote my notes to *Ludwig Feuerbach*. It says there, among other things, that the appearance of the object depends upon the organisation of the subject. "I do not know how a snail sees," I say there, "but I am sure it does so differently from man." Then I set forth this consideration: "What is a snail *for me*? Part of the external world that is acting upon me in a way determined by my organisation. So if I assume that the snail in some way 'sees' the external world, I am forced to admit that the 'appearance' in which the external world presents itself to the snail is itself determined by the properties of this real, existing world."

To you as a Machist, this consideration seems to have no rational basis. When you quote it, you underline the word "properties" and shout:

"Properties! Why, the 'properties' of objects which include also their 'form' and their 'appearance' generally—these 'properties' are obviously 'the result of the action on us of things-in-themselves; they have no "properties" apart from this action on us'! Surely the concept 'properties' has the same *empirical* origin as the concepts 'appearance' and 'form'? It is their generic concept and comes from experience by the same way of abstraction. Whence come the 'properties' of things-in-themselves? Their properties exist only in the consciousness of those subjects on which they act."*

You know already, Mr. Bogdanov, how careless you were in proclaiming "appearance" to be a synonym of "form". Now I have the honour to bring to your notice that you have acted just as carelessly in identifying the "appearance" of the object with its "properties", and in confronting me with the ironical question: whence come the "properties" of the "things-in-themselves"? You think that this question will bowl me over, since it is to me you ascribed the idea that the "properties" of things exist only in the consciousness of those subjects upon which they act. The fact is, however, that I have never voiced this idea, which is one worthy only of subjective idealists of the calibre of Berkeley, Mach, and their followers. I said something quite different, as you yourself should know, by the way, having read, and even quoted, my notes to *Ludwig Feuerbach*.

---

* *Empiriomonism*, Book III, p. XV.

When I said that a snail sees the external world differently from the way it is seen by man, I remarked: "From this, however, it does not follow that the properties of the external world have only subjective significance. By no means! If a man and a snail move from point A to point B, the straight line will be the shortest distance between those two points for both the man and the snail; if both these organisms went along a broken line *they would have to expend a greater amount of labour for their advance.* Consequently, *the properties of space* have *also objective significance,* although they are 'seen' differently by different organisms at different stages of development."*

Now, what right did you have to ascribe to me the subjective-idealist view on the properties of things as something existing only in the consciousness of the subject? You will now tell us, perhaps, that space is not matter. Let us assume that this is true, and speak about matter

Since in discussing philosophy with you it is necessary to speak in a popular way, I shall take an example: if, to use Hegel's words quoted above, the thing-in-itself has colour only when it is being looked at, and smell only when it is being smelled and so on, it is as clear as daylight that by ceasing to look at it or smell it, we do not deprive it of the capacity to evoke in us again the sensation of colour when we look at it again, or the sensation of smell when we again carry it to our nose, and so forth. This capacity is the property of the thing as a thing-in-itself, that is to say, a property *independent* of the subject. Is that clear?

Whenever you feel inclined to translate that into philosophical language, turn to Hegel—he is also an idealist, but not a subjective one, and *in this case* that's the whole point. This old man of genius will explain to you that in philosophy the word "properties" also has two meanings: the properties of the given thing are manifested, first of all, *in its relation to others.* But the concept of properties is not exhausted by this. Why is it that one thing discloses itself in one way in its relation to others, while another thing will disclose itself differently? Obviously, because this other thing-*in-itself* is not the same as the first one.**

And that's how it really is. Although the thing-in-itself has colour only when it is being looked at, then, taking this condition

---

* *Ludwig Feuerbach,* Notes, pp. 112-13.[154]
** "Ein Ding hat *Eigenschaften;* sie sind *erstlich* seine bestimmten Beziehungen auf *anderes....* Aber *zweitens* ist das Ding in diesem Gesetztsein *an sich....* Ein Ding hat die Eigenschaft, dies oder jenes im Andern zu bewirken und auf eine eigenthümliche Weise sich in seiner Beziehung zu äussern" (Hegel, *Wissenschaft der Logik,* Erster Band, Zweites Buch, S. 148, 149). ["A Thing has *properties.* These are, *first,* its determinate relations to *others....* But, *secondly,* in this positedness, the Thing is *in itself....* A Thing has the property of effecting this or that in another, and of disclosing itself in a peculiar manner in its relation."]

for granted, if the rose is red and the corn-flower blue, it is clear that the reason for this distinction must be sought in the distinctiveness of the properties possessed by the thing-in-itself, either the one we call a rose or the one we call a corn-flower, quite independently of the subject looking at them.

By acting upon us, the thing-in-itself arouses in us a series of sensations on the basis of which we form our conception of it. Once we have this conception, the thing-in-itself takes on a two-fold character: it exists, first, in itself, and, secondly, in our conception of it. Its properties—let us say, its structure, exist in exactly the same way: first, in itself, and, secondly, in our conception of it. That is all there is to it.

When I stated that the "appearance" of the thing was only the result of its action on us, I had in mind the properties of the thing as they are *reflected in the conception of the subject* (im Subjectiven Sinne aufgefasst, as Hegel would have said, but in the words of Marx: "as they exist translated into the language of human consciousness"). However, in stating the above, I was far from affirming that the properties of things exist only in our conception. On the contrary, that is just why you do not like my philosophy—because it unhesitatingly recognises (besides the existence of the object in the conception of the subject) the existence of the "object-in-itself" independently of the subject's consciousness, and maintains, *in this—extremely rare—case, in the words of Kant*, that it is absurd to conclude that a phenomenon exists without that which appears in it.*

"But this is dualism," we are told by people who are favourably disposed to the idealist "monism" à la Mach, Verworn,** Avenarius, and others. No, dear Sirs, we reply, there is not even a smell of dualism here. True, it might be possible justly to reproach us with dualism if we separated the subject with its conception from the object. But we do not commit this sin. I said earlier that the existence of the subject presupposes that the object has reached a certain stage of development. What does this mean? Nothing more and nothing less than that *the subject itself is one of the constituent parts of the objective world.* Feuerbach aptly remarked: I feel and think, not as a subject opposed to the object, but as a *subject-object*, as a real material being. For me the object is not only an object of conception; it is also the basis, the necessary

---

* *Critique of Pure Reason*, p. XV.
** [Note from the collection *From Defence to Attack*.] Now some of those who think like Mach, for example, J. Petzoldt, wish to dissociate themselves from Verworn, themselves admitting his idealism. Verworn is indeed an idealist, but he is the same kind of idealist as Mach, Avenarius and Petzoldt. He is only more consistent than they are; he is not scared of the idealist conclusions which frighten them and which they try to evade by the most ridiculous sophisms.

condition, of my conception. The objective world is to be found not only outside myself; it is also within me, in my own skin. Man is but a part of nature, a part of being; there is no room, therefore, for contradiction between his thinking and being."*

Elsewhere (*Wider den Dualismus von Leib und Seele, Fleisch und Geist*). he says, "To myself, I am a psychological object; to others, I am a *physiological* object."**

Finally, he reiterates: "My body, as a whole, is my 'self', my true essence. What thinks is not the abstract being, but this real being, this body." Now, if this is the case (and from the materialist point of view, it is the case precisely), it is not difficult to understand that subjective "experiences" are really nothing else but the self-consciousness of the object, its consciousness of itself, as well as of that great whole ("the external world") to which it itself belongs. The organism which is endowed with thought exists not only "*in itself*", and not only "*for others*" (in the consciousness of other organisms), but also "*for itself*". You, Mr. Bogdanov, exist not only as a given mass of matter, and not only in the mind of the Blessed Anatoly, who regards you as a profound thinker, you exist also in your own mind conceiving that mass of matter of which you are composed as nobody else but Mr. Bogdanov.*** So our sham dualism turns out to be an unmistakable monism. And that's not all. It is the only true, that is to say, the only possible monism. For *how* is the antinomy of subject and object resolved in idealism? Idealism proclaims that the object is only the subject's "experience", or, in other words, that the object does not exist in itself. However, as Feuerbach said, this is not *solving* the problem; it is simply *evading its solution*.****

All this is as simple as ABC. Nevertheless, not only does it remain "*unknown*" to you, Mr. Bogdanov, it is also "*unknowable*" for you. You were spoiled in your early youth by your philosophical wet-nurse Mach, and ever since then you have been quite incapable of comprehending even the most simple and most clear truths of contemporary materialism. So when you encounter one or other of these simple and clear truths, say, in my writings, it immediately acquires a misshapen "appearance" in your mind, causing you under the influence of this "experience" to cackle like

---

*   *Werke*, X, S. 193.
**   *Werke*, II, S. 348-49.
*** [Note from the collection *From Defence to Attack*.] According to Spinoza, the thing (res) is the body (corpus) and at the same time the idea of the body (idea corporis). But since he who is conscious of himself, also is conscious of his own consciousness, the thing is a body (corpus), the idea of a body (idea corporis) and finally the idea of the idea of the body (idea ideae corporis). It can be seen from this how close Feuerbach's materialism is to Spinoza's teaching.
**** Cf. *Fundamental Problems of Marxism*, p. 9 et seq.[155]

the goose that saved the Capitol and to start raising against me objections that spread the most tiresome confusion of ideas and the most pernicious tedium for miles around.

In Shakespeare's *Merchant of Venice*, Bassanio says of Gratiano: "His reasons are as two grains of wheat hid in two bushels of chaff: you shall seek all day ere you find them; and when you have them, they are not worth the search."

The truth must be told, Mr. Bogdanov: you bear no resemblance to Gratiano: *your* "chaff" does not conceal even one grain of wheat. Moreover, it has been rotting on the philosophical thresh-ing-floor for more than a hundred and fifty years and mouse-eaten long since into the bargain. Yet you shamelessly pass it off as though it had come from the very last harvest of "natural science". Is it pleasant to poke among the leavings of mice? And you were puzzled as to why I was not in a hurry to engage in polemics with you....

But I was forgetting that you are not only an *unsuccessful* "crit-ic"... of Marx and Engels, but also one *lacking in courage*. While "criticising" their philosophical views, you now try to convince your readers that your disagreement is, strictly speaking, only with me, presenting me on that score as a pupil of Baron Hol-bach's. Your present, shall we say, lack of frankness, forces me to remind you once more of the good old times—and, perhaps, not so old—of 1905, when you were still artless enough to acknowledge me as one who shared Engels' philosophical views. You yourself know, dear Sir, that you were then much nearer the truth. And just in case any naive reader does not know of this, I shall make fairly long extracts from Engels' *Über historischen Materialismus*, which I already quoted in my first letter. In the first section of the article Engels, among other things, defends materialism against the agnostics. We shall concentrate on this defence.

Leaving aside, as being irrelevant here, Engels' critical remark concerning the views of the agnostics on the existence of God, I shall quote almost fully what he says on the question of the "thing-in-itself" and the possibility of it being known by us.

According to Engels, the agnostic admits that all our knowl-edge is based upon the information (Mitteilungen) which we receive through our senses. But, admitting this, the agnostic asks: How do we know that our senses give us correct representations of the things-in-themselves which we perceive through them? Engels replies to this by citing the words of Faust: *Im Anfang war die That* (In the beginning was the deed). Then he continues: "From the moment we turn to our own use these objects, accord-ing to the qualities we perceive" (Wahrnehmen) "in them, we put to an infallible test the correctness or otherwise of our sense-perceptions. If these perceptions have been wrong, then our estimate of the use to which an object can be turned must also be wrong, and our attempt must fail. But if we succeed in accomplishing our aim, if we find that the object does agree with our idea of it, and does answer the purpose we intended it for, then that is positive proof that our perceptions of it and of its qualities, *so far*, agree with reality outside ourselves" (mit der ausser uns bestehenden Wirklichkeit).[156]

Errors in our judgements concerning the properties of the things perceived are caused, in Engels' opinion, by the fact that the perceptions upon which we acted were either superficial or incomplete, or combined with the results of other perceptions in a way not warranted by reality (durch die Sachlage). Engels continues: "So long as we take care to train and to use our senses properly, and to keep our action within the limits prescribed by perceptions properly made and properly used, so long we shall find that the result of our action proves the conformity of our perceptions "(übereinstimmen)" with the objective nature of the things perceived. Not in one single instance, so far, have we been led to the conclusion that our sense-perceptions, scientifically controlled, induce in our minds ideas respecting the outer world that are, by their very nature, at variance with reality, or that there is an inherent incompatibility "(Unvertraglichkeit)" between the outer world and our sense-perceptions of it."[157]

However, the "neo-Kantian agnostic" does not give up. He replies that while we may correctly perceive the properties of a thing, we cannot by any sensuous perception or mental process grasp the thing-in-itself, which is thus beyond our knowledge. But this argument, as alike as two peas to what Mach thinks of the thing-in-itself, does not disturb Engels. He says that Hegel long since replied to this: "If you know all the qualities of a thing, you know the thing itself; nothing remains but the fact that the said thing exists without us; and when your senses have taught you that fact, you have grasped the last remnant of the thing-in-itself, Kant's celebrated unknowable *Ding an sich*." To this Engels added that in Kant's time our knowledge of material things was so fragmentary that, behind each of them, a mysterious thing-in-itself might well be suspected. "But one after another these [...] things have been grasped, analysed, and, what is more, *reproduced* by the giant progress of science; and what we can produce we certainly cannot consider as unknowable."[158]

I have the honour to inform you, Mr. Bogdanov,—if you have really not noticed it—that here Engels, in a few words, sets forth the principles of the same theory of knowledge which I have been defending till now and shall go on defending. I declare in advance my readiness to renounce all my views on the theory of knowledge which would prove to be in contradiction with these principles—

so firmly convinced am I of their unshakeable truth. If you think that some details of second- or third-rate importance in my theory of knowledge really differ from Engels' teaching, then please prove it. No matter how tiresome it is to be disputing with you, in this case, you would not have long to wait for an answer. Meanwhile, I invite you to "drop your allegories" and give all of us, both your willing and unwilling readers, an answer to the following; question: *do you share the materialist views of Engels as expressed in the above quotations?*

But remember that we want a "plain" answer to this "cursed question" without any "allegories" or "empty hypotheses".[159] And since you are very much addicted to "empty hypotheses" and unnecessary "allegories", I warn you not to seize on separate words, but to speak to the point. *Only* on this condition can we discuss the matter with any advantage to the reading public. But if this condition is fulfilled the whole controversy will be simplified to the last degree.

I have my reasons for saying this; I have a fair idea of your method of "philosophical" (hm!) thinking, and I foresee the possibility of such a diversion, for example, as the following.

Engels said that it is no longer possible to believe—as was permissible in Kant's time—that behind each thing forming part of nature around us there is concealed some kind of mysterious thing-in-itself which is beyond our knowledge. In view of this, Mr. Bogdanov, you are capable of placing the great theoretician of Marxism in the same category as Mach for having *denied* the existence of the thing-in-itself. But a sophism like this is so pitiful that it is really not worth resorting to.

It is strikingly clear from Engels' categorical admission of "the reality outside ourselves", *which may or may not correspond to our idea of it*, that according to his teaching the existence of things *is not confined* to their existence in our perception. Engels denies the *existence only of the Kantian thing-in-itself*, that is to say only one which is alleged not to be subject to the law of causality and is beyond our knowledge. Here again I am in complete agreement with Engels, as you may easily verify by scrutinising my articles against Conrad Schmidt, which were reprinted in *A Critique of Our Critics*, and which you referred to in your controversy with me.[160] Consequently, there is no need to "quibble" in this respect.

All the more so, since, in accordance with the views of Engels, quoted at the beginning of my letter, the real unity of the world existing independently of our ideas is precisely in its materiality. This is exactly the standpoint which I advanced in my disputes with the neo-Kantians, and which served as a pretext for your ill-conceived attacks upon my definition of matter.

Logic has its own rules, and all "empty hypotheses" are impotent before them. If you, Mr. Bogdanov, really wish to be a Marxist, you will have above all to revolt against your mentor, Mach, and "bow" to what he is trying to "burn" after the example set by the bishop of blessed memory, Berkeley of Cloyne. You will have to confess that "bodies" are not just the logical symbols of complexes of sensations, but that they are the basis of these sensations and exist independently of them. There is no other way out. One cannot be a Marxist yet reject the philosophical basis of Marxism.

He who, like Mach, considers that bodies are simple logical symbols for complexes of sensations must share the fate that inevitably befalls all subjective idealists: he will arrive at solipsism, or, in an endeavour to avoid this, will get entangled in insoluble contradictions. That is what happened to Mach. Don't you believe that, Mr. Bogdanov? I shall prove it to you all the more willingly, since in revealing your teacher's weaknesses, I shall at the same time be revealing *your own* "philosophical" weaknesses; no copy is ever better than the original. And after all it is more pleasant to deal with the original than with the copy, and particularly such a dim one as your "empiriomonist" exercises.

II

So, I part with you, dear Sir, and go on to Mach. Well, that's a load off my shoulders; and I'm sure the reader will also breathe a sigh of relief.

Mach wishes to combat metaphysics. The very first chapter of his book, *Analysis of Sensations*, is devoted to "preliminary remarks against metaphysics". However, it is just these preliminary remarks which show that the survivals of idealist metaphysics are too tenacious in him.

He himself describes what exactly impelled him to philosophic reflections, and the character they took. He writes:

"When I was very young (I was fifteen years old at the time) I once found in my father's library Kant's work: *The Prolegomena to Every Future Metaphysic*, and I have always looked upon this incident as a happy one for me. This work made a great and lasting impression on me, the equal of which I did not again experience in the reading of philosophical works. Two or three years later, I suddenly realised what a superfluous role was played by the 'thing-in-itself'. One fine summer day, when I was strolling in the open air, the whole world all at once seemed to me to be *one* complex of interconnected sensations, and my 'ego' a part of this complex, a part in which these sensations were only more strongly connected. Although I did not reflect upon this properly until later, this moment had decisive importance for the whole of my world-outlook."*

We can see from this that Mach's thought followed the same direction as Fichte's, who at one time also took Kant's transcendental idealism as his starting point and soon came also to the same conclusion that the thing-in-itself played a quite "superfluous" role. However, Fichte had a good knowledge of philosophy, whereas Mach says of himself that he could devote time to philosophy only on his Sunday walks (doch nur als Sonntagsjäger durchstreifen).** Therefore, Fichte's philosophical views shaped into a fairly orderly system, though suffering from internal contradictions, while Mach's "anti-metaphysical" Sunday walks "in the open air" had quite sad consequences.

Judge for yourself. The whole world round Mach "all at once" seemed to him to be one complex of sensations, and his "ego" part of this complex. But if the "ego" is only part of the world, it is clear that only an insignificant part of the worldly complex of sensations falls to the share of the "ego", while the remaining and incomparably greater part exists "outside of the ego", and is the external world in relation to him, the "non-ego". What is the outcome of this? It is a case of "ego" and "non-ego", or subject and object, or that selfsame antinomy which, as Engels justifiably remarked, is the fundamental question of all modern philosophy, and which Mach, imbued with a sovereign contempt for "metaphysics", wished to transcend. Indeed, not at all a bad result of his Sunday walks. However, this was not the only result, as we shall see presently, of Mach's meditations "in the open air". There were other no less remarkable results.

Once the antinomy of the subject and the object (the "ego" and the external world) is given, it must be resolved somehow; and for this it is certainly necessary to explain what exactly are the relationships between the two elements composing the antinomy. Mach declares that the whole world is *one* complex of interconnected sensations. Obviously, he believes this is the answer being sought to the question of the relationships between the "ego" and the external world and the external world and the "ego". But I ask, in the words of Heine:

Is that the answer, really?

Let us assume that the sensations of which the "ego" consists are indeed "connected" with the sensations that constitute the external world.

But in this assumption there is not even a hint of the *character* of this connection. Mach, for instance, does not approve of solip-

---

* Ernst Mach, *Analysis of Sensations*, p. 34, Note.
** *Erkenntnis und Irrthum*, Leipzig, 1905, Vorwort, S. VI-VII.

sism. He says: "es gibt keinen isolierten Forscher" (there is no such thing as an isolated investigator),* and, of course, he is right. But it will suffice us to assume that there are only *two* investigators to find ourselves besieged on all sides by those very metaphysical questions that Mach was anxious to abolish by means of the now famous coup d'état "in the open air". We shall call our two "investigators": A and B. Both A and B are connected with that great complex of sensations which—we are assured by Mach, although he does not prove his assurance in any way at all—constitutes the universe, the "whole world". It may well be asked: can A and B know of each other's existence? At first glance, the question appears to be almost superfluous; of course, they can know of each other, because if they could not then each would be in relation to the other an inaccessible and unknowable thing-in-itself and such a thing was pronounced non-existing on that Sunday when the whole world appeared to Mach as one integral complex of sensations. But the matter is more complicated precisely by the circumstance that "investigator" A can become known to "investigator" B, and contrariwise. If A has learned of B's existence, it means he must have had a definite notion of him. And since this is the case, then B exists not only *in himself*, as a part of the great world complex of sensations, but also in the mind of A, who is also no more than a part of this complex. In other words, investigator B is in relation to investigator A an *object*, external to A, and producing a certain impression on him. Thus, we are confronted not only with the antinomy of the subject and object, but also with some idea of how it is resolved: the object exists outside the subject but this does not hinder the object from arousing certain sensations in the subject. The thing-in-itself, which we thought we had written off once and for all as a result of Mach's Sunday discovery, has turned up again. True, Mach waged war on the unknowable thing-in-itself, but now we have to deal with a thing which is fully accessible to our consciousness: "investigator" B can be "investigated" by "investigator" A, and B on his part can do the same good turn to A. And this shows that we have made a step forward. But it is a step forward only in relation to Kant's transcendental idealism, and not at all in respect to materialism, which *denies* that the thing-in-itself is unknowable, as you and I, Mr. Bogdanov, are perfectly well aware after all that has been said above. What then distinguishes Mach's "philosophy" from materialism? Let me explain.

The materialist will say that each of our two investigators is none other than a "subject-object", a real material being, a body, possessing the capacity to sense and think. Whereas the rebel

---

* *Erkenntnis und Irrthum.* S. 9.

against metaphysics, Mach, will raise the objection that since bodies are but the "logical symbols for complexes of elements (complexes of sensations)", we have no logical right to admit that our investigators are material beings, we are obliged to regard them as parts of the world complex of sensations. Meantime we shall neither dispute nor contradict this. For the moment, we shall agree that our "investigators" represent, so to speak, small complexes of sensations. But our tractability does not remove the obstacles in our way; we are still in a state of complete ignorance regarding the way A gets to know of the existence and the properties of B. If we had assumed from the standpoint of materialism that B, by his organism and his acts, arouses definite sensations in A, which then become the basis of definite conceptions, the result would be sheer nonsense: one complex of sensations arousing certain sensations in another complex of sensations? This would have been even worse than the famous "philosophy" which explains that the earth rests on whales, the whales swim on water, and the water is on the earth. Why, even Mach himself, as we shall see later, protests against such assumptions.

However, let's not stray from our interesting subject.

The assumption that B becomes known to A by arousing certain sensations in the latter, has led us into absurdity. And we are led into the same absurdity, as we saw earlier, by the assumption that B is beyond the reach of A's knowledge. What are we to do now? Where are we to find the answer to our importunate question? Someone may advise us to recall Leibnitz and appeal to his "pre-established harmony". Since we happen to be very amenable at the moment, we might, perhaps, have accepted such advice, but the implacable Mach has deprived us of this last way out: he pronounces pre-established harmony to be a monstrous theory (monstruose Theorie).*

All right, we agree to reject it; what good is a monstrous theory to us! But, unfortunately, on page 38 of the Russian translation of *Analyse der Empfindungen*, we come across the following:

"Independent scientific research is easily rendered unintelligible where a view suitable for a special, strictly limited aim is made beforehand the basis of *all* investigations. This happens, for instance, when we regard all experiences as "actions" of the external world reaching our consciousness. This brings us up against a whole series of metaphysical difficulties that appear to be absolutely insoluble. But these evaporate directly we look at the problem in a mathematical sense, so to speak, i.e., when we realise that what is valuable for us is only the establishment of *functional relationships*, the elucidation of the *dependence existing*

---

* *Erkenntnis und Irrthum.* S. 7.

between our experiences. Then it becomes first of all clear that the establishment of a connection between them and some kind of unknown and unspecified primordial variables (things-in-themselves) is a matter that is purely fictitious and without purpose."

Mach categorically declares that it is absurd to consider our experiences as the result of the action of the external world reaching our consciousness. We take his word for it and say to ourselves: if at a given moment we have the "experience" of hearing another person's voice, we should be very much in error if we thought to explain this "experience" by the action upon us of the external world, or, strictly speaking, that part of it consisting of the person speaking. Every assumption of such action, Mach assures us, is obsolete metaphysics. It remains, therefore, for us to suppose that we hear the other person's voice, not because he is speaking (and acting upon us through air vibrations), but because we have an "experience" of him thanks to which he seems to us to be speaking. And if he hears our reply, this also is not to be explained by the fact that the air vibrations caused by us are exciting in him certain auricular sensations, but by his "experience", the purport of which is that it seems to him we are replying. This, indeed, could not be more lucid, and here there are really no "metaphysical difficulties". But isn't this—by your leave!—again that same theory of "pre-established harmony" that Mach described as monstrous?*

Mach proves to us that the only valuable thing for us is to establish functional relationships, that is to say, to elucidate the dependence of *our* experiences on one another. Again we accept his word for it, and again say to ourselves: since the whole matter is one of establishing the functional dependency of *our* experiences upon one another, we have no right to recognise that the existence of other people is independent of these experiences. Such recognition would give rise to a whole tangle of "metaphysical difficulties". But still this is not all. The same consideration leads us to believe that we cannot, without sinning against logic, acknowledge the existence of those "elements" which do not belong to our "ego", and comprise the "*non-ego*", the external world. In general, nothing exists *except our experiences*. Everything else is invention, "metaphysics". Long live solipsism!**

---

* Mach says in another part of *Analysis of Sensations* (p. 265, Russ. ed.): The various sense-perceptions of *one* person, as well as the sense-perceptions of *various* people, are dependent *on each other* in conformity to law. This is what matter consists of." Perhaps. However, the whole question here is: is there, from Mach's point of view, another dependence besides that which corresponds to established harmony?

** Hans Cornelius, whom Mach regards as a person holding the same views as himself, admits outright that he knows of no scientific way out of

If Mach believes he can get over this undoubted "difficulty" by distinguishing between "*ego*" in its narrowest sense* and "*ego*" in a wider sense,** he is terribly mistaken. His extended "*ego*" does, in fact, include, as he himself indicates with a reassuring mien, the external world, in the composition of which there are also, by the way, other "*egos*". But this distinction was made already by Fichte, with whom "*ego*" is contrasted to "*non-ego*" (and this "*non-ego*" embraces other individuals).*** However, this did not prevent Fichte from remaining a subjective idealist — and for a very simple reason: with him, as with Berkeley and Mach, "*non-ego*" existed *only in the conception of the* "*ego*". Since the way out of the boundaries of "*ego*" was closed ⟨very firmly⟩ to Fichte by his denial of the existence of the thing-in-itself, all theoretical possibility of his escaping solipsism vanished. But neither is solipsism a way out; Fichte, therefore, sought safety in the absolute "*ego*". "It is clear that my absolute '*ego*'," he wrote to Jacoby, "is not the individual ... but the individual must be deduced from the absolute '*ego*'. My *Doctrine of Science* will do this in the doctrine of natural right." Unfortunately, the *Doctrine of Science* did not do this. Fichte never succeeded in coping theoretically with solipsism. Neither does Mach. But Fichte, being a great master in the treatment of philosophical conceptions, was, at least, aware of the weaknesses in his own philosophy. Mach, who is ⟨probably⟩ a good physicist, is ⟨undoubtedly⟩ a bad thinker, and is completely unaware that his "philosophy" is overflowing with the most unacceptable and glaring contradictions. He strolls in and out of these contradictions with an ⟨imperturbable⟩ calmness of spirit that is truly worthy of a better cause.

Here, look at this, Mr. Bogdanov! A question occurs to Mach: does inorganic matter also experience sensations? He has this to say regarding it:

"The question is natural enough, if we proceed from the current widespread physical notions according to which matter is the *immediate* and indisputably given *reality*, out of which everything, inorganic and organic, is constructed. Then, indeed, sensation must suddenly arise somewhere in this structure consisting of matter, or else must have previously been present in the foundation. From *our* standpoint, the question is fundamentally a false one. For us, matter is not what is primarily given. Rather, what is

---

solipsism. (See his *Einleitung in die Philosophie*, Leipzig, 1903, S. 323, especially the Note.)

  * See *Erkenntnis und Irrthum*, S. 6.
  ** Ibid., S. 29.
  *** [Note to the collection *From Defence to Attack*.] This much must be added: of course, *Fichte was not the only one* to make this distinction. It *foisted itself*, so to speak, *not only on all idealists, but even on solipsists.*

primarily given are the *elements*, which in a certain definite relation are designated as sensations."*

To give Mach his due, he is quite logical here. He is no less logical, too, on the following page, where, after repeating that matter is nothing else than a definite kind of connection between elements, he rightly deduces: "Consequently, the question of sensation in matter should be formulated in this way: does a definite kind of connection of elements experience sensations (elements which in a certain relationship are the selfsame sensations)? No one will put this question in such a form."**

That is so. But the following passage, which immediately precedes Mach's logical (*from Mach's point of view*) argument on matter just quoted, is completely illogical. "If, while I experience some sensation, I or someone else could observe my brain with all possible physical and chemical appliances, it would be possible to ascertain with what processes of the organism particular sensations are connected. Then, at least by analogy, we might come nearer to a solution of the oft-raised question: how far does sensation extend in the organic world, do the lower animals have sensations, do plants have sensations?"

Far be it from me to raise the question once again here: where the "someone else" to observe "my" brain would come from. We already know that in Mach's "philosophy" there is positively nowhere he could come from. But we are already accustomed to *this* lack of logic in our "philosopher"; it no longer interests us. We have something more important in mind. Mach told us that "the question of sensation in matter should be formulated in this way: does a definite kind of connection of elements experience sensations (elements which in a certain relationship are the selfsame sensations)?" And we agreed with him that it was absurd to put the question in this form. Now if this is true, it is no less absurd to pose the question as to whether the lower animals have sensations and the plants have sensations. Mach, however, has not lost hope of "coming nearer" to a solution of this question, which, from his standpoint, is absurd. How to approach a solution? "At least by analogy." By analogy with what? With what goes on in my brain when I experience certain sensations. And what is my brain? Part of my body. And what is body? Matter. And what is matter? "Nothing else than a definite kind of connection of elements." Therefore, we have to deduce as Mach did: consequently, the question of what goes on in my brain when I experience a certain sensation should be formulated thus—what goes on in a definite kind of connection of a definite kind of "elements" composing the

* *Analysis of Sensations*, p. 197.
** Ibid.

"*ego*", "which in a certain relationship are the selfsame sensations", when the "*ego*" experiences sensations? This question is as impossible logically (from Mach's point of view) as the question regarding sensations in inorganic matter. Yet, we run into this question in one form or another on almost every page of *Analyse der Empfindungen*. Why is this?

Here is the reason. As a naturalist, Mach is constantly compelled to adopt the *materialist standpoint*, though he is quite unaware of it. And every time he does this, he comes into logical conflict with the *idealist basis* of his own "philosophy". Here is an example. Mach says: "Together with a vast number of physiologists and contemporary psychologists, I ... am convinced that the phenomena of will must become comprehensible exclusively—to put it briefly, and in generally understood terms—from organic-physical forces."* This sentence, "to put it briefly, and in generally understood terms", makes sense only when it comes from the pen of a materialist.**

Another example. "The adaptation to chemical and living conditions," we read on page 91 of the same book, "expressed in *colour*, demands a great deal more *movement* than adaptation to the chemical living conditions manifested in taste and smell."

This is a very apt way of putting it, but it is still a completely materialist idea.***

---

* *Analysis of Sensations*, pp. 141-42.

** [Note from the collection *From Defence to Attack*.] I say "only from the pen of a materialist", since this phrase of Mach's assumes that consciousness, that is to say, by the way, also "the phenomena of will", is defined by "being" (the material structure of those organisms in which the phenomena referred to are observed). It is nonsense, therefore, to say that this being is only being in the perception, or in the sensation of beings revealing the "phenomena of will"; being is certainly also "being-in-itself". With Mach it appears, on the one hand, that matter is but one of the conditions ("experiences") of consciousness and, on the other hand, that matter, that is to say, the material structure of the organism, determines those of his "experiences" which our thinker calls phenomena of will.

*** [Note from the collection *From Defence to Attack*.] Certain "chemical and living conditions" exist. The adaptation of the organism to them is "manifested", by the way, in "taste and smell", or, in the character of the sensations peculiar to this organism. It may well be asked: can one now assert, without lapsing into the most glaring contradiction, that the above-mentioned "chemical and living conditions" are only a complex of sensations peculiar to that organism? Apparently, no. But, according to Mach, this not only may, but must, be said. Mach holds stolidly to the "philosophical" proposition that the earth rests on whales, and the whales swim on water, and the water is on the earth. It is to this conviction that he is obliged for the great discovery which so delighted my young friend, Friedrich Adler (see his pamphlet: *Die Entdeckung der Weltelemente*, Sonderabdruck aus N₀. 5 der Zeitschrift *Der Kampf*, Wien, 1908). Incidentally, I have not lost hope that one day my young friend will ponder somewhat more deeply the basic questions of philosophy, and will himself smile at his present naive infatuation with Mach.

16*

Third example. Mach writes: "If some kind of process is going on in both inorganic and organic bodies, a process fully determined by the circumstances of the given moment, and limited to itself so that no further effects arise from it, we can scarcely speak of an aim; such a case, for example, as when irritation causes a sensation of light, or a muscular contraction."* It is impossible not to agree with this. But the case analysed by Mach presupposes such irritation (of an organ of the given subject) the *effect* of which is sensation. This is a purely materialist view on the origin of sensations, and as such it simply does not tally with Mach's teaching that the body is but the *symbol* (of some aggregate of sensations).

The naturalist in Mach tends towards materialism. It could not be otherwise; there cannot be a *non*-materialist natural science. But the "philosopher" in Mach tends towards idealism. This is also perfectly understandable. The public opinion of the contemporary (conservative) bourgeoisie, at grips with the contemporary (revolutionary) proletariat, is too hostile to materialism for it to be anything but exceedingly rare that a naturalist should declare himself outright, as Haeckel did, on the side of materialist monism. Mach has two souls in his breast. Hence his inconsistency.**

For all that, I must again give him his due. He is *not only* ill-informed on the question: idealism *or* materialism? It is not only that he does not understand materialism. He does not understand idealism either.

You do not believe this, Mr. Bogdanov? Read on. Mach complains that it was considered possible to convert him either into an idealist—a follower of Berkeley (Berkeleyanei) or into a materialist. He considers such an accusation to be groundless. "To this charge, I plead not guilty," he says.*** On page 288 (of the Russian translation) the same "protest" is repeated. But on page

---

* [Note from the collection *From Defence to Attack*.], p. 85.
** [Note from the collection *From Defence to Attack*.] For the "penetrating reader", with whom N. G. Chernyshevsky fought at one time in his novel: *What Is To Be Done?*, I shall add the following qualification. I do not at all wish to say that Mach and like-minded thinkers *consciously* adjust their would-be philosophical views to the "spiritual" needs of the contemporary bourgeoisie. In cases such as this, the adaptation of social (or class) consciousness to social (or class) being takes place for the most part unperceived by individuals. Besides, in the present case, the adaptation of consciousness to being was accomplished a long time before Mach began his "Sunday walks" in the domain of philosophy. Mach's guilt lay only in the fact that he did not have time to take a critical attitude to the predominant philosophical trend of his time. But this sin is committed by many, even more gifted people than he.
*** *Analysis of Sensations*, p. 49 of the Russian translation. In the fourth German edition the passage concerned is on p. 39.

292, Mach, defining his "very peculiar" relationship with Kant, writes: "Kant's critical idealism was, as I must acknowledge with the deepest gratitude, the starting point of all my critical thought. But I found it impossible to remain faithful to it. Very soon I returned to the views of *Berkeley*, which are maintained in more or less hidden form in the works of *Kant*. Through research in the field of the physiology of the sense-organs, and the study of *Herbart*, I arrived at views akin to those of *Hume*, although at that time I was not acquainted with *Hume*'s own works. And even today I cannot help regarding *Berkeley* and *Hume* as far more consistent thinkers than *Kant*." It follows, then, that there is no smoke without fire. And what a fire! One might say we have a real blaze here! In fact, *Machism is only Berkeleyism refashioned a little and repainted in the colours of "twentieth-century natural science"*. It was not by chance that Mach dedicated his work: *Erkenntnis und Irrthum* to Wilhelm Schuppe, who, say what you like, is an idealist of the purest water, a fact that can be easily verified by reading his: *Erkenntnistheoretische Logik*.

But—it is impossible to speak of Mach's philosophy without numerous "buts"—our philosopher does also hold views which, perhaps, draw him away from Berkeley. Thus he says: "It is true that some species have perished, just as there is no doubt that some species have come into being. Therefore the sphere of action of will, striving after pleasure and avoiding suffering, must extend beyond the bounds of the preservation of the genus. Will preserves the genus when it is worth preserving, and destroys it when its further existence ceases to be useful."*

What "will" is this? Whose? Where did it spring from? Berkeley would have replied, of course, that it is the will of God. And such a reply would have ended many misunderstandings in the mind of a religious person. It would also have had the advantage that it might have provided a new argument in favour of the religious views of that friend of yours, Mr. Bogdanov—the Blessed Anatoly. However, Mach does not say a word about God; therefore, we shall reject the "hypothesis of God" and turn our attention to the following words of our "thinker"—Mach. "One may accept Schopenhauer's idea of the relationship between will and power without perceiving anything metaphysical in either of them."** Now, as you see, Schopenhauer has stepped on to the stage, and the question inevitably arises: how can one perceive nothing metaphysical in Schopenhauer's idea of the relationship between will and power? Mach has no reply to this question, nor is he likely ever to have one. Be that as it may, the fact remains that when he began to

---

* Mach, *Analysis of Sensations*, p. 74.
** Ibid.. Note.

talk about the will which preserves the genus that is worth preserving and destroys it when it is not worth preserving, Mach has plunged into metaphysics of the very lowest order.

There is still more of it. On page 45 of his *Analysis of Sensations*, Mach speaks of the "nature of *green in itself*" (his italics), a nature which remains immutable, no matter from which angle we may look at it. In the German original, in the corresponding passage, we read: "das Grüne an sich"—"green-in-itself".* But how can there be "green-in-itself"? Did not the same Mach assure us that there could not possibly be any thing-"in-itself"? Just imagine, the thing-in-itself turns out to be stronger than Mach. He drives it out through the door, and it flies in again through the window, having assumed the utterly absurd appearance of "colour-in-itself". What an invincible power!

One may exclaim involuntarily (as L. Büchner did):

> *O Ding an sich,*
> *Wie lieb'ich dich,*
> *Du, aller Dinge Ding!***

How can this possibly be? What kind of philosophy is this after all? That's just the point, gentlemen, it isn't a philosophy at all. Mach himself declares this: "Es gibt vor allem keine Mach'sche Philosophie" (above all, there is no Machist philosophy), he says in the preface to *Erkenntnis und Irrthum*. The same statement occurs in *Analysis of Sensations*: "Again I repeat, there is no philosophy of Mach."***

Well, there's no denying the truth! There is really no Machist philosophy. And there is none, because Mach was quite unable to digest the philosophical concepts with which he wanted to operate. However, the position would have been little better even if he had been seriously prepared for the part of philosopher. Subjective idealism, which was his point of view, would then have led him either to solipsism, which he does not want, or to a whole series of insoluble logical contradictions and to reconciliation with "metaphysics". There is no Machist philosophy. This is very important for us, the Russian Marxists; for some years now we have had this "philosophy" of Mach thrust upon us, and have been urged and pressed to combine this non-existing philosophy with the teaching of Marx. But still more important is that this philosophy à la Mach—or more truly, à la Berkeley or Fichte—cannot be relieved of its incurable contradictions. Especially at

---

* P. 36 of the fourth edition.
** [Oh, thing-in-itself,
   How I love you:
   You, thing of all things!]
** Ibid., p. 203.

the present time: even in the eighteenth century, subjective idealism was the still-born child of philosophy. Now, in the atmosphere of contemporary natural science, there is hardly any room for it to breathe. Therefore even those who would fain revive it have to be continuously renouncing it. I repeat, logic has its own rules.

I think I may now part with you, Mr. Bogdanov. I shall make only one further remark. In your open letter to me, you complain that my associates in philosophy in Russia are spreading all kinds of cock-and-bull stories about you. You are wrong. I am not going to assure you that the people you are accusing of *deliberate*—so I understand you—distortion of your ideas have a greater sense of morality than to stoop to such conduct. I look on the question from the purely practical point of view, and ask: *why should anyone distort your ideas when to tell the truth about them can be far more damaging than any lie?*

I express my sincere sympathy with you over this—alas— undoubted possibility.

G. Plekhanov

THIRD LETTER

"Tu l'as voulu, Georges Dandin!"

Dear Sir,

A whole year has passed since I finished my second letter to you. I thought that I should never again have any dealings with you; however, I have to take up my pen once more to write you this *third* letter. This came to pass in this way.

I

You are unquestionably a pupil of Mach's. But not all pupils are alike: some are modest and some immodest. The modest ones hold dear the interests of truth and are never anxious to extol their own virtues; the immodest ones think only of how to procure the limelight for themselves, and are indifferent to the interests of truth. The history of thought shows that a pupil's modesty is almost always in direct proportion to his talent, while immodesty is in inverse proportion. Take, for example, Chernyshevsky. He was modesty personified. In expounding Feuerbach's philosophical ideas, Chernyshevsky was always willing to give full credit to Feuerbach, even for ideas that were Chernyshevsky's own. If he did not mention Feuerbach by name, this was only because of the censorship; he did everything he could to let the reader know whose philosophical principles *Sovremennik*[161] was defending. He was just as modest in other fields apart from philosophy.

In the domain of socialism, Chernyshevsky was a follower of the
brilliant West European Utopians. Consequently, with his innate
modesty, when presenting and defending his socialist opinions,
he constantly made it clear to the reader that these opinions were,
strictly speaking, not his own, but those of his "great Western
teachers". But for all that, Chernyshevsky displayed great wealth
of intellect, logic, knowledge and talent both in his philosophical
works and in his socialist articles. To repeat: a pupil's modesty
is almost always in direct proportion to his talent, while immodesty in inverse proportion. You belong to the category of immodest students. When spreading Mach's "philosophy" throughout
Russia, you reveal qualities that are exactly the reverse of those
shown by Chernyshevsky in disseminating Feuerbach's philosophy: yet you claim independence and originality of mind. You
expressed surprise because, in my second letter where I refuted
your would-be critical remarks concerning some of my philosophical conceptions, I confined myself to dealing with the insoluble
and really ludicrous contradictions in which Mach entangled
himself, and did not think it necessary to take up your own concoctions. Any one who is not utterly bereft of logic knows that
when the *foundation* of some philosophical doctrine collapses, the
superstructures that might be erected by the pupils of the thinker
who proclaimed this foundation, is bound to collapse too. And if
everybody were acquainted with your own relationship to Mach,
all would grasp at once that with the collapse of Machism, nothing
could remain of your own "philosophical" constructions but dust
and debris. But like the immodest student you are, you took
every precaution to conceal from your readers your true relationship to Mach. Consequently, there may still be people today
who will be impressed by that attitude of studied   carelessness
with which you try to prove—as, for instance, you did at one public meeting soon after my second letter to you came out—that
the objections to Mach's "philosophy" are no concern of yours.
It is for the benefit of such people as these that I again take up the
pen; I wish to free them from their delusions. When I wrote my
first two letters to you, I had comparatively little space at my
disposal, and could not deal both with original and copy. Naturally, I preferred to analyse the original. Now I am not so cramped
for space, and, besides, I have a few days of leisure. So I may deal
with you.

II

You are pleased to remark: "I learned a great deal from Mach.
ı think that Comrade Beltov could also learn much of interest
from this outstanding scientist and thinker, this great destroyer
of scientific fetishes. My advice to young comrades is not to be

disturbed by the argument that Mach is not a Marxist. Let them follow the example of Comrade Beltov, who learned so much from Hegel and Holbach, who, if I am not mistaken, were not Marxists either. However, I cannot own myself a 'Machist' in philosophy. In the general philosophical conception, there is only one thing I borrowed from Mach—the idea of the neutrality of the elements of experience in relation to the 'physical' and 'psychical', and the dependence of these characteristics solely on the *connection* of experience. In all that follows—the theory of the genesis of psychical and physical experience, the doctrine of substitution, the teaching regarding the 'interference' of complex-processes in the general world picture founded on all these premises—in all of these I have nothing in common with Mach. In short, I am much less of a 'Machist' than Comrade Beltov is a 'Holbachian', and I hope that this does not prevent either of us from being good Marxists."*

I shall not follow your example by paying compliments either to myself or to my opponent. As far as the latter is concerned, that is, you, dear Sir, I am afraid, I must again be unkind and remind you of what I said in my previous letters, namely, how utterly impossible it is for any one who rejects the *materialist* basis of the world-outlook of Marx and Engels to be a "good Marxist".** You are not only very far removed from "being a good Marxist", but you have the bad luck to attract all those who, while claiming the title of Marxist, want to adapt their outlook to suit the palate of our contemporary little bourgeois supermen. But that by the way. I quoted your words only to show what a large dose of self-conceit you have injected into the explanation of your attitude to your teacher, Mach. If you are to be believed, it would seem that you have very little in common with Mach on a whole series of propositions that are highly important from the standpoint of "empiriomonism". The trouble is that we cannot believe you in the present case. You are blinded by self-conceit. To become convinced of this, one need only take into consideration the incontestable and very simple circumstance that even where you imagine yourself to be

---

* A. Bogdanov, *Empiriomonism*, Book III, St. Petersburg, 1906, p. XII.
** Here I shall add just one small point: in the preface to the second edition of *Anti-Dühring*, Engels said: "Marx and I were pretty well the only people to rescue conscious dialectics from German idealist philosophy and apply it in the materialist conception of nature and history" (F. Engels, *Philosophy, Political Economy, Socialism*, St. Petersburg, 1907, p. 5).[162] As you see, the materialist explanation of *nature* was to Engels as equally necessary a part of a correct world-outlook as the materialist explanation of *history*. This is too often and too readily forgotten by those with an inclination to eclecticism, or, what is almost the same thing, to theoretical "revisionism".

independent of your teacher you only spoil the teaching you borrowed from him. What's more, you do this *while remaining quite true
to his spirit*, so that all your "empiriomonism" is nothing more
than making *distinctly* absurd what was absurd only *potentially*
(absurdum an sich, as Hegel would have said) in your teacher's
doctrine. What kind of independence is this? Where is there even
a hint of independence here? Enough, our most esteemed friend.
Your ridiculous pretensions collapse like a house of cards at the
least breath of criticism.

You consider me unjust? That is understandable. I repeat, you
are blinded by self-conceit. But the case is just as I have stated it.

Proofs? There is no lack of them. I take for the time being the
first on the list of your contributions to the philosophy of "empirio-criticism" which you detailed above, your "theory of the genesis of physical and psychical experience". Nothing could be more
characteristic of you than this theory, so it deserves every attention. What does this theory consist of? Of this:

In presenting the world-outlook of Mach and Avenarius as
"deeply-rooted in the acquisitions of contemporary science",*
you add: "If we call this outlook critical, evolutionary, coloured
sociologically with positivism, we shall indicate at one stroke
the main currents of philosophical thought which merge in it
into one stream."** Then you proceed:

"Resolving all that is physical and psychical into identical
elements, empirio-criticism does not permit the possibility of any
kind of dualism whatever. But here arises a new critical question:
dualism has been refuted, eliminated, but has monism been
achieved? Does the standpoint of Mach and Avenarius really
free our thinking from its dualistic nature? We have no choice
but to answer this question in the negative."***

Further on you explain why you find yourself "compelled"
to be dissatisfied with your teachers. You state that these writers
still have two connections, distinct in principle and not susceptible
of being united under any higher law. These are: connection of the
physical series on the one hand, and connection of the psychical
series on the other. Avenarius finds duality here, but not dualism.
You consider this idea of his to be wrong.

You argue: "The fact is that laws, distinct in principle and
irreducible to unity, are but little better for integral and orderly
knowledge than realities, distinct in principle and irreducible
to unity. When the domain of experience is divided into two
series, with which knowledge is forced to work quite differently,

---

* Naturally, dear Sir, I disclaim all responsibility for your original
style.

** *Empiriomonism*, Book I, Moscow, 1908, p. 18.

*** Ibid., pp. 18-19.

knowledge cannot feel itself whole and harmonious. Inevitably we are confronted with a number of questions aimed at eliminating duality, at replacing it by a higher unity. Why can there be two laws that are distinct in principle in the united stream of human experience? And why precisely two? Why is the dependent 'psychical' series to be found in close functional relationship precisely with the nervous system and not with some other 'body'; and why are there not in the field of experience countless numbers of dependent series connected with the 'bodies' of other types? Why do some complexes of elements appear in both series of experiences—both as 'bodies' and as 'notions'—while others are never bodies and belong always to one series, and so forth."*

Since the world-outlook of Mach and Avenarius, "deeply-rooted in the acquisitions of contemporary science", cannot furnish the answer to your numerous and profound "whys", you, with your characteristic self-confidence, undertake "the task of overcoming this duality".** And it is just here, in your battle with "this duality", that your philosophical genius is displayed in all its glory.

First of all, you try to elucidate wherein lies the distinction between the two series of experience, the physical and the psychical; and then you wish, "if it appears feasible, to examine the *genesis* of this distinction".*** Thus, the problem you set yourself falls into two separate problems. The first of these is solved in the following way.

According to you, a constant character of everything physical is its *objectivity*. The physical is always objective. Therefore, you try to find a definition for the objective. It is not long before you are convinced that the following definition must be accepted as the most correct:

"We term those data of experience objective which have the same vital meaning for us and for other people, those data upon which not only do we construct our activities without contradiction, but upon which, we are convinced, other people must also base themselves in order to avoid contradiction. The objective character of the physical world consists in the fact that it exists not for me personally, but for everybody, and has a definite meaning for everybody, the same, I am convinced as for me. The objectivity of the physical series is its *universal significance*. As for the 'subjective' in experience, it is that which does not have universal significance, that which has meaning only for one or several individuals."****

---

* Ibid., pp. 19-20.
** Ibid., p. 20.
*** Ibid.
**** Ibid., pp. 22-23.

Having found this definition, which reduces itself to objectivity being universal significance and universal significance the coordination of the experience of various people, you believe you have solved the first of the two secondary problems into which you had subdivided your principal problem. Now you proceed to the second. "Where," you ask, "do we get this coordination, this mutual conformity? Should it be regarded as 'pre-established harmony' or as the result of development?"* It is easy to guess in which sense you solve these questions: you stand for "development". You say:

"A general characteristic of the 'physical' domain of experience, as we have learned, is objectivity, or universal significance. To the physical world we relate exclusively that which we regard as objective.... The coordination of collective experience which is expressed in this 'objectivity' could appear only as the result of the progressive coordination of the experience of various people by means of mutual utterances. The objectivity of the physical bodies we encounter in our experience is in the last analysis established by the mutual verification and coordination of the utterances of various people. In general, the physical world is socially-coordinated, socially harmonised, in a word, *socially organised experience.*"**

This is sufficiently lucid in itself. But you are afraid of being misunderstood. You assume that someone may ask: must a person, who has bruised his leg on a stone wait for some stranger's utterance to be convinced of the objectivity of the stone? To forestall what is indeed a far from idle question, you reply:

"The objectivity of external objects is always reduced to the exchange of utterances *in the last analysis*, but is by far not always *directly* founded on it. In the process of social experience certain general relationships are created, general law-regulated relationships (abstract space and time are among these), which characterise the physical world which they embrace. These general relationships, socially formed and consolidated, are for the most part connected by the social coordination of experience, and are for the most part *objective*. Every new experience which entirely agrees with these relationships, which fits entirely in the bounds of these relationships, we identify as objective, without waiting for anybody's utterances. New experience, naturally, receives the characteristics of the old experience in the forms of which is has crystallised."***

You see, dear Sir, that in expounding your opinions, I have readily afforded you the right to speak for yourself, as the one

---

* *Empiriomonism*, p. 23.
** Ibid., pp. 32-33.
*** Ibid., p. 33.

most competent to deal with what some readers, for instance Mr. Dauge, naively regard as "A. Bogdanov's philosophy". You cannot say that by presenting your ideas in my own words I have thereby changed their content. That is a great convenience. Therefore, I again invite you to speak for yourself in order to dispel any misunderstandings that might have arisen concerning your example with the stone. You said that the stone confronts us as something objective because it is to be found amidst the spatial and temporal consistency of the physical world. But it may be objected that even ghosts haunt the spatial and temporal consistency of the physical world. Really, are ghosts "objective", too? You smile condescendingly and remark that the objectivity of phenomena comes under the control of developing social experience, and is sometimes "revoked" by it: "The hobgoblin that smothers me in the night has for me the character of objectivity, perhaps not a bit less than the stone against which I bruise myself; but the utterances of others take away this objectivity. If this higher criterion of objectivity is forgotten, systematic hallucinations could create an objective world with which healthy people could scarcely agree."*

III

Now I shall cease to trouble you for a while. You have said enough; I want to ponder your words. Now that we have, thanks to you, a "higher criterion of objectivity", I should like to examine just how "objective", that is to say, alien to subjectivism, is your own "theory" concerning it.

Speaking personally, no hobgoblin ever smothers me in the night. But it is said that this quite often happens to the stout wives of Zamoskvorechye merchants who like to have a hearty meal just before bedtime. To these worthy ladies the hobgoblin is no less objective than the stones which pave (unfortunately, not always) the streets of Zamoskvorechye. The question arises: is the hobgoblin objective? You warrant it isn't, since the utterances of other people take away objectivity from the hobgoblin. This, to be sure, is very pleasant, since everyone will agree that life would be more peaceful without hobgoblins than with them. Here, however, we come up against a small, but rather nasty, "snag". Nowadays, there are quite a few people indeed who express themselves categorically in the sense that there are no devils in general and hobgoblins in particular. Nowadays, all these "evil spirits" have been deprived of the hallmark: "universal significance". But there was an epoch—an extremely protracted one at that—when this hallmark belonged wholly and completely

---

* Ibid., p. 34.

to the "evil spirits" and when it would never have entered anybody's head to deny the "objectivity" of the hobgoblin. What
follows from this? That the hobgoblins displayed all the distinctive features of objective existence? If we argue from the standpoint of your "higher criterion of objectivity", we should answer
in the affirmative. This alone is quite sufficient for us to see how
highly absurd this "higher criterion" is, and to reject your theory
of objectivity as the most inept handiwork of a most inexpert
pedant.

Somewhat further on you give the question still another twist:
you say: "Social experience is far from being all socially organised
and always contains various contradictions, so that certain of its
parts do not agree with others. Sprites and hobgoblins may exist
in the sphere of social experience of a given people or of a given
group of people—for example, the peasantry; but they need not
therefore be included under socially organised or objective experience, for they do not harmonise with the rest of collective experience, and do not fit in with its organising forms, for example,
with the chain of causality."*

Sprites and hobgoblins do not harmonise with the rest of collective experience! Really, dear Sir, with the rest of *whose* experience,
if the *whole* of the given people believes in the existence of sprites
and hobgoblins? It is clear the sprites and hobgoblins do not in the
least contradict the collective experience of this particular
people. You will perhaps retort that in speaking of the rest of
collective experience you had in mind the social experience of
more developed peoples. If so, I beg you to tell us how matters
stood when even the most developed peoples believed in sprites
and hobgoblins. There was really such a period; you yourself
know that (primitive animism). Consequently, in the period of
primitive animism sprites and hobgoblins and all other kinds
of spirits in general had objective existence. And as long as you
hold on to your "higher criterion of objectivity", no reservation
will ever save you from this conclusion.

And the chain of causality? By what right do you cite it here?
Didn't you yourself declare some pages before this that "Hume
had every reason to deny the *absolute universal significance* of
causal connection?"** This is fully understandable when looked
at from the angle of your doctrine of experience. According to
this doctrine, causal connection is but a comparatively "late
product of socially cognitive development". Besides, in a certain
period of the evolution of this product (the period of animism)
the notion of sprites and hobgoblins was perfectly at home with

---

  * *Empiriomonism*, Book I, p. 41, Note.
 ** Ibid., p. 34, Note.

the concept of causal connection. It is clear, therefore, that *from your standpoint* causal connection cannot serve as a "higher criterion of objectivity".

No, Mr. Bogdanov, no matter how you twist and turn you will never shake off the hobgoblins and sprites, as they say, neither by the cross, nor by the pestle. Only a correct doctrine of experience can "relieve" you of them, but your "philosophy" is as far removed from such a doctrine as we are from the stars of heaven.

Guided by the clear and incontestable meaning of your theory of objectivity, we must reply to the question of the existence of the hobgoblin in this way: the time was when the hobgoblin had objective existence; subsequently this "granddad" (as our peasants used to call him only recently) lost objective being, and now exists only for the wives of Zamoskvorechye merchants and for other personages who have the silly habit of making "utterances" in the same sense as they do.

What a "development" the hobgoblin has passed through! And why "passed through"? Because people began to make "utterances" against it. It must be admitted that one hears on occasion some truly remarkable "utterances". Indeed, contemporary "utterances" against the hobgoblin completely deprive it of objective existence, whereas in the Middle Ages one could only be "delivered" from them by incantation and exorcism. By this method, a particular merchant's wife might chase away the hobgoblin, but did not do away with it altogether. Nowadays things are much better!

And there are still people who doubt the force of progress!

If there was a time when the hobgoblin had objective existence, it may be assumed also that this same objective existence extended simultaneously to witches, for example. That being so, what are we to think of those judicial proceedings by means of which mankind in the Middle Ages hoped to put an end to some unpleasant machinations of the devil, then existing "objectively"? It would appear that these proceedings, later denounced as infamous, had some "objective" basis. Isn't that true, Mr. Bogdanov?

It is clear that the entire history of human thought must take on a quite new appearance after being investigated with the aid of your "higher criterion of objectivity". That in itself is an excellent thing. It is enough to win one the title of philosophical genius. But the question is not yet exhausted, not by a long chalk. Viewing matters from the standpoint of your "higher criterion of objectivity", the entire history of the earth appears in a completely new light. In the course of the last seventy years, natural science in general has been striving to master the idea of development. But, after listening to you, Mr. Bogdanov, we are forced to confess that the idea of development that is gradually being mastered by modern natural science has nothing in common with the idea of development you have advanced, while leaning, as you say, on the same natural science. In this respect, you have unquestionably accomplished yet another revolution. You are a genius twice over!

All we profane people who clung to the old theory of development were firmly convinced that the emergence of man and, consequently, man's "utterances", were preceded by a very long period in the development of our planet.

Then you appeared and, like Molière's Sganarelle, Vous avez changé cela.* Now we are compelled to see the march of events completely in reverse.

There cannot be the slightest doubt that our planet belongs to the objective, "physical" world. Likewise, there cannot be the least shadow of doubt that the process of development of this planet is part and parcel of the same world.

But we have been informed by you, Mr. A. Bogdanov, that "in general, the physical world is socially-coordinated, socially-harmonised, in a word, *socially organised* experience".** It follows, therefore, that the existence of men preceded the existence of our planet: first came men; men began to give "utterance", while socially organising their experience; out of this happy circumstance came the physical world in general and our own planet in particular. This, of course, is also "development", but it is development in reverse: or more correctly, *development inside out*.

It might seem to the reader that if the existence of men preceded the existence of the earth, people must have been, as it were, suspended in the air for some time. But you and I know, Mr. Bogdanov, that this is simply a "misunderstanding"—the consequence of a certain inattention to the demands of logic. You see, the air too belongs to the physical world. So that at the time under discussion there was no air either. In general, there was nothing in the objective, physical sense, but there were people, who "uttered" their experiences to each other, coordinated their experience and thus created the physical world. All this is plain and above board.

I shall remark in passing that it now becomes quite clear why your like-minded friend, Mr. Lunacharsky, felt his religious vocation, and invented for us a religion "without God". Only those people believe in God who think that He created the world; but you, Mr. Bogdanov, have clearly demonstrated to all of us, and especially to your colleague, Mr. Lunacharsky, that the world was created by men and not by God.

---

* [You have changed all that.]

** See above. I remind you, dear Sir, that this profound thought was expressed by you on page 33 of the third edition of Book I of *Empiriomonism*.

Some reader will observe that the "philosophy" which claims that the physical world was created by men is the most thorough-going, though of course very confused, *idealist* philosophy. And he may add, perhaps, that only an eclectic is capable of attempting to make such a philosophy agree with the teaching of Marx and Engels. But you and I, Mr. Bogdanov, will again say that this is just a "misunderstanding". The philosophy that pronounces the physical world to be the result of socially organised experience is more able than any other to make deductions in the spirit of Marxism. Socially organised experience is really the experience gained by man in the struggle for existence. And man's struggle for existence presupposes the economic process of production; the economic process of production presumes the existence of certain relations of production, that is to say, a certain economic order of society. The concept of an economic order of society opens before us the wide field of "economic materialism". We have only to gain a foothold in this field in order to acquire the untrammelled right to call ourselves convinced Marxists. And, besides, what Marxists! The most extreme of all those who existed both before the appearance of the earth as the outcome of socially organised experience, and after that gratifying event. We are not just ordinary Marxists, we are super-Marxists. Ordinary Marxists say: "On the basis of the economic relationships and the social existence of men which they determine, corresponding ideologies arise." But we super-Marxists add: "Not only ideologies, but the physical world as well." The reader can now see that we are much better Marxists than Marx himself, better even than Mr. Shulya-tikov, and that's saying something!

Naturally, Mr. Bogdanov, you are going to shout about our exaggeration; but you will be wasting your breath. There is not the least exaggeration in my words. I have given a completely accurate account of the obvious meaning of your, it is true, quite incredible, theory of objectivity, as well as of the motive behind your theory. You imagined that by identifying the physical world with socially organised experience, you had opened before economic materialism a quite new and ever so broad theoretical perspective. Generally naive, you are probably most naive of all on the subject of economic materialism. When speaking about you, I keep to Newton's rule: hypothesis non fingo.* But here I shall make a small exception to this general rule. I confess to having a strong suspicion that you were primarily attracted to Mach through your extreme simple-mindedness. You say: "Where Mach outlines the connection between cognition and the social-labour process, the coincidence of his views with Marx's ideas

---

* [I do not invent a hypothesis.]

occasionally becomes really striking."* To substantiate this, you
cite the following from Mach: "Science arose from the needs of
practical life ... from technique." Now that is just this "technique"
combined with the word "economy"—also often used by Mach—
that has brought about your undoing, Mr. Bogdanov. You thought
that by combining Mach and Marx you would approach the theory
of cognition from a new direction altogether, and proclaim "unut-
tered words" to us. You thought you were called upon to correct
and supplement both the teaching of Marx and Engels and the
teaching of Mach and Avenarius. But this was a misunderstanding—this time without quotation marks. First of all, you reduced
Mach to absurdity; secondly, you demonstrated before the eyes
of all how grossly you erred in considering yourself a "good Marxist". In short, the results you achieved were quite different from
what you expected.**

IV

Hold on a minute, though. After I had written the foregoing
chapter, I asked whether I had indeed quite accurately presented
your idea by asserting that it follows from your theory of "objectivity" that *at first* there were men, and *later* the physical world
was created by them. I admit frankly that after turning the matter
over in my mind, I saw that things were not quite, or, perhaps,
not at all as I had written. The expressions "at first" and "later"
show how facts relate to one another *in point of time*. If there were
no such thing as time, these expressions would be meaningless.
But you have it that time itself, like space, was created by the
process of the social organisation of human experience. Here are
your own words: "*Coordinating his experiences with the experiences of
other people, man created the abstract forms of time*."*** And further:
"Thus, what do the abstract forms of space and time in the last.

---

* *Empiriomonism*, Book I, p. 8.
** You know very little about the history of the views that were prevalent in the social sciences of the nineteenth century. If you knew it, you
would not bring together Mach and Marx on the sole grounds that the Austrian
professor of physics explains the origin of science by "the needs of practical
life ... technique". This is a long way from being a new idea. Littré said as
early as the 1840s: "Toute science provient d'un art correspondant, dont elle
se détache peu à peu, le besoin suggérant les arts et plus tard la réflexion
suggérant les sciences; c'est ainsi que la physiologie, mieux dénommée biolo-
gie, est née de la médecine. Ensuite et à fur et à mesure les arts reçoivent des
sciences plus qu'ils ne leur ont d'abord donné." [Every science originates from
a corresponding art, from which it is detached little by little; the need suggests the art and then later reflection suggests the science. In this way, physiology, more exactly called biology, was born of medicine. Then, gradually,
the arts receive from science more than they initially gave to it.] (Quoted
by Alfred Espinas, *Les origines de la technologie*, Paris, 1897, p. 12.)
*** *Empiriomonism*, Book I, p. 30. Your italics.

analysis signify? They express *socially organised* experience. While exchanging countless utterances, people constantly mutually eliminate the contradictions of their social experience, harmonise it, organise it into generally significant, that is to say, objective forms. The further development of experience now proceeds on the basis of these forms and is necessarily confined within their limits."*

As you see, we are now coming to the conclusion that there was a time when there was no time. This is somehow strange. Evidently, I am using the wrong terminology, which is very difficult for those of us who are profane in regard to empiriomonism to get rid of. It is impossible to say there was a time when there was no time. It is impossible for the obvious reason that when time *did not exist* there was no *time*. This is one of those truths the discovery of which does the greatest credit to the human mind. But such truths are blinding, like lightning, and a blind person is easily lost among terms. I shall think and express myself otherwise, *abstracting myself from time*: there is no socially organised experience, neither is there time. What then is there? There are people from whose experience time *"is developing"*. Very good. But if time "is developing", it means, therefore, that it will have developed. Which brings us to the point that there *will be* a time when there will be *time*. Here again I have returned involuntarily to the old terminology. But what is to be done, Mr. Bogdanov, when I am so obviously incapable of thinking of *development outside time*?

This reminds me of the retort made by Engels to Dühring on this very doctrine of time. Dühring contended that time has a beginning and based this idea on the consideration that formerly the world was in an unchanging and self-equal state, i.e., in a condition in which there were no successive changes. And when there are no successive changes, he argued, the concept of time necessarily transforms itself into the more general notion of being. Engels was thoroughly justified in replying to this as follows: "In the first place we are here not in the least concerned with what ideas change in Herr Dühring's head. The subject at issue is not the *idea of time*, but *real* time, which Herr Dühring cannot rid himself of so cheaply. In the second place, however much the idea of time may convert itself into the more general idea of being, this does not take us one step further. For the basic forms of all being are space and time, and being out of time is just as gross an absurdity as being out of space. The Hegelian 'timelessly past being' and the neo-Schellingian 'unpreconceivable being'" (unvordenkliches Sein) "are rational ideas compared with this being out of time."**

* Ibid., p. 31.
** Engels, op. cit., p. 39.[163]

That is how matters stand from the point of view of Marx and
Engels, with whom you, dear Sir, would like to be "treated as one
of the family". Being outside time is just as gross an absurdity
as being outside space. You affixed both these absurdities to
Mach's "philosophy" and on that really not very firm basis you
imagined that, thanks to your enlightened efforts, *"empirio-criticism"* had been transformed into *"empiriomonism"*. And when
I criticised your teacher, Mach, you didn't turn a hair, as they
say. That, you implied, is no concern of mine; I am obliged to
Mach for much, but, after all, I am an independent thinker. Indeed
what a thinker you are! Indeed, what fine independence you
show! It resembles Russia before the Varangians. True, it is not
large, but it is fertile (fancy, two whopping absurdities!) and ...
there is no order in it either.[164]

But, once again, accuracy before everything! In the interests
of accuracy, I shall add that you, following Mach's example,
"strictly distinguish" geometrical, or abstract, space, from physiological space. And you adopt exactly the same attitude to the
concept of time. Let us see if this distinction saves you from the
two absurdities which threaten to immortalise your name.

In what way is physiological space related to geometrical space?

"Physiological space," you say, "is the result of development; in
the life of a child it only gradually crystallises out of the chaos
of visual and tactile elements. This development continues beyond
the first years of life: distance, size, as well as the forms of objects
are more stable in the perception of the adult than in that of the
child. I distinctly recall that, as a five-year-old boy, I conceived
the distance between the earth and the sky two or three times the
height of a two-storey house, and was very much surprised when,
from roof level, I found I was not noticeably nearer to the canopy
of heaven. That is how I became acquainted with one of the *contradictions* of physiological space. These contradictions are less
in the perception of the adult, but they are always there. Abstract
space is *free of contradictions*. In it, one and the same object, not
subjected to sufficient action, never proves to be larger or smaller
than another definite object, of this or that form, and so on. This
is space conforming strictly to law, everywhere completely uniform."*

Now what have you to say about time?

"The relationship of physiological and abstract time is, in general, the same as the relationship of the forms of space we have
examined. Physiological time as compared to abstract time lacks
uniformity. It flows unevenly, sometimes quickly, sometimes
slowly; sometimes it appears as though it had ceased to exist for

---

* *Empiriomonism*, Book I, p. 25.

consciousness, namely, during deep sleep or a fainting fit. Besides, it is restricted by the limits of personal life. Corresponding to all this, the 'temporal magnitude' of one and the same phenomenon, taken in physiological time, is also variable. One and the same process, not experiencing any external action, may flow for us 'quickly' or 'slowly' and now and then seems to be completely outside our physiological time. Not so with abstract time ('the pure form of contemplation'): it is strictly uniform and constant in its flow, and in it phenomena conform strictly to law. In both its directions (past and future) it is infinite."*

Abstract space and time, you say, are products of development. They arise from physiological space and time, by the lack of uniformity characteristic of the latter being eliminated, by continuity being introduced into them, and, finally, by their mental extension beyond the bounds of every given experience.** Very good. But physiological space and time are also products of development. Therefore we are again confronted with importunate questions: 1) does a child in whose life physiological space is only gradually crystallised from the chaos of visual and tactile elements exist in space? 2) does the child in whose life physiological time develops but gradually exist in time? Let's assume that we are entitled—although, strictly speaking, we are not—to answer these questions as follows: the child in whose life physiological space and time are formed only gradually, exists in abstract, space and abstract time. But obviously such a reply makes sense only if we assume that abstract space and time have *already appeared* as a result of development (i.e., social experience). Therefore it is still not clear how matters stood *before* they *appeared.* Common sense inevitably suggests that prior to the appearance of abstract space and time the child existed outside space and outside time. To us, the profane, or even to *your* "modern natural science", children existing outside space and time are inconceivable. We can only conjecture that in those truly sombre days before the formation of abstract space and time children were, to be more precise, not children, but angels. It is probably a great deal easier for angels to exist outside space and outside time than it would be for children. However, in saying this, I am not sure that I have not committed heresy. According to the Bible, even angles seem to exist both in space and in time.

There is still one more equally confounded question closely connected with the foregoing. If abstract time and abstract space are objective forms created by people through "countless utterances", is this process of "countless utterances" accomplished outside

---

* *Empiriomonism*, pp. 26-27.
** Ibid., p. 28.

time and outside space? If the answer is *yes*, again it does not make
sense; if the answer is *no*, it means that we have to distinguish
not two types of space and time (physiological and abstract time
and physiological and abstract space) but three.   And then all
your wonderful "philosophical" construction disperses like smoke
and you enter, albeit somewhat unsteadily, on the sinful ground
of materialism, according to which space and time are not only
forms of contemplation, but also forms of being.

No, Mr. Bogdanov, here things do not turn out well with
you at all. Of course, it is very, very touching that at the tender
age of five, when, perhaps, your physiological space had not yet
fully "crystallised" and your physiological time had not yet fully
"developed", you engaged in measuring the distance between the
earth and the sky. Such measurements belong more to astronomy
than to philosophy. It would therefore have been better for you
if you had remained an astronomer. You were not born for philosophy, if one may say so without being either complimentary or
ironical. In this "subject" you attain nothing but the most incredible discomfiture.

Here is an example. You write: "We are so accustomed to conceive all other people of the past, present, and future—and even the
animals—as 'living in the same space and time as ourselves'.
But custom is not proof. It is incontestable that *we* conceive these
people and animals in *our* space and time, but there is nothing
to show that they conceive themselves and us *in exactly the same*
space and time. Of course, in so far as their organisation in general
resembles ours, and in so far as their utterances are comprehensible
to us, we may presume that they have similar, but not identical,
'forms of contemplation' to ours."*

Earlier in this letter, I deliberately reproduced your lengthy
"utterance" concerning the distinction between physiological space
and time and abstract space and time in order to contrast them
with the passage I have just cited. Do not think that I want to
catch you out in a contradiction. There are no contradictions here,
your propensity for them notwithstanding; this passage is fully
corroborated by those "utterances". These and others make clear
even to the most short-sighted that you do not distinguish, and
indeed, while you continue to uphold your "empiriomonism", you
cannot distinguish, between the *"forms* of contemplation" and
its *objects*. You admit as incontestable that *"we"* conceive people
and animals in *"our"* time and space, but you question whether
"they" can conceive of themselves in the same time and space.
As an inveterate and incorrigible idealist, it just does not occur
to you that the question might be put quite differently, that you

---

* *Empiriomonism*, p. 32, Note.

might be asked: do those animals which do not conceive of themselves in any kind of time or any kind of space exist at all in any kind of time and space? And how is it with plants? I doubt very much whether you would attribute to them any form of contemplation, although they also exist both in time and in space. But they exist not only "*for us*", Mr. Bogdanov, because the history of the earth leaves us in no doubt at all that they existed *before us*. In developing further his objection to Dühring which I mentioned earlier, Engels wrote: "According to Herr Dühring time exists only through change; change in and through time does not exist."* You repeat Dühring's mistake. To you, time and space exist only because living beings perceive them. You refuse to admit the being of time independent of anybody's thinking—of that time in which organisms developed, raising themselves little by little to the level of "thinking". The objective, physical world to you is only a conception. And you are offended when you are called an idealist. It is indisputable that everybody has the right to be a crank, but you, Mr. Bogdanov, are obviously and constantly abusing this unquestionable right.

V

Indeed, and what exactly are these animal "utterances"? Let us leave the mammals, for instance, the donkey, who sometimes makes very loud "utterances" although not entirely pleasing to "our ears"; let us get down again to the level of the amoeba. I invite you, Mr. Bogdanov, to make a resolute "utterance" on this: can the amoeba "give utterance"? In my view, scarcely. But if it cannot "give utterance", then, taking into consideration that the physical world is the result of utterances, we again reach this absurdity: when organisms were at the stage of development corresponding to that of the amoeba, the physical world did not exist. Further. Since matter enters into the composition of the physical world, which had not yet come into being in the period concerned, it must be acknowledged that the lower animals were immaterial, on which I congratulate with all my heart both these interesting animals and you, dear Sir!

But why lower animals? Human organisms, too, belong to the physical world. And since the physical world is the *result* of development ("utterances" and so forth) we shall never and in no way avoid the conclusion that *prior to the manifestation of this result* human beings also had no organisms, that is to say, that the process of coordinating experience must, at the very least, have been started by creatures who were incorporeal. This, of course, is not bad in the sense that human beings lose any reason to envy the

---

* Engels, op. cit., p. 40.[165]

amoebas, but this can hardly be convenient for the "Marxism" professed by you, dear Sir, and those who think like you. In fact, while rejecting the materialism of Marx and Engels, you try to persuade us that you support their materialist explanation of history. But tell us, for the sake of Mach and Avenarius, can there be a materialist explanation of *such* history which is preceded by the "pre-historical life"... of incorporeal creatures?*

Later, when I come to analyse your theory of "substitution", I shall have again to touch upon the question of what the human body is, and how this body originates. Then it will become as clear as crystal that you are "supplementing" Mach in the spirit of a distorted idealism. Just now, consider this. You think fit to deduce the physical, obective world out of people's "utterances". But where did you find these people? I assert that in recognising the existence of other people, you, dear Sir, are being frightfully inconsistent, and have knocked the feet from under your "utterances" in the domain of philosophy. In other words, that you have not the slightest logical right to repudiate *solipsism*. This is not the first time I have had to reproach you with this, Mr. Bogdanov. In the preface to your Book III of *Empiriomonism*, you tried to reject this reproach, but failed. Here is what you wrote in this regard:

"Here I have to focus attention on yet another circumstance that is characteristic of the school: in the 'criticism' of experience it regards intercourse between people as a previously given moment, as a sort of 'a priori', and in striving to create the most simple and most exact picture of the world, this school also has in mind the general applicability of this picture, its practical suitability for the greatest possible number of 'fellow-men' for the longest possible length of time. It is already clear from this how mistaken Comrade Plekhanov is in accusing this school of a tendency to *solipsism*, to acknowledging only individual experience as the Universum, as the 'all' that exists for the cogniser. The recognition of the *equivalence* of 'my' experience and the experience of my 'fellow-men', in so far as their experience is accessible to me by way of their 'utterances', is characteristic of empirio-criticism.

---

* In an article that was not to your liking: "A New Variety of Revisionism" Lyubov Axelrod reminded you, Mr. Bogdanov, of Marx's jocular remark that no one had yet devised the art of catching fish in waters where there were none to be found (*Philosophical Essays*, St. Petersburg, 1906, p. 176). Unfortunately, this reminder did not cause you to change your mind. Right up to the present you go on maintaining that people, coordinating their experiences in the sphere of fishing and "making utterances" to one another regarding this useful occupation, have created both fish and water. Very fine historical materialism!

Here we have something in the nature of an 'epistemological democratism'."*

It is obvious from this that you, Mr. "Epistemological Democrat", simply did not understand the charge "Comrade Plekhanov" made against you. You regard the intercourse between people as a previously given moment, as a sort of "a priori". But the question is: have you the logical right to do this? I denied it, but instead of advancing reasons for your claim, you put forward as proof that which has yet to be proved. An error such as this is called in logic petitio principii. You must agree, dear Sir, that petitio principii cannot serve as a support for any kind of philosophical doctrine.

You continue: "It appears that out of all this school, the one whom our native philosophers suspect most of 'idealism' and 'solipsism' is the true father of the school, Ernst Mach (who, by the way, does not call himself an empirio-criticist). Let's see how he pictures the world. To him, the Universum is an infinite network of complexes consisting of elements that are identical with the elements of sensation. These complexes change, unite, disintegrate; they enter into various combinations, according to various types of connection. In this network there are what might be called 'key points' (my expression), places where the elements are connected with each other more compactly and densely (Mach's formulation). These places are called human 'egos'; there are less complicated combinations similar to them—the psyche of other living beings. Various complexes enter into the connection of these complicated combinations—and then they turn out to be 'experiences' of various beings: then this connection is broken— the complex disappears from the system of experiences of the given being; it may then enter into the system anew, may be in a changed form, and so on. But, in any case, as Mach emphasises, this or that complex does not cease to exist if it disappears from the 'consciousness' of one individual or another; it appears in other combinations, perhaps in connection with other 'key points', with other 'egos'...."**

In this "utterance", dear Sir, you again reveal with irrepressible energy a longing to lean upon petitio principii. Once more you accept as proven a basic proposition that has still to be proved. Mach "emphasises" that this or that complex does not cease to exist if it disappears from the consciousness of this or that individual. That is so. But what logical right has he to acknowledge that "these or those" individuals exist? That is the whole question. Yet in spite of all your verbosity, you give no answer at all to this

* *Empiriomonism*, Book III, St. Petersburg, 1906, pp. XVIII-XIX.
** *Empiriomonism*, p. 19.

basic question, and, as I said previously, you cannot furnish an answer to it so long as you cling to the views on experience that you have borrowed from Mach.

What does this or that person, "this or that individual" represent for me? A certain "complex of sensations". That is how your theory (i.e., of course, your teacher's theory) explains it. But if, according to this theory, this or that individual is for me but a "complex of sensations", the question arises: what logical right have I to assert that this individual exists *not only* in my perception, which is based on my "sensations", *but also outside my conception*, that is to say, that he has independent existence quite apart from my sensations and perceptions? Mach's doctrine on "experience" denies me this right. This doctrine lays it down that if I assert that other people exist outside myself, I pass beyond the boundaries of experience, I "utter" a *proposition that is above experience*. And you, my dear Sir, call a proposition that is above experience, or, to use your own exact term: met-empirical, a *metaphysical* proposition. So it turns out that you and Mach are metaphysicians of the purest water.* That is very bad. But what is even worse is that, though you are *a metaphysician of the purest water*, you are quite unaware of the fact. You swear by all the gods of Olympus that you and your tutors, Mach and Avenarius, always stay within the orbit of experience, and from there you look down on "metaphysicians" with the greatest contempt. When reading your works, and also of course, the works of your teachers, one involuntarily recalls the Krylov fable:

A Monkey in a mirror viewing form and face
Nudged with her leg a Bear who chanced near the place.[166]

Not only do you violate the most elementary requirements of logic, but you make yourself extremely ridiculous by simulating the "critical attitude" of the monkey. If the Dauges, Valentinovs, Yushkeviches, Bermans, Bazarovs, and other long-winded wise-acres whose names are known to the Lord, if all this philosophical rabble (to use Schelling's energetic expression) accept you as a more or less serious thinker (although not always agreeing with you), everyone who knows the subject, everyone who has studied philosophy not just in currently popular books, must smile ironically when reading your onslaughts on the "metaphysicians", and repeat to himself the lines from the same fable:

---

* In the article: "Self-knowledge of Philosophy", you say: "Our Universum is above all the *world of experience*. But this is not only a world of *immediate* experience,—no, it is much wider." (*Empiriomonism*, Book III, p. 155.) Really, "much wider"! So much wider that a "philosophy" supposedly based on experience relies, in fact, on a purely dogmatic doctrine of "elements" that is very closely connected with idealist metaphysics.

To count thy friends though thou dost yearn,
T'were better, gossip, on thyself thy gaze to turn!

At any rate, you renounce solipsism. You admit the existence of "fellow-men". I take note of this and say: if "these or those individuals" both exist in my perception and at the same time have separate being independent of my perception, then surely this means that they exist not only "for me", but also "in themselves". "This or that individual" thus turns out to be but a particular case of the notorious "thing-in-itself", which has created such a furore in philosophy. And what have you to say, honoured Sir, about the "thing-in-itself"?

Among other things, this: "Each particular part of the complex may be lacking in our experience at the given moment, but we nevertheless recognise the 'thing' for *the very same* as a whole complex would be for us. Does this not mean that all 'elements', all 'features' of a thing may be discarded, and it will still remain, not as a phenomenon, but as 'substance'? Of course, this is only an old error in logic. Pluck each hair off a man's head separately, the man will not be bald; pluck all the hairs together, the man will be bald. Such is also the process by which 'substance' is created, the 'substance' which Hegel called, not without reason, the 'caput mortuum' of abstraction. If all the elements of the complex are discarded, there will be no complex; nothing will remain but the *word* denoting it. The word—that is the 'thing-in-itself'."*

Thus the "thing-in-itself" is but an empty word, devoid of all content, a caput mortuum of abstraction, as you repeat after Hegel, whose name, however, you decidedly take in vain here. Well, I shall agree with you: after all, I am an easy-going "individual". The "thing-in-itself" is an empty word. But if this is the case, the individual "in himself" is also an empty word. And if an individual "in himself" is an empty word, these or those "individuals" exist only in my perception, and if so, "I" am quite alone in the world and ... inevitably arrive at solipsism in philosophy. Solus ipse! Yet you, Mr. Bogdanov, reject solipsism. How is it possible? Doesn't it again follow that in the mouthing of empty, meaningless words it is precisely you, "above all", who are guilty, and not other "individuals"? You crammed these empty words, devoid of all meaning, into a lengthy article which you entitled, as if in mockery of yourself: "The Ideal of Cognition". An extremely lofty ideal!

Speaking between ourselves, Mr. Bogdanov, you are entirely at sea in regard to philosophical matters. Therefore I shall try to explain my thoughts to you by means of a graphic example. You have probably read Hauptmann's play: *Und Pippa tanzt!*

* *Empiriomonism*, Book I. pp. 11-12, Note.

In Act II, Pippa, on regaining consciousness after a fainting spell, asks: "Wo bin ich denn?"* To which Hellriegel replies: "In Meinem Kopfe!"**

Hellriegel was right. Pippa really did exist in his head. But the question now arises: was it *only* in his head that she existed? Hellriegel, who on seeing her thought he himself was delirious, at first assumed that Pippa did indeed exist *only* in his head. Of course, Pippa cannot agree with this and protests:

"Aber sieh doch, ich bin doch von Fleisch und Blut!"***

Hellriegel gradually yields to her argument; he places his ear against her chest (like a doctor, says Hauptmann) and exclaims:

"Du bist ja lebendig! du hast ja ein Herz, Pippa!"****

Now, what happened here? To begin with, Hellriegel had a "complex of sensations" which led him to think that Pippa existed only in his perception, and then a number of new "sensations" (heart-beats, etc.) were added to this "complex" and at once turned Hellriegel into a metaphysician in the sense in which you, Mr. Bogdanov, mistakenly use this word. He admitted Pippa's existence outside the bounds of his "experience" (again in your meaning of the word, Mr. Bogdanov), that is to say, that she had separate existence quite regardless of his sensations. It is as simple as ABC. Let us proceed.

As soon as Hellriegel had recognised that Pippa had not been created by his sensations, combined in a certain way, but that his sensations had been sparked off by Pippa, he fell at once into what you, Mr. Bogdanov, not understanding what it is all about, call *dualism*. He began to think that Pippa existed not only in his perception but also in herself. Now, Mr. Bogdanov, perhaps you too have guessed that there is no dualism here at all, and that if Hellriegel had continued to deny Pippa's existence in herself he would have arrived at that same solipsism which you so strongly and so vainly strive to disavow.

That's what speaking popularly means! Having used this example from Hauptmann's play, I am beginning to think that I shall at last be understood even by many of those readers thanks to whom several editions of your "philosophical" works are dispersed over the broad face of the Russian land. What I say is extremely simple. All that is needed to understand me is a little effort.

> *O, children, learn your ABC,*
> *ABC, and learn it right,*
> *We shall all be happy,*
> *When we can read and write!*

---

* [Where am I then?]
** [In my head!]
*** [Don't you see, I am made of flesh and blood!]
**** [Yes, you are alive, you have a heart, Pippa]

VI

You say, dear Sir, that the thing-in-itself, deprived of all meaning by Kant, has become cognitively useless.* And having said
this, you imagine yourself, as usual, to be a profound thinker.
However, it is not hard to understand that the truth you expressed
here is a very cheap one. Kant taught that the thing-in-itself is
inaccessible to knowledge. If it is inaccessible to knowledge, no
one, even those who know nothing about empiriomonism, should
have the least difficulty in guessing that it is cognitively useless.
After all, isn't it one and the same thing? What then follows?
Not at all what you think, dear Sir. Not that the thing-in-itself
does not exist, but only that *Kant's teaching about it* was wrong.
But you have so badly digested the history of philosophy, and
especially of materialism, that you constantly forget that one can
accept some other teaching about the thing-in-itself than Kant's.
Meanwhile, it is clear that if "these or those individuals" exist not
only in my head, they represent things-in-themselves *in relation
to myself*. And if this is clear, it should also be obvious that we
have to take into account the mutual relationship of subject and
object. In as much as you spurn solipsism—although, as I have
already pointed out, you are always being drawn involuntarily
(i.e., unnoticed by you) to its melancholy shores by some mysterious force—in as much as you are *not* a solipsist, you too try to
resolve the question of the relationship of object and subject.
Your absolutely incongruous theory of objectivity, which I
analysed above, is just such an endeavour to solve this question.
But, in doing so you restricted the scope of the question. You excluded from the objective world all people in general, and, consequently, "these or those individuals" to whom you referred in
talking yourself out of solipsism. Again you had no logical right
whatever to do this, since the objective world for every separate
person is the whole external world, to which also belong, incidentally, all other persons, to the extent that they exist not only in
this person's mind. You forgot about this, for the very simple reason that the point of view of the doctrine you have accepted concerning experience is the point of view of solipsism.** But I again

---

* *Empiriomonism*, Book II, St. Petersburg, 1906, p. 9.
** When I say "experience", I have in mind one of two things: *either* my
personal experience *or* not only my personal experience, but also the experience of my "fellow-men". In the first instance I am a solipsist, because in
my personal experience I am always alone (solus ipse). In the second instance,
I steer clear of solipsism, because I cross the bounds of personal experience.
But by accepting the existence of "fellow-men" independent of myself,
I thereby affirm that these have *being in themselves*, separate and apart *from
my perception of them, from my personal experience*. In other words, by recognising the existence of "fellow-men", I, or better to say: you and I, Mr. Bog-

meet you halfway. I again admit you are right in maintaining that "these or those individuals" do not belong to the objective world. I only beg you to explain to me what is the relationship of "these or those individuals" one to another and how they communicate with one another? This question will not embarrass you, I hope, but on the contrary will make you happy, since it offers you the chance to reveal before all of us one of the most "original" features of your world-outlook.

You *naturally* (to use your own expression) take as the starting point of the investigation of this question the concept of man as a definite "complex of immediate experiences". But for another person man appears "above all as a *perception* amidst other perceptions, as a definite visual-tactile-acoustic complex amidst other complexes".* Here I might make the point again that if for person A person B is above all nothing more than a definite visual-tactile-acoustic complex, person A has the logical right to recognise the independent, separate existence of person B only in the case when he, person A, does not adhere to your (or rather Mach's) teaching on experience. If he adheres to it, he must, at least, have the honesty to admit that in declaring person B to have separate existence from him, "individual" A, he is "uttering" a met-empirical, i.e., a metaphysical (I am using these terms in the sense you understand them) proposition; otherwise he is rejecting the whole basis of Machism. But I shall not insist on this, since I suppose the reader now understands well enough this aspect of your inconsistency. The important point for me now is to ascertain how one "complex of immediate experiences" (person B) "appears to another" "complex of immediate experiences" (person A), as a "perception amidst other perceptions", or as a definite visual-tactile-acoustic complex amidst other complexes. In other words, I I should like to understand *how the process of the "immediate experience" of one "complex of immediate experiences" by another "complex of immediate experiences" is accomplished.* The matter appears "above all" to be obscure to the last degree. True, you try to shed some light on it by explaining that one person becomes for another a coordination of immediate experiences *thanks to the fact* that people understand each other's "utterances".** But I have to confess that I find it impossible to thank you for this "thanks to the fact", since "thanks" to it the matter is not any clearer than it was before. In view of this, I once again resort to my system of

danov, declare to be sheer nonsense that which you, Mr. Bogdanov, say *against* being-in-itself, that is to say, we overthrow the entire philosophy of "Machism", "empirio-criticism", "empiriomonism", etc., etc., etc.

* *Empiriomonism*, Book I, p. 121.

** "Finally, thanks to the fact that people mutually 'understand' one another's 'utterances' man becomes also for others a coordination of immediate experiences, a 'psychical process'," etc.—*Empiriomonism*, Book I, p. 121.

making lengthy excerpts from your articles. They may perhaps assist me in ascertaining what are your "independent" discoveries in the sphere I am now interested in.

Between complex A and complex B certain relationships are established, a *mutual influence*, as you say.* Complex A is directly or indirectly reflected in complex B; complex B is reflected, or, at least, can be reflected in complex A. At the same time, you give the quite timely explanation that although, any given complex may be directly or indirectly reflected in other analogous complexes,** "it is not reflected in them as it is, in its immediate form, but in the form of this or that series of alterations of these complexes, in the form of a new grouping of the elements entering into the complexes, complicating their 'inner' relationships".***

We shall keep these words of yours in mind; they contain an idea which is absolutely necessary for the comprehension of your theory of "substitution". At the moment, let's turn to the elucidation of another circumstance, which you, Mr. Bogdanov, consider very important.

This is as follows:

The interaction of "living beings", you say, is not accomplished directly, immediately; the experiences of one being do not lie within the orbit of another's experience. One vital process is "reflected" in another only indirectly.**** And this is accomplished through the intermediary of the environment.

This is not unlike a materialist theory. Feuerbach says in his *Vorläufigen Thesen zur Reform der Philosophie*, "Ich bin Ich—für mich, und zugleich Du—für Andere" (I am "I" for myself, and at the same time "Thou" for others).[167] But in his theory of cognition, Feuerbach remains a consistent materialist: he does not separate "*I*" (nor those "*elements*" into which "*I*" could be divided) from body. He writes: "I am a real and sensuous being, my body belongs to my being: it might be said that my body in its totality" (in seiner Totalität) "is my ego, my very being."***** Therefore, from Feuerbach's materialist standpoint, the interaction of two people is "above all" the interaction of two bodies organised in a definite way.*⁾ This interaction sometimes takes place directly, for

---

* *Empiriomonism*, Book I, p. 124.

** On the following page of the same book, you state the contrary, as I have said above, that the interaction of "living beings" (and of the complexes) does not take place directly and immediately. This is one of your innumerable contradictions that are not worth examination.

*** Ibid., p. 124.

**** Ibid., p. 125.

***** *Werke*, II, 325.

*⁾ "Nicht dem Ich, sondern dem Nicht-Ich in mir, um in der Sprache Fichtes zu reden, ist ein Objekt, d.i. anderes Ich gegeben; denn nur da, wo ich aus einem Ich in ein Du umgewandelt werde, wo ich leide, entstehet die

example, when person A *touches* person B, and sometimes through
the intermediary of the *environment*, for example, when person
A *sees* person B. It need hardly be said that for Feuerbach the environment of men could be only a *material* environment. But this
is much too simple for you: vous avez changé tout cela.* So tell
us, please, what is that environment through the intermediary of
which there occur, according to your "original" teaching, the reciprocal actions of those complexes of immediate experiences which
we profane creatures call *people*, and which you, making allow-
ances for our weakness, but not wishing to be infected by it yourself, call "*people*" (i.e., people in empirio-critical quotation marks).
    We need not wait for your reply. It is already here:
    "But what is 'environment'? This concept has meaning only in
contrast to that which has its own 'environment', or, in the present instance, to the life process. If we regard the life process as
a complex of immediate experiences, the 'environment' will be
all that does not enter into this complex. But if this is that 'environment' thanks to which some life processes are 'reflected' in
others, it must represent the totality of elements not entering into
the organised complexes of experiences—totality of unorganised
elements, a chaos of elements in the proper meaning of the term.
This is what appears to us in our perceptions and cognition as
the 'inorganic world'."**
    Thus, the reciprocal actions of the complexes of immediate ex-
periences are accomplished through the intermediary of the
inorganic world, which in turn is nothing else but a "chaos of elements in the proper meaning of the term". Good. But the inorganic
world, as everyone knows, is part of the objective, physical world.
What then is the physical world? Now we know this excellently,
owing to your revelations, Mr. Bogdanov. You have told us (and
we have not forgotten) that "in general, the physical world is socially-coordinated, socially-harmonised, in a word, *socially organised experience*".*** Not only have you said this, but you have
repeated it with the stubbornness of Cato insisting that Carthage
must be destroyed. Now before us there "naturally" arise five torturing   questions.

_____

Vorstellung einer *ausser* mir seienden Aktivität, d.i. Objektivität. Aber
nur durch den Sinn ist Ich—Nicht-Ich." (*Werke*, II, 322.) [The object, that
is to say, the other "*I*", is not given to the "*I*", but to the Non-"I" in me,
if this may be expressed in Fichte's language; indeed, it is only where I am
transformed from "I" into "Thou", where I suffer, impressions are formed
of activity *outside me*, that is to say, of objectivity. But it is only through
the faculty of sensation that "*I*" am Non-"*I*".]
    * [You have changed all that.]
    ** *Empiriomonism*, Book I, p. 125.
    *** This passage will be found on page 33 of Book I of *Empiriomonism*,
and the italics are yours, Mr. Bogdanov.

First: Under which category of "experiences" falls that fearful catastrophe as a result of which "socially-coordinated, socially-harmonised, in a word, *socially organised experience*" has been transformed into a "chaos of elements in the proper meaning of the term"?

Second: If the reciprocal actions of people (whom for the sake of variety you call living beings—of course, in empirio-critical quotation marks) are not accomplished directly and immediately, "*but only*" through the intermediary of the environment, i.e., the inorganic world which is part of the physical world; if, further, the physical world is socially organised experience and as such is a product of evolution (as we have also heard from you many times) how were the reciprocal actions of people feasible *before this product of development originated*, that is to say, prior to experience being "socially organised", that experience which is the physical world, including the *inorganic world*, that is to say, that same environment which, according to you, is necessary in order that the complexes of immediate experiences, or people, may influence one another?

Third: If the inorganic environment did not exist prior to experience being "socially organised" how could the *beginning* of the organisation of this experience have been brought about? Have we not been told that "the reciprocal actions of living beings are not accomplished directly and immediately"?

Fourth: If the reciprocal actions of people were out of the question before the formation of the inorganic environment as the *result* of the development indicated, how could any kind of world processes have come about; how could anything of any kind arise apart from the isolated complexes of immediate experiences which appeared from the Lord knows where?

Fifth: What in fact could these complexes "experience", at a time when absolutely nothing existed and when, consequently, there was nothing to "experience"?

VII

You yourself feel that here is something "not quite right" again and find it necessary "to eliminate possible misunderstandings". How do you eliminate them?

"*In our experience*," you write, "the inorganic world is not a chaos of elements, but a series of definite space-time groups; *in our cognition*, the inorganic world is even transformed into an orderly system, united by relationships in continuous conformity to law. But 'in experience' and 'in cognition' means in somebody's *experiences*; unity and order, continuity and conformity to law belong precisely to experiences as the organised complexes of ele-

ments; when regarded separately from this organised state, regarded 'an sich', the inorganic world is indeed a chaos of elements, a
complete   or   almost   complete   indeterminateness.   This is by
no means metaphysics, it is simply the expression of the fact that
the inorganic world is not life, and of that fundamental monistic
idea that the inorganic world is distinguished from living nature,
not by its material (those same 'elements' that are the elements
of experience), but by its unorganised state."*

Not only does this "utterance" not eliminate any misunderstandings; it does the exact opposite: it has produced some that were
not there before. In referring to the "fundamental monistic idea",
you revert to the distinguishing of *two* forms of being which, following the example of Mach and Avenarius, cost you so much effort
to criticise. You distinguish being "an sich" from being in our cognition, or, to put it another way, experienced by somebody, i.e.,
in "experience". But if this distinction is correct, then your theory,
in accordance with your own definitions, is met-empirical, i.e.,
metaphysical. You yourself sense this and therefore you declare,
without the least vestige of proof, "this is by no means metaphysics". No, dear Sir, in the light of your doctrine of experience—
and on this doctrine is founded the whole of "empirio-criticism",
the whole of Machism, and the whole of "empiriomonism"—as well
as in the light of your criticism of the "thing-in-itself", this is
the pure unmistakable metaphysics.   But you could not avoid
becoming a "metaphysician" here, since you got yourself entangled
in hopeless contradictions by remaining under the spell of your
doctrine of experience. What can be said of a "philosophy" which
only acquires some hope of salvation from absurdity when it repudiates its own basis?

But you also feel that, in acknowledging a distinction between
being "in experience" and being "an sich", your "philosophy" is
cutting its own throat. Therefore, you resort to what might be
described as a terminological trick. You distinguish the world
"in experience" not from the world in itself, but from the world
"an sich" and fence in this latter world with quotation marks. If
"this or that" individual points out that here you are citing being-
in-itself, which you yourself declared to be "cognitively useless",
you will reply that although you did use the old term signifying
a "cognitively useless" concept, you gave it an entirely new meaning by placing it in quotation marks. Very smart! It was no accident that in my first letter I likened you to cunning monk Gorenflot.

By divesting being-in-itself of its Russian dress and investing
it in a German costume, and putting a screen of quotation marks

* *Empiriomonism,* pp. 125-26.

round it, you wished to forestall objections from "this or that" inopportunely shrewd individual; this is revealed in the note you made somewhat later, to be exact, on page 159.* You "recall" there that you by no means used the expression "an sich" in a metaphysical sense. And you prove this in the following way:

"For certain physiological processes of other people, we substitute the 'immediate complexes'—consciousness; criticism of psychological experience compels us to extend the domain of this substitution, and we regard all physiological life as the 'reflection' of immediate, organised complexes. But the *inorganic processes* are not distinct in principle from the physiological, which are only their organised combination. Being in one continuous series with the physiological processes, the inorganic processes must also, obviously, be regarded as 'reflection'. But of what?—of immediate *unorganised* complexes. We are *as yet unable* to carry out this substitution concretely in our consciousness. What of it! We are often unable to do this in relation to animals as well (the experiences of the amoeba) and even in relation to other people ('incomprehension' of their psychology). But in place of concrete substitution, we can formulate the *relationships* of these cases ('life an sich'—immediate, organised complexes, 'environment an sich'—unorganised complexes)."

The significance of this new reservation of yours will be fully disclosed only when we come to determine the use-value of your theory of "substitution" which, as we have seen, is one of the foundations of your claim to originality in the field of philosophy. However, it may already be said that this reservation is "cognitively useless". Think it out for yourself, Mr. Bogdanov. What significance can your formulation of the *"relationships"* of the "cases" you have indicated have here? Let us assume that this formulation: "life an sich" is immediate, organised complexes, "environment an sich" is the unorganised, is quite correct. What then? After all, the question is not how "life an sich" relates to "environment an sich", but how "life an sich" and "environment an sich" relate to life and environment "in our experience", in our "cognition". Absolutely no reply can be found to this question in your new reservation. Therefore, neither that reservation nor the artful device of changing the clothes of being-in-itself from a Russian dress to a German costume will prevent shrewd "individuals" from exercising their right to declare that, if momentarily you evade the irreconcilable contradictions inherent in your "philosophy", it is only by admitting the "cognitively useless"

---

* *Empiriomonism*, article "Universum" ("Empiriomonism of the Separate and Continuous").

distinction between being-in-itself and being-in-experience.* Like your tutor Mach, out of the most elementary logical necessity, you burn that which you invite us to adore, and adore that which you invite us to burn.

VIII

Just one last word, and then I shall be able to wind up the list of your mortal sins against logic. I go on to your theory of "substitution". It is this particular theory which must explain to us, the profane, how one man "appears to another" as a definite "visual-tactile-acoustic complex amidst other complexes".

We are already aware that there is interaction between the complexes of immediate experiences (or, to put it simply, people). They influence one another, "are *reflected*" in one another. But how are they "reflected"? That is the whole question.

Here we shall have to recall that idea of yours, which I noted already, that although each given "complex" can be reflected in other analogous complexes, it is reflected in them, not in its immediate form but in the form of certain alterations of these complexes, "in the form of a new grouping of elements entering into the complexes, complicating their inner relationships". I remarked that this idea is absolutely necessary for the comprehension of your theory of "substitution". The time has now come to deal with it.

Expressing this important idea in your own words, Mr. Bogdanov, I shall say that the reflection of complex A in complex B is reduced to "a definite series of alterations of this second complex, alterations connected with the content and structure of the first complex by functional dependency".** What does "functional dependency" mean in this instance? Only this, that in the interaction between complex A and complex B, the content and structure of the first complex corresponds to a definite series of alterations of the second complex. No more and no less. This means that when I have the honour to converse with you, my "experiences" come

---

* I say you evade irreconcilable contradictions *momentarily* because you are not destined to evade them for any length of time. Actually, if the inorganic world "an sich" is a chaos of elements, whereas "*in our cognition* it is even transformed into an orderly system, united by relationships in continuous conformity to law", it is a case of one of two things: *either* you yourself do not know what you are talking about, *or* you, who imagine yourself to be an independent thinker of the latest pattern, revert in the most disgraceful way to the point of view of old Kant, who asserted that reason prescribed its laws to external nature. Truly, truly I say unto you, Mr. Bogdanov: until the end of your days you will continue to drift without rudder or sail from one contradiction to another. I am beginning to suspect that your "philosophy" is that very chaos of elements of which, you tell us, the inorganic world is composed.

** *Empiriomonism*, Book I, p. 124.

into conformity with yours. How is this conformity explained? There is nothing to explain it apart from those same words "functional dependency"—and these explain absolutely nothing. So I ask you, Mr. Bogdanov, is there really anything to distinguish this "functional" conformity from that "pre-established harmony" which you reject with such supreme contempt, following your teacher, Mach? Think again and you will see for yourself that there is absolutely no difference between them and that, therefore, you have been insulting old granny "pre-established harmony" for no reason at all. If you really wish to be frank (although I have little hope of that) you will tell us that your reference to "environment" stemmed from a vague consciousness of a (for you) embarrassing resemblance between the old theory of "pre-established harmony" and your "functional dependency". But after what I have said above, it is hardly necessary to explain that in the present difficult case environment is "cognitively useless", if only for one reason that, since in your theory it is the *result* of the interaction of complexes, it does not explain how such interaction is *possible*, apart from "pre-established harmony".

To proceed.

Having expounded the clearly "met-empirical" (i.e., "metaphysical") proposition that the inorganic world "an sich" is something totally distinct from the inorganic world "in our experience", you continue:

"If the unorganised 'environment' is the intermediate link in the interactions of vital processes, if through its intermediary the complexes of experiences are 'reflected' in one another there is nothing new and strange in the fact that through its intermediary the given vital complex is 'reflected' also in itself. Complex A, acting on complex B, can, through the intermediary of B, exert influence on complex C as well as on complex A, that is to say, on itself.... From this point of view, it is perfectly understandable that the living being can have 'external perception' of itself, can see, feel, hear itself, and so on, that is to say, among the series of its own experiences can find those that represent an indirect (through the intermediary of 'environment') reflection of this selfsame series."*

To translate all this into everyday language, it means that when a man perceives his own body, he "experiences" some of his own "experiences", which take on the form of a "visual-tactile complex" because they are being reflected through the intermediary of environment. This is utterly incomprehensible "an sich". Just try to understand how a man "experiences" his own "experiences" even if through the intermediary of "environment", which, as we

---

* *Empiriomonism*, p. 126.

know already, explains absolutely nothing.* Here, Mr. Bogdanov, you become a metaphysician in the sense attributed to the word by Voltaire, who averred that when a man says something he himself does not understand, he is dealing in metaphysics. But the idea you have expressed, incomprehensible "an sich", may be reduced to this: our body is nothing else but our psychical experience reflected in a certain way. If this is not idealism, what is?

You have supplemented Mach splendidly, Mr. Bogdanov, I am not saying this for fun. Mach as a physicist none the less occasionally wandered into materialism. I demonstrated this in my second letter to you with the help of some graphic illustrations. In this sense, Mach committed the sin of dualism. You have corrected his error. You have made his philosophy idealist from A to Z. We cannot but praise you for this.**

Please do not think I am mocking you over this, Mr. Bogdanov. Quite the contrary; I am about to pay you a compliment—perhaps even a very big compliment. The arguments of yours that I have just been quoting remind me of Schelling's teaching about the creative intellect which contemplates its own activity but is not conscious of this process of contemplation, and therefore conceives of its products as objects coming from outside. Of course, with you this teaching of Schelling has changed considerably and, indeed, has assumed the aspect, one may say, of a caricature. But it must already be some consolation for you that you are at least the caricature of a great man.

You should note, however, that in paying you this compliment, which, I confess, may seem doubtful to you, I have no wish to infer in any way that, in making your own supplement to Mach's "philosophy", you were aware that you were only changing someone else's idealist doctrine and a fairly old one at that. No, I suppose that this old doctrine, thanks to some properties of your "environment", was "reflected", quite without your knowledge, in your head as a "complex" of philosophical conclusions from the main acquisitions of "modern natural science". But idealism is still idealism, no matter whether he who preaches it is conscious of its nature or not. While developing after your own fashion, i.e.,

---

* We can "experience" our own "experiences" only by recollecting something that we have undergone previously. But you, Mr. Bogdanov, are talking about something *quite different*.

** You found that the recognition by Mach and Avenarius of the "psychical" and "physical" as two separate series was tantamount to the recognition of a certain "duality". You wished to eliminate this duality. Those numerous and profound "why's" with which you pestered Mach and Avenarius were very transparent hints that you knew the secret of how to get rid of the embarrassing duality. In fact, you said so outright. Now we know the secret: you declare the "physical" to be the other-being of the "psychical". This is, indeed, *monism*. Unfortunately it is *idealist* monism.

distorting, the idealism you have unconsciously assimilated, you "naturally" arrive at a purely idealist view of matter. And although you reject the supposition that, in your opinion, the "physical" is only the "other-being" of the "psychical",* in point of fact this assumption corresponds fully to the truth. Your view of matter, and of everything physical, is, I repeat, saturated through and through with idealism. To become convinced of this, it will suffice to read, for instance, your most profound observations relating to the domain of physiological chemistry. "In a word, it should be regarded as most probable that the organised living albumen is the physical expression ('or reflection') of immediate experiences of a *psychical* character and, of course, the more elementary they are, the more elementary is the organisation of this living albumen in each given instance."** It is obvious that the chemist and physiologist who wished to take this point of view would have had to create purely idealist "disciplines", to return to Schelling's "speculative" natural science.

Now it is not difficult to understand what exactly takes place when one person perceives the body of another person. But first of all we must revert to the inverted commas which have such an outstanding part to play in your "philosophy", Mr. Bogdanov. One person does not by any means see the body of another person—that is a materialism unworthy of "modern natural science"! He sees the "body", i.e., the body in inverted commas, although he notices the inverted commas only if he belongs to the "empiriomonistic" school. And the body in inverted commas means that "this has to be understood spiritually", as the Catechism puts it, or psychically, as you and I put it, Mr. Bogdanov. "Body" is nothing else but the peculiar reflection (reflection through the intermediary of inorganic environment) of one complex of experiences in another such complex. The psychical (in inverted commas and without them) precedes both the "physical" (and the physical) and the "physiological" (and the physiological).

There, Mr. Bogdanov, is your book-learning.

There is the meaning of all your philosophy!

---

* I have placed these three words in inverted commas because they were thus enclosed by you in the hope of foiling any attempt by the reader to understand them in a direct, that is to say, a correct sense. See *Empiriomonism*, Book II, p. 26.

** *Empiriomonism*, p. 30. Elsewhere you say: "To every living cell there corresponds, from our point of view, a certain, even though insignificant, complex of experiences" (*Empiriomonism*, Book I, p. 134). Those who would have thought that in saying this, you were alluding to the "cellular souls" of Haeckel, would have made a serious error. In your view, the conformity between the "living cell", and even an insignificant complex of experiences consists in this, that the cell is but the "reflection" of this complex, i.e., once again its other-being.

Or to express it more modestly, there is the meaning of what bears your grandiloquent title of *systematised, reformed substitution.*

"From the point of view of systematised, reformed substitution," you announce, "all nature appears as an infinite series of 'immediate complexes', the *material* of which is the same as the 'elements' of experience, while their *form* is characterised by the most varying degrees of organisation from the lowest, corresponding to the 'inorganic world', to the highest, corresponding to man's 'experience'. These complexes influence one another. Each individual 'perception of the external world' is a reflection of some one of these complexes in a definite, formed complex—the living psyche, while 'physical experience' is the result of the collectively organising process, harmoniously uniting such perceptions. 'Substitution' gives a kind of reverse reflection of reflection, more resembling the 'reflected' than the first reflection: thus the melody *reproduced* by a phonograph is the second reflection of the melody *perceived by it*, and bears a much greater resemblance to the latter than the first reflection—the indentations and dots on the cylinder of the phonograph."*

It is useless to engage in a philosophical discussion with anyone who doubts even for a moment the idealist character of *such* a philosophy, for he is quite hopeless from the point of view of philosophy.

I might describe you as the enfant terrible of Mach's school, if such a ponderous "complex of immediate experiences" could be compared to a frolicsome and mischievous child. But, in any case, you have blurted out the school's secret, saying openly what the school was too shy to speak about in public. You have put the idealist "dots" over the idealist "i's" that have stamped Mach's "philosophy". And, I repeat, you did this because Mach's (and Avenarius') "philosophy" seemed to you to be insufficiently monistic. You sensed that the monism of this "philosophy" was idealist monism. So you resolved to "supplement" it in the idealist spirit. In this case, your work-tool was the theory of objectivity constructed by you. With its help, you easily fashioned all your other philosophical—shall we say, acquisitions. You yourself admit this in the following passage, which, unfortunately for you, is distinguished by a remarkable clarity, quite unlike the other passages that have come from your ponderous pen:

"Since the history of psychical development shows that objective experience, with its connection with the nervous system, and its orderly conformity to law, is the result of prolonged development, and is crystallised only step by step from the torrent of im-

---

* *Empiriomonism*, Book II, p. 39.

mediate experiences, it remained for us only to accept that the *objective* physiological process is the 'reflection' of the complex of immediate experiences, and not the other way round. The question further remained: if it is 'reflection', then in what exactly? The reply we gave corresponds to the social-monistic conception of experience we had adopted. Recognising the universal significance of objective experience as an expression of its socially organised state, we arrived at the following empiriomonist conclusion: physiological life is the result of the collective harmonisation of 'external perceptions' of the living organism, each of which is the reflection of one complex of experiences in another complex of experiences (or in itself). In other words, *physiological life is the reflection of immediate life in the socially organised experience of living beings.**

This last phrase: "physiological life is the reflection of immediate life in the socially organised experience of living beings" vouches both for you being an idealist, and for you being an "original" idealist. Only an idealist can regard physiological processes as the "reflection" of immediate psychical experiences. And only the most muddled of idealists can assert that "reflections" pertaining to the domain of *physiological life* are the result of socially organised experience, that is to say, the product of *social life.*

But having let out the secret of "empirio-criticism", you added absolutely nothing to this "philosophical" doctrine apart from some utterly incongruous and irreconcilably contradictory fantasies. Reading these fantasies, one goes through almost the same as Chichikov had to "experience" when he took a night's lodging in Korobochka's house.[168] The feather-bed was so skilfully made up for him by Fetinia that it almost touched the ceiling. "When, by standing up on a chair, he clambered into the feather-bed, it sank under him almost to the floor, and the feathers, crowded out of their confining covering, flurried to every corner of the room." Your "empiriomonist" fantasies too rise almost to the ceiling, they are so stuffed with various learned terms and sham wisdom. But at the first touch of criticism the feathers from your "philosophical" feather-bed start flying in all directions, while the astonished reader, swiftly falling, feels himself descending into the murky depths of the most vapid metaphysics. Just because of, that, it is very easy to criticise you: but it is an extremely dull business. That is why I left you alone last year and undertook instead the criticism of your teacher. But since you claimed to have your independent importance, I was compelled to deal with your claim. I have demonstrated how inconsistent your "theory of objectivity" is, and to what extent your doctrine of "substitution" distorts

---

* *Empiriomonism*, p. 136; your italics.

the natural connection of phenomena. That is sufficient. To pursue you further would be a sheer waste of time; the reader sees what your "independent" philosophy is worth.

I shall say just one thing more in conclusion. The regrettable thing is not that such a "complex of immediate experiences" as yourself, Mr. Bogdanov, could appear in our literature, but that this "complex" could play some part in it. Your books were read, some of those on philosophy ran into several editions. One could even be reconciled to that, were your books bought, read, and approved only by obscurantists,* who do not deserve a better spiritual fare. But we cannot be reconciled to the fact that people of an advanced mode of thought read and accepted you seriously. That is a very bad sign. It shows that we are passing through a period of unprecedented intellectual decline. To accept you as a thinker capable of furnishing a philosophical justification of Marxism, one would need to have positively no knowledge either of philosophy or of Marxism. Ignorance is always a bad thing. It is dangerous to all men at all times, but it is especially so for those who wish to go forward. And for them it is doubly dangerous to be ignorant during periods of social stagnation, when they are called upon to do "battle with spiritual weapons" with increased energy. The weapons you have forged, Mr. Bogdanov, are quite unsuitable for advanced people; such weapons assure not victory but defeat. Worse than that. Fighting with such weapons, advanced people are themselves transformed into knights of reaction, opening up the way for mysticism and all varieties of superstition.

Those abroad who hold the same views as ourselves are very much mistaken in thinking, like my friend Kautsky, that there is no need to cross swords over that "philosophy" which is disseminated in Russia by you and similar theoretical revisionists. Kautsky does not know the relationships existing in Russia. He disregards the fact that the theoretical bourgeois reaction which is now causing real havoc in the ranks of our advanced intellectuals is being accomplished in our country under the banner of philosophical idealism, and that, consequently, we are threatened with exceptional harm from such philosophical doctrines, which, while being idealist to the core, pose as the last word in natural science, a science foreign to every metaphysical premise. The struggle against such doctrines is not only not superfluous, it is obligatory, just as obligatory as it is to protest against the *reactionary* "reval-

---

* William James, in trying to substantiate his religious point of view, says: "Concrete reality is composed exclusively of individual experience." ("L'expérience religieuse", Paris-Geneva, 1908, p. 417.) This is equivalent to the assertion that "complexes of immediate experiences" underlie all reality. James is not mistaken in thinking that such assertions throw the door wide open to religious superstitions.

uation of values" which the prolonged efforts of Russian *advanced* thought have produced.

I had intended to say something about your pamphlet: *The Adventures of One Philosophical School*. (St. Petersburg, 1908), but I am now pressed for time and must renounce this intention. Besides there is no great need to analyse this pamphlet. I hope that my three letters will be quite sufficient to elucidate how the philosophical views of the school to which I belong relate to your views, dear Sir, and particularly to the views of your teacher, Mach. That is all I want. There are more than enough people ready to carry on useless arguments, but I am not one of them. Therefore I had better wait until you write something against me and in defence of your teacher, or at least in defence of your own "objectivity" and your own "substitution". Then we shall have another talk!

G. Plekhanov

ON Fr. LÜTGENAU'S BOOK

Fr. Lütgenau, *Natural and Social Religion.*
The Theory of Religion from the Materialist Point of View.
St. Petersburg, 1908

It is not consciousness that determines being, but being that
determines consciousness. When applied to the development of
mankind, this means that it is not the social man's "psyche" that
determines his way of life, but his way of life that determines his
"psyche". That is very well known to us at the present time. But
this still does not mean that in each particular case we know the
process leading to the formation of the particular psyche on the
basis of the particular form of social being. Not by a long way.
Very, very many aspects of this multiform process are *only as yet
becoming subjects of scientific investigation*. The materialist explanation of history is *only a method* leading to the comprehension
of truth in the field of social phenomena, and is in no way a con-
glomerate of ready-made, final conclusions. He who wishes to
prove himself a worthy follower of this method, cannot be content
with a simple repetition that it is not consciousness that determines being but being that determines consciousness. On the
contrary, he must try to find out for himself how in fact this determination of consciousness by being comes about. And there is no
other way of doing this than by studying facts and discovering
their causal connection.

As far as the particular question of *religion* is concerned, here
too, naturally, there can also be no doubt that being is not determined by consciousness; but here too the process of the determination of consciousness by being is still obscure to us in very many
respects. Hence every serious attempt to explain this process
should be welcomed. In its time, Fr. Lütgenau's book, which
appeared in German nearly fourteen years ago, undoubtedly
deserved great attention from everyone interested in historical materialism. Yet even then it was possible to indicate many real shortcomings in the book. Today, apart from having these many shortcomings, the book is pretty well *out of date*. Had we been asked
by Mme Velichkina, whom we know to be a serious and conscientious translator, whether this work was worth translating, we should

at first have found difficulty in answering, but on reflection, we should perhaps have said no.

However, among the blind the one-eyed is king. Mr. Lütgenau's book is practically unique in the Russian language. So in spite of all, we recommend it to the Russian reader. And for the same reason we cannot but regret that Mme Velichkina has not translated the book as well as she once translated von Polenz. Her latest translation is ponderous and, in places, unsatisfactory. In addition, it is distorted by numerous regrettable misprints. This is all the more inconvenient to readers as they are less informed on the subject, i.e., the more in need of intelligible guidance.

But let us now proceed to the content of the book. A philologist by education, Mr. Lütgenau set himself the praiseworthy task of discussing the problem of the origin and development of religion from the point of view of historical materialism. Unfortunately, he was not well enough equipped to fulfil his task satisfactorily. He was not even quite clear as to what exactly is known as historical materialism. Many philistine prejudices still marred his views on the subject. He says: "Marx and Engels proved the erroneousness of idealism and founded the dialectical-materialist world-outlook, according to which we now see in economic conditions the foundation of legal and political institutions as well as moral and religious concepts" (p. 249). But how is that? Is men's *world-outlook*, that is to say, their views *on the whole system of the world*, really exhausted by their views *on the relation of "economic conditions" to legal institutions and moral and religious concepts*? In other words: is *historical* materialism a whole *world-outlook*? Of course not. It is only *one part* of a world-outlook. Of what kind of world-outlook? Well, it is clear—the *materialist* world-outlook. Engels said that he and Marx applied materialism to the interpretation of history. Exactly. But Mr. Lütgenau does not want to hear about materialism, which for some reason he calls *"cognitive-theoretical"** and concerning which he talks a whole lot of indigestible nonsense on pages 249, 250 (footnote), 252, 253 and several others. All of which shows that he has not the least notion of "cognitive-theoretical" materialism, and that in speaking of it he uses the words of those same theologians—or the words of the philosophers influenced by those theologians—whose views he himself, of course, repudiates in so far as they affect the historical field proper and touch upon the religious question. This does him very grave harm even when, as we might say, he is on his home ground—discussing religion. He thinks, for instance, that "religion begins on the borders of cognition or experience" and that "the wider the field of knowledge becomes, the narrower is

* My italics.

the field of religious belief" (p. 247). This might be acceptable
with a very big reservation. The fact is that when the field of
religious belief becomes considerably contracted under the impact
of experience, to the succour of religion comes that philosophy
which teaches that science and religion lie in completely different
planes, since religion has to do with the other world, whereas
science, experience, has to do only with phenomena, and that,
therefore, the widening of the field of experience *cannot* narrow
the field of religion. To the *extent* that the preaching of this philosophy influences men's minds, the field of religious belief ceases
to contract under the impact of experience. It is true that philosophy of this kind can arise and exert influence only in a particular
social situation, only at a certain stage in the development of
class society. But this does not alter matters. On the contrary,
an analysis of the influence of this philosophy and its relationship
to religion would have furnished Mr. Lütgenau with the opportunity to shed a much clearer light on the connection between social
development (cause) and the historical fate of religious beliefs
(effect). Mr. Lütgenau did not avail himself of this opportunity.
He *could not* do so for the simple reason that he was incapable of
adopting a critical attitude to the—supposedly critical—philosophy we are speaking about here. And he was incapable of this
because he *himself* had fallen under the influence of that philosophy. Its effect on him is to be seen in the undiluted nonsense
he has poured forth in his book concerning "cognitive-theoretical"
materialism. But, having piled up this undiluted nonsense, he
himself goes over to the materialist viewpoint in his attitude to
religion. That might of course have been to the good if the nonsense he had talked had not clouded his vision, and hindered him
from making this change-over consciously and without sinning
against logic.

If he had done so consciously, the proposition we have just
cited, viz., that experience brings about the contraction of the
field of religious beliefs, would have assumed in his writings a
much more correct form. It would have read that the accumulation
of knowledge removes the ground from under religious beliefs,
but only in the measure that the prevailing social order does not
prevent the dissemination of knowledge and its utilisation for
the criticism of views inherited from earlier times. This is exactly
what contemporary *materialism* says, and it is partly accepted
by our author as *historical* materialism, and partly rejected by
him under the name of *cognitive-theoretical* materialism.

And it is rejected by him, one might say, in blithe ignorance.
Thus, for example, in discussing Hegel, he writes: "For Hegel,
things and their development were still only the materialised
reflections of 'ideas' existing somewhere, before the world, and

not the results of his own thinking, the more or less absolute reflections of real things and processes" (p. 249). We do not know what is meant by "*absolute*" reflection, and in general we find this whole passage very clumsily written. One thing is clear: Mr. Lütgenau does not agree with Hegel, and believes that things and their development are essentially "reflections of real things and processes". But surely this is nothing else than the "cognitive-theoretical materialism" which is not to his liking. What a mess! After that, just try, if you please, to discuss materialism with Mr. Lütgenau. Why, he himself does not know what it is.

It might not have been necessary to go into all this, but for the following interesting circumstance. At one time, Mr. Lütgenau belonged to the German Social-Democratic Party. His book, written in German, was published, if my memory serves me right, in 1894, that is, not long before the so-called "*revision of Marx*", began. His statements regarding the relationship of *historical* materialism to "*cognitive-theoretical* materialism" showed that he was under the influence of the philosophical ideas which then prevailed, and still prevail, among the ideologists of the German bourgeoisie. But we have no recollection of any one of the theoreticians of the party to which Lütgenau then belonged paying even the slightest attention to his statements. Apparently, to them it was a matter of little importance, or, perhaps, something perfectly natural. But when the "revision" of Marx began, the gentlemen who took on the job (the "revisionists") based themselves, by the way, on those very philosophical ideas which infected Mr. Lütgenau, and, of course, other people too. This is evidence of how revisionism was *prepared*, how it was finding its way into the minds of members of the party at a time when Mr. Bernstein did not as yet express any doubts about the correctness of Marx's teaching. It would repay our Russian Marxists to reflect upon this; there are quite a few people among them today who are engaged in trafficking the philosophical contraband which at one time was smuggled into the minds of the German Social-Democrats by Mr. Lütgenau and other inconsistent thinkers like him.* It goes without saying that there is only one guard capable of doing anything in the struggle against this contraband:—*logic*. But *this* guard, in any case, is never redundant, and he in particular must keep wide awake.

In passing on to the examination of Mr. Lütgenau's views on the origin and development of religious beliefs, we have to recognise that even here our author has only partly coped with his truly very difficult task of providing a materialist explanation of that

---

* Someone like Mr. Yushkevich or Mr. Valentinov, who, as they say, are *no worse* than Mr. Lütgenau.

origin and development. If in philosophy, Mr. Lütgenau was ready to supplement Marx and Engels with *Kant*, now on the question of religion he is supplementing them with *Max Müller*. And, just as in the first instance, he thereby only spoils it all.

He says: "The myth originates simply from language" (p. 12). He then explains this idea of his (or that of his authority—Max Müller) by quoting the latter's words: "We know that Eos (in Greek, the dawn) corresponds to the Sanskrit Ushas, and we know that Ushas is derived from the root Uas, which means shines. So Eos meant originally 'shining-it', or 'shining-he', or 'shining-she'. But who was he, or she, or it? Here you have at once the inevitable birth of what we call a myth. What our senses perceive and what we are able to name is only an effect, it is the specific illumination of the sky, the brightness of the coming morning, or, as we now would say, the reflection of the rays of the sun on the clouds of the sky. But that was not what the ancient people thought. Having formed a word such as Eos which meant shining, or light, they would go on to say Eos has returned, Eos has fled, Eos will come again, Eos rises out of the sea, Eos is the daughter of the sky, Eos is followed by the sun, Eos is loved by the sun, Eos is killed by the sun, and so on. What does all this mean? You may say that it is language, it is of course a myth, and an inevitable myth at that" (p. 13). Mr. Lütgenau adds to this discourse of Müller's by saying: "The question as to the essence of the myth may, consequently, be answered thus: it is a natural and necessary stage in the development of language and thought. But this of course is a far from adequate definition" (same page). It is, indeed, quite "inadequate". But the main point is that even this inadequate definition could have suggested to Mr. Lütgenau a certain pertinent question. He could have—in fact, he should have—asked himself: is it not possible to *condense* this definition, and simply say: the myth is a necessary stage in the development of thinking?

If he had thought about this question without prejudice he would have seen that that was in fact possible. Like our very, very remote ancestors, we say nowadays: the sun sets, the moon has risen, the wind has died down, and so on. But when we express ourselves in this fashion, we do not think, as those very, very remote ancestors did, that the sun, the moon, the wind, etc., are really living beings endowed with consciousness and will. The expressions are similar, but the notions connected with them have become quite different. Formerly, the nature of these notions and thinking in general *facilitated* the development of myths; now that nature is completely *unfavourable* to the promotion of myths, which means that the origin of myths is to be found in the nature of primitive man's thinking. There is no reason to repeat what exactly was the nature of primitive thinking: we have said already that primitive man *animated* the world surrounding him. The whole question now is only to ascertain why this was so. Why is such thinking peculiar to primitive man? The question is not a difficult one to answer. In the final analysis, the nature of thinking is determined by the store of experience at man's disposal. With primitive man, this store was quite insignificant. But in so far as it existed, it was related principally *to an animal world*; primitive man became a *hunter* and a *fisherman* at a very early stage. Of course, even at that very early stage of its existence mankind had also dealings with "inanimate" nature; at that time too, man experienced on himself the effect of heat, moisture, light, etc. But in experiencing this action on himself and endeavouring to *understand* and *explain* it, man had of necessity *to judge the unknown by the known*. And to him the known, as has been stated, was primarily the animal world of so-called *animated* objects; it is not surprising that primitive man regarded all the rest of the much lesser known part of nature as being animated. The less he knew of this side of nature, which by necessity he already conceived of as animated, the more scope there was for the exercise of his imagination. His imagination created a whole series of tales explaining great natural phenomena by the activity of this or that animated creature.

It is of these tales that what we know as *mythology* consists. However, it must be remarked that Mr. Lütgenau errs greatly in averring that primitive man always spoke of *gods* as of *people* (p. 17). He is no less mistaken when he adds that "we" know *why* natural phenomena deified by men were represented in the form of human beings (same page). *This* cannot be known, since *this never happened*. In explaining great natural phenomena by the action of living creatures, the savage, for the most part, envisaged these creatures in the form of *animals*, and not at all as *human beings*. This is such a well-known truth, it would seem, that it is downright surprising how Mr. Lütgenau could not know about it, or could lose sight of it. Let us assume that as a *philologist* he has, in general, no inclination to *ethnology*; indeed he says so himself in his book; but surely there is a limit to all things. To say that the great phenomena and forces of nature were conceived of by primitive man only in the form of people is to close the door to the understanding, for example, even of what was by no means a primitive religion—the Egyptian religion at the time of the Pharaohs.

Max Müller was of little help to Mr. Lütgenau in his attempt at a materialist explanation of religion. On the contrary, *philology* rather prevented our author from paying the proper attention to *technology*, that is to say, to how mythology is modified by the growth of the productive forces and by man's increasing power over nature. We strongly advise those who intend to read Lütgenau's book not to forget this gap in it.*

Another of the book's defects is the unnecessary *schematism* of the presentation. Mr. Lütgenau portrays the course of development of religious beliefs in such a way that it appears as though "natural" religion—"the reflection of man's dependence on nature" —could be separated by a sharply defined boundary from "social" religion, which is a reflection of the same dependence "on social forces, the essence and character of whose action is unknown to him" (i.e. to man—*G.P.*). But there is no such boundary. This may be easily proved by means of the very observations and definitions advanced by Mr. Lütgenau. Thus, for example, he is quite correct in saying that the sphere of *religion* is much narrower than that of *mythology*. "Not all mythology is religion," he writes, "and only those objects that are capable of influencing man's moral character have the right to be called religious" (p. 38). Here an idea which in itself is correct is stated very badly; religion in the broad and, of course, much more exact sense of the word really arises when social man begins to seek sanction for his morality, or in general for his actions and institutions, from a god or gods.** But morality is a *social* phenomenon. Therefore in sanctifying the rules of morality, and in general the existing social relations of men, religion thereby acquires a *social character*. Mr. Lütgenau himself is conscious of this. He says: "From the very beginning already there is the inevitable social element of religion in the analogy between the human and the divine way of life, between the relationship of the father to his child and that of God to man, etc." (p. 133). Precisely. And since this is the case, "natural" religion *cannot* be portrayed as though it were a separate phase of religious evolution. It *may*, if you wish, be so portrayed, but only, for example, by Tylor, in whose opinion religion (in its *minimal* variant) existed *even where* myths had not yet begun to sanctify moral instruction. As for Mr. Lütgenau, to whom religion exists *only where* the unification of mythology and morality has

---

* This gap is in no way bridged by what our author has said, for example on the influence of *exchange* on religious notions. We are speaking now not about *economy*, but about the *technique* of production. The influence of the latter on primitive *mythology* was probably no less strong than its influence on primitive *art*. This particular aspect of the matter is hardly touched upon in Lütgenau's book, and we can blame this primarily on the author's contemptuous attitude to the materials collected by contemporary ethnology.

** By religion *in its narrow sense* we understand what Tylor calls the *minimum of religion*, that is to say, a general belief in the existence of spirits. Originally, such a belief had no influence whatever on man's actions, and at the time, had absolutely no significance as a "factor" of social development. Therefore it could be termed religion only with a very substantial reservation.

already been accomplished, he should have tried from the very
first pages of his exposition to discover the link between men's
social relationships on the one hand, and the forms of their *religious*
beliefs on the other. The discovery of such a connection would
have been useful to him also to elucidate what might be described
as the role of the religious "factor" in the history of mankind.
But Lütgenau did not see the need to elucidate this connection
thoroughly either for the reader's benefit or for his own. Therefore,
and despite his own opinion, "natural religion", in his exposition,
is apparently independent of the "social" form. The same must be
said of "anthropological" as well as "psychological" religion. These
"religions" too are presented by our author as something quite
separate and independent. In the interests of analysis, he breaks
the living, mutual connection of phenomena, and then forgets to
restore it in the interests of *synthesis*. Not surprisingly, his exposition proves to be almost devoid of any inner connection. His
book represents, in its individual chapters, a collection of more
or less valuable data for the materialist explanation of "the
religious phenomenon" (as it is now called by French investigators
in this field) but we find no *systematic explanation* of the "phenomenon".

However, we repeat, among the blind the one-eyed is king.
There is such a poor selection of literature on this subject available to the Russian reader unacquainted with foreign languages
that even Mr. Lütgenau's book will make a useful addition to it.
In any case, it will do no harm to read it.

A couple of words more. In the chapter "Religion and Ethics",
Mr. Lütgenau makes some very apt objections against the idea
that morality must always be founded on religion. He says—
as Diderot, incidentally, did long before him—that the use
brought by religion to man is like that of a crutch: "He who does
not need a crutch is better off" (pp. 240-41). Very true. But the
truth of Diderot's brilliant remark would have become even more
evident if Mr. Lütgenau had buttressed it with the incontestable
fact that, in the history of the development of mankind, morality
appeared *before* man had begun to sanctify its principles by reference to the will of supernatural beings. Mr. Lütgenau, of course,
was well aware of this, but it has not received the proper treatment in his book and consequently cannot throw its full light
on the question of the relation of morality to religion.

Commenting on the well-known proposition that "religion is
a private matter", Mr. Lütgenau says: "To be a member of the
Party, it is sufficient for a person to be convinced that he shares
the views and demands laid down in the Party programme. Thus,
in the Reichstag elections of 1893, a Christian theologian could
have stood as an official Party candidate" (p. 289). That, of course,

19*

is true. But it should nevertheless be noted that the Party programme is based upon the totality of those principles to which the
members of the Party attach serious scientific importance. Every
member of the Party is morally obliged, according to his powers
and opportunities, to engage in *propaganda* of these principles.
The question arises: what should he do if in his propaganda work
he clashes with the system of views which, with the aid of "social"
religion, offers an explanation of what he himself cannot explain
clearly other than by means of scientific socialism? Should he
speak against his own convictions? That would be hypocrisy.
Should he say *nothing* about some part of his views? That would
be semi-hypocrisy i.e., essentially the same hypocrisy. The alternative is to *speak the truth*, but to do so without rubbing the audience the wrong way unnecessarily, by approaching them tactfully,
perhaps even in the manner of a teacher, but all the same to speak
the truth. Again we have to make the same reservation which we
have had to make more than once in this review: Mr. Lütgenau
agrees with us: he says so himself.* But he mentions it only in
passing; and when he has to formulate his opinion conclusively,
he seems inclined to take the opposite view. Thus, on pages 274-
75, he writes: "The most effective agitation here too is: *speak of
what is*. The natural origin of religion; the subsequently appearing
dependence of religious concepts on the economic structure of
society; the facts of Church history; the scientific investigation of
the essence of phenomena, failure to understand which gave rise
to religious interpretations—all these are truths, certainties,
which do away with every doubt and every fantasy stemming
from uncertainty." Very well said. But the author proceeds to
argue in such a way that agitation appears to be unnecessary, and
this for the reason that the "fantasy" in question is rooted in our
contemporary economic reality and will disappear with it. But
it is a very bad argument indeed. It is reminiscent of the arguments
used by the anarchists and the syndicalists: *since* political institutions are founded on relations of production, *then*, so long as
these relations exist, the political struggle is either quite useless
or even harmful to the working class. Actually, the very course
of *economic* development of present-day society furnishes the
necessary fulcrum for fruitful *political* activity by the proletariat.
It would be sheer extravagance not to utilise this fulcrum, indeed
it would be simply nonsensical; and the same must be said about
"fantasies".

The following example will make this idea more intelligible.
Some years ago in the French Party there was a Negro named

---

* That is to say, he agreed and said so while he was a member of the
Party; but what he thinks now, nobody knows.

Legitimus, a Deputy from the island of Martinique. The malicious tongues of his enemies spread the story that during the election campaign Legitimus not only spoke at meetings, but resorted to *sorcery* to ensure his victory at the polls. This, we repeat, was nothing more than a malicious invention. But assume for a moment that it was true. In that event, what attitude should the French Party have taken towards this comrade? Expel him from the Party? But that would have been an exhibition of harmful, impermissible and, in addition, ridiculous intolerance, because belief in sorcery must also be recognised as a private matter. We hope no one will raise objection to this. On the other hand, which of the white comrades of this coloured Deputy would not have considered himself morally bound to inform him of a more correct view of the real causes of political victories and failures? Which of them would not have tried to help extricate him from his gross delusions? Only ill-intentioned or frivolous people would have refused to help him. Yet belief in sorcery also undoubtedly has its materialist interpretation! That is just the point: to find a materialist explanation for a particular historical phenomenon does not at all mean that one has to become reconciled to that phenomenon, or to maintain that it cannot be removed by the conscious activity of men. It is not consciousness that determines being; but being that determines consciousness. That is correct; it is historical materialism, but it is not the whole of historical materialism. To this must be added that, having arisen on the basis of being, consciousness for its part promotes the further development of being. Marx was fully aware of this when he expressed his well-known view on the great importance of "criticism of religion".[169]

HENRI BERGSON

Henri Bergson, *Creative Evolution*.
Translated from the Third French Edition by M. Bulgakov.
Moscow, 1909

Hegel, in his *Lectures on the History of Philosophy*, called the Greek sophists *experts in the treatment of ideas*. This description could with complete justification be applied to Henri Bergson. He is a real expert in this field. In this respect he leaves very far behind him Ernst Mach who is now fashionable here in Russia. Mach is clumsy in most things, even when he is right. H. Bergson almost always astonishes us with his adroitness even when he is in the wrong. It is impossible to read him without pleasure, just as it is pleasing to watch the performance of a gymnast at the top of his profession.

H. Bergson also resembles the sophists in this respect that the *positive* result of his exceptionally skilful exercises in logic is extremely meagre. More than that: this result is a *negative quantity* when Bergson tries to look at the fundamental questions of metaphysics and epistemology from a *new* point of view. At first glance this may appear strange. Naturally one wonders why a man endowed with great flexibility of thought and possessing in addition extensive and varied knowledge should be intellectually so unproductive. But on closer examination, the reason for this becomes quite clear.

Bergson has no love for the beaten paths; he strives to blaze his own trail, and undoubtedly displays no little originality. But non the less his originality is confined to *matters of detail* only, although sometimes his efforts here are truly remarkable. *In general*, however, he is incapable of freeing himself from the *tendency to idealism*, now prevalent among philosophers. This tendency to idealism, from whose influence Bergson cannot escape in spite of all his originality, finally reduces to zero all the results of his investigations quite remarkable in their own way. He is truly a victim of his own inability to make an end of his idealism. In this sense, his example is extremely instructive.

In order better to explain the significance of this example, we shall draw the reader's attention to what might be described as the *materialist* element in Bergson's views.

Here, for instance, on page 99 of his *Creative Evolution*, we read: "The vegetable manufactures organic substances directly with mineral substances: as a rule this aptitude enables it to dispense with movement and consequently with feeling. Animals, which are obliged to go in search of their food, have evolved in the direction of locomotor activity, and consequently of a more and more ample, more and more distinct consciousness" (p. 99). This means that the development of *consciousness* is conditioned by the needs of *being*. Apply this remark which, incidentally, is only the translation into the language of contemporary biology of one of Aristotle's most profound thoughts, to the explanation of the development of *social* thought and you will get the *theory of historical materialism*. Bergson, indeed, comes quite close to this theory, it might even be said that he is one of its followers. He writes: "As regards human intelligence, it has not been sufficiently noted that mechanical invention has been from the first its essential feature, that even today our social life gravitates around the manufacture and use of artificial instruments, that the inventions which like milestones mark the road of progress have also traced its direction" (pp. 118-19). This is one of the basic principles of historical materialism. But as will be seen by the reference in the footnote on page 119, Bergson was familiar only with the very vulgar variety of historical materialism represented by P. Lacombe in his book *Sociological Foundations of History*.* Marx's historical materialism has remained quite unknown to Bergson, otherwise he would not have credited Lacombe with something that had been done much earlier and better by Marx. Being unfamiliar with historical materialism in its classical formulation, Bergson could not grasp the proper significance of the *changing succession of relations of production in the process of development of human society*. He thought that, "in thousands of years, when, seen from a distance, only the main lines of the present age will still be visible, our wars and our revolutions will count for little, even supposing they are still remembered; but the steam engine, and the procession of inventions of every kind that came in its train, will perhaps be spoken of as we speak of the bronze or of the chipped stone; it will serve to define an age" (p. 119). This is too narrow a view. No two revolutions are alike. But as for revolutions in relations of production, *characterising in their totality different modes of production*, these are such "main lines" in the history of social development that they will not by any means "count for little" to any serious historian. However, that by the way. The main point here is that

---

* On Lacombe's book see Appendix III to the last edition of my book *The Development of the Monist View on History*.[170]

Bergson defines complete "intelligence" as the *"faculty of making and using inorganic instruments"* (p. 120, Bergson's italics). This means that the idea of the implements of labour playing a decisive role in the development of mankind has for Bergson an *epistemological*—and not just a *sociological*—significance. There is nothing surprising in this. If in all animals in general *consciousness* is the product of *activity*, as we have seen above, then it is natural that in man in particular the *faculty of understanding*, as Bergson expresses it, is simply *"an appendage of the faculty of acting"* (p. 3, our italics). It cannot be otherwise, for the second idea is no more than a particular case of the first.* However, it is also very natural that the theory of cognition acquires a materialist form from this materialist point of view. "Action cannot move in the unreal," says Bergson quite rightly (p. 5). Therefore such current arguments as that we do not know and cannot know the essence of things, that we must stop at the unknowable, and so on, prove to be groundless. "A mind born to speculate or to dream," says Bergson, "I admit, might remain outside reality, might deform or transform the real, perhaps even create it—as we create the figures of men and animals that our imagination cuts out of the passing cloud. But an intellect bent upon the act to be performed and the reaction to follow, feeling its object so as to get its mobile impression at every instant, is an intellect that touches something of the absolute" (p. 5). The expression "absolute" may give rise to misunderstanding. We believe it to be out of place here. But as we have no desire to enter into terminological argument with Bergson, we readily grant that he is right. We could not act upon external nature if it were beyond the reach of our knowledge. This was explained very well a long time ago by the materialist philosophy of Marx and Engels.** Let us proceed. Bergson affirms that knowledge "becomes relative" where activity is directed to "industry" (as with man—*G.P.*) (same page). This is also perfectly true. Here again the conclusions to be drawn are fully materialist. If Bergson had wished to draw such conclusions and follow them through to the logical end, there is no doubt that, with his strong inclination to and outstanding ability for dialectical thinking, he could have thrown a vivid light on the most important problems of the theory of cognition. But he did not have the least desire to do so. He is a convinced idealist, to whom physics is merely a *"reflection of the psyche"*. Consequently, his very promising arguments on the theory of knowledge end in hackneyed nonsense,

---

* One other point should be noted here: By domesticating *animals*, man acquired for himself *organic* instruments of labour, yet their domestication is also partly the business of the "intellect". This is very important.

** See my polemic with Conrad Schmidt in the work: *A Critique of Our Critics.*[171]

and instead of new results we receive from him only the old, so familiar idealist petitio principii.

Bergson's overpowering prejudice in favour of idealism thwarts the very principles he succeeds in shaping when relying upon his materialist premises. Thus, having stated our faculty of *understanding* to be a simple appendage of our faculty of *acting*, he hastens to add on the plea of further analysis that "*in reality there are no things, there are only actions*" (p. 211, our italics). That is very radical. But if it is true, it goes without saying that Bergson has nothing left but to appeal to *consciousness*, and that is what he does. To him, "consciousness" is "the basic principle" (p. 202). True, he qualifies this by saying that he uses the term "consciousness" for want of a better word. "But we do not mean the narrowed consciousness that functions in each of us" (same page). Such a qualification, however, contains absolutely nothing new and so does not improve matters; indeed, it confuses them still more. Consciousness of the super-individual type is a myth; reference to it may satisfy the *religious feelings* of a believer, but it is positively worthless as the basis for a *philosophy* which, in fact, is *alien to dogmatism*.

Returning to his idealist harbour from his materialist excursions, Bergson avers that the *intellect* has the faculty of knowing reality only from its *outward* aspect and that this is not true knowledge (see, for example, p. 167). True knowledge, knowledge of reality from its *inward* aspect, may be obtained only from a philosophy which steps beyond the limits of the intellect and relies on *intuition*. There is little need to point out that such thinking opens wide the door to *fantasy*. Advancing the reason that "the philosopher must go further than the scientist" (p. 317), he makes up a philosophical story whose nature and content may be gathered from the following passage:

"Let us imagine a vessel full of steam at a high pressure, and here and there in its sides a crack through which the steam is escaping in a jet. The steam thrown into the air is nearly all condensed into little drops which fall, and this condensation and this fall represent simply the loss of something, an interruption, a deficit. But a small part of the jet of steam subsists, uncondensed, for some seconds; it is making an effort to raise the drops which are falling; it succeeds at most in retarding their fall. So, from an immense reservoir of life, jets must be gushing out unceasingly, of which each, falling, is a world. The evolution of living species within this world represents what subsists of the primitive direction of the original jet, and of an impulsion which continues itself in a direction the inverse of materiality" (p. 211).

Should you remark that this comparaison n'est pas raison, like any other, Bergson will at once agree with you. "But let us not

carry too far this comparison," he says, "it gives us but a feeble
and even deceptive image of reality, for the crack, the jet of steam,
the forming of the drops, are determined necessarily, whereas
the creation of the world is a free act, and the life within the
material world participates in that liberty. Let us think rather
of an action like that of raising the arm; then let us suppose that
the arm, left to itself, falls back, and yet that there subsists in
it, striving to raise it up again, something of the will that animates it. In this image of a *creative action which unmakes itself*
we have already a more exact representation of matter" (same
page).

*Life is a creative action, an "élan". Matter is the halting of the
élan, the cessation of the creative action.* We are sure that nowadays
many Russian readers will find this both easy to comprehend and
profound. We congratulate them heartily, and wish them further
penetration, under Bergson's guidance, into the essence of life
seen from its *internal* aspect. To those who are not attracted to
the present philosophical fashion for idealism, we shall, in ending
this long review, offer the remark that Bergson in his intuitive
philosophy makes two great errors.

First, the attempt to observe the process of the formation of
reality from its internal aspect is condemned in advance to dismal
failure; nothing has ever, or can, come out of it but a dense fog
of mysticism. Why? Spinoza gave the answer already in Proposition 23 in Part II of his *Ethics.**

Secondly, the *process of becoming*, about which Bergson has
such a lot to say, is understood by him very one-sidedly: *the
element of existence is utterly missing.* This, of course, facilitates
the decomposing of "the material world" into a simple "jet",
which he advocates in the interests of his mystical idealism:
but thereby he *transforms dialectics into simple sophistry*, as has
been made clear from the history of *Greek* philosophy.

Bergson sympathises with *Plotonius*, which is quite natural
and could not be otherwise. But that Bergson has an attraction
for certain *theoreticians* of French *syndicalism* is one of the most
ludicrous misunderstandings known in the history of philosophical
thought, so rich in misunderstandings. It demonstrates the low
theoretical level reached by the theoreticians of French syndicalism, *so low that, in fact, they cannot fall any lower.*

---

* "The mind has no knowledge of itself, except in so far as it perceives
the ideas of the modifications of the body." *Ethics*, Part II, p. 84.

ON MR. V. SHULYATIKOV'S BOOK

V. Shulyatikov, *Justification of Capitalism in West
European Philosophy (From Descartes to Mach).*
Moscow Book Publishers.
Moscow, 1908

Mr. Shulyatikov writes: "A traditional attitude to philosophy
has been established in intellectual circles, where it is regarded
as a kind of Privatsache, as something in the nature of a domain
where one may exercise individual judgement, individual apprais-
als, and individual creativeness. It is asserted in these circles
that even the most radical divergences in philosophical questions
are by no means evidence of the existence of social antagonisms;
philosophical ideas are represented as being too inadequately
and too weakly linked with any class substratum. The defence
of a particular class position does not, therefore, predetermine,
in the generally held view, support for a particular philosophical
school. On the contrary in this case a wide freedom of choice is
permissible (!)" (p. 5). According to the author, similar views
are held by very many Marxists too.

"They are convinced that in the ranks of the proletarian van-
guard a motley variety of philosophical views is permissible,
that it is of no great importance whether the proletarian ideologists preach materialism or energetics, neo-Kantianism or Machism. It is thought that philosophy is a quite innocent affair"
(p. 5).

Mr. Shulyatikov positively rejects the idea that philosophy is
"innocent"; he thinks such a belief is a naive and very lamentable
mistake. "Philosophy is not the happy exception," he says; "on
the speculative 'heights' the bourgeoisie remains true to itself.
It speaks about nothing else but its own immediate class interests
and aspirations, but it speaks in a very peculiar language, difficult to understand. All philosophical terms and formulas without
exception that are employed by the bourgeoisie, all these 'concepts', 'ideas', 'views', 'notions', 'sensations', all these 'absolutes',
'things-in-themselves', 'noumena', 'phenomena', 'substances',
'modes', 'attributes', 'subjects', 'objects', all these 'spirits',
'material elements', 'forces', 'energies', serve to designate social
classes, groups, nuclei, and their interrelationships. To know the
philosophical system of any one of the bourgeois thinkers is to

have a picture of the class structure of society, drawn with the aid of conventional signs and reproducing the social profession de foi of a certain bourgeois group" (p. 6).

In these remarks of our author, a grain of truth is mixed with much "naive" error. Of course, it would be foolish to think that philosophical ideas are not connected with a "class" substratum. But we are completely in the dark as to why the bourgeoisie on the speculative "heights" "speaks about nothing but its own *immediate* class interests and aspirations". Besides meditating upon these immediate matters what is there to prevent the intellectual representatives of the bourgeoisie, perched on these heights, from also pondering over somewhat more *remote* interests and aspirations? It is true that the investigator's task is very much *simplified* if he presupposes that the philosophical ideas of the given class always express only the *immediate* interest of that class. *But simplicity is far from always being a virtue.* We shall see this presently from the example of Mr. Shulyatikov himself.

Mr. Shulyatikov, who considers himself to be a "Marxist philosopher", assumes, "therefore" (i.e., obviously because philosophy expresses the *immediate* interests of the bourgeoisie), that "the question must be put resolutely". He says: "The task of a Marxist philosopher must not be reduced to altering the details of such a type of pictures. These pictures cannot be accepted as something that could be utilised and co-ordinated with the proletarian world-outlook. This would mean lapsing into opportunism, an attempt to combine that which cannot be combined. In our view, the task confronting the Marxist philosopher is something quite different. It requires, prior to engaging in philosophical constructions, revaluation of philosophical concepts and systems, proceeding from the point of view we have outlined above" (p. 7).

You observe that our "Marxist philosopher" intends to carry through a whole revolution. This is commendable. But the road to hell is known to be paved with good intentions. We shall see how Mr. Shulyatikov manages to fulfil his laudable intentions.

Applying himself to the assessment of philosophical values, he remarks that very little has been done in this respect, although "the first brilliant attempt at such a revaluation took place some years ago". Here he has in mind Mr. A. Bogdanov's article "Authoritarian Thought" published in a collection of his articles, *The Psychology of Society.* Mr. Shulyatikov is convinced that the article concerned opens up a new era in the history of philosophy. According to him, "following the appearance of this article, speculative philosophy lost all right to operate with its two fundamental concepts of 'spirit' and 'body'; it was established that these concepts took shape on the background of authoritarian relationships and the antithesis between them reflected the social antithesis—the antithesis of the organising 'upper strata' and the executing 'lower strata'. With amazing consistency, bourgeois critics have turned a deaf ear to the work of this Russian Marxist"... (same page).

We shall discover shortly how valuable were the ideas which Mr. Shulyatikov extracted from Mr. Bogdanov's "brilliant" article. At the moment we feel the reader's attention ought to be focussed on the following circumstance. In Mr. Shulyatikov's opinion Mr. Bogdanov's article deprived speculative philosophy of the "right" to operate with the concepts of "spirit and body". Let us take for granted that it really did. But surely Marx also "operated" with these two concepts? Undoubtedly he did so in his own way, regarding them from the standpoint of a *materialist*, but none the less he "operated" with them. Therefore, the question arises: what fate befell Marx's materialist philosophy with the appearance of Mr. Bogdanov's shattering article? Was this philosophy also deprived of the "right" to operate in its own materialist fashion with the concepts "spirit" and "body"? If not, it is clear that Mr. Bogdanov's article did not open up a new era at all. If the answer is yes, it is no less clear that the "Russian Marxist" on whom Mr. Shulyatikov relies has distinguished himself in philosophy by overthrowing, in passing, the philosophy of Marx himself. But the Marxist whose philosophical work is to overthrow Marxist philosophy is a Marxist of a very special cut. His Marxism consists not in *following* Marx, but in *refuting* him. And that is actually the case; the "Russian Marxist" who has inspired Mr. Shulyatikov is among the followers of that same Ernst Mach whom Mr. Shulyatikov lists among the bourgeois ideologists (see the chapter: *Empiriocriticism*, pp. 132-47).

Now let us see what this strange *Marxist*, who follows a *bourgeois* philosopher, has taught Mr. Shulyatikov.

"The leader-organiser and the rank-and-file member of society executing his commands—such is the first social antithesis known to history. At the beginning it amounted to no more than a simple contrasting of roles. With the passing of time it came to signify something more. Economic inequality made its appearance; the organisers were transformed gradually into owners of the instruments of production which had formerly belonged to society. And parallel with this, like an echo of the progressing social stratification, the concept of the contrasting principles of spirit and body took shape" (p. 11).

First of all, it is quite untrue to say that the first social antithesis known to history was that between the leader-organiser and the rank-and-file member of society executing the leader's commands. The first social antithesis originated as a contraposing between man and woman. In saying this, I am, of course, not referring to the *physiological but to the sociological* division of labour between them. This division of labour put its stamp upon the whole structure of primitive society and the whole of its world-outlook. But the notion of *spirit*, or, more correctly, of *soul*, did not spring from this division of labour. Modern ethnology has ascertained the genesis of this notion pretty well. All the new data obtained by this science confirm the correctness of Tylor's theory of "*animism*", according to which primitive man animates all nature, and the soul, whose presence or absence explains all natural phenomena, is conceived by him as something which in ordinary conditions is inaccessible to his senses. Death, sleep, and swooning are among the phenomena which most facilitated the appearance of the concept of soul. But sleep, death and swooning are not the outcome of social contrasts, but of man's physiological make-up. So that to explain the origin of the concept of soul—and, consequently, of spirit—by social contrasts is to misuse a method which promises extremely valuable discoveries in the future, but the use of which in practice presupposes two indispensable conditions: first, a certain capacity to think logically, and secondly, knowledge of the facts. Unfortunately, we must recognise that these two conditions are conspicuously absent from Mr. Shulyatikov's work.

We have just seen how badly he knows the facts relating to the primitive history of mankind, while his clumsy meditations on the "innocence" of philosophy show how ill-equipped he is for logical thinking. After all, to assert that "all philosophical terms without exception" serve to designate social classes, groups, nuclei, and their relationships, is to reduce an extremely important question to a simplicity that can only be characterised by the epithet: "Suzdalian".[172] This word denotes neither a "social class", nor a "group", nor a "nucleus", but simply a vast wooden-headedness. There is not the least shadow of doubt that the division of society into classes had a decisive influence on the course of its intellectual development. And it is just as incontestable that the division of society into classes was the outcome "in the last instance" (Engels' expression) of its economic development. However, *influence* is one thing, and *immediate reflection* is another. Besides, to say that the economic development of society conditions "in the last instance" all other aspects of its development is to recognise, precisely by these four words, "in the last instance", the existence of *many other intermediate "instances"*, each of which influences all the others. Thus, as you see, we get a very complicated system of forces at work, in the investigation of which "Suzdalian" simplicity can yield nothing except the most comical results. Mr. Shulyatikov has already shown us a sample of this "Suzdalian" simplicity. According to him, when Kant wrote

иное, какъ представленія вторыхъ". *) Мы убѣждены, что бѣлый столъ, находящійся въ данную минуту передъ нами, является чѣмъ-то внѣшнимъ по отношенію къ нашей душѣ. Но современные философы, заявляетъ Юмъ, не оспариваютъ того, что всѣ чувственныя качества—бѣлизна, твердость и пр. качества вторичныя и существуютъ не въ объектахъ: „они—наши представленія, не имѣющія соотвѣтствующаго внѣшняго архетипа или модели". То же самое слѣдуетъ сказать и о такъ называемыхъ первичныхъ качествахъ. Идею протяженія, напр., мы получаемъ исключительно изъ ощущеній осязанія и зрѣнія. Путемъ отвлеченія, абстрагированія, подобной первичной идеи создать мы не можемъ. Протяженіе, недоступное ни зрѣнію, ни осязанію, не можетъ быть представлено; точно такъже недоступно человѣческому представленію такое протяженіе, которое было бы и осязаемо и видимо, но не было бы ни твердымъ, ни мягкимъ, ни чернымъ, ни бѣлымъ. Пусть кто-нибудь попробуетъ представлять себѣ треугольнымъ, который не будетъ ни равно,—ни разносторовнимъ и стороны котораго не будутъ имѣть предѣльной длины, и также не будутъ стоять другъ къ другу въ отдѣльномъ отношеніи; это лицо вскорѣ убѣдится въ недѣлости всѣхъ схоластическихъ понятій объ абстракціи и общихъ идеяхъ". Юмъ идетъ по пути, намѣченному Беркли, выдвигаетъ понятіе объ индивидуализированныхъ „комплексахъ". Не существуетъ человѣка вообще; существуетъ или Петръ или Иванъ или Яковъ. Не существуетъ для мануфактуры разъ навсегда опредѣленнаго типа рабочаго, „рабочаго вообще", а существуетъ или лондонскій квалифицированный рабочій или ка-

*) Давидъ Юмъ: „Изслѣдованіе человѣческаго разумѣнія", пер. С. И. Церетеля, стр. 176.

Plekhanov's notes on the margins of V. Shulyatikov's book *Justification of Capitalism in West European Philosophy* (1908)

about noumena and phenomena, he not only had in mind various social classes, but also, to use the expression of the old wife of one of Uspensky's bureaucrats, he "aimed at the pocket" of one of these classes, namely, the bourgeoisie. The outcome is something like a caricature of human thought, a caricature which would justly arouse much indignation were it not so utterly comic.

There is not enough space to offer other samples: we shall be content with one more. Mr. Shulyatikov writes:

"To Avenarius, the world appears as an agglomeration of central nervous systems. 'Matter' is thoroughly stripped of all 'qualities', whether 'primary' or 'secondary', formerly considered its inalienable attributes. Positively everything in matter is determined by 'spirit', or, in the terminology of the author of *The Critique of Pure Experience*, by the central nervous system" (p. 114). Why does Avenarius think this? Here is the reason: "Contemporary capitalism is extremely 'elastic': to the owners of capital there is not just one type of worker given once for all, but *today* there are workers of a certain profession and a certain skill, *tomorrow* of another profession and another skill, today Ivan, tomorrow Paul or Jacob...." Enough! This is so good that we ask ourselves: is Mr. Shulyatikov, by some chance, joking? Maybe he is writing a *parody of Marxism?* As a parody, his book is very biting, and even talented but, of course, quite unfair.

In conclusion, we have to remark that we are still in utter darkness as to whether the materialist philosophy of Karl Marx and Frederick Engels is "permissible" among class-conscious proletarians.

ON THE SO-CALLED RELIGIOUS SEEKINGS IN RUSSIA

FIRST ARTICLE

ON RELIGION

I

⟨The question we are about to discuss concerns what is known as the religious seekings which are now going on in Russia. If I am not mistaken this is one of the most topical subjects. Not long ago—one may say, only the other day—Mr. Alexander Yablonovsky wrote in *Kievskaya Mysl* (No. 151) that "in our country the attention of society is at present split into three parts, and concentrates on god-seeking, pornography, and wrestling". Unfortunately, this looks very much like the truth. I have never been interested in wrestling, and I have never had a passion for pornographic literature. But our contemporary "god-seeking" does seem to me to warrant serious attention, and I should like to express the reflections which this trend has suggested and still suggests to me.

Here it will be useful to make the following reservation.

One of our better known god-seekers, S. N. Bulgakov, renowned for his spiritual retreat from "Marxism to idealism" (and even much further, as far as the Sarovskaya hermitage desert, in fact) writes in the magazine *Vekhi*,[173] the third edition of which has recently been issued, and which undoubtedly has had the "success of a scandal" and perhaps not only of a scandal:

"The most striking thing about Russian atheism is its dogmatism, one might say the religious flippancy with which it is accepted. Until recent times, religious problems in all their immense and exceptional importance and urgency, were simply not noticed and not understood by Russian 'educated society', which was generally interested in religion only in so far as it had to do with politics or the propagation of atheism. Our intelligentsia show a startling ignorance of religious matters. I say this not as an accusation because there may perhaps be sufficient historical justification for it, but to diagnose their mental condition. On the question of religion, our intelligentsia have not yet emerged from adolescence, they have not yet thought seriously about religion."*

---

* С. Н. Булгаков, «Героизм и подвижничество», *Вехи.* стр. 32. [S. N. Bulgakov, "Heroism and Dedication", *Vekhi*, p. 32].

Г. В. Плехановъ.

Отъ обороны
къ нападенію.

Отвѣтъ г. А. Богданову, критика итальянскаго
синдикализма и другія статьи.

Мы никогда не должны оставаться
на оборонительной позиціи, а всегда
переходить къ нападенію.

Каммиль Демуленъ.

Складъ изданія: Масякъ, Моховая, домъ Бенкендорфъ,
книжный магазинъ А. Д. Друткахъ.

Title page of the collection *From Defence to Attack*
(1910)

It must be confessed that that is so. And for that reason I did not hesitate to make this long quotation. Our atheism is really very flippant, and our intelligentsia do, indeed, act like adolescents in regard to religion. What Mr. Bulgakov says is the truth, but not the whole truth. He has forgotten to add that ignorance in religious matters is displayed in our country not only by those who profess atheism, but also by those who engage in one way or another in "god-seeking" and "god-building". Our "god-seekers" and "god-builders", too, have not as yet thought seriously of religion, and their religious preaching is not such a stranger to politics (in the broad sense of the word) as it might appear at first glance. Like Mr. Bulgakov, I am not accusing anyone, but only diagnosing the mental condition of those who preach the now fashionable doctrine of "religious self-determination". This mental condition might be best described by the words: an irresistible disposition to religious dogmatism. My task, incidentally, is to determine the social causes of that disposition. But whatever those causes may be, there is no doubt that the disposition is there and makes itself felt almost in the same degree in the writings of "god-seekers" whose "divine" findings to all appearances most strongly differ from one another. Whether we turn to Mr. Minsky's book *Religion of the Future*, or to Mr. Lunacharsky's *Religion and Socialism*; whether we listen to the "anti-bourgeois" Mr. Merezhkovsky, or to the frankly bourgeois Mr. Gershenson; or reflect on the "divine word" of Mr. P. B. Struve—everywhere we shall encounter the same dogmatism that is so distasteful to Mr. Bulgakov, and the same ignorance in religious matters against which he so stoutly revolts. By the by, these shortcomings are not alien either to the religious arguments of Mr. Bulgakov himself. He sees the mote in the other's (the atheist's) eye, but does not notice the beam in his own. An old, but evergreen story!

Be that as it may, the truth is still the truth. Russian "advanced people" have never given serious thought to religion. At one time, this was no great loss, but now the time has come when the neglect of religious questions may lead to very grievous consequences. It is necessary now to think and speak about religion very seriously.

For our part, we do intend to think and speak about it seriously. With this aim in view, and before criticising the religious discoveries of our "god-seekers", we shall try to form a correct conception of *what religion is.*

To understand a particular phenomenon means to ascertain how it develops. We have not the opportunity here to study the history of religion. Therefore, only one way out of the difficulty remains: *to study the most general and characteristic features of the process which we cannot now study as a whole.* We shall proceed along that line.)

II

Religion may be defined as a *more or less orderly system of conceptions, sentiments, and actions*. The conceptions form the *mythological element* of religion; the sentiments belong to the domain of *religious feelings*; the actions to the sphere of *religious worship*, or, as it is otherwise called, of *cult*. We shall have to dwell first and foremost on the mythological element of religion.

The Greek word "*mythos*" means a *story*. Man is startled by some phenomenon, whether real or imaginary is all the same. He tries to explain to himself how it happened; the myth is born. An example: the ancient Greeks believed in the existence of the goddess Athena (Minerva); how did this goddess come to be? Zeus had a headache which pained him so severely that he sought the help of the surgeon. The role of surgeon fell upon Hephaestus (Vulcan) who armed himself with a poleaxe and whacked the king of the gods so vigorously on the head that the head split in two and out sprang the goddess Athena.* Another example: a Jew of antiquity asked himself: where did the world come from? In response to his question, he was told the story of the world having been created in six days and of man having been formed from the dust of the earth. A third example: a contemporary Australian of the Arunta tribe wants to know the origin of the moon. His curiosity is satisfied with this story: in the olden days, when there was as yet no moon in the sky, a man by the name of Opossum died and was buried.** Soon afterwards he rose from the dead in the form of a boy. Seeing this happen, his kinsmen took fright and started to run away from him; he followed them, shout-

---

* [Note from the collection *From Defence to Attack*.] In connection with my reference to the myth telling of the *origin* of the goddess Athena, Mr. V. Rozanov in *Novoye Vremya*[174] of October 14, 1909, reproached me with apparently having forgotten to describe the particular phenomenon which the Greeks explained by means of Pallas Athena and the special mode of her birth. But my wonderful critic, who himself made quite clear to his readers that he had not taken the trouble to read my article, simply did not understand what I was talking about. I related the story of the birth of Athena from the head of Jupiter as a myth explaining *how the goddess Athena came to be....* But *why* she came about that way, and not some other way is quite a different question, which is answered *not by myths but by branches of science— the history of religion or sociology*. As for the compliments Mr. Rozanov pays me, they are not worth talking about: *one does not take offence at half-wits, especially* when they write in *Novoye Vremya*. From a psychological standpoint, one thing is interesting here: is Mr. Rozanov aware of how contemporary science explains the particular features of the myth regarding the origin of Pallas Athena? I may be forgiven for expressing very strong doubts in this respect [p. 187].

** Opossum—a small animal found in Australia, belonging to the Marsupialia. We shall yet see how, in the eyes of savages, one may be both man and opossum or any other animal.

ing: "Don't be afraid, don't run, or else you'll die altogether. I shall die, but I shall rise again in the sky." So the boy grew to be an old man and finally died; then he appeared again in the form of the moon and ever since then he has been dying and rising again periodically.* Thus not only the origin of the moon is explained, but also its periodic disappearance and appearance. I am not sure if this explanation will satisfy any of our present-day "god-seekers"; probably not. But it satisfies the Australian native, just as the Greek of a certain period was content with the story of Athena emerging from the head of Jupiter, or the Jew of ancient times swallowed the tale of the world's creation in six days. *The myth is a story which answers the questions: Why? How? The myth is the first expression of man's awareness of the causal connection between phenomena.*

One of the most prominent German ethnologists of our day says: "The myth is the expression of a primitive world-outlook" (Mythus ist der Ausdruck primitiver Weltanschauung).** That is quite right. One has to have a very primitive world-outlook to believe that the moon is a man called Opossum who rose from the dead and ascended to the sky. What is the main distinguishing feature of this primitive world-outlook? It is that the *person adhering to it animates the phenomena of nature.* All natural phenomena are interpreted by primitive man as the actions of particular beings who, like himself, are endowed with consciousness, needs, passions, desires, and will. Already at a very early stage of development, these beings whose actions are supposed to cause certain natural phenomena assume the nature of spirits in the conception of primitive men. Thus is formed what Tylor called *animism.* This research scientist says: "Spiritual beings are held to affect or control the events of the material world, and man's life here and hereafter; and it being considered that they hold intercourse with men, and receive pleasure or displeasure from human actions, the belief in their existence leads naturally, and it might almost be said inevitably, sooner or later to active reverence and propitiation. Thus animism, in its full development, includes the belief in souls and in a future state, in controlling deities and subordinate spirits, these doctrines practically resulting in some kind of active worship."***

---

* A. van Gennep, *Mythes et légendes d'Australie*, Paris, p. 38.
** Dr. P. Ehrenreich, *Die Mythen und Legenden der südamerikanischen Urvölker und ihre Beziehungen zu denen Nordamerikas und der Alten Welt*, Berlin, 1905, S. 10.
*** Edward B. Tylor, *Primitive Culture*, Vol. II, Russian edition, St. Petersburg, 1897, p. 10. See also Elisée Reclus, *Les croyances populaires*, Paris, 1907, pp. 14-15 and Wundt, *Völkerpsychologie*, II. Band, 2-er Theil. S. 142 et seq.

That is also correct, but it must not be forgotten that there is a world of difference between *believing* in the existence of spirits and *worshipping* them; the *myth* is one thing, *religion* is another. Primitive man believes in the existence of numerous spirits, but worships only some of them.* Religion arises from the combination of the *animistic ideas* with certain *religious acts*. Of course, we cannot evade the question of how this combination is brought about, but at the same time we must not run ahead of our subject. Now we have to find out something about the origin of animism. Tylor remarks correctly that primitive animism embodies the very essence of spiritualistic as opposed to materialistic philosophy.** If that is true, the study of animism will have a two-fold value for us: it will not only help to clear up our ideas on primitive myths, but will also reveal to us the "essence of spiritualistic philosophy". And we cannot afford to ignore this at a time when so many people are striving to resurrect philosophical spiritualism.***

_____

* "Vermenschlichung und Personifizierung von Naturerscheinungen," said Ehrenreich justifiably, "bedingen an sich noch kein religiöses Bewusst-sein" (op. cit., p. 25). The humanising and personifying of natural phenomena does not by itself give rise to religious consciousness.

** Tylor, op. cit., p. 8.

*** It is interesting to note that animism was vividly expressed in one of Y. A. Baratynsky's poems. Here it is (Signs):

Ere man put nature to the wheel
Of survey, scale or crucible;
Attending as a child to Nature's signs,
Man met with faith all her designs.
While he loved Nature,
She answered him with love,
Pregnant, bountiful love and
Finding tongue for man.
In times when danger threatened near,
The raven croaked to still his fear;
His future left to fate forbearing,
Temperate yet e'en in his daring.
When on his path a wolf from forest strayed,
Circling, with anger rising, his victory foresaid.
Stoutly his host he'd throw
At the war-band of the foe.
While overhead in whirling flight two doves
Foretold the bliss of coming loves.
And man stood not alone in lonely land,
Life friendly breathed on every hand.

Baratynsky lamented with simple candour the fact that man's intellectual growth deprived him of his animist illusions:

But, disdaining sense, man gave trust to brain,
Surrendering his future to researches vain;
And Nature closed her heart to faithless worth,
While prophecies vanished from the earth.

This, of course, is rather funny, as Belinsky noticed. None the less, animist notions were never more clearly portrayed than in Baratynsky's poem.

III

Mr. Bogdanov tried to establish the presence of a "special connection between animistic dualism and authoritarian social forms".* Without rejecting out of hand the theory of animism now generally accepted by ethnologists, and which I set forth above, Mr. Bogdanov finds, however, that it is unsatisfactory. He thinks that it "might correctly indicate that psychical *material* which served at least partly for the construction of animistic views; but the question remains, why did a form of thinking which is *fundamental* and *universal* at a certain stage of development originate from this material".** Mr. Bogdanov replies to this question by acknowledging a special connection between animistic dualism and authoritarian forms. In his opinion, animistic dualism is the reflection of social dualism, the dualism of the upper and the lower classes, the organisers and the organised. He says: "Let us envisage a society in which the authoritarian relations embrace the whole system of production, so that each social-labour action breaks up into active-organising elements and passive-operating elements. Thus, a whole vast field of experience—the sphere of immediate production—is of necessity cognised by the members of the society *according to a definite type, a type of homogeneous duality*, in which the organising and the operating elements are constantly combined."*** And when man becomes accustomed to comprehending his labour relations to the external world as the manifestation of an active, organising will which influences the passive will of the operatives, he begins "to discover the selfsame process in every phenomenon". It is then that he conceives the notion that things have souls. "He observes the movement of the sun, the flow of water, hears the rustle of leaves, feels the rain and the wind, and it is all the easier for him to perceive all this by the same means as he perceives his own social-labour life; behind the external force that is acting upon him directly, he assumes a personal will guiding it; and although this will is invisible to him, nevertheless it is immediately authentic since without it the phenomenon would be incomprehensible to him."**** That is very good; so good, in fact, that Mr. Shulyatikov wrote a whole history of modern philosophy on the basis of this idea of Bogdanov's. There is only one thing wrong with Mr. Bogdanov's good idea—it is contrary to the facts.

---

* А. Богданов, «Из психологии общества», СПБ, 1904, стр. 118. [A. Bogdanov, *From the Psychology of Society*, St., Petersburg, 1904, p. 118.]
** Ibid., same page; Mr. Bogdanov's italics.
*** Ibid., pp. 113-14. Mr. Bogdanov's italics.
**** Ibid., p. 115.

It is quite possible, even probable, that animism was not the very first step in the development of man's conception of the world. It is likely that Mr. Guyau was right in supposing that "the initial moment of religious metaphysics lies in a kind of vague monist view not in respect of the divine principle, not of the *deity* ... but of soul and body which at first are a single entity".* If that is correct, then animism must be regarded as the second step in the development of man's conception of the world. Mr. Guyau actually says as much: "The nearest to this conception is the conception of distinct souls, of breaths animating bodies, spirits capable of leaving their abode. This conception is known to historians of religion by the name of *animism*. The remarkable thing about it is its dualistic character. In embryo in it is the opposition between soul and body."** Be that as it may, the fact remains that animism develops among primitive peoples to whom "authoritarian" organisation of society is quite foreign. Mr. Bogdanov is very much mistaken in asserting, with his own brand of bravado: "It is known that at the very earliest stages of social development, in tribes standing at the very lowest level, animism has not yet appeared, the conception of a spiritual principle is completely absent."*** No, that is not "known" at all! Ethnologists are deprived of the possibility of observing those human tribes which adhered to the "kind of vague, monist view"; they know nothing of them. On the contrary, the very lowest of all tribes accessible to ethnological observation—the so-called lower hunting tribes—adhere to animism. Everyone knows that one such tribe is, for example, the Ceylonese Veddas. However, according to Paul Sarrazin, they believe in the existence of the soul after death.**** Another investigator, Emile Deschamps, expresses himself even more categorically. He avers that in the opinion of the Veddas every man turns into a "demon" or spirit after death, and, consequently, spirits are very numerous. The Veddas blame their misfortunes on these spirits.***** The same traits may be observed among the Negritos of the Andaman islands, the Bushmen, the Australian aborigines, in a word, among all the "lower hunters". The Hudson Bay Eskimos, who are not much further advanced than these hunters, are also convinced animists; they have water-

---

* M. Guyau, *Irreligion in the Future*, Russian edition, St. Petersburg, 1908, p. 60.
   ** M. Guyau, ibid., same page.
   *** A. Bogdanov, op. cit., p. 118.
   **** "Über religiöse Vorstellungen bei niedrigsten Menschenformen", in *Actes du II-ième Congrès International d'Histoire des Religions à Bâle*, 1904, p. 135.
   ***** E. Deschamps, *Au pays des veddas*, Paris, 1892, p. 386.

spirits, rain-cloud spirits, wind-spirits, cloud-spirits, and so forth.*
If we wish to know what stage of development has been reached
by "authoritarian" relationships among the Eskimos, we are told
that they have no chiefs, that is to say, no "authority". ("Among
these people there is no such person as chief").** True, even these
Eskimos have leaders, but their power is insignificant and in
addition, they are usually dominated by those whom British
investigators call the "medicine-men", i.e., sorcerers, or people *who
have contact with spirits*.*** In the Eskimos' way of life there are
strong traces of a primitive type of communism. As far as such
of the lowest tribes as the Veddas are concerned, they must be
recognised as real, and in their own fashion irreproachable, communists. So where are the authoritarian relations of production
here? It goes without saying that there is some element of materialism in the conceptions of the primitive hunting tribes regarding
spirits. The spirits of these tribes do not yet possess that immaterial nature which is characteristic, for example, of the God of
our contemporary Christians, or of those "elements" which play
such an important part in the "natural-science" philosophy of
Ernst Mach. When the "savage" thinks of a spirit, he often pictures
it in the form of a small person.**** There is, of course, much that is
"material" about such a picture. But, in the first place, it was also
characteristic of the work of the fourteenth-century artist (whether
Orcagna or somebody else) who painted the famous fresco, "The
Triumph of Death", on one of the walls of the Pisa cemetery.
Let Mr. Bogdanov have a look at that fresco, or even a photograph
of it. He will see that human souls are depicted there as small
people, with all the signs of materiality, including a tonsure of
the plump soul of the Catholic priest whom the angel is hauling
along by the hand, intent on taking it to paradise; while the
devil (also showing all the signs of materiality) grasps the priest's
soul by the leg with the obvious aim of installing it in hell.
Mr. Bogdanov may well tell us that real animism was also unknown in the fourteenth century. In that case, when exactly did
it first appear? Surely not at the same time as the so-called
"empiriomonist philosophy"!

Secondly, the following must be borne in mind. By simple
necessity, all our concepts have a "material" nature. It is all a

---

* Lucien Turner, *The Hudson Bay Eskimo*, Eleventh Report of the
Bureau of Ethnology, p. 194.
** Ibid., p. 193.
*** Ibid., same page.
**** The kaffirs believe that the shades of the departed live underground,
only they then selves as well as their cattle and huts, i.e., the shades of
their cattle and huts, are very tiny. (*Völkerkunde* von Dr. F. Ratzel, erster
Band, Leipzig, 1888, S. 268.)

question of the number of "material" signs attached to the given concept. The fewer there are of these signs, the more abstract the concept, and the more we are inclined to impart an immaterial nature to it. Here there is a kind of distillation of the concepts forming in man in the course of his acting upon external nature. It cannot be denied that this distillation of concepts is already very much advanced among the lower hunters. If their concept of spirit is firmly entwined with their concept of breathing (and, as is known, not only theirs), this is because, on the one hand, one of the effects of breathing—the motion of the exhaled air—undoubtedly exists, and, on the other, it is almost completely beyond the reach of our senses.* In order to conceive the idea of spirit, the "savage" tries to imagine something that does not act upon the senses. Looking into the eye of a companion, he will sometimes see on the cornea the tiny image of a man. He takes this image to be the soul of the man conversing with him.** He accepts the image as a soul, because he believes it is completely immaterial, that is to say, elusive and impervious to any kind of influence on his part. He forgets, of course, that he *saw* the image, and that, in fact, it *acted on his eye*.*** The question of why the animistic form of thinking is "*fundamental and universal* at a certain stage of development" makes real sense only when formulated quite differently. It should read: why is the belief in gods still extant even in those civilised societies where the productive forces have reached a very high level of development, and which have thus acquired considerable power over nature? The founders of scientific socialism gave the answer to this question long ago, and I presented it in one of my open letters to Mr. Bogdanov. But to grasp the full meaning of this reply, we must once and for all elucidate the problem before us of the origin of animism with which we are faced.

In this respect we can get some interesting pointers from one of the founders of scientific socialism, namely Frederick Engels.

---

* Another cause of this combination of concepts is that the cessation of breathing is the cessation of life.

** Tylor called this image the "pupil image". E. Monseur (*Revue de l'histoire des religions*, 1905, 1-23) speaks of the custom of closing the eyes of the deceased because of the belief that the "pupil image" was a soul.

*** Mach says: "We naturalists look askance at the concept of 'soul', often making fun of it. But matter is an abstraction of exactly the same sort, no better and no worse than the other abstraction. We know just as much about the soul as we do about matter" (E. Mach, *Principle of the Conservation of Work*, St. Petersburg, 1909, p. 31). Mach is very much in error; spirit is an abstraction of a quite different "sort". The concept of spirit is the outcome of the effort *to abstract oneself from the conception of matter*. This is an abstraction of a secondary order, negating the real basis upon which the abstraction of the first order—matter—grows.

In his remarkable work, *Ludwig Feuerbach*, he wrote: "The great basic question of all philosophy, especially of more recent philosophy, is that concerning the relation of thinking and being. From the very early times when men, still completely ignorant of the structure of their own bodies, under the stimulus of dream apparitions came to believe that their thinking and sensation were not activities of their bodies, but of a distinct soul which inhabits the body and leaves it at death—from this time men have been driven to reflect about the relation between this soul and the outside world. If upon death it took leave of the body and lived on, there was no occasion to invent yet another distinct death for it. Thus arose the idea of its immortality, which at that stage of development appeared not at all as a consolation but as a fate against which it was no use fighting, and often enough, as among the Greeks, as a positive misfortune. Not religious desire for consolation, but the quandary arising from the common universal ignorance of what to do with this soul, once its existence had been accepted, after the death of the body, led in a general way to the tedious notion of personal immortality."*

Thus, when people do not know the structure of their own bodies and are at a loss to explain dreams, they form the concept of a soul. In confirmation of this, Engels, quoting Imthurn, makes the following quite true remark: "Among savages and lower barbarians the idea is still universal that the human forms which appear in dreams are souls which have temporarily left their bodies; the real man is, therefore, held responsible for acts committed by his dream apparition against the dreamer."**

The question is not one of authoritarian organisation of production, which is not known among savages and is to be observed only in embryonic form at the lower level of barbarism; it is a question of the technical conditions under which primitive man struggles for existence.

His productive forces are very poorly developed; his power over nature is insignificant. But in the development of human thought *practice* always precedes *theory*; the wider the scope of man's action upon nature, the wider and more correct is his understanding of it. And conversely: the narrower that scope, the weaker his theory. And the weaker his theory, the more readily man turns to the realm of fantasy for an explanation of those phenomena which for some reason have attracted his attention. Underlying all such fantastic explanations of natural life is judgment by analogy. In observing his own actions, primitive man sees that they were preceded by definite wishes, or, to use an expression more like his own way of thinking, that they were *caused* by these

---

* F. Engels, *Ludwig Feuerbach*, St. Petersburg, 1906, pp. 40-41.[175]
** Ibid., page 40, footnote.[176]

wishes. Therefore when he is struck by some natural phenomenon, he puts it down to someone having willed it. The beings whom he assumes to be causing such striking phenomena of nature are beyond the reach of his senses. Therefore he thinks of them as similar to the human soul which, as we already know, is immaterial in the sense described above. The assumption that natural phenomena are caused by the will of beings who are inaccessible to his senses, or accessible only in the very smallest degree, develops and is reinforced under the impact of his hunting way of life. This may seem paradoxical, but it is nevertheless true: the hunt as a means of livelihood disposes man to spiritualism.

Engels says in his book *The Origin of the Family, Private Property and the State*, that exclusively hunting people "figure" only in books, and have never existed, for the fruits of the chase are much too precarious to make that possible.* That is quite correct. The so-called lower hunting tribes fed not only on the meat of animals killed in the chase, but also on the roots of plants and tubers, to say nothing of fish and shell-fish. Yet for all that, contemporary ethnology more and more convinces us that the whole mode of thought of the "savage" is conditioned by the hunt. His conception of the world and even his aesthetical tastes are the world-outlook and tastes of a hunter. In my essay on art[178] (see my collection *For Twenty Years*), expressing the same view with regard to the world-outlook and tastes of the "savage", I quoted von den Steinen who has given a first-rate account of the life and customs of the Brazilian Indians. I shall now repeat that quotation:

"We can only understand these people," he says, "when we regard them as the product of the hunter's way of life. The most important part of their experience is associated with the animal world, and it was on the basis of this experience that their world-outlook was formed. Correspondingly, their art motifs, too, are borrowed with staggering uniformity from the animal world. It may be said that all their wonderfully rich art is rooted in their life as hunters."** All of their mythology is rooted in the same hunting life. Continuing to describe the psychology of the Brazilian Indians, von den Steinen says: "We must erase from our minds completely all distinction between man and animal. Of course, the animal does not have a bow and arrow, or a beetle to crush the grain of the maize, but in the eyes of the Indian that is the principal difference between him and the animal."*** But

---

* *Der Ursprung der Familie, des Privateigenthums und des Staats*, 8-te Auflage, Stuttgart, 1900, S. 2.[177]
** *Unter den Naturvölkern Zentral-Brasiliens*, Berlin, 1894, S. 201. Cf. Frobenius, *Die Weltanschauung der Naturvölker*, Weimar, 1898.
*** Ibid., p. 351.

if there is no distinction between man and animal, and if man possesses a soul, then evidently the animal must have one too. Thus, when the "savage" wonders about natural phenomena, reasoning by analogy, he does so with reference not only to himself, but to the whole animal world.

Like men, animals die. Their deaths, just as with men, are explained by their souls having left their bodies. In this way, the domain of animistic notions is extended even more. Little by little—but, in spite of Mr. Bogdanov, long before the authoritarian organisation of production comes into existence—the whole world turns out to be populated with spirits, and each natural phenomenon that attracts the attention of primitive man has its own "spiritual" explanation. In order to understand how animism originated, there is no need at all to refer to the authoritarian organisation of production, since it was completely non-existent at the first stage of social development.

It is incontestable that the authoritarian organisation of production—and not only of production, *but of the whole of social life*—once it had arisen, began to wield an enormous influence on religious beliefs. This is but a particular case of that general rule according to which, in class-divided society, the development of ideologies proceeds under the most powerful influence of interclass relations. I have mentioned this rule several times in writing of art. But like all rules, it may be understood rightly, and it may also be interpreted in the form of a caricature. Unfortunately, this is how Mr. Bogdanov preferred to interpret it, and consequently ascribed a decisive role to authoritarian relationships even in a society where they did not exist.

Now we may leave Mr. Bogdanov and return to Tylor.

IV

Tylor says: "The early animistic theory of vitality, regarding the functions of life as caused by the soul, offers to the savage mind an explanation of several bodily and mental conditions, as being effects of a departure of the soul or some of its constituent spirits. This theory holds a wide and strong position in savage biology."* Tylor brings forward many examples to reinforce his opinion. Natives of South Australia say that a man in a state of unconsciousness is without soul. The Fiji natives hold the same view. Besides this, they believe that if a soul that has left a body is called upon to return it may do so. It happens that a Fijian stricken with illness and lying on the ground will be heard shouting loudly for his soul to return to his body. The Tatar races of North-

---

* Tylor, op. cit., p. 17.

ern Asia keep strictly to the theory of the departure of the soul
from the body during sickness, and in Buddhist tribes the lamas
use solemn incantations for the return of the soul which has been
abducted from the body of a sick person by an evil spirit.* Tylor
and other researchers have many similar examples, and they are
undoubtedly very convincing. But the instance of the Buddhist
lamas who by their incantations compel the evil spirit to return
the sick man's soul which it has enticed away, does inspire such
questions as: can there be a power then, which is capable of subjecting spirits to its will? And if there is such a power, does it
not follow that the theory of animism, even to the minds of the
savages, does not by any means explain all natural phenomena?

Both these questions must get affirmative replies. Yes, primitive man recognises the existence of a power that is capable of
subjecting even spirits to its will. Yes, the animistic theory does
not explain everything even in the physics and biology of primitive man.

Why? Simply because animism—like spiritualism in general—
in point of fact cannot explain a *single* natural phenomenon.

Let us take one of Tylor's examples.

The sick Fijian calls upon his soul to return. He blames his
illness on its departure. But until he is well again, his illness
will take its course, and since his soul has forsaken him, it is
clear that the further course of his illness will be determined by
some other power and not by the presence of the soul in his body:
the latter is obviously only an explanation of the normal state
of his health.

Further. The sick Fijian's loud calls for the return of his soul
are of no avail and he dies, his soul having spurned the invitation
to re-enter his body. The dead man's corpse starts to decompose.
If the man's death is to be explained by the soul having abandoned
the body, it is again clear that the process of the decomposition
of the corpse has to be explained by some other causes and not
by the action of the departed soul. Facts such as these are legion.
Their undoubted existence is also reflected in the consciousness
of primitive man in the form of a belief that there is some kind
of power (or powers) with the ability to influence even the will
of spirits. Out of this belief come the incantations of the Buddhist
lamas which, in his opinion, must compel the evil spirit to return
the soul it abducted from the human body. These incantations are
part and parcel of the extensive practice of *primitive magic*.

Some modern investigators regard magic as something in the
nature of the natural science of primitive man. In it they see
the embryonic conviction that natural phenomena are governed

_____
* Ibid., pp. 17-18.

by laws. Frazer, for instance, writes: "Thus its fundamental conception is identical with that of modern science; underlying the whole system is a faith, implicit but real and firm, in the order and uniformity of nature."* Thus, Frazer considers that magic as well as science stands in fundamental antagonism to religion, which assumes that the uniform course of nature can be changed by a god or gods at man's request.** There is quite a lot of truth in this. Magic is opposed to religion in the sense that the religious believer explains natural phenomena as the product of the will of the subject (spirit, god), whereas the man who turns to magic for assistance is trying to discover an objective cause behind this will. The antagonism noted by Frazer between religion on the one hand and magic and science on the other is the antagonism between the subjective and objective methods of interpreting phenomena. This contrast was undoubtedly revealed already in the conceptions of savages. But it must not be forgotten that there is a highly important distinction between science and magic. Science aims at discovering the causal connection between phenomena, whereas magic is content with a simple association of ideas, a mere symbolism, which itself may be founded only on an insufficiently clear distinction between what is going on in a man's mind and what is being accomplished in reality. To give an example: to call for rain, the magician of the American Redskins scatters water in a certain way from the roof of his hut.*** The sound and appearance of the water falling from the roof remind him of rain, and he is convinced that this association of ideas is sufficient to cause rain to follow. If it should happen to rain after water has been scattered on the roof, he credits this to the working of his magic. This will suffice to show the immeasurable gap that exists between science and magic.

Magic makes the same mistake as that which, to a high degree, is characteristic of modern empirio-monism. It mixes up objective and subjective phenomena. And just because of this, the ideas that are characteristic of magic exclude those that are associated with animism. Magic is supplemented by animism; animism is supplemented by magic. This is to be seen at every step in absolutely all religions.

Magical acts are a component part of every religious worship. But it is still too soon to speak of this aspect; there are some other sides of primitive man's world-outlook which require elucidation.

---

* J. G. Frazer, *Le Rameau d'or*, Paris, 1903, t. I, p. 64.
** Ibid., p. 66.
*** D. G. Brinton, *Religions of Primitive Peoples*, New York-London, 1899, pp. 173-74.

V

We have seen that animism by its very nature is incapable of furnishing any kind of satisfactory explanation of phenomena, and that even the savage, although a firm believer in animism, does not by any means always resort to animistic explanations. Now it is time to ask ourselves: what particular forms do these explanations take, then, where people are satisfied with them?

A man is convinced that a given phenomenon is the action of some spirit. But just how does he conceive the process whereby the spirit concerned brought about the given phenomenon? It is self-evident that this process will certainly be reminiscent of the processes by which man himself brought into being something he wished to happen.

Here is a vivid example. The question: where did the world come from? is answered by some Polynesians as follows: Once upon a time, God was sitting on the seashore fishing and suddenly pulled out on his hook the world instead of a fish. The primitive fishermen conceived God's actions in the likeness of their own, and such beliefs are shared not only by fishermen. But the actions of the "savage" are confined within the very narrow limits of an extremely low level of technical development. The Bible says: "And the Lord God formed man *of* the dust of the ground, and breathed into his nostrils the breath of life: and man became a living soul."* And when Adam had sinned the Lord God said unto him: "For dust thou *art*, and unto dust shalt thou return."** The belief that man was created by God from "dust", or more exactly, from "*earth*", or still more exactly, from "*clay*", is very widespread among primitive peoples. But this very widely held view implies a particular level of technical development, namely, man's knowledge of pottery. But this knowledge was not acquired by primitive man all at once; far from it. Even to this day, the Veddas of Ceylon do not know the art of pottery.***

Therefore, it would never occur to them to think of man as having been created by God from "earth", in the same way as a potter fashions his articles from clay. The nature of primitive theory regarding the origin of the world is, in general, determined by the level of primitive technique.

It must be remarked, though—and this is exceptionally important for elucidating the causal dependence of thinking on being— that the creation of the world and man is rarely mentioned in

---

* Genesis 2:7.
** Genesis 3:19.
*** "Töpferei ist den Weddas unbekannt." Paul Sarasin (op. cit., p. 129). [Pottery is unknown to the Veddas.]

primitive mythology. The savage "creates" comparatively little; his production is limited chiefly to procuring and appropriating, with as little or as great an effort as may be needed, that which nature provides apart from his own productive efforts. While the man fishes and hunts, the woman gathers wild roots and tubers. The "savage" does not create the animals that sustain him. But his sustenance does depend on his knowledge of the animals' habits, their usual haunts, and so on. This is why the fundamental question answered in his mythology is not *who created* man and the animals, but *where did they come from?* Once the primitive hunter has thought of a reply to this fundamental question, he is satisfied, and his curiosity suggests no further questions. Before his curiosity is again aroused about this matter, he has to make fresh progress in the sphere of technical development.

As an example, here is a myth current among the Australian Dieri. "In the beginning, the earth opened in the middle of lake Peregundi and out of it came one animal after another: the Kaualka—the raven; Katatara, a species of parrot; Warukati-Emu (Australian ostrich) and so on. As they were not fully formed, being without limbs and sense organs, they lay on the dunes surrounding the lake. While they lay stretched out in the sun their strength grew; they at last rose as Kana (i.e., real people) and went away in all directions."* That is all. As you see, God does absolutely nothing; the earth opens of its own accord and the creatures come forth, true, not fully formed, but developing of themselves with the beneficent aid of the sun. The modern Christian would contend that this theory could have been invented only by an atheist, and, indeed, it must be numbered among the theories which claim to explain the evolution of living creatures without resorting to the "hypothesis of God".

This, too, may appear to be paradoxical, but it is also indisputable—the primitive hunter is predominantly an evolutionist. All the really primitive myths known to us are concerned with the development rather than the creation of man and animals. Here are some examples: since I have just quoted Australia, I shall finish with that country by citing one more instance. It is a story told among the Narrinyeri of South Australia, a story of how some fish came into being. Once upon a time there were two hunters: Nurundere and Nepelle. One day they were fishing together in the same lake. Nepelle caught an enormous fish, which his comrade took and cut into small pieces, which he threw into the water: from each of the pieces emerged a particular breed of fish. Some other breeds of fish had a different origin, coming out of flat stones which one of the two fishermen

---

* Van Gennep, op. cit., p. 28.

had thrown into the water.* This is a very far cry from the Christian theory of creation, but not unlike the Greek myth according to which men came from stones.

If we now move from the eucalyptus groves of Australia to the sandy deserts of South Africa, we shall find there an evidently very ancient myth of the Bushmen revealing to us that man and beast came forth from a cave or a crack in the earth's surface somewhere in the north, where, as those well-versed in the matter will tell you, traces left by the first men and animals are still visible. This myth was related by Moffat, a missionary, who thought it to be perfectly absurd. But Moffat admits that the Bushmen found his account of the world's creation equally absurd. They pointed out that since Moffat had never been in paradise, he could not know what went on there, whereas, they said, we can find traces of the first man in the sand.** History is silent as to whether the worthy Christian was able to give a sufficiently convincing answer to this argument, which, after all, is not entirely lacking in wit.

Not far from these Bushmen live (it would be more correct now to say lived) the Ovaherero tribe, against whom the Germans recently waged such an inhuman war of extermination. The Ovahereros are much more developed than the Bushmen; they are not hunters, but typical cattle-breeders. They recount that the first man and the first woman came out of the Omumborombonga tree. From the same tree came neatcattle, and sheep and goats sprang from a flat rock.*** Some Zulus think that men first came out of a bed of reeds, while others believe that they issued from under the ground.****

The tribe of Navajo Indians in New Mexico narrate that all Americans at first lived in a cave, later burrowing their way out into the open, accompanied by all the animals.*****

It is true that these last myths are concerned not so much with the evolution of living beings as with their coming into the world fully developed. However, this in no way contradicts what I have said. The main point for me here is not whether all living creatures first appeared as the outcome of the process of evolution, or always existed in their present form. It is rather: were these beings created by some spirit or other? We have seen that not one of the myths I have related speaks of the creation of living beings. More than that. Ehrenreich, who made a basic study of the South American Indians, says that in those places

---

* Ibid., p. 7.
** A. Lang, *Mythes*, etc., pp. 161-62.
*** Ibid., p. 162.
**** Ibid., pp. 164-65.
***** Ibid., p. 170.

where it is generally believed that men and animals came out of the earth, no one ever asks how they got there in the first place.* The same author remarks in another part of the same book that where the myths have it that man first emerged from under the ground, there is never any mention of his creation. He himself, though, somewhat qualifies this remark. He says that the natives of South America believe that people have always existed, only that they were very few in number at first, and so all the same the need arose subsequently to create new people.** This is undoubtedly a transition from the old mythology to a new one, reflecting the advance of technique and the corresponding increase in man's creative labour in obtaining the means of life. The same Ehrenreich refers to another instance which demonstrates most lucidly how closely mythology is associated with the initial, hesitant steps in technical progress. He tells us of a myth current in the Guarayo tribe, that man was formed out of clay, but that the effort to create him in this fashion succeeded only after several vain attempts.***

Thus the myth regarding the creation of man did not arise all at once. It presupposes some progress in technical development, which, though not very great from our point of view, is nevertheless extremely important in reality. The more technique is perfected, the greater the growth of the productive forces, the more man increases his power over nature, the more established becomes the myth of the world having been created by God.**** This continues until the dialectics of human progress has raised man's power over nature to such a height that the "hypothesis of God" creating the world is no longer necessary. Man then abandons this hypothesis—in the same way as the adult Australian native abandons the hypothesis of the spirit chastising the child for mischief-making—and returns to the point of view of evolution that was characteristic of one of the first stages in the development of his thought. But now he substantiates this hypothesis by recourse to the vast store of knowledge he has acquired in the course of his own development. In this respect, the last phase resembles the first, except that it is immeasurably richer in content.

---

* P. Ehrenreich, *Die Mythen und Legenden*, etc., p. 33.
** Ibid., p. 55.
*** Ibid., same page.
**** In a locality of Ancient Egypt, the god Khnum is portrayed as a potter shaping an egg. This was the first egg, out of which the whole world developed. This is an eclectic myth, combining in itself the primitive theory of evolution and the doctrine of the creation of the world by God. In Memphis it was said that the god Phtah built the world as a mason would erect a building. In Sais they believed that the world was *woven* by a goddess, and so forth. (P. D. Chantepie de la Saussaye, *Manuel d'histoire des religions*, Paris, 1909, p. 122.)

VI

Primitive man thinks of himself as being very close to the animal. The seemingly strange circumstance that tribal savages consider themselves connected with animals *by ties of blood relationship* therefore becomes quite understandable.

Totemism is characterised by a belief in kinship between a certain blood-related group of people and a particular species of animal. Here, I have in view the so-called *animal* totemism. Besides it, there is *vegetable* totemism, a belief in mutual relation between men and *plants*. I shall not dilate upon the last-named here, since its nature will be sufficiently clear to any one who can correctly grasp the meaning of animal totemism. Moreover, there is every reason to believe that vegetable totemism arose much later, and was formed on the basis of concepts connected with animal totemism.*

For greater clarity, let us take an example. We shall assume that the totem of a particular clan is the turtle. In this case, the clan believes that the turtle is a blood relative; consequently, it will not only do him no harm, but, on the contrary, it will take the clan members under its protection. For their part, the clan members must not harm the turtle. Killing the turtle is considered in the clan to be a heinous offense; should one of the clan happen by chance on a dead one, he is obliged by clan custom to bury it with the same rites observed at the burial of members.** Should he be forced by extreme necessity—say, famine—to kill a turtle, the clansman must solemnly beg its forgiveness for having shown such patent disrespect. When scarcity of food compels a Redskin with a bear totem to kill one of these animals, he does not simply ask forgiveness, but he invites the bear to eat of its own flesh at the feast which usually accompanies a happy hunt.*** I do not know if the bear is always mollified by such unusual politeness, but the fact is that the animal totem is capable of taking terrible revenge upon its blood relatives for its killing. Thus, the natives of Samoa who have the turtle as their totem believe that if any one of them eats the flesh of the turtle he will

---

* See Frank Byron Jevons, *An Introduction to the History of Religion*, Third edition, London, p. 115.

** Similarly, the Greeks considered it impermissible to eat the lobster. On one of the islands in the Aegean Sea, it was customary to weep over lobsters that were accidentally found dead, and to give them a ceremonial burial. Some scientists think that the wolf enjoyed similar privileges in Athens (Frazer, *Le totémisme*, Paris, 1898, p. 23). Since this book was published, Frazer has modified his view on the *origin* of totemism, but his *characterisation* of it remains the most comprehensive yet. More on totemism can be read in *Wundt's* work on the question, Vol. II, Part 2, p. 238 et seq.

*** Frazer, op. cit.

certainly grow ill. Moreover, they add that more than once a voice
has been heard coming from the inside of a sick man, saying:
"He ate me; I am killing him."* The voice is obviously that of
the spirit of the eaten turtle. But, on the other hand, where
people respect their totem animal, it will be well disposed towards
them. In Senegambia, for instance, the Negroes of the Scorpion
clan are never bitten by these creatures, which are of a very deadly
kind in that locality.** But that is not all. In the same Senegambia, members of the Serpent clan have the enviable capacity
to heal by their touch persons who have been bitten by serpents.***
In Australia the animal totem, for example the kangaroo, warns
its blood relations of an approaching enemy. The Kurnai tribe,
also of Australia, have as their totem the crow, which answers
their questions by cawing.**** In Samoa, the natives of the Owl
clan watched the flight of the owl when marching to war; if it
flew before them in the direction of the enemy, that was taken
as a signal to go on; if it flew backwards, it was a sign to retreat,
and so on. Some of these tribes kept tame owls on purpose to
give omens in war.*****

Sometimes the totem-animal renders, so to speak, meteorolog-
ical service. During a fog the men of the Turtle subclan of the
Omahas in North America draw the figure of a turtle on the ground
with its head to the south, placing some tobacco on the drawing.
In this way they hope to make the fog disappear.*)

Without going into the question of totemism in greater detail,
I shall add this. When a particular clan is subdivided into
two parts, the totem also takes on a split character. Among the
Iroquois there thus appeared, for instance, the Grey Wolf and
Yellow Wolf clans and the Great Turtle and Little Turtle clans,
and so on.**) And when two clans merge, their totem animals
take the form of something in the nature of the Greek chimera:
it is formed from two different animals.***)

Primitive man does not only admit the possibility of kinship
between himself and a species of animal, but also quite often
takes his own ancestry from this species and attributes to it
all his cultural acquirements, however poor. Here again modern
ethnologists do not see anything surprising. Von den Steinen,
whom I have time and again cited, says: "Indeed, the Indian

---

* Frazer, p. 26.
** Ibid., p. 30.
*** Ibid., p. 33.
**** Ibid., p. 34. Incidentally, in Australia they do not use the
American word *totem*; they use the word *kobong*.
***** Frazer, p. 35.
*) Ibid., p. 36.
**) Ibid., p. 89.
***) Ibid., p. 92.

is obliged to the ... animals for the most important part of his
culture.... The teeth, bones, shells of animals are his working
tools, without which he could not produce his weapons or utensils.... Every child knows that the animals, the hunting of which
is the essential precondition for that production, shall provide
the most indispensable things."* Ehrenreich makes exactly the
same point: "Animals supply man with the instruments of his
labour and with cultivated plants, and their myths relate how
man received these boons from their animal brothers."** In
North America, according to A. Krause, a reliable authority,
the entire mythology of the Tlingit Indians revolves round El
the raven, credited with having created the world and being the
benefactor of mankind.*** Andrew Lang tells us that in the mythology of the Bushmen, who undoubtedly belong to the lowest
stage of hunting tribes, animals play an almost exclusive role,
the chief figure being Cagn who is a creative grasshopper.****
Animals also dominate the mythology of native Australian tribes;
it is not without interest to note that some of them play the part of
Prometheus, trying to bring fire for the use of man.***** True, in
Australian mythology there are animals which try to conceal
the use of fire from man. But this, of course, makes no difference
to the main point. And it all shows in the clearest possible way
that in the savage's conception of the world there is, indeed, no
dividing line between himself and the animals, and all this makes
explicable for us why he initially conceives his gods in the form
of animals. The Greek philosopher Xenophanes was mistaken
when he said that man always creates his god in his own image
and likeness. No, at the beginning he creates his god in the image
and likeness of an animal. Man-like gods appeared only later,
as a consequence of man's new successes in developing his productive forces. But even for a long time afterwards deep traces
of zoomorphism are preserved in man's religious ideas. It is
enough to recall the worship of animals in ancient Egypt and
the fact that statues portraying Egyptian gods very often had
the heads of beasts.

VII

But what exactly is a god? We know that primitive man believes
in the existence of numerous spirits. But not every spirit by far
is a god. For a long time people believed, and many still do, in

---

  * Von den Steinen, op. cit., p. 354.
 ** Ehrenreich, op. cit., p. 28.
 *** Dr. Aurel Krause, *Die Tlinkit-Indianer*, Jena, 1885, S. 253, 266-67.
**** A. Lang, *Mythes, cultes et religions*, Paris, 1896, pp. 331-32.
***** There is the example of the part played by the falcon in the mythology
of one of the tribes of Victoria (Arnold van Gennep, *Mythes et légendes d'Aust-
ralie*, Paris, p. 83. Year of publication not indicated; preface written in 1881).

the existence of the devil. But the devil is not a god. What are the features that distinguish this latter concept?

Payne defines a god as "a benevolent" (to man—*G.P.*) "spirit, permanently embodied in some tangible object, usually an image" (an idol—*G.P.*), "and to whom food, drink, and so on, are regularly offered for the purpose of securing assistance in the affairs of life."*

This definition must be recognised as correct in application to a very prolonged period of cultural development. But it is not quite correct when applied to man's first steps on the road of culture.

While man conceived of his god in the form of a beast, he regarded the god as embodied, not in some inanimate object, but in that species of particular animal. The totem animals must be regarded as the very first gods ever worshipped by man.

Besides, Payne's definition presupposes a stage of the individualisation of gods which is reached only after a lengthy period of time. In the epoch of totemism, what serves as god is neither an individual nor a more or less numerous group of individuals, but a whole animal species or animal variety: the bear, the turtle, the wolf, the crocodile, the owl, the eagle, the lobster, the scorpion, and so forth. The human personality has not yet completely separated from its blood kinship, and the process of the individualisation of gods has accordingly not yet begun. In this first period, we encounter the remarkable phenomenon that god, or, more exactly, the divine clan, is not concerned about human morals, as are, for instance, the gods of the Christians, the Jews, the Mahommedans, etc. The primitive divine clan metes out punishment only for sins committed against it personally. We are aware that if the Samoan islander consumes his turtle totem he is punished by illness and by death. But, here too, at first it is not the individual that is subject to punishment, but his entire kindred. Blood feud is the basic rule of the primitive Themis. I should point out, by the way, that it is precisely because of this that primitive man is not at all disposed to what is nowadays called religious liberty: god punishes him for the sins of his kinsmen, sometimes, as Jehovah did, to the fourth generation, so that even the most simple prudence on the part of primitive man impelled him to note carefully how his blood relations conducted themselves in respect to their god. Consciousness is determined by being.

Psychology of this variety gives rise to facts such as the following.

---

* Quoted by Andrew Lang in his book *The Making of Religion*. London. 1900, p. 161.

Spencer and Gillen inform us that some of the natives of Central Australia bring up their children "in the fear of God", as we would call it now, that is to say, inculcate them with the belief that they will be punished by certain spirits for misbehaving. When the young people reach the age of maturity and become fully-fledged members of the tribe, they are informed by the elders during the performance of rites in connection with their coming of age that such spirits do not exist and that the tribe itself will punish them for any misconduct. W. S. Berkeley tells us exactly the same about some natives of Tierra del Fuego. They persuade their children that they will be chastised if they get up to mischief by the forest-spirit (something in the nature of the Russian wood-goblin), or it might be the hill-spirit or the cloud-spirit, and so on. To convince the children that there really are such spiritual pedagogues, the parents dress up as make-believe spirits, decorate themselves with twigs, or smear themselves with white paint: in short, they assume a terrifying appearance to put fear into the children. But when the children (properly speaking, the boys) reach the age of fourteen and are recognised as adults, the elders, after teaching them the entire code of morals, confess that the terrifying spirits were really their fellow-tribesmen, and for greater emphasis the elders acquaint the boys with the methods used in imitating the spirits. Having been initiated into this important secret, the boys are then sworn sacredly to preserve the mystery from the women and the children. Breach of this law is punishable by death.*

The Australian aborigines and the natives of Tierra del Fuego belong to the very lowest of the now known savage tribes. They do not question the existence of spirits, but they think that only a child would believe that spirits are interested in human morality. At this stage of social development, morality exists quite independently of animistic notions. Later, morality and animism fuse firmly together. We shall soon see the social causes that give rise to this interesting psychological phenomenon. Now we must dwell on some instructive survivals of totemism.

Despite the widespread practice of prohibiting the slaughter of totem animals, there is a custom allowing the animal to be used for food, providing certain rituals are observed. This seeming paradox may be explained by the fact that the clan, although feeling bound by the closest ties of kinship with the animal concerned, hoped, and, indeed, thought it essential to strengthen these ties by ceremonially consuming the flesh of their totem animal. When carried out for this motive, the slaughter of the

---

* J. G. Frazer, "The Beginnings of Religion and Totemism among the Australian Aborigines" (*The Fortnightly Review*, July 1905, pp. 166-67).

sacred animal is not considered sinful, but, on the contrary, an act of piety. Primitive religion, which forbade the killing of the god, stipulated that his flesh must be eaten from time to time. At a higher level of religious development, this custom was replaced by human sacrifices to the god. Thus, the inhabitants of ancient Arcadia periodically made human sacrifices to Zeus, they themselves eating the flesh of the sacrificed victim, believing thereby that they were transformed into wolves; whence they called one another wolves (lykoi) and Zeus wolf-like (Zeus lykaios).* Here it is clear that the human sacrifice has taken the place of the former recurrent feasting on the flesh of the totem wolf.

The Arcadian "wolf"-folk, at one time ceremonially eating wolf-meat, began later to eat human flesh, that of the victim brought to Zeus as a sacrifice. Zeus then was portrayed as wolf-like (lykaios), proving that he had taken the place of the old wolf-god, growing from the wolf after a prolonged period of social development. If man believed in a blood relationship between himself and the animal, it is not surprising that his god, when adopting human form, still retained memories of his old kinsmen—the animals. When the animal-like (zoomorphic) conception of god gives way to the man-like (anthropomorphic) conception, the animal which formerly was a totem becomes a so-called attribute. We know, for example, that among the ancient Greeks the eagle was an attribute of Zeus, the owl an attribute of Minerva, and so on.

VIII

Why did totemism disintegrate? As a result of changes in the material conditions of human life.

The changes in the material conditions of life are expressed above all in the growth of the productive forces of primitive man: in other words, in the increase of his power over nature And this brings a corresponding change in his attitude to nature Marx said that by acting on the external world and changing it man changes his own nature.[179] To this might be added that in changing his own nature, man also changes his ideas about the world around him. But when this happens, a more or less radical modification of his religious conceptions naturally takes place. We already know that at one time man did not contrast himself to animals; on the contrary, in very many cases he considered himself to be inferior to them. This was the time of the origin of totemism. Later the time gradually came when man began to realise

---

* S. Reinach, *Cultes, Mythes et religions*, Tome I, Paris, 1905, p. 16.

his superiority over animals, and to draw a contrast between himself and them. Then totemism had necessarily to disappear. The most extreme point of the contrasting of man to animal was reached in the Christian religion,* although, of course, the process itself began very much earlier. To explain the origin of this process, I shall quote Mr. Bogdanov (suum cuique!). His theory of "authoritarian organisation" of primitive production is a caricature. But the idea which Mr. Bogdanov offered us in the form of a caricature is absolutely correct. Where there are "authoritarian relations" the master looks down on his subject; therefore, he does not try to liken himself but rather to contrast himself to the subject. We have therefore only to assume the existence of "authoritarian" relations between men and animals in order to grasp the psychological background of the contrast between them with which we are concerned. Such relations are, indeed, to be found where man has domesticated an animal and uses it for his own needs. It may, therefore, be said that man's exploitation of the animal is the cause of his becoming inclined to set himself in contrast to it. However, this inclination did not come about all at once; far from it. Many pastoral tribes, such as the African Batokas on the upper reaches of the Zambezi river, exploit their bulls and cows, of course, but at the same time, to use Schweinfurth's expression, almost idolise them, slaughtering them only in extremity, and using only their milk.** The man of the tribe doesn't object to making himself resemble the cow, even to the point of extracting his top incisors. This is a far cry from man being in contrast to the animal.*** But when the man harnesses the ox to the plough or the horse to the cart he is hardly

---

* Elsewhere—see my article "On Art" published in the collection *For Twenty Years*—I said that this contrast was reflected also in aesthetic tastes. I quoted Lotze's opinion, which it will not be out of place to repeat in part here: "In dieser Idealisierung der Natur liess sich die Sculptur von Fingerzeigen der Natur selbst leiten; sie überschätzte hauptsächlich Merkmale, die den Menschen vom Thiere unterscheiden." (Lotze, *Geschichte der Aesthetik in Deutschland*, München, 1868, S. 568.) [In its idealisation of Nature, sculpture was guided by the finger of Nature itself; it chiefly overvalued features which distinguish man from the animal.]
** Schweinfurth, *Au Coeur de l'Afrique*, Paris, 1875, t. I, p. 148.
*** The primitive religion of the Persians, i.e., their religion in the epoch before Zoroaster, was the religion of a pastoral people. Both the cow and the dog were treated as sacred and even divine. They played a big part in ancient Persian mythology and cosmogony, and left their imprint even on the language. The expression "I gave the cow plenty to eat" meant in general: "I have fulfilled my duties completely". The expression "I have bought a cow" meant: "By my good deeds I have earned myself glory in heaven", and so on. It is scarcely possible to find a more vivid example of how man's consciousness is determined by his being (Cf. Chantepie de la Saussaye, op. cit., p. 445).

likely to feel any great similarity with these animals.* The farmer treasures his cattle and is proud of their good condition. He is ready to place them under the protection of a special god. There are cases in some parts of Russia where Frol and Lavr are looked up to as the guardians of domestic animals, and where special prayers are offered up to them under the open skies and in the presence of the cattle driven in from the surrounding villages by the supplicating peasants. G. I. Uspensky says in one of his sketches that the word "Sabaoth" is pronounced by the peasants as "Samoov" [Samo-ov—"Sheep himself"—Tr.] and is understood by them in the sense of the sheep's god, i.e., the most trustworthy guardian of the sheep. But naturally this "most sheepish" god did not have the actual form of a sheep in the minds of the peasants Uspensky was writing about. Agricultural life is not particularly favourable for the zoomorphism of religious ideas. True, religion is always very conservative; it always clings tenaciously to the obsolete. But the ancient ideas that arose in the conditions of primitive hunting life scarcely conform to the nature of agricultural labour, and disappear more or less rapidly. Numerous relics of the growth of man-gods from animal-gods have been preserved for us from ancient Egypt in the form of gods with animal and bird heads.

Now I shall ask the reader to recall the famous words: "If bulls had a religion, their gods would be bulls." Xenophanes believed that the idea of man also conceiving his god in the form of a bull is unthinkable. He maintained the views that sprung up on the train of agricultural life, and which, after reaching a considerable degree of development, presuppose the existence of "authoritarian" relations between man and bull. But what is the source of such relations? How is the domestication of animals generally accomplished?

Modern ethnologists find the answer in causal connection with totemism. When men undertake to care for a particular species or a particular variety of animal, it is plain that they will domesticate those which by nature are capable of being domesticated—

---

* The domestication of animals is still far removed from their being used for work. It is not so easy to see, either, how man, even if a "savage", decided to put his own blood relative—god—to work. But first of all, the idea of utilising the domesticated god for labour could have arisen in other tribes, which did not regard the animal as a sacred relative. Secondly, in primitive religion there are also "arrangements avec le bon Dieu". Thus some tribes of New South Wales will not themselves kill the animals that serve them as totems, but entrust this to strangers and then do not consider it a sin to eat their flesh. The Narrinyeri hold a different view in their religious casuistry, abstaining from the use of their totem as food only if it is an emaciated specimen, while they eat plump specimens without a twinge of conscience (Frazer, op. cit., p. 29).

different animals, of course, have different natures. But from
the domestication of animals there is a direct though long way
to their exploitation, and also to their use as a labour force.
What follows from this?

When man begins to utilise animals as a labour force he thereby
increases his productive forces quite significantly. And the growth
in the productive forces gives an impetus to the development of
socio-economic relations. It seems that we have reached a conclusion not in keeping with the basic thesis of historical materialism, viz., that consciousness is determined by being, and not
being by consciousness. Now I have advanced a fact which apparently makes out that men's being—their *economic* being, the development of their economic relations—is, contrary to the above
thesis, determined by their religious consciousness. Totemism
leads to the domestication of animals; the domestication of animals brings opportunities to exploit some of them as a labour
force, and the beginning of this exploitation signalises an epoch
in the development of the productive forces of society, and, consequently, in its economic structure. What can be said about
this?

Ten to fifteen years ago, some German scientists averred in
this connection that the advances in modern ethnology refuted
Marx's historical theory. I shall cite one book only, that of E. Hahn,
Die Haustiere, etc., published in 1896. Hahn wrote a very valuable
work, full of most precious factual material, but betraying his
very meagre knowledge of historical materialism: no better knowledge, incidentally, than that of the "revisionists" who appeared
some years afterwards and imagined that the theory of historical
materialism does not allow for man's consciousness exerting
influence on social being. The "revisionists" regarded this as a sign
of the "one-sidedness" of the historical theory of Marx and Engels.
When they were confronted with extracts from the works and
letters of Marx and Engels proving the falsity of this charge, the
"revisionists" said that the extracts cited dated from a later period
in the life of the founders of scientific socialism, a period when
Marx and Engels themselves had noted and were trying to correct
this one-sidedness. Elsewhere,* I exposed, I make bold to say,
the utter absurdity of this argument. In an analysis of the *Manifesto*, written by Marx and Engels in the early period of their
literary activity, I demonstrated that in expounding historical
materialism they always recognised that human consciousness,
stemming from the given social being, in turn influences this
being, thereby promoting its further development, which intro-

---

* In the preface to the second edition of my translation of the *Manifesto
of the Communist Party.*[180]

duces new modifications again in the field of ideology. Historical materialism does not deny the interaction of human consciousness and social being. All it says is that the fact of this interaction does not solve the problem of the origin of both these forces. In regard to the latter question, the theory of historical materialism establishes the causal dependence of the given content of consciousness on the given content of being.

The domestication of animals—if it was in fact a consequence of totemism*—may serve as a graphic illustration of this theory. On a particular economic basis—that of primitive hunting life— there grows up a primitive form of religious consciousness, totemism. This form of religious consciousness engenders and consolidates relations between the primitive hunters and certain species of animals which promote a quite significant increase in the productive forces of the hunting tribes. The increase in the productive forces modifies man's attitude to Nature and, in particular, his conception of the animal world. Man begins to contrast himself to animals. This gives a very strong impetus to the development of anthropomorphic conceptions of gods; totemism has outlived its day. Being gives rise to consciousness, which, in turn, influences being and thereby prepares the way for its own further modification.

If one compares the so-called New World with the Old World, it will be seen that totemism had much greater vitality in the New than it did in the Old. Why was this? Because in the New World, apart from the llama alone, there were no animals which, when domesticated, could have had any great significance in the economic life of man. Thus one of the most important conditions of the disappearance of totemism was absent there. On the other hand, such conditions were at hand in the Old World and so totemism sooner disintegrated there, leaving the way open for new forms of religious consciousness.**

But in pointing out what to me is a most important fact, I have as yet discovered only one side of the dialectical process of social development. Now we must look at the other side.

IX

Lewis H. Morgan, in his well-known work *Ancient Society*, notes that the religious rites of the ancient Romans seem to have had their primary connection with the gens rather than

---

* I say "if" because we are concerned here with a hypothesis—a very clever one, but as yet still a hypothesis. In any case, it is very difficult to believe that totemism was the *only* source of the domestication of animals.
** Cf. Frank Byron Jevons, *An Introduction*, etc., pp. 182-88.

the family.* This is incontestable, and is explained by the fact that the system of consanguinity, or blood relatives, preceded the family system and not vice versa. The Roman patriarchal family originated comparatively very late from the break-up of the gens life under the impact of agriculture and slavery.** But with this family there also appeared family gods (Dii manes) and family divine service in which the part of the priest was played by the head of the family.*** Social being here, too, determined religious consciousness.

The gods of the patriarchal family were ancestral gods. And inasmuch as the members of the family had filial attachment to its head, they accorded the same sentiment to the ancestral gods. Thus the psychological groundwork was laid for the idea that man must love God as children do their father. Primitive man did not know his father as a particular individual. To him, the word "father" designated every one of his blood relations who had reached a prescribed age. Therefore, primitive man knew nothing of a son's duties as we know these. In place of such duties, he was conscious of a bond of solidarity with all his blood relation. We have seen already how his consciousness of this solidarity extended into a consciousness of solidarity with the divine animal-totem. Now we are witnessing something different. The evolution of sentiment is conditioned by the evolution of social relations.

But the disintegration of the system of consanguinity leads to more than the formation of the family. *Tribal* organisation is replaced by *state* organisation. What is meant by the state?

The state, like religion, is variously defined. The American ethnologist Powell describes it this way: "The state is a body politic, an organised group of men with an established government, and a body of determined laws."**** I think this definition could do with some changes and additions. But at the moment I am quite satisfied to leave it as it is.

The institution of government implies certain relations between governors and governed. The governors assume the obligation to look after the welfare of the governed, and the governed recognise a duty to submit to the governors. Moreover, where there are

---

* See page 245 of the German translation of his book, *Die Urgesellschaft*, Stuttgart, 1891. [Lewis H. Morgan, op. cit., Chicago, Charles H. Kerr & Company. S. d. p. 297.]

** Morgan, op. cit., pp. 396-97. [P. 477, p. 478.]

*** F. B. Jevons writes: "It is still a much disputed question what was the original form of human marriage, but in any case the family seems to be a later institution than the clan or community, whatever its structure and family gods consequently are later than the gods of the community" (Jevons, *An Introduction*, etc., p. 180). [Quoted in English by Plekhanov.]

**** [Quoted in English by Plekhanov.]

determined laws, there naturally are also people who guard these laws professionally: legislators and judges. All these relations among people find their fantastic expression in religion. The gods become celestial governors and celestial judges. If the aborigines of Australia and Tierra del Fuego think that the belief that spirits punish for misbehaviour is only for children, this belief becomes very widespread and very deep-rooted with the formation of the state. Thus, animistic notions become firmly merged with morality.

Primitive man believes that after death his existence will be just as it was before death. If he does allow for any differences, these bear no relation at all to his morality. If he believes that his clan issued from the turtle, he will not be averse to the idea that after death he himself will become a turtle. To him, the expression "Rest in the Lord" would mean: "Once more adopt the form of a beast, or a fish, or a bird, or an insect, and so forth". We have a relic of this belief in the doctrine of the transmigration of souls which is very widespread even among civilised peoples. For example, India is a classical country of this doctrine. But among civilised nations the belief in the transmigration of souls is closely united with the conviction that after death comes the judgment of man's conduct on earth. "The rules are set forth in the book of Manu," says Tylor, "how souls endowed with the quality of goodness acquire divine nature, while souls governed by passion take up the human state, and souls sunk in darkness are degraded to brutes. Thus the range of migration stretches downward from gods and saints, through holy ascetics, Brahmans, nymphs, kings, counsellors, to actors, drunkards, birds, dancers, cheats, elephants, horses, Sudras, barbarians, wild beasts, snakes, worms, insects and inert things. Obscure as the relation mostly is between the crime and its punishment in a new life, there may be discerned through the code of penal transmigration an attempt at appropriateness of penalty and an intention to punish the sinner wherein he sinned."*

The belief in the transmigration of souls is a survival from that extremely remote period when there was still no dividing line in man's perception between him and the animal. This survival was not equally strong everywhere. We come across only very weak allusions to it in the beliefs of the people of ancient Egypt. But its absence did not prevent the Egyptians from being convinced that in the other world there are judges who punish

---

* Tylor, op, cit., p. 82. Cf. also L. de Milloué, *Le brahmanisme*, Paris, 1905, p. 138. [Edward B. Tylor, *Primitive Culture. Researches into the Development of Mythology, Philosophy, Religion, Language, Art, and Custom*, Vol. II, London 1903, pp. 9-10.]

or reward men according to their behaviour in life. As everywhere else, in Egypt this conviction was not elaborated all at once. In the first period of the existence of the Egyptian state, it was evidently considered that man's conduct in life had no influence on his existence beyond the grave. Only subsequently, in the Theban epoch, did the opposite view prevail.*

According to the Egyptian faith, man's soul was committed to judgment after death and the sentence passed upon it determined its further existence. But it is noteworthy that this perspective of divine justice did not eliminate the conception among the Egyptians that people of different social classes would also lead different lives beyond the grave.

Egypt is an agricultural land, depending wholly for its existence on the Nile floods. To bring order into this flooding, a whole system of canals was created already in the depths of antiquity. Work on these canals was a natural obligation upon the Egyptian peasants. But the people of the upper classes escaped this obligation by appointing proxies. This circumstance was reflected also in the ideas of the Egyptians about life after death.

The Egyptian peasant was convinced that when he died he would be called on to dig and clean canals in the other world too. He reconciled himself to this proposition, probably consoling himself with the consideration that he could "do nothing" about it. The people of the upper classes did not relish this prospect at all and a very simple method was devised to reassure them. Dolls (Ushabti) were placed in their graves, whose souls were to work for them in the other world. But the most prudent people were not content with this safeguard alone; they wondered: "But what will happen if the souls of these dolls refuse to work for me and go over to my enemies?" To prevent this happening, some of them—probably the more wise and inventive—ordered this edifying inscription to be put on the dolls: "Hearken only to the one who made you, hearken not to his enemies."**

If we turn now from the Egyptians to the ancient Greeks, we shall see how their ideas on life after death also combined only gradually with the conception of punishment in the future life for earthly sins. True, Ulysses meets "Minos, glorious son of Zeus", in Hades; Minos sits in judgment on the shades of the dead:

> *Wielding a golden sceptre,*
> *giving sentence from his throne to the dead,*
> *while they sat and stood around the prince*
> *asking his dooms through the wide-gated house of Hades.*

---

* Chantepie de la Saussaye, op. cit., pp. 106-107.
** *La religion égyptienne*, par A. Erman, Traduction franç. par. Ch. Vidal, Paris, 1907, pp. 201-02, 266. [Adolf Erman, *Die ägyptische Religion*.]

But, in describing further his stay among the shades of the deceased, Ulysses recalls the torment only of such outstanding sinners as Tityos, Sisyphus, and Tantalus culpable mainly of sinning against the gods; in their ways of life in Hades, the remaining shades are indistinguishable from one another. The "lady mother" of Ulysses, Anticleia, is in exactly the same spot as the hateful wife Eriphyle

who took fine gold for the price of her dear lord's life.

This is quite different from *The Divine Comedy*, in which Dante apportions torment or bliss in strict conformity to man's earthly behaviour. Moreover, in the Greek heroic period, the shades of the rulers who descend into the house of Hades remain as rulers, and the shades of the subjects remain as subjects. In *The Odyssey* Ulysses says to Achilles:

*We Argives gave thee one honour with the gods
and now thou art a great prince among the dead.
Wherefore let not thy death be any grief to thee, Achilles.*

But by Plato's time there was evidently a widely-held belief that life after death was fully determined by man's conduct on earth. Plato taught that people must expect rewards in the other world for good deeds and punishments for sins. In the Tenth Book of his *Republic* he makes Er the Pamphylian, whose soul has visited the other world, depict the frightful torment of the sinners, especially patricides and tyrants.

It is interesting that the torments are inflicted by terrifying, apparently fiery monsters. In these monsters it is not difficult to recognise ancestors of the Christian devils.

X

I said that religion represents a more or less orderly system of ideas, sentiments, and actions. After what we have learned of the religions of various tribes and peoples, we should have no difficulty in realising how the first two of the three elements, viz., ideas and sentiments, originated.

Religious ideas are animistic in character and are the outcome of man's inability to comprehend natural phenomena. Subsequently, the ideas arising from this source are joined by those animistic conceptions by means of which people personify and explain their relations among themselves.

As far as religious sentiments are concerned, they are founded on the feelings and aspirations of men which stem from particular social relations, and they change parallel with the changes in these relations.

Both one and the other—ideas and sentiments—can be explained only with the help of the proposition which runs: it is not consciousness that determines being, but being that determines consciousness.

It now remains for me to say something about the actions that are associated with religious ideas and sentiments. We already know in part how these actions are related to such ideas and sentiments. At a certain stage of cultural development, animistic ideas and the sentiments connected with them coalesce with morality in the broadest sense of the word, that is to say, with the conceptions people have of their reciprocal obligations. Man then begins to regard these obligations as commandments of God. But although the conception of these obligations merges with animistic ideas, it does not by any means spring from them. Morality appears prior to the start of the process whereby ideas related to morality are knitted together with belief in the existence of gods. Religion does not create morality. It only sanctifies its rules, which grow out of a particular social system.

There are actions of another kind. They are inspired not by the relations between men, but by the relationship between men and gods or God. The totality of these actions is known as religious worship, or *cult*.

There is no need for me to dwell at length in this article on religious worship. I shall remark only that if man creates his god in his own image and likeness—and we now know that, within certain limits which I have indicated, that is quite correct—it is clear that he will conceive of his relationship with the "higher powers", too, in the image and likeness of the relationships prevailing in the society to which he belongs, and which are familiar to him. This is also confirmed, by the way, by the example of totemism. It is further confirmed by the fact that in the eastern despotisms the chief gods were conceived of in the form of eastern despots, while in the Greek Olympus there prevailed relationships which were very reminiscent of the structure of Greek society in the Heroic age.

In his worship of the gods (in his cult) man performs those actions which appear necessary to him for the fulfilment of his obligations to the gods or God.* We already know that in return man expects certain services from the gods as a reward.

---

* Gods are stronger than men. (Daniel Brinton says: "The god is one who can do more than man." [Quoted in English by Plekhanov.]—*Religions of Primitive Peoples*, New York-London, 1899, p. 81.) But it is very difficult, and perhaps impossible, for them to do without the help of men. The gods are, first of all, in need of nourishment. The Caraibes build special huts in which they lock up the sacrifices they bring for the gods. And they even hear the champing of the gods' jaws as they devour the food. (A. Bros, *La religion des peuples non civilisés*, p. 135.) Many

At the beginning, the relations between god and man resemble relations based on a mutual covenant, or, more exactly, on blood relationship. In the measure that social power develops, these relations change in the sense of man's ever-growing consciousness of his subordination to God. This subordination reaches its most advanced stage in despotic states. In modern civilised societies, alongside the efforts to limit the powers of kings, came the trend towards "natural religion" and to deism, that is, to a system of ideas wherein the power of God is restricted on all sides by the *laws of Nature*. Deism is celestial parliamentarism.

However, it is unquestionable, too, that even where man imagines himself to be the slave of his god, his worship always leaves a more or less considerable scope for magic, i.e., for actions aimed at *compelling* the god to render certain services. We already know that the objective viewpoint of magic is the opposite of the subjective viewpoint of animism. The magician appeals to necessity in order to influence the *arbitrariness* of gods.

These, then, are the conclusions which we have drawn from an analysis of the component parts of religion. (They will help us to comprehend the real nature of the religious seekings now going on in Russia. In studying these seekings, we shall see that some of them are an attempt to revive now dying animistic ideas. Those being conducted by Messrs Bulgakov, Merezhkovsky, Struve, and Minsky are of this nature. The representatives of other searches would like to eliminate the animistic conceptions in religion, while keeping its other elements intact. Such are Mr. Lunacharsky, and partly also Leo Tolstoy.

We shall also try to clear up the theoretical and practical value of the diverse searches of this kind. We shall see how these attempts themselves confirm by their very existence the correctness of the fundamental proposition of historical materialism:

---

gods are very fond of feasting on human flesh. Human sacrifices are known to be quite common among primitive tribes. When the Iroquois made a human sacrifice to their god, they used to say the following prayer: "We bring Thee this sacrifice so that Thou mayest feed on human flesh and so that Thou wilt help us to win happiness and victory over our enemies" (A. Bros, ibidem, p. 136). Nothing could be more explicit: do ut des, I give to Thee, so that Thou wilt give to me. But gods do not live by food alone; they also like to be entertained by dancing, which explains the origin of the sacred dances. When the gods become settled in their way of life—together with the people who worship them—they feel the need for a permanent abode; then comes the building of temples, etc., etc. In brief, gods have the same requirements as men, and these requirements change as the faithful advance along the road of cultural development. The greater the heights reached by man's moral development, the more disinterested their gods become. The prophet Hosea (6:6) has Jehovah saying: "For I desired mercy, and not sacrifice; and the knowledge of God more than burnt offerings." Kant thought it was possible to reduce religion to a view of moral duties as divine commandments.

it is not being that is determined by consciousness, but consciousness that is determined by being. But already at this stage I feel justified in asserting that⟩ any attempt to eradicate the element of animism from religion contradicts the very nature of religion and is therefore doomed to failure. To eliminate animism from religion is to leave us only with morality in the widest meaning of the term. But morality is not religion. Morality appears before religion and can get along without its sanction.

Hydrochloric acid is a combination of chlorine and hydrogen. Take away the hydrogen and you are left with chlorine, but you will no longer have hydrochloric acid. Take away chlorine, and you will have hydrogen, but again no hydrochloric acid.

⟨True, someone may point to Buddhism, which many investigators believe to be utterly alien to animism. If they were correct, my view would not stand up to criticism. Buddhism has about 500 million followers. In this respect—the numbers of its adherents—all other religions are far behind Buddhism. If Buddhism were alien to animism, it would mean that the most widely supported religion in the world would, by its example, prove not only the *possibility*, but the incontestable *reality* of that which I consider *impossible* and which could, therefore, have no place in real life. But that is not the case. We shall see that Buddhism is not at all alien to animistic ideas, but that these ideas do not have in it the same form as in other religions. Buddhism does not refute my view; it confirms it.⟩

SECOND ARTICLE

ONCE MORE ON RELIGION

> "*Religious* questions of the day have at the present time a *social* significance. It is no longer a question of *religious* interests as *such*. Only the *theologian* can believe it is a question of religion as religion."[181]
>
> K. Marx

1. AN ESSENTIAL RESERVATION

In the first article, I said that religion is a more or less orderly system of ideas, sentiments, and actions, that is to say, a system more or less free of contradictions. Besides this, I said that religious ideas are *animistic* in character. So far as I am aware, there is no exception to this general rule. True, many people regard Buddhism as an *atheistic* religion. Since an atheistic religion—a "religion without God"—may be easily taken to be a religion completely free of animism, I may, perhaps, be told that Buddhism is a highly important exception to the general rule indicated above. I will readily agree that if Buddhism had indeed no trace of animism, my general rule would prove to be seriously shaken. I will express myself even more strongly and say that in such circumstances my rule would no longer hold good. Actually, Buddhism has more believers than any other religion. And if it could be shown that Buddhism was a *religion without animism*, it would be strange, indeed, to maintain the view that animism was an inevitable component part of religion.

But can we really consider Buddhism to be a religion which is alien to animistic ideas? Some quite authoritative writers in this field say yes. Thus, for example, Rhys Davids writes: "Now the central position of the Buddhist alternative to those previous views of life was this—that Gotama not only ignored the whole of the soul theory, but even held all discussion as to the ultimate soul problems with which the Vedanta and the other philosophies were chiefly concerned, as not only childish and useless, but as actually inimical to the only ideal worth striving after—the ideal of a perfect life, here and now, in this present world, in Arahatship."* I cannot argue with Rhys Davids; perhaps Gotama did indeed approach the question of the soul in that way. It is also possible that his conception of the soul was one in which there was no room for animism. It is beyond dispute, however, that not far from this "central position" the matter took quite a different turn. To substantiate this, I shall refer to the same Rhys Davids. Here is what we read on pages 48-49 of his book on Buddhism: "Of Gotama's childhood and early youth we know next to nothing from the earlier texts. But there are not wanting even there descriptions of the wonders that attended his birth, and of the marvellous precocity of the boy. He was not born as ordinary men are; he had no earthly father; he descended of his own accord into his mother's womb from his throne in heaven; and he gave unmistakable signs, immediately after his birth, of his high

---

* Rhys Davids, St. Petersburg, 1899, p. 21. [Plekhanov is quoting from the Russian translation of T. W. Rhys Davids' *Buddhism. Its History and Literature.*] It is interesting to compare this with the following opinion of P. Oltramare, author of one of the most recent works on Buddhism: "Par sa conception du monde et de la vie le bouddhisme s'est placé aux antipodes du vieil animisme populaire. Celui-ci voit partout des êtres autonomes, et son univers se compose d'une infinité de volontés plus ou moins puissantes; le bouddhisme a poussé jusqu'aux derniéres limites son explication phénoméniste et déterministe des choses." (P. Oltramare, *La formule bouddhique des douze causes*. Genève, 1909.) [In its conception of the world and its view of life, Buddhism is the antipode of ancient popular animism. The latter sees autonomous beings everywhere, and its universe is composed of an infinite number of more or less powerful wills; Buddhism pushes its phenomenist and determinist explanation of things to the extreme limit.]

character and of his future greatness. Earth and heaven at his birth united to pay him homage; the very trees bent of their own accord over his mother, and the angels and archangels were present with their help." What is this, if not the most obvious animism?

Rhys Davids continues by quoting a very important text entitled *The Discourse on Wonders and Marvels*: "In it," he writes, "is laid down as true of each Buddha (and therefore also of the historical Buddha) that the universe is illumined with brilliant light at the moment of his conception; that the womb is transparent so that his mother can see the babe before it is born; that the pregnancy lasts exactly 280 days; that the mother stands during parturition; that on the birth of the babe it is received first into the hands of heavenly beings, and that supernatural showers provide first hot and then cold water in which the child is bathed; that the future Buddha walks and speaks at once, and that the whole universe is again illumined with a brilliant light. There are other details, but this is enough to show—as the collection of dialogues is certainly one of the very oldest texts we have—how very short is the time (less than a century) required for such belief in the marvellous to spring up."*

The details expounded by Rhys Davids are, indeed, more than enough to demonstrate the strength of the Buddhist belief in the miraculous. But where there is the miraculous there is animism too. We see how the angels and archangels performed the role of midwives at the birth of Buddha. Here is what Rhys Davids has to tell us—again on the basis of ancient texts—of how the Buddha was wont to spend part of his nights: "And in the evening he would sit awhile alone ... till his brethren ... began to assemble. Then some would ask him questions on things that puzzled them.... Thus would the first watch of the night pass, as the Blessed One satisfied the desire of each, and then they would take their leave."**

Again I ask: is this not obvious animism?

Buddhism is in no way alien to animism. It recognises the existence of "innumerable gods" and spirits. But the relation between men and gods and spirits is depicted in this religion quite differently from what it is, for example, in Christianity. And this explains the error of those who regard Buddhism as an atheistic religion. Why, for instance, does Chantepie de la Saussaye speak of the "atheism" of the Buddhists? Because, according to Buddhist teaching, Brahma with all his greatness is powerless before the

---

* [Rhys Davids] op. cit., p. 50. Chantepie de la Saussaye also confirms that in its fundamental views, Buddhism is "absolutely atheistic". Yet the same author simultaneously admits that this religion populates heaven with innumerable gods (*Manuel d'histoire des religions*, pp. 382-83).

** Op. cit., p. 58.

one who has achieved Arahatship.* But when the medicine-men of the primitive hunting tribes resort to witchcraft, they perform acts which in their opinion force the gods to do their will; in other words, they make man in some senses stronger than the gods. However, this does not give us any right to call these medicine-men atheists. I am prepared to admit that in the Buddhist religion the conception of men's relationships to the gods took a highly original form. But to attribute to this complex conception highly original form does not mean eliminating one of its two component parts: the notion of gods and spirits in general. Even if we assumed that Gotama himself was an atheist and as such was simply an advocate of morality, we should nevertheless have to acknowledge that after his death—and perhaps even in his lifetime—his followers introduced into his teaching an abundance of animistic elements, thus furnishing his doctrine with a *religious* character. Rhys Davids in relating the story of the Buddha's childhood and early youth, cited by me above, adds that similar legends are told of all the founders of great religions and that "in a certain stage of intellectual progress it is a necessity of the human mind that such legends should grow up".** That is absolutely correct. But at which stage precisely? Precisely at the one which is characterised by the appearance and consolidation of *animism*. Since religions originate exactly at this very wide stage of development, it is strange to think that even one of the religions could remain free of animistic notions; it is strange to hear of the "atheism" of the Buddhists.

Religion alien to animistic notions has never yet existed, and, as I said, cannot exist.

2. OUR CURRENT ATTEMPTS TO FOUND A RELIGION FREE OF "SUPERNATURAL" ELEMENTS

a) Leo TOLSTOY

I do not intend to make an analysis here of Leo Tolstoy's teaching. It would be inappropriate and, in any case, unnecessary since it has been very well analysed in L. Axelrod's *Tolstoi's Weltanschauung und ihre Entwicklung*. I wish only to touch on Tolstoy's religion and that only in so far as it concerns the question of animism which I am interested in.

Leo Tolstoy himself considers his religion to be free of all "supernatural" elements. To him, the supernatural is synonymous

---

* Chantepie de la Saussaye, op. cit., p. 383.
** Op. cit., p. 49.

with the senseless and irrational. He pours scorn on those who are accustomed to think of the "supernatural otherwise the senseless" as the principal distinguishing mark of religion. "To assert that the supernatural and irrational constitute the basic properties of religion," he says, "is just the same as though someone who knew only rotten apples asserted that the flaccid bitter taste and the harmful effect on the stomach were the basic properties of the apple."* What, in Leo Tolstoy's opinion, is religion?

Answer: "Religion is the definition of man's relationship to the beginning of all and of the purpose of man flowing from this and of the rules of conduct flowing from this purpose."**

In another part of the same work, Leo Tolstoy gives the following definition of religion: "*True religion is the establishment by man of a relationship based on reason and knowledge with the infinite life surrounding him, a relationship which binds his life to this infinity and guides his conduct.*"***

At first glance, these definitions of religion, which are in essence completely identical, appear rather strange. The question inevitably arises: then why is this called religion? To determine one's relationship to "the beginning of all" or (as in the second definition) to "the infinite life" surrounding man, does not mean to lay the foundations of a religious world-outlook. Similarly, to be guided in one's behaviour by a view on "the beginning of all" (on "infinite life") does not mean to be religious. There is the example of Diderot, who very assiduously determined "his relationship to the beginning of all" and built his system of ethics on this definition; but in that period of his life when his view on "the beginning of all" had become the view of a convinced materialist, he was not at all religious. What then is the point here? It seems to me that the whole point lies in the word "*purpose*". Leo Tolstoy thinks that man, by determining his relationship to "the beginning of all", thereby determines his "purpose" in life. But this "purpose" presupposes, first, the subject or being for whom it *is laid down*—in this case, man—and, secondly, the being or power who *gives* man his "purpose". This being or power obviously possesses consciousness; otherwise it could not give man his "purpose", place a definite task before him. How are we to conceive of this conscious being? Tolstoy provides a clear reply to this question too. He does not like the present-

---

* Л. Н. Толстой, «Что такое религия и в чем сущность ее», изд. «Свободного Слова», 1902, стр. 48. [Leo Tolstoy, *What Is Religion, What Is Its Essence*, Free Word Publishers, 1902, p. 48.]
  ** Op. cit., pp. 48-49.
  *** Ibid., p. 11, Tolstoy's italics.

day teaching of religion. In his opinion, we should not inculcate children with and confirm in adults "the belief that God sent His own Son to atone for the sins of Adam, and established His Church to exact obedience".* He believes it would be incomparably better if the children were "inculcated with and confirmed in the belief that God is a spirit whose manifestation is within us and whose power we can increase by our way of life".** But to suggest to children that God is a spirit whose manifestation is within us is to put *animistic* ideas into their minds. So, as it turns out, the conscious being who furnishes man with his purpose in life is a *spirit*. What is a spirit? I said enough about this in my first article. Here I shall confine myself to the remark that if a spirit is, as we know, a being by whose volition natural phenomena are occasioned, it must stand *above nature*; in other words, it must be regarded as a *supernatural* being.*** Which means that Leo Tolstoy is mistaken in thinking that his religion is free of "supernatural" beliefs.

What led him to make this mistake? In his conception, the "supernatural" is identical with the "senseless" and irrational. But his own personal belief in the existence of God, who "is a spirit", did not seem to him to be senseless and irrational; on the contrary, he regarded it as a display of sound common sense and of the highest intelligence, and therefore he decided that there was no place in his religion for the "supernatural". He either forgot or did not know that belief in the "supernatural" simply means the recognition of the existence of spirits or a spirit (it is all the same which). In various historical epochs, the belief in spirits (animism) acquires such highly different forms that the people of one epoch describe as senseless the belief in the "supernatural" which was regarded as a manifestation of the highest intelligence during another epoch, or even during several epochs. But these misunderstandings among people holding the animistic point of view did not in the least alter the fundamental nature of the belief common to them all: the belief in the existence of one or several "supernatural" powers. It is only because this

---

* Ibid., p. 50.
** Ibid., same page.
*** "Der Glaube, dass ein Gott ist, oder, was dasselbe, ein Gott die Welt macht und regiert, ist nichts anderes als der Glaube, d.h., hier die Überzeugung oder Vorstellung, dass die Welt, die Natur nicht von Naturkräften oder Naturgesetzen, sondern *von denselben Kräften und Beweggründen* beherrscht und bewegt wird, als der Mensch." (L. Feuerbach, *Works*, IX, p. 334.), ["The belief that there is a God, or what is the same thing, that God created the world and governs it, is nothing more than a belief, that is to say, a conviction or conception, according to which the world, nature is directed not by natural forces or natural laws, but *by the same forces and motive powers as man*."]

belief was common to all of them that they could be said to have religion. Religion alien to animistic ideas has never yet existed, nor can it exist; the conceptions inherent in religion always have a more or less animistic nature. The example of Leo Tolstoy's religion may serve as a further illustration of this truth. Leo Tolstoy is an animist, and his moral aspirations have a religious colouring only to the extent that they are combined with belief in a God, who is a "spirit" and who has determined man's purpose on earth.

b) A. LUNACHARSKY

As for Mr. A. Lunacharsky, I shall be compelled to dwell upon his religious "seekings" in greater detail. This seems to me to be necessary, firstly, because his "religion" is very much less known than Leo Tolstoy's and, secondly, the more so since he had, and may still have, a certain positive attitude to Russian Marxism.

Unfortunately, in examining Mr. A. Lunacharsky's religious "seekings", I shall have to speak partly about myself. The circumstances are such that lately many Russian writers engaged in refuting one or other principle of Marxism thought fit to direct their "critical" weapons against my "humble self" (meine Wenigkeit, as the Germans say). It does enter my head occasionally that I have some cause to be gratified with this. Still, it is very tedious.

Mr. A. Lunacharsky takes me on, one might say, first and foremost, by translating into Russian and criticising my reply to the questionnaire on the future of religion sponsored by *Mercure de France* in 1907.[182] To give him his due, he summarises the content of my reply accurately. "Thus," he says, "Plekhanov maintains that religion is, above all, a definite and *animistic* explanation of phenomena. Subsequently, 'spirits' were called upon to guard the moral laws, the source of which was seen in their volition. Now phenomena have received another explanation. Spirits are no longer at hand, and 'this hypothesis is not required any more for the pursuit of knowledge', as Laplace said, so that morality must reject supernatural sanction and find a natural one. The supernatural is thrown out by scientific realism and there is no further room for religion."* That is indeed my opinion. True, I did not use the expression "scientific realism" which seems to me to be somewhat indeterminate. But that is not important here. Mr. Lunacharsky has even greater regard for the truth when he adds: "Engels held the same point of view

---

* А. Луначарский, «Религия и социализм», часть первая, СПБ, 1908, стр. 24. [A. Lunacharsky, *Religion and Socialism*, First Part, St. Petersburg, 1908, p. 24.]

as Plekhanov.* Although on the following pages he forgets my
solidarity with Engels, and takes me alone to task, it is all to
the good that he does not deny that solidarity. Mr. A. Lunacharsky's friend, Mr. Bogdanov, takes another line: he is forever
striving to drive a wedge between Engels and myself, and to put
me down under the heading of eighteenth-century "bourgeois
materialism". That is a lot worse. However, be that as it may,
the fact is that Mr. A. Lunacharsky is not satisfied with my view
on religion. He offers to it the definition of religion given by Vandervelde.[183] This definition, says Mr. Lunacharsky, is "more profound than Plekhanov's, less narrow, less rationalist".** However
later he announces that Mr. Vandervelde, too, mixes truth and
error; and some lines further on it turns out that in his definition
of religion the celebrated Belgian socialist relies on "pure Kantianism". And that is true. But it is useless for Mr. Lunacharsky
to remark after that: "In the present instance, we appear to be closer
to comrade Plekhanov."*** That is quite untrue. "Pure Kantianism" did not hinder E. Vandervelde from providing a definition
of religion which, in Mr. Lunacharsky's opinion, is more profound
and less narrow than "Plekhanov's". Thus, when all is said and done,
Mr. A. Lunacharsky is closer to E. Vandervelde than to
Plekhanov.****

That too by the way. The main consideration is that Mr. Lunacharsky wants a religion without God. "Yes," he exclaims, "the
needs of 'practical reasons', that is to say, of man's longing for
happiness can neither be declared non-existent or unimportant,
nor answered by science as such; but to conclude from this that
these needs will always be met by fables that are irrefutable only
because their sources are outside the limits of sensual nature, is
to present humanity with a certificate of poverty of 'spirit'."*****
Mr. A. Lunacharsky is confident that "modern man" can have religion without God, and "to prove that this is possible is to deal
the final blow at God."*) Since our author is very anxious "to
deal the final blow at God", he takes it upon himself to prove
"that this is possible", and with this in mind he turns to Feuerbach.

---

* Ibid., same page.
** Ibid., p. 28. We are already aware that to be "more profound" (and
so on—*G.P.*) "than Plekhanov" is also to be more profound than Engels. But
we must understand also that, "these days", it is more expedient to criticise
Plekhanov while rebelling against Marx and Engels. Who wants the reputa-
tion of being among "Marx's critics"?
*** Ibid., p. 29.
**** It is not inappropriate to remind the reader again that in this case
"to Plekhanov" means also "to Engels", and also that it is not convenient for
our author to speak of Engels, because he does not want to be included among
the theoretical "revisionists".
***** Ibid., pp. 28-29.
*) Ibid., p. 29.

He thinks that "there is not one materialist who has dealt such a shattering blow at religion, *positive religion* and any belief in God, the other world, and the supernatural as Ludwig Feuerbach did.* After Feuerbach, the religion of God was philosophically dead."** Later we shall verify by the example of Mr. A. Lunacharsky himself whether the "religion of God" is really dead. In the meantime, let us see what Mr. A. Lunacharsky likes about Feuerbach (apart from the "killing of God").

"Feuerbach's definition of religion is nowhere formulated quite satisfactorily," he says, "but the reader will feel at once the vast difference between Feuerbach and the social-democratic rationalists and enlighteners when reading the lines: 'Religion is the solemn revelation of the treasures hidden in man, the acknowledgment of his inner thoughts, the open confession of the secret of his love.' Here Feuerbach has grasped religion by the heart and not by the clothes as comrade Plekhanov does."***

After citing another passage from Feuerbach, in which he voices the thought that in all religions man worships his own essence, Mr. A. Lunacharsky then considers it possible to oppose the philosophical profundity of Feuerbach to the "scientific superficiality of Tylor, from whom comrade Plekhanov borrowed his definition."****

But no matter from whom "comrade Plekhanov" borrowed his definition of religion, we already know that on the question now under discussion this "comrade" held the same view as Engels, as Mr. A. Lunacharsky himself has admitted. It follows, therefore, that the contrasting of Feuerbach with his "philosophical profundity" to Tylor with his "scientific superficiality" is manifestly a blow—*if* it really is one—not only at "comrade Plekhanov" but also at "comrade Engels". Do not imagine, reader, that in constantly bringing this up, I am trying to shield myself from my dread critic by hiding behind one of the founders of scientific socialism. Not in the least. It is not a matter of my being afraid— *if* I am afraid— of Mr. A. Lunacharsky, but of what he has to say. Here is some of it:

"I think that from a religious-philosophical point of view Marx brilliantly continued the work of elevating *anthropology to the level of theology,* i.e., he finally helped human self-consciousness to become human religion."*****

This thought of Mr. A. Lunacharsky's was prompted by some-

---

* It is obvious from this that Mr. Lunacharsky, no doubt following the example of F. A. Lange, does not look upon Feuerbach as a materialist. I have proved more than once that this is a great error. (See, among others, the first page of my pamphlet *Fundamental Problems of Marxism.*)[184]
  ** *Religion and Socialism*, p. 31.
  *** Ibid., p. 32.
  **** Ibid., same page.
  ***** Ibid., p. 31.

thing Feuerbach said: "I reduce theology to anthropology and thereby *elevate anthropology to the level of theology*." Look what we have got now. Marx, brilliantly continuing the work started by Feuerbach, "finally helped human self-consciousness to become human religion". But it is well known that Engels constantly shared Marx's views and was his unfailing collaborator. Never at any time did he have any differences with Marx on the question of religion; which means that at least part of the credit which Mr. A. Lunacharsky gives to Marx belongs to Engels; which means that Engels also was by no means a stranger to comprehension of the profound Feuerbachian view on the "heart" of religion. Yet on the other hand, "Engels held the same point of view as Plekhanov". And Plekhanov in his views on religion reveals narrowness, an unnecessary rationalism, shallowness of thought and approximates to Tylor, who, if we are to believe Mr. A. Lunacharsky, gives a definition of religion "current among bourgeois and social-democratic free-thinking publicists".* Where and what is the truth here?

Come, reader, let us look for the truth ourselves. We have little hopes of Mr. A. Lunacharsky.

Marx, who "finally helped human self-consciousness to become human religion", says in the article on Proudhon written immediately after the latter's death: "Nevertheless his attacks on religion the church, etc., were of great merit locally at a time when the French Socialists deemed fit to be superior in religiosity to the bourgeois Voltairianism of the eighteenth century and the German godlessness of the nineteenth. If Peter the Great defeated Russian barbarism by barbarity, Proudhon did his best to vanquish French phrasemongering by phrases."**

These words of Marx give grounds for thinking that he looked on all talk of transforming "human self-consciousness into human religion" as phrasemongering. And that in fact was Marx's position, nor could it have been otherwise. Marx's attitude to religion was completely negative, as any one will easily realise who takes the trouble to read his well-known article "Zur Kritik der Hegel'schen Rechtsphilosophie".

When he wrote this article, he still agreed with Feuerbach's views on religion and accepted fully, *in its essentials*, Feuerbach's criticism of religion. But, and in spite of Feuerbach himself, Marx drew some "*irreligious*" conclusions from this criticism. He said: "The basis of irreligious criticism is: *Man makes religion*, religion does not make man. In other words (und zwar), religion is the self-consciousness and self-esteem of man who has either

---

* Ibid., p. 32.
** This article was published as a supplement to *Poverty of Philosophy*, translated by V. I. Zasulich and edited by myself.[185]

not yet found himself or has already lost himself again (der sich selbst entweder noch nicht erworben, oder schon wieder verloren hat). But *man* is no abstract being encamped outside the world. Man is *the world of man*, the state, society. This state, this society, produce religion, an *inverted world-consciousness*, because they are an *inverted world*. Religion is the general theory of that world, its encyclopaedic compendium, its logic in a popular form, its spiritualistic *point d'honneur*, its enthusiasm, its moral sanction, its solemn complement, its universal source of consolation and justification. It is the *fantastic realisation* of the human essence because the human essence has no true reality. The struggle against religion is therefore indirectly a fight against *the world* of which religion is the spiritual *aroma*.... Religion is only the illusory sun which revolves round man as long as he does not revolve round himself."*

Judge for yourself now how splendidly Mr. A. Lunacharsky has understood Marx in declaring his teaching to be "the fifth great religion formulated by Judaism",** and taking upon himself the role of modern prophet of this "fifth religion". Apparently Mr. Lunacharsky does not in the least suspect that he is saying the exact opposite of what Marx said. To Marx, religion is inverted world consciousness produced by inverted social relations. Therefore, concludes Mr. A. Lunacharsky, we must attempt to invert human world consciousness even if social relations cease to be inverted. According to Marx, religion is the self-consciousness and self-esteem of man who has either not yet found himself or has already lost himself again. So that—our eloquent and sensitive author deduces—religion must certainly exist even when man has "found" himself. Marx says that religion is only the illusory sun which revolves round man because he has not yet learned to revolve round himself. So—concludes our modern prophet of the "fifth religion"—the illusory sun must exist even when man has learned to revolve round himself. What staggering conclusions! What iron logic!

And Engels?

In replying to Carlyle's attempt to perform almost the same operation on human self-consciousness as Mr. A. Lunacharsky would now like to perform, Engels wrote: "Religion by its very essence drains man and nature of substance, and transfers this substance to the phantom of an other-worldly God, who in turn then graciously permits man and nature to receive some of his superfluity."*** True, Mr. A. Lunacharsky tells us that he wishes

---

* *Gesammelte Schriften von Karl Marx und Friedrich Engels, 1841 bis 1850,* Erster Band, Stuttgart, 1902, S. 384-385.[186]
** A. Lunacharsky, op. cit., p. 145.
*** *Gesammelte Schriften,* I, S. 483.[187]

to create a "religion without God". Perhaps Engels would have condoned such a religion? No, Engels disapproved of such a religion too. He found that now all possibility of religion had disappeared ("alle Möglichkeiten der Religion sind erschöpft") and that to man must now be returned the content which had been transferred to God: but it must be returned not as divine, but as purely human. "And this whole process of giving," he wrote, "is no more than simply the awakening of self-consciousness."* Here we should note that in this, his own view, Engels was much more true to the teaching on religion which constitutes Feuerbach's real service. Indeed, according to this teaching, religion is the fantastic reflection of the human essence. Therefore, when human self-consciousness reaches that stage of development where the fog of fantasy is dispersed by the light of reason, all possibility for religion will of necessity prove to have disappeared. Feuerbach himself did not draw this conclusion, since he considered it possible and necessary to propagate the religion of the heart, love.** But, in spite of what Mr. Lunacharsky has said, we have to see in this not Feuerbach's merit, not his profundity, but his weakness, the concession he made to idealism. This is how Engels understood it, and here, of course, he was once more in complete agreement with Marx. He could not have expressed himself more definitely on this point than he did in his pamphlet on Feuerbach.

"The real idealism of Feuerbach," we read there, "becomes evident as soon as we come to his philosophy of religion and ethics. He by no means wishes to abolish religion; he wants to perfect it. Philosophy itself must be absorbed in religion.... Feuerbach's idealism consists here in this: he does not simply accept mutual relations based on reciprocal inclination between human beings, such as sex love, friendship, compassion, self-sacrifice, etc., as what they are in themselves—without associating them with any particular religion which to him, too, belongs to the past; but instead he asserts that they will attain their full value only when consecrated by the name of 'religion'. The chief thing for him is not that these purely human relations exist, but that they shall be conceived of as the new, true religion. They are to have full value only after they have been marked with a religious stamp."*** Further, after pointing out that the noun "religion" is derived from the word religare, so that it is thought by some that every mutual bond between people is religion,**** Engels

---

* Op. cit., pp. 484-85. [188]
** Although it is he that uttered the magnificent expression: "Religion is the sleep of the human spirit."
*** F. Engels, *Ludwig Feuerbach*, St. Petersburg, 1900, pp. 51-52. [189]
**** Mr. Lunacharsky actually says: "Religion is a bond" (op. cit., p. 39).

continues: "Such etymological tricks are the last resort of idealist philosophy."[190] It would be as well for Mr. Lunacharsky not to forget these words; even though he is extremely hostile to materialist philosophy, he still claims to be a supporter of the theory of historical materialism.

In the same passage, Engels makes mocking reference to Feuerbach's attempt to constitute a religion without God—the attempt that has so delighted Mr. A. Lunacharsky: "If Feuerbach wishes to establish a true religion upon the basis of an essentially materialist conception of nature, that is the same as regarding modern chemistry as true alchemy. If religion can exist without its god, alchemy can exist without its philosopher's stone."*

A very just remark. However, we must remember that the religion composed by Lunacharsky does not remain long "without God". On page 104 of his book we already discover that it was not in vain that Strauss recognised in allegory the existence of a power that works miracles. "Because," our exalted author proclaims, "there are being accomplished before our eyes miracles of the victory of reason and will over nature, the sick are healed, mountains are moved, stormy oceans are navigated with ease, thought flies on the wings of electricity from one hemisphere to another, and gazing on the successes of Genius, should we not say: who is this to whom even the turbulent seas submit? Do we not feel how the God born between the ox and the ass grows stronger?"**

This eloquent tirade, which would probably have aroused stormy applause at the recent congress of missionaries, heavily underlines my contention that religion is impossible without animistic notions. When a man who wanted to invent a religion without God "feels how the God born between the ox and the ass grows stronger", it proves that I am right: there is no religion without a god; where there is a religion there must be a god. And not only a god, but perhaps even a goddess, since it is not good even for a god to be alone. Here is what Mr. Lunacharsky writes on page 147 of his divine book, addressing himself to nature: "Perfidious, soulless Nature, mighty, resplendent in the beauty, extravagantly rich: thou shalt be the most obedient slave; in thee man shalt plumb the depths of happiness. The very outbursts of thy rebellion and the depth of thy fatal indifference, thy perfidy of a being unreasonable, enchanting and great goddess, the perils of love alone with thee—will enrapture the male heart of man."

Religion is impossible without animistic notions. That is why Mr. Lunacharsky, the preacher of a "religion without God", em-

---

* F. Engels, *Ludwig Feuerbach*, p. 52. [191]
** A. Lunacharsky, op. cit., p. 104.

ploys a language that is appropriate only where there is at least one god and at least one goddess. That is perfectly natural. But precisely because it is natural, we should not wonder why our author is more and more at variance with the founders of scientific socialism, and more and more in agreement with ... the apostle Paul. According to Mr. Lunacharsky, the apostle Paul "brilliantly approaches the essence of religion" when he says: "For I reckon that the sufferings of this present time *are* not worthy *to be compared* with the glory which shall be revealed in us. For the earnest expectation of the creature waiteth for the manifestation of the sons of God. For the creature was made subject to vanity, not willingly, but by reason of him who hath subjected *the same* in hope. Because the creature itself also shall be delivered from the bondage of corruption into the glorious liberty of the children of God. For we know that the whole creation groaneth and travaileth in pain together until now. And not only *they*, but ourselves also, which have the first fruits of the Spirit, even we ourselves groan within ourselves waiting for the adoption, *to wit*, the redemption of our body." (Romans: 8: 18-23.*)

In another passage, to which I shall return later, Mr. Lunacharsky writes: "We, together with the apostle Paul, can say: 'we are saved by hope.'"** I am very glad for Mr. Lunacharsky's sake if it really is so. But has it not occurred to him that he has produced the following, somewhat unexpected combination: Engels has the "same point of view as Plekhanov, while the apostle Paul is "saved by hope" together with Mr. A. Lunacharsky? Personally, I have nothing against such a combination, but does it suit our author, who has claimed, and still claims, to be a follower of Marx and Engels? I have strong doubts about it.

Having indicated how the apostle Paul "brilliantly approaches the essence of religion", Mr. Lunacharsky then presents his own definition of religion. Here it is: "*Religion is such thinking about the world and such world-sensation as psychologically resolves the contrast between the laws of life and the laws of nature.*"*** He does not regard this definition as conclusive. He says: "This is a general definition of religion that does not embrace all its essential aspects." But he hopes that the other properties of religion may be extracted from this definition.**** Don't his hopes beguile him?

Religion is a certain kind of "thinking about the world" and a certain "world-sensation". Good. And what is the distinguishing feature of this thinking which is peculiar to religion? Mr. Lunacharsky tells us that this thinking changes with the progress of

---

   * Op. cit., p. 40.
  ** Ibid., p. 49.
 *** Ibid., p. 40, Lunacharsky's italics.
**** Ibid., same page.

the intellectual development of mankind: "Mythological creation gave way to metaphysics and, finally, to exact science; the belief in magic collapsed and was replaced by belief in labour. In place of animism, there is now scientific energetics; in the place of magic, there is now modern technique."* Let us assume for a moment that energetics is precisely the world-outlook which must now take the place of "magic" and animism. But, I ask, how will religion affect the thinking of people who uphold the mode of thought referred to as "energetics"? If these people could *deify* energy, the question could be answered very simply: deification presupposes a religious relationship to one's subject. But to deify is to personify, and to personify is, in the present instance, to have recourse to animism, in the place of which there now stands, according to Mr. Lunacharsky, scientific energetics. But where is the way out of all this? It is not visible in the direction of "thinking". Mr. Lunacharsky is himself more or less vaguely aware of this. He has no sooner pointed out that animism has now been replaced by scientific energetics, and magic by modern technique, than he adds: "But has this changed anything in the religious essence of the human soul? Has man really attained happiness? Are there really no great desires still alive in his soul? Have his dreams of true happiness become dimmer and his ideals more lacklustre and closer? If this were the case, Hartmann would be right: humanity would, indeed, have become "positive", i.e., commercially calculating, easily satisfied, sluggish and decrepit."**

Mankind in the person of the advanced class in modern society has become neither easily satisfied, sluggish, nor decrepit. It has not yet attained happiness; it is still filled with many desires, its dreams of happiness are undimmed and its ideals bright. This is all true. And, if you like, it is all connected with "world-sensation". But I ask again: where does religion come in? Mr. Lunacharsky himself sees that it has nothing to do with the case; so he thinks further explanations are required.

"Despondency is alive in man," he writes, "and he who cannot conceive the world religiously is foredoomed to pessimism unless he be a common philistine ready to repeat with Chekhov's teacher: 'I'm happy, I'm happy'.[192] If despondency in primitive man was a pining for life to continue, a yearning for protection from his menacing surroundings, the modern form of despondency is a craving *to dominate nature*. This is the great change that has taken place in man's religious sensations."**

Thus, despondency is alive in man, and religion is an escape

---

   * Ibid., pp. 40-41.
  ** A. Lunacharsky, op. cit., p. 41.
 *** Ibid., same page.

from it, since "he who cannot conceive the world religiously is foredoomed to pessimism unless he be a common philistine". It is not easy to find anything to object to this; it is all a matter of personal "world-sensation". There are people whose state of despondency drives them to drink. There are others whose despondent condition (more truly, a different variety of despondency) goads them to seek consolation in one of the *old religions*. Finally, there are those with still another variety of despondency which impels them to dream of some *new religion*. I am very well aware of all that. But I shall risk being called a "common philistine" and admit that I am quite unable to understand why "the craving *to dominate nature*" must inevitably take the form of despondency, and, moreover, a despondency predisposing to religion. I believe Mr. Lunacharsky is sincere and, consequently, do not doubt that in him the said "craving" has turned into "despondency". Besides, I assume that our prophet of the "fifth religion" has a certain retinue who are also transforming "craving" into "despondency", and "despondency" into religion. There are many despondent people—and more who spread despondency—in present-day Russia. And this has its own social cause. But here I envisage this phenomenon for the moment only from the point of view of logic, and would like to know what logical principles permit Mr. A. Lunacharsky, with a skill close to that of a military man, to deduce *the said* "despondency" from *the said* "craving". The answer is contained in the words: "*contrast between the laws of life and the laws of nature*" contained in Mr. A. Lunacharsky's definition of religion which I quoted above. What is this contrast?

Mr. A. Lunacharsky, who is known to adhere to the "philosophical" theory of Mach and Avenarius, quite suddenly refers to himself as a materialist in a certain sense of the word. He says: "We are not idealists; we are materialists in the sense that we find nothing in common between the laws of the physical world and our truths and ideals, our moral world."* Theoretically that is false, "in the sense" that since not one serious materialist has ever posed the question as to whether there was anything *in common* between the laws of the physical world and our truths and ideals.** To pose such a question is to commensurate the incom-

---

* Op. cit., p. 46.
** And in general, very few have ever concerned themselves with this problem. What is there in common between the law of nature which runs: the intensity of light is in inverse proportion to the square of the distance, and Mr. A. Lunacharsky's socio-political ideal? It is hardly likely that there are many thinkers who would undertake to solve this question. There was one who could have solved it with the greatest ease, but he is now dead. I am talking of the late Dr. A. M. Korobov, one of the "seekers" after religion at the end of the 1870s and the beginning of the 1880s. Dr. Korobov published

mensurable. It is a fact, though, that in the opinion of all serious
materialists, a person can discover the truth by studying nature's
laws (in the broadest sense of the term) and fulfil his ideals by
relying upon these laws. Mr. A. Lunacharsky knows nothing
at all of materialist literature. This is obvious from the nonsense
he has talked about the materialism of Diderot and Holbach
in the article "Atheism", published in the collection *Essays on
the Philosophy of Marxism.**[193] Only as a consequence of his complete ignorance of materialism could our prophet of the "fifth
religion" call himself a materialist in the sense he indicated.
But by this vain attempt to line up in the materialist camp he
wished only to reinforce the proposition that "moral powers supposedly ruling the world do not exist".** This proposition is
correct, in spite of its childishly naive basis: the powers he talks
about do not exist. It is a pity only that this proposition, correct
in itself, takes on a very peculiar tang when propounded by Mr.
A. Lunacharsky. Citing the "splendid" work of Harald Höffding
on religion, and trying to put us in a religious frame of mind,
Mr. A. Lunacharsky writes:

"Science brings us to the law of eternal energy, but this energy,
remaining quantitatively equal to itself, may vary in the sense
of its value to man. The death of a man, let us say, for example,
Lassalle, or Marx, or Raphael, or Georg Büchner, changes nothing
in the equations of energetics, but it is considered a misfortune,
a loss in the world of feeling, in the world of values. Progress
is above all the growth of the quantity and the height of cultural
values. Is progress an immanent law of nature? If we answer—
"yes", we are pure metaphysicians, since we confirm that which
is not guaranteed to us by science."***

These observations open the door to religion, which is regarded,
according to the definition given by Höffding, as concern for the
destinies of values. But for religion understood in this sense to
afford us some kind of consolation in misfortunes of the sort mentioned by Mr. Lunacharsky, we have to recognise the existence of

---

a collection of his writings under the title of *The Allalphabet or the Tetragram-
maton*. He solved there, incidentally, the profound problem of the number of
atoms embodied in divine justice. If my memory serves me right, he found
by calculations and geometrical constructions that divine justice consisted
of some 280,000 atoms. I think Mr. A. Lunacharsky would have easily come
to an understanding with Dr. Korobov, though it might seem that they were
looking at the subject from opposite points of view.

* Judging by the content of this collection there seems to be an important misprint in the title. Evidently it should read: *Essays on the Philosophy
of Machism*. But it is not my business to correct misprints in books I am
quoting. I am not a proof-reader.

** *Religion and Socialism*, p. 46.

*** Op. cit., pp. 46-47.

"moral powers", which stand above nature and whose laws are expressed in the equations of energetics; otherwise our "concern for the destiny of values" will, in the religious sense, lead to a dead end. But then Mr. Lunacharsky does not admit the existence of "moral powers supposedly ruling the world". Consequently, he can do nothing but contradict himself: and he does this with striking success.

As we have only just seen, Mr. Lunacharsky declares in his book that he who answers "yes" to the question: is progress an immanent law of nature, is a pure metaphysician. But in his article "Atheism" mentioned above he asserts categorically:

"*Material evolution and spiritual progress coincide.* There is the great truth which the proletariat sensed and discovered in philosophy."*

The same truth, although not so "highly colourful", is also repeated, incidentally, in Mr. A. Lunacharsky's book—which, in general, limps badly from the standpoint of logic. Consequently, the reader would be mistaken if he thought that the contradiction I have mentioned is only between what Mr. A. Lunacharsky writes in his book and what he writes in his article. No, the book also contradicts itself. Here is an example.

After remarking that science never provides certainty but always only probability, though this probability is often practically equal to certainty, Mr. A. Lunacharsky fortifies this remark even more by the following observation: "That which applies to science in general applies in an incomparably greater measure to complex scientific predictions: the destiny of the world, of the earth, of humanity."** But we scarcely have time to grasp the importance of this observation and to say to ourselves: so "in an incomparably greater measure" we cannot have the certainty, for instance, of the triumph of socialism, before Mr. A. Lunacharsky hastens to reassure us: "Socialism as the future," he says, "thanks to the Marxian analysis of the trends of capitalist society, possesses probability bordering on certainty."*** Again we take the word of our prophet for granted and say to ourselves, with a sigh of relief: "In that case, we have nothing to fear for the destiny of that 'value' which we call socialism, and we have no need to call upon the help of religion; science will vouch for socialism." But if we were completely reassured on this point we would no longer need a prophet. Therefore, the prophet puts fear into us again. He says: "Science is more likely to be against us in the more general

* «Очерки по философии марксизма» СПБ, стр. 148. [*Essays on the Philosophy of Marxism*, St. Petersburg, 1908, p. 148.] The italics are Mr. Lunacharsky's.
** *Religion and Socialism*, p. 47.
*** Op. cit., p. 48.

question of whether life, organic matter, reason—in their self-assertion confronting insensate matter, nature" (as if organic matter were not a part of nature!—*G.P.*) "which like Cronus is ready to devour her own children will be victorious.* We tremble again and exclaim: "Mr. Lunacharsky, give us a religion which is concern for the destinies of our 'values'! But in supplying us with religion, do take the trouble to explain just how this concern is manifested." It goes without saying that our prophet has a ready answer to this. He goes off into an eloquent harangue, which I feel myself bound to reproduce in almost all its completeness for the edification of non-believers.

"There are no limits to knowledge and the technique founded on it. Think of the psychical life of the Mollusca—our ancestors—and then of wireless telegraphy. Yet the psychical life of our descendants, not so remote perhaps, in the run of progress will just as miraculously surpass ours as the brain-power of Faraday or Marconi excels that of the nerve-cell of the Protozoa." (There they are, the supermen predicted by Nietzsche!—*G.P.*) "There are no limits to the power of thoughts, that is to say, the expedient self-organisation of the social cerebro-nervous system, and together with it, no limit to the progress of technique. We can say only that there is struggle ahead. This struggle will commence on a new, unheard-of scale precisely after the victory of the social principles of socialism. Socialism is humanity's organised struggle with nature for its complete subjection to reason; in the hope of victory, in aspiration, in the straining of all our forces, there is a new religion. Together with the apostle Paul we may say: 'We are saved by hope.' The new religion cannot lead to passivity, which is the upshot of every other religion giving an absolute guarantee of the triumph of good—the new religion passes wholly into action. 'Man was born not for contemplation,' says Aristotle, 'but for action'; and the principle of delighted contemplation is now being ousted from religion and replaced by the principle of ceaseless activity. The new religion, the religion of mankind, the religion of labour, gives no guarantees. But I suppose that even without God and without guarantees—the mask of the selfsame God—it remains a *religion*."**

So there is no limit to the progress of technique. Therefore, "we can say only that there is struggle ahead". Quite true. But *since* we can say "*only*" that there is struggle ahead, we must, *therefore*, say that there must be and will be a new religion. Logical! Further: religion is concern about the destinies of "values". This concern makes sense only if it provides some form of guarantee.

---

  * Ibid., same page.
 ** *Religion and Socialism*, pp. 48-49.

From this we deduce along with Mr. Lunacharsky that what we need is a religion which gives no guarantee of any kind: namely, one that is bereft of all sense. That again could not be more logical!

But that is still not all. Do you really think Mr. A. Lunacharsky's religion has no god? You are mistaken. I have already pointed out that this religion has the irrepressible desire to give birth to at least one god ("between the ox and the ass") and to at least one goddess. If the reader felt sceptical about this, he shall do penance by listening to the prophet himself:

"But is it true that we now have no God?" Mr. Lunacharsky reflects. "Does not the conception of God signify something eternally beautiful? Is it not in this image (when this idea is conveyed in image) that everything human is exalted to the highest potentiality—hence its beauty?...."* Then, after a long and not very clever wrangle with Dietzgen, the prophetic lover of beauty repeats: "And I am left without God, because he is neither in the world nor outside it." Here again it looks as though the prophet has at last decided, not without regret, to invent his promised "religion without God". But yet again we are deceived by appearances. Mr. Lunacharsky once more lapses into meditation. "But, however...," he remarks, and in a tone giving us clearly to understand that his religion, notwithstanding his clear promise to us, will, after all, have a God. Recollecting, and in passing berating Sorel's "vile doctrine" of the general strike as a social myth, the prophet continues:

"But the theory of the social myth was never more applicable than in the domain of the new religious consciousness (proletarian, and not in the aristo-Berdayev style). God as Omniscience, Beatitude, Omnipotence, the Universal, Eternal Life, is really all mankind in the highest potentiality. Then let us say it: God is mankind in the highest potentiality. But mankind in the highest potentiality does not exist? That is sacred truth. However mankind does exist in reality, concealing its potentialities within itself. Let us then worship the potentialities of mankind, our potentialities, and conceive of them in the crown of glory in order the more strongly to love them."**

Having finally invented a God, the prophet, comme de raison, falls into a prayerful mood, and then and there séance tenante composes a prayer: "Let the Kingdom of God prevail," he implores. Regnum gloriae, the apotheosis of man, the victory of reasonable being over sister nature, beautiful in her unreason. "His Will shall be." The Will of the Master from limit to limit, i.e., without limit. "Holy be His Name." On the throne of worlds

---

* *Essays on the Philosophy of Marxism*, **p.** 157.
** Ibid., p. 159.

shall take his seat Someone in the image of man, and the well-organised world, through the lips of living and dead elements and by the voice of its beauty, exclaims: "Holy, Holy, Holy; Heaven and Earth abounds with Thy Glory."*

Mr. A. Lunacharsky feels fine after his prayer. "And the man-God will look round and smile," he prophesies, "for everything is very good."** Who knows, perhaps it might be like this; if so it will be a great comfort. There is only one fly in the ointment: not everything by far in our prophet's dissertations is "very good". His recitals leave very much to be desired. The religion devised by Mr. Lunacharsky has only one "value", true, a quite big one: it may put the serious reader into a very cheerful mood. And the more serious-minded the reader, the more fun he will get out of reading the prophet's book and article.

None the less, the new religion, so well-argued (hm!) in these comic works, must command attention as an index of the social mood. Marx did not speak idly when he said that religious questions now have social significance and that only theologians could think of religion as such. In composing his religion, Mr. Lunacharsky was simply adapting himself to the social mood now prevailing in our country. At the present time, for many reasons of a social character, there is in Russia a great demand for "religion".*** And where there is demand there is supply. Mr. Lunacharsky generally keeps a very close eye on what is in demand. When there was the demand for syndicalism, he hastened to air himself in our literature arm-in-arm with the well-known Italian syndicalist Arturo Labriola, whom on this suitable occasion he presented as a Marxist. When the demand for religion arose, he took the stage as a prophet of the "fifth religion". If the reading public were to respond unfavourably to religion, he would find it opportune to remember that his religion was planned at first as a religion without God, and would make the timely conjecture that such a religion was really not a religion at all, but a play upon words. Verily, verily, I say unto you: Mr. A. Lunacharsky is like a coquette—he wishes to please, no matter what the cost. Unfortunately, there have always been such people around. But why does he think that he will please precisely in the role of prophet of the "fifth religion"? What particular social reason promises him some success in this role? To put it briefly: why is there now in Russia a demand for religion?

I shall reply by using Mr. Lunacharsky's own words: "De-

---

* Ibid., same page.
** *Essays on the Philosophy of Marxism*, same page.
*** [Note from *From Defence to Attack*.]—There is being repeated now, but with much greater emphasis, what we went through in the period of reaction in the 1880s. [194]

spondency is alive in man." By this I wish to say: in the Russian of *today.* "Alive" and very strong. The explanation lies in the great events that have occurred in Russia in recent years. Under the impact of these events, many many "intellectuals" have lost faith in the triumph of any more or less advanced social ideal in the near future. This is now all too familiar a situation. When people lose hope in the victory of a social ideal, the first "concern" which then arises is for their own precious personality. And uppermost is their "concern" about what is to become of that personality after its "earthly covering" has passed away. Science, with what Mr. Lunacharsky calls its equations of energetics, gives a fairly comfortless reply to this question: it utters a threat of personal non-existence. Therefore the good gentlemen who are concerned about their precious personality do not exactly relinquish the scientific viewpoint altogether—that is just not done these days— but adopt a system of double book-keeping. They say: "Knowledge is one thing and faith is another; science is one thing and religion is another. Science does not secure my personal immortality, but religion does. Long live religion!" That is how the matter is argued, for example, by Mr. Merezhkovsky, whose religious seekings will be examined in my next article. Mr. Merezhkovsky's "religion" is thoroughly saturated with uncompromising individualism. To Mr. Lunacharsky's credit it should be said that he does not suffer from an excess of that individualism. True, without noticing it, he often uses that tone himself. As an example of this, I recall his (theoretically very strange) observation that "we find nothing in common between the laws of the physical world and our truths and ideals". This observation, which is absurd from a theoretical standpoint, makes sense only to the degree that it expresses the state of split mind usual in a man who has lost faith in a social ideal and is now utterly absorbed in his own precious person. In speaking this way, Mr. Lunacharsky is making a concession to prevailing public opinion. He could not accommodate himself to it otherwise. But having made the concession, he at once makes the reader understand that he, Mr. A. Lunacharsky, as a "true socialist", has penetrated deeply the essence of the relationship between the individual and the species. To him, reality is the species, humanity, while the individual is but a partial expression of that essence.* His "religion" and his preaching of love are based upon this thought. "The individual ends with death," he says; "but another device elaborated in struggle furnishes the reply to this fact: reproduction, connected with love. This removes the living organism outside the boundary of narrow individual existence; it expresses itself in

---

* *Religion and Socialism,* p. 45.

the presence therein at first of ultra-individual instincts, and later in specific self-consciousness, in love for the species."* The same aim of struggle with the extremes of despondent individualism compels Mr. Lunacharsky to expatiate on co-operation as the basis of ultra-individual life: "Society is co-operation, the whole, embracing individuals and groups and opening up horizons in the domain of knowledge and technique which are completely inaccessible to separate individuals.... Socialism moves in the direction of world development which, by way of struggle and selection, creates ever more complex and mighty individualities of a higher calibre."** All Mr. Lunacharsky's "colourful" prophesies have the aim of doctoring the moral ulcers of the all-Russia "intellectual" who has been stricken with despondency. This is the imprint on his religious seeking. Our prophet willingly talks about the proletariat, the proletarian viewpoint, the proletarian struggle, etc. But with the proletariat as such, the proletariat für sich, with the working class which has achieved self-consciousness, Mr. Lunacharsky has nothing "in common". He is a typical Russian "intellectual", one of the most impressionable, most superficial and therefore least steadfast among them. These peculiarities of his type of intellect explain all his metamorphoses which he naively imagines to be a sign of advance. The fact that it occurred to him to invest socialism in a religious habit and even compose an amusing litany to the god-humanity, could only have happened because the low-spirited Russian "intelligentsia" had taken to religion. I. Kireyevsky once used the expression: "the padded-jacket of modern despondency". Many people thought this expression rather droll. But droll subjects should have droll titles. When I read the book *Religion and Socialism*, I said to myself: Mr. Lunacharsky has made himself a padded-jacket of modern despondency. And I still think that my first impression was not deceptive.

Now let us turn our attention to the other side of the same question. Like the one we have just considered it is extremely instructive.

At the end of his article "Atheism", Mr. Lunacharsky writes: "Let us discard the tattered mantle of grey materialism. If our materialists are men of courage and action ... it is *in spite* of their materialism and not because of it. That was the case with their true teachers, the Encyclopaedists.[195] But in a bourgeois, destructive way, materialism was an acute antithesis to the pernicious mysticism of the old régime. The proletariat needs a harmonious synthesis that will raise both opposites, convert them to itself and destroy them. We are all still searching for

---

* *Essays on the Philosophy of Marxism*, p. 151.
** Ibid., pp. 151-52.

this synthesis to the best of our ability. We may be mistaken, but we are searching joyfully and diligently. The annoyed shouts of the honoured veteran corporals will not stop us:

Yes, in our time the men were men,
Soldiers, not lads like you—were then
Heroes indeed! [196]

grumble the corporals. "But, uncle, they're dead and we need to use our own brains." The corporals command:

"Now children, learn your ABC,
—and learn it right."

"Uncle, why do we always have to repeat the alphabet, isn't it time we went on to syllables?"*

This is written glibly and amusingly, but, unfortunately, not very intelligently. Allegro, ma non allegro con spirito. And for the very simple reason that it reveals Mr. Lunacharsky's total lack of understanding of the part he is playing in Russian socialist literature. He is carried away by his fantasies on the excuse of moving forwad and in the name of the further development of the fundamental ideas of Marxism. But as I have already demonstrated, his attitude to religion is in direct opposition to that of Marx and Engels. Now I shall add this: in cutting out a religious costume for socialism, he is moving backwards like a crayfish, returning to the very view on religion held by the vast majority of the utopian socialists. Take the example of France. There Saint-Simon and his followers preached the "New Christianity". Cabet invented *"true* Christianity". Fourier thundered against the irreligious spirit of the people of modern times ("esprit irréligieux des modernes").**
Louis Blanc was a staunch upholder of deism. Pierre Leroux waxed indignant at people who thought that religion was done for, and exclaimed with emotion: "I am a *believer.* Even though I was born in an era of scepticism, I was such a believer by nature that I collected (such, at least, is my conviction) the faith of humanity at a time when that faith was in a state of latency, when it seemed that mankind believed in nothing, and I have the ambition of restoring that faith to humanity." The same Leroux proudly declares that he came into the world not in order to display literary talent, but "to find the most useful truth, religious truth" ("mais pour

---

* Ibid., pp. 160-61.
** In one of the manuscripts published after Fourier's death, we read: "Tous les travers de l'esprit humain se rattachent à une cause primordiale: c'est l'irréligion, le défaut de concordance avec Dieu, d'étude de ses attributions et révélations." ["All the failings of the human intellect are connected with one primordial cause: irreligion, the absence of concord with God, of study of his attributes and revelations."] Quoted by H. Bourgin in *Fourier.* Paris, 1905, p. 272.

trouver la vérité la plus utile—la vérité religieuse").* We see therefore that our Russian prophet had many predecessors in France.
Or take the case of Germany. Who is not aware how Wilhelm
Weitling liked to dabble in religion? Which Marxist does not recall Marx's polemics with the prophet of a "new religion" Hermann
Kriege, who has gone to live in New York? Who does not still
remember Engels' humorous characterisation of the prophet Albrecht (at the beginning of the 1840s) and the prophet George Kuhl-
mann from Holstein, who published a book in German in Geneva in
1845 under the title: *The New World or the Kingdom of the Spirit
on Earth. Annunciation.* See how many prophets there were! We
Russians are very backward in this respect as compared to Germany, and if we are starting to pick up a little now we have to
thank Mr. A. Lunacharsky and those who think like him. But for
one like myself, who is very disposed to wear what Mr. Lunacharsky describes as the tattered mantle of grey materialism, what is
most interesting in this historical information is the fact that some
German utopian socialists were capable of regarding materialism
with the same splendid contempt which we now hear from our
Russian empiriomonist and prophet of the "fifth religion", Mr.
Lunacharsky. He has already told us that "if our materialists are
men of courage and action ... it is *in spite* of their materialism and
not because of it". Now listen to what the Utopian Karl Grün prophesied to the world in the summer of the Year of our Lord 1845:
"The materialist who becomes a socialist perpetrates an appalling
inconsistency; happily, man is always worth more than his system." ("Ein Materialist, der Sozialist wird, begeht eine furchtbare
Inkonsequenz; glücklicherweise ist der Mensch immer mehr werth,
als sein System.")** You are late, frightfully late, blessed Anatoly,
with your disdainful condemnations, your exalted prophecies and
your "harmonious synthesis"!

But I am nevertheless very grateful to you, holy father, that
having promised us a religion without God, you could not refrain
from fabricating a "God"—mankind, and composing a suitable
litany for his glorification. In doing so you confirmed—though

----

* See *Oeuvres de Pierre Leroux* (1825-1850), t. I, Paris, 1850, Avertis-
sement, p. XI. See also pp. 4, 15, 41 and 44 of the text.
** Karl Grün, *Die soziale Bewegung in Frankreich und Belgien*, Darmstadt,
1845, S. 392. This is the same Karl Grün who is mentioned in the following
passage from Marx: "In the course of lengthy debates, often lasting all night,
I infected him to his great injury with Hegelianism.... After my expulsion
from Paris Herr *Karl Grün* continued what I had begun. As a teacher of German philosophy he had, besides, the advantage over me that he understood
nothing about it himself." (See "Karl Marx on Proudhon" in Supplement to
The Poverty of Philosophy translated by V. I. Zasulich and edited by myself.) [197]
He was, as you see, a worthy predecessor of Lunacharsky.

of course against your will—my thought that religious conceptions always have an animistic character. Your religion is no more than a fashionable game. But it, too, is no stranger to the logic found in all religions: people who play this game willy-nilly prattle in the language of animists, despite the fact that they have none of the beliefs peculiar to animists. The logic of religion compels them!

c) M. GORKY'S "A CONFESSION"
AS THE PREACHING OF "NEW RELIGION"

Maxim Gorky is a remarkable and brilliant artist. But even artists of genius are frequently utterly helpless in the domain of theory. There is no need to go far for examples: Gogol, Dostoyevsky, Tolstoy, these giants in the field of literary creation revealed infantile weakness every time they took up some abstract question. Belinsky often said that artists' minds went into their talents. There are not many exceptions to this rule. In any case, M. Gorky is not one of them. His mind also went into his talent. Hence the failings in those of his works where there is a high publicist element, for example, his essays on American life and his novel *Mother*. Those who encourage him to adopt the part of thinker and preacher are doing Gorky a very bad service; he is not cast for such parts. New proof of this may be found in his *A Confession*.

The book undoubtedly contains some wonderful pages dictated by a poetical sense of the unity of man and nature; pages in which one feels strongly the Goethe motif. These marvellous pages however cannot hide in the last analysis the weakness of *A Confession*. M. Gorky, who in his *Mother* made himself an advocate of socialism, appears in *A Confession* as an advocate of Mr. A. Lunacharsky's "fifth religion". And it is this circumstance that spoils the whole book. Because of it, *A Confession* becomes excessively lengthy, artificial, and, in places, downright dull. The hero—Matvei the novice, who tells the story, Yehudiil (Iona) the wanderer, and the factory teacher Mikhailo engage in the most nonsensical discussions. Gorky could not be blamed for this if his attitude to them had been that of an artist: but instead he approaches them as a preacher, using them to express his own personal thoughts. Therefore the reader has no alternative but to accept as Gorky's views what comes out of the mouths of his heroes. And the more these heroes go on talking nonsense, the more vexing it becomes, reminding one of the moral in Krylov's fable which tells how

The pike with jagged teeth one thought how nice
To set up as a cat and catch some mice.[198]

But it is not my intention here to analyse the story *A Confession*.
My purpose is not to deal with Gorky the artist, but with Gorky
the religious advocate, who is preaching in the same cause as Mr.
Lunacharsky. But he knows less than Mr. Lunacharsky (and by
that I do not mean to say that Mr. Lunacharsky knows much);
he is more naive than Mr. Lunacharsky (I do not mean by that that
Mr. Lunacharsky is not naive); he is less conversant with contemporary socialist theory (that does not mean that Mr. Lunacharsky
is so very conversant with it himself). Therefore his attempt to
clothe socialism in the vestments of religiosity proves an even big-
ger failure. The fitter from the local factory, Pyotr Yagikh, is saying to his nephew, Mikhailo:

"You, Mishka, have been picking up church ideas, like pilfering cucumbers from someone else's garden, and you only confuse
people."*

I need hardly say that I shall not repeat the word "pilfering"
here, even as a joke. That would be quite out of place. I must,
however, confess that M. Gorky's religious ideas do give me the
impression of being cucumbers from someone else's garden; they
certainly never grew in the soil in which the ideas of contemporary
socialism grow and ripen. M. Gorky tries to provide us with a philosophy of religion, but succeeds only in showing ... how badly he
is acquainted with that philosophy.

The most experienced of the god-seekers in this story, Mikhailo,
says for the edification of Matvei: "Slaves never had a God, but
made a god of human law forced on them from without, and slaves
will never have a God, for He is born from the flame of the sweet
consciousness of spiritual kinship of each with all!"** In fact that
is not true. We saw in the first article that God is not formed in
the flame of sweet consciousness of spiritual kinship of each with
all. He comes into existence when a given group of people linked
by blood relationship comes to conceive of their close tie with
a given spirit. Little by little the members of this group begin
to show love and respect towards the spirit, that is to say, they
begin to apply to the spirit the social feelings which are engendered
and consolidated in their common struggle for existence. It can
now be said with confidence that these feelings arise much earlier
than the appearance of gods. Hence the obvious error of all those
who, like Gorky, give the name of *religion* to every *social* feeling.
As far as slaves are concerned, their gods were the gods of the
tribes to which they belonged, unless, of course, the slaves adopted
the religion of their masters. That is my first reply to Gorky when

---

* «Исповедь» М. Горького [M. Corky's *A Confession*]. page 163 of the
Berlin edition to which all my references relate.
** *A Confession*, p. 164.

he speaks through the mouth of Mikhailo, after cleansing his words of the holy oil with which they are so plentifully covered. But looking more closely at Mikhailo's utterances, cleansed of the holy oil, I see, to use a well-worn expression, that they have to be "understood spiritually". Mikhailo's God is not just one of the numerous gods that were or are worshipped by savages, or barbarians, or for that matter, civilised peoples. No, this is a God of the future, that God which, Gorky is convinced, will be "constructed"* by the proletariat on reaching self-consciousness in collaboration with the whole of the people.** If that is so, it can be said right away that there never has been such a god and "for the rest of time" there never will be such a god, not only among slaves, but also among all those who do not take to the faith composed by the Blessed Anatoly. That is the gospel truth. No matter how thickly M. Gorky smears this sacred truth with holy oil, it will still be as lean as the most lean of Pharaoh's kine. It will add absolutely nothing new either to our conception of the world or to our understanding of the psychology of the proletariat.

Wait, though. In saying that Mikhailo's God is not one of the numerous gods that were or are worshipped by tribes and peoples

---

* This expression is very characteristic of our god-seekers today they aim consciously to "construct" god from previously prepared plans, just as an architect would build a house, an outhouse or a railway station.

** "It is the people that create gods," says Gorky through his character Iona (alias Yehudiil), "the world multitude which no man can number—holy martyrs greater than those whom the Church extols. That is the God that works miracles. I believe in the spirit of the people—the immortal people, whose might I acknowledge. It is the only origin of life that does not admit of doubt—the only parent of gods that have been and are yet to come!" (p. 140.) Mr. A. Lunacharsky, who has written a commentary to *A Confession* (see his article on the XXIII collection of the *Znaniye* in the 2nd book of *Literary Decadence* [Literaturny Raspad] was afraid that the reader might suspect Gorky of being "Socialist-Revolutionary",[199] and hastened to allay this suspicion. "While in no way adopting the turbid muddle of Socialist-Revolutionism," he says, "we can and must take the view that the influence of the proletariat on the popular masses is no empty phrase but a matter of the first importance. And Gorky portrays this in *A Confession*. Light starts to penetrate the darkness; it spreads throughout the villages where the "power of darkness" is still strong, around every town and every factory" (*Literary Decadence*, p. 92). Now we understand. This is something in the nature of the notorious "dictatorship of the proletariat and the peasantry" in application to religious creation. Mr. Lunacharsky says so outright: "That political hegemony, that revolutionary collaboration, the programme of which was indicated in outline, and the possibility of which was proved by ever such a 'narrow orthodox' writer (as some see him) as Kautsky, will undoubtedly have as its parallel the influence of proletarian ideology on the petty bourgeoisie" (ibid., p. 91). Isn't that splendid! Now it should be clear to everyone that in speaking of the "people", the old man, the elder Yehudiil does not in the least spurn the tactics of Mr. A. Lunacharsky and his like-minded associates. It will probably be realised by everyone that the story *A Confession* was not written without the influence of these tactics.

at various stages of their cultural development. I again (and again not at all by my own fault) did not exactly convey Gorky's thought. At the end of the story it turns out that the "god-creating people" are the people not of some more or less distant future, but of the present, represented by the throng of believers that follow in religious ecstasy the miraculous picture of the Blessed Virgin. This "people" of the present day performs even the miracle of healing the sick, as a consequence of which Matvei the novice turns to it with this prayer:

"Thou art my God and creator of all gods which thou hast formed from the beauties of thy spirit in the travail and torture of thy quest",etc.*

Evidently Mikhailo was wrong when he said "with a smile": "God is not yet created." And he was also wrong when he "obstinately" insisted:

"The God of whom I am speaking began to exist when men unanimously created Him out of the substance of their mind, in order to lighten the darkness of their life; but when the people were divided into slaves and lords, into bits and pieces, and tore asunder their thought and will, then God perished, then he was destroyed."**

To tell the truth, I do not know how on earth I should have found my way through this maze of contradictions without the Commentary. In his Commentary Mr. Lunacharsky explains everything which is unclear in the story itself.

"The might of the collective, the beautiful ecstasy of collective life, the wonder-working power of the collective," we read in the Commentary, "that is what our author believes in, that is to what he calls us. But did he not say himself that the people are now divided and oppressed? Did he himself not say that collectivism is to be sought only in the people reborn, in the factory?—Yes, only there, only in the assembly of the class collective, in the slow building of the all-proletarian organisation, is the real work of transforming people into mankind, though it may be only preparatory work. This does not signify that there will not be impulses, moments when the collective mood will blaze up, and that sometimes and somewhere by chance the masses of humanity will not merge into a single-willed whole. And now, like a symbol of the future, like a pale image—pale compared with what is yet to come, but vivid in comparison with our present surroundings—comes Gorky's miracle."***

Very good. The miracle of healing the sick is a symbol of the future. But here is the point. If those moments when "the collec-

---

* *A Confession*, p. 194.
** Ibid., p. 162.
*** *Literary Decadence*, Book 2, pp. 96-97.

tive mood blazes up" and when the "masses of humanity merge into a single-willed whole" are to be regarded as moments of the creation of God, the "worker of miracles", it must be said that the God who, according to Mikhailo, has still to be born, has been born countless times at the most varied stages of cultural development. He was not only born at those times, but he is born each time a deeply believing crowd takes part in a religious procession. I have never been to Lourdes, [200] but it seems to me that if l did go there, even for a short time, it would be vouchsafed to me to witness perhaps more than one "symbol of the future" perfectly resembling that described in Gorky's story. And this means that in Gorky's symbol there is nothing symbolic. More than that. The "masses of humanity" merge into a"single-willed whole" not only in the performance of religious rites. They thus merge also, for example, in war dances. Stanley gives an excellent description of one of those dances he observed in central Africa. One would indeed have to be overflowing with goodwill to discover in such manifestations of collective life the prototype of future religious creation. I do not know if that is how M. Gorky feels about it? Apparently not. But Mr. A. Lunacharsky senses that things are not quite right here, and tries to amend them. "What is important here is the presence of a *common* sentiment, a *common* will," says he in his Commentary. "The collective, true, is created here artificially, and its power is a fetish in the minds of the participants; but it is nevertheless created and the power is there. It is not a question of *denying* it completely, a priori, but of comprehending it and evaluating it."* Just so. The question is, of course, not to deny it "completely", "a priori", but to evaluate and comprehend it. But does Mr. Lunacharsky properly evaluate and comprehend all he has said in his Commentary? I am afraid he does so badly. That the class-conscious proletariat, in carrying out its great historic task, will on many occasions manifest its "common sentiment" and "common will" is so clear as to require no explanation. But it does not follow in the least that this "common sentiment" and "common will" will have a religious character. The only people who are likely to agree with Mr. Lunacharsky about such an eventuality are those who are content with the "etymological trick" by which the word "religion" is identified with the word "bond". But we already know how one of the founders of scientific socialism regarded this trick, and Mr. Lunacharsky will not put us off the point by repeating it in the name of Marx. Further: it is true that in the case we are now discussing "the power of the collective is a fetish in the minds of the participants" but the whole question is, will it remain so? A. Lunacharsky and

---

* Ibid., p. 97.

24*

M. Gorky would like it to be always so. They have noticed that
old fetishes have partly outlived, and are partly outliving their
time, and they have decided to make humanity itself a fetish by
placing the stamp of divinity upon it. They imagine that they are
being guided in this by their love for humanity. But this is a
simple, and even grotesque, misunderstanding. They begin by recognising that God is a fiction and end by declaring that humanity
is God. But humanity is no fiction. Then why call humanity God?
Why should mankind be flattered to be identified with one of its
fictions? No, whether you like it or not, I prefer Engels to the
novice Matvei and the elder Yehudiil. Engels said:

"We have no need to begin with the creation of an abstract God
in order to ... understand the greatness of man; we have no need
to take this roundabout way; we have no need to place the stamp of
divinity on man in order to be imbued with respect for man."[201]

Engels praises Goethe because he was reluctant to have recourse
to the deity and even avoided using the word: "Goethe's greatness lies in this humanity, in this emancipation of art from religion."* How good it would be if the study of Marxism could help
Gorky to understand the greatness of Goethe in that respect!

However, I still have to examine the blunders made by Gorky
in believing in the greatness of Mr. A. Lunacharsky.

Here is another blunder which does not yield in importance to
the first. The wanderer Iona, alias Yehudiil, "talking in a loud
voice as if he were arguing with someone", shouts: "God was not
created by man's weakness, but by his superfluity of strength, and
he lives not outside us, brother, but within us; but, for fear of
the questions of the spirit, they have fetched him out of us and
set him over us, in the desire to curb our pride, and our will, which
never brooked any limitations. I tell you that you have turned
strength into weakness, in holding back its growth by force. The
ideals of perfection are being created in too much of a hurry. This
is a cause of grief and mischief to us. Men are divided into two
tribes: those of the first are eternally building god, those of the
other are for ever the slaves of a dominant striving to lord it over
the first and over the whole world. They have seized on this power
and used it to establish the existence of God outside man—a god
who is the enemy of man and the judge and ruler of the earth.
They have defaced the image of Christ's soul, rejected His commandments, because the living Christ is against them, against
the dominion of man over man."**

That is a truly astonishing philosophy of history. It divides
people into two groups: one of them "eternally" engaged in build-

---

 * *Gesammelte Schriften*, B. I, S. 487.[202]
** *A Confession*, p. 139.

ing gods, and the other "ever" trying to subject the eternal god-builders to their will. The mutual relations between these "tribes" are supposed to explain the origin of the concept of God existing outside man. This again is factually incorrect. The concept of God existing outside man owes its origin, not to the division of people into "tribes", or classes, but to primitive animism. It is therefore also not true that "God was created by man's superfluity of strength". Finally, there is no basis whatever for the view that "Christ was against the dominion of man over man". True, it is extremely difficult for us to judge what that doctrine was exactly in its original form, and just because of this we must be careful in our approach to it and not colour it with our own aspirations. It would be as well, in any case, to remember the saying: "My Kingdom is not of this world." As for the early Christians, almost the most prominent one among them wrote: "Servants, obey your masters!" Why distort historical truth? In formulating these objections against M. Gorky, I keep the Commentary in mind (it is a very useful thing, this Commentary; one should always have it at hand when reading A Confession!). In it I find the following passage: "The hero of A Confession is not a Social-Democrat and not a worker, but a semi-peasant. That has to be kept well in mind."* The reference here is to Matvei the novice. "I keep this so well in mind" that I would have no objection to applying it to the old man Iona—Yehudiil who prattles so much nonsense about God, about Christ and the two eternal "tribes" of people. How are we to know? Maybe he talks nonsense only because he is not a Social-Democrat, not a worker, but a "semi"-something else? My doubts have been dispelled by Mr. A. Lunacharsky himself, who on the occasion of Matvei's meeting with Iona says in his Commentary (I repeat: keep this Commentary beside you when you are reading A Confession!): "The ideological force and perfect novelty of Gorky's story is in the grandiose picture: an exhausted people, portrayed in the person of Matvei, its spokesman, its seeker, comes face to face with the "new faith", with the truth which the proletariat is bringing to the world".** If this is the case, if the elder Iona is expounding to the exhausted Matvei the truth which the proletariat is bringing to the world, then we shall have to be strict: we have no right to take into account extenuating circumstances like the fact that Iona is not a worker but a "semi"-who-knows-what. And we must demand of Gorky who "created" Iona that he tells us the new truth in all its fulness. However, as I have already said, the great artist Gorky is a very poor thinker and an ineffectual preacher of the new truth. And there's the rub.

---

* *Literary Decadence*, Book II, p. 90.
** Ibid., p. 91.

I shall be frank to the end; in criticising such an outstanding artist as M. Gorky, one is obliged to speak out "straight, without evasion". M. Gorky himself has had extreme difficulty in digesting the truth which the proletariat is bringing to the world. This is the root of many of his literary errors. If he had digested this truth well, his American essays would have been written in a completely different vein: he would not have come before us like a Narodnik cursing the advent of capitalism. If he had digested this truth well, those of his heroes whom he has appointed to propagate this truth would not talk ambiguous nonsense at every conceivable opportunity. Finally—and this is the most important—if he had digested this truth, he would have seen clearly that at the present time there is neither the theoretical nor the practical need to warm up Feuerbach's old error and put the stamp of religion on human relationships, on human feelings, moods, and aspirations in which there is absolutely nothing religious. Then he would never have committed the greatest error of all, called *A Confession*. But ... many things could happen if ifs and ans were pots and pans.... "The pike with jagged teeth once thought how nice to set up as a cat and catch some mice." Gorky wanted to set up as a teacher, when in point of fact he has not completed his own education. The lad Fedyuk says to Matvei, whom he is seeing off at night: "They all say the same thing; such a life as they lead is worthless, it hampers you. Before I heard such talk as that, I lived quietly enough. Now I see that I haven't grown any higher, yet I have to bow my head. So its true—it hampers you!"* Add a few phrases to this: that truth must prevail on the earth; that man must not rule over man; and that, consequently, the proletariat must combat the bourgeoisie—and you will have exhausted M. Gorky's entire socialist world-outlook. I must say quite categorically that M. Gorky said nothing apart from this in his novel *Mother*, where he assumed the role of propagandist of socialism before he had as yet dressed it up in a priestly cassock. But that is not quite enough to make one a socialist, impervious to the utopias of the good old days. That is why Gorky has been unable to withstand the most incongruous of these utopias, the utopia of a new God, created by Mr. A. Lunacharsky for the correction, instruction, and encouragement of despondent "intellectuals".

However, to get back to *A Confession*. There is one very interesting passage in it which sheds light on the psychology of our present-day *god-inventor*. Matvei is describing the effect on him of his meeting with Mikhailo, who asserted that man ought to know everything.

---

* *A Confession*, p. 183.

"So I buried myself in books; I read the whole day long. I was troubled in mind and angry withal. Books don't argue with me; they just don't want to have anything to do with me. One book caused me great torment; it spoke of the development of the world and the life of man. It was written against the Bible. It was all very simple, intelligible, and necessary, yet I found no place for myself in that simplicity, for I felt surrounded by all sorts of forces, and I was like a mouse in a trap amidst them. I have read the book twice; I read it in silence, and I've tried to find a gap in it through which I might escape to freedom. But I don't find it."*

We have learned already from the Commentary that the hero of Gorky's story is neither a Social-Democrat nor a worker, but a semi-peasant, and that this should be "kept well in mind". But whether Matvei is a semi-peasant or not has nothing to do with the matter. The theoretical difficulty which nonplussed the "semi-peasant" Matvei has almost floored his teacher Mikhailo too, whom it seems we must regard as a Social-Democrat ... with a religious lining.

"I said to my teacher:
'How is that? Where does man come in?'
'It seems to me, too,' said he, 'that that is incorrect; but I can't explain where the error lies. But, as an attempt to explain the plan of the universe, it is very beautiful.'"**

Clearly, the book was materialist, and inspired in Matvei the same question around which much ink was spilt during the disputes between the Marxists and the subjectivists, viz.: how to reconcile the conception of natural necessity with the conception of human activity. It is known that the subjectivists were unable to solve this question and, like Matvei, they struggled around like a mouse in a trap. Again like Matvei, the subjectivists used to ask the Marxists: "Where does man come in?" The Marxists replied by indicating the answer already furnished by Hegel and assimilated by Marx and Engels.*** Needless to say, this reply did not satisfy the subjectivists. The matter was further complicated by the fact that even among the Marxists only those who held the viewpoint of modern dialectical materialism could grasp this solution correctly. Those who were inclined towards Kant's teaching—and to our shame there were then quite a few of them—or who were generally careless about philosophy, were without the theoretical means to reconcile the concept of freedom with the concept of

---

* Ibid., p. 161.
** Ibid., pp. 161-62.
*** See *Anti-Dühring*, published by Yakovenko, the chapter on "Freedom and Necessity."[203] Also the relevant pages of my book *The Development of the Monist View of History*.[204]

necessity; therefore, sooner or later, in one way or another, they returned to the theoretical positions of the subjectivists. Thus the question remained obscure even for many of those who, with complete sincerity, sympathised unreservedly with the contemporary movement of the class-conscious proletariat. Among these, it now turns out, was M. Gorky.

He has long interested himself in this question. Already in his story "Despondency" (1896) the armless Misha carries on the following very remarkable conversation with the drunken merchant Tikhon Pavlovich:

"'I once had a different opinion about life; I was very worried about myself and others, too ... like, as they say, what's the sense of it, what's it all about, what's it for, why?... Now, to hell with it. Life goes on in a certain way; well, let it go. That is as it should be. I have nothing to do with it. There's the laws.... You can't go against them .... no point to it; even the man who knows everything knows nothing. Oh, believe me, I've talked to the wisest people—students and many ministers of the church.... Ha, ha!'

"'So there's nothing a man can do?'

"'Not a thing!'"—said the armless, his eyes flashing, and turned himself squarely towards Tikhon Pavlovich and in a constrained voice added severely: 'Laws! Mysterious causes and powers— understand?' Raising his eyebrows, he shook his head importantly. 'Nobody knows anything—we're all in the dark!' He screwed himself up, drew in his head, and it seemed to the miller that, if his companion had had arms, he would have shaken a finger at him. 'So it means this: live, but don't complain, show humility! That's all!'"*

When this story first appeared, one wanted to think and might have thought that its author knew the weak side of the armless Misha's arguments. After the publication of *A Confession*, it is no longer possible, unfortunately, to believe this. Mikhailo, who, according to the Commentary, represents in this story the truth the proletariat is bringing to the world, admits with praiseworthy candour that he cannot answer the question, "Where does man come in?", that is to say, to solve the antinomy between natural necessity and human freedom. And it would be fruitless for us to seek in these conversations—in general very verbose—of the characters in the story even the slightest hint of a solution of this problem. There is no hint of it, and there could not be any. Gorky has finally decided that if the materialist view on the universe is to be maintained, it is necessary to accept the gloomy views of Matvei and the armless Misha on the question of human freedom.

* М. Горький, «Рассказы», т. I, СПБ, 1898, стр. 310—11. [M. Gorky, *Stories*, St. Petersburg, 1898, Vol. I, pp. 310-11.]

The "fifth religion" has become for him a means of escape from this hopeless conclusion. True, this religion by itself has apparently no direct relation to the question of how to combine the concept of freedom with the concept of necessity. But it is very closely connected with that "philosophy" on which the "fifth religion" is based; at least, that is what Mr. Lunacharsky says, after inventing a new God and writing his Commentary to the story *A Confession*. In his article "Atheism",* he assures the reader at great length that "grey materialism" seemingly does not leave any room for human freedom, whereas the philosophy of "empiriomonism" gives it a stable theoretical basis. In general, it may confidently be said that the "fifth religion" could have been formulated and adopted only by those "Marxists" who have been unable to cope with the principal theoretical tenets of the teaching of Marx and Engels. This is also something which "should be kept well in mind".

In passing, I should add that Mr. D. Merezhkovsky paid greater attention to the verbiage of the armless Misha, and described it as coming from a "scientific ignoramus—we don't know—which has sunk to the 'lower depths' of the vagabond."** In his evaluation of materialism (the "mechanical world-outlook") and the moral conclusions flowing from it, Mr. Merezhkovsky closely and touchingly agrees with Mr. Lunacharsky. "And it will do no harm to keep this well in mind." Our contemporary god-invention has its several varieties, each of which portrays a particular psychological mood and particular social "seekings". But all of them together have one feature in common: a complete inability to solve the antinomy between freedom and necessity.

It is not social consciousness that determines social being, but the other way round: social being determines social consciousness. Social movements and social moods are not occasioned by the theoretical errors made by the people taking part in these movements or experiencing these moods. But once a certain social movement is present, or—to express it more exactly—once a certain state of society is present and with it the social mood that corresponds to it, then theory, too, enters into its rights. Not every theoretical construction corresponds to a given social mood. Dialectical materialism is absolutely no help in god-invention. He who succumbs to the mood prevailing among our contemporary "intelligentsia" and takes to god-invention, must of necessity renounce dialectical materialism and commit certain errors in theory. However, this

---

* In the contents of the collection decorated by it this article is entitled "Atheists".

** Д. С. Мережковский, «Грядущий хам», СПБ, 1906, стр. 61. [D. S. Merezhkovsky, *Barbarian at the Gate*, St. Petersburg, 1906, p. 61.]

does not happen to everyone. Certain preliminary data are also necessary, and in the present instance they are reduced chiefly to incapacity to overcome the theoretical difficulty I have indicated.

It is time to finish. I should like, though, to say a few words more about M. Gorky's unfortunate story.

In it Mikhailo preaches to Matvei:

"This deplorable life, unworthy of human intelligence, began on the day when the first human personality tore itself adrift from the miraculous power of the people, from the mass its mother, and out of the dread of isolation and its own impotence it hunched itself up into a wicked bundle of petty desires—a bundle which was christened 'ego'. This 'ego' is man's worst enemy. For the sake of its self-defence and self-assertion on earth, it has fruitlessly killed all the forces of the spirit and all the great faculties for creating spiritual wealth in mankind."*

This reminds me forcibly once again of Marx's polemic with Hermann Kriege. Kriege, who was preaching a new religion, wrote: "We have more to do than be concerned with our own wretched 'ego'" (Wir haben noch etwas mehr zu thun, als für unser lumpiges Selbst zu sorgen). Marx replied with the cutting remark that Kriege's religion, *like every religion*, ends in servility to a metaphysical or even religious fiction which is humanity separated from "self".[205] Mikhailo and his creator, M. Gorky, would be well advised to ponder over these words of the author of *Capital*.**

Yes, it is worth thinking about. The question of "ego", when applied to the relationships between people, is frequently resolved according to the metaphysical formula: "either—or": *either* "non-ego" is sacrificed for the sake of "ego" (solution in the spirit of Nietzsche), *or* "ego" is declared to be unworthy of attention in view of the interests of "non-ego" (solution in the spirit of Kriege and Mikhailo). The dialectical solution of this problem, offering a logical possibility of reconciling both sides of the antinomy, was already indicated by Hegel and, incidentally, was borrowed from him by our Herzen and Belinsky. But the pity is that many of the most valuable attainments of West European thought during its historical development, up to and including Marx and Engels, are a closed book to our god-inventors. This is something they have in common with the "critics of Marx". Gorky's Iona declares: "You can't say to a man: stop there! but—from here or further!" The "formula of progress" which the "critics of Marx" and our con-

---

* *A Confession*, p. 154.
** *Gesam. Schriften von K. Marx und F. Engels*, II, S. 425.

temporary god-inventors have mastered for their own use, runs: "You can't say to a man: stop there (at Marx): but—from here go backwards, to where human thought was before Marx, or even before Hegel: there a whole series of brilliant discoveries are waiting for you."

Gogol, Dostoyevsky, Tolstoy, Gorky—all these are vast artistic talents. And all these vast talents have stumbled over religion, bringing unutterable harm to their artistic work. They are all much alike in this respect. But only in that. Each of them has created in his own way, as should follow from the possession of great talent. Even in religion each has his own particular way of stumbling. What is Gorky's way?

It is easy to say that M. Gorky made such-and-such a theoretical mistake. It still has to be explained why his thoughts turned along the theoretical path that led him into error. It is easy to say that M. Gorky succumbed to the influence of some god-inventor or other, if you like, Mr. A. Lunacharsky. We have yet to discover his state of mind which made it possible for this god-inventor to influence him. For what is Mr. A. Lunacharsky in comparison with M. Gorky? A haystack compared to Mont Blanc. But why did Mont Blanc submit to the influence of a haystack? Why has our poetical "Stormy Petrel" begun to speak in the mystical language of a sanctimonious humbug?

The significance of M. Gorky in Russian literature consists in this, that in a series of poetical sketches he introduced at the appropriate historical moment the idea he expressed through the old woman Izergil: "When a man yearns to do brave deeds, he will always find an opportunity. Life is full of such opportunities...." But the lyrical singer of exploits that quicken the heart-beats of Russian readers with their power, has badly understood the historical conditions in which the advanced man of present-day Russia has to perform his feats of endeavour. Theoretically speaking, M. Gorky is fearfully behind the times; rather let us say that he has not yet caught up with them. Consequently, there is still room in his mind for mysticism. His bold Malva was fascinated by the life of the man of God, Alexei. Gorky is not unlike his Malva. While admiring the beauty of heroic feats, he is not averse to glancing at them from the viewpoint of religion. That is a great and vexing weakness. And it was precisely because of this great and vexing weakness that the little haystack was able to subordinate to its influence the highest of mountains.

THIRD ARTICLE

THE GOSPEL OF DECADENCE

> "*Religious* questions of the day have at
> the present time a *social* significance. It
> is no longer a question of *religious*
> interests as *such*. Only the *theologian*
> can believe it is a question of reli-
> gion as religion."[181]
>
> *K. Marx*

I

Messrs Lunacharsky and Gorky proclaim that man is God on
the ground that there is not and cannot be any other God. But the
majority of our religious authors are opposed to this pronuncia-
mento. Mr. D. Merezhkovsky rebels against it with special passion. He says: "Conscious Christianity is the religion of God who
became man; conscious vagabondage, anti-Christianity, is the
religion of man who wants to become a god. The latter is, of course,
deception. The whole starting point of the vagabondage—"*only*
man exists," there is no God, God is nothing; and consequently
"man is God"—means that man is nothing. The illusory deification of man leads to his actual destruction."
    We shall see shortly why Mr. Merezhkovsky has talked about
"conscious vagabondage". Meanwhile, I must confine myself to the
remark that Mr. Merezhkovsky is fully justified in objecting to
"the religion of man who wants to become a god".* In my second
article, I noted the poor logic of those who first of all declare God
to be fiction and then acknowledge man as God; after all, man is
no fiction, no figment of the imagination, but a real being. But
if Mr. Merezhkovsky—and with him the majority of our god-
seekers—correctly indicate the shortcomings of the "man-deity"
religion, this does not yet mean that he himself has found a correct
viewpoint on religion. No, Mr. Merezhkovsky is no less mistaken
than Mr. A. Lunacharsky. But he is wrong in a different way, and
now we have to find out exactly where lies the particular distinctive feature of his own mistake. This will enable us to understand
one of the most interesting phenomena (from the standpoint of
social psychology) in our contemporary god-seeking.
    Mr. D. Merezhkovsky has a very flattering opinion of his own
education. He numbers himself among those who have penetrated
the innermost depths of European culture.** This flattering and

---

* See *Barbarian at the Gate*, etc., 1906, p. 66.
** See his article "Religion und Revolution" in the collection *Der Zar
und Revolution*, München und Leipzig, 1908, S. 161.

modest opinion of himself is, of course, very very much exaggerated. He is a long way from the depths of European culture, although it must be admitted that, in his own fashion, he is a very well educated person. And this very well educated man belongs to none of the reactionary or even conservative social groups.

Certainly not! On the contrary, he considers himself to be a supporter of such a revolution as must make prosaic and philistine Western Europe grow pale with fear. Here, too, of course, there is tremendous exaggeration. We shall see for ourselves that there is not the slightest reason why Western Europe should grow pale when confronted with such revolutionaries as Mr. Merezhkovsky and his fellow-religionists. Nevertheless, it is a fact that Mr. Merezhkovsky is not happy about the existing order of things. It might seem that this circumstance ought to earn him the sympathy of all ideologists of the proletariat. And yet it is difficult to imagine any such ideologist of the proletariat taking any attitude to Mr. Merezhkovsky other than one of ridicule. Why?

Of course, it is not because Mr. Merezhkovsky has a weakness, in season and out, for mentioning the devil. That kind of weakness is very funny, but it is quite harmless. That is not the point at all. The point is that even where Mr. Merezhkovsky desires to be extremely revolutionary, he reveals aspirations that could never be supported by ideologists of the proletariat. It is just these aspirations that are voiced by him in his religious "seeking".

The theoretical pretensions with which Mr. Merezhkovsky approaches the question of religion are astonishingly out of conformity with the theoretical resources he has at his disposal. This is most perceptible where he takes to task what he calls conscious vagabondage. See for yourself. He writes: *"Human, only human"* reason, renouncing the only possible affirmation of absolute freedom and absolute being of human personality *in God*, thereby affirms the absolute slavery and absolute nonentity of this personality in the world order, makes it a blind instrument of blind necessity—"a piano keyboard or an organ-stop" on which the laws of nature play in such a way as, having played, to destroy. But man cannot be reconciled to this destruction. Thus in order to affirm *at any cost* his absolute freedom and absolute being he is compelled to deny that which denies these, that is to say, the world order, the laws of natural necessity and, finally, the laws of his own reason. In saving his human dignity, man runs from reason to unreason, from world order to "destruction and chaos".*

What is this "absolute freedom", which man wishes to affirm, according to Mr. Merezhkovsky, *"at any cost"*? And why must man, deprived of the opportunity to affirm his absolute freedom, think

---

* *Barbarian at the Gate*, p. 59. Italics in the original.

of himself as a blind instrument of necessity? We are not told. If,
indeed, Mr. Merezhkovsky had managed to penetrate the depths
of European culture, he would have displayed greater care in his
handling of such concepts as "freedom" and "necessity". For Schelling long ago said that if a given individual were absolutely free,
all other people would be absolutely unfree, and freedom would
be impossible. In application to history, this means—as Schelling explains in another of his works—that the *free* (conscious)
activity of man presupposes *necessity* as the basis of human actions.
In a word, according to Schelling, our *freedom* is not an empty
formula only where the actions of our fellow-men are *necessary*.
This implies that European "culture" in the persons of its most
profound thinkers had already solved the antinomy now raised
by Mr. Merezhkovsky in his criticism of "conscious vagabondage".
It did this, not today or yesterday, but more than one hundred
years ago. This one fact is all we need to judge the enormous gap
between Mr. Merezhkovsky's theoretical pretensions and his theoretical resources: our would-be man of profound culture is lagging
behind the philosophical thought of cultured Europe by more than
a whole century. Nothing could be funnier!

II

Mr. Merezhkovsky states that the common metaphysical starting point of the intellectual and the tramp may be reduced to
a mechanical world-outlook, that is to say, "to the affirmation,
as of the only reality, of that world order which denies the absolute freedom and absolute being of human personality in God
and which makes man 'a piano keyboard or an organ-stop of blind
forces of nature'". In confirmation of this, he cites the argument
which I myself quoted (in the second article) from one of Gorky's
tramps: "There are laws and powers. How can we oppose them if
the only weapons we have are in our mind and that, too, must obey
those laws and powers? Very simple. Just live and make the best
of it, or power will soon make mincemeat of you." His companion
asked: "So there's nothing a man can do?" The tramp replied with
unswerving conviction: "Not a thing! Nobody knows anything—
we' re all in the dark!" Mr. Merezhkovsky imagines that this answer is as alike as two peas to that final conclusion arrived at by
the "mechanical world-outlook". He says: "But this is the scientif-
ic-ignoramus—we don't know—which has sunk to the 'lower
pepths' of the vagabond. Here, 'in the lower depths', it will have
exactly the same effects as at the intellectual surface." However, in
making this point, Mr. Merezhkovsky—obviously quite unconsious-
ly—demonstrates not that the "scientific ignoramus" coincides
with the arguments of the tramp, but that he himself is a tramp
in questions of this type.

The men whose labours created the elements of the "mechanical world-outlook", i.e., the natural scientists, were very often quite indifferent as regards philosophy. Inasmuch as they were indifferent in this respect, they were utterly uninterested in matters concerning the relationship of the concept of human freedom to the concept of natural necessity. But inasmuch as they did interest themselves in philosophy and especially in the question of the interrelations of these two concepts, they came to conclusions that had nothing in common with the verbal expansiveness of Gorky's unhappy inebriate. The celebrated ignoramus—more correctly, ignorabimus—of Du Bois-Reymond relates to the question of why the vibrations of matter organised in a certain way are accompanied by so-called psychical phenomena. The fact that science is unable to find the answers to *such* questions does not give Mr. Merezhkovsky the least right to attribute to the thinking, i.e., the philosophically developed representatives of science, the absurd contrasting of "man" to the forces of nature. The natural scientists of the time found it sufficient to grasp the attainments of classical German idealism, namely, the conclusions of Schelling and Hegel, to look upon such contrasting as one of the most vivid examples of the most childish nonsense. Already since the time of Bacon and Descartes, natural scientists envisaged man as a possible master of nature: tantum possumus quantum scimus (we can do as mush as we know). This yardstick of man's power over nature by knowing its laws is a far cry from the *"so there's nothing a man can do"* which Mr. Merezhkovsky foists on science as its final conclusion. The fact that Mr. Merezhkovsky could foist this ridiculous conclusion on science is yet another indication of the wide gap between his theoretical pretensions and the theoretical means at his disposal.

Mr. Merezhkovsky believes that every one who upholds the "mechanical world-outlook" *must* regard man as a "piano keyboard" or an "organ-stop" of the blind forces of nature. That is nonsense. But nonsense also has its causes. Why did our "deeply cultured" author think up such nonsense? Because he cannot get away from the standpoint of animism.

III

From the standpoint of animism which has reached a certain stage of development, man and all the universe were created by a god or gods. Once man has learned to look upon god as his father, naturally he begins to think of the God as the fountain-head of all good. And since freedom in all its varieties is conceived of by man as a boon, he believes accordingly that his God is the source of his freedom. Therefore there is nothing surprising in the fact that to him the denial of God is the denial of freedom. This psychological aberration is quite natural at a certain level of man's intellectual development. Nevertheless, it is no more than an aberration. To base a criticism of the mechanical world-outlook on it is simply to misapprehend its nature and to reveal a naivety quite unworthy of a "deeply cultured" person.

Mr. Merezhkovsky continues: "First of all—the conclusion: there is no God; or more correctly, man has no need of God, between man and God there is no unity, no bond, no religion, for *religio* means a bond between man and God."*

It goes without saying that if there is no God there cannot be any bond between man and God other than that existing between man and his invention. In this "conclusion", as such, there is nothing at all to be afraid of.

Why then is Mr. Merezhkovsky so frightened of it? He replies:

"This dogmatic positivism (because positivism too has its dogmas, its metaphysics and even its mysticism) leads inevitably to dogmatic materialism: 'Man's belly is the main thing. When the belly is replete, it means the soul is alive: every human activity comes from the belly.' Utilitarian morality is but a transitional stage at which one cannot stop somewhere between the old metaphysical morality and the extreme but unavoidable conclusion which Nietzsche draws from positivism—frank *amoralism*, which negates all human morality. The intellectual has not drawn this extreme conclusion because he was restrained by unconscious survivals of metaphysical idealism. There was nothing to restrain the tramp: in this respect as in many others, he was in advance of the intellectual: the tramp is a frank and almost conscious amoralist."**

Here, by dogmatic positivism, Mr. Merezhkovsky understands materialism proper: as is known, positivism in its modern sense (the positivism of Mach, Avenarius, Petzoldt) denies the mechanical interpretation of nature. Consequently, I can confine myself to examining how far Mr. Merezhkovsky's idea, just quoted, can be applied to materialism. This question has hardly occurred to me when I recollect the following passage from Engels, known to be one of the most notable materialists of the nineteenth century:

"By the word materialism the Philistine understands gluttony, drunkenness, lust of the eye, lust of the flesh, arrogance, cupidity, avarice, covetousness, profit-hunting and stock-exchange swindling—in short, all the filthy vices in which he himself indulges in private. By the word idealism he understands the belief in virtue, universal philanthropy and in a general way a 'better world', of which he boasts before others but in which he himself at the utmost believes only so long as he is having the blues

---

* *Barbarian at the Gate*, p. 61.
** Ibid., pp. 61-62.

or is going through the bankruptcy consequent upon his customary 'materialist' excesses. It is then that he sings his favourite song, What is man?—Half beast, half angel."*

In citing this passage from Engels, I have no wish to imply that Mr. Merezhkovsky is only infrequently disposed to idealism, i.e. that he only now and then believes in virtue, has love for humanity, etc. I fully and readily believe in his sincerity. I cannot help noticing, though, that his view on materialism was borrowed from the very philistine of whom Engels was speaking. And naturally this point of view does not become better founded by passing from a philistine to Mr. Merezhkovsky. Mr. Merezhkovsky thinks he has been called upon to reveal to the world a new religious word. That is just why he criticises our sinful materialist views. But the trouble is that in his criticism he confines himself to repeating very old errors.

In the present case, his errors are again closely bound up with animism. Already in my first article I explained that, at the earliest stages of social development, man's moral ideas were quite independent of his belief in the existence of spirits. Later these ideas fused solidly with the conceptions of those spirits which play the role of gods. Then it begins to appear that morality was based on belief in the existence of gods, and that with the collapse of this belief must also come the collapse of morality. The late Dostoyevsky was firmly convinced of this, and our author obviously shares this conviction. Here too we are dealing with the kind of psychological aberration which, while being perfectly understandable, is no less *only* an aberration, that is to say, it does not acquire the importance of being a *reason*.

We can doubtlessly come across people who will repeat sincerely the famous phrase: "If there is no God, anything is permissible."[207] But the example of such people proves nothing. Though, on second thoughts, I have put the matter wrongly: this example does not at all prove the proposition in defence of which it is usually advanced. But it is fairly convincing proof of the opposite proposition. Here is how that happens.

IV

If man's moral concepts are so closely bound up with belief in spirits that the ending of that belief threatens to be the end of morality, this constitutes a *great social danger*. Society cannot be indifferent to the fate of morality being dependent on a given fiction. To avoid such a dangerous situation, society would have to see to it that its members learned to regard the requirements of

---

* *Ludwig Feuerbach*, St. Petersburg, 1906, p. 50.[206]

morality as *something completely independent of any kind of supernatural beings*. Some may reasonably ask me: but what is society
if it is not the aggregate of its members? Can society take a different attitude to morality from that taken by its members? I readily accept this as a correct objection: society cannot look at any
single question differently from ist members. But a real society
is never homogeneous; one of its parts (group, estate, class) can
have some views, while another part has other views. When groups
are formed within it whose moral concepts do not correspond to
belief in the existence of spirits, it is in vain that other groups
which still cling to the old habits of mind charge them with immorality. In these groups society for the first time has grown up to
moral concepts which are able to stand on their own feet, without
any kind of outside support.

It is quite true that Nietzsche drew a conclusion from "positivism" which was tantamount to a denial of all human morality.
But the blame for this should not be placed on "positivism" or
materialism but only on Nietzsche himself. It is not thinking that
determines being; it is being that determines thinking. In his amoralism, Nietzsche expressed a mood peculiar to bourgeois society
in a period of decline, and this mood made itself felt not only in
the works of the German Nietzsche. Take the works of the Frenchman Maurice Barrès. Here is how he formulates the content of
one of them: "There is only one thing which we know, and which
really exists among all the false religions offered to you.... This
sole tangible reality is my ego (c'est le moi),* and the universe is
only a more or less beautiful fresco painted by it. Let us attach
ourselves to our "ego" and protect it from strangers, from the barbarians." That is sufficiently expressive. When people get into such
a mood, when the "sole tangible reality" is their precious "ego",
they have become true amoralists. Should these sentiments not
always prompt them to *immoral theoretical conclusions*, this is solely because *immoral practice* is far from always in need of an *immoral theory*. On the contrary, an immoral theory can frequently
be a hindrance to immoral practice. That is why people who are
immoral in practice often have a weakness for moral theory. Who
wrote *Anti-Machiavelli*? That Prussian king who, perhaps more
zealously than any other prince, abided in practice by the rule
laid down in the book *Il principe*[208]; and that is why the contemporary bourgeoisie, with all their involuntary sympathy towards
Nietzsche, will always consider that the disavowal of his amoralism
is a sign of good breeding. Nietzsche gave voice to what goes on
in bourgeois society, but which it is not the thing to admit. There-

---

* *Le culte du moi. Examen de trois idéologies* par Maurice Barrès, Paris,
1892, p. 45.

fore contemporary society cannot accord him more than *half-recognition*. Be that as it may, Nietzsche is a product of certain *social* conditions, and to ascribe his amoralism to positivism or to the mechanical world-outlook is to fail to comprehend the reciprocal connection of phenomena. The French materialists of the eighteenth century, if my memory serves me right, were also adherents of the mechanical world-outlook, and yet none of them preached amoralism. On the contrary, they spoke so often and so warmly about morality that in one of his letters Grimm jokingly referred to them as the *Capuchins of virtue*. Why did their mechanical world-outlook not induce them to amoralism? Solely because, in the then prevailing social conditions, the ideologists of the bourgeoisie, among whom the materialists of the day were the "extreme Left wing", could not but appear as defenders of morality in general and civic virtue in particular. The bourgeois were then in the *ascendant*, they were the *advanced* social class, they engaged in struggle with the immoral aristocracy and thereby learned to value and cherish morality. But now the bourgeoisie have themselves become the ruling class, now this class is moving in a *downward* direction, now its own ranks are being permeated more and more with corruption, and now the war of all against all more and more becomes the conditio sine qua non of its existence. It is not surprising, therefore, that the ideologists of this class are arriving at amoralism—that is to say, strictly speaking, those of them who are *frank*, and not prone to the hypocrisy so habitual nowadays among the bourgeois theoreticians. This is all perfectly understandable. But of necessity it can never be understood by anyone who holds the extremely childish view that the moods and actions of men are determined by whether they believe or do not believe in the existence of supernatural beings.

Here again I recall the splendid passage from Engels which I quoted in my second article: "In its essence, religion is the devastating of man and nature, denuding them of all content, the transferring of this content to the phantom of the other-worldly god, who then again gives to man and nature someting from his abundance."[209] Mr. Merezhkovsky belongs to the most diligent of the "devastators" of man and nature.* All that is morally exalted, everything noble, all that is truly human belongs, in his opinion, not to man but to the other-worldly phantom which man has created. Consequently, this phantom is to him an essential prerequi-

---

* Mr. N. Minsky says: "Men worship God not only because without God there is no truth, but also because without God there is no happiness" («Религия будущего», СПБ, 1905, стр. 85 [*Religion of the Future*, St. Petersburg, 1905, p. 85]). His words demonstrate that Mr. Minsky too will do yeoman service in the role of a devastator. It is no accident that he occupies one of the leading places among the founders of decadent religion.

site for the moral regeneration of mankind and for all social progress. He preaches revolution, but we shall see presently that only
in the spiritually devastated soul could there arise an inclination
towards the kind of revolution which he preaches.

V

"The question on which the fate of all the Russian intelligentsia depends," says Mr. Merezhkovsky, "was foretold in the fate
of Herzen, that greatest of Russian intellectuals: will they understand that only in the Christianity of the future is there the power
capable of overcoming philistinism and the approaching barbarian-
ism? If they understand this, then they will be the first confes-
sors and martyrs of the new world; if not, then, like Herzen, they
will only be the last warriors of the old world, the dying gladia-
tors."*
   At first, these words seem incomprehensible—what has all this
to do with Herzen? But here is how the matter is explained.
   "Positivism, or to use Herzen's words, 'scientific realism', is
the ultimate limit for all contemporary European culture, as a
method not only of particular scientific, but also of general philosophical and even of religious thinking. Engendered in science and
philosophy, positivism has grown from scientific and philosophical consciousness into an unconscious religion, which is striving
to abolish and take the place of all previous religions. In this broad
sense, positivism is the affirmation of the world open to sensual
experience, as the only real world, and the rejection of the super-
sensual world; the denial of the end and the beginning of the world
in God, and the affirmation of the continuance of the world without end and without beginning, in an environment of phenomena itself without beginning or end and inscrutable for man; the
affirmation of the *average*, of mediocrity, of that absolute conglo-
merated mediocrity, perfectly compact like a Chinese wall, that
absolute philistinism, of which Mill and Herzen spoke without
themselves realising the ultimate metaphysical depth of what
they were saying."**
   Now it is clear. Herzen was very much perturbed by the "philistinism" of the Western Europe of his day. Mr. Merezhkovsky
proves that Herzen was unable to answer the question: "how will
the people overcome philistinism?"*** and that he was unable to do
so because he was afraid of the "religious depths even more than
he was of the positivist shallows".**** Herzen sought God uncon-

---

  * Ibid., p. 20.
 ** Ibid., p. 6.
*** Ibid., p. 10.
**** Ibid., p. 15.

sciously, but his consciousness rejected God, and therein lay his tragedy. "This is not the first prophet and martyr of the new world, but the last warrior, the dying gladiator of the old world, of the old Rome."* The Russian intelligentsia of today must learn the lesson from Herzen's fate, and must consciously take the side of that "Christianity of the future" which has been invented for them with such solicitous care by Mr. Merezhkovsky.

The main link in all this chain of argument is our well-known play upon words: yearning for the good is the search for a God. Since dislike of "philistinism" is undoubtedly conditioned by yearning for the good, Herzen, who hated "philistinism", was an unconscious god-seeker. And since he did not want to hold religious views, he committed the sin of inconsistency, and this led him into "split-mindedness". After all that has been set forth above, it is not necessary to prove that the play upon words in which our author indulges has no more theoretical value than a a bad pun. But it will do no harm to examine more closely Mr. Merezhkovsky's firm conviction that "positivism" leads fatally to "absolute philistinism". On what is this conviction based—one that, incidentally, is not the prerogative of Mr. Merezhkovsky alone, as we shall soon see? He himself explains this as follows:

"In Europe, positivism is only now becoming, in China it has already become a religion. The spiritual basis of China, the teaching of Lao-Tze and Confucius, is perfected positivism, religion without God, 'earthly religion, religion without heaven', as Herzen described European scientific realism. No mysteries, no profundities or aspiration to 'other worlds'. All is simple, all is flat. Invulnerable common sense, unconquerable positiveness. There is that which there is, there is nothing more, and nothing more is needed. The world here is all, and there is no other world than the one here. The earth is all; there is nothing except the earth. Heaven is not the beginning and the end, but the continuation of the earth without beginning and without end. The earth and heaven *will not be one*, as Christianity affirms, but *are essentially one*. The greatest empire of the earth is also the Celestial empire, Heaven on earth, the Middle kingdom, the kingdom of the eternal average, of eternal mediocrity, of absolute philistinism— 'kingdom not divine, but human', as Herzen again defined the social ideal of positivism. To the Chinese worship of ancestors, to the golden age in the past, there corresponds the European worship of descendants, the golden age in the future. If we do not, then our descendants will see the earthly paradise, Heaven on earth— asserts the religion of progress. And both in the worship of ancestors and in the worship of descendants, there is equally sacrificed

* Ibid., p. 19.

the unique human person, personality—to the impersonal, the
numberless species, the people, humanity, 'the caviare, compressed
out of a myriad of petty philistines', the future universal
polyp and antheap. Disavowing God, disavowing the absolute
divine personality, man unavoidably disavows his own human
personality. Renouncing his divine hunger and divine birthright
for the sake of the mess of pottage, of frugal satiety, man falls
inevitably into absolute philistinism. The Chinese are the completely yellow-faced positivists; the Europeans are not yet completely white-faced Chinese. In this sense, the Americans are more
perfect than the Europeans. There the extreme West meets the
extreme East."*

Our "deeply cultured" author appears here in all the majesty of
his amazing argumentation. He takes it for granted, obviously,
that *to prove* a certain idea, all that is required is to repeat it,
and the more often it is repeated the more convincingly it is proved.
Why must "positivism" lead immediately to philistinism?
Because "in disavowing God, man unavoidably disavows his own
human personality". It is not the first time we have heard this from
Mr. Merezhkovsky, and not once has he taken the trouble to adduce even the slightest hint of proof. But we are already aware that
people who are accustomed to devastating the human soul for
the sake of an other-worldly phantom cannot conceive the matter
in any other way: they cannot but think that with the disappearance of the phantom there will be a "desolation of all feeling"
in the human heart, as it was with Sumarokov's Kashchei.[210] Well,
where there is desolation of all feeling, there is naturally the installing of all vices. The whole question now before us is what exactly does Mr. Merezhkovsky mean by "philistinism", and why
exactly does "philistinism" come under the heading of vices?

We have been told that man will fall into absolute philistinism
if for the sake of frugal satiety he renounces his divine hunger
and his divine birthright. And some lines before this, our author
gave us to understand that renunciation of the divine hunger and
the divine birthright takes place where the human person is sacrificed "to the impersonal, the numberless species, the people, humanity". Let us assume that our author is giving us a correct definition of "absolute philistinism", and ask him where, all the same, he
came across this; was it really in Europe of today? We know that in
contemporary Europe the bourgeois system holds sway and that the
basic bourgeois law of that system is the rule: each for himself
and God for all. It is not hard to understand that those who follow
that rule in their practical lives are in no way disposed to sacrifice
themselves (and consequently, their "person") to "the species, the

---

* Ibid., pp. 6-7.

people, humanity". What is this our "deeply cultured" author is
telling us?

But that is not yet all.

<h1 style="text-align:center">VI</h1>

According to his definition, "absolute philistinism" consists
in the human person being sacrificed "to the species, the people,
humanity", for the sake of *the golden age in the future*. It is precisely
this sacrificing of the person for the sake of the golden age in the
future that characterises contemporary Europe, whereas the "yellow-faced positivists", the Chinese, worship the golden age in the
past. Again we ask: is it not in Europe of today that the bourgeois
order prevails: Where then did Mr. Merezhkovsky get the idea
that the bourgeoisie ruling in Western Europe aspires to the golden
age in the future? Whose portrait is he painting? Where did he
hear this kind of talk? Was it not from the socialists who, after all,
were the first to speak of the golden age in the future.

That is just how it is. Mr. Merezhkovsky says that socialism
"involuntarily embraces the spirit of the eternal average, philistinism, the inevitable metaphysical consequence of positivism,
as a religion upon which it itself, socialism, is constructed".*
Leaving metaphysics aside, let us look at the matter from the
standpoint of social psychology.

"The hungry proletarian and the sated philistine have different
economic interests, but the same metaphysics and religion,"
Mr. Merezhkovsky tells us, "the metaphysics of moderate common
sense, the religion of moderate philistine satiety. The war of the
fourth estate against the third estate, though economically real, is
just as unreal metaphysically and religiously as the war of the
yellow race against the white. In both cases it is force against
force and not God against God."**

"That war in which there is not God against God is metaphysically and religiously unreal." Let it be so. But why does our author think that the hungry proletarian has no other moral interest
apart from moderate satiety even when he sacrifices his personal
interests to the advantage of "the unconditionally golden age"?
That remains a secret. But it is not a difficult one to uncover.
Mr. Merezhkovsky took his characterisation of the hungry proletarian's psychology from the gentlemen of whom Heine said:

---

* Ibid., p. 11. Z. Hippius, who is of the same mind as Mr. Merezhkovsky,
expresses herself much more decisively. She assures West European readers
that socialist teachings are based "auf einem krassen Materialismus". (See
her article "Die wahre Macht des Zarismus" in the collection *Der Zar und die
Revolution*, p. 193).

** Ibid., p. 10.

Sie trinken heimlich Wein
*Und predigen öffentlich Wasser.*****[211]

That is an old song. Every time the "hungry proletarian" places certain economic demands before the sated bourgeois, he is charged by the latter with "crude materialism". The bourgeois in his well-fed narrowness does not and cannot understand that to the hungry proletarian the realisation of his *economic* demands is tantamount to guaranteeing him the possibility of satisfying at least some of his *"spiritual"* needs. Nor does it occur to him that the struggle for the realisation of these economic demands can inspire and inculcate in the spirit of the hungry proletarian the most noble sentiments of courage, human dignity, selflessness, devotion to the common cause, and so on and so forth. The bourgeois judges by his own standards. He himself is daily engaged in economic struggle, but never experiences in it the slightest moral inspiration. Hence his contemptuous smile when he hears of proletarian ideals: "Tell it to the marines, you can't fool me!" And, as we have seen, Mr. Merezhkovsky fully shares this sceptical view, even while imagining himself the hater of the sated "philistine". Is he the only one? Unfortunately, no; not by any means. Read, for instance, what N. Minsky writes:

"Don't you see that the socialist-worker and the capitalist-dandy have the same aim in life? Both of them pay homage to articles of consumption and the comforts of life, both strive to increase the quantity of goods they consume. The only one is on the bottom rung of the ladder and the other on the top rung. The worker tries to raise the minimum of living standards, the capitalist the maximum. Each is within his rights and the struggle between them is simply a contest for which rung of the ladder has to be taken first—the top one or the bottom one."****

Further: "If the fourth estate is gaining victory after victory before our very eyes, this does not arise because this estate has more sacred principles on its side than the other, but because the workers prosaically organise their forces, collect capital, put forward demands, and support them by force. Understand that, my friend. With all my heart I sympathise with the new social force, if only for the reason that I consider myself to be a worker. I am even prepared to admit that it has justice on its side, for justice seems to me to be nothing but a balance of real forces. Therefore I believe that conservatism is a betrayal of justice. However, I cannot help noticing that by its victories the new social force is not only failing to create a new morality, but is drawing us still further into the jungle of goods-worship. I cannot fail to see that

---

* [They drink wine in secret and in public preach the virtues of water.]
** *Religion of the Future*, p. 287.

the ideal of the socialists is the same philistine ideal of prosperity in goods, continued downwards, in the direction of a universally accessible minimum. They are right for themselves, but no new truth comes from them."*

Finally, in a recently published book *On Social Themes*, Mr. Minsky says:

"We, the Russian intellectuals, would be committing an act of spiritual suicide were we to forget our vocation and common human ideal, and accept in full the teaching of European Social-Democracy with all its philosophical basis and psychological content. We must constantly keep in mind that European socialism was begotten in the same original sin of individualism as were the European nobility and bourgeoisie. At the root of all the claims and hopes of the European proletariat is not general love for all men but the same longing for freedom and comfort which in its day inspired the third estate, and has led to the present discord. The claims and hopes of the workers are more legitimate and human than those of the capitalists, but, since they have a class nature, they do not correspond to the interests of humanity."**

Mr. Merezhkovsky could make nothing of the antinomy of freedom and necessity. Mr. Minsky stumbled over the antinomy of general human love and freedom accompanied by comfort. The second is even funnier than the first. As an incorrigible idealist, Mr. Minsky just cannot understand that the interests of a given class at a given period of historical development of a given society may coincide with the general interests of humanity. I have not the slightest desire to lead him out of this difficulty, but I do think it would be useful to point out to the reader that this description of modern socialism as an expression of the "philistine" aspirations of the proletariat contains absolutely nothing new, apart maybe from a few particular figures of speech.*** Thus, for example, Renan wrote in the preface to his *l'Avenir de la science*: "A state which would guarantee the greatest happiness of the individual would probably end in a condition of profound decay from the point of view of the noble aspirations of mankind". Is this con-

---

* Ibid., p. 288.
** *On Social Themes*, St. Petersburg, 1909, p. 63.
*** Incidentally, on page 10 of his book, *Barbarian at the Gate*, Mr. Merezhkovsky portrays matters as though his view on the psychology of the "hungry proletarian" was merely a development of Herzen's view. That is quite wrong. True, Herzen assumed that the Western proletariat "will all pass through philistinism". But this seemed inevitable to him only if there were not a social revolution in the West. Whereas Mr. Merezhkovsky says that it is the social, i.e., at least the socialist, revolution which must lead to philistinism. For Herzen's views on philistinism and how these are distorted by our present-day supermen, see my article, "The Ideology of Present-Day Philistinism" (*Sovremenny Mir*, 1908, May and June).

trasting of the happiness of the individual to the high ideals of
mankind not the prototype of the contrasting of the general love
for mankind to freedom, accompanied by comfort, which
Mr. Minsky presents to us as the main outcome of his critical and, of
course, original reflections on the nature of contemporary socialism? The same Renan, who partly understood the significance of
the class struggle as the mainspring of mankind's historical development, could never rise to the height of viewing this struggle as
the source of the moral perfecting of its participants. He believed
that the class struggle aroused in people only envy and, in general,
the lowest instincts. According to him, people taking part in the
class struggle, at least those on the side of the oppressed—an
especially interesting point for us in the present case—are incapable of rising higher than Caliban, hating his master Prospero.[212]
Renan consoled himself with the thought that flowers may spring
from dung, and that the basest instincts of those taking part in
the people's emancipation movement do ultimately serve the cause
of progress. Compare his conception of the class struggle with
what we have read in Messrs Merezhkovsky and Minsky about the
psychology of the militant proletariat, and you will be astonished
by the resemblance of this old pseudo-philosophical twaddle to
the new *gospel of decadence*. Yet Renan was not the only one to
indulge in this pseudo-philosophical twaddle: he only expressed
more vividly than others the sentiment already revealed by some
French Romanticists, which becomes the ruling passion among
the French "Parnassians" (parnassiens).[213] The fanatical adherents
of the theory of art for art's sake, the "Parnassians", were convinced
that they had been brought into the world "not for worldly agitation, nor worldly greed, nor worldly strife",[214] and with very few
exceptions, were quite incapable of understanding the moral
grandeur of that "worldly agitation" which stems from historic
class "strife". Sincere, and "in their own fashion" honest and noble
in their aversion to "philistinism", they put into the same compartment of "philistinism" positively all civilised humanity of their
time, and with truly comical indignation hurled the charge of
"philistinism" at the great historical movement which is called
upon to root out *philistinism* in the moral field, by putting an end
to the philistine (i.e., the bourgeois) mode of production. From
the Parnassians, this comic contempt for the imaginary philistinism of the emancipation struggle of the proletariat passed to
the Decadents—first the French and then the Russian. If we take
into account the circumstance that our modern evangelists, for
example selfsame Messrs Minsky and Merezhkovsky, studied with
great diligence and excellent success in the Decadent school,
we shall realise at once where their views on the psychology of
the hungry West European proletariat originated, a psychology

which they portray in such truly philistine colours for the spiritual edification of the Russian intellectual.

<h2 style="text-align:center">VII</h2>

Alas, there is nothing new under the sun! All the gospels of Messrs Merezhkovsky, Minsky, and their ilk prove—at least in their negative attitude to the imaginary philistinism of the West European proletariat—to be but a new copy of a much worn original. But this is only half the sorry tale. The real tragedy is that the original which our half-baked denouncers of proletarian philistinism reproduce is itself saturated through and through with the spirit of the bourgeoisie. It is a kind of mockery of fate, and, one must admit, a very bitter, malicious mockery. While reproaching the "hungry proletarians" engaged in bitter struggle for the right to a human existence with philistinism, the French Parnassians and Decadents themselves not only did not turn up their noses at worldly goods, but, on the contrary, were incensed with contemporary bourgeois society, by the way, for failing to assure an adequate supply of the good things of life to them, the Parnassians and Decadents, the sensitive votaries of beauty and truth. Regarding the class movement of the proletariat as the offspring of a base feeling of envy, they had no objection whatever to society being divided into classes. Flaubert wrote in one of his letters to Renan: "I thank you for having risen against democratic equality, which seems to me to be an element of death in the world." It is not surprising, therefore, that with all their hatred of philistinism, the "Parnassians and Decadents" took the side of the bourgeoisie in its struggle against the innovative aspirations of the proletariat. Nor is it less surprising that before locking themselves "*in their ivory tower*" they spared no effort to improve their own material position in bourgeois society. The hero of Huysmans' famous novel *A rebours* is so revolted by philistinism that he decides to build his entire life the opposite way to what it is in bourgeois society (hence the title: *The Other Way Round*, inside out). He begins, however, by putting his own financial affairs in order, making sure of an income, I think, of some 50,000 francs. With all his heart and soul he detests philistinism, but it does not enter his head that it is only thanks to the philistine (capitalist) mode of production that he can receive his large income without lifting a finger and indulge in his anti-philistine extravagances. He wants the cause, but hates the consequences inevitably flowing from this cause. He wants the bourgeois economic order but despises the sentiments and moods it creates. He is an enemy of *philistinism*; but this does not prevent him from being a *philistine to the very core*, since in his rebellion against philistinism he does not once raise his hand against the foundations of the philistine economic order.

Mr. Merezhkovsky speaks of the tragedy which Herzen experienced under the influence of the impressions he had formed of "philistine" Europe. I shall not dilate here upon this tragedy. I shall only say that Mr. Merezhkovsky has understood it even less than the late N. Strakhov, who wrote about it in his book *The Struggle with the West in Our Literature*.* But I should like to draw the reader's attention to the tragic conflict which must inevitably arise in the mind of a man who sincerely despises "philistinism" and at the same time is utterly incapable of abandoning a philistine view of the basis of social relations. Such a man will become a pessimist in his social views whether he likes it or not: he has really nothing to expect from social development.

But it is not easy to be a pessimist. It is not everyone who can bear the burden of pessimism. And so he who finds "philistinism" repulsive averts his gaze from the earth, soaked through and through and for ever with "philistinism", and turns it towards ... heaven. There takes place that "devastating of man and nature" of which I spoke earlier. The phantom of the other world presents itself in the form of an inexhaustible reservoir of every kind of antiphilistinism, and thus prepares the most direct route into the domain of mysticism. It was no accident that the sincere and honest Huysmans lived his own works so profoundly that he ended his days as a thorough-going mystic, almost a monk.

Taking all this into account, we shall have no trouble in determining the sociological equivalent of the religious seekings which are making themselves felt so strongly in our country, in an environment more or less—and even more than less—involved in Decadence.**

---

* My view on this tragedy is presented in my article "Herzen the Emigrant" in Book 13 of *The History of Russian Literature in the 19th Century*, published by the Mir Co-operative and edited by D. N. Ovsyaniko-Kulikovsky.

** Mr. Merezhkovsky understands quite well that his religious seekings are connected with decadent "culture". (See the collection *Der Zar und die Revolution*, S. 151 et seq.) As one of the representatives of Russian Decadence, Mr. Merezhkovsky seriously overestimates its social significance. He says: Die russischen Dekadenten sind eigentlich die ersten russischen Europäer; sie haben die höchsten Gipfel der Weltkultur erreicht, von denen sich neue Horizonte der noch unbekannten Zukunft überblicken lassen" [the Russian Decadents are essentially the first Russian Europeans; they have reached the highest peaks of world culture, from which new horizons of the as yet unknown future open up], etc. This is really funny in the full meaning of the word, but quite understandable, when one considers that Mr. Merezhkovsky, with all his modern gospel, is bone of the bone and flesh of the flesh of Russian Decadence.

VIII

Those who belong to that environment, *seek a way to heaven for the simple reason that they have lost their way on earth.* The greatest historical movements of mankind seem to them to be deeply "philistine" in nature. Hence the reason why some of them are indifferent to these movements or even hostile to them, and others, while attaining some sympathy towards them, find it essential to sprinkle them with holy water, in order to wash off the curse of their "material" economic origin.

However, I shall be told that I have myself admitted that, among our Decadents who are seeking a way to heaven, there are people who sympathise with modern social movements. How can this be reconciled with my contention that all these people are themselves imbued with the spirit of the philistine?

Such an objection not only *can* be made, it had *already been* made even before I expressed my thoughts on the matter. It was made by none other than one of the prophets of the new gospel — Mr. Minsky.*

It is known that in the autumn of 1905 Mr. Minsky, who in the same year published his book *The New Religion*,[215] from which I made long extracts earlier on the question of the "philistine" spirit of the contemporary labour movement, attached himself to one of the factions of our Social-Democratic party.[216] This naturally aroused much derision and perplexity. Here is how Mr. Minsky replied to that derision and perplexity. I shall make a very long extract, since in his explanation Mr. Minsky touches upon most important problems of contemporary — Russian and West European — social life and literature.

"First of all, I should remark that a good half of the bewilderment and the charges directed against me are related to that primary misunderstanding which has established itself in our liberal criticism in regard to symbolical and mystical poetry, and which consists in the belief that the poets of the new sentiments, if they are not open enemies of political freedom, are at the very least politically indifferent. The Messrs Skabichevskys and Protopopovs have not descried the most important element — that the whole symbolist movement was nothing else than a yearning for freedom and a protest against conventional trends imposed from without. But when, instead of verbal calls to freedom, there

---

* I should put it more exactly: one of the prophets of one of the modern gospels. Mr. Minsky thinks that his new gospel bears no resemblance to Mr. Merezhkovsky's new gospel (see his article "Absolute Reaction" in the collection *On Social Themes* [«На общественные темы»]). That is his right. But I too insist on my right, just as incontestable as his, to notice the features of an astonishing *family resemblance* in the two gospels.

swept over Russia the living breath of freedom, something took place which, from the standpoint of liberal criticism, was incomprehensible, but was in fact necessary and simple. All—I emphasise this word—all the representatives of the new sentiments without exception: Balmont, Sollogub, Bryusov, Merezhkovsky, A. Bely, Blok, V. Ivanov proved to be songsters in the camp of the Russian revolution. In the camp of reaction were those poets who were hostile to symbolism and loyal to the old traditions— the Golenishchev-Kutuzovs and the Tsertelevs. The same thing happened among the Russian painters. The refined aesthetes of The World of Art[217] created a revolutionary satirical journal in alliance with the representatives of the extreme opposition, [218] while the old knights of tendentious painting, the pillars of the Mobile Exhibitions, at the first thunder of the revolution, hid themselves in the nearest corners. What a curious comparison: the healthy realist Repin, Rector of the Academy, painting a picture of the State Council, and the impressionist Serov, from the window of the same Academy, jotting down a sketch of the Cossack attack upon a crowd of workers on the morning of January 9. There is nothing to be surprised at here, however. Events already familiar in European life were being repeated in our midst. Was not the sincerest aesthete, the friend of the Pre-Raphaelites— Morris—simultaneously the author of a social utopia and one of the leaders of the labour movement? Were not the most talented of the contemporary symbolists—Maeterlinck and Verhaeren— the apostles of freedom and justice? The union of symbolism with the revolution was an event of inner necessity. The artists with the most sensitive nerves could not help being the most responsive to the voice of truth. The innovators in the field of art could not but stand shoulder to shoulder with the transformers of practical life."

In this long extract, the most remarkable point (the one "emphasised" by Mr. Minsky) is that all our representatives of the new literary sentiments without exception proved to be "songsters in the camp of the Russian revolution". This is indeed a very interesting fact. But in order to grasp the importance of this fact in the history of the development of Russian social thought and literature, it will be worth while giving a little historical information. In France, whence Decadence came to us, the "representatives of the new trends" also sometimes appeared as songsters "in the camp of the revolution". And it is instructive to recall some characteristic peculiarities of this phenomenon. Take Baudelaire, who in many very important respects may be regarded as the founder of the latest literary trends which attracted the said Mr. Minsky.

Immediately following the February revolution of 1848, Bau-

delaire together with Champfleury founded the revolutionary journal, *Le Salut Public*. It is true that the journal soon ceased: only
two issues appeared, for February 27 and 28. But this did not
happen because Baudelaire had ceased to sing the praises of the
revolution. No, for in 1851 we still find him among the editors of
the democratic almanac, *La République du Peuple*, and it is well
worth noting that he sharply disputed "the infantile theory of art
for art's sake". In 1852, in the preface to Pierre Dupont's *Chansons*,
he proved that "art is henceforth inseparable from morality and
utility" (l'art est désormais inséparable de la morale et de l'utili-
té). And several months before this he had written: "The excessive enthusiasm for form is being carried to monstrous extremes ...
the concepts of truth and justice are disappearing. The unbridled
passion for art is an ulcer consuming everything around it.... I
understand the frenzy of the Iconoclasts and the Moslems against
religious images.... The crazy enthusiasm for art is tantamount to
abuse of the intellect", and so on. In a word, Baudelaire spoke in
almost the same language as our destroyers of aesthetics. And all
in the name of the people, in the name of the revolution.

But what had the same Baudelaire been saying before the revolution? He said—no further back than 1846—that whenever he
happened to witness a republican outbreak and saw a policeman
striking a republican with the butt of his rifle, he was ready to
shout: "Hit him, hit harder, hit again, dear policeman.... I adore
you for beating him up, and regard you as akin to the supreme
judge Jupiter. The man you are beating is the enemy of roses and
fragrance, the fanatic of household utensils; he is the enemy of
Watteau, the enemy of Raphael, the desperate foe of luxury, fine
arts, and belles-lettres, an inveterate iconoclast, the executioner
of Venus and Apollo.... Beat that anarchist about the shoulders,
and do it with religious fervour!" In short, Baudelaire used the
strongest language. And all in the name of beauty, all in the name
of art for art's sake.

And what did he say *after* the revolution? He said—and not
so long after the events of the early 50s, to be precise, in 1855—
that the idea of progress was ridiculous and a sign of decline. According to him then, this idea is "a lantern, that sheds nothing but
darkness on all questions of knowledge," and "he who wishes to
see history clearly must first of all extinguish this treacherous
light". In short, our former "songster in the camp of the revolution", did not mince his words on this occasion either. And once
again in the name of beauty, once again in the name of art, once
again in the name of the "new trends".*

---

* See Albert Cassagne, *La théorie de l'art pour l'art en France chez les
derniers romantiques et les premiers réalistes*, Paris, 1906, pp. 81 et suiv.,
113 et suiv.

IX

What does Mr. Minsky think? Why was it that Baudelaire, who in 1846 was imploring the dear policeman to club the republican, two years later turned up as a "songster in the camp of the revolution"? Was it because he had sold himself to the revolutionaries? Of course not. Baudelaire appeared "in the camp of the revolution" for a reason that was a great deal less shameful: quite unexpectedly for himself he was projected into the revolutionary camp by the waves of the people's movement. Being as impressionable as a hysterical woman, he was incapable of swimming against the stream; and when "in place of the verbal calls for freedom", there swept over France "the living breath of freedom", he who had not long before mocked so crudely both at the calls for freedom and the active struggle for freedom, was blown like a piece of paper in the wind into the camp of the revolutionaries. But when reaction triumphed, when the living breath of freedom had been stifled, he began to find the idea of progress ludicrous. People of this calibre are utterly untrustworthy as allies. They cannot help turning out to be "responsive to the voice of truth". But they are not usually responsive for long; they do not have enough character for that. They dream of supermen; they idealise strength; but they do so not because they are strong, but because they are weak. They idealise not what they *have* but what they *do not have*. That is just why they cannot swim against the stream. They are, rather, borne along by the wind. So is it surprising that the revolutionary wind sometimes blows them into the camp of the democrats? It still however does not follow from their being sometimes blown by that wind that "the union of symbolism with the revolution is an event of inner necessity", as Mr. Minsky assures us. Not at all! This union is brought about—when it is brought about—by causes that have no direct relationship either to the nature of symbolism or to the nature of revolution. The examples of Morris, Maeterlinck, and Verhaeren which were advanced by Mr. Minsky prove at best * only that talented people, too, can be inconsistent. But this is one of those truths which require no proof.

I shall put it bluntly: I should have a great deal more respect for our representatives of "modern trends" if during the revolutionary storm of 1905-1906 they had shown some ability to swim against the stream, and had not been in such a hurry to take up their revolutionary lyre. Surely they themselves must realise now that in their unaccustomed hands that lyre gave forth not very

---

* I say "at best" because quite frankly I must confess that I do not know in what Maeterlinck showed himself as "an apostle of freedom and justice". Let Mr. Minsky enlighten me on this point, and I shall be very grateful to him.

harmonious notes. It might have been better had they just continued in the service of pure beauty. It would have been better to
have composed new variations, for instance, on such an old theme:

> *Thirteen, figure of baleful   meaning,*
> *Portent of evil, mockery, revenge:*
> *Treachery, knavery and degradation*
> *Into the world with Serpent creeping.*[219]

I do not wish to assume the role of a prophet, to predict that
our decadent "songsters in the camp of the Russian revolution"
will go through all the zigzags of the road which Baudelaire followed in his time. But they themselves are quite well aware that
they have left quite a few zigzags of their own behind them. Mr.
Minsky writes: "How long is it since Merezhkovsky was preening
himself in the garb of a Greek, a superman? How long since Berdayev wore the costume of a Marxist, a neo-Kantian? Yet here they
are, surrendering themselves to the power of spontaneous, invincible, the latest sincerity, serving the undisguised absurdity of
a miracle, participating with ecstasy in a rite of superstitious sectarianism, taking with them, we trust, not many." I too hope that
Messrs Berdayev and Merezhkovsky—as well as Mr. Minsky—
will attract "not many". But I beg Mr. Minsky to tell us how, knowing so well the amazing vacillations of the Decadent representatives of "modern trends", he can with an air of triumph point
out that the same vacillation brought them into "the camp of the
Russian revolution" as well?

But even in their vacillations these people remain steadfast
in one respect: they never fail to look down on the working-class
liberation movement.* Mr. Minsky himself, in relating the story
of his comic editorship, confesses—of course, in his own way—

---

* Incidentally, Mr. Minsky, who is so well versed in foreign literature,
should have known that its modern trends came into being as a reaction
against the liberation efforts of the working class. This truth is now universally accepted in the history of literature. For instance, here is what Léon
Pineau says about the evolution of the novel in Germany: "Socialism had had
as its result Nietzsche, that is to say, the protest of personality refusing to be
dissolved in anonymity, against the levelling and all-conquering masses;
the revolt of genius refusing to submit to the stupidity of the crowd and—
in opposition to all the great words of solidarity, equality and social justice—
the bold and paradoxical proclamation that only the strong have the right
to live, and that humanity exists only to produce from time to time some
supermen, to whom all others must serve as slaves."
  This anti-socialist tendency was reflected, according to Pineau, in the
modern German novel. Assert after this that modern literary trends do not
conflict sharply with the interests of the proletariat! But it appears as if
Mr. Minsky has never heard of *this* aspect of the modern trends. "Oh, deafness, thou art a vice!"[220] (See *L'Evolution du roman en Allemagne au XIXe siècle*,
Paris, 1908, p. 300 et seq.)

that when he joined up with the Social-Democrats, he wanted to
sprinkle their revolutionary aspirations with the holy water of
his new religious faith. Now that he has long been convinced that
his efforts in that direction were foredoomed to failure, he is ready
without a tremour to accuse his former allies of the most grievous
sins against "all the higher spiritual values".*

X

Enough of that. In a characterisation of Mr. Merezhkovsky,
Mr. Minsky writes:

"Merezhkovsky reveals to us with great naivety the reasons why
he believes in the resurrection of Christ. 'In comparison with
an undoubtedly putrefying mass, what is a questionable immortality in glory, in the memory of man?'—he asks. 'Surely that
which is most precious, most unique in me, that which makes me
what I am—Peter, Ivan, or Socrates, or Goethe—will not exist
in a burdock?' In short, the reason is clear: Merezhkovsky is afraid
of death, and wants immortality."**

A fact is a fact, and there is no getting away from it! Mr. Merezhkovsky is really afraid of death and hopes for immortality. And
as science does not guarantee immortality, he turns to religion,
from the standpoint of which life after death appears to be incontestable. As he sees it, immortality there must certainly be, because if it were otherwise the time would surely come when that
which is most precious and unique, that which makes Mr. Merezhkovsky Mr. Merezhkovsky, would no longer be. From the point
of view of logic, this argument would not withstand even the most
tolerant of criticism. One cannot prove the existence of a given
being or object by the consideration that, if this being or that
object did not exist, it would be most unpleasant for me. Khles-
takov says that he must eat, because if he does not he will waste
away. As you know, this argument of his did not convince anyone.
But no matter how weak Mr. Merezhkovsky's argument is, the fact
remains that consciously or unconsciously many are resorting
to it. Among these is Mr. Minsky, too. Here is his disdainful way
of referring to what he calls those of "scanty intellect" who solve
too artlessly, in his opinion, the eternal questions of being:
"Death? Ha, ha! We shall all be there.... The beginning of life?
Ha, ha! The monkey.... The end of life? Ha, ha! The burdock....
Desiring to cleanse Russian reality of the corruption of illusory
values, these jolly fellows, all these 'smart' pillars of *Sovremyen-
nik*, *Dyelo*, *Otechestvenniye Zapiski*,[221]—the Pisarevs, Dobrolyu-

---

* *On Social Themes*, pp. 193-99.
** Ibid., p. 230.

bovs, Shchedrins, Mikhailovskys—without noticing it themselves made life cheap, and with the best intentions created a colourless reality and a second-rate literature. Realism, denying the divinity of life, degenerated into nihilism, and nihilist hilarity has ended in boredom. The soul finds itself constricted between the monkey and the burdock, and matters are not made better either by the dissection of frogs, or by going to the people, or by political martyrdom".*

Mr. Minsky assures us that in order to dispel the boredom caused by "nihilist hilarity" we have no alternative but to assimilate his "religion of the future". I do not propose to argue the point with him. But why does this "nihilist hilarity" irritate him so? Obviously because jokes are unseemly where the eternal questions of existence are being decided. Does he really think those who showed a hilarity that he does not approve of *solved* these questions *with the aid of jokes*? They are known to have solved them, on the contrary, by the serious exercise of their intelligence; suffice it to recall Turgenev's story of the absorbing interest with which Belinsky studied the question of the existence of God. But once they had resolved these serious questions thanks to the serious application of their intellects, and turned to the old solutions inherited from their fathers and grandfathers, they acquired a "hilarious", that is to say, strictly speaking, a mocking attitude of mind. It is the recollection of this mocking mood that irritates our serious author. This serious author does not want to understand that, as Marx aptly remarked, when I laugh at a joke that is a sign that I take it seriously. The whole question, therefore, may be reduced to this: were the solutions of the "eternal questions" arrived at by the "hilarious" advanced people of the 1870s and 1880s serious solutions? Mr. Minsky, in characterising these solutions with the words: "the monkey", "we shall all be there", "the burdock", considers that they are not serious at all. But here he himself sins very much by lack of a serious attitude to the subject.

"We shall all be there", "the monkey", and "the burdock", point to a very definite world-outlook which may be characterised by the words: unity of the cosmos, the evolution of living beings, eternally changing forms of life. What here is lacking in seriousness? It would seem, nothing. It would seem that it was just this world-outlook for which the way was prepared by the whole course of scientific development in the nineteenth century. What is there here to annoy Mr. Minsky? He is irritated by the "ha, ha's" which— the truth must be told —far too often accompanied references to "the burdock" and "the monkey". But we have to be just. We must understand that, from the standpoint of the world-outlook mentioned above, the solutions of the eternal questions accepted by our

* Ibid., p. 251.

grandfathers cannot but strike one as funny. These solutions have
an animistic character, that is to say, they are rooted in the world-
outlook of the savage, as I showed earlier (see my first article "On
Religious Seekings"). But very often and very naturally civilised
people laugh at the savage's view of the world.

It is utterly useless for Mr. Minsky to think that the "boredom"
from which he and those like him are trying to find an escape in
the gospel of Decadence stems from nihilist hilarity. I already explained that this "boredom" is conditioned by the particular psychological state of the present-day "superman", which has the closest possible connection with philistinism and could not possibly
be further removed from nihilism. It is just as vain for him to des-
pise "hilarity". There is "hilarity" and "hilarity". The "hilarity"
of Voltaire, the celebrated "ha, ha's" with which he so severely castigated fanaticism and superstition, rendered a most *serious*
service to humanity. In general, it is very strange that our contemporary religious seekers do not like laughter. Laughter is a great
thing. Feuerbach was right when he said that laughter distinguishes man from the animal.

XI

I fully believe that the soul of Mr. Minsky finds itself constricted "between the monkey and the burdock". How could it be otherwise? He holds such a world-outlook that it compels him to look
down on both the "burdock" and the "monkey". He is a dualist.
He writes: "In himself each individual represents not a monad as
Leibniz taught, but a complex biune dyad, i.e., an indissoluble
unity of two separate and indivisible elements—spirit and body,
or, more correctly, a whole system of such dyads, just as a large
crystal is composed of small crystals of the same form."*

This is the most indubitable dualism, except that it is veiled
in pseudo-monistic terminology. It is this dualism alone which
opens the door for Mr. Minsky to his religion of the future, although
on this door is written "*spirit*", and not "*body*". As a religious man,
Mr. Minsky sees the world from the angle of animism. Indeed, only
a man holding this view could repeat after Mr. Minsky the following deathbed prayer.

"In this grievous hour of death, in departing for all eternity
from the light of the sun and from all I held dear on earth, I
thank Thee, O God, that out of Thy love for me Thou didst sacrifice Thyself. As I look back on my short life, its forgotten joys
and memorable sufferings, I see that there was no life, just as now
there is no death. Only Thou alone didst live and die, and I,
in the measure of the power Thou didst grant me, reflect Thy life,

* *Religion of the Future*, p. 177.

as I now reflect Thy death. I thank Thee, Lord, that Thou didst let me witness Thy unity".*

Mr. Minsky asserts that "science investigates causes, and religion aims". Having created himself a God in the way prescribed by animism, that is to say, in the final analysis, in his own image and likeness, the question quite naturally comes up of the aims God is supposed to have pursued when creating the world and man. Spinoza drew attention to this aspect of the matter a long time ago. He then elucidated in excellent fashion that many prejudices depend "upon this one prejudice by which men commonly suppose that all natural things act like themselves with an end in view, and ... assert with assurance that God directs all things to a certain end (for they say that God made all things for man, and man that he might worship him)".**

Once having established definite aims for the activity of the phantom he has created, man may then conveniently devise whatever he pleases. Then it is no trouble to convince oneself that there is "no death" as Mr. Minsky asserts, and so forth.

It is remarkable, though, that the modern religious seekings revolve predominantly around the question of personal immortality. Hegel once remarked that in the world of antiquity, the question of life beyond the grave attained exceptional importance when, with the decline of the ancient city-states, all the old social ties were dissolved and man found himself morally isolated. We are faced with something of the kind today. Bourgeois individualism, pushed to the extreme, has reached the point where man seizes upon the question of his personal immortality as the primary question of being. If Maurice Barrès is right, if "ego" is the sole reality, the question as to whether this "ego" is destined to have eternal existence or not truly becomes the question of all questions.*** And since, if we are to believe the same Barrès, the universe is nothing but a fresco which, badly or well, is drawn by

---

* Ibid., p. 301.

** Benedict Spinoza, *Ethics*, translated into Russian by Modestov, St. Petersburg, 1904, p. 44.

*** Mme Z. Hippius says: "Are we to blame that every 'ego' has now become separate, lonely and isolated from every other 'ego', and therefore incomprehensible and unnecessary to it? We all of us passionately need, understand and prize our prayer, we need our verse—the reflection of an instantaneous fullness of our heart. But to another, whose cherished 'ego' is different, my prayer is incomprehensible and alien. The consciousness of loneliness isolates people from one another still more. We are ashamed of our prayers, and knowing that all the same we shall not merge in them with anyone, we say them, we compose them already in a whisper, to ourselves, in hints that are clear only to ourselves" («Сборник стихов», Москва, книгоиздательство «Скорпион», 1904, стр. III [*Collected Verse*, Moscow, Scorpion Book Publishers, 1904, p. III]). So that's how it is! Starting with that, you will discover "philistinism" willy-nilly in the greatest movements of humanity, and can't help plunging into one of the religions of the future!

our "ego", it is quite natural to see to it that the fresco proves to
be as "entertaining" as possible. In view of this, one need not be
surprised either by Mr. Merezhkovsky's "devil", or Mr. Minsky's
"dyad" or anything else.*

"The question of immortality, like that of God," says Mr.
Merezhkovsky, "is one of the main themes of Russian literature
from Lermontov to L. Tolstoy and Dostoyevsky. But no matter
how thoroughly the question is gone into, no matter how its solution wavers between *yes* and *no*, it still remains a question." **
I quite understand that Mr. Merezhkovsky saw in the question of
immortality one of the main themes of Russian literature. But
I do not understand at all how he overlooked the fact that Russian literature has provided at least one circumstantial reply to
this question. This reply came ... from Zinaida Hippius; it is not
very long, so I shall quote it in full.

EVENING

July thunder has clattered on its ways
And frowning clouds disperse in scudding haze;
The azure, dimmed, shines out anew
On sodden woodland path as we drive through.
Pale gloom descends upon the earth,
From chinks of cloud peeps out new moon at birth.
Our steed moves on with lessening pace,
The fine reins trembling like shimmering lace.
Time is still: thunderless lightning thins
The clouds of lulling darkness.
Lightly the undulating wind does start
Urging the vagrant leaves caress my heart.
From wheels on forest path no sound is heard;
Branches heavy droop as tho' their fate demurred.
From field and meadow rises vapour fine.
Now, as ne'er before, I sense that I am Thine,
O dear and orderly Nature!
In Thee I live and I shall die with Thee,
*My soul resigned and passing free.****

Here there is one note that does not ring true—even very untrue. What does this mean: "I shall die with Thee"? That when I

---

* Mr. Merezhkovsky's "devil" is known to have a tail, long and smooth,
like a Great Dane's. I venture to propose this hypothesis: that as the necessary antithesis of this *godless* tail there exist *devout wings*, invisibly adorning
Mr. Merezhkovsky's shoulders. I imagine these wings to be short and covered
with down, like those of an innocent chick.
** *Barbarian at the Gate*, p. 86.
*** *Collected Verse*, pp. 49-50.

die, Nature dies with me? But that is wrong. Nature does not live within me, but I within Nature, or, to put it more correctly, Nature lives in me only as a consequence of my living in her, that I am one of her countless parts. So when this part dies, that is to say, decomposes, yielding place to other combinations, Nature will as before continue her eternal existence. But for all that, Mme Z. Hippius notes with extreme delicacy the *sense of freedom* growing out of the sense of unity of Nature and man, *despite the idea of the inevitability* of death. This feeling is directly opposed to the feeling of slavish dependence on Nature which, in Mr. Merezhkovsky's opinion, must possess every soul that does not lean upon the crutch of religious consciousness. It is quite astonishing that this poem, "Evening", could come from the pen of a writer capable of appealing to the number thirteen:

> *The first creator willed that Thou,*
> *Thirteen, art necessary now.*
> *By worldly law Thou dost portend*
> *To bring the world to direst end.**

The sense of freedom, generated by the consciousness of the unity and kinship of man and Nature and in no way weakened by thoughts of death, is the most glorious and gratifying possible. But it has nothing in common with the "boredom" which seizes upon Messrs Minsky and Merezhkovsky every time they recall their brother the "burdock" and their sister "the monkey". This sense is in no way afraid of the "burdock immortality" which so frightens Mr. Merezhkovsky. Moreover, it is based on the instinctive consciousness of that immortality, so distasteful to Mr. Merezhkovsky. Whoever has this sense will not be afraid of death, while where it is absent that person will not get rid of his thoughts of death by conjuring up all sorts of "dyads" or "religions of the future".

XII

The contemporary religious seekers address themselves to the phantom of the other world precisely because this sense of freedom is either absent from their devastated souls, or is an extremely rare visitor. They seek in religion the consolation which others— sometimes, by the way, they themselves—seek in wine. And the view is very widely held that religious consolation is especially necessary to man when, in one way or another, he has to pay his tribute to death.

---

* *Collected Verse*, p. 142. This poem demonstrates, in line with the "Revelation" of Zinaida, that the world will end on one of the 13ths, while on the next day, the 14th, nothing more will exist. What wisdom!

But is everyone consoled by such a consolation? That's just the
point, they are not.

Feuerbach asks: "What is religious consolation? Simply an appearance. Am I consoled by the thought that a loving father in Heav-
en has deprived these children of their father? Can a father be
replaced? Can this misfortune be made good? Yes, in a human way
it can, but through religion, no. How? Will the notion of a loving
Father help me if my poor child lies ill for years on end? No....
My heart rejects religious consolation....*

What has Mr. Merezhkovsky to say about that? It seems to me
that such speeches inspire recollections of proud titans rather
than pitiful drunken vagrants.

Mr. Merezhkovsky speaks of "burdock immortality" with supreme contempt. It is plain that he is alien to that cheering sense of
kinship with nature so poetically described in Mme Hippius's
poem "Evening". He thinks that only so-called crude materialists
could be content with "burdock immortality". However, for an
adequate characterisation of the crude "materialists" it has to
be said that their conception of immortality is not covered by the
notion of "burdock immortality" They also say that a dead man may
live on in the memories of other people. There is Feuerbach's excellent phrase: "Das Reich der Erinnerung ist der Himmel" (the
kingdom of recollection is heaven). Only Feuerbach could reason
thus, since, no matter what anyone says, he was nevertheless
a materialist. But the fine gentlemen of the Decadence are not
satisfied by such a thought. To refer to life in recollection produces on them the impression of wicked mockery. These fine gentlemen, generally speaking, so attached to idealism which sees the
world only as our conception of it, are deeply insulted when they
hear that a time will come when they themselves will live only in
the conception of other people. Their one thought is to preserve
their cherished "ego"; a world without that "ego" seems to them
to be a world without freedom, a world of gloomy chaos.

Feuerbach said that only people who regarded mankind with
indifference or even with contempt could not be satisfied with the
idea of the continued existence of man in man: "The doctrine of celestial, superhuman immortality is the doctrine of egoism, the
doctrine of the continued ... existence of man in man is the doctrine of love."** There is no doubt about the justness of this remark.
Our fine and exalted Decadents see in the question of personal
immortality the fundamental question of life just because they are
individualists to the very marrow. The individualist, it may be
said, by his very title, is bound to be an egoist.

---

* See *Ludwig Feuerbach in seinem Briefwechsel und Nachlass*, dargestellt
von Karl Grün, B. I, S. 418.
** Karl Grün, op. cit., Vol. I, p. 420.

Am I wrong? Do I exaggerate? I shall cite Mme Z. Hippius again: "I think," she writes, "that should a poet appear today, in our difficult and bitter times, essentially like ourselves, but a genius—he would find himself alone on his narrow summit; only the peak of his rock would seem to be higher—closer to heaven—and the litany he sang would appear even less distinct. Until we find a common God, or at least until we understand that we all aspire to Him, to the One, our prayers, our poems, alive for each of us, will be incomprehensible and unnecessary to anyone."*

Why should "our poems", "alive for each of us", be and unnecessary incomprehensible to anyone? Simply because it is the outcome of extreme individualism. When the poet finds the human world around him unnecessary and incomprehensible, he himself becomes unnecessary and incomprehensible for the surrounding human world. But consciousness of solitude lies heavily: this can be felt even in the words of Mme Hippius. And so, as it is impossible to get away from this loneliness with the aid of notions concerning the real, earthly life of our sinful humanity, the individualists, exhausted by their spiritual solitude, turn towards heaven to seek a "common God". They hope that the "common God" they have invented will cure them of their old sickness—individualism. Rise, o God![222] Vain call! No heavenly potion is there against individualism. A sad fruit of man's earthly life, it will vanish only when the mutual (earthly) relations of men are no longer expressed in the principle: "Man to man is wolf."

XIII

Now we know the psychology of the decadent type of "god-builders" well enough to realise, once and for all, just how inconceivable it is for these gentlemen to sympathise with the liberation movement of the working class. They see only philistinism in the psychology of the hungry proletarian. I have pointed out already that this is explained above all by their invincible, though perhaps unconscious, sympathy with that same "philistine" economic order which so considerately frees them from the tiresome necessity of living by the work of their own hands. In their contempt for the "philistinism" of the hungry proletarian is disclosed the philistinism—the true, genuine philistinism—of the sated bourgeois. Now we see that their philistinism comes to the surface also in another sense. It is expressed in that extreme individualism which renders impossible not only sympathy on their part with the proletariat, but even their mutual understanding among themselves. The precious "ego" of each one of them rea-

* Op. cit., p. 6.

lises Leibniz's philosophical ideal: it becomes a monad "which has no windows on the outside".

Imagine now that such a monad, having turned devout under the influence of the intolerable dullness of life and the unconquerable fear of death which threatens to destroy the precious "ego", decides at last to abandon its "ivory tower". Busied up till then with "the number thirteen" and the propagation of art for art's sake, it now turns benevolently to our vale of tears and takes up the aim of reconstructing anew the reciprocal relationships of men. In brief, imagine that a monad "which has no windows on the outside" is thrown by the burst of a historical storm into the "camp of revolution". What will it do there?

We already know that it will sprinkle the economic aspirations of present-day struggling humanity with the holy water of its modern piety, and fumigate it with the incense of its "modern" mysticism. But not content with this, it will wish to refashion the said aspirations in conformity with its own spiritual mould.

The contemporary working-class emancipation movement is a movement directed against the exploiting minority. The *strength* of the participants of this movement lies in their *solidarity*. Their *success* presupposes in them the capacity to sacrifice their private interests to the interests of the whole. The *pathos* of this struggle is *self-abnegation*. But the monad "which has no windows on the outside" does not know the meaning of self-abnegation. The subordination of private interests to the interests of the whole seems to it to be an act of violence against personality. It is antipathetic to the mass, which, in its view, threatens it with "anonymity". Consequently, it never concludes sincere and lasting peace with the socialist ideal. It will reject that ideal, even when involuntarily yielding to it.

We see this from the example of Mr. Minsky. In words he makes many concessions to contemporary socialism, but in practice all his sympathy is for so-called revolutionary syndicalists, whose *theory* is the bastard daughter of anarchism. Socialism of the Marx school seems to him to be too "fond of power". It is true that he does not approve of the Benjamin Tucker school of anarchists— those extreme individualists. They appear to him to be too "fond of themselves". So he resolves that "the socialists' love of power and the anarchists' preaching of self-love makes them akin, not only with the ideology but also with the psychology of the bourgeoisie which they hate".* On this basis you may think, perhaps, that Mr. Minsky is as far removed from socialism as he is from anarchism. You are wrong. Listen further:

"The libertarian socialists prove to be fully radical in simul-

---

* *On Social Themes*, p. 90.

taneously denying both private property and organised power and are thus entitled to consider themselves fully cured of the poison of the philistine conception of life and way of life."*

Who are these "libertarian" socialists who are so much to the taste of our author? They are the anarchists of the Bakunin and Kropotkin school, i.e., the anarchists who call themselves communists. Taking into account the fact that there are scarcely any other anarchists in Europe—the few followers of Tucker there are will be found mostly in the United States of America—we see that Mr. Minsky's sympathy goes to the West European anarchists. These anarchists, as he says, reject both private property and organised power. Since the anarchists do not of course recognise unorganised power either, our author would have been more exact had he said that the "libertarian socialists" deny all restrictions on the rights of the individual. Such a denial seems to him to be very radical, especially as the "libertarian socialists" also deny private property. Quite carried away by this radicalism Mr. Minsky is ready to declare that the "libertarian socialists" are "fully cured of the poison of the philistine conception of life and way of life". It turns out, therefore, that the only movement hostile to philistinism is today the one which carries in Western Europe the banner of anarchism. Could one speak more favourably of it? Our author, so favourably disposed towards communist anarchism, has not noticed that the "*radicalism*" of this trend can be reduced simply to *paralogism*: in fact, one cannot oppose any restriction of the rights of the individual and *at the same time* denounce private property, namely the right of the individual to acquire for himself certain objects. But the brain is often silent when the heart speaks. An individual from the decadent camp cannot but feel the most cordial sympathy for individualists from the camp of "libertarian socialism".** The funniest thing about it all is that Mr. Minsky tries to put the blame on someone else. He hurls the reproach of individualism at contemporary socialism, or, to use his own words, social-democratism. "It is quite possible," he says, "that the conception of the world process as a struggle for economic interests is normal and true for the individualist. But for those of us who have worked out in suffering a different attitude to the world, perhaps a morbid one, but still one that is near and dear to us,

---

* Ibid., same page.
** By the way, why does Mr. Minsky think that we Marxists speak of the bourgeois nature of anarchist doctrine only under the influence of "polemical fervour"? Fervour has nothing to do with it; we simply state a fact, viz., that the ideologists of anarchism are even more extreme individualists than the ideologists of the bourgeoisie. One can dispute this fact only if one is indeed influenced by polemical fervour.

of universal love and self-sacrifice,—for us the normal and true conception of the world process is the mystery of universal love and   sacrifice."*

Here the first thing to be remarked is that it would never enter the head of a single sensible Marxist to regard the whole "world process", i.e., for example, the development of the solar system as well, as a struggle for economic interests. That is nonsense which we could expect only from some of our half-baked empirio-monists (Bogdanov and Co). But that is not the point. As has been said above, it is very characteristic of our contemporary philistine to contrast "universal love and self-sacrifice" to the struggle for economic interests—note: *the struggle for the economic interests of the economically exploited class.* Only someone who knows nothing either of self-sacrifice or of all-embracing human love would be capable of making such a contrast. It is precisely because Mr. Minsky understands neither one nor the other that he feels the irresistible need to smother them in a dark cloud of religious "mystery".

And Mr. Merezhkovsky?

As for him, he can understand socialism even less than Mr. Minsky does; therefore he is inclined towards that "eternal anarchy", which, according to him, is the hidden soul of the Russian revolution.** And he is not alone: the whole trinity of D. Merezhkovsky, Z. Hippius and D. Filosofov are, as we see, inclined to eternal anarchy. In the unsigned preface to the triune work *Der Zar und die Revolution* it is said—obviously on behalf of the whole trinity—that the conscious empirical aim of the Russian revolution is socialism, but its mystical and unconscious aim is anarchy.***

Here the Russian revolution is *identified* with anarchy ("Die russische Revolution oder Anarchie", S. 1); and it is foretold that sooner or later "Europe as a whole" will come into conflict with the anarchist Russian revolution. And in order that Europe as a whole should know with whom it will have to deal in the coming conflict, it is informed that, whereas for the European politics is a science, for us it is a religion**** and that "we", deep down at the bottom of our being and will, are mystics. Moreover, "our mystical essence" is characterised, incidentally, in this: that "we do not walk, we run; we do not run, we fly. We do not fly, we fall".***** A little further on, "Europe as a whole" reads

---

* *On Social Themes.* p. 70.
** *Der Zar und die Revolution,* S. 153.
*** Ibid., p. 5. As is obvious, the trinity finds that socialism "prescribes" the complete subordination of personality to society (this last "prescription" is particularly good!).
**** Ibid., p. 2.
***** Ibid.

with the greatest astonishment that "we fly" in the most unusual way—namely, "mit in die Luft gerichteten Fersen".* In Russian this expression means: head downwards, or vulgo: upside down.

This admission by the triune author of the collection seems to me to be the most valuable element of all the varieties of the decadent "religion of the future". These worthy mystics, in fact, neither walk nor run—one can walk or run only on the earth, but *we* are not concerned with the earth—they fly, and what's more, they fly upside down. This new mode of transport has the effect of making their blood flow to their heads, with the result that their brains do not function too well. This circumstance throws an extraordinarily bright light on the origin of decadent mysticism.

The religion without God invented by Mr. Lunacharsky and the gospel of Decadence do not by any means exhaust the varied types of our contemporary religious "seekings". In the original plan for my series of articles on this subject, a place was also set aside for a detailed analysis of the religious revelation which comes to us from the group of writers who have published the much acclaimed collection *Vekhi*. But the more carefully I delved into this work, and the more I listened to the discussions it has aroused, the more surely I was convinced that the gospel of Struve, Gerschensohn, Frank and Bulgakov requires a special work to be devoted to it, examining it, as the Germans say, in another connection. I shall do this in the coming year in an article, or perhaps a series of articles, devoted to investigating how a part of our intelligentsia moved backwards from "Marxism to idealism" ... and still further back—to *Vekhi*. I do not deem it necessary to hide the fact that one of the main themes of my future work will be the question of how and why a certain variety of our religious seekings serves as a spiritual weapon for the Europeanisation of our bourgeoisie. Marx was indeed right: "Religious questions now have social significance." And it is really being naive to think that when Mr. P. Struve, for example, attempts to refute with the aid of religion some "philosophical principles" of socialism, he is acting as a *theologian*, and not as a *publicist* who holds the viewpoint of a definite class.

---

* Ibid., p. 4.

ON M. GUYAU'S BOOK

M. Guyau, *Unbelief of the Future. A Sociological Investigation. With a Biographical Note by A. Fouillee and a Preface by Professor D. N. Ovsyaniko-Kulikovsky*. Translated from the French (11th Edition), Edited by Y. L. Saker, St. Petersburg.

Religion is a widely discussed topic nowadays in Russia. For the most part, those who are discussing it show themselves to be completely uninformed about this social phenomenon, which, in any case deserves the serious attention of a sociologist. M. Guyau's book has therefore arrived at an opportune moment; it will help to disperse the dense fog of ignorance surrounding the religious question in Russia.

The book opens with a preface by Prof. D. N. Ovsyaniko-Kulikovsky. In it the esteemed professor touches on our contemporary religious searches, which appear to him to be "at the very least, unnecessary". We could not agree more with him on this point. In his words, the great majority of these searches "are more like a religious game, an infantile exercise on religious themes, and there is in them something at once scholastic, dilettante and fantastic" (p. IX). This is severe but just criticism. No less just is D. N. Ovsyaniko-Kulikovsky's remark that in these searches "there is noticeable an endeavour to furnish a religious basis to social phenomena," (IX)—for example, our emancipation movement—and that there is not the slightest need for it. "This is a feature of an archaistic nature," he says, "contradicting the general and ever-growing tendency of progress towards freeing social phenomena from the religious ferule.... It is true that our religious reformers and Utopians do not introduce new rituals but they seek a new religious sanction for such 'secular' affairs as liberalism, socialism, the emancipation movement, and so on. This would be a step backward, into the depths of the archaic stages of both religion and culture, if it, in fact, could be called a 'step', and not just an intellectual game and empty 'fancy'" (IX-X). We shall add that among the reformers and Utopians D. N. Ovsyaniko-Kulikovsky includes Mr. Lunacharsky, who "has launched an attempt to create a 'Social-Democratic' religion, for which there is hardly any need" (IX). In this case, it might be remarked that our author is expressing himself too mildly; actually, one is fully justified in declaring that there was positively no need at all for Mr. Lunacharsky's attempt.

But—we are very sorry to have to use this "but"—we do not entirely agree with D. N. Ovsyaniko-Kulikovsky. Frankly speaking, we see no necessity either for the "coming religiosity" to which he pays homage in his preface. He writes: "The progress of positive science and philosophy brings man face to face with the unknowable—and it is here that that *religion* begins which, in contrast to past religions, *does not bind* ('religio' means 'bond') the human soul but frees it from the bonds that chain it to time and place, to the problems of the day, to the worries of the age, as it was always chained by past religions, so closely connected were they with history, with culture, with society, with the state, with classes and the interests of human groups. In comparison with them the religion of the future seems to us, *not a religion*, but in it man's *religiosity* will ascend to the highest peak of that *rational contemplation* which, ennobling the human spirit, accumulates and frees man's energy for non-religious cultural activity and struggle for humanity and the highest ideals of mankind" (X-XI).

This argumentation seems to us not very convincing. We think that "rational contemplation" has nothing to do with religiosity. Moreover, D. N. Ovsyaniko-Kulikovsky himself seems to support our opinion with some remarks of his own. Indeed, from what he says it emerges that underlying the coming religiosity will be "the idea of the infinite and eternal Cosmos"(X). This idea "transcends the bounds of human understanding; though conceived in a rational manner, it is irrational or supra-rational, in other words, mystical" (X). Let us assume that this is so. But then the coming religiosity also must be "irrational or supra-rational, in other words, *mystical*". But in that case, as we have said, it has nothing to do with "*rational contemplation*". Besides, what is inaccessible to scientific knowledge cannot be called *mystical*. We know that the moon always turns the same side towards the earth. The other side of the moon will, therefore, forever remain inaccessible to scientific investigation. (In saying this we have in mind, of course, the scientists living on the earth.) But does it follow from this that the other side of the moon is irrational, supra-rational, or mystical? In our opinion, it does not follow at all. It will, of course, be objected—and perhaps our author may be among the objectors—that it is one thing when something is unknown or inaccessible to knowledge as a consequence of some special conditions, but absolute unknowability is quite another matter. Our reply is, yes, that may be so ... from the viewpoint of the Kantian theory of cognition, or of one of its modern varieties. But for a reference to that theory of cognition to be convincing, that theory must first be proved correct and that is not such an easy task. In addition, the suggestion that the "mystical" is identical with the unknowable will just not hold water.

M. Guyau says in the book under review: "The universe is, without doubt, infinite; consequently the *material* for human science is also infinite; nevertheless, the universe is governed by a certain number of simple laws which we are more and more becoming aware of" (pp. 358-59). That is very true. And it contains the answer to D. N. Ovsyaniko-Kulikovsky, who considers the idea of the infinity and eternity of the Cosmos "mystical". Once a man has finally become convinced that the infinite universe is governed by a certain number of simple laws, *there is no room* in his world-outlook *for mysticism*. The esteemed professor, in characterising the late M. Guyau's views, says that this French philosopher foresaw "not a decline of morality and religion, but the opposite, *the blossoming of moral and religious creativity*, inspired not only by the external guarantees of freedom of conscience and thought, but also by the *inner freedom* of man from the shackles of dogmatism in questions of religious and moral consciousness" (VI). Just so: but it would not be out of place to add that by the religion of the future M. Guyau understands something that has no resemblance to religion. Thus, he writes: "We have said that science is likewise a religion, which returns to reality, resumes its normal direction, finds itself again, so to speak. Science says to living beings: penetrate one another, know one another. Religion says to them: unite with one another; conclude among yourselves a close, solid union. These two precepts are one and the same" (186). If "science is a religion", then, undoubtedly, in the future religious creativity will wax greatly in strength, since the scientific activity of civilised man grows apace. But in other places—for instance, in the first and second chapters of the first part of his book—Guyau himself explains very well that the religious viewpoint is directly opposed to the scientific viewpoint; science considers nature as a chain of phenomena, interdependent on one another; religion, or more exactly, the theory underlying religion, sees nature as the manifestation of "wills more or less independent, endowed with extraordinary powers and capable of acting on one another and on us" (p. 50; see also p. 51). Thus any identification of science with religion becomes logically inconsistent. Guyau remarks that "Spencer's supposed reconciliation of science and religion springs only from ambiguity of expression" (p. 361). He might well have applied this remark to himself. Only by using ambiguous expressions can one assert that "science is a religion", and so on.

But however ambiguous Guyau's expressions may sometimes be, it is none the less plain that he understands the blossoming of religious creativity in the future as, strictly speaking, the blossoming of science, art, and morality. To be assured of this, it is enough to read but chapter II of the Part Three of his work (pp.364-95). This chapter has the characteristic title: "Association. — What Will Remain of Religion in Social Life?" It turns out that nothing will remain. We are not joking. Guyau says: "If religion is regard ed as the popularisation of man's first scientific theories, there is reason to believe that the most reliable means to combat the errors and preserve the good sides of religion will be the popularisation of the true theories of modern science" (369). For our part, we repeat that the popularisation of the true theories of science will, of course, increase greatly in the future, but this is no guarantee at all for the preservation of even the good sides of religion, since its viewpoint is directly opposed to that of science. Some pages further on we read: "The object of enthusiasm changes from epoch to epoch; it applies itself to religion, but it can also apply itself to scientific doctrines and discoveries, and especially moral and social beliefs. From this follows a new consequence, that the very spirit of *proselytism*, which appears to be peculiar to religions, will by no means disappear with them; it will merely be transformed" (374). Here again it is clear that the only religion which will "remain" will not be at all the religion that we know, and it would be a great mistake to confuse it with the old religion.

M. Guyau is an inconsistent thinker, and we considered it our duty to warn the reader in advance about his inconsistency. Nevertheless, he is a thinker, and not afflicted by religious hysterics like; our "god-seekers". Therefore, in spite of his inconsistencies, there are in his book many elements which, as we have said, will help to disperse dense fog of ignorance surrounding the religious question in Russia. Most of these elements are to be found in the first part of his book; we strongly recommend this part to the attention of our readers.

Unfortunately, we can recommend even this part only with reservations; we can agree in an absolute sense with hardly anything Guyau says in it. Take, for instance, his definition of religion. His opinion is that "religion is a *physical, metaphysical, and moral explanation* of all things by analogy with human society, in imaginative and symbolic form. In short: religion is the *universal sociological explanation of the world in mythical form*" (XIX). In fact, religion does explain much by analogy with human society. But not everything. We know already that a religious person sees in nature the manifestation of the will of divine beings. This view represents that animistic element which has always had its place in every religion. But animism arose not by analogy with human *society*, but by analogy with the *indiviolual* as a being endowed with consciousness and will. Primitive man explained all phenomena of nature by analogy with himself;

he personified nature, assuming the presence of consciousness
and will everywhere. This personification of nature was connected
in the closest possible way with the state of primitive technique.
We think it necessary to point this out because Guyau's characteristic view of religion as *universal sociomorphism* has prevented
him from assessing at its full value the most important influence
of technique on the development of primitive mythology.

In general, it should be noted that the ethnological material
on which Guyau based his work is now largely out of date. Suffice
it to say that, in regarding religion as universal sociomorphism,
he says nothing about totemism, which is such an eloquent example
of the explanation of phenomena, i.e., of *some aspects of them*,
by analogy with human society.

It is useful to read Guyau's book, but a mistake to think that
it has even approximately exhausted the question. It is a very,
very long way from that!

ON W. WINDELBAND'S BOOK

Wilhelm Windelband, *Philosophy in the Spiritual Life of Nineteenth-Century Germany.* Authorised Translation from the German by M.!M. Rubinstein. Zveno Publishers. Moscow, 1910

This book comprises a series of lectures delivered in 1908 in the Free German Higher Institute at Frankfort-on-the-Main. The task of the lectures was, "in the context of the general historical development of the German nation during the nineteenth century to elucidate the elements of a world-outlook which play a definite role in this development, and in which life itself is reflected". Obviously a very interesting and important task. But in order to fulfil it, in order to elucidate how German social life in the nineteenth century was reflected in the German world-outlook of that period, it is necessary, first of all to master thoroughly the basic proposition of materialism: that it is not thinking which determines being, but being which determines thinking. Wilhelm Windelband is a talented writer, but he is far from having grasped this proposition. His views on materialism in general and historical materialism in particular are the views of a prejudiced idealist who remains blind to the most important and strongest sides of the theory he is trying to refute. Consequently, first, all the pages of his book which deal with materialism are totally unsatisfactory. Secondly — and this is even more important—the task set in the study remains unfulfilled. As a matter of fact, Windelband furnishes only a few more or less apt hints as to how the development of the German world-outlook in the nineteenth century must be explained by the development of modern Germany's social life. But he provides no explanation which is to any degree consistent and cohesive; and as for the development of German social thought during the last third of the nineteenth century, his exposition, as we shall see in a moment, suffers from quite serious errors. It could not be otherwise. Whoever takes up the study of the history of social thought in one or more of its manifestations cannot now with impunity ignore materialism.

However, we shall deal first of all with what we have called our author's more apt hints. Here are the most noteworthy of them. Windelband says: "We have the right to see at all times the most noble task of philosophy precisely in this, that it forms the self-consciousness of developing cultural life. It does this indirectly and involuntarily, unconsciously and semi-consciously even where the thinker, to all appearances, follows—and thinks that he follows—exclusively his individual yearning for knowledge, the motives, as free as possible from all the requirements of the surrounding world, of his own intellectual satisfaction. Precisely because of this, the significance of philosophical systems lies, in the last analysis, not in the transient formulas of their conceptions, but in those contents of life which find their explanation in it...." "Similarly also here, in observing the course of development through which our people passed in the nineteenth century, we must everywhere regard theories as the sedimentary deposit of life — and this is not only permissible, it is even imperative, the more so since this is one of the pivotal questions of that development itself" (pp. 5-6). Nothing could be more true. And since this is the case, one must regard as particularly naive those people who wonder at the terms: "bourgeois philosophy", "proletarian theory" and the like. For if philosophy does represent "the self-consciousness of developing cultural life", it is natural that in the period of cultural development characterised by the predominance of the bourgeoisie in social life, philosophy itself—all its dominant trends—bears the stamp of the bourgeoisie. That goes without saying. No less understandable is the fact that when the proletariat begins to revolt against the rule of the bourgeoisie, theories expressing its anti-bourgeois aspirations begin to spread in its midst. Of course, every scientific view may be understood superficially and one-sidedly. Its superficial and one-sided understanding by particular individuals or whole groups of people can produce distorted, ludicrous, caricatured conclusions. We know this, having seen it in the examples of our Shulyatikovs, Bogdanovs, Lunacharskys, etc., etc. But is there, can there be, any scientific view that is proof against wrong understanding by people ill-prepared to assimilate it? There is not and there cannot be such a view. No matter how ridiculous are the Shulyatikovs, Bogdanovs, and Lunacharskys, no matter how much they distort Marx's teaching, this teaching still remains correct. No matter how this or that "mind still unripe, fruit of yet scant learning",[223] misuses expressions such as proletarian theory, bourgeois philosophy, and the like, these expressions do not cease to be theoretically valid; proletarian theories as well as bourgeois philosophy really do exist as distinct aspects of "the self-consciousness of developing cultural life". There is nothing one can do about this, beyond accepting it for information and guidance. To take it for guidance means to understand that the contemporary philosophy of Western Europe, in which the bourgeoisie hold such powerful sway, cannot but be the self-consciousness of the bourgeoisie. The pity is that this very simple truth finds great difficulty nowadays in penetrating the minds of even those who, generally speaking, take the side of the working class. Hence the reason why such people both in Russia and in Western Europe, very often disseminate with great zeal philosophical theories that are the last word of bourgeois reaction against the proletariat's strivings for emancipation. This is a very sorry spectacle which we are forced by the very course of European cultural development to contemplate.

But to get back to Windelband with his more or less apt hints. Here is yet another one of them: "When reading the arguments on the basis of which Schiller, in his letters on the aesthetic upbringing of man and in his treatise on naive, sentimental poetry, extolls, in accordance with his aesthetic theory, the Hellenic world as the true humanity, one clearly feels throughout an action of contrasts, in which everything which the present lacks in terms of the ideal is asserted as reality in antiquity. Escaping into the past is, properly speaking, the same as escaping into the ideal" (p. 30). This again is very true and very well put. The "action of contrasts", which Hegel spoke of in his day, explains very much in the history of the intellectual development of every society divided into classes. It is so great that he who does not sufficiently take it into account risks making the most crude errors in study of such history. Unfortunately, Windelband himself is not always able to define correctly the "action of contrasts" he acknowledges. Needless to say, this reduces the "value" of his investigation quite considerably.

Here is a vivid example to confirm what I have just said. In characterising the social life of Western Europe in the nineteenth century, Windelband writes: "Hegel's words have come true: the masses are moving forward. They have entered into the historical movement which, in essentials, was previously playing itself out above their heads, in the thin upper layers of society. The masses are asserting their rights not only in political development, but in all spheres of spiritual history, in the same measure as in the economic sphere. All strata of the body politic are demanding for themselves, with all seriousness and energy, full participation in all the benefits of society, both spiritual and material, launching out in every sphere of social life with the claim to participate in it and to assert their interests. Thus, our life has been given a completely new cast, and this social expansion forms the most important basis for the extensive and intensive enhancement of life which mankind experienced in the nineteenth century" (pp. 136-37). This is true, of course. Contemporary social life in Western Europe has, in fact, been given a "completely new cast" as a result of the "masses moving forward". But the

author forgot that this onward movement of the popular masses
has encountered, and continues to encounter, strong resistance
from the upper classes. Once having forgotten this, naturally
he also lost sight of the fact that the resistance of the upper classes
to the onward movement of the masses was bound to find its
reflection in the whole course of Europe's intellectual development,
and especially in the history of literature, art and philosophy.
Consequently, he has given a quite incorrect interpretation of that
preaching of individualism which brought fame to the name of
Friedrich Nietzsche. Windelband says: "Thus, we are undergoing a levelling down of historical distinctions, and the establishment of a uniformity of life, about which not one of the
previous ages in human history had the faintest notion. But from
this there now emerges the grave danger that we shall thereby
lose what is most valuable, that which, strictly speaking, first
constitutes and at all times constituted culture and history, viz.:
the life of personality. The sense of this danger pervades deep
down the whole spiritual life of the last decades, and bursts
out from time to time with passionate energy. Alongside this
outwardly magnificently developing material culture there is
growing a fervent need for one's own inner life, and together
with the democratising and socialising life of the masses there
is springing up an ardent opposition of individuals, their upstriving
against suppression by the mass, their primitive striving to dis-
burden their own personality" (pp. 142-43). The question arises:
how can "individuals" be suppressed by the "mass" who themselves
are suppressed in class-divided capitalist society? It would be
a waste of time searching in the book under review for the answer
to this inevitable question. Windelband does not want to understand that in so far as modern individualism, which found its
most brilliant representative in the person of Friedrich Nietzsche,
is a protest against the forward movement of the *mass*, it voices
not fear for the rights of *personality*, but fear for *class privileges*.
This is not only *true*; it is gradually becoming *common knowledge*.
Take literature, for example. Prof. Leon Pineau in his book:
L'Evolution du roman en Allemagne au XIX-e siècle, Paris, 1908,
portrays modern individualism—the individualism of the "neo-
Romanticists"—as a reaction against the contemporary socialist
movement (see, in the book mentioned, chapter XV—"Le roman
néo-Romantique: symbolique, réligieux et lyrique"). There is no
doubt at all about his being right. But the contemporary socialist
movement is not directed against "personality" at all. Quite the
reverse. It strives to defend those rights —which are being constantly violated as a result of the dependent position of the enormous majority,—of "personality" in contemporary society, i.e., of
the proletariat. Therefore contemporary individualism cannot

be considered in any respect a movement in favour of the rights of the individual in general. It is a movement in favour of the rights of the individual belonging to a particular class. And it very well understands—for example in the person of the same Friedrich Nietzsche—that the interests of *such personality* can be protected only by suppressing the "personality" of another and incomparably more numerous class, viz.: the proletariat. But Windelband remains blind to all this. This may seem strange, but it is explained by the fact that his own philosophical views reflect some negative aspects of social life today.

Mr. M. Rubinstein has translated Windelband's book not at all badly, which is surprising, since we seldom find even moderately tolerable translations.

COWARDLY IDEALISM

Joseph Petzoldt, *The Problem of the World from the Standpoint of Positivism.* Translated from the German by R. L. Edited by P. Yushkevich. Shipovnik Publishers. St. Petersburg, 1909

I

This book is apparently destined to have conspicuous success among certain circles of our reading public. First, it provides an exposition of a philosophy now fashionable in these circles. According to J. Petzoldt, the aim of the book is "to explain the usually falsely construed central point of the positivist understanding of the world, substantiated by Wilhelm Schuppe, Ernst Mach, and Richard Avenarius, and to comprehend this world-outlook as historically necessary, logically inevitable and therefore, most probably, final in its essential features".* That will suffice at present to attract the attention of numerous readers to the work concerned; and apart from this, Petzoldt knows how to write with great clarity. True, it is not that scrupulous clarity which helps one to overcome the difficulties of the subject, but that deceptive clarity which tends to conceal them from the reader. It is the clarity of very superficial thinking, which brings its work to a halt just where its main task begins. But this is not a bad thing. A very superficial philosophy is just what we need at present. The reading public which is buying up the works of the Bogdanovs, Valentinovs, and Yushkeviches, and leaving unsold in book stores such a splendid work as Engels' *Ludwig Feuerbach,*—this reading public does not have and never will have the slightest need of profound philosophical works. Hence there is every reason to expect that Petzoldt's *The Problem of the World* will quickly run into several editions.

But since I do not share the philosophical infatuation fashionable just now, and since I am not content with the sort of clarity that conceals the difficulties of a subject instead of helping to overcome them, I consider it worth while subjecting to criticism the principal ideas set forth in Petzoldt's book. Who can tell? Perhaps I shall find a reader who prefers to use his own brains for thinking rather than to follow the latest fashion in philosophy. Anything can happen in this world!

---

* P. VI.

The fundamental idea of Petzoldt's whole book is expressed by the author himself in the following words: "There is no world-*in-itself*, there is only a world *for us*. Its elements are not atoms and not other absolute beings, but the 'sensations' of colour, sound, touch, space, time, etc. In spite of this, things are not only subjective, not only phenomena of consciousness—on the contrary, we must conceive of the parts of our environment, composed of these elements, as existing in the same manner both at the moment of perception and when we no longer perceive them."*

I leave aside for the time being the question of what is meant exactly by the proposition that "sensations" must be regarded as fundamental elements of the world. I will dwell at present on the following: "There is no world-*in-itself*, there is only a world *for us*." So Petzoldt assures us. We believe him and say: "Since there is no world-in-itself, there is nothing objective; all things are subjective and the world is only our idea of it." We wish to be consistent, but Petzoldt does not want that. No, he objects, in spite of there being only the world *for us*, this world is not only our idea of it, and things are not only subjective; they are not only phenomena of our consciousness. Let us admit that too: we believe Petzoldt. But what is the meaning of: things are not only subjective, they are not only phenomena of our consciousness? It means that in spite of there being only the "world for us", there is also the "world-in-itself". But if there is the world-in-itself, then Petzoldt is wrong in proclaiming that the world-in-itself does not exist. What are we to do now? What are we to believe? To extricate us from this difficulty, our author advises us, as we know, to conceive of the parts of our environment as "existing in the same manner both at the moment of perception and when we no longer perceive them". But unfortunately this advice does not in the least get us out of our difficulties. The question here is not *what* things are like at the moment we do not perceive them, but whether they exist independently of our perception. According to Petzoldt, this question can only be answered affirmatively; yes, things exist independently of our perception, that is to say, they do not cease to be when we stop perceiving them. But this reply does not correspond to what *Petzoldt himself* thinks and says. To say that a thing does not cease to exist even when we cease to perceive it is the same as saying that it has being which does not cease even when the thing no longer exists "*for us*". Then *what sort* of being is this? The answer is as clear as twice two are four: it is *being-in-itself*. But Petzoldt assures us that there is no being-in-itself. Again I ask: what are we to do,

* P. V.

which Petzoldt are we to believe? The Petzoldt who reiterates that there is "no world-in-itself" or the one who proves that the world exists even independently of our perception of it, i.e., that there is a world-in-itself? This is a question truly in the mood of Hamlet! Let us work out the answer for ourselves, since it is useless to expect help from our author—he himself does not "sense" the contradiction in which he is so *ludicrously* struggling.

II
THESIS

There is no world-*in-itself*, there is only the world *for us*; there is not only the world *for us*, there is also the *world-in-itself*. Such is the antinomy in which Petzoldt is entangled. In order to see where exactly he committed his sin against logic, we shall have to examine separately what he says in favour of each of the two sides of the antinomy.

There is no world-*in-itself*, there is only the world *for us*. Why does Petzoldt think so?

Because he believes the *doctrine of substance* to be completely untenable. He says: "The idea of substance contradicts experience. Not in a single thing do we find such a something that underlies the thing, something that would constitute its inner essence and remain unaltered in it under all changes determined by time and circumstances.... We can only resolve things into a number of exclusively changeable qualities—which psychology calls sensations, into what can be seen, what can be touched, what produces sound, what has taste, and so on, which in the course of time are replaced in everything by something else which can be seen, touched, and so on; but never, even with the most perfect instruments, do we discover a part which is undefinable by its quality, to say nothing of such an undefinable something underlying all things. It is a pure thought-thing about which reality knows nothing.*

Further, in characterising the development of the philosophy of antiquity, Petzoldt asserts that the notion of substance leads inevitably to dualism: "Heraclitus and Parmenides, however differently they conceived of *what* properly speaking, that is which only is present in appearance—being in a state of rest, or *becoming* which knows no rest—nevertheless agreed that it is the eye and the ear and the senses in general which conjure up before us a false picture of the world and are the cause of all error...; that we can expect truth from reason only. This dualism also

---

* Pp. 60-61.

is an inevitable consequence of the idea of substance."* Somewhat
further on it appears that the idea of substance, developing in the
most logical way, changes into the idea of something which is
within things much in the same way as the soul is within the
body according to the views of the animists. "...Since substance,
in the final analysis, is everything, then it must also contain
the principle of motion and of change in general; and as it, generally speaking, cannot be perceived by the senses—on the contrary,
visual appearance, appearance perceived by the senses conceals it
from us, but since it nevertheless is the essential in every thing,
then it is hidden in the thing, as the soul, as it were, of the thing."**

This, of course, is quite untrue. But the important point to
me is not that it is untrue but that it seems to Petzoldt to be
true. I set myself the task of expounding in his own words the
principal arguments he advances in favour of the thesis: there
is no world-*in-itself*, there is only a world *for us*. To accomplish
this task, I shall have to make one more extract in which the
question of substance is also dealt with.

"The knowledge of the real world could have developed in
a straight line after Protagoras only if we had been able to free
ourselves completely from the idea of substance, if we had realised
that the strong tendency of philosophical teachings to diverge
was based only on fruitless efforts to find an imaginary absolute
world, only on the unjustified belief in an absolute being, an
absolute truth, not dependent upon anything subjective, on the
delusion that behind the many there must lie a one, behind the
heterogeneity of being and reality—something homogeneous,
immutable, persistent. Had Protagoras omitted or been unable
to cast this conception, which he had arrived at more by brilliant
intuition than by logical analysis, into propositions unassailable
in all respects and thereby made it relatively easy to pass them
on, it would have been the task of his wise followers to elevate
the new knowledge to the full light of consciousness and think
it out to the end."***

Now we are sufficiently well acquainted with the arguments
advanced by Petzoldt in defence of his thesis. It must be admitted
that within the limits of this defence our author is logical after
his own fashion. Actually, to say that there is no such thing
as substance is to assert that there is no world-in-itself, but only
a world for us, for the perceiving subjects. But who exactly are
these "we", these perceiving subjects? Should we not attach
substantial significance to them? Must we not assume that the
human ego is the *substance* underlying *phenomena*? If Petzoldt

* P. 93.
** Pp. 113-14.
*** P. 110.

would say "yes" to these questions, that tiny word would mean the total renunciation of all he has said *against* the existence of substance. But, like his teachers—Mach, Avenarius, and Schuppe— he will not pronounce that tiny word. He will not accord substantial significance to the human ego. He says:"Protagoras knew already that the soul is nothing outside of its content and, consequently, this content does not require a special vehicle. He was also aware that the sensual perceptions are the basis of the spiritual elements, with which everything else is associated. Thus he held in principle the point of view of our contemporary 'psychology without the soul', and thus the prerequisites were provided for fruitful investigation of the facts of the soul."* Here again he is logical; but if there is no "ego" as a substance *undergoing* sensations, and no thing-in-itself as a substance *causing* these sensations, what are we left with? We are left with nothing but these sensations, which are thus transformed into the basic elements of the world. He who denies the conceptional substance comes logically to "Machism".

Having substantiated his *thesis*, Petzoldt breaks into a song of victory. He says: "Once science has fully overcome the idea of substance, a whole period of thought, stretching over many thousands of years, has been brought to an end. Philosophy's main previous task has been resolved. The history of philosophy in its former sense has ended, since it was primarily the history of the idea of substance, the history of metaphysics." ***

In a certain sense, this is true. If the concept of substance has been eliminated, then by the very fact the most important of the problems with which philosophy had struggled so long has also been eliminated. Among these first place is held by the problems of the subject, the object, and their mutual relationship. If Petzoldt's "positivism" entitles us to dispense with these most difficult problems as empty "metaphysical" concoctions, it lifts a considerable load off the shoulders of the philosopher. Unfortunately, it does not and cannot entitle us to disregard these problems. We very clearly see this from the example of Petzoldt himself, whose *thesis* is followed by an *antithesis*.

III
ANTITHESIS

There is not only a *world for us*; there is also a *world-in-itself*. Our author proves this at least as successfully as he has substantiated his thesis.

---

* P. 111.
** Pp. 211-12.

He rejects decisively Kant's concept of reason dictating its laws to nature. "It is not thinking that is determined by things, but things by thinking," he exclaims. That is the proud and fateful Copernican reversal through which the rationalistic passion, held in check in Kant by his wide knowledge of and interest in the natural sciences, was to be unfettered anew in his successors of theological origin."* That is quite true. And Petzoldt's following remark is no less true: "...If the laws governing phenomena originated only in the brain, then we are at a loss to answer the question: how was the development of organisms possible before the formation of the brain? From this it is clear that whoever holds that things are determined by thinking delivers himself body and soul to the devil of transcendentalism, of that metaphysics which Kant most earnestly wished to see banished from all genuine science, although he himself had completely fallen to it."** But if it is absurd to say that things are determined by *thinking*, it is no less absurd to assert that they are determined by *sensation*; and if he who says that they are determined by thinking delivers himself "body and soul to the devil of transcendentalism", then he who contends that things are determined by sensation cannot hope to escape the same terrible fate. To the first of these two rather poor thinkers, it is indeed necessary to put the question:"How was the development of organisms possible before the formation of the brain?" But it is also necessary to ask a similar question of the second of our poor thinkers: how was the development of the universe possible before the formation of organisms capable of having sensations? He can have only one answer to this question: the universe then consisted of those elements which later, in the organism, were to become sensations. But this is nothing more than the height of "transcendentalism"!

However, that by the way. My task here is not to refute Petzoldt but to indicate the arguments he uses to prove the correctness of his antithesis. Let us follow him.

The most important of these arguments is contained, in my opinion, in the following remarkable passage:

"Let us try then to draw as clear a picture as possible of what results when we cease to believe in the existence of things independent of ourselves. I have only to close my eyes, and all the objects I now see before me will vanish not only from the sphere of my perception but vanish altogether. I have only to open my eyes again and they are there anew; they arise again. In deep sleep the universe is annihilated, and when I awake it arises again out of absolute nothingness. Is it not clear that ideas of such possibili-

---

* P. 181.
** P. 182.

ties can enter the head only of one accustomed to think of every-thing in terms of ideas which come and go? Could anyone lend himself to such fancies who, from the very beginning, ascribes just as much independent existence to the physical, corporeal, "non-ego" as he does to the psychical, the soul, the "ego"? Where in this case is the consideration for the fact that independently of whether my eyes are open, things always appear again either where they were or in another place independent of my thinking, for the fact that there is a fully consistent and law-regulated con-nection between the things perceived?"*

This is a triumphant refutation of the views of people who refuse "to believe in the independent existence of things", that is to say, in the existence of the world-in-itself. But Petzoldt does not rest on his laurels. He gives no quarter to the idealism he has vanquished, and finishes it off with arguments that combine over-whelming logical thoroughness with the acidity of malicious satire.

"Of course," he continues, "the true idealist cannot be content with his experience alone. In fact, the present moment is all that he is sure of. It is in no way established for him that the world and human history exist, that something must develop, that he himself was once a child and grew up physically and mentally, that he lived yesterday—more than that, that he was living a moment ago—all this might perhaps be but a delusion, only a chain of ideas being lived through at the given moment, a clever hypothesis created for the sole purpose of interpreting logically that which is being perceived at the present moment—just try to prove to him the opposite!"**

Whoever does not wish to get lost in this labyrinth of absurdi-ties must certainly recognise that things exist independently of our notions of them, that is to say, not only for us, i.e., also in them-selves. Which is what was to be proved. But if the antithesis is proved, what about the thesis? If the world exists also in itself, if it existed already prior to the coming of man, i.e., if it exists *not only for us*, how can Petzoldt claim that it exists *only for us*? We now know how the thesis is proved and how the antithesis is proved: we are familiar with both sides of the antinomy, but we do not see any way out of it. There is not even a hint of syn-thesis, and this absence of a way out is a bitter reproach to our logic. A way out must be found, cost what it may!

IV

"All the difficulties of conceiving of the range of elements of the optical and tactile qualities (such as red, blue, round, angular, prismatic, conical, hard, soft, rough, etc.) as existing outside of

* P. 197-98.
** P. 198.

our perceptions of them," says Petzoldt, "spring from the difficulty
we have in detaching ourselves from the concept of absolute being
and immersing ourselves sufficiently in the idea of relative existence. Until recent times, the great idea of Protagoras exerted
only very insignificant influence. Even Hume failed because
he could not find a way to relativism in principle. In his works
(as in those of Hobbes before him) we find only feeble rudiments
of relativism, and only *Mach* and *Avenarius* rediscovered the
deeply buried truth and made it the main factor in their world-
outlook."*

This passage gives us to understand that the way out of the
antinomy wherein we have lost ourselves must be sought, not
in the direction of the antithesis, but in that of the thesis. The
world also exists independently of us, but this existence can in
no way be acknowledged as being-in-itself. The world exists
not only for us, but its existence *not only for us* is identical with
its existence *only for us*. We assert the antithesis but we do so
only for the greater glory of the thesis. Such is the solution implicit
in the passage just quoted from Petzoldt. Do you think it is an
impossible solution? You are mistaken. You are not well enough
acquainted with "modern" positivism.** Listen to Petzoldt:

"Imagine observer A standing before a blossoming apple-tree
and describing to us what he sees. His description coincides with
our own observations. Let us assume that he turns away from
the tree, and that he no longer perceives it. This does not affect
in the least our own perception of the tree. The tree goes on existing
for us, and in its existence for us it is independent of A's perception. Moreover, by eliminating the concept of substance we cease
to make a distinction between our perception, the "image" of the
tree in our perception, and the perceived part of the tree itself:
in perception we apprehend the object immediately in its perceptible parts. If we now assume that observer A is in principle entirely like ourselves, that he is sensitive and thinking person like
ourselves, and that in principle we find ourselves exactly in the
same position in relation to the tree as he, we at the same time
also assume the existence of the tree independently of our own
perception of it; just as the tree continued to exist after A had
turned away from it, so it will go on existing if we ourselves turn
away from it. But if we deny or doubt this independent existence,

---

* Pp. 199-200.

** I call Petzoldt's positivism *modern* because he severs connection with
the old positivism of Auguste Comte and Mill. "Alongside of the Kant variety
of idealism," we read on page 195 of the book under review, "there is also
positive idealism. It knows no a priori conditions of experience (Comte,
Mill) but, as pure phenomenalism, is as untenable as the first." I earnestly
beg the reader to note the reason given by Petzoldt for the rupture of the
"modern" positivism with the old.

we also deny or doubt the existence of other people. So long as we do not decide to do this, we have no possibility of denying the continued existence of things even if we no longer perceive them."*

Now you see *how* the contest between thesis and antithesis is brought to an end. You understand also *why* it ends in favour of the thesis. Having eliminated the concept of substance, we cease to make any distinction between our "image" in the perception of the tree and the part of the tree perceived. The dualism of being-in-itself and being-for-us has given way to the kind of monism in which being-in-itself is indistinguishable from being-for-us. True, this monism smacks strongly of extreme subjective idealism: if we do not differentiate being-in-itself from beingin-our-perception, the existence of the "blossoming apple-tree" must be considered to cease as soon as we turn our backs on it, i.e., when we cease to perceive it. However, this would hold true only in the case when we denied the existence of other people or, at least, had doubted it. But we do not commit this sin at all. Quite the contrary! Without a moment's hesitation, we "imagine" observer A who perceives the "blossoming apple-tree" on our behalf while we stand with our backs to it. Since the tree continues to exist in his perception of it, it follows that it exists independently of us; which means that we have maintained all the lawful rights of the antithesis. But, on the other hand, since the tree's existence independently of "us" is no more than its existence in the perception of observer A, that is to say, existence only for "us", it follows that the tree has no being-in-itself. In other words, it turns out that, although the antithesis seems to have maintained all its lawful rights, so brilliantly defended by Petzoldt, the contest was won, not by the antithesis, but by the thesis. How easily this truly perplexing affair has been resolved! All that was required was the use *in one and the same argument* of the word "*we*" in two different senses: at first (in proving the antithesis) in the sense of a pronoun in the first person singular, i.e., instead of "*I*", and then (from the moment observer A came on the scene) in the sense of the same pronoun in the first person plural, i.e., in the sense of the proper "*we*" signifying not one person but many. Eins, zwei, drei, Geschwindigkeit ist keine Hexerei!

But no matter how amazing our author's Geschwindigkeit, I take the liberty of reminding him of the terrifying question he asked when defending his antithesis and which he used like the cudgel of some hero of old to strike down the idealists: "How was the development of organisms possible before the formation

* P. 200.

of the brain?" In the present instance this question takes on the following form: "How was the development of 'blossoming' trees possible before the appearance of observer A, who went on looking at one of them at least, while 'we' and Mr. Petzoldt turned our backs on it?" There can only be two possible answers to this terrifying question. One of them runs: before "we" and observer A appeared there were no trees. This reply has the great disadvantage of being in contradiction to the conclusions of geology, or to be more exact, of paleophytology; but on the other hand it also has the great advantage of being fully in accord with the fundamental principle of Petzoldt's book, viz.: there is no being-in-itself, the world exists only for us. The other possible reply has a meaning directly opposite to the first: the tree existed already at the time when "we" did not yet exist. This reply is fully confirmed by the conclusions of paleophytology but causes "us" and Mr. Petzoldt this unpleasantness, that it knocks down like a house of cards the whole doctrine of "modern" positivism. For if trees really did exist at the time when we did not, that means that the world exists not only for us but also in itself.

Incidentally, if we recognise the independent existence of the world *only* because we believe in the existence of other people, we continue to stand with both feet on the ground of "pure phenomenalism". But on the admission of Petzoldt himself, "pure phenomenalism" is nothing else than one of the varieties of idealism (see above our author's contemptuous reference to Auguste Comte and Mill). Therefore, Petzoldt himself must be placed among the idealists.* But his idealism does not acknowledge its own existence and is afraid of its own essence. This is unconscious and cowardly idealism.

This cowardly idealism is imagined to be *monism*, since it thinks it has eliminated the *"dualism"* of being-in-itself and being-for-us. But by what manner of logic was this imaginary dualism "eliminated"? By admitting that the existence of the object independently of our perception is but its existence in the perception of other people. The blossoming apple-tree exists independently of me: this is proved by its existence not only in my perception but also in that of "observer A" and of other egos. But if it exists in the perception of each of these individuals, without having any "being-in-itself", it must have as many existences as "we" have observers. In place of *monism*

---

* Indeed, in his attempt to solve the antinomy we are discussing he does not pass beyond the limits of *Schuppe*'s well-known, purely idealist principle: Kein Gegenstand ausserhalb des Bewusstseins. ["There is no object outside of consciousness."]

28—01230

we arrive at something in the nature of a parody of *pluralism*. But again "we" do not notice this "turn of events", since "our" idealism is not only cowardly but unconscious.

Not without reason is it said: know thyself. Petzoldt's unconscious idealism has the shortcomings characteristic of idealism in general. But to the shortcomings characteristic of all brands of idealism, Petzoldt adds particular defects caused by its being unconscious. Conscious idealism does not refuse to solve the fundamental question of all modern philosophy, that of the mutual relation of subject and object, although the solution it offers is a bad one. Petzoldt's unconscious idealism evades the examination of this question on the excuse that the question loses its meaning as soon as we renounce the concept of substance. But just because Petzoldt's unconscious idealism, which calls itself modern or real positivism, evades the problem of the mutual relation of subject and object, the problem makes itself felt in the most unexpected and unceremonious fashion in the arguments of his followers. Drive it out of the door and it flies in through the window.

Indeed, the reader will recall that, on Petzoldt's invitation, we imagined observer A to be "in principle entirely like ourselves", and standing beside a blossoming apple-tree. We did so hoping that this gentleman would extricate us from the difficult situation in which we found ourselves, stuck fast in the antinomy between Petzoldt's thesis and his own antithesis. Now we know that he did us a very doubtful service by taking us directly into the domain of idealism, which Petzoldt and we were repudiating with all our might. But this did not by any means exhaust the unpleasantness caused us by his appearance "beside the apple-tree". His seemingly so innocent appearance there meant, in fact, that we were unexpectedly confronted with the very same question concerning the mutual relations of subject and object which Petzoldt and we were hoping to evade. His appearance demonstrated to us that serious philosophical problems, like things, exist quite independently of whether men wish to consider them or not.

Observer A is "in principle entirely like ourselves"; he is just as sensitive and thinking person like ourselves. That is splendid. But one asks: does he exist only "*for us*" or does he exist also "*in himself*"?

To answer this question, let us assume for a minute that observer A exists only in our imagination (Petzoldt's invitation to "imagine" observer A did not come by chance). In that case, observer A has, of course, only being "*for us*" and any being "*in himself*" is alien to him. He bears no resemblance at all to any kind of substance. That is also good. But what is bad is that in that event his appearance (in our imagination) does not offer us even that illusory solution of the antinomy torturing us which our author had hoped to find in inventing this gentleman; for in this case observer A exists, true, for us, but in no way independently of us. But what is still worse is that if all "other people", like gentleman A, exist only in our imagination, we prove to be incurable solipsists; and then we have not the least right logically to believe in the existence (i.e., the real existence, and not as the products of our imagination) of "other people". But even Petzoldt himself, of course, would not dream of agreeing that solipsism can solve a single question of philosophy, or represents anything more than a mockery of philosophy.

It remains for us now to assume that gentleman A exists *not only* in our imagination. But in making this hypothesis, we recall the sad consequences that followed from the duality of the tiny word "we" when used by Petzoldt. Therefore, we should like, to begin with, to get agreement on terminology.

The word "we" signifies here all people apart from gentleman A. The assumption that gentleman A exists not only in our imagination means that he would exist even if we had *no* idea of him. Are we entitled to make such a hypothesis? We are not only entitled, we are obliged to make it because, as we have seen, the contrary hypothesis is utterly untenable. But what is the upshot of our now being able to make this hypothesis? The upshot is that gentleman A has not only being "*for us*" but also being "*in himself*".

The problem is now solved, but in quite a different way from that planned by Petzoldt. He sought a solution proceeding from the idea that being-in-itself was impossible. It turned out that the question could be solved—short of resorting to the absurdities of solipsism—only on the basis of the idea that it is essential to assume being-in-itself. In other words, if you want to find the truth, you should proceed in the opposite direction to that in which the "positivist" Petzoldt is calling you.

We shall bear that in mind. Now let us go on. What exactly is this being-in-itself which we were compelled to recognise in spite of our author's arguments? To whom does it apply? It applies, as a matter of fact, to me, to you, to observer A, who, according to Petzoldt, is "just as sensitive and thinking person like ourselves", and, lastly, to all "other people". Now tell me, do you and I and all other people represent something that is beyond the reach of knowledge? It would seem not. Why then did Petzoldt think that being-in-itself is an attribute only of unknowable substance? Simply because he has a wrong notion of being-in-itself. He would like us to believe that he is a positiv-

28*

ist in its newest sense, but in fact turns out to be an idealist who clings to an utterly obsolete, utterly bankrupt theory of cognition. This seems improbable, but it only seems so because "philosophers" of the school to which Petzoldt belongs have been shrieking themselves hoarse about their positivism. They were taken at their own valuation, which was very very imprudent.

We have assumed that observer A exists, in spite of the fact that all the rest of mankind have not the foggiest notion of him. Now let us assume that "we" have finally discovered that he does exist. In consequence of this, he has begun to exist "*for us*". Do "we" have any reason to think that on account of this he has ceased to exist in himself? No, since to discover the existence of gentleman A does not mean to destroy him. If this is so, it turns out that our gentleman now exists in dual form: 1) *in himself*, 2) *for us*. In the first instance, he is a thing-in-itself, and in the second instance, he is a phenomenon. Nor can it be otherwise. All that I assert here in regard to observer A, I assert also in regard to you, reader. First of all, you exist in yourself, and, secondly, for me, that is to say, in my imagination. Am I right? Perhaps, if you are a "positivist" in the newest sense, you will find my assertion to be "metaphysical" and will tell me that such duality is "unnecessary"?* Maybe you will demand that I repudiate your being-in-itself and acknowledge that you exist only for me, that is to say, in my imagination? I say in advance that I will never agree to this, because if I did, I should arrive at solipsism, and both Petzoldt and I reject solipsism decidedly.

What does all this mean? It simply means that Petzoldt is hopelessly entangled in contradictions and that his "positivism", which promised radically to eliminate the very question of the mutual relation of subject and object, has quite unexpectedly run up against this important question and smashed itself to smithereens.

VI

Now I invite the reader to recall the arguments our author used to defend his thesis.

He said (see above) that the idea of substance contradicts experience, since "we can only resolve things into a number of exclusively changeable qualities—which psychology calls sensations ... but never, even with the most perfect instruments, do we discover a part which is undefinable by its quality...." This reasoning, which he believes to be irrefutable and to which he returns on

---

* "If, in this way, Kant does not break with the unnecessary duality of the world into the thing-in-itself and phenomenon," says Petzoldt, "if he even goes backward in comparison with his predecessors..." etc. (P. 188 of the book under review).

almost every page of his book, in fact proves that he himself has not yet emerged from the sphere of an obsolete and truly scholastic theory of cognition.

For people who have outgrown this scholastic theory—for example, the materialists, at whom Petzoldt turns up his nose without the least justification—the question is not whether anything remains after we have "resolved" a thing into its "qualities". According to their doctrine, it is quite ridiculous to pose the question in this way. The quality of a thing is by no means a component part of it. This may be easily verified if we take the example of, say, such a commonly known thing as water. If we resolve this water into its component parts we shall get oxygen and hydrogen. These two elements are component parts of water. But can we describe them as *qualities*? This would really be excusable only on the part of Gogol's Poprishchin.[224]

What do we mean when we refer to the qualities of a thing? Its qualities—or, to use a more common and, in this case, more exact term, its properties—we materialists describe as the capacity of a thing to modify itself in a certain way, under certain conditions, and to induce corresponding modifications in other things connected with it in one way or another. For example, water at 0°C. freezes. That capacity to freeze at the temperature mentioned is undoubtedly one of the properties of water. Further: frozen water (ice) coming into contact with one's body produces certain changes in the condition of the body, frequently leading to illness, for instance, inflammation. This capacity of ice to promote certain processes in one's body under conditions of more or less continuous contact must also be regarded as its property. Those changes in the state of the body which are produced by contact with ice are accompanied by a *sensation of cold*. The capacity of ice to arouse this sensation is again called its property. To Petzoldt, all properties of all bodies are "reducible" to sensations. He thinks so because, as we know already, he takes the standpoint of idealism, although he is afraid to admit it either to himself or to others. In fact, sensation is but the subjective side of the process which begins when a given body— shall we say, ice—starts to influence another body organised in a certain way, for example, the human body. For a very long time past, the idealists have been advancing the proposition, in opposition to the materialists, that man is "given" only his sensations and ideas, and that therefore he can know only his sensations and ideas; whereas the things-in-themselves, which, in the opinion of the materialists, are the cause of sensations, are beyond the reach of knowledge. The idealists look upon this proposition as of paramount importance. However, it cannot withstand the faintest breath of serious gnosiological criticism.

What does it mean to know a given thing? It means that one must
have a correct idea of its properties. This idea of its properties
is always based on the sensations we experience when subjected
to its influence. Knowledge, like sensation, is always subjective,
because the process of cognition is nothing more than the process
of forming certain ideas in the subject. One must have a great
deal of naivete in philosophical matters to believe that the discovery of what is presupposed in the very concept of knowledge
is a highly important gnosiological revelation. To repeat that
our knowledge is subjective is simply tautology. The question
is not whether knowledge is subjective: that is self-evident. The
question is: can knowledge be true? To put it another way: can
the ideas of the properties of a thing formed in the subject correspond to, i.e., not contradict, its real properties? This question
presents little difficulty when we remember that our ideas of
a thing are created on the basis of the sensations we experience
when we come into contact with it in some way or other. On the
basis of our previous contact with a thing we may have formed an
idea of its properties that does not conform to reality; in that
case, sooner or later we shall feel this lack of conformity when
we again come into contact with the thing. Thus if we thought
that water could not solidify—the savage natives of the tropical
countries actually have no idea of this property of water—we
should realise our mistake at our first opportunity of seeing
water freezing. Experience is the judge which decides in the
last resort whether the idea of an object formed in the mind of
a subject corresponds to the properties of the object. Sometimes
the judge needs much time to solve one or other of the innumerable
questions of this sort. The old man is sometimes exasperatingly
slow. But, generally speaking, the older our judge becomes the
more he sheds this defect. Besides, no matter how long he takes
to "go into it", he must none the less be recognised as a quite
reliable judge. Should the subject's conceptions, say those of our
friend observer A, of the world surrounding him not correspond
even to a part of the real properties of the world, he simply could
not exist; he would perish in the struggle for existence, in the
same way as all other incompatible organisations perish in it.
Thus the very fact that subjects *exist*, i.e., exist in reality and
not in the heads of some philosophising super-subjects or other—is
our guarantee that their knowledge is not only "subjective" but
is also true, at least partly, or in other words, that it, at least
partly, corresponds to the real properties of the world. This
thought could be expressed in another way: *the very fact that
there exist thinkers who proclaim the unknowability of the external
world* (i.e., the world lying beyond sensations) *is our guarantee
of its knowability.*

Completely at a loss on this question, Petzoldt, being nurtured on idealist prejudices, decided that, if the subject is "given" only his sensations, there is absolutely no need to assume the existence of any kind of external cause for these sensations. He repudiated the existence of things-in-themselves. But after doing so he admitted, as we have seen, the existence of "other people". And by admitting the existence of "other people", he *thereby admitted* the existence of things-in-themselves, because each given person is, as we have seen, a person (and, consequently, a thing) in himself, and at the same time is a person (and, consequently, a thing) for another, i.e., for his fellow-man. There is no dualism of any kind here, no unnecessary duality, since from the time other people came to be, not even one of them, as far as we know, "doubled" himself as a consequence of existing not only in himself (and as a conscious being, for himself) but also for others.* If Petzoldt got himself involved in contradictions, it was precisely because he knew nothing of the materialist theory of cognition. He knew only that idealist gnosiology which claims that knowledge based on sensations is not real knowledge, since it supposedly does not reveal to us the true nature of things, but tells us only about their external appearance. He was simple enough to believe that all thinkers who recognise the existence of things-in-themselves, must be agreed among themselves "that it is the eye and the ear and the senses in general which conjure up before us a false picture of the world and are the cause of all error". In clinging to the utterly mistaken conviction that things which had the property of being-in-themselves could not be perceived by the external senses ("on the contrary, appearance perceived by the senses conceals them from us") he took up arms against the doctrine of being-in-itself, making the struggle with this doctrine the principal task of philosophy. After what I have said above, reader, about your and my being-in-ourselves, I see no necessity to prove that Petzoldt was mistaken in attributing to all thinkers who acknowledge such being the striving "to find an imaginary absolute world", accompanied by the belief in some kind of absolute being, in some kind of absolute truth that is dependent on nothing subjective. This enormous error, extremely unfortunate in its results, arose from the fact that Petzoldt, as I have already remarked, had a very poor understanding of the materialist theory of cognition, and knew only the idealist gnosiology which, indeed, has committed from time to time—

---

* "Das Ding ist hiernach für sich, und *auch* für ein anderes, ein *gedoppeltes* verschiedenes Sein; aber es ist auch *Eins*" (Hegel, *Phänomenologie des Geistes*, Bamberg und Würzburg, 1807, S. 51). [The Thing is, hence for itself and *also* for another, a Being that has difference of a dual kind. But it is also *one*.] See my remark above on Petzoldt's *pluralism*.

for example, in the person of Plato—all the sins he himself refers
to.* And only because he knew so little about the materialist
theory of knowledge, which had already acquired a systematised
form in the works of Feuerbach, did he turn to Protagoras, whose
well-known principle "Man is the measure of all things", won
him over by its deceptive simplicity and obviousness. But we
already know that this proposition of Protagoras' was not fated
to guide our author out of a maze of insoluble and often highly
comic contradictions.

VII

In characterising the philosophy of Parmenides, Petzoldt says
reproachfully that it did not even consider the question, "whether,
and how, the world of appearance, which after all exists in some
manner and is governed by laws, is related to the real world
of the one which has being".** Yet, adds our author, anyone who
did not think formally would regard this question as most important. I am very pleased to be able to agree with Petzoldt, if only
on this point. The question is, in fact, one of cardinal importance.
But it is a pity that, as we have seen, Petzoldt himself was not
only unable to cope with this question, but could not even approach
it. It does not occur to him either that man's sensations and ideas
can be related in a law-governed manner to the external world.
I shall not go as far as to say that Petzoldt could not even approach
this question because he has one of those "minds that think formally". Of course, his thinking is distinguished by a strange
formalism, but the matter does not end there. Petzoldt's formal
mind, in addition, did not have the proper information. Quite
unconsciously, he continued to be under the influence of the idealist
theory of knowledge *even while he was rebelling against it.* And it
was only because he remained under its influence that he could main-

---

* To be just, I should mention, however, that even materialists have
sometimes not refused to repeat idealist phrases about the unknowability of
things-in-themselves. Holbach, for instance, was sometimes not innocent
of this. But what was simply inconsistency on the part of materialists, was
the foundation of the entire idealist gnosiology. Quite a big difference.
Let me add that the difference between idealist gnosiology and the materialist theory of knowledge was apparent already in ancient philosophy.
W. Windelband, in elucidating the "main distinction" between Plato and
Democritus in respect to theory and knowledge, says: "The last-named also
demanded, together with knowledge gained through perception (σκοτίη
γνώμη) understood and evaluated in Protagoras' sense, also true knowledge
(γνησίη γνώμη) obtained by thinking; but he believed that one could be
deduced from the other; he established a difference between them only of
degree, but not in essence. Thus by thinking, operating with concepts ... he
found, not a new incorporeal world, but only the fundamental element
of the same corporeal world—the atom" (W. Windelband, *Plato*, St. Petersburg, 1904, p. 84, footnote).
** P. 85.

tain the belief that if the world exists not only *"for us"*, but also *"in itself"*, then its being-"in-itself" is beyond the reach of our external senses. This is just the same belief he chides Parmenides for holding: the belief in the absence of any relation conforming to law between being "in itself" and being "for us". By clinging to this belief, he naturally discerned dualism where in fact there was none. To get rid of this illusory dualism, and lacking knowledge of the materialist theory of cognition, he could think of nothing better than to deny "being-in-itself". And this was tantamount to reconciliation with idealism. The only difference was that one idealist theory of cognition was replaced by another still less satisfactory and still more contradictory. He wanted to move forward, but instead he moved backward, extremely pleased with himself and imagining that his retreat practically solved the most difficult philosophical question "once and for all". All the arguments advanced by Petzoldt in defence of his thesis are constructed on a proposition borrowed from the idealists, viz., that "being-in-itself" cannot be accessible to our external senses. The more often he repeats this proposition, the more clearly revealed is the kinship of "modern" positivism with idealism of the purest water. True, Petzoldt is afraid to admit this kinship, but fear is not a reason, and not even an extenuating circumstance. Idealism, having turned cowardly, has not then ceased to be idealism.

How poorly Petzoldt is acquainted with materialism may be seen, incidentally, from the following passage in his book. While noting that "the preservation of spiritual substance only", which is characteristic of spiritualism, is empirically and logically impossible, he proceeds: "Matters are no better with the corresponding materialist reduction, the elimination of the spiritual substance in favour of the material. To assert that the perception of a colour, a sound, a pain, or the concepts of loyalty, valour, science, war are identical with the process of motion within the brain, that these sensations are one and the same as this motion and not merely caused by it, is just as insufferable as to assert that the world is only an idea, something without extension."*

Our author would find himself in a real quandary if we were to ask him which materialist exactly and in which work asserted that perception and thought *are identical* with motion within the brain. True, two pages further he writes that Hobbes "explicitly denies spiritual phenomena, as being immaterial". But that is a very inept reference. Hobbes looked upon spiritual processes as the inner states of matter in motion and, of course, appropriately organised. Anyone who goes to the trouble of reading his books

---

* Pp. 162-63.

may confirm this for himself. Petzoldt would apparently have
been far more justified had he cited the well-known dictum:
"thought is matter in motion". But, first of all, this phrase was
coined by someone who was by no means an authority on questions
of materialist philosophy,[225] and nothing similar to that assertion
will be found in the works of any one of the classical materialists
of the seventeenth, eighteenth or nineteenth centuries. Secondly,
even this awkward phrase did not suggest the identity of thought
and motion but that motion is a necessary and adequate condition of thought.* Thirdly, how does Petzoldt himself not understand that one cannot flay the same ox twice, and that in reproving
the materialists for dualism on the ground that they distinguish
"being-in-itself" from being-in-perception, he had not the slightest
logical ground for accusing them at the same time of making
these two concepts identical? Fourth: "What need acquaintances
to reckon, when you within the mirror writhe and beckon?"
If anyone is guilty of identifying sensation and motion—or
more exactly, identifying motion with sensation—it is precisely
the modern "positivism" of Mach, Avenarius, and Petzoldt. To
reproach the materialists with having identified sensation and
thought with motion is to thrust on them that "*doctrine of identity*"
whose bankruptcy was so well exposed by Feuerbach, who also
demonstrated that this doctrine is a necessary component part
of idealist "philosophy".

To cap everything, Petzoldt himself believes it is necessary
to include among the materialists those scientists "who regard
spiritual experiences as the products or physiological functions
of material substance, without however identifying them with
material phenomena".** But if this be true, to what then is "reduced"
the reproach hurled at materialism that "it eliminates spiritual
substance in favour of the material"? Simply to a failure to understand what the materialists are talking about.

---

* Regarding a similar expression of Vogt's, "the brain secretes thought
as the kidneys secrete urine", even Lange, who was never kindly disposed
towards the materialists. remarked: "Es ist bei den zahlreichen Erörterungen
von *Vogts* berühmtem Urin-Vergleich wohl klar genug geworden, dass man
nicht den 'Gedanken' als ein besonderes Produkt *neben* den stofflichen Vor-
gängen ansehen kann, sondern dass eben der subjektive Zustand des empfin-
denden Individuums *zugleich* für die äussere Beobachtung ein objektiver,
eine *Molecularbewegung* ist." (F. A. Lange, *Geschichte des Materialismus und
Kritik seiner Bedeutung in der Gegenwart*. Zweites Buch. siebente Auflage,
Leipzig. 1902, S. 374.) [Vogt's much discussed comparison of thought with
urine clearly reveals that "thought" cannot be regarded as a special product
on a level with material processes, but that the subjective state of the perceiving individual is *at the same time* objective for external observation, is
molecular movement.] True, in other parts of his work Lange writes as though
he never even suspected the possibility of such a remark. But that has to do
with his logic, which we are not discussing at the moment.
** P. 165.

Petzoldt corrects himself: "It would be even better to define the essence of the problem by the following delimitation. If the fundamental ideas or concepts which have been developed to explain or describe natural phenomena are applied to explain or describe spiritual processes then we are dealing with materialism."*

This correction only makes matters worse. If spiritual phenomena cannot be described or explained by means of the ideas or concepts which were developed to explain or describe *natural* phenomena, then the dualists are right, since we then have, first, natural phenomena and, secondly, spiritual phenomena not included in the first-named. In short, we then have the dualism of nature and the soul or spirit. A fine "monism" this is, that so frequently and so unwittingly lands in the domain of "ideas or concepts" that are typical of dualism! But let us assume that Petzoldt is simply expressing himself badly, and that when he speaks of natural phenomena he is thinking of motion in the proper meaning of the word. The question then arises: which of the prominent representatives of materialism has explained or described spiritual phenomena with the help of ideas or concepts that were developed to explain or describe motion? Not one of the materialists of modern times! All the foremost materialists of these times said that spiritual phenomena and motion are two aspects of the one and the same process taking place in the organised body (belonging, of course, to nature). One may or may not agree with this. However, it cannot but be recognised, without committing the most glaring injustice, that in this there is neither the identification of one series of phenomena with another, nor the admission that it is possible to explain or describe one series of phenomena by the ideas or concepts "developed" to explain or describe another. Petzoldt defines materialism badly because he knows it badly. As a result, it is not surprising that he makes laughable errors every time he takes to criticising it.**

VIII

Petzoldt has no better reason either for the reproaches he levels at Spinoza. He says: "Spinoza ... understands both substances, not as products of God's creation, but as aspects of his being. God does not only think, he also has extension; he has not only

---

* Ibid.

** I may be told that this very concept of matter must be changed radically in view of the striking discoveries in physics during recent years. There is a point there. But not one of these discoveries vitiates the definition of matter according to which matter is that (in "itself" existing) which directly or indirectly acts, or in certain circumstances can act, on our external senses. That is good enough for me at the moment.

a soul, but also a body; he is identical with nature, i.e., for Spinoza, with the world. This pantheism signifies the lessening and perhaps the complete elimination of the power of the anthropomorphic conception of God, but it leaves untouched the main problem of the theory of cognition. For if to our philosopher matter and spirit are really not two distinct substances, but only attributes of the one and only substance of God, then for our problem this is essentially only a mere renaming of old concepts. We still do not know how material brain processes give rise to immaterial spiritual processes and vice versa, or how relationships conforming to law are established between these aspects which, even according to Spinoza, have nothing in common; and for the elucidation of all this it is a matter of indifference whether they are called substances or only attributes."*

No, it is not a matter of indifference; far from it. Difference in name is of no significance only where it is not accompanied by difference in the corresponding concept. To Spinoza, the new name means a new concept. In eliminating the doctrine of two substances, Spinoza expelled from the domain of philosophy that animism to which Descartes had paid such heavy tribute, to which every idealist pays equally lavish tribute, and which, in Petzoldt's opinion (a justifiable one this time), constitutes one of the greatest errors of human thought. Further. It is strange to reproach Spinoza with not having explained how material brain processes give rise to immaterial spiritual processes. Did not the author of *Ethics* say outright that the second kind of processes *are not caused* by the first kind, but only *attend* them. "The soul and the body," said Spinoza, "are but one and the same thing, conceived now under the attribute of thought, now under the attribute of extension."** Take stock of these words of Spinoza and see if there is even an iota of sense left in the question of how spiritual processes are *caused* by corporeal processes. You see that the question is absolutely devoid of all meaning. The attribute of thought is *not caused* by the attribute of extension, but is simply the reverse side of "one and the same thing", one and the same process. Petzoldt's censure of Spinoza is tantamount to blaming this brilliant Jew for not explaining *how* one and the same process, conceived of from the angle of varying attributes, may present itself quite differently. But Spinoza never undertook this task. The fact that extension and thought are essentially two attributes of one and the same substance was for him an established fact, which explains many other facts, but is not itself subject to explanation. It is remarkable that the same Petzoldt credits

* P. 141.
** Spinoza, *Ethics*, St. Petersburg, 1894, p. 121.

Spinoza with eliminating "the so-called interaction of body and spirit". He says that having got rid of this interaction, Spinoza thereby prepared the ground for the latest views.* But surely it must be clear that Spinoza could only have postulated the question of how material brain processes *give rise* to immaterial spiritual processes if he had recognised the interaction of body and spirit. Petzoldt reproves Spinoza for not tackling this question, and simultaneously praises him for having refuted the interaction of body and spirit. A wonderful power of logic!

Petzoldt avers that "already in Spinoza's works we encounter the idea to which Leibniz later gave the appelation: pre-established harmony".** As a matter of fact, Spinoza was spurned by the theologians of all countries, to use Lessing's phrase, "like a dead dog", because he had left no room in his philosophy for a being who could establish "harmony".*** Petzoldt calls Spinoza's teaching on the mutual relationship of thought and extension the doctrine of pre-established harmony. "Thus, two series of completely independent processes flow side by side.... When a physical phenomenon recurs, there will recur with it the spiritual phenomenon which previously manifested itself together with it, and vice versa."**** Well, isn't it true? Is it a "metaphysical" invention by Spinoza? A man drinks a bottle of vodka: that is a "physical phenomenon". He gets drunk and all sorts of nonsense comes into his head: that is a "spiritual phenomenon". Some days later he drinks another bottle of vodka: again a "physical phenomenon". Once again he gets drunk, and again his head is filled with all kind of nonsense: this again is a "spiritual phenomenon". "When a physical phenomenon recurs, there will recur with it the spiritual phenomenon which previously manifested itself together with it." Surely everybody knows that? But what do the words "and vice versa" mean which Petzoldt attaches to the sentence I have just quoted? I must confess their meaning is beyond me. It must be that we have to see the example of the drunken man like this: the man gets drunk and the full bottle is found to be empty. Otherwise "and vice versa" is meaningless.*****

---

  * P. 141.
  ** P. 142.
  *** Theologians were not satisfied, and could not be, with Spinoza's use of the word "God", since by this word he meant Nature. He said so: "God or Nature" (*Deus sive natura*). From the point of view of terminology, it was of course incorrect, but that is another question which does not concern us here.
  **** P. 142.
  ***** The influence of the physical condition upon the physiological processes is often spoken about. Nowadays, the medical profession dilate much and readily on this influence. I think that the facts prompting this idea are often quite correctly *indicated*. But they are altogether wrongly *explained*. Those who talk much of the influence of the "psychical" upon the "physical"

But however that may be, it is a fact that certain relationships conforming to law exist between psychical phenomena on the one hand and physiological phenomena on the other. Petzoldt himself, of course, does not deny this. But he finds that Spinoza explained these relationships badly. Let us agree with him for the time being and ask: are these relationships explained any better in idealist philosophy? Petzoldt will say no. What remains? "Modern" positivism! We turn to "modern" positivism.

Petzoldt contends that the mistake of all philosophical teachings prior to this positivism consisted in the following: "They could not conceive of any other mutual dependence of natural phenomena than that of sequence in time: *first* A, *then* B; but not as in geometry: *if* A, *then* B. According to the geometrical method, if the sides of a triangle are equal, then the opposite angles are also equal.... If attention is directed to this completely general functional dependence of both geometrical and physical determining elements, then it is not difficult to conceive as analogous the relationships between spiritual and bodily phenomena (or determining elements), thereby bridging the gulf separating the two worlds. But Spinoza, although he set forth the basic principles of his main work and proved them, following strictly the model of Euclid's geometry, and although he weakened the contrast between the two substances, reducing them to the level of two aspects of one and the same substance, nevertheless was very far from the aforesaid analogy. He was unable to think of parallelism between the spiritual and bodily processes in the form of the interrelation between x and y in the equation: y equals f (x), but needed a connective member between the two variable quantities, namely the conception of substance."*

So there we are: *if* A, *then* B; if the sides of a triangle are equal, then the opposite angles are also equal. That is indeed very simple.

---

forget that each particular psychical condition is only *one* side of the process, the *other* side being physiological, or to be more accurate, a whole combination of physiological phenomena in the proper meaning of the term. When we say that a particular psychical condition has influenced in a certain way the physiological functions of a particular organism, we have to understand that this influence we speak of was caused, strictly speaking, by those phenomena (which are also purely physiological) the *subjective side* of which constitutes this psychical condition. If it were otherwise, if this or that psychical conditions could serve as the real cause of physiological phenomena, we should have to renounce the law of the conservation of energy. This has already been adequately dealt with by F. A. Lange in his [*History of Materialism*], Vol. II. p. 370 et seq. See also note 39 on pages 440-42 of the same Volume. True, Ostwald's pupils would revolt against my remark concerning the law of the conservation of energy, but I cannot start wrangling with them here. I hope soon to devote a special article to analysing Ostwald's theory of knowledge.

* Pp. 142-43.

If a man has drunk a litre of vodka, *then* he has become intoxicated: which was to be proved. But does it answer the question with which Petzoldt has just been pestering Spinoza? Do we now know—thanks to "modern" positivism—"*how*" the given relationships conforming to law are established between A and B? Do we now know *what determines* the reciprocal relationship of spiritual and bodily phenomena? No, we do not. And it is all too clear that *if* we in turn began to worry Petzoldt with these questions, *then* he would decline to answer, on the ground that science discovers that phenomena are regulated by laws, but does not explain *why* there is this conformity to law. And he would be right. However, as the Germans justifiably say, *was dem einen recht, ist dem anderen billig.** Here also is a sort of "if—then". *If* Petzoldt cannot be reproached for having an inclination towards the doctrine of pre-established harmony, *then* neither can Spinoza; for both of them leave one and the same question unanswered.

The only difference is that Spinoza "needed a connective member between the two variable quantities, namely the conception of substance", and Petzoldt did not. But it is now clear from what has been said that the difference is not at all in Petzoldt's favour.

In analysing Hume's views on the relationship of the "inner world" to the external world, Petzoldt thus formulates his own theory on this subject: "Both worlds emerge from indifferent elements in the process of mutual differentiation and interrelationship. And this already indicates that they exist in relations of mutually functional dependence, while at the same time having a common independent root."**

Whatever these "indifferent elements" may be, the differentiation of which leads, in Petzoldt's words, to the emergence of the external world on the one hand, and the inner world on the other, one thing is clear: these two worlds have no sooner emerged than a relationship is established between them which is usually referred to as the relationship of the object to the subject. We already know just how badly the "new" positivism explains—or it would be better to say: how much it confuses—the conception of this relationship. Consequently, I shall not enlarge upon it. I will only remark that, here also, our author does not explain to us *why* certain reciprocal relationships are established between the "inner" world and the "external" world: that is to say, he is guilty— if one can speak of guilt in this case—of doing exactly the same thing he accused Spinoza of doing. However, there is a morsel of truth in the remark cited above. The two worlds really "do have a common root". To the degree that this is correct, it comes

---

* [What is right for one, is right for another.]
** P. 172.

nearer to Spinoza's doctrine that thought and extension are essentially two attributes of one and the same substance. Petzoldt is not in error only when he repeats the materialist doctrine of Spinoza which he has repudiated, albeit presenting that doctrine in an extremely muddled form.

IX

But most interesting of all is the "conclusion" our author draws from Spinoza's teaching. It is so incredible that I cannot expound its underlying argument in my own words, and must leave that to Petzoldt himself.

"This conclusion consists first of all in this: that the souls of two people, A and B, cannot communicate anything to each other and are completely isolated from each other. Only their bodies, in particular the cerebra, are in mutual contact by means of their motions of expression, in particular, the motions of the speech organs. The sounds produced by A set the air in vibrations; the airwaves strike B's ear-drum, and its vibrations are transferred to the auditory nerve which, in turn, communicates its impulses to the cerebrum. There, all kinds of complicated changes occur, which finally lead to movements of subject B's organs of speech; and these movements, traversing now the return journey, reach A's cerebrum. But at no time does any of these manifestations touch the souls of the two subjects. Their cerebra alone carry on the conversation; their souls know nothing about it."*

One would have to know nothing whatever of Spinoza's philosophy to believe this. The author of *Ethics* must, apparently, have foreseen his Petzoldt and tried to anticipate this preposterous "conclusion". Theorem XII of Part II of Spinoza's main work reads: "*Whatever comes to pass on the subject of the idea, which constitutes the human soul, must be perceived by the human soul, or there will necessarily be an idea in the human soul of the said occurrence. That is, if the object of the idea constituting the human soul be a body, nothing can take place in that body without being perceived by the soul.*"** After that one may judge how profound is the conclusion reached which has its culminating point

---

* Pp.146-47.
** *Ethics*, p. 66, Spinoza's italics. It would be useful to contrast this with Theorem XIV in the same Part: "*The human mind is capable of perceiving a great number of things, and is so in proportion as its body is capable of receiving a great number of impressions.*—Proof: The human body (*by Post. III and VI*) is affected in very many ways by external bodies, and is capable in very many ways of affecting external bodies. But (*Theorem XII in the same Part*) the human mind must perceive all that takes place in the human body; the human mind is, therefore, capable of perceiving a great number of things, and is so in proportion, etc.—which was to be proved." (Ibid., p. 75.)

in the words: "Their cerebra alone carry on the conversation; their souls know nothing about it." If Spinoza had taught that "brains" could carry on a conversation about which the "soul" knew nothing, he would have been a dualist and not a monist, and we should again be confronted with the two independent substances, with one of them—the "soul"—having allotted to it all psychical phenomena, while the other—the "body"—would be regarded as incapable of either sensation or thought, in which case it would be beyond all comprehension how such material things as brains could "carry on a conversation". To get out of this difficulty, it would only remain for us to assume that matter can think, that is to say, to go back to the teaching of the same Spinoza for whose refutation there was invented the "conclusion" about conversing "brains" and "isolated" souls.

Petzoldt himself feels that his conclusion is directly opposed to what Spinoza said, and consequently hastens to put things right by the following consideration: "If, in spite of this, simultaneously with the brain processes there occur processes in the soul corresponding to those of the brain—and therefore to one another—the cause of this is that pre-established harmony, that mathematical magical term which, at the proper moment, substitutes itself for the missing concept and makes things so different, in the sense of their premises, as soul and body, only *aspects* of one and the same thing."* But I said already that the doctrine of pre-established harmony is being foisted on Spinoza by Petzoldt without the slightest justification. As for love of mathematical magical terms, this is the distinguishing feature of precisely the "modern" positivists. We have seen this from Petzoldt's example. Was it not he who told us that the mathematical concept of functional dependence enables us to bridge the gulf separating spiritual from bodily phenomena? But there's the rub: Petzoldt has a flair for putting the blame on someone else. On page 143 of his book, he refers to the concept of functional dependence, claiming that it will help us to "bridge", etc., while on page 147 he accuses Spinoza of having a love for "mathematical magical terms". Willy-nilly, we recall Krylov's bear advising the monkey to look at itself in the mirror, instead of counting up its acquaintances.

Someone will tell us, perhaps, that to Petzoldt the "mathematical term" *signifies* a certain concept, whereas this concept is absent in Spinoza's teaching, having been replaced by this mathematical term. It is obvious that this is exactly what Petzoldt himself wishes to convey. But this reproach has no more basis than any of the others. First, one may disagree with Spinoza's

---

* P. 147.

doctrine of the two attributes of a single substance, but it is decidedly out of the question to describe this doctrine as lacking in content. Secondly, we have seen that Petzoldt himself, in his theory of the relationship between psychical and physical phenomena, avoids falling into contradictions only when he reproduces Spinoza's idea, though in a distorted form. Finally—last but not least*—notwithstanding Spinoza's geometrical method of *presentation*, he very seldom had recourse to "mathematical terms" in his *reasoning*, as is known to all who have read his *Ethics*. Why throw the blame on someone else? I pass over such logical conclusions from Spinoza's teaching as these: "Souls are isolated both in relation to each other and in relation to the external world. Just as in fact they cannot hear, neither can they see or have any kind of perception of the world around them."** We already know that *such* conclusions may be drawn from Spinoza's teaching only with the aid of that strange logic which makes itself felt on every page of Petzoldt's book. But I cannot resist the temptation to point to the following "inevitable conclusion from Spinoza's teaching". This conclusion winds up the chapter devoted to the author of *Ethics*, and I should like to leave the reader with a happy memory of this chapter.

"I myself am a soul, completely cut off from the external world. What, then, gives me the right to speak at all of a world existing outside myself? Nothing, absolutely nothing. The world *may* exist—that cannot be denied. It could be, however, that I alone exist in the world, that I myself am this world, a world composed exclusively of ideas coming and going. And even if a world outside myself did exist, there is nothing I could presume regarding its arrangement. I shall never know whether there exist other beings like myself. I know now that those whom I formerly took to be beings like myself are only my ideas. But even if I did know that there were such beings, it would not make things easier for me. I could never really have intercourse with them. It must, therefore, be to me a matter of extreme indifference whether they exist or not. In my world I am alone—the world is my own."***

As an example of the "logical conclusions" to be drawn from Petzoldt's *thesis*, that is not at all bad. And since we are aware that the antinomy between the antithesis and the thesis was resolved in favour of the thesis, the above passage may be described as a caricature by Petzoldt of his own philosophical theory. Painters are often known to paint their own *portraits*. But as far as I know philosophers have hitherto not drawn *caricatures*

---

  * [These words are in English in the original.]
 ** P. 147.
*** P. 148.

of their own views. Petzoldt is a real innovator in this respect, and therein lies the true originality of his book. It deserves great and sympathetic attention.

X

Mr. P. Yushkevich has written his own preface to this book, heading it *On the Question of the World Enigma*. It is worthwhile saying a few words about this preface.

Mr. P. Yushkevich finds Petzoldt's book interesting because it is devoted to "one of the fundamental questions of philosophy", the question of the existence of things independently of us. Generally speaking, he is satisfied with the reply given to this question by Petzoldt; but he thinks it needs some "correction", since without this Petzoldt's solution "does not by any means eliminate all doubts".* We know by now that this is indeed so, even more so; in fact, Petzoldt's "solution" does not eliminate a *single* doubt. But why is Mr. P. Yushkevich not fully satisfied with it? In his book, Petzoldt frequently refers to Protagoras' proposition: "To each man the world is as it appears to him."** It is in respect of this proposition that Mr. P. Yushkevich suggests his correction. "If we are to proceed from Protagoras' principle," he says, "it must be taken in the most general and, therefore, the most relative form: to each man the world is as it appears to him *at each given moment....* A tree to me is not simply green. At such and such a moment it has such and such a shade of green; at another moment—a different shade.... If at different moments t_1, t_2, t_3, ... t_n I have different images of the tree: A_1, A_2, A_3, ... A_n, and if I do not take their arithmetical mean, do not take their end image A ($=$"the tree is green"), then at which of these images must I stop when I am speaking of the existence of trees outside myself? At none in particular, which means at them all."*** From this Mr. P. Yushkevich draws the justifiable conclusion that absolute relativism devours itself. What then? Mr. P. Yushkevich says that relativism too has to be regarded from a "relativist" point of view; relativism must restrict itself, otherwise it will degenerate into absurdity. Mr. P. Yushkevich writes: "Heraclitus taught that one cannot swim in one and the same river twice.

---

* Pp. 17 and 28.
** This proposition of Protagoras' is interpreted by Petzoldt in the sense of extreme subjectivism, even though the latest historians of ancient philosophy are advancing arguments which cast doubt on the correctness of such an interpretation. (See, for example, Théodore Gomperz, *Les penseurs de la Grèce. Histoire de la philosophie antique*, Lausanne, pp. 464-501, especially pp. 483 et seq.) Mr. P. Yushkevich says nothing about Petzoldt's views on Protagoras; evidently he agrees with them.
*** Pp. 17, 18, 19.

One cannot swim in the same river once, taught Cratylus, elevating his dynamism into a certain absolute. Since everything is fluid, is constantly changing, there is nothing recurring. There is no 'one and the same thing', there is only diversity: nothing can be said about anything, since a word is also 'one and the same' and when we use a word we are fixing something which recurs, that is to say, which does not exist. A thought, once spoken, is a lie. But this thought, too, being spoken, is a lie—it negates itself."*

Mr. P. Yushkevich is speaking the truth here, but it is a truth, incidentally, that was much better expressed by Hegel who said that existence (Dasein) is the first negation of negation. But to state this incontestable truth still does not mean that we have solved the question of things existing independently of ourselves. Mr. P. Yushkevich is quite right when he says: "Extreme relativism coincides with extreme solipsism—a solipsism of the moment, knowing only the one present moment.** More than once we have had occasion to witness how Petzoldt's illusory positivism leads fatally to solipsism. But what exactly is the correction which, in Mr. P. Yushkevich's opinion, could lead us out of the blind alley of solipsism?

He asserts that the question of the existence of the objective world, independent of our perceptions, presupposes the existence of "some fairly significant community of organisation". He repeats Protagoras' phrase: man is the measure of all things, and goes on: "By the same right, we could say that 'a worm is the measure of all things'—'the amoeba is the measure of all things', and so on. If we do single out man in this connection, it is only because he is a measure which is *conscious* of being a measure. This consciousness is the product of the social elaboration of experience, presupposing a high degree of agreement between human organisations. 'Social man is the measure of things.' Only this social man, who has recognised himself to be a measure, later endows each separate personality, every living creature, with its special individual measure of being."***

That is truly a brilliantly simple solution. In order to get out of the blind alley of solipsism, all we have to do is to imagine that we are not in this dreary alley, but in the pleasant company of human beings like ourselves. All our troubles have disappeared as with the waving of a magic wand. There is but one regret: we still do not know by what logical right we give such freedom to our imagination. But if we do not insist upon this painful question, everything will go swimmingly.

---

     * Pp. 19-20.
    ** P. 21.
   *** Pp. 23-24.

"Confronting us," Mr. P. Yushkevich reassures us, "are most diverse individual pictures of the world, some similar, some different; before us also is the collective system of experience, the social image of the world, derived from these similarities. This social picture of the world is, of course, not an 'absolute' one. It changes in accordance with the acquisitions of knowledge, to the extent that the constantly widening collective experience discovers new diversities for us, but also new and more profound similarities between the diverse individual experiences. But no matter how far from the absolute the social human conception of the world is, in our eyes it has its special importance alongside the individual images of the world. It is precisely to this that we refer when we speak of the 'real', the 'independent', the 'objective', etc., world."*

This is, perhaps, a slight improvement on absolute relativism. But what is new in Mr. Yushkevich's "correction"? Absolutely nothing. It is an old idealist tune: that which exists in the minds of all people is objective. But to exist in the minds of all people is to exist in a conception common to all. And if our "picture of the world" is objective only because it exists in the minds of all people, we are idealists, regarding the world as a conception. Meanwhile, Petzoldt, with whom Mr. P. Yushkevich is in full agreement, apart from the exception indicated, categorically declares that "the doctrine of the world as a conception" is a "colossal absurdity".** Try and understand that! Amazing compliments these gentlemen of "modern" positivism pay one another.

A word or two more. Mr. P. Yushkevich admits that, if man is the measure of things, then a worm is a measure of things too, an amoeba is a measure of things, and so on. Man is singled out "by us" in this respect "only because he is a measure which is *conscious* of being a *measure*". We have to suppose that neither the worm nor the amoeba are in fact conscious of themselves as measures, and do not study philosophy. But although in this respect they do not resemble man, a fact is still a fact and is admitted as such even by Mr. P. Yushkevich: the "worm" does not have the same "picture of the world" as the "amoeba", and the "amoeba" has not the same picture that man has. How does this come about? It is because the material organisation of man does not resemble the material organisation of the other two "measures of things". What does this mean? It means that *consciousness* ("the picture of the world" peculiar to each particular "measure of things") is determined by *being* (the material organisation of that "measure"). And that is pure materialism which our "modern" positivists refuse to have anything to do with. Against this, of course, it

* Pp. 24-25.
** P. 146.

may be objected, as is done in no uncertain fashion by all adversaries of materialism, that the amoeba and the worm, as well
as the material organisation of one and the other, are nothing
more than our conceptions. But if this is true, where does logic
come in? For then it will turn out that to explain the character
of "our picture of the world", that is to say, the totality of "our"
conceptions systematised in some way or other, we and Mr. Yushkevich are referring to the difference between all of this picture,
on the one hand, and the "picture of the world" as seen by some
of its component parts—in this instance, the worm and the amoeba.
Our imagination is first of all our imagination, and then the imagination of the picture of the world peculiar to the worm. In other
words, we imagine to ourselves an image peculiar to some of our
imaginations—and this is what constitutes "our entire scientific
method", and everything that we can oppose to materialism reduces itself to this "scientific method". It isn't very much! But
Petzoldt imagines that the "world-outlook" elaborated by this
method, absurd in the true sense of the word, may perhaps be
recognised as "final in all its main features". To be sure, he has
thought of a fine ending to the history of philosophical thought!*

However, I repeat: Petzoldt's book is evidently assured of great
success among some circles of our reading public. In it is enunciated the very miserable philosophy of cowardly idealism.
But this miserable philosophy is well suited to our miserable
times. Hegel justly remarked that any philosophy is but the ideological expression of its time. The Russian people has expressed,
if you like, that same thought, but in a more general form by
saying: "Senka has the cap that fits him!"

---

* Mr. Yushkevich's "worm" and "amoeba" remind me of the question once
put by F. A. Lange: "If a worm, a beetle, a man, and an angel look at a tree,
do we have *five* trees?" He replied that we should have, in all probability,
four very distinct *conceptions* of the tree, but that all four of these would
relate to one and the same *object* (op. cit., Vol. II, p. 102). Lange was right,
although it cannot be said that his correct reply could have been very well
substantiated with the aid of his (Kantian) theory of cognition. What will
Mr. Yushkevich reply to this question? How many trees will *he* have? I suppose he will have as many as Petzoldt would have got; we already know that
Petzoldt aspires towards monism but arrives at pluralism. In passing I shall
add this: if the tree "in itself" does not exist, whereas the worm, the beetle,
the man and the angel have simultaneous, though distinct impressions of it,
we have a highly interesting case of "pre-established harmony".

ON THE STUDY OF PHILOSOPHY

In an interesting letter to me a comrade makes a rather flattering proposal which I think should be answered in print. This is what he writes.

Pointing to the strong interest in belles lettres and philosophy among the class-conscious proletarians, he proceeds:

"It seems to me that thought on philosophical questions is being stimulated not only by the gloomy political conditions, but also by the concrete material which is forcing itself on the consciousness of the masses. This has to be put in order. That is why they are taking so eagerly to philosophy, why such facts are possible. I am told in a letter from Kazan: 'above all, they are interested here in philosophical questions,' and he adds in inverted commas: 'it's the topic of the day....' In Vienna, a report is to be delivered at the Russian emigrants' May Day meeting on no other subject than philosophy.

"Now political interests are awakening again, but philosophical matters will still predominate for a long time and, of course, will remain to a significant extent, also in the new conditions, one of the most valuable conquests of our present gloomy epoch.

"It is interesting to do everything possible to encourage these quests and to capture the interest of the masses in favour of a more real world-outlook.

"Recently, a worker (from hereabouts) wrote to me: 'I try to read about philosophy; I try all I know. I think and I can't understand. And I have little time. The factory takes it all. Haven't you intellectuals written anything simpler, easier to understand....'

"An 'introduction to philosophy' is needed, which on the basis of scientific Marxism and the natural sciences, is systematically ... if not setting forth, then at least posing all the most essential questions of this subject.

"No one could do this better than you, if you are not already working at it, or something similar. Then those who now have to grope their way through the Paulsens and the Wundts and the like will begin with Marxist works.

"That is my proposal and the desire of my friends."

I shall begin with the proposal made by my correspondent expressing the wish of his friends. However flattering it is to me, unfortunately, because of numerous other obligations, I cannot accept the proposal at present. And then is it necessary that I should be the one to do it? For more than two years an *Introduction to the Philosophy of Dialectical Materialism*, written by a very competent comrade, has been lying here. In spite of all my efforts I cannot find a publisher for it.[226] Why? Evidently because the publishers whom I have approached—and I have approached very many—have no hope of selling an *Introduction* written by a materialist. But if a publisher could be found, the demand which my correspondent rightly notes would be satisfied to a considerable extent. I say "to a considerable extent" and not completely, because the *Introduction* which is lying here may not be as popularly written as my correspondent wishes. But I can guarantee that it would dispel a multitude of harmful prejudices. If any of the comrades interested in philosophy could find a publisher for this work, we should have less reason for complaint about the absence of a proper handbook on philosophy.

The publishers are well acquainted with the reading public. They know that materialism is not an advantageous proposition at the present moment. But if the publishers, in their own way, are right, we Social-Democrats—those of us who purchase books on philosophy—are partly to blame. Here is an interesting example. In the summer of 1892, I published abroad a Russian translation of Engels' classic work, *Ludwig Feuerbach*, together with my notes to it and, as an appendix, a chapter of the famous book, *The Holy Family*. By the summer of 1905, another edition was required. At almost exactly the same time, my translation (with the exception of some footnotes) was published in St. Petersburg. This was a period when the reading public hungrily bought up every printed work bearing the name of a more or less well-known socialist writer. I was confident that *Ludwig Feuerbach*, which had been issued in a fairly limited quantity in St. Petersburg, would be sold out in no time. It turned out that there was very little demand for it. The only explanation I can find for this is that even socialist readers were seeking something "more up-to-date" than the philosophy of dialectical materialism. So that when comrades bemoan the absence of authoritative philosophical works in the Russian language, I invariably ask them: "And have you read Engels' *Ludwig Feuerbach?*" More often than not they reply: "No, I haven't." This kind of reply is often given even by people well acquainted with the "philosophical" works of some Bogdanov or other. When I hear these replies, I lose all inclination to talk about what to read on philosophy.

What the author of the letter says is the honest truth. Our reading public will be devoting almost their main attention to philosophical matters for a long time to come. That is understandable. Today, philosophy is the most reliable weapon we have in Russia for adapting our social consciousness to our social being. This being, after all, is assuming a bourgeois character. Consciousness, too, must assume the same character. And philosophy is actively assisting in this.

But not every philosophy is suitable for adapting bourgeois social consciousness to bourgeois social being. Just now only *idealist* philosophy can serve this purpose. Hence the absence of demand for philosophical works written by *materialists*.

But surely there are *socialists* too among the reading public? Of course, there are. Are they, too, turning their backs on materialist works? As we have already said, they are. But why? Obviously because they themselves are coming under bourgeois influence.

This influence is the clue to why Frederick Engels' *Ludwig Feuerbach* lies on the shelves at the publishers, while the wretched Bogdanov is printed in many editions.

And Engels is not the only one selling badly. L. Axelrod's splendid *Philosophical Essays* are hardly any better, and all for the same reason, all through the fault of the socialist readers. This is something well worth thinking about. It is our business as socialists, not to adapt social consciousness to bourgeois social being, but to prepare the minds of the workers for the struggle against that bourgeois being. In this cause, Engels and L. Axelrod will be much more useful, not only than the ridiculous and archfoggy Bogdanov, but also than any of the most prominent philosophical representatives of the bourgeois world-outlook.

It is a shame to have to say so, but it would be a sin to hide it: we make it extremely difficult for ourselves to acquire sound philosophical conceptions. How do our comrades study philosophy? They read, or I will say, for politeness' sake, they "study" the now fashionable philosophical writers. But these philosophical writers who are now in fashion are thoroughly saturated with idealism. It is quite natural that our comrades "studying" these works become infected with idealist prejudices. And those same Socialists who are fairly well acquainted with the Machs, Avenariuses, Windelbands, etc., etc., have not the slightest notion about the philosophy of Engels, Marx and Feuerbach. So the process finally leads to attempts to build a new "philosophical foundation" for the theoretical structure of Marxism.

In other words: we must begin to study philosophy from a different end altogether. Neither Mach nor Avenarius, neither Windelband nor Wundt, nor even Kant must lead us to the sanctuary of philosophical truth, but only Engels, Marx, Feuerbach, and

Hegel. Only from these teachers can we learn what we need to know.

I shall speak of this in more detail some other time. Now I want to reply, even if briefly, to the interesting letter from the comrade who honoured me with the proposal mentioned above.

P. S. All the same, I cannot conceal from this comrade that his proposal is very, very attractive for me. A year or two ago I toyed for a long time with the idea of writing in as popular a way as I could a criticism of the philosophical works of Max Vervoern. It seemed to me that such a criticism would lay a direct and not very difficult path to the understanding of the fundamental truths of materialist philosophy. I should like to think that I shall still carry out that intention.

SCEPTICISM IN PHILOSOPHY

Raoul Richter, *Scepticism in Philosophy. Volume I.*
Translated from the German by V. Bazarov and
B. Stolpner
Library of Contemporary Philosophy. Issue No. Five.
Shipovnik Publishers. St. Petersburg, 1910

I

This is a very interesting book. It should be read and reread and that more than once. It deals with the very latest questions in knowledge, and presents these very well. But it also suffers from at least one substantial shortcoming: the proffered solutions of these well-presented questions are unsatisfactory. Therefore, in reading and rereading the book, one has to be constantly on the alert. The more so as the author possesses intelligence and no little knowledge and readers can be easily influenced by him.

The author's work is still unfinished; this is only the first volume. R. Richter says: "The final solution concerning the measure of truth contained in the realist or idealist views must be held over till Volume II. Here we have been concerned first of all to show in both these views ways out which have not been obstructed by the scepticism of antiquity and permit us at least to discern the properties of things" (p. 281). That must be kept in mind. However, judging by the contents of Volume I, we may already say with all justification that R. Richter, if he does not exactly uphold the point of view of idealism, has assimilated many of its arguments; and this fact has brought a very noticeable and very annoying element of confusion into his world-outlook. The translators, Messrs V. Bazarov and B. Stolpner, have not noticed this weak point of the German writer. It is clear why: idealism has regrettably wrought even greater havoc in their world-outlook too. But an unbiased person, capable of thinking consistently and of reading the book carefully, will easily find where R. Richter has gone wrong. His work is concerned with the question of scepticism. The sceptics used to say: we do not know the criterion of truth. Anyone agreeing with them on this point must admit that their position is unshakeable. But R. Richter does not agree with them. How does he refute the proposition that is the key to the whole of their position? What, in his view, is the criterion of truth, and, finally, the famous question which Pontius Pilate put to the arrested Jesus—what is truth?

"Truth," replies R. Richter, "is a *concept of relationship*, expressing the relationship of judgments to the senses of the subject"

(p. 347). Elsewhere he says: "Truth ... is a concept the source of which is the human spirit; to find it is a task set by the human spirit alone, and therefore to be resolved by it alone; it is a knot tied by the human spirit and therefore to be unravelled by it alone.... A truth in itself is ... an utterly unrealisable thought" (p. 191). It follows from this that, according to Richter, only the relationship of the truth to the subject is possible. He is not a bit afraid of this conclusion. He declares categorically:

"It goes without saying that we reject the ordinary definition of truth as 'agreement between the conception and its object', and this for two reasons. First, the sense of the evident attaches only to judgments and not conceptions. Secondly, the assumption of the relationship between conceptions and objects—and this assumption is the basis of the definition given above—is either a petitio principii or a remote result—and one, moreover, disputed by all idealists—of applying criteria of truth. Both characteristics are circumstances that are fatal precisely for a definition of truth" (p. LVI).

Let us examine this. A particular person seems to me to be pale. Is that true? A stupid question! Once a particular person seems to me to be pale, there is nothing to argue about; that is undoubtedly how he seems to me. It is quite another matter if, on this basis, I utter the judgment: "That man is ill." It may be true, or it may be false. In which case is it true? In the case when my judgment corresponds to the actual state of the person's health. In which case is it false? That is self-evident: when the actual state of the person's health and my judgment on it do not correspond. That means that truth is precisely correspondence between the judgment and its object. In other words, it is the definition rejected by R. Richter which is correct.* To put it another way: our author says that truth is related only to the subject. On this point he is strongly influenced by idealism. The idealist denies the existence of the object outside human consciousness. Therefore he cannot define truth as a certain relationship between the judgment of the subject and the actual state of the object. But being reluctant to contradict idealism, R. Richter comes into conflict with the most legitimate requirements of logic. His view on the criterion of truth is a great, one may say an unpardonable, mistake. I considered it my duty to draw the attention of Russian readers to this error which Messrs Bazarov and Stolpner failed to notice, and could not notice, because they too, regrettably, are infected with idealism.

---

* What is true is that, as we have just seen, not the concept but the opinion may be true or false: but this does not change the essence of the judgment. All the same Richter's proposed criterion of truth is quite untenable.

II

R. Richter thinks that once we accept the existence of a relationship between conception (more correctly, judgment) and object, we are committing a petitio principii. But where is the petitio principii in what I have said about the necessary and adequate conditions for the truth of the judgment: that pale man is ill? In what I said on this subject there is no sign of the logical error which so frightens our author that he wards it off by an obvious and gross blunder—as the saying goes, jumping out of the frying pan into the fire.

We already know what is the matter. In saying: "my judgment of a particular person's state of health is correct only if it agrees with the actual state of the particular person", I am assuming something which is unacceptable to idealists and which. as R. Richter says, they dispute. This assumption is that the object exists independently of my consciousness. But an object existing independently of my consciousness is an object-in-itself. In assuming that objects have such existence, I am rejecting the fundamental tenet of idealism that esse = percipi, that is to say, that being is equal to being-in-consciousness. But R. Richter wants none of this. True, the object mentioned in my example is such a special one that only very few idealists venture to apply to it their principle of esse = percipi. I ask, how may one be sure that a particular *man* is ill? But what do these words: esse = percipi mean in their *application to man*? They mean that there are no other people than the person who at that particular moment is proclaiming the principle. The consistent application of this principle leads to *solipsism*. The overwhelming majority of idealists, despite the most inexorable demands of logic, do not venture to go as far as to land in *solipsism*. Very many of them stop at the point of view which is now called *solohumanism*. This means that, for them, being remains being-in-consciousness, in the consciousness, however, not of an individual but of all the human race. To agree with them, one would have to answer the question: "Is there an external world?" by saying: "Outside myself, that is to say, independently of my consciousness, there is only the human race. Everything else—the stars, the planets, plants, animals, etc.— exist only in human consciousness."

The reader will recall the conversation between the sotnik and the philosopher Khoma Brut.[227]

"Who are you, where do you come from, and what is your calling, good man?" asked the sotnik.

"A seminarist, student of philosophy, Khoma Brut...."

"Who was your father?"

"I don't know, honoured sir."

"Your mother?"

"I don't know my mother either. It is reasonable to suppose, of course, that I had a mother; but who she was, and where she came from, and when she lived—upon my soul, good sir, I don't know."

Obviously, the philosopher Khoma Brut was far from averse to criticism. Only sound reasoning convinced him that he had had a mother. But he nevertheless admitted her existence. He did not say: "my mother exists (or existed) only in my consciousness." If he had said so (considering himself born of a woman who existed only in his consciousness), he would have been a *solipsist*. Though he was no stranger to criticism, he did not go the length of drawing such a conclusion. Therefore, we may presume that he took his stand, for example, on *solohumanism*. If this presumption is correct, he did not confine himself to admitting his mother's existence alone, but in general recognised the "plurality of individuals". He did deny, however, the existence independently of consciousness of those objects on which these individuals act in the process of social production. So that if his mother was, shall we say, a baker, he would have had to confess that she existed independently of his consciousness, whereas the buns she baked existed only in her and his mind and in the minds of the individuals who bought and ate them, naively imagining that these buns had existence in themselves, independently of human consciousness. If he saw a herdsman driving his cattle, as a solohumanist he would have had to admit that the herdsman existed independently of his consciousness, while the herd of cows, sheep and pigs existed only in his mind and in that of the herdsman tending those conceptual animals. He would have had to utter a similar "judgment" when he saw protruding from the pocket of his worthy fellow-traveller Khalyava the huge tail of the fish that had been filched by the learned theologian. The theologian exists independently of the consciousness of the philosopher Khoma Brut, but the pilfered fish has no other existence except in the consciousness of these two learned men, and, of course, the ox-cart driver from whom Khalyava had filched it. Philosophy of this sort is, as you see, distinguished by its great profundity. There is only one thing wrong: on the very same day and at the very same hour when the philosopher Khoma Brut recognised that the theologian Khalyava (or the rhetorician Gorobets, it's all the same) had being apart from his consciousness, he would have run into irreconcilable contradiction with the principle of esse=percipi: he would have had to admit that the concept *being* is in no way conveyed by the concept *being-in-consciousness*.

The erudite R. Richter looks down on simple-minded realists with the lofty disdain of the "critical" thinker; but he himself is so thoroughly infected with idealism that he is completely blind to the comical artlessness which, to a greater or lesser extent, is characteristic of all varieties of this philosophical trend. He takes seriously those arguments of idealist philosophy which deserve only to be laughed at, and in consequence he gives a wrong definition of truth. Here is how he formulates the theoretical-cognitive credo of "extreme" idealism.

"...There exist no things, objects, realities, bodies, independent of the conceptions of them in a consciousness, and the things perceived by the senses are completely dissolved in the subjective and ideal parts of which they are composed" (p. 247).

Let us assume that this is true—that no things, objects and bodies exist independently of the conceptions of them in consciousness. But if every particular person exists independently of the consciousness of other people, it positively cannot be said that there are no "realities" independent of consciousness. Surely every person existing independently of other people's consciousness must be regarded as an indisputable reality, even though at the same time—in accordance with our first assumption—we regarded him as an incorporeal being. The penetrating R. Richter does not realise this. Further. If an incorporeal man named Ivan exists independently of the consciousness of an incorporeal man called Pyotr, he may express certain judgments about Pyotr. These opinions will be true only if they correspond to reality. In other words, the incorporeal Ivan's judgments about the condition of the incorporeal Pyotr are true only if Pyotr is in fact what Ivan considers him to be. This must be admitted by every idealist, except, of course, the solipsist, who denies the plurality of individuals. And whoever admits this, by the same token also admits that truth consists in a judgment conforming to its object.

III

Richter says: "Deeply penetrating research is fathoming more and more the *law-governed relationships* between things and within them, and less and less the things themselves; these it is simply dissolving in the complex of such relationships. Consequently, the results of this research may for the most part be easily formulated in the language of any particular philosophical trend provided it does not attack these relationships, though it may have its own opinion about the concept of the thing. When the historian writes of a ruler possessing a noble or base soul, he merely wishes to say that the ruler concerned usually responded to such and such events with morally high or low thoughts, feelings, and

volitional impulses, and it is irrelevant to the historian whether
the soul exists or not" (p. 289).

Of course, for a historian it is a matter of indifference whether
the *soul* exists or not. But it is by no means a matter of indifference
to him whether the *"ruler"* about whose actions he is forming
a judgment exists or not. And it is precisely the "ruler" who
plays here the part of the disputed *"thing"*. Let us admit for
a moment that natural science is in fact dissolving things more
and more in the complex of relationships. Can the same be said
of the social sciences? Where is the sociologist who would base
his judgments on the proposition that people do not exist, that
there are only social relationships ... of people? Such a sociologist
could be met with only in a mental institution. If that is so,
it is evident that not every "philosophical trend" can be reconciled
with scientific research, at least into social phenomena. For
example, the concept of evolution plays a titanic part in contemporary sociology. Can this concept be reconciled with those
philosophical trends under whose influence our author elaborated
his definition of the criterion of truth? If what we call the external
world exists only in people's consciousness, can we speak without
an augur's smile of those periods in the earth's development
which *preceded* the coming of the zoological species we call homo
sapiens? If space and time are only forms of contemplation (Anschauung) that I myself possess, it is clear that when I did not
exist these forms did not exist either, that is to say, there was
no time and no space, so that when I assert, for instance, that
Pericles lived long before me, I am talking arrant nonsense.
Is it not obvious that the "philosophical" trend bearing the name
of solipsism can in no way be reconciled with the concept of evolution? It may be objected, perhaps, that if this is true as regards
solipsism, it is untrue in relation to *solohumanism*; since solohumanism recognises the existence of the human race, then, while
this race is still around, there will exist both forms of contemplation which are peculiar to it, i.e., space and time. However, the
following must be remembered. First, solohumanism, as we have
seen, totally excludes the view of man as a product of zoological
evolution. Secondly, if time does not exist independently of the
consciousness of the individuals making up the human race, it is
quite incomprehensible where we get the right to assert that one
of these individuals lived earlier than another, for example, that
the celebrated Athenian Pericles lived prior to the notorious
Frenchman Briand. Why can we not put it the other way round,
namely, that Briand preceded Pericles? Is it not because our
judgments adapt themselves here to the objective sequence of
events, which does not depend upon human consciousness? And
if that is indeed the reason, is it not clear that those thinkers

were right who averred that although space and time as *formal elements of consciousness* exist not outside us, but within us, nevertheless to both these elements there correspond certain objective (i.e., independent of consciousness) relationships of things and processes? Is it not plain, finally, that only by admitting the existence of these objective relationships do we have any possibility of constructing a scientific theory which will explain the emergence of the human race itself with the forms of consciousness peculiar to it! Being is not determined by consciousness, but consciousness by being.

Nowadays, some people like to dilate on the distinctions between the "sciences of nature" and the "sciences of culture". The writers who enjoy discussing this theme are all without exception more or less inclined to consistent idealism. They are trying to find a refuge for their idealist notions in the "sciences of culture". But, in fact, these sciences, i.e., the social science in the broad meaning of the term, are even less reconcilable with idealism than the natural science. The social science presupposes society. Society presupposes a plurality of individuals. A plurality of individuals makes inevitable the distinction between the individual as he exists "*in himself*" and the same individual as he exists in the consciousness of other people, as well as in his own.* And that returns us to that theory of cognition against which representatives of various trends of philosophical idealism have raised their differing voices. The solohumanist is bound to accept the cardinal principle of this theory, which says that apart from being-in-consciousness there is also being-in-oneself. But the solohumanist denies the existence of all "things" and "bodies". To him, people are essentially nothing more than the bearers of consciousness, i.e., nothing more than incorporeal beings. Hence it follows that everyone interested in "the last word" in knowledge, yet desirious of steering clear of solipsism, is faced with a dilemma. To regard himself as an incorporeal being, or to agree with the materialist Feuerbach: "Ich bin ein wirkliches, ein sinnliches Wesen, ja der Leib in seiner Totalität ist mein Ich, mein Wesen selbst." ("I am a real, sensual being, a body; it is this body, taken in its totality, which is my *ego*, my essence.")

If R. Richter had taken all this into consideration, his interesting book would have been even more interesting and incomparably richer in correct philosophical content. But if he had taken account of it, he would have been an exception among present-day German writers on philosophical matters. But to

---

* An individual in a deep swoon does not exist in his own consciousness but, as long as he is alive, he exists "in himself". Thus, there is certainly a distinction here too, between existing "*in oneself*" and existing *in consciousness*.

his misfortune, there is nothing exceptional about him just as, to their misfortune, there is nothing exceptional about his Russian translators, who failed to notice the weakness of their author's arguments.

IV

I stated, and I trust have proved, that R. Richter is deeply infected with idealism. Now I think it would be useful to add that the most profound and most orderly system of idealism— Hegel's philosophy—has obviously much less attraction for him than other less profound and less orderly systems of idealism. I would say more. It is very plain that he has not bothered himself trying to understand Hegel. Here is a vivid example.

At the beginning of his book, having examined the historical prerequisites of Greek scepticism, R. Richter hastens to caution his readers:

"However, it would be quite wrong to conclude from this that the achievements of the sceptical philosophers we are about to discuss were insignificant, as though all they had to do was skilfully to select and methodically to compare the ideas of their predecessors, as though, in the Hegelian sense, according to the reasonable development of the world they were bound to come when and as they did. We hope, on the contrary, that by our exposition of the philosophy of scepticism we shall succeed in proving its complete originality—an originality that is quite astonishing. Historical prerequisites are not yet spiritual causes. The spiritual father of philosophical scepticism was the genius of Pyrrho, and not the philosophers before him nor world reason, about which we know absolutely nothing" (pp. 60-61).

That passage could never have been written by anyone who had taken the trouble to read Hegel's *Vorlesungen über die Geschichte der Philosophie.* Did the demands of "self-developing world reason" induce Hegel to exclude the "complete originality" of the creators of the most important philosophical systems? By no means. Did Hegel ever oppose world reason to the genius of individual thinkers? Decidedly never. But that is just the trouble: contemporary German authors of philosophical treatises know Hegel very badly. They are idealists, but the content of their idealism is infinitely poorer than that of Hegel. Of course, Hegel loses nothing at all by being ignored by present-day German writers; it is they who are the losers. Hegel was a great master of the "treatment of ideas", and he who desires to "treat ideas" must pass through his school, even if he does not share Hegel's idealist views. Conversely, present-day German writers who are occupied with philosophical questions treat ideas very clumsily. This is especially noticeable where they need most of all to display their intellectual powers, namely, when they are called upon to defend their idealist standpoint. It is precisely this point then that these people, who speak so contemptuously of "naive dogmatists", themselves produce in their arguments some real pearls of naive dogmatism.*

V

The first volume of Richter's work is a study of Greek scepticism. The first chapter outlines the history of this school of philosophy, the second sets forth its teaching, while the third is a criticism of the doctrine of scepticism. Let us dwell for a moment on the third chapter.

Greek scepticism posed three fundamental questions: 1) what is the nature of things? 2) what should be our attitude to things? 3) what will result for us from this attitude? Its answer to the first question was that every thesis on the nature of things may be opposed by an equally well-founded antithesis: i. e., that their nature is unknown to us. To the second question, scepticism replied that our attitude to things must be one of unconditional scepticism, always abstaining from making a judgment of any kind (sceptical "Ἐποχή"). Lastly, the third question was answered in the sense that abstention from expressing judgment gives one imperturbability of mind (ataraxia) and the absence of suffering (apatheia) that make for happiness. What has Richter to say in his criticism of scepticism regarding these replies?

Let us take the reply to the first question. In his analysis of it, Richter distinguishes the following fundamental theoretical and cognitive positions: first, extreme realism; second, extreme idealism; third, moderate realism, which he also calls moderate idealism or ideal-realism. According to him, scepticism is capable of mastering only the first of these positions, namely, that of extreme realism; the other two are quite beyond it (p. 199).

But we have already seen that the philosophical trend to which Richter gives the title of extreme idealism (i. e., in fact, more or less consistent idealism) leads to insoluble and ludicrous contradictions. One would have to be very partial to "extreme idealism" to imagine that it could possibly be regarded as an at all lasting philosophical position. Therefore, I shall not enlarge

---

* *Robert Flint* noted long ago, in his *Philosophy of History in France and Germany,* that of all varieties of idealism Hegel's system was the closest to materialism. In a certain sense this is true. It is only one step from the absolute idealism of Hegel to the materialism of Feuerbach. This is more or less clearly recognised by present-day German thinkers and is one of the causes of their invincible dislike of Hegel. They find various forms of *subjective* idealism more to their liking. Hegel is too *objective* for them.

upon it further, but shall turn my attention to "extreme realism" and "ideal-realism".

The Greek Sceptics, for example, posed the question: is honey sweet or bitter? To the majority of people it is sweet; but there are certain invalids to whom honey seems bitter. The sceptics concluded from this that we cannot know the true nature of honey. It is easy to notice that, in posing the above question, the Sceptics believed that honey could be either sweet or bitter in itself, quite apart from the person tasting it. But when I say that honey is sweet (or bitter) I only mean that it gives me the sensation of sweetness (or bitterness). Sensation presupposes a subject who is experiencing it. When there is no such subject, there is no sensation. To ask whether honey is sweet or bitter in itself is as absurd as to ask what a particular sensation is when there is no one to experience it. Yet this question, absurd as it may be, is perfectly legitimate from the viewpoint which Richter calls extreme realism. This viewpoint identifies the properties of the object with the sensations these properties stimulate in us. Richter gives a good illustration of the standpoint of extreme realism when he says: "The tree whose leaves I see green, whose bark I see brown, whose hard trunk I touch, whose sweet fruit I taste and the rustle of whose topmost branches I hear, also has *in itself* green leaves, brown bark, a hard trunk, sweet fruit, and rustling branches" (p. 200). Richter also notes correctly that, so far as science is concerned, *such* realism died long ago. The materialist Democritus was already able to distinguish the properties of an object from the sensations aroused in us by those properties. If the Sceptics could confound their adversaries by posing such questions as: is honey sweet or bitter in itself?—one may only conclude that both they themselves and their adversaries, who were apparently unable to stand up to them, were (to use the terminology R. Richter has assimilated) "extreme realists", that is to say, they held a quite untenable theory of cognition. In this regard, Richter is not mistaken.

VI

I pass on to ideal-realism. By ideal-realism (or real-idealism, or moderate realism) R. Richter understands that view which acknowledges the existence of things independent of the subject, but "does not ascribe to these real things, as their objective properties, all the component parts of perception, but only some of them" (p. 221).

He points out correctly that this theory of cognition enjoys the widest recognition among contemporary naturalists. According to this theory, definite sensations *correspond* to definite properties or conditions of things, but do *not resemble* them in any way. A definite sound corresponds to definite vibrations of the air, but the sensation of sound does not resemble the vibrations of the atmospheric particles. This can also be said of sensations of light, produced by vibrations of the ether, and so on. Thus this theory distinguishes the *primary* properties of bodies from their *secondary* properties, or the properties of the first order from the properties of the second order. The properties of the first order are sometimes called the physico-mathematical qualities of things. These include, for instance, density, shape, extension. Pointing out the distinction between the primary properties of things and their secondary properties, Richter remarks that this distinction completely invalidates the argument of the Sceptics which was based on the relativity of sensual perception, e.g., on the fact that honey seems sweet to one person and bitter to another. From this relativity, the Sceptics deduced that things were unknowable. But to the "moderate realists" this deduction is quite wrong. Indeed, colour exists only in relationship to light, and changes with changing light. This also applies exactly to the temperature of a given body, which induces in us sensations of either heat or cold, according to the temperature level of our blood, and so on. But from this it follows only that sensations are not primary properties of things, but the effects of the action of objects possessing certain primary properties upon the subject. That is all quite true. Here Richter is once again quite right. But then he goes on to say:

"If, finally, the moderate realist cannot come to irreconcilably contradictory judgments on the secondary properties of things because, in his view, it is not through sensations at all that the properties of things become known, *on the other hand, he can get to know very well* the real properties which correspond to the purely subjective sensations, that is to say, which, like irritants, arouse these sensations. For these irritants are always of a spatial, material, and consequently in principle knowable nature" (p. 241).

It is impossible to accept this without a very serious reservation. Take note of Richter's argument with which he attempts to prove, in refutation of the Sceptics, that the moderate realist "cannot come to irreconcilably contradictory judgments on the secondary properties of things". And why not? "Because, in his view, it is not through sensations at all that the properties of things become known." That is not true. Though it is true that many "moderate realists", submitting to the influence of idealist prejudices, imagine that the properties of things cannot become known through sensations. But how, indeed, can they not become known? A thing excites a particular sensation. This capacity to arouse a sensation in us is the property of the thing. Consequently once the particular sensation is known, this particular property of the thing also thereby becomes known. Therefore we must say the exact opposite to what Richter said: according to "moderate realism" (we shall call it this for the time being), in general, it is through sensations (it would be more exact to say: by means of sensations),that the properties of things are known. This seems to be clear. Only one argument could really be advanced against this: that the sensation aroused by the particular property of a thing changes with the changing condition of the subject. But we have already seen that this objection will not stand up to criticism. Sensation is the *result* of interaction of object and subject. It is quite natural that this result should depend *not only* on the properties of the object, not only on the properties of what is becoming known, but also on the properties of the knowing subject. However, this quite natural circumstance does not in any way prove the unknowability of things.* Quite the contrary. It proves their knowability. The sensual and knowing subject not only can, but in certain circumstances must, be regarded as an object, for example, when we are referring to an invalid in whom particular things produce unusual sensations. If honey tastes sweet to a man in good health and bitter to an invalid, only one conclusion may be drawn from this, viz: that in certain circumstances the human organism is capable of reacting in an unusual fashion to a definite irritant. This capacity is an objective property which can be studied, that is to say, known. Which means—and there is no need to be afraid of repeating this—that in accordance with the correctly understood view of "moderate realism", *in sensations generally the properties of things become known.* This, in turn, signifies that those who contend that things are unknowable, citing in support of this the complete dissimilarity between a sensation (e.g., sound) and the objective process that produces it (in this case, the wave-like motion of the air) are making a great mistake in the domain of the theory of knowledge. Incidentally, all that was said against the knowability of things by Kant and his followers is based upon this mistake.

---

* With his customary depth and clarity of thought Hegel said: "Ein Ding hat die Eigenschaft dieses oder jenes im Andern zu bewirken und auf eine eigenthümliche Weise sich in seiner Beziehung zu äussern. Es beweist diese Eigenschaft nur unter der Bedingung einer entsprechenden Beschaffenheit der andern Dinge, aber sie ist ihm zugleich eigenthümlich und seine mit sich identische Grundlage." (*Wissenschaft der Logik*, I. Band, 2-er Buch S. 149.) [A Thing has the property of affecting this or that in another, and of disclosing itself in a peculiar manner in its relation. It manifests this property only under one condition—the other Thing must have a corresponding nature: but it is also peculiar to the first Thing, and is its own self-identical foundation.]

It was also at the bottom of Greek scepticism. We see that Richter himself is far from being free from it. This is also because, as we stated above, he is deeply infected with idealism. Looking at his "case" from the angle of my theory of cognition, I would say that in succumbing to the influence of idealism, Richter acquired the "property" of comprehending incorrectly the true meaning of the "moderate realist" view. His subjective state distorted in a definite (and moreover most undesirable) way the effect upon him of the logic of this view. But this has not rendered either Richter or the doctrine of "moderate realism" unknowable.

VII

In making his remarks regarding the unknowability of the properties of things in sensations, Richter admits, as we have seen, that "on the other hand, the 'moderate realist' *can get to know very well** the real properties which correspond to the purely subjective sensations". This expression: "to the purely subjective sensations" is very characteristic of Richter as well as of all those philosophising writers who, like him, have more or less succumbed to idealism. We shall recognise it as even more characteristic if we turn our attention to the conclusion which Richter finally reaches on the matter under discussion.

"*In so far as the elements of perception can be traced back to properties of things, these properties are basically knowable. In so far as the component parts of perception as properties of things would be unknowable, they are in general not properties of things*" (p. 241, author's italics).

What does Richter mean here by the component parts of perception which are unknowable as properties of things? Sensations. Why? Because sensations are *"purely subjective"* (my italics); they do not belong to the properties of the object which arouses these sensations in the subject. Good. Let us take this for granted, keep it in mind, and ponder the following example taken from Überweg—if my memory serves me right.

In a cellar there are a barrel of meal and two mice. The cellar is locked, there are no chinks in the floor, on the ceiling or in the walls, so no other mice can get in. Finding themselves in the happy possession of a whole barrel of meal, our two mice set about bringing into the world little mice who are also imbued with the lust for life thanks to the abundant food supply. In due course they too reproduce a generation of mice, who then go on to repeat the same story. Thus the number of mice continues to increase and the store of food decreases. Finally the moment ar-

---

* Author's italics.

rives when the barrel is completely empty. What is the outcome? It is that a definite quantity of an object which is *devoid* of sensation (meal) has been transformed into a definite quantity of objects *that have sensations*; for example: they suffer hunger now that all the meal has gone (mice). The capacity to have sensations is just as much a property of certain organisms as is their capacity to stimulate in us, say, certain visual sensations. Therefore, from this point of view too, Richter is wrong in saying that everything "purely subjective" is beyond the meaning of the concept: properties of things. I am *I*—for myself and at the same time *Thou*—for another. I am a subject and at the same time an object. The subject is not separated from the object by an impassable gulf. Consistent philosophical thought convinces us of the unity of subject and object. "That which for me, *subjectively*," says Feuerbach, "is a purely spiritual, insensible act, is in itself, *objectively*, a material, sensible act." This conception of the unity of subject and object is the heart of contemporary materialism. It is in this that we find the true meaning of "moderate realism" (or ideal-realism). From which it follows that "moderate realism" is nothing but materialism, but a materialism that is timid, inconsistent, hesitating in pursuing its conclusions to the very end and making more or less significant and (in any case) illegitimate concessions to idealism.

VIII

So far we have dealt with, strictly speaking, the first question posed by the Sceptics, namely, are things knowable? And we have seen that our author, infected with idealist prejudices, has not an entirely correct view of this question. But what does he say about the other two basic questions posed by Greek scepticism? As regards these, he argues as follows:

"The Sceptics' reply to Timon's last two basic questions: What should be our attitude to things? and: What will result for us from this attitude? only draws the conclusions from the solution of the first and most important problem concerning the nature of things. Criticism after examining this solution: 'things are unknowable', and rejecting it as unjustified, no longer needed to investigate the negative and positive consequences of the basic viewpoint of scepticism *in isolation*, since they claim validity only presupposing that viewpoint" (p. 370).

Quite so. If criticism found the Sceptics' assertion that things are unknowable to be erroneous, it must recognise as no less erroneous the belief that we should refrain from forming any judgments about things, and equally erroneous the claim that such abstention is essential for our happiness. That is all true. But since it is true, I again cease to understand Richter. He has admitted that only an "extreme realist" would find the Sceptics' arguments irrefutable. "Moderate realism" and even "extreme idealism", in his opinion, refute these arguments easily. As has been already said, so far as idealism is concerned, Richter is in this case wrong. Idealism is quite incapable of refuting scepticism for the simple but fully adequate reason that it itself suffers from insoluble contradictions. However, I have no intention of returning to that subject here. I shall repeat just one thing: if the "moderate realist" and the "extreme idealist" are quite capable of refuting the Sceptic's arguments, neither of them requires to make any concession whatever to the sceptical mode of thought. Yet Richter himself makes some very important concessions to it. He says that "from the very first" a dose of scepticism has been circulating in the blood of modern man (pp. 348-49) and beseeches us to show some "resignation" regarding questions of cognition (p. 192). Why resignation? With what object? Well, just listen to this:

"We must ... whether we like it or not, learn from the sceptics and admit that the truth which is undoubtedly accessible to us is truth pertaining only to man, and that truth which we, in general, can conceive, is truth pertaining to beings similar to ourselves. We must not, on the other hand, be carried away as a result of this to the premature conclusion that we must, for this reason, despair of ever finding the truth.... But this resignation will be made much easier for us by the fact that everything we cannot in any way conceive also does not pertain to us, does not concern us, can leave us indifferent. Only he who has partaken of the apple feels the urge to do so again, and is distressed if denied this enjoyment. But he who cannot form any conception of this sensation of taste will not miss the apple. Only those who have lost their sight are unhappy; those born blind are not. As regards extra-human knowledge—if there is such a thing—we are all born blind" (pp. 192-93).

Throughout all the foregoing there is a very obvious and nasty note of philistinism. A fine consolation indeed that we did not lose our sight but were born blind! Why did Richter have to drag in this "consolation"?* He only wished to console us because we, humans, cannot know "extra-human" truth. According to him, this is not a very great misfortune. I could not agree more with him; in fact, as I see it, it is not a misfortune here at all. I shall go further: the very thought that it is misfortune, even if only a tiny one, is rooted in the mistaken theory of cognition I spoke about earlier. The process of the subject getting to know the

---

* [The word "consolation" is in English in the original.]

object is the process whereby the former arrives at a correct opinion of the latter. The object becomes known to the subject only because it is capable of influencing the subject in a certain way. Therefore, we cannot speak of cognition where there is no relationship between the subject and the object. But those soft-hearted people who, like Richter, find it necessary to console us because extra-human truth is beyond us, do admit (perhaps unnoticed by themselves) that knowledge of an object is possible even where there is no subject getting to know it. They even imagine that such knowledge—knowledge independent of the subject, that is to say, that notorious knowledge of "things-in-themselves" spoken of by Kant and other "critical" philosophers in contemporary philosophy—is the only real knowledge. If we could have knowledge of *that* kind we should not be born blind, and would not need Richter's proffered consolation.

Messrs Bazarov and Stolpner might, perhaps, object that their author does not admit the possibility of such a knowledge of "things-in-themselves". But they would not be right at all.

Let us assume that, indeed, Richter does not admit this possibility. But why? Precisely because, and only because, he thinks that it is inaccessible to man. He does not realise that *knowledge*, independent of the person knowing it, is a contradictio in adjecto—a logical absurdity. One person is convinced that the creature which the Greeks called a chimera does not and cannot exist. Another thinks that there is such a creature but we cannot know anything about it owing to the special way our bodies are constituted. What do you think, can one assert that both these men have the same view of the unknowability of the chimera? It is clear that they have not. If I think that the chimera does not and cannot exist, I can only laugh at those who are worried because it is inaccessible to their cognition; all talk of resignation would here be an insult to common sense. And yet Richter considers it necessary to preach such resignation. How is it possible to avoid feeling that he resembles the man who admits the existence of the chimera, but believes it to be inaccessible to his cognition?

IX

Richter's inclination to extreme idealism in his teaching on the criterion of truth arises out of his inability to shed his idealist prejudices in the theory of cognition. According to him, it would appear that truth for man is truth of some kind of secondary, lower category. Hence his recommendation that we should show "resignation", that is to say, be reconciled with the impossibility of knowing higher truth, truth of the first category.

We have seen that his teaching on the criterion of truth must be rejected as utterly unsound. Truth is related not only to the subject but also to the object. That opinion of the object, which corresponds to its real state, is a true opinion. That which is true for man is also true in itself, precisely because a correct opinion truly depicts the actual state of things.* Therefore there is no point in our talking of resignation.

If we throw a man into the fire, he will be burnt; that is truth for him. And if we throw a cat into the fire? It too will be burnt. That is truth for the cat. Does truth for the man in this case resemble truth for the cat? They are as like as two peas! What does that mean? It means that truth for man has an objective significance that is not confined to the human race. Naturally, there are truths which are applicable only to the human race. These truths are the judgments that correspond to the actual state of all particular human feelings, thoughts, or relationships. But this does not affect the main point. The important thing is that true judgments regarding the natural laws are true not only for man, although man alone is capable of forming such judgments. Systematic cognition of the natural laws became possible only when "social man" emerged, having reached a certain level of mental development. A natural law which man has got to know is truth for man. But natural laws were operating on the earth before the appearance of man, that is to say, when there was no one capable of studying these laws. And only because these laws were operating at that time did man himself appear, bringing with him the systematic cognition of nature.

No one who understands this will accept, as Richter does, the legitimacy of that dose of scepticism which, he says, from the very first has been circulating in the blood of modern man. Modern man in a "certain social position" has indeed a good dose of scepticism. But this is adequately explained by the state of modern society.

X

That brings us to the question: *what is the source* of scepticism?

Richter rightly says that the Sceptics of antiquity were, in the majority of cases, passive people, of "tired, enfeebled, broken will" and devoid of passion (p.377). He is no less correct in linking these traits of the sceptics of antiquity with the course of development of ancient Greek society, and in looking on Greek scepticism as the fruit of the decay of that society. Well, if that

---

* It is raining. If this is indeed true, it is a truth for man. But it is truth for man only because, and solely in the sense that, it is indeed true.

is the case, it is quite natural to assume that the dose of scepticism which, he says, circulates in everyone's blood may also be explained by social decay. True, we have no ground for saying, as the Slavophiles[228] used to say, that the advanced countries of the civilised world are now falling into decay. Taken as a whole, any one of the present-day civilised nations represents not a regressing but a progressing society. But what may be right in relation to the whole may be wrong in relation to its parts. Richter points to the scepticism that was widespread at the end of the eighteenth century, and reiterates that it is just as widespread today as it was then. But what explains the spread of scepticism in the eighteenth century? The explanation is that the system of social relations that had for long held sway in European society was then rapidly falling into decay. Taken as a whole, society at that time was also progressing, not regressing. But this cannot at all be said of the then upper class, the temporal and spiritual aristocracy. This class had long outlived its best days, and existed only in the form of an unwanted and therefore harmful relic. Something quite like this we see today. Only now the declining class is not the aristocracy, but the bourgeoisie.* Our century, like the eighteenth, represents the eve of a great social upheaval. All such periods of decline of the old ruling class provide exceptionally fertile soil for the development of scepticism. This is what explains that dose of scepticism which, in Richter's words, circulates in the blood of modern man. It is not a question of extra-human truth being inaccessible to man, but of social revolution approaching, and of this approach, realised instinctively by the bourgeoisie, arousing in its ideologists a feeling of profound discontent, taking the form of scepticism, pessimism, etc. This discontent is, however, noticeable only among the bourgeois ideologists. The proletarian ideologists on the contrary are full of hope for the future. All of them are ready to repeat with Ulrich von Hutten his well-known exclamation: "How good it is to be alive in our times!"[230] And that is why they are sceptical only, say, when it is a question of the advantages of the present-day social order or of certain beliefs which have grown up on the basis of this social order and others preceding it in historical development, or perhaps, when the bourgeoisie begins to extol its own virtues. Then scepticism is perfectly legitimate. Generally speaking, however, there is no room for scepticism in the mood and world-outlook of the proletariat. It is not consciousness that determines being, but being that determines consciousness.

---

* For the benefit of Russian readers with a certain way of thinking: I am speaking here of countries with a *fully developed* capitalist economy.[229]

Richter has grasped this incontestable truth very badly indeed, although, as has been remarked already, he understands fairly well that Greek scepticism was brought about by the decline of ancient Greece. How muddled he is here may be seen from the following.

He repudiates the Sceptics' principle of isostheneia, that is to say, the proposition that to every *thesis* on the nature of things there can be opposed an equally well-founded *antithesis*.* He is willing, however, to acknowledge that isostheneia is an incontrovertible fact in relation to much *"sham knowledge"*,** both in daily life and in science. He instances the question of parties to prove his point, and his example is worthy of attention.

"Here," he argues, "they unconditionally accept and jealously insist upon a whole series of solutions to the latest questions, that are still not theoretically ripe for discussion. Here the right and left often really confront each other, like thesis and antithesis, like 'yea' and 'nay'. But he who desires to take an objective decision will often enough have to say to himself that the liberal is no less justified than the conservative, the modernist in aesthetics no less than his classic opponent, the atomist no less than the energeticist, that, to use the language of the Sceptics, it's a complete isostheneia" (p. 178).

And so, if one wishes to be objective, one must agree fairly often that the conservative is as right as the liberal, the modernist in aesthetics as the classicist, etc. Here our critic of the Sceptics has himself become a sceptic.

The Sceptics held that we have no way of knowing truth. Richter says the same about this sort of questions. It was not without good reason that he recognised that modern man has a good dose of scepticism in his blood.

XI

However, let us see with what criterion of truth we have to judge, for example, who is right: the "conservative" or the "liberal". Let us suppose that it is a question of electoral rights. The "liberals" demand their extension. The "conservatives" are against it. Who is right? Richter says that both are right. Indeed, this is partly true. The "conservative", *from his point of view*, is quite right; the extension of electoral rights would, generally speaking, be harmful to his interests, since it would weaken the political power of those of his own circle. The "liberal" is no less right *from his point of view*. If implemented, the reform of the electo-

---

* Recall the question as to whether honey was sweet or bitter.
** My italics.—*G.P.*

ral system which he demands would strengthen the power of
the social group he represents and thus enable him to promote
its interests better. But if everyone is right from his own point
of view, is there really no sense in asking who should be judged
more correct? Richter believes that this question is, in many
cases, insoluble. That is not to be wondered at. Actually, he
should have said that this question is insoluble in general, and
not just fairly often. In his view, truth is relative only to the
subject. Consequently the question of truth must be decided by
him sceptically whenever the contesting subjects *are* each *right
from their point of view*. But his decision is not binding on us.
We consider that Richter's criterion of truth is basically wrong.
Therefore we argue differently.

The "conservative", *from his point of view*, is fully justified in
opposing the extension of electoral rights.* But what arguments
does he advance against it? He asserts that it would be harmful
to the whole of society. Here is the logical error made by the conservative who *is right from his point of view*: he identifies his own
interests with the interests of society. And the "liberal"? Oh, he
does exactly the same. He, too, identifies his interests with those
of society. But if they are both wrong *in one direction*, it does not
follow that they are both wrong *to the same extent*. In order to
judge which of them is committing the smaller mistake, it suffices to determine whose interests are less at variance with the
interests of society. Is there really no objective criterion by which
such a question could be solved? Will the historian never be able
to decide who was right in Russia on the eve of the peasant reform: the conservatives who did not wish to abolish serfdom
(there were, of course, such people) or the liberals who sought
for this change? In my opinion, the historian will have to record
that the liberals were right, although they, too, did not forget
their own interests at the time. The interests of their party were
less at variance with the interests of society than were the conservative interests. To prove this, it is sufficient to recall the harmful influence of serfdom on all aspects of social life at that time.
History is the process of social development. In its development
society finds advantageous all that promotes this development
and rejects as harmful all that retards it. Stagnation was never
useful to society. This incontestable fact provides the objective

---

* Bismarck, although a conservative, introduced universal suffrage in
Germany. This was of advantage to the interests he was defending. But such
cases are exceptional, and we are not going into them here. Neither shall we
deal with the case when liberals do not support an extension of the franchise.
What is important for us at the moment is not the sociological but the logical
aspect of the matter.

criterion by which to judge which of the two disputing parties is less mistaken, or not mistaken at all.*

It seems as though our author suspects nothing of this, becoming a sceptic where there is no sufficient reason at all for scepticism. He writes:

"A motivation in favour of a cause with which we sympathise 'convinces' us more than one differently oriented but no less conclusive. The instinct of life compels the urge for knowledge to serve it and obscures its view to such a degree that it cannot take cognisance of the logical isostheneia of arguments and counter-arguments. Otherwise, how would it be possible that, for example, in adopting a political position which theoretically presupposes a decision in respect of most delicate questions of sociology, political economy, ethics and the understanding of history, the parties by and large coincide with the social classes? Does the same solution of the questions raised occur, so to speak, by chance to people who by chance belong to the same circle? Their motives here are certainly not their motives. Just count the Social-Democrats among the aristocracy and the convinced conservatives among the factory workers, the supporters of the sharing out of fortunes among the capitalists and of the centralisation of fortunes among the poor! They all represent not the interest of truth, but of their own person (p. 179).

Richter is vexed because people who belong to different classes defend their own interests, and not the interests of truth. But did he not say that truth always relates to the subject? Now he wants a truth which is independent of the subject. He is inconsistent. Further. The fact that the limits of acceptance of varying political convictions, by and large, coincide with class limits is by no means an argument in favour of the sceptics' principle of isostheneia. It proves only that being determines consciousness. It is only by grasping this truth that one is able to understand the course of development of the various ideologies. Richter is hopelessly bewildered by it. The reason for this is that it is difficult for anyone who does not take his stand solidly on the proletarian point of view to understand and fully assimilate this truth at the present time. Richter himself rightly says that the instinct of life often compels the need for knowledge to serve it and considerably obscures its view. He who is convinced that it is not consciousness that determines being, but being that determines consciousness, thereby recognises that the ideas formed and feelings experienced by a particular class in the period of its domination have at best the significance only of

---

* There are cases when the interests of a particular class coincide with the interests of the whole of society.

temporary, transient truths and values. And it is not easy for one belonging to that class to realise this. That is why the best people of the modern bourgeoisie are more easily reconciled to the idea that the domain of disputed social problems is dominated by the sceptical principle of isostheneia than they are to the assertion that the viewpoint of the class of "factory workers" *is becoming* the truth just when the viewpoint of the capitalists *is ceasing* to be truth.* Richter, too, cannot reconcile himself to this idea. Hence his scepticism in social questions. The position of people of this way of thinking is a very unenviable one. Just as Buridan's ass could not make up its mind which of the two bundles of hay to eat, neither can such people attach themselves to one of the two great classes of our time struggling with each other. This creates a special psychological mood, in which it is necessary to seek the explanation of all the trends now prevailing among the ideologists of the upper classes: both the latest aesthetical theories to which Richter alludes and the subjective idealism with which he is infected. It is not consciousness that determines being, but being that determines consciousness.

This is what I thought it essential to tell the reader in recommending Richter's interesting book to him. I am very sorry that the translators of this interesting book did not see the need for such a warning. However, the explanation for this is that they themselves are strongly influenced by those very ideologies which spring from the psychological mood I have just mentioned.

---

* There is no need to prove here that the class-conscious factory workers of our time have no intention of "sharing out all property". Richter thinks this only because he is very badly acquainted with their aspirations. I trust that in this case, at least, his translators will agree with me.

ON MR. H. RICKERT'S BOOK

H. Rickert, *Sciences of Nature and Sciences of Culture.*
Translated from the Second German Edition.
Edited by S. Hessen. Obrazovaniye Publishers.
St. Petersburg, 1911

There is a saying: tell me your friends, and I will tell you who you are. By the same token it might be said: I will determine who you are if you tell me your enemies. There are extraordinarily characteristic types of hostility. Among them is one which many representatives of social science feel nowadays towards the materialist explanation of history. Don't think that I am expressing myself inexactly: I mean precisely hostility, and not a calm denial arising from some more or less correct theoretical considerations. In other words, in rejecting the materialist explanation of history, many of our present-day social scientists are, for the most part, obeying the dictates of their hearts instead of listening to the voice of their intellects, which usually remain in a state of considerable vagueness about what they are rejecting. In proof, I shall cite Heinrich Rickert, the author of a small book, or, if you like, a large pamphlet, entitled *Sciences of Nature and Sciences of Culture* and highly recommended by Mr. S. Hessen.

Rickert discerns in historical materialism an attempt "to transform all history into economic history and then into natural science" (p. 159). One would require to be almost completely in the dark about this subject to believe anything like that. First of all, the adherents of historical materialism have never attempted to "transform all history into economic history". Secondly, it has even less entered their heads "then" to transform economic history into natural science. Rickert would have known this has he taken the trouble to familiarise himself with the views of the men who founded historical materialism—Marx and Engels. Marx used to state categorically that "natural-scientific" materialism was utterly inadequate to explain social phenomena. But while Rickert thinks nothing of repudiating Marx's historical theory, he does not consider it necessary to get to know it. He is guided by his heart and not by his head, as is crystal-clear from all his subsequent argumentation.

The alleged attempts to transform all history into economic history and then into natural science are based, he says, "on a quite arbitrarily selected principle of separating the essential

from the non-essential, a principle which moreover owed its
preference initially to a completely unscientific political prejudice. This may be observed already in the works of Condorcet,
and the so-called materialist conception of history, which represents only the extreme apex of this trend, may serve as a classic
example of this. A very great part of it is dependent on specifically Social-Democratic aspirations. As the guiding cultural ideal
is democratic there is an inclination to consider [the great personalities of the past] too as 'non-essential' and to take account
only of that which comes from the masses. Hence the idea of
'collectivist' history. From the standpoint of the proletariat,
or from the standpoint which the theoreticians regard as the
standpoint of the masses, moreover, it is mainly the economic values which come in for consideration and consequently
only that is 'essential' which has a direct bearing on them, that
is to say, economic life. Hence, too, history becomes 'materialist'"
(pp. 159-60).

Whoever has read the celebrated book: *Esquisse d'un tableau
historique des progrès de l'esprit humain* will be very surprised
to hear from Rickert that Condorcet tried to transform all history
into economic history. True, in Condorcet one does find materialist explanations of some individual historical phenomena. He
also has a propensity to regard the first stages in the cultural
development of mankind from the angle of the development
of the productive forces. But that is due to the fact that he is
unable to discover an adequate level of knowledge at these stages.
Starting approximately with Greece, a purely idealist view of all
subsequent history prevails in Condorcet's book. Idealism was so
predominant in all the historical writings of the eighteenth
century that even the materialists of that day were purely idealist
in their historical outlook, although some of them, for example
Helvétius, sometimes also very shrewdly explained some particular historical phenomena by materialist considerations. It is
strange, indeed, that the learned Mr. Rickert and the enlightened
Mr. Hessen do not know about this (or, perhaps, they do not
want to know about it?). Further. The adherents of historical
materialism are, in fact, very much concerned with what "comes"
from the masses. But, to begin with, this is not their "only"
concern; they pay exceptionally great attention also to what
comes from the upper classes. Marx's *Capital* proves this splendidly by its mere existence. Secondly, the practice of taking
into consideration what comes from the masses—and of doing
so deliberately—was begun already by the French historians at
the time of the Restoration (for instance, Augustin Thierry)
to whom "Social-Democratic aspirations" were utterly alien.
Again it is very strange that neither the enlightened Mr. Hessen

nor the learned Mr. Rickert wish to hear of this. Finally, is it not ludicrous to affirm that, from the standpoint of the proletariat, or, as Rickert puts it, from the standpoint which the theoreticians regard as the standpoint of the masses, attention is turned mainly to economic values. If anyone is paying chief attention to these values nowadays it is surely the bourgeoisie in its opposition to the proletariat. Those who uphold today the materialist explanation of history are quite well aware of this and never lose sight of it. Consequently what Rickert says about them does not make sense from that standpoint either.

Rickert interprets historical materialism in such an astonishing fashion that F. Tönnies, a man, who, as far as we know, has no connection with Social-Democracy, asks him mockingly (in *Archiv für system. Philos.*, Bd. VIII, S. 38): "From which swamp did he borrow his so characteristic exposition of the materialist conception of history?" (quoted by Rickert in a footnote to page 161). And, indeed, there is a strong smell of the swamp about Rickert's exposition. However, the question of what particular swamp he borrows from is fraught with some complexity. The fact is that Rickert and other scientists like him do not have the foggiest notion of historical materialism, not for any *personal* reason, but because their intellectual field of vision is clouded by prejudices that are peculiar *to a whole class*. It might truly be said of them that the rubbish they offer as an exposition of historical materialism is determined by "a completely unscientific political prejudice". Their aversion to historical materialism speaks most eloquently of their fear of "specifically Social-Democratic aspirations". And since the materialist explanation of history is the sole scientific explanation of the historical process (as is revealed by the fact that even those scientists who close their ears to the very word materialism have recourse to it more and more often in their specialised works), those writers whose class prejudices render them incapable of comprehending and assimilating it, when they attempt to elaborate a general theory of history, necessarily find themselves in a blind alley of more or less clever but always arbitrary and, therefore, barren theoretical constructions. Rickert's theory can be listed in the category of such arbitrary constructions.

This theory amounts to the division of the empirical sciences into two groups: the generalising sciences of nature and the individualising sciences of culture. The natural sciences, says Rickert, "see in their objects existence and occurrence, free of anything pertaining to value; their interest is to study the general abstract relationships, and as far as possible the laws, whose significance affects this being and occurrence. The individual case is for them only a 'copy'." Elsewhere he follows Kant in advancing the concept of nature as the existence of things, in so far as it is determined by general laws (p. 38). To this concept he opposes the concept of historical phenomena.

"We have no one suitable word corresponding to the term 'nature', which could characterise them [these sciences] from the standpoint of their object as well as from the standpoint of their method. We must, therefore, select two expressions that correspond to the two meanings of the word 'nature'. As sciences of culture, they study objects pertaining to universal cultural values; as historical sciences, they portray their unique development in its distinctiveness and individuality. And the fact that their objects are essentially processes of culture imparts to their historical method at the same time the principle of concept formation, for what is essential to them is only that which in its individual originality has significance for the guiding cultural value. Therefore, by individualising, they select from reality as 'culture' something quite distinct from the natural sciences which examine in a generalising way the same reality, as 'nature'. For the significance of a cultural process, in most cases, rests precisely on the originality which distinguishes it from other processes, whereas, on the other hand, that which it possesses in common with other processes, that is to say, that which constitutes their natural-scientific essence, is non-essential to the historical science of culture" (pp. 142-43).

These passages strikingly reveal the weakness of Rickert's theory. Leaving aside for the moment the question of cultural values, I will remark, first, that if the importance of every particular historical process lies in its originality—and that is correct—this by no means justifies the contrasting of natural science to history, or, as Rickert puts it, the sciences of nature to the sciences of culture. The fact is that among the natural sciences there are sciences which do not cease to be *natural* sciences while at the same time being *historical* sciences. Such, for example, is *geology*. The special subject it is concerned with cannot at all be regarded as "only a copy". No. Geology studies the history of the earth and not some other celestial body, just as the history of Russia is the history of our fatherland and not the history of some other country. The history of the earth is "individualised" not a whit less than the history of Russia, France, and so forth. Consequently it cannot be fitted at all into the framework of the division that Rickert tries to establish. Our author himself feels that in this respect things are not at all right with him. He tries to remedy this by acknowledging the presence of "intermediate spheres" in which the historical method passes over to the domain of natural science (p. 147 et seqq.). But this acknowledgement gets him absolutely nowhere.

As an example, he takes phylogenetic biology. "Although it operates exclusively with general concepts," he agrees, "these concepts are, however, constituted in such a way that the investigated whole which it examines is considered from the standpoint of its singleness and peculiarity" (p. 148). But in his opinion this is no argument against his principles for the division of the sciences: "Similar mixed forms, on the contrary, become comprehensible as mixed forms precisely because of this" (p. 150). The trouble is that history represents a form *absolutely as mixed* as phylogenetic biology or geology. If these two last-named sciences belong to the "intermediate sphere", history is also part of it. And if that is so, it shatters the very concept of this sphere, since, according to Rickert, it lies *between* history and natural science.

Rickert also hopes to save the situation by pointing out that "in general, interest in phylogenetic biology is evidently dying out" (p. 152). That may be so. But that is beside the point. The point is what method was used by scientists while they were still interested in this science. And it was the same method which is used by the scientists concerned with universal history. Besides, the interest in geology, for example, is not "dying out" at all. The very existence of this science alone is sufficient to refute Rickert's principle of the division of the sciences.

Our author also refers to such concepts as "progress" and "regress" being used in phylogenetic biology, although they have meaning only from the standpoint of value (p. 151). But this circumstance by no means settles the question of which *method* is used by phylogenetic biology. It may, in truth, be said of geology too that it is of interest to man principally as the history of the planet on which the development of human culture is taking place. And one could probably agree with that. But even having agreed with it, we shall nevertheless have to recognise that what is "essential" in the eyes of the geologist, *as such*, is not that which pertains to any kind of cultural value, but that—and only that—which enables him to understand and depict the objective course of the earth's development.

The same with history. Undoubtedly, every historian arranges his scientific material—separating the essential from the non-essential—from the viewpoint of a certain value. The whole question is: *what is the nature* of this value? It is quite impossible to answer this question by asserting that, in this particular case, the value concerned is in the category of *cultural values*. Not at all. As a man of science—and *within the framework of his science*—the historian considers as essential that which helps him to determine the causal connection of those events the aggregate of which constitutes the individual process of development he is studying: and as non-essential that which is irrelevant to this theme. Consequently what is involved there is not at all the category of values spoken of by Rickert.

With Rickert, generalised natural science is contrasted to history which depicts the particular processes of development in their individualised forms. But apart from history, in the broad sense, there is also sociology, which is concerned with "the general" to the same degree as natural science. History becomes a science only in so far as it succeeds in explaining from the point of view of sociology the processes it portrays. Therefore history is related to sociology in exactly the same way as geology is related to "generalised" natural science. And hence it follows that Rickert's attempt to *oppose* the sciences of culture to the sciences of nature has no serious basis.

It is not without interest that some theoreticians of syndicalism at present have a weakness for Rickert. This gives a fair assessment of the "value" of their own teaching.

ON E. BOUTROUX'S BOOK

E. Boutroux, *Science and Religion in Contemporary Philosophy.*
Translated by V. Bazarov with a Preface by the Translator.
Library of Contemporary Philosophy. No. Three.
Shipovnik Publishers. St. Petersburg 1910

In his preface to the work of E. Boutroux, Mr. Bazarov says that some fifty years ago, in reply to the question, what gives rise to the conflict between religion and science and will this conflict find its ultimate solution sometime and in some way, every "enlightened" person would simply have shrugged his shoulders contemptuously. At that time, such a question was thought to be absurd, since it was believed that science contradicted the conceptions underlying every religion. Now it is different. Now truly "cultured" people would never dream of such an opinion. They think it is absurd even to speak of such a conflict, not because religion has allegedly *been refuted already* by science, once and for all, but because, they say, science and religion "revolve" on quite different planes. "In the past," Mr. V. Bazarov tells us, "theoretical concepts contended with religious dogmas. Now scientific ideas supplanted religious beliefs and took their place—and then men of science said that traditional religion had been 'refuted', that the time had come to create a 'scientific religion', and so on. Now, on the contrary, science appeared to be 'bankrupt', incapable of solving 'the riddles of the universe' and then the adherents of traditional religion raised their heads and with fresh ardour exalted their own solution of the secrets of the universe. And in each instance the very *content* both of science and religion respectively engaged in battle. The presence of common ground between them, and consequently of ground for conflict, was never doubted.... At the present time, another point of view is steadily and stubbornly coming to the fore.... This view recognises that in past conflicts both these opposing forces were right, and in the most extreme, most irreconcilable of their conclusions at that.... If all religious notions are absurd from a scientific point of view, if all scientific concepts are impious—or, at best, indifferent from the standpoint of religion, this simply means that between the first and second spheres, in point of fact, conflict or contradiction of any kind is unthinkable.... People of the old stock were mistaken, not in that they considered religious and scientific ideas to be incompatible,—here they were quite right—but in that, despite of this, they still tried at any cost to combine them..." (pp. 5-8).

That is very interesting. There is just one thing wrong with it: *it is completely at loggerheads with historical truth.* "Formerly" theoretical concepts were *far from always* contending with religious dogmas. Really, has the "cultured" Mr. V. Bazarov never heard of the so-called *"dual truth"*? This doctrine first saw the light of day in the Middle Ages and reached maturity in the Renaissance period. The whole meaning of it is that the truths of science "revolve" in quite a different plane from that of the truths of religion. Thus, if "cultured" people assure us *at the present time* that there is essentially no room for conflict between science and religion they are only warming up something very much of "the past".* On the other hand, how long is it since the "bankruptcy of science" was loudly and triumphantly proclaimed by, for example, Brunetière? Everyone knows that this was only a short time ago. So it is strange to refer an argument on the theme of this supposed bankruptcy of science only to a period "of the past". It follows from all this that the "cultured" person who wrote the preface to Boutroux's book is badly versed both in the *history* of philosophical thought and in *present-day* "philosophical" trends.

An impartial observer will readily discern the obvious social causes prompting the present-day "philosophers" of a certain type to warm up the *old* doctrine of "dual truth" and serve it with a *new* sauce.** E. Boutroux is one of those warmers-up whose works constitute what might justifiably be called *twentieth-century scholasticism.* He has an excellent knowledge of the literature on his subject. But there is not an atom of originality and not a shred of literary talent in his work. It is, therefore, insufferably dull. Beware, Russian reader!

Here is a sample of Boutroux's arguments. "Man must be permitted to examine the conditions not only of scientific knowledge, but also of his own life" (p. 324). That "but" is really matchless!

---

* G. H. Lewes in his *History of Philosophy* alleges that Francis Bacon was one of the first to enunciate the "doctrine of dual truth". That is inaccurate.[231] But notice how Lewes himself, who recognises this truth, formulates it: "Philosophy may be occupied about the same problems as Religion: but it employs altogether different criteria, and depends on altogether different principles...." [G. H. Lewes, *History of Philosophy*, Series I, Conclusion]. This is word for word the same as what we are offered *"at the present time"* by Mr. Bazarov, from the writings of E. Boutroux and those who share his views on this question. Yet Lewes is undoubtedly a writer of *"the past"*.

** See the excellent article by L. I. Axelrod: "Dual Truth in Contemporary German Philosophy". *Collected Philosophical Essays*, St. Petersburg, 1906.

It assumes that man's investigation of "his own life" cannot be *scientific*; but it goes without saying that this assumption is utterly unjustified. Yet, it is on this utterly unjustified assumption that Boutroux constructs his whole defence of the rights of the religious mode of thought. A remarkable defence of religion! When one gets to know the arguments of such defenders of religion, one ceases to wonder at the Pope almost excommunicating them. The Roman Catholic Church knows perfectly well that religion has many friends who, in fact, are worse than enemies.

"Each one of my actions," continues our luckless defender of the faith, "each word of mine, each thought of mine signifies that I attribute some reality and some value to my personal existence, its preservation, its role in the world. I know absolutely nothing concerning the objective value of this judgment; I do not need to have it proved to me. If I do happen to reflect upon it, I find that this opinion is but the expression of my instinct, of my habits and my prejudices.... In conformity with these prejudices, the thought suggests itself to me to attribute to myself a tendency to persevere in my own being, to believe myself capable of something, to consider my ideas as serious, original, useful, to work to spread them and have them adopted. Nothing of all this will bear the slightest scientific scrutiny. But without these illusions} I could not live, at least, like a man; and thanks to these lies, I occasionally alleviate some unhappiness, encourage some of my fellow-men to bear or to love life, love myself and seek to make a tolerable use of it" (same page).

There is the whole of Boutroux, with all his amazing instability and all the revolting immorality of his sickly-sweet arguments. It does not even enter his head that he who lives "thanks" to some sort of "*lies*", and without them cannot "make a tolerable use of his life" does not by any means live "*like a man*". This sensitive person does not understand how dirt-cheap is the value of the alleged help he renders to his fellow-men, consisting as it does of bolstering up their "*illusions*"! He does not even suspect that it is precisely his wretched attempt to find a theoretical justification for the "*illusions*" that "will not bear the slightest at all scientific scrutiny". And why does he imagine that it is only thanks to auto-suggestion that he has "the tendency to persevere in his own being"? Actually, this tendency is a property of all organisms. It is an inevitable consequence and expression of life. To point to it as proof that there are phenomena beyond the reach of "scientific scrutiny" is simply to play with words. Nor is there anything surprising in the fact that "I believe myself capable of something". As long as "I" am *alive*, "I" have certain *powers*, and the presence of these powers induces me to consider

myself *capable* of doing this or that. Of course, "I" may exaggerate
my capabilities: not without reason has it been said that to err
is human. We do not need to look far for an example. E. Boutroux
errs very much in regarding the considerations he advances in
defence of religion as "serious" and "useful" (I shall say nothing
about their "originality" for that is out of the question). But it
does not at all follow from the fact that he is mistaken that the
hopes people naturally place on their capabilities require any
mystical explanation and that they cannot be explained otherwise
than with the help of "dual truth".

Errors are governed by their own laws. Boutroux's error in
believing his defence of religion is "serious" and "useful" is conditioned by his role as an ideologist of a declining social class,
the *present-day* French bourgeoisie. Here, too, there is absolutely
nothing inaccessible to scientific scrutiny. The fact is that every
social class, like every individual, defends itself *as* it can and *as
long* as it can....

It will be useful to add to what has been said an analysis of the
following argument advanced by our author:

"Practice presupposes, first, faith; secondly, an object assumed
by that faith; thirdly, love of the object and the desire to realise
it" (p. 331).

If I "assume" there is a she-wolf in a nearby wood, there is not
the slightest need to "assume" also *faith* in that she-wolf before
going out to hunt her. E. Boutroux *multiplies by two what ought
to be left in the singular*. Why? There is only one possible answer
to this, in my opinion; it is to accustom himself and his readers
to the misplaced use of the word "*faith*". Anyone convinced that
practice is inconceivable without "faith" will be very much disposed
to accept "dual truth". In other words, Boutroux is resorting to
a little cunning. But it does not matter. We have already been
told by him that "*illusions*" and "*lies*" are essential to "*human*"
existence.

Further. Practice assumes love for the object. This is not always
the case. The hunt of the she-wolf assumes not love for her, but
love of hunting. However, let us not be too severe. Let us assume
that practice always demands a love for the object we are "assuming". What follows from that? According to Boutroux, that
practice is impossible without religion, since "if one goes deeper
into love, it plunges beyond nature in the proper sense of the
word" (p. 333). Very convincing. Even more so than Boutroux
himself thinks. In fact, as the female predatory animals undoubtedly love their young, it follows that our "assumed" she-wolf
is also not impervious to religious sentiment.

One cannot but admit that things are in a very bad way indeed
with the social class whose ideologist is constrained to "deceive"

himself (or only others?) by such wisdom. In the eighteenth century, on the eve of the revolution, the French bourgeois ideologists were much more "serious". But that time has gone, never to return.

And what about Mr. V. Bazarov, who once imagined himself to be an ideologist of the proletariat? Things are in a still worse way with him; he knows not what he does.

Once again: beware, Russian reader!

FRENCH UTOPIAN SOCIALISM
OF THE NINETEENTH CENTURY

The various systems and doctrines of nineteenth-century French *utopian* socialism differ very much from one another on many important questions.* Nevertheless, all of them have several basic features in common that distinguish them from international *scientific* socialism as we know it today. Had they not had these features in common it would have been impossible for me to present here a characterisation of French utopian socialism as a whole; a detailed exposition of its various teachings and systems could not have been undertaken in this article, and, in any case, would have been irrelevant.

Before one can ascertain the features common to all shades of French utopian socialism in the period mentioned, it is necessary to recall its historical origin.

I

In his polemic with Bruno Bauer and his associates, Marx wrote: "There is no need for any great penetration to see from the teaching of materialism on the original goodness and equal

* The word "*socialism*" first appeared in English and French literature in the 30s of the nineteenth century. The author of the article "Socialism" in the *Encyclopaedia Britannica* (Vol. XXII, p. 205) states that the word owes its origin to The Association of All Classes of All Nations formed in England in 1835. On the other hand, Pierre Leroux contends that it was used for the first time in an article written by him in 1834, "De l'individualisme et du socialisme" (see *Œuvres de Pierre Leroux*, t. I, 1850, p. 376, footnote). It should be remarked, however, that in this article Leroux uses the word only in the sense of "exaggerating the idea of association". Some time later it came to mean any striving to reconstruct the social system with the aim of raising the well-being of the lower classes and guaranteeing social peace. In view of the extremely vague meaning of the term, the word *communism* was often contrasted to it, as defining the much more definite aim of establishing social equality by transforming the means of production, and sometimes also the articles of consumption, into social property. Nowadays, the word "socialism" has almost replaced the word "communism", but as recompense it has lost its initial vagueness. Its present meaning approximates to the original meaning of the word "communism".

intellectual endowment of men, the omnipotence of experience, habit and education, and the influence of environment on man, the great significance of industry, the justification of enjoyment, etc., how necessarily materialism is connected with communism and socialism."[232] Incidentally, Marx proceeds to confirm this remark with the consideration that if man draws all his knowledge, sensations, etc., from the world of the senses and the experience gained from it, as was taught by the eighteenth-century materialists, then the empirical world must be arranged so that in it man experiences and gets used to what is really human and that he becomes aware of himself as man. That is quite correct. Marx was also quite right in asserting that Fourier, for example, "proceeds directly from the teaching of the French materialists".[233] If any one doubts this, he would be well advised to compare Fourier's teaching on the passions with what is said about them in the first chapter of the first part of Holbach's *Système social.* It would be no less interesting in this respect to compare Fourier with Helvétius. But it is important to remember the following.

Although Fourier* proceeds immediately from the teaching of French materialism, at the same time he has a completely negative attitude to the whole of the eighteenth-century French philosophy of Enlightenment. This attitude made itself felt already in his first work, *Théorie des quatre mouvements et des destinées sociales*, published in Lyons in 1888.** We read there:

"From the time when the philosophers revealed their impotence in their very first experiment, the French Revolution, all agreed among themselves that their philosophy should be regarded as an error of the human intellect. And the streams of political and moral enlightenment were found to be streams of illusion. And could anything else be found in the works of scholars who, after spending two thousand five hundred years in perfecting their theories and uniting all ancient and modern enlightenment, at their first attempt gave birth to no fewer calamities than they had promised blessings, and caused the civilised world to decline to a state of barbarism? Such were the consequences of the first five years during which philosophical theories were put to the test in France. After the catastrophe of 1793, the illusions were dispelled...."*** In another part of the same work, Fourier recalls with indignation the scholastic quarrels over equality (querelles scolastiques sur l'égalité) which wrecked thrones, altars and the laws of property, and thanks to which, he says, Europe was moving towards barbarism.

---

* Fourier was born at Besançon on April 7, 1772, and died in Paris on October 10, 1837.
** "Leipzig" is printed on the cover.
*** Op. cit., p. 3.

Fourier was never at any time a supporter of the old order. On the contrary, it is most probable that, in common with the entire third estate of the time, he did not approve of that order and wished to see an end of it. But the revolutionary struggle of the various classes of French society at that time assumed such a violent character—especially in 1793—that Fourier along with the majority of his contemporaries took fright. Since he considered that the eighteenth-century philosophy of Enlightenment was responsible for the "catastrophe of 1793",[234] he declared that philosophy to be totally bankrupt. In his opposition to it, he went to the length of working out two rules of procedure for himself: 1) "absolute doubt" (le doute absolu) and 2) "absolute digression" (l'écart absolu). "Absolute doubt" consisted in regarding with scepticism even the most widespread opinions of his time. For example—and this is his own example—all the various philosophical trends were agreed in their attitude of respect for civilisation. But Fourier, in applying here his rule of "absolute doubt", questioned the "perfection" of civilisation. He asked himself: "Can there be anything more imperfect than this civilisation which is attended by so many calamities? Can there be anything more doubtful than its necessity and the inevitability of its future existence? Is it not probable that it represents but a stage in social development?"* Having set himself these questions, he soon became convinced that "civilisation", that is to say, those social relations which prevail in the civilised nations, must give way to other forms of community; and he began to ponder over the nature of those future forms.

As far as Fourier's "absolute digression" is concerned, it consisted of his deciding "never to walk the paths laid down by the uncertain sciences", i.e., by the selfsame eighteenth-century philosophy. It is interesting to note that, in justification of this rule of procedure, Fourier adduced the circumstance that the "uncertain sciences", in spite of the enormous successes of industry, were unable even to "prevent poverty".

However, the very application of these two rules demonstrated that, in rebelling against eighteenth-century philosophy, Fourier none the less remained very strongly influenced by it. As we know, that philosophy was essentially *progressive*. One of its most important distinguishing traits was a deep belief in progress, in the perfectibility (perfectibilité) of man and of human society. Fourier habitually sneered at this belief. But it should be noted that in applying the rule of "absolute doubt" to civilisation, strictly speaking, he was casting doubt not on civilisation itself, but only on the inevitability of the existence of certain serious

---

* Ibid., p. 7.

defects in the social structure of the civilised nations. When he finally reached the conclusion that these serious defects could be eliminated, when he had elaborated a plan of the new social system, he himself became an active worker in the cause of perfection, although he did not cease to sneer at the doctrine of the "uncertain sciences" concerning the capacity of man and human society to perfect themselves. No less remarkable is the fact that this *"absolute digressionist"* from the paths laid down by the "uncertain sciences" immediately encountered the *problem of poverty.* The man who reproaches eighteenth-century French philosophy for not preventing poverty, himself remains loyal to its spirit, since that philosophy constantly reiterated: salus populi—suprema lex (the welfare of the people is the supreme law).

But if this is true, and if Fourier, while sharply opposing and malevolently sneering at eighteenth-century philosophy, did remain essentially its loyal follower and made its teaching the basis of his own theoretical constructions, it may well be asked: where did his "absolute doubt" and his "absolute digression" lead him to?

First, they led him into many theoretical *eccentricities,* which for a long time provided a target for the witticisms of socialism's adversaries. "Absolute doubt" led Fourier to disregard rules of theoretical reflection which no one can disregard with impunity. When he dilates upon "disyllabic immortality" and erects a "general ladder of metempsychoses" (échelle générale des métempsycoses);* when he assures us that "he who gave us lions will give us anti-lions upon which we may ride at great speed";** when he describes the good qualities of the future anti-whales, anti-sharks, anti-hippopotami, and anti-seals,*** he is obviously abusing the "digression" which resulted from his revolt against all former philosophers. If he had not rebelled in this way, he would probably not have revealed so much of the self-assurance of the self-taught and would have tried to curb his flights of fantasy.

Secondly, in obeying the rule of "absolute digression", Fourier, in his own words, tried to take up only those problems that eighteenth-century philosophy had not touched upon. Since this philosophy had been greatly occupied with *politics* and *reli-*

---

* See *Œuvres complètes de Ch. Fourier,* Paris, MDCCCXLI, tome II, p. 319.
** Ibid., Vol. IV, p. 254. Fourier would have us believe that by travelling mounted on an anti-lion one could breakfast in Paris, lunch in Lyons, and dine in Marseilles; one need only change these good animals when they tire.
*** Ibid., p. 255.

gion, Fourier felt bound in contrast "to seek social well-being only in measures that had nothing to do with the administration and the priesthood and extended only to industry and domestic life, and would be compatible with any government, without any need for its interference."* *This largely defines the nature of his social system; it is, in fact, devoid of any political aspirations.*

But there is still more to it than that. Since Fourier's revolt against French eighteenth-century philosophy was caused by his conviction that it was responsible for the "catastrophe of 1793", not only did he stress at every convenient opportunity (and, perhaps, at some not so convenient) that his system *had no revolutionary aspirations*, but he recommended it as the sole reliable means of struggle against such aspirations. In the first volume of his book, *La fausse industrie, morcelée, répugnante, mensongère et l'antidote, l'industrie naturelle, combinée* etc., there is an interesting chapter entitled "Notice sur les intérêts du Roi.—Moyens d'en finir des conspirations" (Notes on the King's interests.— Means to put an end to conspiracies). In it, Fourier points out that since the infernal machine is the conspirators' new weapon ** it is essential "to test an invention that will avert conspiracies by creating general well-being and good morals" (p. 337). Then follows a fairly detailed exposition of his new social system. In the second volume of the same work, published a year later, this thought is repeated in a note: "Thème général, appliqué aux attentats régicides" (General theme, in its application to attempted regicide). In it Fourier blames the philosophy of the Enlightenment for these attempts. "In the course of the last forty-eight years," he says, "kings have been at war with philosophy, but they only use against it half-measures which strengthen it; they are incapable of creating an effective opposition to it, of exposing its false knowledge by opposing to it an exact science of the industrial mechanism and the destiny of society."*** It goes without saying that this exact science is Fourier's system, recommended to Louis Philippe as the best means against conspiracies.

We shall see shortly that in this respect Fourier was not an exception among socialists of those days. On the contrary, such appeals were very typical of nineteenth-century French utopian socialism. Therefore, it would be useful if we ascertained their general psychological background.

---

* The book was issued in 1808, that is to say, during the reign of Napoleon I, who, as is known, did not show indulgence to "agitators".

** The book was published in 1835 and the note was obviously written under the influence of Fieschi's attempt on the life of Louis Philippe (on July 28 of that year).

*** This page is not numbered, but the one following it is marked: M-616.

II

See how Fourier portrays (in the book already mentioned — *Théorie des quatre mouvements*) — the revolutionary condition of society which, he says, may be got rid of only by putting into effect his plan for social reform.

"Yes," he exclaims, "the civilised order* is becoming more and more shaky; the volcano created by philosophy in 1789 is only in its first eruption; others will follow as soon as a weak rule favours the agitators;** the war of the poor against the rich was so successful that the intriguers of all countries dream only of resuming it. It is useless to try to avert it; nature ridicules our enlightenment and our foresight; it will be able to bring forth revolution out of the same measures which we adopt to ensure social tranquillity."***

All this is worthy of the greatest attention. Already in 1808, Fourier sees in the Great Revolution an episode of the class struggle: *the war of the poor against the rich.* As though in regret, he announces that this war was successful. It might be thought from this that he sympathised with the old order; but, as has been said above, that is not the case. He had no sympathy with the old order; he simply *rejected the class struggle in general and the revolutionary class struggle in particular.* He maintained that France could have escaped the Great Revolution if the discoveries which he made *after* the "catastrophe of 1793" had been made by some other genius under the old order, and made timely use of as the basis of social reform. But now the discoveries had been made; social upheavals could be forestalled and the war "of the poor against the rich" avoided, if only those interested in the preservation of social tranquillity would understand the advantages of the social system that Fourier had thought out. Therefore, in his appeal to them, he spared no colours in depicting the upheavals that would be the price civilised society would pay for failing to heed his voice.

Such were his "tactics". They were characterised, first, by *indifference to politics*; second, by a completely negative attitude to the class struggle. There was a very obvious and close connection between these two most important features of his system. The connection consisted in the second begetting the first.

Fourier's negative attitude to the class struggle was the outcome of the "catastrophe of 1793". And since politics is a weapon

---

* We have noticed already that this is Fourier's way of referring to the social structure of civilised societies.
** Op. cit., p. 388.
*** *Théorie des quatre mouvements*, p. 8.

of the class struggle, it is natural that with Fourier negation of
this struggle was followed by negation of politics.

Do not think that this is simply a special case in the history
of utopian socialism. No! There are so many similar cases that
we are fully entitled to speak of a general rule. Here is another
example, perhaps less vivid, but no less important.

Saint-Simon* also regarded the French Revolution as a class
struggle: to be exact, the struggle of the non-possessing class
against the propertied class, and, like Fourier, he was very unfavourably disposed towards this struggle. In his brochure *Lettres
d'un habitant de Genève à ses contemporains*, published in 1802,
that is to say, six years before the appearance of Fourier's first
book, he calls the French Revolution the most terrifying explosion
and the greatest of all scourges.** He writes at length of "frightful
atrocities caused by this application of the principle of equality",***
and in an appeal to the non-possessing class, says: "See what
happened in France when your comrades held sway there; they
brought forth famine."**** It is plain that the "catastrophe of
1793" made the strongest impression on Saint-Simon too. If
Fourier laid the blame for this "catastrophe" at the door of
eighteenth-century philosophers, Saint-Simon explained it by
the ignorance of the non-possessing class. But this is only an
apparent difference, since "the application of the principle of
equality" was, in Saint-Simon's opinion, nothing more than the
practical application of the extreme conclusions reached by the
philosophers of the Enlightenment. Thus, Saint-Simon's teaching
reveals the same indifference to politics that we have seen in
Fourier's.***** In a practical sense, Saint-Simonism (of the
first style) is no more than a study of the measures required to
put an end to revolution (sur les mesures à prendre pour terminer
la révolution). The degree to which Saint-Simon was averse to
all thought of revolution may be gauged from the following
passage taken from his book *Du système industriel*. To the ques-

---

  * Born in Paris on October 17, 1760; died there on May 19, 1825.
  ** See *Œuvres choisies de C.-H. de Saint Simon*, t. I, Bruxelles, 1859,
pp. 20 et 21.
   *** Ibid., p. 31.
   **** Ibid., p. 27.
  ***** Where Fourier thunders against the "philosophers", Saint-Simon
fulminates against the "legists". In his opinion, their "metaphysical doctrines" explain the unsuccessful outcome of the French Revolution. See *Du
système industriel, par Henri Saint-Simon*, with the epigraph: "Dieu a dit:
aimez-vous et secourez vous les uns les autres", Paris, 1821, Préface, pp. I-
VIII. [God said: Love and help one another.] Saint-Simon's concept of
"legist", or *representative of "metaphysical doctrine"* is analogous to Fourier's
concept (which we know from his book) of "philosopher", or representative
of "uncertain sciences". To us, this concept is now conveyed by the words
revolutionary intelligentsia.

tion, which force will produce the changes he is contemplating in social relationships and who will guide this force, he replies:

"These changes will be accomplished by the force of moral feeling, and this force will have as its prime mover the belief that all political principles must be deduced from the general principle given to humanity by God." ("Love one another."—G. P.). *"This force will be directed by philanthropists who, as they were at the time when Christianity was being formed, will be the immediate agents of the Eternal."*

A little further on Saint-Simon writes: *"The sole means to which the philanthropists will have recourse will be oral and printed preaching."**

Like Fourier, Saint-Simon was horrified at the very thought of the class struggle and sometimes liked to intimidate his readers with "the propertyless class", the "people". In his Fourth Letter to Messrs the Industrialists, in demonstrating the undesirable turn which their struggle with "Bonaparte's feudalism" might take, he writes: "Besides, gentlemen, one cannot contemplate without trepidation that in case of open battle it" (Bonaparte's feudalism—G. P.) "could momentarily attract the people to its side. Although you are the natural and invariable leaders" (chefs) "of the people and although it acknowledges you as such, experience has shown you that it could be rallied for a time to the banner of the military and the legists. You think rightly that the influence which the agitators could have on the people has now" (in comparison with the period of the Great Revolution—G.P.) "diminished considerably.... But it has not been altogether destroyed. The dogma of Turkish equality**... may still, unless you take precautions, make great ravages.... What means have you to fight against the seductions of this dogma, unless you previously offer the people clear and precise notions of their true interests?"***

This passage shows most convincingly that the propertyless class was not at all the class which Saint-Simon counted upon

---

* The italics are Saint-Simon's. See his *Adresse aux philanthropes* in the aforesaid book, pp. 297, 298, 299, and 302. I make the point for those interested in the evolution of Saint-Simon's ideas that the expressions: "le nouveau christianisme", and "le christianisme définitif", are to be met with already in this book, and that he sometimes speaks in it in the style of the Scriptures, summonsing to himself les hérétiques en morale et en politique, and so on (p. 310). Later we shall see how we must understand Saint-Simon's attempt to rely on religion.

** This is what Saint-Simon called the equality for which the communists were striving. He affirmed that such equality was possible only in Eastern despotisms.

*** *Du système industriel.* pp. 205-07.

to realise his practical plans. Saint-Simon's views, like Fourier's, were by no means the views of the proletariat.

The followers of these two great founders of French utopian socialism were completely loyal to them in the extremely important respects I have indicated. They repudiated indignantly any idea of making the class struggle going on in society the basis of their social-reforming aspirations. As an example, I shall mention one of Fourier's most talented followers—Victor Considérant.*

III

In his brochure *Débâcle de la politique en France*, issued in 1836, that is to say, while Fourier was still alive, Considérant defines politics as *"the totality of contending opinions and theories relating to the fundamental principles of government or to the various administrative systems that wrangle over portfolios for the sake of the greatest good of the nation."*** The last words in this definition have a very noticeable touch of irony about them. and show that, in Considérant's eyes, politics was of no great value; far from hiding this opinion, he notes with satisfaction that, in comparison with recent times, interest in and respect for politics in general had fallen considerably in France.*** Why? In consequence of some theoretical errors of politics (erreurs théoriques de la politique). What were these errors? Reply: "Instead of bothering about the means necessary for realising the *unity of interests* (l'alliance des intérêts), which would be profitable to all interests, people" (of the various political parties—*G.P.*) "are taken up exclusively with *supporting and strengthening their struggle*, which is profitable only to those who traffic in that struggle (qui trafiquent de cette lutte)."****

Politics is a weapon of the class struggle; like his teacher Fourier, Considérant does not want the class struggle. Consequently—again like Fourier—he turns his back on politics. This could not be more logical. In another part of the same brochure, Considérant puts forward as a truth that admits of no denial the following proposition:

*"All of us are interested in everyone without exception being happy; and for each class the best means of ensuring its material interests is to link with its own interests the interests of the other classes."*****

---

      * Born in 1808; died in 1893.
    ** My italics.
   *** Op. cit., pp. 2 and 52.
  **** Op. cit., p. 16. Considérant's italics.
 ***** Ibid., p. 63, Considérant's italics.

Considérant is as completely disapproving as Fourier in regard to eighteenth-century French philosophy. He calls it *subversive*, and says that when the fundamental idea of this philosophy, that is to say, the idea of overthrowing feudalism and the Catholic religion, began to be realised, great social upheavals occurred. He gives us to understand that at the end of the eighteenth century, in his opinion, the means were available to improve the social order without resorting to revolutionary struggle.* As far as his own epoch is concerned, he has not the slightest doubt about the possibility of a peaceful transformation of society. This possibility is fully assured by Fourier's discoveries, which offer the most reliable means of reconciling the interests of all social classes. The revolutionaries who take so readily to acts of violence do not wish to understand this.** Hence his very severe condemnation of the revolutionaries. True, he gives no quarter either to the authorities, who, he says, compromise their own cause by their clumsiness.*** But for all that, he is convinced that "at the present time, the party that is interested in the preservation of order, is less anti-social (moins anti-social) than the party that is striving to overthrow it". Why? "Since it is evident from the contemporary condition of society," he replies, "that now it is necessary not to fight, but to improve and organise, *the party whose very position provides it with a love for order is less unfavourable* (moins défavorable) *to the action which must be taken now than the party that still wants to expel, smash, overthrow.*"****

Here in Russia, the late Leo Tolstoy reasoned in exactly the same way: he too, out of the selfsame considerations, was more sympathetic to the authorities than to the revolutionaries.

All this is, I trust, sufficiently characteristic. But Considérant's views are even more vividly expressed in this passage:

"Any uprising of one element against another is unlawful; only concord, harmony, free and full development, Order, are lawful."*****

---

* Ibid., p. 147.
** I will recall that Considérant's brochure was published in 1836, i.e., at the most stormy period of Louis Philippe's reign.
*** He says they are always ready to attach a policeman to every noble sentiment (ibid., p. 24). That is truly and strikingly apt.
**** Ibid., p. 57. Considérant's italics.
***** Ibid., p. 91. Cf. his *Principes du socialisme, manifeste de la démocratie au XIX siècle*, 2-me édition, Paris, 1847. In this work, written at a time when Considérant was already less disposed to deny politics, the *revolutionary party* is otherwise called *reactionary democracy*, since only peaceful democracy is progressive (p. 45). Of all the revolutionaries, Considérant's most severe condemnation is reserved for the "*political* communists", who "resolutely adopt a great material Revolution" (p. 46). I shall have something to say about these communists later.

These words illustrate the whole tactics of utopian socialism.*
I am not saying that the tactics never changed. That would
have been completely unnatural in the feverish public life of
France in those days. But in spite of modifications, the tactics
of utopian socialism in general retained this character to the
very end. No matter how numerous were the individual features
distinguishing one school of utopian socialism from another, all
of these schools—again with some few exceptions which I shall
deal with later—were indifferent to politics, and all of them,
again apart from a few exceptions, were against the class struggle.

Take the Saint-Simonists. In expounding their doctrine, they
refer to the class struggle which has been taking place in history
and to the exploitation of "man by man". They say that in modern
society the workers (les travailleurs) are exploited by the idle
(les oisifs). Already in their first publication, *Le Producteur*,
appearing in 1825-1826, they state that it is already now "*impossible to imagine that the interests of the idle are the same as those
of the workers*".** The aim of social development, they say, is the
elimination of class antagonisms and the triumph of "association". But when the question is raised of how to bring about the
triumph of "association", they point to the *reconciliation of classes*.
This can all be read in the interesting collection of their lectures:
Doctrine saint-simonienne. Exposition (see the first volume especially).[235] But these views are presented with particular clarity
in the *Report on the Work of the Saint-Simonist Family*, submitted
by Stéphane Flachat to the "fathers"[236] Bazard and Enfantin.

Stéphane Flachat not only recognises the division of contemporary society into two classes, but expresses himself much more
precisely than most of those who shared his views. Whereas to
the enormous majority of Saint-Simonists contemporary society
is divided into a class of "idle" and a class of "workers", Flachat
speaks of the opposition between the *bourgeoisie* and the *proletariat*, naively supposing at the same time, however, that behind
the difference in terms there is no difference in social relationships. He notes that after the 1830 revolution the bourgeoisie

---

* Another of Fourier's pupils, the former Saint-Simonist A. Paget says
that his associates "abandoned the field of politics in order to exercise their
intellect in the more fertile ground of social questions" (*Introduction à l'étude
de la science sociale*, Paris, 1838). Here *politics* is sharply contrasted with activity in the domain of *social* questions. This contrasting of politics with social
questions is a common trait of the overwhelming majority of utopian socialists. We shall see later what explains the exceptions to this general rule. But
it is precisely the rule and not the exception which is characteristic of utopian
socialism. This opposing of politics to social activity, borrowed from the
West, predominated also in Russian literature until the victory of Marxism.
** See the article by Enfantin, *Opuscules financiers* in Vol. II of *Producteur*.
p. 479.

did not see any necessity of giving serious thought to the interests of the proletariat. And for all his readiness to excuse this error of the bourgeoisie, he does, nevertheless, think it is high time the error was corrected, since otherwise society is threatened with "upheavals more prolonged and more profound than those that marked the struggle of the bourgeoisie and feudalism".* It is obvious from this that recollections of the class struggle in the period of the Great Revolution are very fresh in the memory of the socialist rapporteur. They compel him to strive for the reconciliation of classes. He quotes Saint-Simon as saying that the English proletarians are ready at the first favourable opportunity to launch a war *of the poor against the rich*,** and then goes on to say:

"It is in these grave circumstances that we appear on the scene. We say to the bourgeoisie: *we are the voice of the people* demanding for them their just share in the association, an *energetic voice* because the demand is just, but *peaceful* because, being heralds of the future, we know from our teacher that violence is retrograde and that its reign is over. To the people we have said, we repeat every day: *we are the voice of the bourgeoisie.* All you who suffer, demand universal association and you will receive it, because it is God's will. But it will be granted to you only if you demand it *peacefully* and *gradually.* For if you try to snatch by force the instruments of labour from the hands of those who now possess them, remember that the strong men who will be directing your fury would not find the mansions and palaces, whose owners they had evicted, too big or too sumptuous for themselves, and you would only have changed masters."***

This warning about the "strong men" may astonish the present-day reader. But there was nothing strange in it for the rapporteur. Flachat believed that the proletariat was incapable "in consequence of its ignorance of clearly formulating its needs and its hopes".**** *Such* a social class was really very easy to lead by the nose. The whole question was whether abstinence from politics would promote the intellectual development of such a class.

The extent to which this mood of conciliation was rooted in the spirit of that time, or, more correctly, in the minds of those people of that time who were interested in social questions, is shown, incidentally, by the following fact.

---

* See *Œuvres de Saint-Simon et d'Enfantin*, Vol. IV, pp. 58-59, Paris, 1865.
   ** Flachat's italics.
   *** Ibid., pp. 70, 71, and 72.
   **** Ibid., p. 58.

When Pierre Leroux*—who is known to have excited great
interest in Russia, in the circle of Belinsky and Herzen, and
out of caution, was referred to by them as *Pyotr Ryzhy*—joined
the Saint-Simonists, he mentioned the peaceful character of
their "doctrine" as the aspect which had had the greatest influence in converting him.**

Louis Blanc*** was another who was utterly opposed to the
class struggle. His famous work, *Organisation du travail*, begins
in this way: "It is to you, the rich, that this book is addressed,
since it is a question of the poor. For their cause is your cause."
Further on, there is another, somewhat modified, version of this
appeal: "This appeal is, I repeat, dedicated to you, the rich....
Yes, it is your cause, this sacred cause of the poor. Their emancipation alone will be appropriate to reveal to you the treasures
you have not yet known of serene joys."****

Even Proudhon,***** whom many even yet, for some reason,
regard as a great revolutionary, in reality rejected the posing of the
social question in a revolutionary way. In a letter to Marx dated
March 17, 1846, he says: "We must not lay down revolutionary
action as a means of social reform, because this pretended means
would be simply an appeal to force, to arbitrary rule, in short,
a contradiction. Therefore I set the problem to myself as follows:
by means of an economic combination to return to society the
wealth taken from it by another economic combination (interest
on capital, land rent, house rent, usury). In other words, to turn
in political economy the theory of property against property,
in order to ensure freedom and equality."*)

This desire to solve the social problem by means of an *economic
combination* spells the negation of *politics* we now know so well.
This negation has always played the decisive part in Proudhon's
views. It led him into anarchism, and passed from him to
M. A. Bakunin, Elisée Reclus, P. A. Kropotkin, J. Grave, and
other theoreticians of anarchism, as well as to the present-day
French and Italian "revolutionary syndicalists".

In 1848 Proudhon, with the magnificent turn of phrase characteristic of him, proclaimed that the Provisional Government
preferred the tricolour to the red flag.[238] "Poor red flag, everyone
is abandoning you! But I kiss you, I press you to my breast....

---

* Born in Paris in 1797; died there in 1871.
** See his Open Letter published in *Le Globe*.[237]
*** Born October 29, 1811; died December 6, 1882.
**** *Organisation du travail*, IV-e édition, Paris, 1845, Introduction,
pp. V et 31-32. The first edition of this work was published in 1840.
***** Born January 15, 1809; died January 19, 1865.
*) Not having Proudhon's correspondence at hand, I am quoting from
Abrégé des œuvres de Proudhon where the letter is printed, though not in full,
unfortunately, on pages 414-15.

The red flag is the federal banner of the human race."* But this ardent devotion to the red flag did not in the least prevent him from preaching the union of the proletariat and the bourgeoisie. Thus, when his candidature was proposed at Besançon, he wrote in his election address: "Workers, offer your hand to your employers, and you, employers, do not reject the advances of those who were your workers."** In his paper *La Voix du Peuple*[239] (issue of March 20, 1850) he wrote: "The union of the bourgeoisie and the proletariat means, today as of old, the emancipation of the serf, a defensive and offensive alliance of the industrialists and the workers against the capitalist and the nobleman, the solidarity of interests of the proletarian and the master."***

The contrasting of the *master* to the *capitalist* shows that by bourgeoisie Proudhon understood, strictly speaking, the petty bourgeoisie: he invited the *master* to unite with the *journeyman* (le compagnon). This is worth noting as material for characterising the views of the utopian socialists on economic relations in the society of their day. I shall have to analyse these views in more detail later. Meantime, I shall add just one point: Proudhon's book *Idée générale de la révolution au dix-neuvième siècle*, which was published in 1851 and left deep traces in the views of the socialists in the Latin countries and Russia for a very long time, was dedicated to the bourgeoisie. The dedication comprised a whole song of praise to that class: "To you, the bourgeois, the homage of these new essays," said Proudhon, "you have in all ages been the most intrepid, the most skilful revolutionaries.... You and you alone—yes, you elaborated the principles, laid the foundation of Revolution in the nineteenth century. Nothing undertaken without you or against you could survive. Nothing undertaken by you was in vain. Nothing prepared by you will fail.... Is it possible that, having accomplished so many revolutions, you have in the end become irrecoverably, in spite of interest, in spite of reason, in spite of honour, counter-revolutionaries?" and so forth. Later, Proudhon speaks of the 1793 revolution, during which the garrulous tribunes of the people could, as he put it, do absolutely nothing, and of the 1848 revolution, which was unable to solve the social question; and winds up by once more calling on the bourgeoisie to be reconciled with the proletariat: "I say to you: reconciliation is revolution." It might be thought from this that in 1851 Proudhon had become a revolutionary; but the content of his book refutes that idea. In the most detailed fashion, he sets out a plan for a quite peace-

---

* See *P. J. Proudhon* par A. Desjardins, Paris, 1896, t. I, p. 90, note.
** Cited from Desjardins, op. cit., p. 99.
*** Quoted by Karl Diehl in *P. J. Proudhon, seine Lehre und sein Leben*, III. Abteilung, Jena, 1896, S. 100.

ful "social liquidation" which he presents as social revolution
only because, in general, he badly misuses terminology.

The utopian socialists' characteristic aversion to revolutionary
action was classically expressed by Etienne Cabet:

*"If I had the revolution in my grasp, I would not open my hand
even if I had to die in exile for it."**

IV

Thus, the utopian socialists admit the existence of the class
struggle in contemporary society. But they do not adapt their
plans of reform to this struggle, and resolutely refuse to take
advantage of it to further their aims. They hope to put their
plans into effect through reconciling the classes. Accordingly,
they reject revolutionary action and turn their back on politics.**

When the July revolution broke out, the Saint-Simonists
decided to take no part in it. Their "fathers", Bazard and Enfantin, wrote in a special message to the Saint-Simonists in the
provinces: "Those who are triumphant today will doubtless be
indignant at what they will call our coldness and indifference;
we are prepared to put up with their insults and their violence....
Dear children, a happier fate is in store for us." This happier
fate consisted in working for "the realisation of the kingdom
of God on earth" (la réalisation du Régne de Dieu sur la terre),
as the authors of the message expressed it.

But to turn one's back on politics does not mean to remove
from the historical arena the political forces acting in it. Even
while eschewing politics, the utopian socialists had to admit
the presence of those political forces. Thus they conceived the
wish somehow to utilise them for their own ends. But how? There
was only one way open to them: to convince some influential
representative of a particular political force that the interests
of his own cause, properly understood, demanded the speediest
realisation of the particular plan for social reform. But how to do

---

* *Voyage en Icarie*, Paris, 1845, p. 565. Italics in the original. Cabet was
born on January 2, 1788, and died on November 8, 1856. The first edition
of his book, *Voyage en Icarie*, was published in March, 1842.[240]

** "Nous sommes *religieux*, c'est-à-dire *pacifiques et aimants* envers *tous
les hommes, toutes les classes, tous les partis....* Nous pensons que la violence
est toujours funeste, toujours *impie*." ["We are *religious*, that is to say, *peaceful and love all people, all classes, all parties....* We think that violence is
always pernicious, always *ungodly*."] So said Charles Lemonnier in a call to
the Saint-Simonists dated July 7, 1832. Further he declared that the Saint-
Simonists loved all parties but associated with none of them, and laid down
his *own* programme which was capable, as he thought, of uniting people of
all political opinions: 1) the immediate construction of a railway from Paris
to Marseilles; 2) the improvement of the water-supply and sewage system
of Paris; 3) the building of a road from the Louvre to the Bastille. And so on.

the convincing? This depended on whom precisely the reformer appealed to and in which particular circumstances the appeal was made. When Saint-Simon wished to draw the attention of Napoleon I to his writings, he gave one of them a title which held the promise of showing how victory over England might be achieved (Moyens de faire reconnaître aux anglais l'indépendance des pavillons), although the actual work itself was devoted to a quite different subject. When Fourier took it into his head to draw Louis Philippe, who was being harassed by conspirators, over to his side, he began repeating that the establishment of phalansteries was the best way of combating the revolutionaries. When the police of the July monarchy arrested the Duchess of Berry for attempting a restoration in favour of her son, the Duke of Bordeaux, and when the rumour spread throughout society that she was to be executed, "Father" Enfantin immediately wrote an open Letter to The Queen, in which, protesting against the death penalty, he proclaimed (*in bold type*) the future emancipation of women ("*la femme s'affranchira!*"). Informing his "children" of this letter, he expressed the hope that it would promote "the introduction of women into politics".* Having departed subsequently for Algiers, Enfantin tried through one of his correspondents to establish contact with the Duke of Orleans. This attempt led to the tragi-comic consequence that the Duke graciously offered the "Supreme Father" of the Saint-Simonists the post of sub-prefect. Unfortunately, this did not sober Enfantin. He did not cease to build far-reaching schemes for preaching to crowned heads ("apostolat princier"). These plans led him to commit some very crude errors, true, much more of a theoretical than a practical nature. Heine is known to have been interested in and sympathetic to the Saint-Simonists. The first edition of his book *De l'Allemagne* was dedicated to "Father" Enfantin, who in reply printed a letter under the heading To Heinrich Heine (A Henri Heine) in which he developed some, to say the least, astonishing political views.

In speaking of Germany, Enfantin revealed a tremendous sympathy for Austria (the Austria of Metternich!). In his opinion, Austria represented order, hierarchy, sense of duty and especially of peace. "Recognising that the dogma of freedom and equality is neither full enough nor perfect enough to guide the peoples, let us bless Austria for resisting the invasion of these

* *Œuvres de Saint-Simon et d'Enfantin*, Paris, 1866, t. VIII, p. 168. The letter is on pages 165 and 166 of this volume. The Duchess of Berry was arrested on November 6, and the letter was written on November 9 (1832). It is clear from this how Enfantin hastened to draw women "into politics". After what has been said it is scarcely necessary to add that the word "politics" had here a very peculiar meaning.

purely revolutionary ideas and repelling them even in the person
of a Joseph II; let us bless the sublime patience of that nation,
incessantly subjected to the sabre thrusts of the revolution as
personified by Napoleon.... Let us bless Austria for providing
a noble refuge to the last representatives of feudal law, our old
Bourbons, since God has not yet said his last word on the form
of the transition by means of which mankind abolishes the old
law and ushers in the new. Finally, let us bless her for extending
across Alps a heavy hand which holds down the Italian peoples
and prevents them from stabbing one another. Surrounded by
nations in which there is a ferment of freedom, Austria constantly
reiterates in her calm and authoritative voice: Children, you
have no love for order, you have not matured for freedom."

Further on, Enfantin confesses that war against the Holy
Alliance[241] and against the "obscurantism of the Cabinets" seems
to him to be a pretty shabby affair, "at least for men of a strong
character".*

Heine silently reacted to this letter by removing the dedication
to Enfantin from the later editions of his book *On Germany*.
This, of course, was in itself his most expressive criticism.**

It is unlikely that Enfantin had any predilection for legitimism.
He simply wanted with diplomatic finesse to conduct his apostolic mission among persons in high places who, by their very
position, were disposed to defend "order".

When Louis Bonaparte, who could never have been accused
of legitimism, carried out his coup d'état in France, Enfantin
started to flirt with this lucky adventurer, and even worked out
a whole programme of action for him. True, it was not a particularly definite programme. Enfantin wanted Louis Bonaparte
to serve the cause of good socialism (bon socialisme). This service
was to consist in renouncing militarism and energetically promoting France's industrial development.***

The reader will perhaps have detected an ironical note running
through my exposition. Needless to say, we can scarcely look back
now on Enfantin's apostolic mission among persons in high places
without a smile. But it would be wrong to see this error as Enfantin's alone. This sort of mistake was the persistent and logical
outcome of the negative attitude taken by the utopian socialists
to politics which I pointed out above. *The rejection of politics
led* logically to *political intrigues* (just as it invariable *does* with

---

* Ibid., Vol. X, pp. 118-19.
** However, the letter was favourably received by even such a prominent Saint-Simonist as Olinde Rodrigues (see *Histoire du Saint-Simonisme*,
par S. Charlety, p. 315, note).
*** On this subject see *Œuvres de Saint-Simon et d'Enfantin*, t. X, pp. 200
et 205.

those who commit the same error today). Of course, some representatives of utopian socialism committed in their intrigues more crude errors than others. But this is a detail. The essential thing is that, once having renounced politics and taken to intriguing, even the most outstanding people could not avoid blundering in a manner that seems to us nowadays to be quite improbable.

Here is convincing evidence of this. The "man-terror" (l'homme-terreur) Proudhon, generally speaking, was very unlike the "Supreme Father" Enfantin. In many respects, he was Enfantin's exact opposite. But even he did not avoid making blunders exactly like those astonishing ones committed by Enfantin.

Proudhon is known to have been the father of French *anarchism.** As an anarchist, he regarded politics with the greatest contempt. And yet his contempt for politics did not keep him out of political intrigues. On the contrary, it drove him into them. In one of his letters he remarks that he who engages in politics must "wash his hands in dung".** This washing of hands in dung is precisely political intrigue. How fervently he indulged in it at times may be seen from his book *La révolution sociale, démontrée par le coup d'état du 2 décembre*, in which he does his utmost to convince the reader and above all, of course, Louis Bonaparte himself that the historical meaning of December 2[242] was "democratic and social revolution".***

When *political intriguing* reaches such a pitch of intensity it is more than the logical outcome of a denial of *politics*. It is also perhaps the best indication of the inconsistency and confusion of the *social* views of the utopian socialists who engage in it.

V

I make haste to remind the reader that in nineteenth-century French utopian socialism there was a trend—one of the varieties of *communism*—which did not spurn the class struggle and did not at all reject politics, though regarding it in a very narrow sense. As I said above, this trend was the exception to the general rule. But to grasp well the meaning of this *exception*, we must first of all scrutinise the *rule* itself from all aspects.

Although they rejected the class struggle, the utopian socialists at the same time understood its historical significance. This may

---

* He derived his theory of *anarchy* from Saint-Simon's idea that the role of government in social life diminishes in the course of historical development, and in time will be reduced to nothing.
** "Se laver les mains dans la crotte." (Desjardins, *Proudhon*, t. I, p. 190.)
*** See the fifth edition of the book mentioned, p. 93.

seem paradoxical, but it is true none the less. The reader already knows that in the eyes of Saint-Simon, Fourier and their followers, the Great French Revolution was "a war of the poor against the rich". Indeed, Saint-Simon expressed this noteworthy view of the French Revolution as early as 1802, subsequently developing it in some detail. He said that the basic law in every country is that which governs property (gouverne la propriété) and the institutions protecting it. The aim of the social alliance is production. Consequently, people who are leaders of production have always headed this alliance and always will. Until the fifteenth century the most important branch of social production was agriculture. The leaders of agriculture were the nobility. The civil power was therefore concentrated in their hands.* Little by little, however, a new social force emerged—*the third estate.* In need of support, this estate concluded an alliance with the monarchy and through this alliance determined all the subsequent development of society. In saying this, Saint-Simon had in mind France in particular, and greatly deplored the fact that in the person of Louis XIV the monarchy betrayed the third estate and went over to the side of the aristocracy. The Bourbons paid very dearly for this mistake, which however did not halt the progress of the third estate. The struggle of the new industrial order against the obsolete feudal system gave rise to the French Revolution and determines the most important social events in our days.

Saint-Simon's views on philosophy and history passed from him to Augustin Thierry. Saint-Simon even thought that Guizot, too, made them the basis of his historical researches. It is possible that the great French historian arrived at these views independently of Saint-Simon; such historical views were then fairly widespread. There is no doubt about one thing: Guizot, Thierry, Mignet and all French historians of that trend held precisely those historical views which were originally preached systematically by Saint-Simon. In studying those views, we are involuntarily and frequently reminded of the theory which later came into existence and became known as historical materialism. Those views were without doubt valuable material for the elaboration of this theory. But for some time they got on very well with the most extreme forms of historical idealism. Later, I will explain this apparently strange circumstance. For my present purpose it will suffice to note that, following Saint-Simon and Fourier, the overwhelming majority of the French utopian socialists saw (true, regretfully, but still saw) in the history of Europe

---

* See *Opinions littéraires, philosophiques et industrielles*, Paris, 1825. pp. 144-45. See also "Catéchisme des industriels" in *Œuvres de Saint-Simon...*, Paris, 1832. p. 18.

a long process of class struggle which at times became extremely acute.

The utopian socialists saw the same class struggle in the society in which they lived; and indeed they never ceased to talk of it. They bemoaned the existence of this struggle and worked to bring the warring classes together.* In their practical part, their various systems were nothing more than an aggregate of measures intended to put an end to the class war and establish social peace. But the very fact that they did bemoan the class war and strive for social peace is evidence that they fully recognised the existence of that war. So the question naturally arises: which classes were, in the opinion of the French utopian socialists, the chief contestants in the war going on in modern society? The answer to this question is extremely important for the history of socialist ideas.

Saint-Simon held the view, as has been already indicated, that the most important events of the internal life of the society of his time were determined by the struggle of the new industrial order with the old feudal system—in short, of the industrialists with the feudalists. To Saint-Simon, this struggle was the most important class struggle of his time. He said: "In the course of fifteen centuries, the feudal system gradually disorganised and the industrial system gradually organised. Tactful behaviour on the part of the main representatives of industry will suffice to establish the industrial system once and for all, and to clear society of the ruins of the feudal structure in which our ancestors at one time lived.** But who were those main representatives of industry? Not the proletarians, of course. They were, first, the bankers and, secondly, the big industrialists. Saint-Simon regarded them as the natural representatives and leaders of the entire class of workers. We have seen already how he sometimes intimidated them with what the workers might do. But he did this only to remind them of their duties as the natural leaders of the working class. It is also known that, at least towards the end of his life, Saint-Simon put as the first of these duties concern for the poorest part of the working class. "All social institutions," he said then, "must aim at the moral, intellectual, and physical improvement (amélioration) of the most numerous and poorest class." This was the dominant idea of his last work *Le nouveau christianisme*. But "the most numerous and poorest class" had to be *under the guardianship* of the representatives of industry placed over it; the *leading role* in social life, Saint-Simon argued,

---

* See, for example, Considérant's *Principes du socialisme*, pp. 20-21.
** *Œuvres*, p. 59.

had to belong to just those higher-placed representatives of
industry—the bankers and industrialists.

In so far as he held this opinion, Saint-Simon was the immediate continuer of the cause of the advanced eighteenth-century
people, who saw the victory of the third estate over the temporal
and spiritual aristocracy as their principal social task. The
reader has, of course, heard of the famous words uttered by Sieyès:
"What is the third estate? Nothing. What must it become? Everything." Saint-Simon was a son of the eighteenth century. True,
during the second half of his life the third estate ceased to be
"*nothing*" and became *very much*. But it was not yet "*everything*"
(I remind you that Saint-Simon died in 1825, in the period of the
Restoration), and he tried to make it "everything" as quickly as
possible. That is why, while persisting in inviting the rich to
display concern for the lot of the poor, he did not analyse the
relationships within the third estate itself, i.e., the relations
between the employers on the one hand and the wage-workers
on the other. His attention was wholly taken up with the mutual
relations established after the Revolution between the representatives of the old order and the "industrialists". He gave a striking
and fairly thorough analysis of these relationships in his celebrated *Parabola.**

His pupils said more than once that, while sharing Saint-
Simon's views, they were simultaneously developing them further.
It has to be admitted that in many respects they considerably
surpassed their teacher. For instance, they were a great deal
more interested in economic questions than he had been. They
tried to define the meaning of the expressions: "idle class" and
"working class" from the point of view of economics. Among
the "idle class" they included the landowners living on land rent,
and the capitalists whose incomes were made up of interest paid
on their capital. Enfantin had a lot to say about these categories
of persons in his articles on economics published in *Le Producteur*.
It is worth noting, though, that he identified the profits of the
industrialists with wages. He says outright, in objecting to Ricardo's theory of rent (with extremely little success, I should add):
"We understand the term 'wages' to cover the employer's profits,
since we regard his profits as payment for his labour."** Such
a conception of the relations between the employers and his wage-
workers precluded altogether any thought of antagonism between
the interests of industrial capital and wage labour. The reader
may not have forgotten that many years later Proudhon's ideas

---

* This was published in 1819 in the *Organisateur* and led to Saint-Simon
being prosecuted. Incidentally, this literary trial ended in a triumph for
the accused, the jury finding him not guilty.
** *Le Producteur*, t. I, p. 245.

suffered from a similar unclarity. Earlier in this article I quoted an extract from an article of his that appeared in 1850, inviting the *bourgeoisie* to join with the proletariat in the struggle against *"the noble man and the capitalist"*.* Invitations of this kind could have come only from the pen of a man who understood capitalists to mean only those who received interest on capital.

In examining the question of interest on capital, Enfantin dwells on the fact that in industrially developed countries, the rate of interest is considerably lower than in the backward countries. He concludes from this that the income of all the "idle class" in general, by the very development of industry, tends constantly to *diminish*. "We think ...," he says, "that the business of the idle man, the inactive owner of property, grows worse and worse and that, like capital, the land is rented out on conditions more and more favourable to those who take the trouble to work it."** This, you can see, is quite an optimistic view of the state of affairs in civilised society. To this should be added that, in Enfantin's opinion, there was a constant increase *not only* of the share in the national income taken by the owners *together* with the wage-workers: he thought that the workers' share, too, was constantly increasing. It is clear that if the total share of the national income received by the *employers together with the workers* constitutes a given sum, the part which goes to the *workers* proper can be increased only at the expense of the share that goes into the pockets of the *employers*. This shows that Enfantin had no grounds for considering that the interests of the wage-worker were at one with the interests of the employer. But he does not dwell on this side of the question at all. He is content with the remark that now the workers are better fed and clothed than they were before.*** It did not occur to him that the improvement of the living conditions of the working class could go hand in hand with a diminution of their share in the national income, that is to say, with an increase in their exploitation by the employers, i.e. with their *relative* impoverishment.

In general, it should be noted that Enfantin's knowledge of economics was very superficial, though he was the chief theoretician in this field in the pages of *Le Producteur*. Ricardo, with whom he disputed much, was evidently known to him only at second hand, and J. B. Say appeared to him to be a great economist. There is nothing surprising in this. The main question for Enfantin as for all utopian socialists was not what *is*, but what *should be*. It was natural, therefore, that he scrutinised with care what *is* only until such times as his views on what *should be*

---

* My italics.
** *Le Producteur*, t. I, p. 245.
*** Ibid., p. 558.

were clearly formed. But, again, as with all other utopian socialists, even this conception was determined primarily by *moral*
considerations. Consequently, Enfantin lectures the bourgeois
economists on morality more often than he criticises their theories.*

Le Producteur was being published at a time when the views
of the Saint-Simonists were still far from completely formed.
It may be assumed that subsequently the economic theories of
this school became more profound in content. In fact, that is not
the case. The lectures delivered by Isaac Pereire in 1831 reveal
the same unclarity concerning the relation between industrial
capital and wage labour and the same quite untenable argument
that "the dues paid by labour to idleness" are constantly decreas-
ing. "As these dues decrease, not only will the workers' happiness increase, but production will be able to become much more
regular."**

Taking into consideration the unclear views of the Saint-
Simonists on the economy of society in their day, it must be
admitted that their *theory*, to say nothing of their peaceful *mood*,
provided them with no grounds whatever for working out plans
of practical activity based on the existence of antagonistic interests of wage labour and business capital. On the contrary, it was
bound to impel them to preach social peace. True, they recognised that the interests of the *working* class and the class of *idle*
owners were antagonistic. To eliminate this antagonism, they
proposed the abolition of inheritance, which they said would
result in the transfer of the means of production to social ownership. In *this* respect they did really go a long way further than
their teacher, who had given no thought to changing the form
of property. But if, as Enfantin asserted, the business of the
idle owner was worsening all the time, in other words, if the
position of this class was becoming more and more difficult
through the reduction of interest rates, the very course of events
would ensure the possibility of a peaceful realisation of the most

---

* One very prominent Saint-Simonist, who later became a famous financier, Isaac Pereire, in one of his lectures on political economy read in 1831,
promising to examine the question of wealth distribution in contemporary
society, said frankly: "Nous examinerons la moralité de cet état de choses."
(*Religion saint-simonienne.—Leçons sur l'industrie et les finances*, Paris, 1832,
p. 3.) [We shall examine the morality of this order of things.] Do not imagine
that the word "moralité" is used here in a figurative sense. Pereire says in the
preface to the volume of his lectures: "In the first two lectures, we set out to
refute (repousser) the concept of *value* as it is taught by present-day economists; we fought it because it is an expression *of the struggle, the antagonism*
prevailing in present-day society." That is nothing else but a lecture on
morality addressed to the bourgeois economists, instead of an analysis of the
bourgeois relations of production.
** Ibid., p. 14.

important of the reforms proposed by the Saint-Simonists—the abolition of inheritance. In this respect too, therefore, the Saint-Simonists could preserve their cherished belief in the peaceful course of social development.

The reader can easily realise that, in advancing the abolition of inheritance, the Saint-Simonists frightened the life out of the philistines of their day. The philistines looked on the Saint-Simonists as communists, and even do so to some extent today. (Only recently, one historian of Russian social thought referred to them as such.) However, there was and is no reason to consider them as communists, a fact which they themselves constantly pointed out in their publications.

According to the teaching of the Saint-Simonists, the means of production which became the property of society would be placed at the disposal of those producers who were most capable of operating them successfully. But there was never any thought in their minds of restoring small-scale industry; they were ardent supporters of large-scale industrial enterprises. How was the income from these enterprises to be distributed? The Saint-Simonists said: *to each according to his ability, to each ability according to its works* (à chacun selon sa capacité, à chaque capacité selon ses oeuvres). How to determine works? We know that Enfantin believed that the industrialist's profit constituted his wages. It is but a simple step from this to the belief that if a particular owner receives an incomparably higher "wage" than his worker, this is a result of the difference in the amount of his work. It is not surprising, therefore, that many socialists of other schools,—for instance, in France the communists, Louis Blanc and others, in Russia N. G. Chernyshevsky—decisively rejected the Saint-Simonist principle of to each according to ability and works. Arguments of this kind may seem quite pointless: what sense is there in disputing how to divide the bear's skin before the animal is killed? And it is easy to observe that the critical methods of Saint-Simonists' socialist opponents were not always satisfactory. Indeed, they mostly repeated the errors of the Saint-Simonists; questions that should have been examined from the angle of *production relations, that is to say, of social economy,* were discussed by them from the standpoint of *morality, justice,* and suchlike *abstract principles.* Yet despite the great error in their method, they were, after their own fashion, right. The Saint-Simonist principle of distribution which they condemned contained all the unclarity we noted already in the Saint-Simonist teaching on the production relations of society of their day. He who confuses the employer's profit with wages when speaking of present-day society runs a very serious risk of retaining in his plan for a future social system a fairly wide place for "the exploitation of man by man". It is all the same to the proletarian who owns the factory in which by his labour he enriches the employers: whether it belongs to the factory owner himself, or to some other private person, or, finally, to society. The Saint-Simonists could claim in their defence that in a society constructed according to their plan industry would be organised and not disorganised as it is now. The place of the present owners would be taken by leaders of industry in the service of society and receiving their remuneration from society. But this would again bring us back to the old question: *how to assess the size of the remuneration to be given to the "leaders of industry"*? In other words, will the Saint-Simonist society not be based upon the exploitation of the vast majority of the producing population by these relatively few leaders? To this, the Saint-Simonists could again give no reply except to refer to his "works", which explains nothing. In fact, they simply could not think out this subject, in *its economic* aspect, to the end.

VI

Other schools of utopian socialism did not share the optimistic views of the Saint-Simonists regarding the course of economic development in modern society. Saint-Simon's great contemporary and rival, Fourier, categorically refused to admit that the position of the working—or, as he expressed it, the poor—class was improving. "Social progress is an illusion," he insisted. "The wealthy class goes forward, but the poor class remains as it was, at zero."* At times he displays even greater pessimism, stating that "the position of the poor in modern society is worse than that of the savage, who has at least the right to kill game and to fish where he pleases, and even to steal from anyone apart from his fellow-tribesmen. The savage, moreover, is as carefree as the animals, a trait that is utterly foreign to civilised man. The freedom granted to the poor man by present-day society is a sham, since while depriving him of the advantages the savage has access to, it does not even guarantee him that minimum means of subsistence that might be a compensation for the loss of these advantages."** Finally, Fourier declares that the position of the people in civilised society, in spite of the sophists who sing the praises of progress, is worse than the lot of the wild beasts.*** True to his habit of calculating and classifying even what does not lend itself to calculation and classification Fourier indicates

---

* "Publication de manuscripts", v. 2, p. 23. Quoted from Bourgin's *Fourier*, Paris, 1905, p. 207.
** *Œuvres complètes de Ch. Fourier*, Paris, 1841, t. III, pp. 163-70.
*** Ibid., t. IV, p. 193.

twelve "disgrâces des industrieux" (misfortunes of industrial workers) to which, for the sake of exactitude, he adds another four. Although this attempt to calculate the misfortunes of civilised man may provoke a smile—the more so since our author apologises for his calculation being incomplete and suggests leaving it to more experienced people to finish—it does reveal a rare perspicacity. As an example, I shall refer to the "second" misfortune, which is that civilised man is engaged in labour that overtaxes his strength, risks undermining his health, on which the existence of his children and his own depend. Then there is Fourier's "tenth" misfortune, which he calls anticipated poverty and which consists of the worker's fear of losing his wage. Lastly, the "seventh" misfortune, caused by the increasing luxury of the rich, at the sight of which the poor man feels himself to be even poorer (the present-day theory of relative impoverishment).* If the Saint-Simonists did not make any distinction between the positions of the wage-workers and the employers, Fourier on the other hand sees that the interests of these two social categories are antagonistic, and asserts that in modern society the success of industrial enterprises is founded upon the impoverishment of the workers, that is to say, the reduction of their wages to the lowest possible level.** Whereas the Saint-Simonists see in the development of banks the last word in progress, Fourier thunders against the bankers and the stock-exchange speculators. Where the Saint-Simonists are enraptured by the development of large-scale industry, Fourier proves that it brings with it the concentration of capital and the restoration of feudalism in a new financial, commercial and industrial form.

His followers express themselves in the same spirit. Considérant says: "The first feudalism, which emerged from military conquest, gave the land to the military leaders and tied the conquered population to the persons of the conquerors by the bonds of serfdom. Since the trade and industrial war, in the form of that competition whereby Capital and Speculation inevitably become the rulers over poor Labour has replaced military war" (sic!), "it has tended to establish and in fact has always established a new serfdom by means of its conquests. Now there comes into being, not *personal and immediate dependence*, but a mediate and collective dependence, mass rule over the destitute classes by the class that owns capital, machinery, and the instruments of labour. In fact, *taken collectively* the urban and rural proletarians are in a position of absolute dependence on the owners of the instruments of labour. This great economic and political

---

* *Œuvres complètes*, t. IV, pp. 191-92.
** "Publication de manuscrits", t. III, p. 4. Quoted from Bourgin's *Proudhon*, p. 231.

fact is expressed in the following formula of practical life: *in order to have a piece of bread each worker must find himself a master.* (I know that you now say *employer*, but in its pristine simplicity the tongue keeps repeating *master*: and it will be justified, until the New Order is established, until the economic relations of the present feudal order, of financial, industrial and commercial feudalism are replaced by new relations)."*

Fourier already called the industrial crises occurring periodically in modern society *crises of plethora*, and asserted that the *poverty* of this society was engendered by its *wealth.* Considérant developed this profound thought further. He pointed to the example of England, "choking from its own plethora", and pronounced absurd and inhuman a social order that "condemns the working class to hunger, and at the same time suffers from a shortage of consumers".

Competition destroy the intermediate social strata, he goes on, and leads to the division of society into two classes, "a few having everything and a large number having nothing".**

Generally speaking, the Fourierists very often took the opposite view to the Saint-Simonists on economic questions, and this was vividly shown in their respective attitudes to the problem of the development of the productive forces in France as she was then, as well as in the whole civilised world. The Saint-Simonists were unreservedly enthusiastic in welcoming the construction of railways, and dreamed of the cutting of the Suez and Panama canals.*** The Fourierists, on the contrary, considered that before building railways it was essential to reconcile the interests of the employers and the workers, and to establish the correct distribution of products between capital, labour, and talent through the establishment of phalansteries.**** Of course the Fourierists were completely in the wrong here; labour and capital in France have not been "reconciled" even up to the pres-

---

* *Le socialisme devant le vieux monde, ou le vivant devant les morts,* Paris, 1849, p. 13. Compare *Principes dusocialisme,* p. 6.
** *Principes du socialisme,* pp. 22-23; 9-11.
*** Enfantin himself took part in the French railway business and apparently helped to improve it. At the end of 1846, he founded the Société d'études pour le canal de Suez, but when the enterprise was well on the way to success, it was taken out of his hands by Ferdinand de Lesseps. In this connection, see Charlety's *Histoire du saint-simonisme,* pp. 372, 398, 399, et seq.
**** See the extremely interesting brochure by Considérant: *Déraison et dangers de l'engouement pour les chemins en fer,* Paris, 1838. In the phalansteries, the product had to be divided out as follows: $5/12$ to labour; $4/12$ to capital, and $3/12$ to talent. So that in spite of all, the Fourierists were at one with the Saint-Simonists in this sense, that in their plan for social construction they also set aside a place for the exploitation of labour by capital, as the communists of all shades pointed out at the time.

ent day. Yet what would France be like today without railways? In reply to the argument that the construction of railways would lead to the strengthening of industrial feudalism, Enfantin said that industrial feudalism was inevitable as a transitional stage of social development. That was right. But at once Enfantin slid back into utopia, adding that, thanks to the discoveries of Saint-Simon and the Saint-Simonists, the secret of peaceful social transformation was now known to mankind, so that the latter was able consciously and without upheavals to put an end to industrial feudalism.* He was also utopian when he maintained that, just as it had been necessary, for example, in the period of the Reformation to go along with Luther and Calvin, so now it was necessary to "fly to Rothschild". The reformers of the nineteenth century had quite a different task. The urge "to Rothschild" was the Saint-Simonist version of: "Let's go for training to capitalism."[243]

Like the Fourierists, Louis Blanc decidedly did not share the Saint-Simonists' optimistic views on the position of hired labour. In his *Organisation du travail*, he wrote that, under the impact of competition, wages tended consistently downwards, with the most serious consequences for the working class: it was degenerating. And—again like the Fourierists—Louis Blanc pointed to the growth of property inequality in contemporary society, and in this respect he also spoke of the concentration of landownership and not only of capital.** Whereas the Saint-Simonists opposed the *industrial* class to the *idle* class, Louis Blanc opposes the *"people"* to the *"bourgeoisie"*. But it is well worth noting that his definition of the bourgeoisie fits the lower strata of this class more than it does the higher. "By the bourgeoisie," he says, "I understand the aggregate of those citizens who, owning either instruments of labour or capital, work with means of their own and depend on others only to a certain extent." That is either very badly put or is very close to Proudhon's conception of the bourgeoisie, that is, to the conception of the *petty* bourgeoisie. No less remarkable is the fact that, in speaking of the "people", Louis Blanc has in mind the *proletarians* proper, "that aggregate of citizens who, having no capital, are entirely dependent on others as regards the primary necessities of life".*** Louis Blanc observes the formation of a new social class, but sees it through the spectacles of old democratic conceptions, and therefore gives this class an old name, dear to the hearts of the democrats.

---

* Charlety, op. cit., p. 368.
** See the second edition of this work, pp. 10, 11, 50, 56, and 64.
*** *Histoire de dix ans, 1830-1840*, 4-me edition, t. I, p. 8, footnote.

I shall refer to two more socialist writers of those days: one of them is still fairly well known, while the other has been completely forgotten, although he fully deserves to be mentioned. I have in mind Pierre Leroux and his friend Jean Reynaud. Both of them went through the school of Saint-Simonism and early on took a critical attitude to this school. However, here I am interested only in their views on the role and position of labour in present-day society.

As early as 1832, when the vast majority of Saint-Simonists discerned in the prevailing society only the antagonism of interests between the working class and the idle owners, and regarded "politics" as the obsolete prejudice of backward people, Jean Reynaud published an article in the April issue of *Revue Encyclopédique* under the heading: "De la nécessité d'une représentation spéciale pour les prolétaires", in which he expounded views that were truly remarkable for that period.

"I say," he wrote, "that the people consists of two classes, distinct both in their situation and their interests: the proletarians and the bourgeoisie. I call proletarians the people who produce all the wealth of the nation; who have nothing apart from the daily wage for their labour; whose work depends on causes outside of their control; who from the fruits of their own labour receive daily only a small part, which is continuously being reduced by competition; whose future depends only on the precarious hopes of an industry that is unreliable and chaotic in its progress, and who have nothing to expect in their old age but a place in hospital or an untimely death." To this vivid description of the proletariat, there is added an equally vivid description of the bourgeoisie. "By bourgeois I understand the people to whose fate the fate of the proletarians is subordinated and chained; the people who possess capital and live on the income from it; those who hold industry in their pay and who raise or lower it according to their whims in consumption; who fully enjoy the present and have no wish for their future except that what they had yesterday should continue, and that there should exist for all eternity the constitution which gives them the first place and the best share."

It might perhaps be assumed on the basis of Reynaud's statement that the bourgeoisie are essentially those who live on the income from their capital, that like all other Saint-Simonists he too had in mind only the *idle owners*, i. e., the *rentiers*. Such an assumption would be wrong. Further on in his article he explains his idea very well. As it turns out, he puts among the bourgeoisie "the 2,000 manufacturers of Lyons, the 500 manufacturers of St. Etienne and all the feudal possessors of industry". This makes it clear that his definition fully includes the *representatives of indus-*

rial capital. He is perfectly well aware that between the classes of the bourgeoisie and the proletariat there may be also intermediate social strata. But he is not dismayed by this. "I may be told," he says, "that these two classes do not exist, since there is no insuperable barrier or indestructible wall between them, and there exist bourgeois who work and proletarians who own property. To this I will reply that between the most sharply distinct shades there are always intermediate shades, and that in our colonies it will not occur to anyone to deny the existence of black and white people, simply because there are mulattoes and half-breeds among them."

Reynaud believed there had been a time when the bourgeoisie, representing their own personal interests, simultaneously represented the interests of the proletariat. That was in the period of the Restoration. But now that the destruction of the feudal nobility, which was prepared by the bourgeoisie, has been completed by the proletariat, the interests of these two classes have parted, making it essential for the proletariat to have special political representation.

It would be difficult to put this more clearly. Reynaud, however, is yet a son of his time. He has not entirely lost the fearful recollections of 1793. He is afraid of civil war; consequently he makes reservations. According to him, although the interests of the bourgeoisie are distinct from the interests of the proletariat, nevertheless they do not contradict each other (ne sont pas contradictoires). Therefore the two classes can work amicably together to improve legislation.*

Pierre Leroux held the same opinions on the relationship of the proletariat to the bourgeoisie.** In the book I have just mentioned in a footnote, *De la plutocratie ou du gouvernement des riches*, he develops this view in detail. But the more detail he provides, the more obvious and even the greater is the unclarity of this view, an unclarity that can already be noticed to some extent in Reynaud's work. It consists of this.

Reynaud had already said: "I call proletarians the workers in the towns and the peasants in the countryside" (les paysans de campagne). One must suppose that in recognising the existence in present-day society of *proletarians owning property*, he was thinking precisely of the *"peasants in the countryside"*. With a wealth of detail, Leroux enlarges on this kind of "proletar-

---

* Reynaud's remarkable article is reproduced in part in *De la plutocratie* by Pierre Leroux, Boussac, 1848, Chapter XXXIV, "Le prolétaire et le bourgeois" and apparently was published in full in Vol. I of the unfinished edition of Pierre Leroux's *Works* (Paris, 1850), pp. 346-64.

** Leroux is quite aware that his views on industrialism differ radically from Saint-Simon's. He even polemises with his former teacher.

ian". He asks: "Is the peasant with a hectare of land a proletarian or a property-owner?" In his opinion, he is a proletarian,
since his hectare of land furnishes him with a livelihood only to
the degree that he *applies heavy manual labour to it daily.* What
does it matter that this peasant is a *landowner,* if his ownership
of land permits him to live only by arduous daily work? It is only
when the instruments of labour have reached a certain limit that
they are sufficiently productive to bring in a rent adequate for
the subsistence of the owner. Within this limit one is a proletarian; one is a property-owner only beyond it."*

Leroux asks whether the man who owns a small plot of land is
a property-owner *or* a proletarian. This question presumes that
one cannot be a proletarian and an owner at one and the same
time. But immediately after this, Leroux goes on to declare that
the man to whom a hectare of land belongs, i.e., the *owner* of one
hectare, is a *proletarian.* Here, the presumption that *one cannot be*
simultaneously a *property-owner* and a *proletarian* is quietly
shelved. Why? Because the owner of the plot *works.* But this suffices only to acknowledge him as a *working-owner.* The identification
of a working-owner with a proletarian is, in any case, arbitrary.
Why did Leroux consider it not only permissible, but, indeed,
inevitable? Only because the man who owns a small plot of land
is often very poor. To Pierre Leroux, *the poor man and the proletarian* are one and the same. This is why he lists among the proletarians all *beggars,* whom he calculates in France to number four
millions, whereas the number employed in industry and commerce,
by his own calculation, is not more than half of that figure.**
So that in France, according to him, out of a population of thirty-
four and a half million there are as many as thirty million proletarians.***

In Reynaud's argument "proletarian-owners" were compared
with mulattoes and half-breeds, who in the colonies occupy a middle position between the black and the white races. Leroux, however, made out that these "mulattoes" and "half-breeds" constituted
the larger part of the French *proletariat.*

Needless to say, from the point of view of economics, Leroux's
calculations would often not hold water. But to understand him
we have to remember that he is arguing not so much from the
standpoint of *economics* as from the standpoint of *morality.* He
saw his task not as having to determine exactly the relations of
production prevailing in France, but to demonstrate how many
French people were living in poverty and by their poverty were

---

* See the second edition of this book (the first edition was published in
1843), pp. 23-24.
** Ibid., pp. 79 and 167.
*** Ibid., p. 25.

a reminder of the need for social reform. And inasmuch as he understood this to be his task he was in the right, although this did not prevent him from making obvious errors in logic: on the contrary, it caused him to make them.

From this angle, Leroux's methods of reasoning remind one very much of our Narodniks' mode of thought.* Be that as it may, it cannot be denied that his book *De la plutocratie* and some of his other works—for example, the articles published later under the title *Malthus et les économistes, ou y aura-t-il toujours des pauvres?*—contain a much deeper analysis of the relations between the wage-worker and the capitalist than what we find in the works of Enfantin and other orthodox Saint-Simonists. And, of course, this is certainly a great credit to him.

However, these first steps in socialist analysis sometimes lead to quite unexpected theoretical results. To Fourier and his pupils, especially Toussenel as well as Pierre Leroux, Désamy and others, the main culprits of financial and industrial "feudalism" were the *Jews.* Fourier protested against equal rights for the Jews. Leroux pointed to them as "the kings of our epoch".** The Fourierist Toussenel, as late as the first half of the 1840s, advocated an alliance between the July monarchy and the people for the struggle against the Jews. "Force to power! Death to parasitism!" he proclaimed. "War on the Jews! There is the motto of the new revolution!"*** These theoretical errors, which, happily, did not do any great practical harm in France, had not been surmounted by some varieties of utopian socialism right to the end of their existence. And this, of course, is no small minus in the algebraic sum of their distinguishing features.

In conclusion, I will add that the *economic* views of the French socialists were far removed from the clarity and orderliness of the economic views expounded by English socialist writers in the 1820s and 1830s: Hodgskin, Thompson, Gray, Edmonds, Bray and others. The reason for this is clear: Britain was very far in advance of France in economic development.

VII

Let us look back. In the person of Saint-Simon, French utopian socialism enters the scene as the direct continuation of the work performed by the ideologists of the third estate in the eighteenth century. It champions the interests of this estate against those of

---

* I think that Mr. Peshekhonov, for instance, would have fully accepted them.

** See the collection of articles *Malthus et les économistes*, t. I, "Les juifs, rois de l'époque".

*** *Les juifs, rois de l'époque. Histoire de la féodalité financière*, t. I, 2-me édition. Paris, 1847, pp. 286-90.

the aristocracy. But in doing so it has two distinctive features. First of all, under the influence of the events of 1793, it rejects the idea of the class struggle.* Secondly, it insists on attention to the plight of the disinherited, proclaiming—even in the form of religious precepts—as a duty the all-round improvement of the condition of "the poorest and most numerous class". The fulfilling of this duty falls primarily on "the leaders of industry", who are ordained to play a directing role in social life. To Saint-Simon and the Saint-Simonists, the interests of the leaders of industry are in complete conformity with the interests of the working class.

Fourier and his followers penetrate much more deeply into the mysteries of the rising capitalist order. Nevertheless, they no less determinedly reject the class struggle; they, too, address themselves to the "rich" and not to the "poor". The great majority of the founders of other socialist systems follow the example set by these first two schools of utopian socialism. The plans of social reform drawn up by these founders represent nothing else but a series of measures promising to reconcile the classes through the establishment of social harmony. The authors of these plans consider that the initiative for their realisation must belong to the upper classes. In other words, the utopian socialists leave no room for the *self-activity of the proletariat*: indeed, the very concept of the latter, at first, does not emerge from their general conception of the "working class". This is in keeping with the comparatively undeveloped state of social relations in France in the first quarter of the nineteenth century. The very rejection of politics, which we know to be one of the main distinguishing features of utopian socialism, is in the closest causal connection with these poorly-developed social relations. Consciousness does not determine being; it is being that determines consciousness. So long as the proletariat had not emerged as an independent social force, the political struggle could signify only the struggle between different sections of the ruling class, who had not the slightest interest in the fate of "the poorest and most numerous class". Consequently the political struggle presented no interest at all for the utopian socialists, inasmuch as they were seeking to better the lot of just that class. Besides, politics spells struggle, while the utopian socialists did not want struggle: their aim was to reconcile all sections of society. Consequently, they declared politics a mistake,

---

* Saint-Simon's rejection of the idea of class struggle was, strictly speaking, a rejection of the *revolutionary* mode of action. He did not reject, but advocated *peaceful* struggle by the third estate against those who **were** defending the remnants of the old order. It was only the thought of a struggle between the workers and the employers which would have met a sharp and positive condemnation from him. In any case, Saint-Simon was less *indifferent to politics* than were his pupils.

and concentrated their attention on the social field. It seemed to them that reforms adopted in this field had no relation to politics, and so social reformers could live at peace with any government.* It is timely to add, finally, that the formation of such a view was facilitated by the reaction against the belief, current in the eighteenth century, that the political activity of the rulers was the *cause* and the social system the *effect*.

The utopian socialists retained their political indifference for a long time. We know already that this indifference explains their sometimes naive and sometimes unattractive political *intriguing*. But as France's economic development advanced, the contradiction of interests between wage-labour and industrial capital became more acute. And as it became more acute, the "*poor class*" of that country became the *proletariat*. I made reference earlier to Reynaud's statement to the effect that the destruction of the nobility had been prepared by the bourgeoisie and completed by the proletariat. These remarkable words show that, already at the beginning of the 1830s, some representatives of French utopian socialism (true, very few), had begun to recognise the enormous *political* importance of the working class. This awakening consciousness was undoubtedly aroused by the impressions of the July revolution. If it did not develop much between July 1830 and February 1848, the collapse of the monarchy of Louis Philippe gave it a powerful impulse. The Fourierists, who had previously declared politics to be a mistake, themselves began to engage in politics. Elected as a "representative of the people", Considérant joined the Montagnards and, in 1849, had to flee the country because of his participaton in the well-known demonstration of June 13.[244] In the revolutionary period of 1848 to 1850, Proudhon, Pierre Leroux, Louis Blanc, Buchez, Vidal and some others were deputies too. Of all the outstanding representatives of utopian socialism, Cabet was the only one occupied in this period mainly with establishing his communist colony "Icaria" in Texas. "Politics" turned out to be stronger than utopia. It imposed itself on utopian socialism, which had erstwhile called it an error.** But even while acting on the political scene, the utopian socialists did not cease to be utopians. In the period of the most acute class struggle, they

---

* This was a mistake characteristic of not only the utopian socialists. In his *Traité d'économie politique* (*discours préliminaire*) J. B. Say asserts that "in essence, wealth does not depend on political organisation. A well-administered state can flourish under any form of government. Examples are known of nations prospering under absolute monarchs, and of other nations ruined under people's governments", etc. We all know that J. B. Say was in science a typical representative of the French bourgeoisie.

** At that time their attitude to the intelligentsia was already more benevolent than in the period of Saint-Simon and Fourier. However, generally speaking, they continued to condemn the revolutionary mode of action.

went on dreaming of the reconciliation of classes. In the pamphlet I have already cited, *Le socialisme devant le vieux monde, ou le vivant devant les morts,* Considérant expressed his sincere regret that the bourgeoisie had given a bad example to the proletariat by forcibly abolishing the privileges of the nobility during the Great Revolution. On April 14, 1849, the same Considérant delivered a big speech before the National Assembly in which he proposed that the Assembly allocate funds to the Fourierists for the setting up of phalansteries. It need hardly be said that the Assembly did not grant any funds. Finally, I will mention the well-known errors committed by Louis Blanc in 1848.

Dragged into the political arena by the very course of events in France, the utopian socialists were unable to work out correct tactical principles for the simple reason that there was no sound theoretical basis to be found for such principles in utopian socialism.* This brings us to the question: what then is the distinguishing feature, the presence of which in a given socialist system imparts to it a utopian character, regardless of whether details of the system are worthy of attention and approval? This question is the more relevant here since anyone with an inadequate knowledge of the subject might imagine that the word "utopian" has no precise theoretical meaning, and when applied to some plan or system simply indicates disapproval. Indeed the word "utopia" was known to the French utopian socialists, and when one of them, say Fourier, wished to express his dissatisfaction with some aspects of some other socialist school, for example, the Saint-Simonist, he called it, among other things, *utopian.* Of course, to proclaim that a particular system was utopian was tantamount to proclaiming it impracticable. But not one of the utopian socialists had a clear conception of the criterion by which the practicability of a given system could be judged. This is why the word "utopia" had only polemical significance in the writings of the utopian socialists. Nowadays, we see this differently.

VIII

In condemning the bad example set the proletariat by the bourgeoisie in forcibly abolishing the privileges of the nobility, Considérant believed that as early as the end of the eighteenth century it was feasible in France to project a plan of social reform which would by degrees win over all Frenchmen, irrespective of title, rank or estate. The whole trouble was that no one had devised such a plan. That such plans could be invented followed from

---

* I recall the plan proposed by Toussenel relating to an alliance of the people and the monarchy against the Jews.

the fact that their appearance depended on chance. Indeed, Fourier wrote a whole dissertation on this theme, in which he related how chance had led him to discover the "calculus of attraction" (calcul de l'attraction). He said that, like Newton, he arrived at his brilliant discovery thanks to an apple he ate in a Paris restaurant. Subsequently he even remarked that "there were four famous apples, two of them noted for the trouble they caused (Adam's apple and the apple of Paris), and the other two for having enriched science". Fourier went so far as to say that these four famous apples were worthy of a special page in the history of human thought.* His artless gratitude to the apple is a good illustration of the fact that Fourier had no idea of *man's knowledge developing in conformity to law*. He was convinced that discoveries depend entirely on "chance". It did not even occur to him that in the history of human thought the action of "chance" itself may be in causal dependence on a course of events in conformity to law. The utopian socialists not only did not recognise that the course of events determines the progress of ideas; on the contrary, they believed that the development of ideas is the cardinal cause of the historical development of mankind. This was a purely idealist view, borrowed by them from the French Enlighteners of the eighteenth century, who stubbornly maintained that *opinion governs the world* (c'est l'opinion, qui gouverne le monde). Reading the profound utterances of Saint-Simon on the role of the class struggle in the internal history of French society, one might think that he was a man who had completely abandoned the standpoint of historical idealism. In fact, he kept to that standpoint firmly to the end of his days. It may be said that he carried the idealist view of history to the extreme. Not only did he consider the development of ideas as the ultimate cause of the development of social relations, but among ideas he attributed the most important place to *scientific ideas*—the "scientific system of the world"—from which flowed *religious ideas* which, in turn, determined man's *moral concepts*. At the first glance, it is not easy to understand how Saint-Simon squared his extreme historical idealism with the idea we know he had that the law on property is the basic law of society. But the fact is that, even though Saint-Simon believed that property relations are at the root of every given social system, he nevertheless regarded them as having been brought into being by human sentiment and opinion. Thus to him, just as to the eighteenth-century Enlighteners, the world was governed, in the final analysis, by "*opinion*". This idealist outlook was transmitted in its entirety to his pupils. The very same outlook is met with among other

* See my article objecting to Bernstein's report on the possibility of scientific socialism.[245]

utopian socialists. We have already seen how little Fourier was able to link the course of development of human thought with the course of development of human life. His most outstanding pupil, Considérant, wrote: "Ideas are the mothers of facts, and today's facts are the children of yesterday's ideas."* Considérant did not ask himself where yesterday's ideas came from. Neither did any of the other utopian socialists. When they were faced with the question of how the ideas of today—say, the ideas of the Saint-Simonist or the Fourierist school—would become the facts of tomorrow, they—again like the eighteenth-century Enlighteners—confined themselves to pointing to the unconquerable force of truth. In upholding this viewpoint, it was natural for them to reject the class struggle and politics as a weapon of that struggle, for once revealed the truth must be equally accessible to all social classes. More than that. The people of the upper classes, having more leisure and a certain education, are more able to assimilate truth. This makes it perfectly clear that the tactics of the utopian socialists were closely bound up with their historical idealism. I should add here that their political intrigues were also not unconnected with this idealism. Take the example of Fourier. If he did discover the truth by chance, thanks to a chance apple, then any kind of chance circumstance could promote its dissemination. Therefore it is equally useful to knock at all doors, to try to influence all and sundry, and, probably, even in particular those who have much money or much power. And so Fourier obstinately tried to bring influence to bear on the mighty of this world, though of course quite without success.

While describing their opponents' systems as *utopian*, the socialists of the period under review with complete conviction referred to their own systems as *scientific*.** What did they take as a scientific criterion? *Whether the given system corresponded to "the nature of man"*. But to take as term of reference human nature, that is to say, the nature of man generally, taken independently of particular social relationships, is to abandon the ground of historical reality and to rely on an abstract conception: and this road leads directly to utopia. The more often these writers appeal to human nature, while accusing their opponents of utopianism, the more clearly is revealed the utopian character of their own theories.

In taking their conception of human nature as the criterion of scientific construction, the utopian socialists naturally deemed it possible to devise a *perfect* social system: the perfect social system being exactly that which conformed fully to the particular reformer's conception of human nature. This was one of the mo-

---

* *Le socialisme devant le vieux monde*, p. 29.
** For instance, the Fourierist journal, *La Phalange*,[246] is known to have been called *"the organ of social science"*.

tives behind the heated arguments that occurred among the utopian socialists, for example, on the principle of the distribution of products in the future society. They lost sight of the point that the mode of distribution would certainly change with the growth of society's productive forces.

Thus, *the utopian is one who endeavours to construct a perfect social system on the basis of some abstract principle.* All socialists in the period we are discussing come under this definition. So there is no cause to wonder that we now call them utopians without in any way being inspired by ill-will towards them. From the viewpoint of science, utopianism is but a phase in the development of socialist thought. This phase came to an end only when the advanced societies of the civilised world had reached a certain level of economic development. Social being is not determined by consciousness, consciousness is determined by social being.

We have seen that this ultimate truth remained beyond the grasp of the utopian socialists. They were convinced that social being was conditioned by "opinion". Only by taking account of this shall we be able to comprehend how, for example, Saint-Simon could arrive at his "religion".

He says that religious ideas flow from the scientific system of the world. It follows that with the change of this system religious ideas must also change. But since the system has changed very much in comparison with what it was in the Middle Ages, the time has now arrived for the emergence of new religious ideas. With this in mind, Saint-Simon invented a *"new Christianity"*. It would be easy to show that he himself was a confirmed unbeliever. So the question arises: why did he create a new religion? The answer to this perplexing question is that Saint-Simon regarded religion from the standpoint of its *usefulness*: religious ideas determine *moral concepts*, consequently, whoever wishes to influence the moral conduct of his contemporaries must turn to religion. That is what Saint-Simon did. If my explanation seems improbable to the reader, I would remind him that Saint-Simon looked on this question too through the eyes of the eighteenth century: that is to say, he believed that religions are instituted by wise "legislators" in the interests of social well-being.*

Approximately the same considerations were probably also behind the work of Cabet, *Le vrai Christianisme suivant Jesus-Christ.*** In inventing his "true Christianity", Cabet desired to imitate the wise legislators of older days, as the eighteenth-century philosophers imagined them.

---

* He strongly approved of a book issued in 1798 by Dupuis, *Abrégé de l'origine de tous les cultes* which contains just such a view on religion.

** The first edition appeared in 1846 and is said to have had a great success among the workers.

By saying this, I do not want to assert that all the socialist writers we are interested in here shared the views of the eighteenth century on religion. That would be an unwarranted exaggeration. Not all of them had the same attitude to religion as Saint-Simon and Cabet. First of all, the Romantic reaction against the philosophical ideas of the eighteenth century, which was widespread among French intellectuals, also had its influence among the socialists of the 1830s and 1840s, that is to say, socialists, so to speak, of "the second generation", and significantly weakened the influence on them of the anti-religious ideas inherited from the philosophy of the Enlightenment. Saint-Simon's own pupils felt the attraction of the new religion invented by their teacher, not with their heads but with their hearts; with the result that their meetings were sometimes conducted in a spirit of real religious ecstasy. We must remember, too, that when socialism acquired great influence among the then French intelligentsia, it attracted even such people as had never at any time or in any way been subjected to the influence of eighteenth-century philosophy. The most outstanding among these was undoubtedly Jean Lamennais.*[247] It was not by chance that George Sand, in her *Histoire de ma vie*, portrayed Lamennais in such vivid and fascinating colours. He was really a very remarkable man. In him were combined the powerful religious eloquence of the ancient Jewish prophets, the temperament of a revolutionary and a warm sympathy for the people in its miseries. After reading his *Paroles d'un croyant* (1834) Chateaubriand said: "This priest wants to build a revolutionary club in his belfry." Very likely he did. But while setting about the building of a "revolutionary club", Lamennais still remained a Catholic priest. Even after he broke with the Church, his ideas did not throw off the yoke of old theological customs; and just because of this his religious views and sentiments cannot be considered as typical of French socialism of those days. The same might well be said of Philippe Buchez,** who, after a temporary infatuation with socialism in his youth, soon returned to Catholicism.

"The religious seekings" of the French utopian socialists of the "second generation" can be characterised only by religions such as those of the Saint-Simonists (but, I repeat, not Saint-Simon), Pierre Leroux, etc. The extent to which these religions were connected with the Romantic reaction against the Enlightenment philosophy of the eighteenth century may be seen, by the way, in the fact that many Saint-Simonists read with enthusiasm the works of Joseph de Maistre and other writers of that trend. This impor-

---

* Born on June 19, 1782; died on February 28, 1854.
** Born in 1796: died in 1865.

tant circumstance shows that the romantic reaction affected French utopian socialism at a time when it itself still had absolutely nothing in common with any kind of aspiration to freedom. Consequently, we are entitled to compare the "religious seekings" of the socialists of that day with their rejection of the class struggle and their endeavours to secure social peace at any price. All this: the "seekings" for a religion, the aversion for the class struggle, and the love of peace which they elevated into a dogma, were nothing else but the result of the disappointment and weariness that followed "the catastrophe of 1793". In the eyes of the utopian socialists, the terrifying year of revolutionary struggle was the most convincing evidence in favour of their belief that the class struggle in general was utterly futile. Indeed, some of them said that the futility of the class struggle was best demonstrated by the example of 1793.* Being unsympathetic to the revolutionaries of the eighteenth century, they began to pay careful attention to what was said and written by the enemies of the revolution. And though the theoreticians of reaction did not succeed in winning them over, although they continued in part the theoretical work of the eighteenth century, and in part took their own separate and, in a sense, new road, nevertheless the reaction left noticeable traces in their views. If this is not kept in mind, some important aspects of French utopian socialism will remain incomprehensible. Among these are its "religious seekings" in the form they took in the 1830s and 1840s.

IX

Now it is time to say at least a few words about the trend in French utopian socialism which I referred to above as being the exception to the general rule. Contrary to the general rule, this trend, first, was thoroughly impregnated with revolutionary spirit; secondly, it did not reject politics; thirdly, it was foreign to "religious seekings". The most notable exponent of this trend was Auguste Blanqui,** who proclaimed the slogan: Ni dieu, ni maître (Neither God nor master).[249] Whence came this trend which so sharply contradicted "the spirit of the times"?

To understand its origin one must remember that it was known initially as *Babouvism*. Those who belonged to this trend consid-

---

* In opposition to them, the conscious bourgeois ideologists—Guizot, Thierry, Mignet and many others, who did not of course in the least approve of the statesmen of 1793, were decided and conscious advocates of the class struggle, so long as it remained a struggle of the bourgeoisie against the aristocracy. They started to preach social peace only after 1848, when the proletariat took action. I have explained this in detail in another place (see my preface to the second edition of my translation of the *Manifesto of the Communist Party*.[248]

** Born in 1805; died in 1880.

ered themselves to be followers of Babeuf, the famous communist conspirator of the end of the eighteenth century.* In the first half of the 1830s, the most influential figure among the French Babouvists was one who had participated in the "Conspiracy of Equals",[250] a descendant of Michelangelo whose name was Filippo Buonarroti, and who wrote the history of this conspiracy.[251] It is generally known that Babeuf and the other participants of the "Conspiracy of Equals" were extreme revolutionaries. "We demand real equality or death," they wrote in their manifesto. "And we shall have it, it matters not at what price. Woe betide those who place themselves between us and it!" and so on. This language bears no resemblance to the language of the nineteenth-century utopian socialists. And those—comparatively very few—French socialists who remained true to the testament of Babeuf and his comrades were in no way disposed to social peace. Auguste Blanqui contemptuously condemned this inclination of the French socialists of his time, and they, for their part, looked with fear at the incorrigible and tireless revolutionary conspirator.**

We see therefore where the trend we are discussing came from. It was a direct continuation of the revolutionary aspirations of the eighteenth century. Since the great revolutionary storm had fatigued the population of France and imbued a large section of the intelligentsia with negative attitude to the class struggle, this trend could not be a strong one: it represented only a tiny ripple in the broad stream of French socialist thought.*** That is why I described it as an exception to the general rule.

The reader will understand that the few representatives of the French intellectuals who were unaffected by the scare due to the "catastrophe of 1793" had no special reason for rejecting the spiritual testament handed down from the eighteenth century. Con-

---

* F. N. Babeuf was born in 1764. He was sentenced to death and died on the scaffold on February 24, 1797. On the eve of the execution he made an unsuccessful attempt to commit suicide.

** He represented that trend of "political communism" which seemed to Considérant to be the most dangerous (see above).

*** I insist that the revolutionary storm at the end of the eighteenth century engendered a negative attitude precisely to the class struggle. This attitude did not exclude now and then an inclination to a revolutionary mode of action. One of the two future supreme fathers of Saint-Simonism, Bazard, belonged at one time to the Carbonari. Buchez and several more of the future socialists were also in the Carbonari. But the aspirations of the Carbonari were purely "political", that is to say, they did not concern themselves with property relations and so did not threaten to sound the call for "the war of the poor against the rich". Socialism did concern itself with property relations and consequently reminded people of that war. This is why the former conspirators, Bazard, Buchez and others, hastened to proclaim themselves *supporters of social peace* as soon as they became socialists. Again: he will not understand the history of French utopian socialism who forgets the effect of the "catastrophe of 1793" on the minds of the French intellectuals.

sequently, their attitude to religion was exactly the same as that which distinguished the most prominent spokesmen of French philosophy of the Enlightenment. Here we have the source of August Blanqui's challenge: "Neither God nor master!" Similarly with regard to their appreciation of politics: here, too, they followed the example of the men of the eighteenth century. And these men did not turn their backs on politics: on the contrary, they attributed an exaggerated importance to political activity. They were simple enough to believe that the "legislator" could reconstruct the whole of social relations, and even the habits, tastes, and aspirations of the citizens, in accordance with his ideal. It is self-evident that the Babouvists and Blanquists of the period we are considering, who had largely adopted this conception of the activity of the "legislator", were not at all disposed to political indifference. Just the opposite: they were bound to strive to put themselves in the position of "legislators" in order to realise their communist ideals. That is what they hoped to achieve by means of secret societies and plots. Thus their tactics, which flowed logically from their conception of the role of the "legislator", were directly opposed to the tactics of the then utopian socialists. But this was not enough to provide a concrete basis for their tactics. The communism of the Babouvists and the Blanquists suffered from utopianism no less than the socialism of Saint-Simon or Fourier, Cabet or Pierre Leroux. *Only it was utopianism of a different colour*. It was precisely belief in the omnipotence of the "legislator", i.e., of politics, which they had inherited from the eighteenth century that made it utopian. *In this respect*, the revolutionary communism of that time lagged far behind socialism, which, although it dreamed of class reconciliation and committed an enormous theoretical error by its negation of politics, nevertheless enriched theory through studies in the *social field*. The consequence was that some utopian socialists, the most numerous, concentrated their attention on *"social" theory*, while others, representing an exception to the general rule, concentrated on *political action*. Both sinned by their one-sidedness. The elimination of such one-sidedness could only be a matter of the future. It presupposed an entire revolution in theory. Only when socialism renounced the *idealist* conception of history and assimilated the *materialist* conception, did it acquire the theoretical possibility of doing away with utopia. But it is outside the scope of this article to relate the story of how the transition of socialism from utopia to science took place in reality.

UTOPIAN SOCIALISM
IN THE NINETEENTH CENTURY

West European literature in the first half of the nineteenth century was, as it is always and everywhere, an expression of social life. Since an important part in the social life of that period began to be played by phenomena the aggregate of which gave rise in social theory to the so-called social question, it seems relevant to preface a review of that literature with a brief outline of the teachings of the utopian socialists. By stepping beyond the limits of the history of literature, in the narrow meaning of the term, such a characterisation will help us to understand the literary trends proper. But for lack of space I shall have to confine myself to indicating the most important shades of nineteenth-century utopian socialism and elucidating the main influences that determined their development.

As Engels pointed out in his polemic with Dühring, nineteenth-century socialism seems at first glance to be but a further development of the conclusions arrived at by the eighteenth-century philosophy of Enlightenment. As an example, I will mention that the socialist theoreticians of that period very readily appeal to *natural law* [252] which held such an important place in the arguments of the French Enlighteners. Besides, there is not the slightest doubt that the socialists took over in its entirety the teaching on man adhered to by these Enlighteners in general and the materialists—La Mettrie, Holbach, Diderot, and Helvétius in France, and Hartley and Priestley in England—in particular. Thus, already William Godwin (1756-1836) proceeded from the proposition worked out by the materialists that the virtues and vices of every man are determined by circumstances which, taken together, constitute the history of his life.* Godwin concluded from

---

* Leslie Stephen finds that in intellectual temperament Godwin, more than any other English thinker, resembled the French theorists of the pre-revolutionary period (*History of English Thought in the Eighteenth Century by Leslie Stephen*, Second Edition, London, 1881, Vol. II, p. 264). Let us assume that is so. But Godwin's theoretical premise was exactly the same as, for example, that of Owen, Fourier, and other outstanding socialists of the European continent.

this that if this set of circumstances were given the appropriate character, vice would be completely eradicated from the world. After this he had only to decide precisely which measures were capable of giving this set of circumstances the desired character. He examined this question in his main work, *Inquiry Concerning Political Justice and Its Influence on General Virtue and Happiness,* published in 1793. The results of his study were very similar to what is known now as anarchist communism. In this respect, many of the nineteenth-century socialists strongly differ from him. But they are at one with him in that they take as their starting point the materialists' teaching on the formation of the human character which they had assimilated.

This was the most important of the theoretical influences under which the socialist doctrine of the nineteenth century took shape. Among the *practical* influences, the most decisive was the influence of the industrial revolution in Britain at the end of the eighteenth century as well as of the political revolution which is called the Great French Revolution—especially the *terrorist* period of that revolution. It goes without saying that the influence of the industrial revolution was most strongly felt in Britain and the influence of the Great Revolution in France.

A. BRITISH UTOPIAN SOCIALISM

1

I am allocating first place to Britain just because that country earlier than all others went through the industrial revolution which for a long time determined the internal history of civilised societies to come. This revolution was characterised by the rapid development of machine production, which affected production relations in the sense that independent producers were replaced by hired workers, employed in more or less large-scale enterprises under the command and for the benefit of capitalists. This change in the production relations brought much severe and prolonged suffering to the working population of Britain. Its harmful results were aggravated by the so-called *enclosures*, which accompanied the change-over from small to large-scale farming. The reader will understand that the "enclosures", i.e., the seizure by the big landowners of the lands belonging previously to village communities and the "consolidation" of small farms into large ones, were bound to lead to the migration of a considerable part of the rural population to industrial centres. It is easy to realise also that the villagers expulsed from their old homes increased the supply of "hands" on the labour market, thereby lowering wages. Never

before had pauperism reached such formidable proportions in
Britain as it did in the period immediately following the "industrial revolution". In 1784, the poor tax reached some five shillings
per head of the population, and by 1818 it had risen to thirteen
shillings and threepence. Exhausted by want, the working people
of Britain were in a state of constant ferment: agricultural labourers set fire to farms, industrial workers smashed factory machines.
These were the first, as yet instinctive, steps on the way of protest
taken by the oppressed against their oppressors. At the beginning
of this period only a very small section of the working class had
reached the degree of intellectual development which enabled it
to begin the conscious struggle for a better future. This section
was attracted by radical political theories and sympathised with
the French revolutionaries. Already in 1792, the London Corresponding Society[253] was formed, in which there were many workers,
artisans, and small traders. Following the fashion of the French
revolutionaries, the members of this society addressed each other
as *citizen*, and displayed very revolutionary sentiments, especially
after the execution of Louis XVI. However thin the democratic
stratum capable of becoming inspired by the advanced ideas of the
time, its threatening mood aroused great alarm in the ruling
circles, which were following with trepidation what was then
taking place in France. The British Government adopted against
its domestic "Jacobins", a series of repressive measures which boiled
down to restrictions on free speech, on the organising of trade
unions, and on assembly. At the same time the ideologists of the
upper classes felt themselves obliged to reinforce the efforts of the
police in maintaining order and to direct the "*spiritual weapon*"
against the revolutionaries. One of the literary monuments of this
intellectual reaction was the much-vaunted investigation by
Malthus into the law of population:[254] it was provoked by Godwin's above-mentioned work on "political justice". Godwin attributed all human miseries to the working of governments and social
institutions, while Malthus tried to show that they were caused
not by governments or institutions, but by an inexorable law of
nature by which the population always grows faster than the
means of subsistence.

Although the British industrial revolution had such severe
repercussions on the condition of the working class, it also meant
an enormous increase in the country's productive forces. This
was strikingly evident to all investigators. It gave many of them
the occasion to declare that the sufferings of the working class
were only temporary, and that in general everything was going
splendidly. This optimistic view however was not shared by
everyone. There were people who could not observe the sufferings
of others with such Olympian calm. The most courageous and

thoughtful of these created the British socialist literature of the first half of the last century.*

In 1805, Dr. Charles Hall (1745-1825) published the results of his investigations [255] into the question of how "civilisation"—he had in view, strictly speaking, the growth of the forces of production in the civilised countries—affected the condition of the working people. Hall proved that the masses grew poorer because of "civilisation": "Hence, the increase of the wealth or power of some is the cause of the increase of poverty and subjection of the others."**

This proposition is very important for the history of theory, since it demonstrates how clearly British socialism in the person of Charles Hall already perceived the opposition of interests between the "rich" and the "poor" classes. And it should be noted that by the "poor" class Hall meant the class of people who live by the sale of their "labour", that is to say, the *proletarians*, while by the "rich" he meant the capitalists and the landowners, whose prosperity is founded on the economic exploitation of the "poor".

As the "rich" live by the economic exploitation of the "poor", the interests of these two classes are diametrically opposed. In Hall's book there is a section (XV) which is headed: "On the Different Interests of the Rich and Poor". The gist of our author's argument is as follows.

Every rich man must be considered as the *buyer*, every poor man as the *seller*, of labour. It is in the interest of the rich man to get as much as he can out of the labour he has bought of the poor man and to pay as little as possible for it. In other words, he wants to get as great a part as possible of the product created by the worker's labour; the worker, on the other hand, endeavours to get as large a part as possible of that product. Hence their mutual struggle. But it is an unequal struggle. Deprived of the means of subsistence, the workers are usually compelled to surrender, just as a garrison short of provisions surrenders to the enemy. Moreover, strikes are often crushed by military force, whereas only in a few

---

* The "enclosures" gave rise to a whole literature devoted to the agrarian reform. This literature, for example, the works of Thomas Spence, William Ogilvie and Thomas Paine, is in its way very remarkable, and played a fairly significant part in promoting the development of socialist theory in Britain. However, I cannot deal with this here, if only because, belonging to the eighteenth century, it is outside the scope of my theme even chronologically.

** British socialist writings of the first half of the nineteenth century are now very rare. Consequently, in speaking of some of them, I am compelled to quote from recently published German translations. B. Oldenberg translated into German Hall's book under the title of *Die Wirkungen der Zivilisation auf die Massen*, Leipzig, 1905. This was the fourth in a series published by the late Professor G. Adler under the general title of *Hauptwerke des Sozialismus und der Sozialpolitik*. The quotation from Hall is on page 29 of Oldenberg's translation.

states does the law forbid the masters to combine for the purpose
of lowering wages.

Hall compares the position of the agricultural labourer with
that of the farmer's ox or horse. If there is any difference, it is not
in the labourer's favour, for the master sustains no loss by the
death of his worker, but he does by the death of his ox or horse.*
The masters show great resolution in defending their economic
interests in the struggle with the workers. As against this, the
workers are not equally resolute in the struggle against the
masters; poverty deprives them of the economic and moral powers
of resistance.** Furthermore, the law takes the side of the masters and severely punishes all violations of the rights of property.***
In view of this, the question arises: how large is that part of the
annual national income which is received by the working class
taken as a whole? Hall calculates that this class gets only one-
eighth of the value of the produce of its labour, the remaining
seven-eighths going to "the masters".****

This conclusion cannot, of course, be accepted as correct. Hall
underestimated the share of the national income received by the
workers. But the reader will understand that there is no need now
to expose our author's mistake. Rather we should note that in
spite of this arithmetical error, he very well grasped the economic
essence of the exploitation of wage labour by capital.

Crime follows in the wake of poverty. Hall considered "all, or
almost all what is called original corruption and evil disposition,
to be the effects of the system of civilisation; and particularly that
prominent feature of it, the great inequality of property".*****
Civilisation corrupts the poor by material privations, but their
"masters" acquire vices common to rich people, and above all,
the very worst of all vices—the propensity to oppress their fellow-
creatures. That is the reason why social morality would gain very
much from the abolition of inequality of property. But can it be
abolished? Hall thinks it can. He cites three instances from
history where equality of property was established; one among the
Jews, another at Sparta, and a third under the government of
the Jesuits in Paraguay. "In all these cases, as far as we know, it
was in a great degree successful."*)

Touching on the question of measures that might be taken to
eliminate inequality of property, Hall insistently recommends

---

    * Ibid., p. 38.
    ** Ibid., pp. 38, 39.
    *** Ibid., p. 47. It should be pointed out that British law then treated
a strike as a criminal offence.
    **** Ibid., p. 40.
    ***** Ibid., p. 76.
    *) Ibid., p. 82.

great caution; and not only caution. It is essential, he says, that the reform be in the hands of persons who are disinterested and dispassionate. Such people cannot be found among the oppressed, who would probably press on too violently. We should rather appeal to the oppressors; for where the matter concerns not us personally but others, we are seldom so hasty and violent in implementing the demands of justice, no matter how highly we value them. "It would be better, therefore," says Hall, "that the redress of the grievances of the poor should originate from the rich themselves."* In other words, the interests of social peace demand that inequality of property be eliminated by those who draw all the advantages from it. This is typical not only of Hall; in essence, the vast majority of the socialists of this period—not only in Britain, but on the continent of Europe—held the same view on the question. In this respect, the greatest of the British utopian socialists, Robert Owen,** was close to Hall.

II

At the beginning of the year 1800, Owen was manager of a large cotton mill in New Lanark, Scotland. The "poor" employed in the mill worked much and earned little, were addicted to drunkenness, were often caught stealing, and generally had a very low level of intellectual and moral development. When he became manager of the mill, Owen hastened to improve the material conditions of his workers. He cut the working day to ten and a half hours,[256] and when the mill was idle for some months owing to a shortage of raw materials, he did not throw the "poor" on to the streets as usually happened, and still happens, during "breakdowns" and crises; instead, he continued to pay them full wages. Along with this he showed great concern for the upbringing and education of the children. He was the first to introduce kindergartens into Britain. The results of these efforts proved in every way excellent. The moral level of the workers improved noticeably: the sense of their human dignity was aroused in them. At the same time the profits of the enterprise increased considerably. All this, taken together, turned New Lanark into something extremely attractive to all those who in their goodness of heart did not mind sparing the sheep so long as the wolves did not go hungry. Owen acquired widespread fame as a philanthropist. Even most highly-placed persons readily visited New Lanark and were touched by the sight of the well-being of the "poor" there. However, Owen himself was by no means happy with what he had achieved in New

* Ibid., p. 49.
** Born on March 14, 1771, in Newtown, North Wales; died on November 17. 1858.

Lanark. He said justly that even though his workers enjoyed comparative well-being, they were still his *slaves*. So the philanthropist, who had moved even the most hardened reactionaries by his benevolent attitude to the workers, gradually became transformed into a social reformer, scaring the wits out of all the "respectable" people of the United Kingdom by his "extremism".

Like Hall, Owen was astounded by the paradoxical situation that the growth of the productive forces in Britain led to the impoverishment of the very people who were using them. He said: "The world is now saturated with wealth—with inexhaustible means of still increasing it—and yet misery abounds! Such at this moment is the actual state of human society." *The means were there* to give wealth, enlightenment and contentment to the people, yet, he went on, the great mass of the world lived in the depths of poverty, in want of a sufficiency of food. Things could not remain like that; a change for the better was needed. And the change will be most easy.* The world *knows* and *feels* the existing evil: it will look at the new order of things proposed—approve—will the change—and it is done."**

But to ensure that the world approve the proposed reform it was necessary first to make clear to it what man is by nature, what he had been made by the circumstances surrounding him, and what he could become under new circumstances corresponding to the demands of reason. According to Owen, man's mind had to be born again before he could be wise and happy.*** In order to promote the rebirth of the human mind, Owen wrote his famous *Essays* on the formation of the human character.****

Like Godwin, Owen was firmly convinced that man's character is determined by the circumstances of his social surroundings, regardless of his will. Man's views and habits are obtained from his environment, and these determine his conduct. Therefore the population of any country, or for that matter of the world at large, can have imparted to it, by the appropriate measures, any kind of character, from the very worst to the very best. The means necessary for this are at the command of the government. The

---

* [The last five words are in English in the original.]
** [The last four words are in English in the original.] See his letter, which was printed in a number of London newspapers on August 9, 1817, and reproduced in *The Life of Robert Owen Written by Himself*, London, 1857, as supplementary to his autobiography. The volume in question is referred to as I A. I shall frequently refer to it below.
*** See *The Life...*, I A, pp. 84, 86.
**** The full title of this work is *A New View of Society; or Essays on the Principle of the Formation of the Human Character, and Application of the Principle to the Practice*. There are four of these Essays; two of them appeared at the end of 1812, and the other two at the beginninng of 1813.

government can act in such a way that people can live without knowing poverty, crime, or punishment, for these are nothing but the consequences of wrong education and government. Since the aim of government is to make both the governed and those who govern happy, the people who hold political power must immediately set about reforming the social system.*

The first step towards this reform should be to bring to the general knowledge that no individual of the present generation will be deprived of his property. Then must follow proclamation of freedom of conscience; the abolition of institutions having a deleterious effect on people's morals, a review of the Poor Law, and finally and most important, the adoption of measures for the education and enlightenment of the people.

"...Every state, to be well-governed, ought to direct its chief attention to the formation of character; the best governed state will be that which shall possess the best national system of education."** The system of education, Owen says, must be uniform for the whole state.

Almost the whole of Owen's subsequent literary and agitational activity boiled down to further developing the views presented above and passionately defending them before public opinion. Thus, adhering to the principle that man's character is determined by the influence of the conditions surrounding him, Owen raised the question of how favourable were the conditions of the British workers of his day from childhood. Knowing the workers' conditions of life well, even if only from his observations at New Lanark, Owen could answer this question only by saying that these conditions were most unfavourable. According to him, the diffusion of manufactories throughout the country spoiled the character of the inhabitants and this spoiled character made them wretched. This moral evil was most lamentable, and could only be checked by legislative interference and direction.*** And this could not be put off indefinitely. If the workers' position was already worse than it had been formerly, with the passage of time it would worsen still more. The export of manufactured goods had probably reached its utmost height; it would now diminish by the competition of other states, and this in turn would have a serious and alarming effect on the condition of the working class.****

---

* Here and elsewhere I am quoting from the 2nd edition of *Essays* (1816); see pp. 19, 90 and 91.

** Ibid., p. 149.

*** See *Observations on the effects of the manufacturing system, with hints for the improvement of those parts of it which are most injurious to health and morals; Dedicated most respectfully to the British Legislature* (1815). Reprinted in *The Life of Robert Owen*, I A. The words mentioned are on p. 38; cf. also p. 39.

**** Ibid., p. 39. It would be too easy to prove that Owen was mistaken

Owen demanded the adoption of a Factory Act by Parliament to reduce the working day to ten and a half hours at establishments using machines. The Act had to provide for the prohibition of child labour under ten years of age, and also of children over that age who were unable to read or write. This was a quite specific demand for *factory legislation*. Owen put this demand forward "in the name of the millions of the neglected poor".* It was granted, finally, in a much curtailed form, by a Parliamentary Act in 1819.[257] Unfortunately even this Act, which had cheesepared Owen's demand, remained a dead letter, as Parliament took no steps whatever to put it into effect. Subsequently the Chief Inspector of Factories reported that "prior to the Act of 1833, young persons and children were worked all night, all day, or both ad libitum".**

Not confining himself to the demand for factory legislation, Owen tried to secure a review of the Poor Law. He wished to have established for the unemployed special villages where they could engage in agricultural and industrial work. Owen called these villages, on which he placed great hopes, "villages of unity and mutual co-operation".*** He thought they would be the medium for the adoption of serious measures for the proper education of the working people and their inculcation with a rational view of life. Believing that these "villages" could easily become prosperous, he saw them as a first step on the road to a social system in which there would be neither "poor" nor "rich", neither "slaves" nor "masters". It was no accident that he proposed to "*nationalise the poor*".**** This was essential to him because, in his initial plan, he had proposed that the system of education, as I mentioned earlier when setting forth the content of his *Essays*, should be uniform throughout the state.

As far back as 1817, Owen drew up a detailed estimate of the expenditure likely to be incurred in building "villages of unity and mutual co-operation".*** It is hardly worth saying now that the government had no intention of granting the money needed for this venture. Later, in 1834, they did indeed change the Poor Law, but not at all in the way the reformer had suggested. Instead of

---

in considering that in 1815 British exports had reached their "utmost height". It is useful to note, however, that in Owen's views the *theory of the markets* was already beginning to play a part not unlike that which was assigned to it in the teaching of our Narodniks in the 1880s.

* [The words in inverted cammas are in English in the original.]
** Karl Marx, *Capital*, published by O. N. Popova, Vol. I, p. 215 [in Russian].[258]
*** *Observations...*, p. 78. [The words in inverted commas are in English in the original.]
**** *The Life...*, IA, p. 60 et seq. [The italicised words are in English in the original.]

"villages of unity and mutual co-operation", the destitute poor were confined to workhouses that were no different from convict prisons.

Meeting with failure in his attempts to move the "governors" to carry out social reform, Owen, though he had not lost faith in their good will, nevertheless felt compelled to attempt to undertake the task of bringing his cherished ideas to fruition with his own resources, and with the assistance of like-minded people. He began to establish communist colonies in the United Kingdom and in North America. These attempts to put the communist ideal into effect within the narrow limits of a single settlement proved a failure and almost ruined Owen. There were many reasons for this failure. One of the most important was revealed by Owen himself when he said that the success of such enterprises presupposed that their participants possessed certain moral propensities, which were far from general among them at a time when the social environment so strongly distorted the human character. It emerged, therefore, that the communist communities were essential in order to give people a proper education and, on the other hand, this education was a necessary preliminary condition for the success of the communist communities. This is the contradiction on which so many good intentions were wrecked during the past century; and it can only be resolved by the historical process of the development of society *as a whole*—the process of *gradually* adapting man's character to the *gradually* forming new conditions of his existence. But utopian socialism took very little account of the progress of historical development. Owen was fond of saying that the new social order might come suddenly "like a thief in the night".

III

At a public meeting in 1817, Owen addressed these remarks to his audience: "My friends, I tell you that hitherto you have been prevented from even knowing what happiness really is, solely in consequence of the errors—gross errors—that have been combined with the fundamental notions of every religion that has hitherto been taught to men. And, in consequence, they have made man the most inconsistent, and the most miserable being in existence. By the errors of these systems he has been made a weak imbecile animal; a furious bigot and fanatic; or a miserable hypocrite."* Words like these had not been heard before in Britain, and they were sufficient to arouse the indignation of all "respectable" men against Owen. He himself saw that "respectable people" had begun to frown on him as a blasphemer. But this did not in any way lessen his frankness or his faith in the good will of the powers

---

* *The Life...*, I A, p. 115.

that be. In October 1830, he delivered two lectures "on genuine religion". These lectures give but a vague idea of the distinguishing features of "true" religious doctrine.* But for all that they are clear evidence of Owen's deep contempt for all "hitherto existing religions". In the first lecture, he declared them to be the sole source of the disunion, mutual hatred and crime that darkened human life. In the second, he said that they had turned the world into one great madhouse. And he demonstrated that it was urgently necessary to take measures to fight them. This again was more than enough to infuriate all the "respectable" gentlemen of the United Kingdom. It might seem that Owen himself ought to have understood that none of them could approve of measures *against* religions. But it was just this that he did not want to understand.

In the second lecture he said that people who had cognised truth were morally bound to help the government to put it into effect. He then invited his audience to petition the King and both Houses of Parliament to fight religions. The draft petition took for granted that the King wished nothing better than the happiness of his subjects, but that their happiness could only be achieved by substituting for the present unnatural religion, in which, unfortunately, they continue to be educated, a religion of truth and nature. Finally, this religion could triumph without danger to society or, at the very most, only with some temporary inconveniences. Hence the King should use his high position to induce his Ministers to examine the role of religion in regard to the formation of the human character. The petition to both Houses of Parliament was couched in the same spirit.** The audience endorsed Owen's draft petitions. Needless to say, the petitions brought no advantage whatsoever to Owen's cause.

Religious concepts formed on a given social basis sanction this basis. Whoever attacks religion shakes its social basis. The guardians of order are therefore never disposed to toleration where the question of religious convictions is concerned. They are even less disposed to *fight* religion. Owen overlooked this. And that meant that he was unable to draw all the practical conclusions following from his own teaching on the formation of the human character.

If the character of every given person is determined by the conditions of his upbringing, it is obvious that the character of

---

* It had evidently to consist of a materialist view of nature, slightly modified by the usual phraseology of deism and supplemented by socialist morality.

** Both lectures are reproduced as a supplement to Owen's *Lectures on an Entire New State of Society*.

each particular social class is determined by its position in society. A class that lives on the exploitation of other classes will always be ready to defend social injustice, and not to rebel against it. In as much as Owen hoped to move the aristocracy and the bourgeoisie to reforms that would have ended the class division of society, without knowing it he came up against the same contradiction that had thwarted eighteenth-century materialist philosophy. This philosophy taught that man, with all his opinions and habits, is the product of the social environment. And at the same time it did not cease to repeat that the social environment with all its properties is determined by people's opinion. "C'est l'opinion, qui gouverne le monde," said the materialists, and with them all the Enlighteners of the eighteenth century. Hence their appeals to more or less enlightened despots, for they firmly believed in the force of "opinion". Robert Owen was just as firm a believer in "opinion". As a follower of the eighteenth-century materialists, he repeated word for word after them that "opinions govern the world".* Following their example, he tried to enlighten the "governors". In regard to the working class, he was evidently guided for a long time by the impressions he had absorbed in New Lanark. He tried with all his might to help the "working poor", but he had no faith in their independent activity. And, having no faith in their independent activity, he could recommend to them only one course: never to enter into conflict with the rich, but to conduct themselves in such a way that the rich would not be afraid of taking the initiative for social reform. In April 1819, he published in the newspapers "An Address to the Working Classes".** Noting with regret that the working classes were filled with anger at their condition, he repeated that the character of man is determined by his social environment. Remembering this, the workers should not in his opinion blame the "rich" for their attitude to the "poor". The rich will but one thing: to retain their privileged social status. And the workers must respect that desire. What was more, should the privileged wish to acquire still more wealth, the workers must not oppose them. It was essential to occupy oneself not with the past but with the future, that is to say, to concentrate all attention on social reform. The reader may well ask what new element could be brought about by a reform that not only preserved privileges but enriched the privileged even more. The point is, however, that according to Owen the colossal productive forces now at the disposal of mankind would recompense the workers for all their concessions, if only these

---

* *Lectures on an Entire New State*, etc., p. 151 (Lecture 11). [The words in inverted commas are in English in the original.]

** Even yet in Britain they speak of the "working classes" instead of the "working class".

35—01230

productive forces were utilised in a planned way. Owen—like
Rodbertus later on—did not insist that the workers should receive
the whole product of their labour, but only their share of the
product should not be too small. As we see, his communism
was reconciled to a certain social inequality; but this inequality
had to be under social control, and should not go beyond the limits
established by society. Owen was convinced that the rich and
the poor, the governors and the governed, had really but one
interest.* Until the very end of his life, he was a staunch advocate
of *social peace*.

Every class struggle is a political struggle. He who is against
the struggle of classes will naturally not attach any importance
to their political actions. It is not surprising that Owen was opposed to Parliamentary reform. He found that, in general, electoral rights were "not desirable"** until such times as the people
received proper education; he did not favour the democratic and
republican aspirations of his time. He thought that if the republicans and democrats ceased threatening the governments there would
in all probability be a beneficial change in the government
of the world.***

Owen was never a member of the Chartist movement,[259] then
fighting for full *political* rights for the workers. But since the
upper classes did not evince the least desire to support his plans
for social reform, willy-nilly he ultimately had to set his hopes
on the workers' movement. In the early thirties, when this
movement broadened out and even became menacing, Owen
endeavoured to use the growing strength of the proletariat to
achieve his cherished ideas. In September 1832, he organised an
"equitable labour exchange bazaar",**** as he called it, in London;
almost simultaneously with this he entered into close relations
with the trades unions. However, here too the practical results
did not measure up to his expectations.

Equitable exchange meant the exchange of goods according to
the utmost of labour expended in their production. But if a particular product did not correspond to social demand, no one
would buy it and the labour spent in its production would have
gone for nothing. In order that products should *always* be exchange-
able proportionally to the sum of labour embodied in each—in
other words, in order that the law of *value* should not operate
through a constant fluctuation of *prices*—planned organisation
of production was essential. Production must be so organised that
the work of each producer be consciously directed to satisfy

* *The Life...*, I A, pp. 229-30.
** [The last two words are in English in the original.]
*** *The Life...*, I A, Introduction, III.
**** [The words in inverted commas are in English in the original.]

definite social needs. So long as this is not the case, fluctuation
of prices is unavoidable which means that "equitable exchange"
is also impossible. But when this planned production is function-
ing, there will be no necessity for "equitable exchange", because
the products will no longer be *exchanged* one for the other; they
will be *distributed* at rates determined by society among its
members. The "equitable exchange bazaars"* were evidence that
Owen and his followers, for all their interest in economic questions, still did not understand the difference between *commodity*
(unorganised) production on the one hand and *communist* (organised) production on the other.

In aligning himself with the trades unions, Owen hoped they
would help him rapidly to build a whole range of co-operatives
throughout the country, which would be the basis of the new social system. In accordance with his constant conviction, the social
revolution had to be accomplished *without struggle of any kind.*
In striving for this, Owen wished to transform an instrument of
class struggle—which the trades unions always are to some extent
or other—into an instrument of *peaceful* social reform. This plan,
however, was quite utopian. Owen soon realised that he and the
trades unions were moving along different paths: the same trades
unions which were most sympathetic of all to the co-operative
idea were then preparing with special energy *for a general strike*,
something that never at any time or anywhere was possible without
infringing *social peace.***

Much greater practical success came the way of Owen and his
followers in the sphere of *consumers'* societies. Owen himself was
not enthusiastic about these societies, which he regarded as very
close to "trading companies".

I have outlined Owen's activity in such detail because it reflects so vividly both the strong and weak sides of utopian socialism. Having done so, I am now able to confine myself to brief
references to these in my further presentation.

Some investigators think that Owen's influence brought no
advantage to the British labour movement. This is an enormous,
strange and unpardonable error. Owen, an indefatigable propagandist of his ideas, awakened the thoughts of the working class, placing before it the most important—*fundamental*—problems of
the social structure and providing it with much data for the cor-

---

* Besides the one in London, another was opened at Birmingham.
** In this essay I have been discussing only the history of certain *ideas*
and not the history of a social *movement*; but in passing I will remark that
the period of Owen's association with the trades unions was one in which
the British workers were rather strongly inclined to practical methods of
class struggle, very highly reminiscent of those dear to the hearts of our
present-day "revolutionary" syndicalists.

ect solution of these problems, at least in theory. If his *practical*
ractivity in general was *utopian* in character, it must be admitted
that here, too, he sometimes gave his contemporaries extremely
useful lessons. He was the true father of the British co-operative
movement. There was absolutely nothing utopian about his
demand for factory legislation. Nor was there anything utopian
about his suggestions on the need to provide at least elementary
schooling for the children and young persons working in the
factories. In turning his back on politics and condemning the
class struggle, he was of course very much in error. It is remarkable, though, that the workers who were attracted by his message
were able to correct his mistakes. In assimilating Owen's co-
operative and, to some extent, communist ideas, the workers simultaneously took an active part in the *political* movement of the
British proletariat at that time. At least the most gifted of them:
Lovett, Hetherington, Watson, and others did so.*

To all this should be added that in his fearless advocacy of
"true religion" and rational relations between the sexes, Owen
influenced the development of the workers' consciousness not
in the social field alone.**

His immediate influence was felt not only in Great Britain and
Ireland but also in the United States of America.***

IV

A zealous adversary of socialism, Professor Foxwell of Cam-
bridge University asserts that it was not Owen but Ricardo who
gave British socialism its most genuine spiritual weapon.****
That is not the case. True, Engels already remarked that, in so
far as the theories of contemporary socialism stemmed from bour-

---

* The recently published book by M. Beer, *Geschichte des Sozialismus in
England*, has more to say of them (p. 280 et seq.). Hetherington's will is
worthy of special note (pp. 282 and 283). Lovett and Hetherington were active
members of the Chartist movement. There is an autobiography of Lovett,
*The Life and Struggles of William Lovett, in his Pursuit of Bread, Knowledge,
and Freedom*, London, 1876.

** Hetherington's will shows how the most talented workers understood
his true religion: "The only religion useful to man consists exclusively of
the practice of morality, and in the mutual interchange of kind actions."

*** See Chapter II, The Owenite Period", in *History of Socialism in the
United States* by Morris Hillquit, New York, 1903. There are both German and
Russian translations.

**** See page LXXI et seq. of his essay "Geschichte der sozialistischen
Ideen in England" which is an Introduction to the German translation of the
now fairly well-known work by William Thompson, *Inquiry into the Principles
of the Distribution of Wealth Most Conducive to Human Happiness*. In referring
to this work, I shall be quoting the German translation by Oswald Collmann
published in Berlin in 1903.

geois political economy, almost all of them leaned on Ricardo's theory of value. There was good enough reason for this. It is, however, beyond doubt that, at least, many of the British socialists whose teachings relied on Ricardo's theory of value were pupils of Owen, and turned to bourgeois political economy precisely because, by utilising its conclusions, they wished to proceed further in the direction taken by their teacher. Those whom it would manifestly be wrong to call Owenites will be found to be closely associated intellectually with the communist anarchist Godwin. They turned to Ricardo only so as to be able through him to expose political economy as being in contradiction with its own—moreover fundamental—theoretical principles. Among Owen's pupils I will refer, first of all, to William Thompson.* In the Introduction to the work that I have just mentioned (see footnote) Thompson asks how was it that a nation abounding more than any other in the raw materials, machinery, dwellings, and food, in intelligent and industrious producers should still pine in privation.** This is the selfsame question which occupied Owen almost from the beginning of the nineteenth century, and was quite definitely formulated by him in some of his published works. Further, Thompson wonders why the fruits of the workers' labour are mysteriously taken from them through no fault of theirs. We meet the same question in almost all of Owen's works. Thompson, however, recognises that it is precisely such questions which induce "us" to take an interest in the distribution of wealth. Thus, if Thompson turned to Ricardo—as he actually did, and indeed borrowed much from him—it was the outcome of Owen's previous influence upon him. Of course, in matters of political economy, Ricardo was very much stronger than Owen. But Thompson approached the problems of political economy from a different side altogether from that of Ricardo. The latter affirmed and demonstrated that labour is the only source of the value of products. But he was quite reconciled with the fact that bourgeois society condemned the workers to subjection and distress. Thompson, on the other hand, could not accept this state of affairs. He desired that the system of distribution of goods should cease to contradict the basic law of their production. In other words, he demanded that the value created by *labour* should go to the *workers*. And in his exposition of this demand he followed in the footsteps of Owen.

All the other British socialists who relied on Ricardo's economic doctrine presented quite the same demand in their criticism of bourgeois society. Ricardo's main work was published in 1817.***

---

* Born in 1785; died in 1833.
** See page 16 of the German translation.
*** It is called *Principles of Political Economy and Taxation*.

Already in 1821 there appeared, in the form of an open letter to
Lord John Russell, a short anonymous pamphlet exposing bourgeois society as being founded on the exploitation of the workers. *Following this came a series of other productions which were
remarkable in their own way. Not all of them owed their origin to
Robert Owen's followers; some of them came from the pens of
people more or less strongly inclined to anarchism. Among Owen's
pupils, besides Thompson, I should include John Gray, John Bray,
and from the writers who were more or less drawn to anarchism—
Piercy Ravenstone and Thomas Hodgskin.**

All these writers were for long completely forgotten. When they
were recalled—partly owing to Marx, who mentioned them already
in his polemic with Proudhon—their works were referred to as the
source from which Marx borrowed his teaching on the surplus product and surplus value. It went so far that the Webbs referred to
Marx as "Hodgskin's illustrious disciple".*** There is absolutely
no truth whatever in this. In the works of the British socialists,
however, we encounter not only theories of the exploitation, of
labour by capital but even such expressions as "surplus produce", "surplus value", "additional value". However, it is not a
question of words but of scientific concepts. As far as the latter

---

* It is entitled *The Source and Remedy of the National Difficulties.
A Letter to Lord John Russell.* Marx mentions it in *Theorien über den Mehrwert.*
Dritter Band, Stuttgart, 1910, S. 281-306.[260]
** *Thompson's* study of distribution came out in 1824; in the following
year he published *Labour Rewarded.* In the same year, *Gray* (1798-1850) published *A Lecture on Human Happiness* and in 1831 *Social System.* John Bray's
book, *Labour's Wrongs and Labour's Remedy; or, the Age of Might and the Age
of Right* is important for the history of economic theory (it was published
in Leeds in 1839). It is remarkable, by the way, for the fact that in it
Bray seemingly showed a tendency to abandon the idealist view of history
common to all the utopians and adopt the standpoint of the materialist
explanation of history (see his argument on page 26 that society cannot at
will change the direction of its opinions). True, this tendency did not impel
Bray to make a serious analysis of the basic causes of social development.
I will mention here, too, T. R. Edmonds' book, *Practical Moral and Political
Economy,* London, 1828. According to Edmonds, the working class receives
only a third of the value it produces; the remaining two-thirds go to the
employers (pp. 107, 116, and 288). This is quite close to the truth for Britain
even today. His views on the social causes of *pauperism* (pp. 109-10) are also
well worth attention. In 1821, Ravenstone published the pamphlet, *A Few
Doubts as to the Correctness of Some Opinions Generally Entertained on the
Subjects of Population and Political Economy.* Among Hodgskin's works the
most important for us here are: 1. *Labour Defended Against the Claims of
Capital,* London, 1825; 2. *Popular Political Economy;* 3. *The Natural and
Artificial Right of Property Contrasted,* London, 1832. Concerning Ravenstone
and Hodgskin, see Marx's work mentioned above (pp. 306-80).[261] There is
also a work on Hodgskin by Elie Halévy, entitled *Thomas Hodgskin (1787-
1869),* Paris, 1903.
*** *The History of Trade Unionism,* London, 1894, p. 147.

are concerned, every well-informed and *unbiassed* person must admit that Hodgskin, for example, was, to say the least, as far removed from Marx as Rodbertus. Marx is no longer named a pupil of Rodbertus; it is to be hoped that we shall soon cease to hear him being named a pupil of the British socialists of the 1820s.* However, enough of that. Although Marx was not a "pupil" of Hodgskin, Thompson, or Gray, the fact that these British socialists attained a clarity of political and economic conceptions rare for their times and, as Marx himself said, made a step forward of no small importance in comparison with Ricardo,[262] is yet of the highest importance for the history of socialist theory. In this respect, they were far ahead of the French and German utopian socialists. If our N. G. Chernyshevsky had been acquainted with them, he would have probably translated one of their works instead of that of John Stuart Mill.

B. FRENCH UTOPIAN SOCIALISM

I

In the second half of the eighteenth century, while the industrial revolution was proceeding in England, a desperate struggle was taking place in France between the third estate and the old regime. The third estate then embraced, to use a well-known expression, the whole of the French people except the "privileged". The struggle against the "privileged" was a *political* struggle. When political power was snatched from the hands of the "priv-

---

* Hodgskin's real relationship to Marx may be seen in the—note, very sympathetic—criticism of Hodgskin's views in Volume III—which I have already mentioned—of *Theorien über den Mehrwert*. In political economy, Marx has the same relation to the British socialists as he has to Auguste Thierry, Guizot or Mignet in the scientific explanation of history. In both cases they are not teachers of Marx but only predecessors, who prepared some—true, very valuable—material for the theoretical edifice later constructed by Marx. As far as Marx's predecessors are concerned, in considering the history of the scientific solution of the question of the exploitation of wage labour by capital, one should not confine oneself to the British socialists of the first half of the nineteenth century. Some English writers of the seventeenth century had already displayed a fairly clear comprehension of the nature and origin of this exploitation. (See, for example, *The Law of Freedom in a Platform: Or, True Magistracy Restored. Humbly Presented to Oliver Cromwell*, by Gerard Winstanley, London, 1651, p. 12; see also *Proposals for Raising a College of Industry of All Useful Trades and Husbandry with Profit for the Rich, a Plentiful Living for the Poor and a Good Education for Youth*, London, 1695, p. 21; and finally, *Essays about the Poor, Manufactures, Trade Plantations, and Immorality, etc.*, by John Bellers, London, 1699, pp. 5-6.) It is strange that no one has yet taken the trouble to discover that Marx borrowed his economic theory from the authors of the above-mentioned works.

ileged" by the third estate, the latter, naturally, used it to abolish all those economic and social institutions which together
formed the basis of the old political order. All the very varied
elements of the population constituting the third estate were vitally interested in the battle against these institutions. Consequently, the advanced French writers of the eighteenth century
were all agreed in their condemnation of the *old* social and political order. But that was not all. They differed very little, either,
in their views of the *new* social order which they desired. Obviously in the advanced camp certain shades of opinion were unavoidable. However, despite these shades of opinion, that camp was
unanimous in its striving to establish that social order which
we now call bourgeois. The strength of this unanimous endeavour
was so great that even people who had no sympathy with the
bourgeois ideal fell in with it. Here is an example.

The then very well-known Abbé de Mably, when polemising
with the physiocrats,[263] declared against private property and
the social inequality it entails. In his own words, he "could not
abandon the pleasing idea of community of property". In other
words, he defended communism. But this convinced communist
believed it was his duty to state that the idea of community of
property seemed to him to be impracticable. "No human power,"
he wrote, "could now attempt to restore equality without causing
disorders much greater than those it wished to abolish."* Such was
the force of things. Even while admitting in theory the advantages
of communism, one had to be content with the idea of the old
order being replaced, not by a communist, but by a bourgeois
order.

When the revolution brought triumph to the bourgeois system,
a struggle at once began among the heterogeneous elements constituting the third estate. The social stratum which was at the
time the embryo of the modern proletariat began war against the
"rich", whom it put into the same bracket as the aristocracy.
Although the most outstanding political representatives of this
stratum—such as Robespierre and Saint-Just—were far from holding communist ideas, communism did nevertheless appear on
the historical scene, in the person of "Gracchus" Babeuf, in the
final act of the great revolutionary drama. The "Conspiracy of
Equals" constituted by Babeuf and his associates was as it were a
sort of prologue to that still unfinished struggle between the proletariat and the bourgeoisie which is one of the most characteristic features of the internal history of France in the nineteenth
century. As a matter of fact, no. It would be more accurate to

---

* *Doutes proposés aux philosophes économistes sur l'ordre naturel et essentiel
des sociétés politiques*, par Monsieur l'Abbé de Mably, A la Haye,
MDCCLXVIII, p. 15.

describe the "Conspiracy of Equals" as the *prologue to the prologue* of this struggle. In the arguments of Babeuf and his comrades we meet only faint and vague hints of an understanding of the historical essence of the new social order which they had condemned to destruction. They knew, and in different ways repeated, the one theme: "In a true society, there must be neither rich nor poor" (Dans une véritable société il ne doit y avoir ni riches, ni pauvres). Since there were both rich and poor in the society created by the revolution, the revolution could not be considered as completed until this society had given way to a *true* society.* How far removed the Babouvists' ideas were from those we met with in our examination of British utopian socialism may be very clearly seen from the following.

The British socialists attributed enormous historical significance to the fact that modern society had at its command powerful forces of production. In their view, the existence of these forces of production had for the first time made it a practical possibility to transform society so that there would be neither rich nor poor. In contrast to this, some of the Babouvists were quite reconciled to the assumption that the realisation of their communist ideals would bring "the destruction of all the arts", including, of course, the technical arts. The Manifesto of "Equals" says outright: "Perish, if it must be, all the arts, provided real equality is left to us."** True, this Manifesto, which was written by S. Maréchal, did not please many of the Babouvists and was not even distributed by them. However, Buonarroti himself tells us that in defending the plan of communist revolution, he, together with Debon, Darthé and Lepelletier, argued as follows: "We were told, moreover, that if it is true that inequality hastened the progress of the really useful arts, it must cease today, that further progress would add nothing to the real happiness of all."*** This meant that mankind no longer had any significant need for the development of technology. Probably Marx and Engels had in mind, by the way, this kind of argument of the Babouvists when they wrote in *The Communist Manifesto* that the revolutionary literature that accompanied the first proletarian movements was reactionary since it preached universal asceticism and the establishment of primitive equality.[264]

The works of the nineteenth-century French socialists do not have this ascetic feature; on the contrary, we find there a highly sympathetic attitude to technical progress.

---

* See *Analyse de la doctrine de Babeuf, tribun du peuple, proscrit par le directoire exécutif pour avoir dit la vérité*. Published as a supplement to F. Buonarroti's famous book, *Gracchus Babeuf et la conjuration des égaux*. I have at hand the Paris edition of 1869, which is somewhat abridged.

** *Gracchus Babeuf*, etc., p. 70.

*** Ibid., pp. 48 and 50.

It may, perhaps, be said that even the strange and—let the truth be told! —ridiculous dreams of Fourier, regarding anti-lions, anti-sharks, anti-hippopotami and other suchlike kind animals which, in due course, would serve man and thus increase his comforts, were no more than a recognition, in extremely fantastic attire, of the importance and boundless magnitude of future technical progress. But for all that—and this is of vast import for the history of theory—the French utopian socialists in the great majority of cases trailed far behind their British counterparts in comprehending the true nature of the direct social and economic consequences of the technical progress of their time.

II

As we are aware, the British socialists believed that the growth of the productive forces deepened · the division of society into two classes—the "rich" and the "poor". At the same time, they saw the opposition between these two classes as opposition between the employers and the wage-workers. The employers appropriate the greater part of the value created by the workers' labour. This was already clear to Charles Hall, but was only gradually being understood by the French socialist writers. And even those French socialists who realised that the most important contradiction of contemporary society is that between the interests of capital and those of wage-labour never grasped this with the same lucidity that we see in the works of Thompson, Gray, and Hodgskin.

Saint-Simon* directly continued the work accomplished by the eighteenth-century ideologists of the third estate. He did not speak of the employers exploiting the workers, but only of the employers and workers *taken together* undergoing exploitation by the "idle" class, who comprised mainly the aristocracy and the bureaucracy. Saint-Simon looked on the employers as the natural representatives and defenders of the workers' interests. His pupils went further. Analysing the concept "idle class", they included in it not only the *landowners* exploiting the "labouring class" by the receipt of land rent, but also the *capitalists*. However, it should be noted that they understood the term capitalists to mean only those whose income was derived from interest on capital. The employer's profit, they held, coincided with the workers' wages.** We find the same unclarity of view in Proudhon's works—and a quarter of a century later at that!*** In March 1850,

---

* Born on October 17, 1760; died on May 19, 1825.
** See *Le Producteur*, Vol. I, p. 245.
*** Born in 1809; died in 1865.

he wrote: "The union of the bourgeoisie and the proletariat signifies now, as previously, the liberation of the serf, the defensive and offensive alliance of the industrialists with the workers
against the capitalist and the nobleman." Louis Blanc* saw
the matter more clearly. To him, the social opposition we are
discussing took the form of an opposition between the *bourgeoisie*
and the *people*. But by bourgeoisie he means "the aggregate
of those citizens who, owning either instruments of labour or
capital, work with means which are their own and depend on
others only to a certain extent". What is meant here by "only"?
And how are we to understand Louis Blanc's idea that the
citizens who in the aggregate make up the bourgeoisie *work* with
means which are their own? Is he thinking here only of the
petty—*artisan*—bourgeoisie? Or are we to understand it in the
sense that Louis Blanc, like the Saint-Simonists, regarded the
employers' profit as payment for their labour? There is no reply
to this. The people are defined by Louis Blanc as "the aggregate
of the citizens who, having no capital, depend entirely on others
as regards the prime necessities of life".** This by itself gives rise
to no objection. But one may "depend on others" in various ways:
therefore Louis Blanc's concept of the people does not coincide
with the far more exact concept of the hired worker used by the
British socialists in their investigations. In any case Louis Blanc
was, in general, little interested in economic concepts. Much
greater attention was paid to them by Jean Reynaud*** and Pierre
Leroux.**** Both of these had belonged previously to the school
of Saint-Simon, but had soon become dissatisfied with its teaching.
Reynaud asserted that the *people* was composed of *two* classes with
opposing interests—the proletariat and the bourgeoisie. He called
proletarians "the people who produce all the wealth of the nation;
who have nothing apart from the daily payment for their labour". The bourgeoisie he defined as "the people who possess capital and live on its income". Recognising the correctness of these
definitions, Pierre Leroux even tried to calculate the number of
proletarians. He estimated that there were in France up to thirty
million of them.***** That figure was, of course, too high. There is
nothing like that number of proletarians in France even at the
present time. The overestimation came about as a result of Leroux
including among the proletariat not only the peasantry but also
the beggars of France, of whom, he reckoned, there were up to four

---

        * Born in 1811; died in 1882.
       ** *Histoire de dix ans, 1830-1840*, 4-me éd., Vol. I, p. 4, footnote.
      *** Born in 1806; died in 1863.
     **** Born in 1797; died in 1871.
    ***** See *De la ploutocratie*, Boussac, 1848, p. 25. The first edition of this
book was issued in 1843.

million. Reynaud committed a similar error when he included the
"village peasantry" among the proletariat, despite his own definition of the concept "proletarian". On this question, the views of
Reynaud and Leroux are very close to those of our *Trudoviks*.[265]

The reader will understand why the economic views of the
French socialists of the utopian period were not distinguished
by the clarity which was a feature of the British utopian socialists'
concepts: the distinctive features of the capitalist relations of
production were more sharply expressed in Britain than in France.

The clarity existing among the then British socialists on economic matters did not prevent them from cherishing the belief
that the proletariat and the bourgeoisie—two classes diametrically opposed to each other in economic interests—could undertake
social reform in complete agreement. The British socialists discerned the existence of the class struggle in present-day society;
but they decisively condemned it, and under no circumstances
would they link with it the realisation of their plans for reform.
Here there was no difference between them and the majority of
the French socialists. Saint-Simon and the Saint-Simonists, Fourier and the Fourierists, Cabet, Proudhon, and Louis Blanc, sharply differing among themselves on many problems, were all fully
agreed that social reform presupposed not the struggle but the
complete reconciliation of classes.

We shall see later that not all the French utopian socialists
rejected the class struggle. For the moment, however, we must
remember that the majority of them were opposed to it and that
this opposition explains why they would have nothing to do with
politics.

In the mid-1830s, Fourier's most outstanding pupil, Victor
Considérant* expressed his satisfaction that interest in politics
among the French population had declined. He attributed this to
the "theoretical" errors of the politicians: instead of trying to find
ways and means to reconcile interests, the politicians gave support to this mutual struggle, which, he said, was "profitable only
to those who traffic in it".**

At first glance, the peaceful sentiments of the majority of the
French utopian socialists appear strange in a country where not
long before the storm of the Great Revolution had raged and
where, it would seem, advanced people should have held revolutionary tradition particularly dear. But on closer examination
it becomes obvious that it was precisely the recollection of the
recent revolution which predisposed advanced ideologists, such
as Considérant, to seek for measures which might put an end to

---

* Born in 1808; died in 1893.
** *Débâcle de la politique en France*, Paris, 1836, p. 16.

the class struggle. Their peaceful sentiments were a psychological reaction to the revolutionary passions of 1793. The great majority of the French utopian socialists were terrified at the thought that the mutual struggle of interests might again reach the acuteness which marked that memorable year. In his first work, *Théorie des quatre mouvements et des destinées sociales*, published in 1808, Fourier spoke with indignation of "the catastrophe of 1793" which had brought civilised society, as he put it, close to a state of barbarism. Saint-Simon, for his part, had still earlier than Fourier described the French Revolution as the most terrible outbreak and the greatest of all scourges.* This attitude to the "catastrophe of 1793" even inspired Fourier with a negative view of the eighteenth-century philosophy of Enlightenment, to which he, however, was indebted for the basic principles of his own theory. Saint-Simon did not approve of that philosophy either, at any rate in so far as it seemed to him to be destructive and responsible for the events of 1793. Saint-Simon considered that the most important task of social thought in the nineteenth century was to study measures necessary *"to put an end to revolution".*** In the 1830s and 1840s his followers tried to solve the same problem. The only difference was that they were concerned, not with the revolution at the end of the eighteenth century, but with the revolution of 1830. One of the main arguments they advanced in favour of social reform was that this ("association", "organisation") would halt the revolution. They intimidated their adversaries with the spectre of revolution. In 1840 Enfantin praised the Saint-Simonists because in the thirties, when the proletariat had just tried out its strength in a successful revolt against the throne, they had shouted: "Voici les barbares!" ("Here come the barbarians!"). And he proudly added that now, too, ten years later, he does not cease to repeat the same cry: "Here come the barbarians!"***

III

Enfantin regarded the appearance of the proletariat on the historical scene as being tantamount to the coming of "the barbarians"; so did the majority of the French utopian socialists.**** This is very typical of their mode of thought in general and their attitude to the political struggle in particular. They warmly defended the interests of the working class; they mercilessly ex-

---

* *Oeuvres choisies de C.-H. de Saint-Simon*, Vol. I, Bruxelles, 1859, pp. 20-21.
** My italics.
*** *Correspondance politique, 1835-1840*. Paris, 1849, p. 6.
**** Echoes of such views on the proletarians may be heard in some of A. I. Herzen's discourses.

posed many contradictions in bourgeois society. Towards the end
of his life, Saint-Simon taught that "all social institutions must
aim at the moral, intellectual and physical improvement of the
most numerous and poorest class". Fourier asserted with noble
indignation that the workers' position in civilised society was
worse than that of wild beasts.* But, while bewailing the sad lot
of the working class and striving in every way to help it, the
utopian socialists did not believe in the independent action of the
working class, and when they did, they were afraid of it. As we
have only just seen, Enfantin regarded the appearance of the
proletariat as being tantamount to an invasion of barbarians.
As early as 1802, Saint-Simon, addressing "the propertyless class",
said: "See what happened in France when your comrades held
sway there; they brought about famine."**

An interesting contrast: right up to the February revolution of
1848 the bourgeois ideologists were by no means hostile to the
political struggle of classes. In 1820, Guizot wrote that the middle
class had to win political power if it wanted to assure its interests in the struggle against the reactionaries who, for their part,
were striving to get power and to utilise it in their own interests.*** And when the reactionaries reproached him that, while
preaching the class struggle, he was thus exciting evil passions,
he told them that the whole history of France was "made" by the
war of classes, and that it was shameful of them to forget that
history simply because "its conclusions" had proved to be unfavourable to them.****

Guizot believed in the independent action of the "middle class",
that is to say, the bourgeoisie, and he was not in the least afraid
of it. That was why he demonstrated the necessity of the political
struggle of classes. Of course, he, too, did not approve of the "catastrophe of 1793"—far from it! But for a time he considered that
its repetition was out of the question. In 1848 he changed his
opinion and became, in his turn, an advocate of social peace.
Thus the course of development of social thought proceeded
and changed in accordance with the course of development of
social life.

It is now time to remind the reader that a *minority* of the socialists in France at that time was in no way opposed either to
politics or to the class struggle. In its mode of thought this minority differed substantially from the majority with whom we have

---

* *Oeuvres complètes de Ch. Fourier*, Paris, 1841, Vol. IV, pp. 191-92.
** *Oeuvres choisies*, Vol. I, p. 27.
*** *Du Gouvernement de la France et du ministère actuel*, Paris, 1820, p. 237.
**** See Avant-propos to the third edition of the above book, *Du
Gouvernement de la France*, etc.

been occupied till now. The minority was descended directly from Babeuf and those who shared his views. One of the active participants of the "Conspiracy of Equals", a descendant of Michelangelo, Philippe Buonarroti,* a native of Tuscany who became a French citizen by decree of the Convention,[266] appeared in nineteenth-century utopian socialism as the bearer of the revolutionary traditions of the Babouvists. His work (which I mentioned earlier), *Histoire de la conspiration pour l'égalité, dite de Babeuf, suivie du procès auquel elle a donné lieu*, was published in Brussels in 1828 and was of enormous importance in shaping the ideas of the revolutionary minority of the French socialists.** The very fact that this minority came under the influence of a former member of the "Conspiracy of Equals" demonstrates that, as distinct from the majority, it was not embarrassed by memories of the "catastrophe of 1793". The most famous representative of this minority, Auguste Blanqui,*** remained until the end of his long life an indomitable revolutionary.

Whereas Saint-Simon insisted on measures which would *put an end to revolution* and the majority of the French socialists quite agreed with him on this, the minority, under the influence of Babouvism, fully shared the view of the "Equals" that the revolution had as yet not been completed, since the rich had seized all the good things of life. Therein lies the cardinal difference between the two trends of French utopian socialism: one aimed to put an end to the revolution, the other wished to continue it.

Those who desired to put an end to the revolution naturally endeavoured to secure agreement among the warring social interests. Considérant wrote: "*For each class the best means of ensuring its particular interests is to link them with the interests of other classes.*"**** All peaceable utopian socialists thought in such a way. They only differed on the measures needed to harmonise the interests of all classes in society. Almost every one of the peaceable founders of socialist systems invented his own special plan to safeguard the interests of the *propertied class*. For example, Fourier recommended that in the future society the product of labour be so distributed that the workers' share be five-twelfths, the capitalists' four-twelfths, and the representatives of talent, three-twelfths of the total product. All the other peaceable utopian plans of distribution invariably made some concession or

---

* Born in 1761 in Pisa; died in 1837 in Paris.
** On this, see Chernov's book *Le parti républicain en France*, Paris, 1901, pp. 80-89, 281-82. It should be noted, however, that Mr. Chernov gives an incorrect description of the attitude of Blanqui to Babouvism and to Saint-Simonism.
*** Born in 1805; died on January 1, 1881.
**** *Débâcle de la politique en France*, p. 63. Considérant's italics.

other to the capitalists; if it had been otherwise, the interests
of the propertied class would not have been assured and, consequently, all hope of a *peaceful solution of the social problem* would
have been lost. Only those socialists who were not afraid of this
contingency, that is to say, those who were in favour of *revolutionary action*, could afford to ignore the interests of the capitalists
and the "rich" generally. Such action was preferred by the "Babouvists" at the end of the eighteenth century and those French socialists of the nineteenth century who were influenced by Babouvists.
Since they saw no need to spare the interests of the "rich",
people of this turn of mind declared outright that they were not
only revolutionaries but also communists. Generally speaking,
the concept "socialism" then differed in France from the concept
"communism" by the fact that in their draft plans of the future
social system the socialists allowed for some—often quite
significant—inequality of property, whereas the communists
rejected it.

As we have just seen, inclination to a revolutionary turn of
mind was to make it easier for French reformers to adopt a communist programme. And, in fact, revolutionaries like Théodore
Dézamy* and Auguste Blanqui upheld the ideas of communism.
However, not all the communists of those days were revolutionaries; the most notable representative of peaceful communism was
Etienne Cabet.** He expressed most vividly the peaceable tendency of the majority of the French socialists when he said: *"If I
had the revolution in my grasp, I would not open my hand even if
I had to die in exile."**** Like the eighteenth-century Enlighteners,
Cabet believed in the omnipotence of reason. He was of the opinion that the benefits of communism could be understood and
appreciated even by the propertied class. The communist revolutionaries did not rely on this and, consequently, preached the
class struggle.

---

* Very little is said about him by the historians of French socialism,
although in certain respects his views are worthy of close attention. I regret
that space does not allow me to present his teaching here. I shall mention
only this. More than any other, it shows how closely connected were the
ideas of the French utopian socialists—and especially of their Left wing,
the communists—with the French materialists of the eighteenth century.
Dézamy relied mainly on Helvétius, whom he referred to as a bold innovator
and an immortal thinker. Dézamy's main work, *Code de la communauté*, was
published in Paris in 1843. In 1841 he published the newspaper *L'Humanitaire*.
It is interesting to note that Marx, in his polemic with the Bauer brothers,
described the Dézamy trend as scientific.[267]

** Born in 1788; died in 1856.

*** *Voyage en Icarie* 1855, p. 565. The italics are Cabet's. This book
(*Voyage to Icaria*) was first published in March 1842. It is the best known of
all Cabet's works; it describes the life of an imaginary communist society.

However, we should not think that their tactics resembled those of the present-day international Social-Democracy, which also of course does not reject either the class struggle or politics. They were predominantly *conspirators*. In the history of international socialism it is hardly possible to find another *conspirator* so typical as Auguste Blanqui. Conspiratorial tactics leave very little room for the independent action of the *masses*. Although the French communist revolutionaries relied more on the masses than their contemporaries—the peaceable socialists, nevertheless, in their conception of the future transformation of society, the masses were only to *support* the conspirators, who were to carry through the main action by themselves.* Conspiratorial tactics are always an unmistakable sign of the inequality of the working class. They become a thing of the past as soon as the working class reaches a definite level of maturity.

IV

The utopian socialists of all shades firmly believed in mankind's progress. We know how much the young M. Y. Saltykov was encouraged by Saint-Simon's idea that the golden age was not behind but ahead of us.[268] The eighteenth-century Enlighteners were also staunch believers in progress. Suffice it to recall the noble Condorcet. The distinguishing feature of socialism is, strictly speaking, not so much belief in progress as the conviction that progress leads to the abolition of the *"exploitation of man by man"*. This theme is constantly to be met with in the speeches and writings of the Saint-Simonists.** "In the past," they said, "the social system was always to some degree or other based upon the exploitation of man by man; today the most important progress will be to put an end to that exploitation, in whatever form it may be conceived."*** The socialists of all other schools also aspired to this end. Their plans of social organisation in many cases stopped short of this aim. As we already know, these plans often did not rule out a certain social inequality which could, in the last resort, be based only on the "exploitation of man by man". The communists alone avoided this inconsistency, which was explained, on the one hand, by the efforts to reconcile the interests of all classes so as to avoid the class struggle and, on the

---

* Regarding F. Buonarroti's attitude to the independent action of the people, see the interesting remark in Paul Robiquet's *Buonarroti et la secte des Egaux d'après les documents inédits*, Paris, 1910, p. 282.

** In the works of Saint-Simon there are but allusions to it; we have already pointed out that in some respects the followers of Saint-Simon went much further than their teacher.

*** See *Doctrine saint-simonienne. Exposition*, Paris, 1854, p. 207.

other hand, by lack of clarity as to what precisely constituted the *economic essence* of that exploitation. Not without reason did the communist Dézamy chide the Saint-Simonists that their "aristocracy of capacities" (l'aristocratie des capacités) and "political theocracy" would in practice lead to almost the same state of affairs then prevailing in society.* However, it was not a question of plans of future social organisation, plans which in any case never came to fruition. The important thing was that the utopian socialists launched into social circulation a great idea which, once it had penetrated the minds of the workers, became the most powerful cultural force of the nineteenth century. The preaching of this idea is probably the greatest service rendered by utopian socialism.

In its various ways of proving the necessity of abolishing the exploitation of man by man, utopian socialism could not but touch upon the effect of this exploitation on social morality. The British socialists, especially Owen and Thompson, had already dilated on the theme that the exploitation of man by man corrupted both the exploited and the exploiters. The French socialists, too, devoted much space in their writings to this subject. That is understandable. If the character of man is determined by the conditions of its development—and this was repeated by all utopian socialists without exception—it is obvious that man's character will be good only where it is allowed to develop in good conditions. In order to make these conditions good, the defects of the prevailing social structure had to be got rid of. The nineteenth-century utopian socialists rejected asceticism, and in one or other way proclaimed the "rehabilitation of the flesh".** On these grounds they were attributed a striving to "unleash evil passions", to assure the triumph of man's *baser* needs over his more exalted ones. This was foolish slander. The utopian socialists never disregarded man's spiritual development. Some of them stated outright that social reform was essential precisely in the interests of man's spiritual growth, being, indeed, its preliminary condition. Already in the writings of the Saint-Simonists there are many strikingly apt illustrations of how poor are the prospects for morality in modern society. This society, they say, is incapable of *preventing* crimes, it can only *punish* them; consequently, the "hangman is the sole authorised professor of morality".*** It is a

---

* *Code de la communauté.* p. 49.
** Sometimes this "rehabilitation" itself was presented in a utopian form: for example, some of Enfantin's fantasies on the relations between the sexes But in essence it meant the intention "here on earth to mount to the kingdom of heaven", as Heine[269] put it somewhat later. (See, by the way, *De l'Humanité*, by Pierre Leroux, Vol. I, p. 176, et seq., 1845 édition.)
*** *Doctrine saint-simonienne,* p. 235.

point of interest that, in repudiating the "hangman", the Saint-Simonists generally repudiated violence as a means of improving human morality. Here again the socialists of all other schools concurred. Even the communist revolutionaries acknowledged violence only as a means of removing the obstacles to social transformation. They were just as energetic as the Saint-Simonists in denying the ability of the "hangman" to be a "professor" of social morality. They, too, understood perfectly well that crimes are prevented not by punishment, but only by eliminating the social causes which incline man's will to evil. *In this sense*, the most extreme revolutionaries, the most indefatigable conspirators, were the convinced advocates of "not opposing evil by force".

V

The views of the utopian socialists on *education* are also extremely important. We already know the close link between Owen's concern for the upbringing of the younger generation and his doctrine on the formation of the human character. This doctrine was shared by the socialists of all countries; so it is not surprising that all of them attached immense importance to education. Among the French utopian socialists, the most profound views on education were expounded by Fourier.

Man is not born corrupt, he is corrupted by circumstances. A child has in embryo all the passions proper to an adult. These should not be suppressed, but given suitable direction. If this is done, says Fourier, the passions will become the source of all that is good, great, useful and generous. But they cannot be given suitable direction under the present social order. Its contradictions put the pedagogue in an impasse, as a result of which education is now but an empty word. The children of the poor cannot be educated in the same way as the children of the rich and privileged. The poor man's son chooses his career at the dictates of necessity; he cannot follow his natural bent. True, the rich man's son has the material means to follow his calling, but his nature is spoiled by the depraving influence of the exclusive position held in society by the privileged class. Education will cease to be an empty word only when "civilisation", as Fourier calls the bourgeois system, gives place to a rational social order. Today work is a heavy burden and a curse to the workers. In a community organised in conformity with the demands of reason, in the phalanstery, work will be an attractive (attrayant) occupation. The spectacle of labour enthusiastically performed by groups of adults will have a highly beneficial effect upon the rising generation. From its earliest years it will learn to love work. This will be all the easier since, in general, children like to work,

36*

and are always eager to imitate the work of adults. This inclination will find its right application only in the phalanstery. There all the children's toys will become simultaneously implements of labour, and every game a productive occupation. Thus, without compulsion, playing and imitating, the child will be taught all the kinds of work for which it feels an aptitude. But that is not enough. *Labour* must find meaning in *knowledge*, and knowledge must be acquired by the young generation in the process of labour useful to society. This means, incidentally, that instruction, in Fourier's opinion, must take the form known in modern pedagogy as the *laboratory system*. And this instruction, which as far as possible will take place out of doors, will have nothing *compulsory* in it. Children and young persons themselves will select freely what they will study and who will teach them.

Only such a system of instruction will, in Fourier's view, provide for the maximum development of the child's natural abilities. Its salutary action will be supplemented by the fact that the abolition of the prevailing social contradictions will broaden the scope for the development of man's social instincts. The productivity of labour will reach its highest peak only when man is able to engage in his favourite occupation *in the society of comrades congenial to him.*

The reader will agree that all these considerations on education are of very great value. Here is another most interesting point. Fourier held that, beginning from three or four years of age, children should be taught by means of various types of joint exercises the mastering *of measured movements*, something in the style of the rhythmical gymnastics of Jacques Dalcroze which now meet with such favour everywhere. In the system of the brilliant French utopian, Fourier, *"measured or material harmony"*, (l'harmonie mesurée ou matérielle) was one of the conditions for harmony of the passions (l'harmonie passionnelle).*

VI

French utopian socialism expressed opinions about art too. The Saint-Simonists wrote a great deal about art, striving to make the *poet* into a prophet, heralding new social truths. But possibly the most thoughtful of all the utopian socialists on questions of art was Pierre Leroux.

Leroux wrote that, as distinct from industry which had the aim of influencing the external world, art was the expression of man's own life. In other words, it was "his life itself, conveying itself

* See *Œuvres complètes de Fourier*, t. V, pp. 1-84. *On Rhythm,* pp. 75-80.

to other men, realising itself, endeavouring to perpetuate itself".*
Proceeding from this thought, Leroux maintained that art is
neither the reproduction of *nature* nor its imitation. Neither can
art imitate *art*, that is to say, the art of a given period cannot
reproduce the art of another period. The true art of every particular historical period reflects the aspirations of that period
alone, and of no other. "Art grows from generation to generation,
like a tall tree that each year adds to its height and raises its top
towards the heavens while simultaneously sinking its roots deeper
into the earth."** The beautiful is called the principle of art: but
that is wrong, since artists quite frequently portray subjects that
are ugly, repulsive and even downright horrific. The domain of
art is much more extensive than that of the beautiful, because
art is the artistic expression of life, and life is not always beautiful."*** But in that case, what does to express life artistically
mean? Leroux believed that it meant expressing life through
symbols. He is quite definite on that score. "The sole principle of
art is the symbol," he affirms (Le principe unique de l'art est le
symbole),**** he asserts. However, by symbolic expression he
understood, in general, the expression of life *in images.* When
V. G. Belinsky said that the thinker expressed his ideas by means
of syllogisms and the artist by images, he was in complete agreement with Leroux.***** In pursuing this idea "Pyotr the Red-
Headed" came to the conclusion that the artist was free, but not
as independent as some believed. "Art is life, which addresses itself
to life." The artist commits a mistake if he ignores the life around
him. *Art for art's sake* is to Leroux "a special kind of egoism".******
All the same, he feels that "art for art's sake" is the fruit of the
artist's discontent with his social environment. Consequently, he
is ready to prefer art for art's sake to the banal art which depicts

---

* See his *Discourse aux artistes,* which appeared for the first time in
the November and December issues of *Revue Encyclopédique* for 1831 and was
reproduced in his *Oeuvres,* Paris, 1850, t. I. The passage quoted is on
page   66.
** Ibid., p. 67.
*** The same thought was expressed later by N. G. Chernyshevsky
and Count Leo Tolstoy.
**** Ibid., pp. 65-67.
***** It is known that the leading Russian "Westerners" of the 1840s[270]
were extremely favourably inclined to Pierre Leroux, whom, for the sake
of caution, they gave the nom de plume of "Pyotr Ryzhy" (Pyotr the Red-
Headed). Of course, their sympathies were not confined solely to his *literary*
views. But it does no harm to point out that they were in agreement with
him, too, on the fundamental questions of aesthetics.
****** From the article "Considérations sur Werther et en général sur
la poésie de notre époque" which appeared in 1839 and subsequently in the
first volume of Leroux's *Works,* pp. 431-51. The remark on the egoism of art
for art's sake is on page 447.

the base—Leroux says: "the basely materialistic"—propensities of bourgeois society. At any rate, Leroux puts a much higher evaluation on the "morbid" poetry which gave birth to the *Werthers Leiden* and *Faust* of Goethe. "Poets!" he exclaims. "Show us hearts, as proud, as independent as those portrayed by Goethe. Only give this independence some purpose, and let it thus turn into heroism.... In brief, show us in all your works the salvation of individual destiny linked with that of universal destiny.... Out of the titans of Goethe and Byron make men, but do not thereby deprive them of their noble character."* In their time, these views played an important role in the history of France's literary development. Everyone knows that they greatly influenced the literary activity of George Sand. In general, if there were people among the French Romanticists who rejected the principle of art for art's sake (for instance Victor Hugo apart from George Sand) it is quite reasonable to suppose that their literary views were not shaped without some help from the socialist literature of the time.

C. GERMAN UTOPIAN SOCIALISM

I

In France and in Britain, utopian socialism was closely related theoretically to the French eighteenth-century philosophy of Enlightenment. This is only partly true of German utopian socialism. Among the German socialists there were some whose views were formed under the *immediate* influence of French *utopian socialism* and, consequently, under the *indirect* influence of French *Enlighteners*. But there were others among them whose social opinions stemmed not from French but from German philosophy. Ludwig Feuerbach more than any other of the German philosophers influenced the course of development of German socialist theory. There was an entire school in German socialism with theoretical structures which are quite incomprehensible without a previous study of the philosophy of the author of *The Essence of Christianity* (so-called true or philosophical socialism). That is why I will touch on this school only in an article on the progress of German philosophical thought from Hegel to Feuerbach.[271] Here I shall deal only with that current of German socialism which kept aloof from German philosophy, and arose from the influence of French socialist literature on German minds.

If France at that time lagged far behind Britain in economic

---

* Ibid., p. 450.

development, Germany trailed a long way behind France. More than three-fourths of the population in Prussia lived in the countryside, and handicraft production was the predominant form in all German towns. Modern industrial capitalism had made significant advances only in a very few provinces, for example, in Rhenish Prussia. The legal position of the German journeyman may be summed up in a few words: complete defencelessness against arbitrary action by the police. "Whoever has even once visited the Vienna police headquarters in the morning," writes Violand, "will remember the hundreds of journeymen who had to stand packed together for hours in a narrow corridor, waiting for their 'road-books', while a policeman with a sabre or baton in his hand kept an eye on them like on overseer watching slaves. It seemed as though police and justice had conspired to drive these poor men to despair."* It was these despairing poor, whom, in Violand's words, the authorities treated like cattle, that were the chief disseminators of the ideas of French socialism throughout Germany during the thirties and forties. From among them came the outstanding communist writer, Wilhelm Weitling (a tailor by trade).** His views will take precedence here. But before proceeding to discuss them, I have a few words to say about one work of the talented Georg Büchner who died early in life.***

This work, published illegally, is entitled *Der Hessische Landbote* (The Hessen Rural Herald). It was printed in July 1834, in a secret printing press in Offenbach, and was addressed primarily to the *peasantry*. This is a remarkable fact. We can find no direct appeals to the peasantry either in English or French socialist literature. Even in Germany, *The Hessen Rural Herald* remained unique. Weitling and his associates wrote for the working class, that is to say, properly speaking, for the artisans. Only the Russian socialists of the 1870s addressed their appeals in the main to the peasantry.

The content of *The Hessen Rural Herald* is also, one might say, Narodnik. It speaks of "the immediate needs of the people" (to use an expression our Narodniks often resorted to). In it Büchner contrasts the free and untrammelled life of the rich man, which, he says, resembles one continuous holiday, to the bitter life of the poor man which he likens to an eternal day of toil. Then he points to the burden of taxation crushing the people and sharply criticises the existing system of government. Lastly, he advises the people to rise against their oppressors and cites examples from

---

* See Bernhard Becker, *Die Reaktion in Deutschland gegen die Revolution von 1848*, Braunschweig, 1873, S. 68.
** Born in 1808; left for America in 1849 and died in 1871.
*** Born in 1813; died in 1837. He was the brother of Ludwig Büchner who became prominent later.

history, notably, the French revolutions of 1789 and 1830, which prove the possibility of a victorious people's uprising.

The revolutionary call to the peasantry stood no chance of success in those days. The peasants handed over to the authorities the copies of *The Hessen Rural Herald* scattered near their huts during the night. The rest of the edition was confiscated by the police, and Büchner had to flee. But the fact that he spoke to the peasantry in the language of a revolutionary is typical of German socialist thought in the 1830s. "Friede den Hütten! Krieg den Palästen!" (Peace to the huts! War to the Palaces!) proclaimed Büchner in his *Landbote*. This was a call to the class struggle. Weitling too addressed the same kind of appeal to his readers. Peaceful moods were revealed and prevailed for a time only in the works of those German socialist writers who had been through Feuerbach's philosophical school.

In preaching the class struggle, Büchner did not, however, realise the importance of politics in this struggle. He set no store by the advantages of a constitutional regime. Like our Narodniks, he was afraid that a constitution, by bringing about the domination of the bourgeoisie, would worsen still further the position of the people. "If our Constitutionalists succeeded in overthrowing the German governments and setting up a united monarchy or a republic,* that would only create a financial aristocracy here, as in France. Better to let things stay as they are." Such a view of a constitution also makes Büchner akin to our Narodniks. Being a revolutionary, he was not, of course, a supporter of the outrageous political system then existing. He also favoured a republic, but not one which would usher in the rule of the financial aristocracy. He wanted the revolution to guarantee above all the material interests of the people. On the other hand, he considered that German liberalism was impotent precisely because it neither desired nor was able to make the interests of the working masses the basis of its political aspirations.

For Büchner the question of freedom was a question of force. This is the same idea which, many years later, was so well developed by Lassalle in his speech on the essence of the Constitution.

Büchner also wrote a play, *Danton's Tod* (The Death of Danton). I refrain from making a literary assessment of the play and shall merely note that its "pathos" lies in the unavailing and therefore tormenting quest for conformity to law in the great movements of history. In one of his letters to his betrothed, evidently dating to the period when he was working on his play,

---

* The Constitutionalists were working for the political unification of Germany.

Büchner wrote: "For several days already I have been taking up my pen every minute, but cannot write a word. I have been studying the history of the revolution, I have felt myself crushed, as it were, by the frightful fatalism of history. I see in human nature the most repulsive mediocrity, and in human relations an irresistible force imparted to all in general and no one in particular. The individual personality is only foam on the crest of the wave, greatness is only an accident, the power of genius only a puppet-show, a ridiculous attempt to fight against an iron law, which at best can only be discovered, but which it is impossible to master." Nineteenth-century utopian socialism, just like the French Enlighteners of the eighteenth century, could not solve the problem of conformity to law in the historical development of mankind. I will say more. The socialism of that period was utopian precisely because it was unable to solve this question. However, Büchner's persistent efforts in this direction show that he was no longer content with the point of view of utopian socialism. When A. I. Herzen was writing his book, *From the Other Shore*, he struggled with the same problem that had much earlier worried Büchner.

II

I have said that the artisan journeymen in Germany were the bearers of French socialist ideas. Here is how this happened. As we know, after finishing their apprenticeship they spent several years in travel. Their travels frequently took them out of Germany, and while residing in more advanced countries they came in contact with progressive social movements there. In France they became acquainted with socialism, and sympathised most with its extreme shade—*communism*. The most notable theoretician of German socialism at the time, the tailor Weitling, whom I have already mentioned, also experienced the influence of the French utopian socialists, and also became a communist.

Utopian socialism did not appeal to the objective course of historical development, but to the better feelings of mankind. As German writers say nowadays, it was *socialism of emotions*. Weitling was no exception to this general rule. He, too, appealed to feeling, reinforcing his calls with excerpts from the Bible. His first work, *Die Menschheit wie sie ist und wie sie sein sollte* (Mankind As It Is and As It Ought to Be), published in 1838, begins with these words from the Gospel: But when He saw the multitudes He was moved with compassion on them.... Then saith He unto His disciples, The harvest truly is plenteous, but the labourers are few. Pray ye therefore the Lord of the harvest, that He sends forth labourers into His harvest.

Weitling explains this passage in the sense that the harvest is mankind ripening to perfection, and its fruit is the community of property on earth. "The commandment of love calls you to the harvest," he says to his readers, "and the reaping to enjoyment. If then you wish to reap and find enjoyment, fulfil the commandment of love."*

Owen proceeded from the teaching on the formation of the human character, that is to say, from the known concept of human nature. The French utopian socialists based themselves on the same concept, modifying it here and there to suit themselves. Weitling was no exception. Following Fourier's example, he proceeded from an analysis of the passions and needs of man; and constructed his plan of future society upon the results of this analysis.** However, he did not attribute any absolute significance to his plan. He said himself that plans of this type are very good in that they prove the possibility and necessity for social reform. "The more such works there are, the more proof the people will have of this. But the best work of all on this subject we shall have to write with our blood."*** Here we feel a more or less vague consciousness of the fact that the nature of the future society will be determined by the objective course of social development, expressed by the way in the revolutionary struggle of classes. Weitling addressed himself, not to the "rich" and not even to the whole of mankind without distinction of title and rank, but only to the "people of labour and affliction". He took Fourier severely to task for making concessions to capital in his plan for the distribution of products. In Weitling's opinion, to make such concessions was to sew old patches on humanity's new clothing and to hold up to ridicule the present and all future generations.**** He said that every replacement of the old by the new was a revolution. Consequently, communists could not but be revolutionaries. However, revolutions would not always be bloody.***** Communistspreferred a peaceful revolution to one accompanied by bloods-

---

* See page 7 of the New York edition of this work, 1854.
** Ten peasants form a "Zug" and appoint a "Zugführer"; ten "Zugführers" appoint an "Ackermann"; one hundred "Ackermänner" appoint a "Landwirtschaftsrath" and so on, and so forth (*Die Menschheit*, p. 32). This is how agricultural work is to organised in Weitling's future society. He goes into similar detail in describing other sides of its life, I see no point in quoting them here.
*** Ibid., p. 30.
**** See his main work *Garantien der Harmonie und Freiheit*, published at the end of 1842. It was republished in Berlin in 1908 on the occasion of the hundredth anniversary of Weitling's birth, with a biographical introduction and notes by Mehring. The reference to Fourier's plan of distribution of products is on pages 224 and 225 of that edition.
***** Ibid., pp. 226 and 227.

hed. But the course of transformation depended not on them, but on the conduct of the upper classes and of governments. "In peaceful times, let us teach; in stormy times, let us act," wrote Weitling.* However, he made reservations to this formula which show that he did not have an entirely clear conception either of the character of proletarian *action* or of what the workers had to be *taught*. According to him, humanity was now mature enough to understand all that might help it remove the knife pointed at its throat. Weitling condemned Marx's opinion that Germany in its historical progress towards communism could not by-pass the intermediate phase of bourgeois rule. He wanted Germany to skip over this stage, just as later our Narodniks desired that Russia should skip over it. In 1848 he refused to agree with the proposition that the proletariat should support the bourgeoisie in its struggle against the remnants of feudalism and the absolute monarchy. Being convinced that everyone was wise enough to wish to remove the knife pointed at his throat, Weitling upheld the theory usually expressed in the words: "The worse, the better." He believed that the worse the position of the working mass became, the more likely it was to protest against the existing order of things. The subsequent development of the European proletariat demonstrated that actually this was not the case. Nevertheless, this theory was repeated in full in the arguments of M. A. Bakunin. Among the measures which Weitling believed could prove to be necessary in certain circumstances of the struggle for social reconstruction, was one that today seems very strange. He thought it possible to recommend to the communists (true), only conditionally, in certain circumstances) that they should appeal to the slum element of the urban population and adopt "new tactics" in keeping with the low moral level of these elements. In his main work, he expressed this thought only in hints, though fairly transparent ones.** Later he came to express it more clearly, building up a theory of the "thieving proletariat" (des "stehlenden Proletariats"). Weitling's associates rejected this theory.*** But M. A. Bakunin subsequently created a theory close to that of Weitling's, the doctrine of the "*brigand*" as the bulwark of the revolutionary movement. To those who may be too unpleasantly surprised by such theories, I would remind that the type of the great-hearted and heroically bold brigand had

---

* Ibid., p. 235.
** See *Garantien der Harmonie und Freiheit*, S. 235-36.
*** On this matter and the attitude of other communists to it, see G. Adler, *Die Geschichte der ersten sozialpolitischen Arbeiterbewegung in Deutschland mit besonderen Rücksicht auf die einwirkenden Theorien*, Breslau, 1885, S. 43-44. I hasten to add that Weitling himself soon ceased to defend his "new tactics".

quite a respectable place in Romantic literature.* And not only in Romantic literature; Schiller's Karl Moor was also a robber. Utopian socialism in general paid a fairly high tribute to the fantastic.

III

In Weitling's main work, which was warmly praised by Feuerbach and Marx, there is much evidence that he understood, more clearly than many of the French utopians, the objective logic of the mutual relations between the classes in capitalist society. The reader will find a number of interesting remarks also in those —first—chapters of his *Garantien* which deal with the *origin* of classes and of class rule. In his conception of the motive forces of social development, Weitling remained unquestionably an idealist. However, one senses that he is no longer satisfied with historical idealism, and that he dwells with pleasure on those conjectures which at times occur to him, and which suggest the possibility of a more profound explanation of at least some aspects of social life. I am sure that it was this particular feature of his main work which was one of the reasons why he won Marx's sympathy and understanding. But for all that, Weitling's *Garantien* shows no sign of its author having taken very much interest in economic theory as such. He was a product of his times: and in his times the German socialists did not as yet study economics. "I do not believe," Engels wrote, in his reminiscences of the German Communist League of the pre-Marxist period, "there was a single man in the whole League at that time who had ever read a book on political economy. But that mattered little; for the time being 'equality', 'brotherhood', and 'justice' helped them to surmount every theoretical obstacle."[272] The German Communists obviously bore no resemblance to the British socialists in this respect. It should not be forgotten, however, that as early as the thirties of the last century there was a socialist in Germany who was deeply interested in economic questions and extremely well versed in the literature of political economy. True, he stood quite apart. His name was Johann-Karl Rodbertus Jagetzow.**

He said of himself that his theory was only "the consistent sequel of the proposition introduced into the science by Smith, and still more profoundly substantiated by the school of Ricardo, the proposition that all articles of consumption, *economically considered, must be regarded only as products of labour, as costing*

---

* See the interesting remarks on this subject in I. Ivanov's preface to the Russian translation of Byron's *The Corsair* (*Complete Works of Byron*, published by Efron-Brockhaus, Vol. I, St. Petersburg, 1904, pp. 274-76 [in Russian]).

** Born in 1805: died in 1875.

nothing apart from labour."* This view of his on labour as the sole source of the value of articles of consumption was expounded in the first of his books, published in 1842 and entitled *Zur Erkenntnis unserer staatswirtschaftlichen Zustände.* A literal translation of this is "Contribution to the Knowledge of Our National Economic Conditions". But in point of fact Rodbertus did not occupy himself with national economic matters in the proper meaning of the term. He studied the position of the worker in capitalist society, and tried to devise measures that would contribute to improving that position. "The main purpose of my researches," he writes, "will be to increase the share of the working classes in the national product, and that on a solid foundation freed from the influences of the vicissitudes of the market. I want to give this class the opportunity also to share in the advance of productivity; I want to abolish that law which otherwise could be fatal for our condition, namely, the law that, no matter how much productivity increases, the workers are always reduced by virtue of the market to a wage-level no higher than the necessary subsistence level; a wage-level which deprives the workers of the possibility of receiving the education of our time ... a wage-level which constitutes the most glaring contradiction with their present legal position, with that formal equality with the other estates proclaimed by our most important institutions."**

As wages in present-day conditions are always being reduced to the workers' basest subsistence level, and since the productivity of labour is constantly increasing, the working class receives an ever-lessening share of the product which it creates by its labour. "I am convinced," says Rodbertus, "that the wages of labour, regarded as a quota of the product, fall in a proportion at least equal to, if not greater than, that in which the productivity of labour rises."*** And if a constant reduction of the workers' wages— as a share of the national product created by their labour—can be proved, then such menacing phenomena as *industrial crises* become quite understandable. As a consequence of the relative reduction of wages, the workers' purchasing power ceases to correspond to the development of the social productive forces. This purchasing power does not increase, or even decreases, while production increases and the markets are glutted with goods. From this arise the difficulties in selling the goods, stagnation in business, and finally

---

* Italicised by Rodbertus.
** *Zur Erkenntnis*, etc. pp. 28-29, footnote.
*** *Zur Beleuchtung der sozialen Frage*, Berlin, 1875, S. 25. This book is a reprint of the *Social Letters to von Kirchmann* published in 1850-51. It contains the second and third letters. Originally there were three letters. A fourth was published after the death of Rodbertus under the title of *Das Kapital*, (Berlin, 1884).

industrial crises. Rodbertus is not daunted by the objection that purchasing power remains in the hands of the upper classes, and so continues to influence the market. "Value is inherent in a product," he says, "but it does not rise above the demand. What in the hands of a worker is still of value, in the hands of others becomes superfluous, i.e., an unsaleable product. A long halt must occur in national production to allow the accumulated mass to be distributed, and only then should a large part of national production be restructured so that what is taken from a worker could amount, in the hands of another, to an increment in the purchasing power in the market."*

The reduction of the share of the working class in the national product signifies its *impoverishment*. Rodbertus does not agree with Adam Smith, who contended that a man was rich or poor to the degree that he was assured the satisfaction of his needs. If this were true, the well-to-do German of today would be richer than the kings of antiquity. "By wealth (of a person or a class) we have to understand the *relative share*" (of that person or class) "in the mass of products determined by the current stage of the cultural development of a people."**

So the growth of social wealth is accompanied by the relative impoverishment of the class whose labour creates that wealth. Five-sixths of the nation not only prove to be deprived of all the blessings of culture, but have at times to endure the most frightful miseries of destitution which hangs over them constantly. In previous historical epochs, the privations of the working masses—let us assume—were essential for the progress of civilisation. That no longer holds good. Now the growth of the productive forces gives every possibility of eliminating these privations. And Rodbertus asks in his first letter to Kirchmann: "Can there be ... a more just demand than that the creators of the old and new wealth also receive some advantage from this increase; than that their income be increased or their labour-time shortened, or that an ever greater number of them enter the ranks of those happy ones who are preferentially entitled to reap the fruits of labour?" Convinced that there is nothing more just than this demand, Rodbertus proposes a series of measures for the improvement of the workers' lot.

All these measures can be reduced to the regulation of wages by law. The state must establish their level for each branch of production, and then alter them in accordance with the rise in the productivity of national labour. Such a determination of

---

* *Zeitschrift für die gesammte Staatswissenschaft*, 1878, erstes u. zweites Heft, S. 345. Rodbertus' pamphlet *Der normal-Arbeitstag* is reprinted there.
** *Zur Erkenntnis*, pp. 38-39.

wages would lead logically to the establishment of a new "scale of value".

Since all articles of consumption, from the point of view of political economy, must be regarded only as products of labour, costing nothing apart from labour, *only labour* can be the true "scale of value". In present-day society, because of the fluctuation of market prices, products are not always exchanged in accordance with the amount of labour expended on their production. This evil must be eliminated by state intervention. The state must put into circulation "labour money", i.e., certificates indicating how much labour had been spent on the production of a given article. In brief, Rodbertus arrives here at the same idea of the organisation of exchange which arose first in Britain in the 1820s and then went from there to France (Proudhon). It would be superfluous to enlarge upon it.

It should be added, however, that all such measures were for Rodbertus only of temporary significance. He said that later—in some five hundred years—communist society would be established, and then the exploitation of man by man would come to an end altogether.

In proposing his solution of the "social question", Rodbertus never tired of repeating that this solution must be *absolutely peaceable*. He believed neither in "barricades" nor in "kerosene", nor yet in the independent political action of the proletariat. He expected everything to come from above, from the royal power which, in his opinion, should and could become "social" (soziales Königthum).

My exposition of Rodbertus' views has been taken from various of his works, starting with *Zur Erkenntnis*, published in 1842, etc. It is worth while noting, however, that he presented all his views in condensed form as early as the late thirties, in an article which he sent to the *Augsburger Allgemeine Zeitung*, but which that paper did not accept. The article was reprinted in *Briefe und sozialpolitische Aufsätze* by Dr. Rodbertus-Jagetzow published by Rudolph Meyer in 1882 in Berlin. (See pp. 575-86 in Volume II: "Fragmente aus einem alten Manuskript." It is interesting in many respects. But the following points deserve the most attention: first, his view of the working class as barbarians ("Barbaren an Geist und Sitte"—barbarians in spirit and morals);* secondly, the fear that the barbarians living within the ranks of civilised society might become its rulers, just as the barbarians of antiquity became the rulers of Rome. Everything went well so long as it was a question of the present-day barbarians being used by the state in its struggle against the bourgeoisie. But on whom

---

* Compare with Enfantin's views given above.

would the state rely in the struggle against these barbarians? Would the latter struggle for long against themselves? In the interests of its self-preservation society will have to carry out social reform.*

Rodbertus was afraid of the working class. If he had been less afraid of this class, he would have been less inclined both to his principal utopia—a "social" monarchy, and his secondary utopias closely connected with it, like "labour money".

Today bourgeois economists are fond of repeating that Marx took his economic theory from the British socialists. Some twenty to twenty-five years ago, when they were hardly acquainted with British socialist literature, they "discovered" that Marx owed his position as an economist entirely to Rodbertus. One argument is as unfounded as the other. Moreover, the greater part of Rodbertus' works appeared at a time when Marx's economic views were already fully formed in their main features. Nevertheless, Rodbertus holds a place of honour among the German economists** whom, be it said in passing, he regarded with profound disdain.

---

* See p. 579 in Vol. II of the R. Meyer publication just quoted.

** On Rodbertus, see Engels' preface to the German translation of Marx's *Misère de la philosophie* (The Poverty of Philosophy originally published in French; there is a Russian translation by V. I. Zasulich edited by myself,)[273] and *Theorien über den Mehrwert*, by Marx, Vol. II, second section of the first part (Die Grundrente).[274] Rodbertus' views were first expounded in Russian at the beginning of the 1880s by the late N. I. Sieber (in *Yuridichesky Vestnik*) and by myself (in *Otechestvenniye zapiski*).[275] My articles on Rodbertus were reprinted in the collection *Over Twenty Years* (under the pen name of Beltov), pp. 503-647. Besides these, see T. Kozak, *Rodbertus, sozial-ökonomische Ansichten*, Jena, 1882, Georg Adler, *Rodbertus, der Begründer des wissenschaftlichen Sozialismus*, Leipzig, 1883; Dietzel, *Karl Rodbertus, Darstellung seines Lebens und seiner Lehre*, Jena, 1886-1887, 2 Teile; Jentsch, *Rodbertus*, Stuttgart, 1899; Gonner, *Social Philosophy of Rodbertus*, London, 1899.

PREFACE TO A. DEBORIN'S BOOK: *AN INTRODUCTION TO THE PHIOLOSOPHY OF DIALECTICAL MATERIALISM*

I

What is the task of philosophy? Its task, says E. Zeller, is "to investigate scientifically the ultimate basis of cognition and being, and to comprehend all existing reality in its connection with that basis."[276] That is correct. However, a new question arises at once: can the "basis of cognition" be considered as something separate from the "basis of being"? That question must be answered decisively in the negative. Our *ego* contrasts itself to the external world (*non-ego*), but at the same time it feels its connection with that external world. Consequently, when man begins to philosophise, that is to say, when he conceives the desire to find a consistent world-outlook for himself, he immediately comes up against the question of what is the relation of *ego* to *non-ego*, of "cognition" to "being", of "spirit" to "nature". True, there was a time when philosophers did not discuss such questions. This was in the initial period of the development of ancient Greek philosophy. For instance, Thales taught that water is the primary substance from which all things come and to which all things return. But he did not ask himself: what relation has consciousness to that primary substance? Nor did Anaximenes ask himself the same question when he averred that the primary substance was not water but air. However, the time arrived when even Greek philosophers could no longer evade the question of the relationship of *ego* to *non-ego*, of consciousness to being. And then the question became the cardinal problem of philosophy. And it remains so even now.

Various philosophical systems give various answers to it. But if we consider the replies given by these various systems we shall see that they are far from being as different as they appear at first sight. All of them can be divided into two compartments.

The first embraces those philosophical constructions which take as their starting point the *object*, or *being*, or again, *nature*. Here, the thinkers have to explain how to the *object* is added the *subject*, to *being—consciousness*, to *nature—spirit*. Since they do not all explain this in the same way, the result is that, in spite of their having the same point of departure, their systems are not quite the same.

The other compartment takes in all philosophical constructions which take as their starting point the *subject, consciousness, spirit*. Obviously, here the thinker has to explain how to the *subject* is added the *object*, to *consciousness—being*, to *spirit—nature*. And according to the *manner in which* they fulfil this task, philosophical systems that come into this compartment differ from one another.

He who takes the object as his starting point, if only he has the ability and courage to think consistently, arrives at one of the varieties of the *materialist world-outlook*.

He who takes the *subject* as his starting point and again if only he is prepared to think the matter out to the end, will turn out to be an *idealist* of one shade or another.

And those people who are incapable of consistent thought stop half-way and are content with a mish-mash of idealism and materialism. Such inconsistent thinkers are called *eclectics*.

To this it may be objected that there are also adherents of *"critical" philosophy*, who are equally far from materialism as from idealism and yet are free of the weaknesses commonly associated with the eclectic mode of thought. I recall such an objection being advanced against me by Professor Chelpanov. But I refer the reader to Chapter Six of Deborin's book ("The Transcendental Method"). There he will see just how unfounded this objection is. Deborin clearly and convincingly demonstrates that the "critical" philosophy of Kant suffers from *dualism*. And since *dualism is always eclectic*, it is only by a misconception that one can cite Kant in refutation of my contention that every consistent thinker is bound to choose between idealism and materialism.

Fichte already pointed out the inconsistency of Kantianism, although it is true that he initially ascribed this to Kant's followers rather than to Kant himself. "Your Earth," he said to them, "rests on an elephant, and the elephant, in turn, rests on the Earth. Your thing-in-itself, which is a pure thought, has to act upon the ego." Convinced that Kant himself was free of this contradiction—indeed an unquestionable and unpardonable one— Fichte declared that the true meaning of the "Kantianism of Kant" lies in idealism (namely, in Fichte's *Theory of Knowledge*). Kant disagreed with this, and protested in print against such an interpretation of his philosophy. He described Fichte's idealist system as resembling an apparition: "When you think you have got hold of it, there is nothing there but yourself, and of this self there is nothing but a hand stretched out to catch."* After that there was

---

* *Kant's Werke*, Ausgabe von Hartenstein, X. Band, S. 577-78. There are more details about this in the article, "Materialism or Kantianism", contained in my collection of articles, *A Critique of Our Critics*.[277]

nothing Fichte could do but reproach Kant himself with inconsistency, which he did, calling him "ein Dreiviertelskopf" (literally, three-fourths of a head).

II

Now let us proceed. It is quite obvious that if each of us is a subject for himself (*I*), to other people he can only be an object (*thou*). It is no less obvious that people do not exist outside nature but within it. It would appear, therefore, that it is precisely nature (being, object) that must be taken as the starting point of all philosophical systems. How can one explain the origin of those philosophical systems in which the starting point is *spirit* and not *nature*?

For an answer to this question we must turn first of all *to the history of culture*.

The famous English ethnologist, Edward B. Tylor, said a long time ago that the very essence of spiritualist philosophy, as opposed to materialist philosophy, stems from primitive animism.* Some might consider this as paradoxical. Then again others may remark that, generally speaking, ethnologists are not very competent in the history of philosophy. To such readers I would say that the ethnologist's opinion in this case is shared, at least partly, by one very famous historian of philosophy. In his very talented work, dedicated to "Greek thinkers", Theodor Gomperz recognises that Plato's doctrine on ideas bears a significant resemblance to the conceptions of some primitive tribes, conceptions which have their origin in animism.** But why resort to authorities? We can see what is going on with our own eyes. What is animism? It is an attempt on the part of the savage to explain natural phenomena. No matter how feeble and ineffectual this attempt may be, it is inevitable in primitive man's conditions of life.

In his struggle for existence, primitive man performs certain acts that bring about certain happenings. Thus he comes to look upon himself as the *cause* of these occurrences. By analogy with himself, he thinks that all other phenomena spring likewise from the actions of creatures who like himself have certain sensations, needs, passions, reason and volition. But as he cannot see these creatures, he comes to accept them as "*spirits*" which in ordinary circumstances are imperceptible to his senses, and act directly upon these senses only in exceptional cases. *Religion*, the subsequent development of which is determined by the course of social development, stems from this animism.

---

* *La civilisation primitive*, Paris, 1876, I, p. 493.
** Not having at hand the German original, I am quoting from the French translation—see pages 414-15 of the Lausanne edition, 1905, Vol. 2.

Gods are those spirits that primitive man believes are disposed towards him and whom he therefore worships. He believes that one or several of these spirits *created* the world. True, what interests primitive hunter is not *who created the animals*, the hunting of which provides him with the means of existence, but *where the animals come from*. The primitive hunter finds the answer to this principal question in his cosmogony. Stories of the world's creation only come later, when with the development of the productive forces man's productive activity extends, and he becomes more and more accustomed to the idea of *creation*. It is quite natural that the activity of the world's creator (or creators) seems to primitive man similar to his own productive activity. Thus, according to the myth of one American tribe, man was fashioned from clay. In Memphis they believed that the god Ptah *built* the world as a mason builds a house; in Sais it was said that the world had been *woven* by a goddess, etc.

We see that *cosmogony* is closely related to *technique*. But that by the way.* Here I have but one remark to make: once belief in the world having been created by some spirit or other was established, this paved the way for all those philosophical systems which have *spirit* (the *subject*) as their starting point, and, hence, in some way or other define the existence of *nature* (the *object*). It is in this sense that we can and must admit that spiritualist philosophy—and every idealist philosophy—in its opposition to materialism, springs from primitive animism.

Needless to say, the creative spirit of the idealists—for example, the absolute spirit of Schelling or Hegel—bears very little resemblance to the god of the American tribe I mentioned above who was said to have fashioned man out of clay. The gods of primitive tribes were completely like people, except that they had greater power. But there is nothing human in Schelling's or Hegel's absolute spirit, apart from consciousness. In other words, the conceptions of spirits which primitive man had underwent a very long process of *distillation* (as Engels expressed it),[279] before merging into the conception of the absolute spirit as formulated by the great German idealists. But the long process of "distillation" could bring no *essential* change in animist ideas: *in essence* they remained unaltered.

III

Animism is the first expression we know of man's consciousness that there is a causal connection between natural phenomena. It explains natural phenomena with the aid of *myths*. But although

---

* For more details of this see my first article, "On Religious Seekings" in the collection *From Defence to Attack*.[278]

such explanations satisfy the curiosity of primitive man, they do not at all increase his power over nature.

Let us take an example. A Fijian falls ill and lies down on the ground, shouting loudly to persuade his soul to return to his body. Of course, the arguments which he addresses to his soul exert no influence at all on the pathological processes taking place in his body. In order to acquire the possibility of influencing these processes in the desired way, man had first to observe organic life from the standpoint of science. To observe natural phenomena from the standpoint of science means to explain them, not by the action of this or that spiritual being, but by the laws of nature itself. Man succeeds in increasing his power over nature only to the extent that he notices the law-governed connection between phenomena. A scientific view of a particular field of natural phenomena completely excludes an animist view of nature. As one historian of Greece correctly remarked, he who knows the true cause of the apparent motion of the sun round the earth will not tell the story of Helios who every morning mounts his fiery chariot to climb the steep celestial path, and in the evening descends into the west to rest. This means that in explaining the cause of the sun's apparent motion round the earth he would take as his starting point not the subject, but the object, and would address himself not to spirit, but to nature.

This is exactly how the Greek thinkers of the Ionian school acted.[280] He who taught that the beginning of all things was water or air, obviously started from the object and not from the subject. In exactly the same way, when Heraclitus said that the cosmos was not created by any gods or men, "but it was forever, it is and always will be eternal fire, regularly flaring up and regularly dying away", even with the greatest will in the world it was impossible to impose on him an animist view of the world as the product of the activity of a spirit or spirits. Recalling E. Zeller's definition of the task facing philosophy, we can say that to the thinkers of the Ionian school the ultimate basis of *cognition* stemmed from the ultimate basis of *being*. This is true to such an extent that, for example, Diogenes of Apollonia, who maintained that all things are varieties of air, believed that this primary matter possesses *reason* and "*knows much*".

The scientific view of natural phenomena has such enormous advantages over the animist view that Greek philosophy had perforce to proceed in its further development from the object instead of the subject, that is to say, to be materialist and not idealist. Yet we know that, at least from the time of Socrates, Greek philosophy quite definitely took the path of idealism. And in our days, idealism has become the dominant philosophy. Nowadays the specialists in philosophy—especially the assistant-professors—

do not even think it necessary to argue with the materialists. They are convinced that to criticise materialism is as superfluous as knocking at an open door. The classical country of this majestic contempt for materialism was and, of course, remains Germany, with its innumerable teachers of philosophy who are described very aptly by Schopenhauer.* And since the vast majority of our Russian intelligentsia are trailing along behind those German teachers of philosophy (for our intelligentsia has an interest in philosophy) it is not surprising that here in Russia the philosophical people** (as Joseph Priestley once called them) have become accustomed to look down on us, the impenitent materialists. This is the explanation of a fact our readers are well aware of, that so many attempts have been made in Russia to provide the teaching of Marx and Engels with a new philosophical basis. All these attempts were dictated by the desire to reconcile the *materialist* explanation of history with one or other of the brands of the *idealist* theory of cognition. These attempts were foredoomed to failure, because eclecticism had always been as barren as the virgin who had devoted herself to God. Apart from this, the writers had neither knowledge nor philosophical talent. It is not worth while discussing them, although their writings deserve mention as being very typical of the period.

IV

Why did idealism triumph over materialism, notwithstanding the obvious advantages of the scientific view of nature over the animist?

There are two main reasons for this.

First of all, for a very long time natural science made such slow progress that it could not eject animism from all its positions. While gradually becoming accustomed to seeing some fields of phenomena from the point of view of science, people continued to cling to their animist views in other more extensive fields. Consequently, their world-outlook in general remained animist. When social life began to grow complex and relations between separate societies became more frequent, there even came into existence a quite new field of phenomena which for a long time would not yield to scientific research, and, consequently, was interpreted animistically by reference to the activity of some god or other. The tragedies of Euripides often end with the words: "In many a shape is the Gods' will wrought, and much They accomplish that none foreknows. What men deemed sure, They bring to naught, and what none dreamed of They dispose...." In the struggle of

---

* *Parerga und Paralipomena*: *Über die Universitätsphilosophie.*
** [Plekhanov here gives the English phrase: the philosophical people].

forces within a given nation, as well as in international wars and in trading relations, that which was considered to be impossible, was and is very often accomplished, while that which was expected remains unaccomplished. This to a very large extent supported and still supports belief in the existence of "celestial powers" and the tendency to seek aid from them. Such belief and such a tendency are to be remarked even among those prominent thinkers who have acted as leaders of civilised mankind in the progress towards a scientific understanding of the world. The fathers of the scientific philosophy of nature—the Ionian thinkers—continued to believe in the existence of gods.*

Besides this, we should bear in mind the following. Although animist conceptions arise and continue to exist for some time, quite independently of the view which the savage may have of his obligations towards the society to which he belongs, nevertheless this view begins to combine fairly early with the animist conceptions. Subsequently, at higher stages of culture, animist conceptions are wrought into more or less orderly systems of religious beliefs and become very firmly welded with people's conceptions of their mutual obligations. People begin to regard these obligations as commandments of the gods. Religion *sanctifies* the morality established in the given society, as well as all its other *"mainstays"*.

In the Laws of Manu, we read that the creator of the universe fashioned people of different social classes out of different parts of his body. From his mouth (said to be the most noble part— *G.P.*) he made the Brahmans; from his arms, the Kshatriya; from his thigh, the Vaisya; and lastly, from his feet, the Sudra.** It is the creator's wish that the lower classes should always be obedient to the upper classes,*** and he goes on to explain that the existing division of society into classes must remain as immutable as the seasonal sequence of the year.****

This sanctification of a given social order by a given religion makes the latter a major conservative force. Consequently, religion is very dear to the heart of all conservatives. And if there are in the ruling class of a given society people studying questions of theory in general and philosophy in particular, they will doubtless be sworn enemies of any philosophical doctrine which, extending the conception of natural conformity to law to the whole understanding of the world, undermines the very foundation of

---

* True, Thales is believed to have said that gods, like everything else, are made from water. This legend shows that Thales' contemporaries thought that his ideas on gods were unlike their own.
** *Book I*, paragraph 31.
*** *Book IX*, paragraphs 313-36.
**** *Book I*, paragraph 30.

religious beliefs. Lucretius made the following rapturous utterance in praise of the materialist Epicurus for rendering harmless
faith in the gods:

> *When human life lay foully on the earth*
> *Before all eyes, 'neath Superstition crushed,*
> *Who from the heavenly quarters showed her head*
> *And with appalling aspect lowered on men,*
> *Then did a Greek first lift eyes to hers—*
> *First brave her face to face. Him neither myth*
> *Of gods, nor thunderbolt, nor sky with roar*
> *And threat could quell....*

Such praise presupposes one of two things: either that he who
utters it is hostile to the prevailing social order, or that he is
firmly convinced in the unshakeable firmness of that order and
considers it superfluous to defend it with "spiritual weapon". Taken
as a whole, not a single ruling class has ever revolted against
its own rule. On the other hand, in present-day European society,
which has undergone so many upheavals, the ruling classes have
not the slightest reason to believe in the unshakeable firmness of
the existing order of things. As a result, they do not scorn the use
of the "spiritual weapon", and their ideologists make every possible effort to purge philosophy of all "destructive" elements.

In transitional periods of social development, when a particular
class has just attained victory, even though incomplete, over the
class above it, and when the excitement of thought aroused by
the struggle has not as yet abated—in such transitional periods of
social development philosophical hypocrisy begins to be considered
a duty which a thinking person owes to "respectable" society.
This, too, may appear incredible, but it is true nevertheless.
Just take the trouble to read the following passage written by a
man who could not have been farther from the materialist explanation of the history of philosophy. He is speaking of England at
the end of the seventeenth century and in the first half of the
eighteenth century.

"If free-thinking had at first to wrest a place from the church
authorities for its own development, with the passage of time
voices were heard within it speaking against the unrestricted rule
of freedom of thought.... The esoteric view withdrew ever further
from positive religion and, partly under the reverse influence of
French literature, even began to adopt the temporal scepticism
inherent in the latter. On the other hand, the exoteric doctrine
adapted itself more and more to the purely political or police
conception of religion.... It was precisely in the upper classes of
English society that this internally self-contradictory situation ...
became apparent."[281]

V

Windelband quite rightly selects Lord Bolingbroke (1662-1751) as the most striking spiritual expression of this situation. Bolingbroke was the author of *Letters on the Study and Use of History*, first published in 1738.

"Being himself as critical and believing as little in the Bible as any deist," we read further in Windelband's book, "he" (Bolingbroke—*G.P.*) "declares all literature disseminating such views to be revolutionary, and calls this literature a plague of society. He does not hide his opinion that free-thinking is a right which belongs solely to the ruling class: and he turns all the egoism of social exclusiveness against ... the popularisation of free thought. He believes that in the salons it is permissible to ridicule the narrowness and absurdity of positive religion, and he himself is not above jibing frivolously at it. But in the life of society, religion is an indispensable force that cannot be shaken without endangering the foundation of the state— the obedience of the masses."*

Windelband found that, in essence, Bolingbroke "had only enough courage to divulge the secret of high society of his time— a secret that was not confined even to this one epoch". And this is true, of course. But this being true, the history of philosophical ideas in a society divided into classes must be seen in the light of the materialist proposition that it is not thinking that determines being, but, on the contrary, being that determines thinking. The present universal triumph of the idealist world-outlook will then be more of an argument *against* that world-outlook than in *favour of it*.

Is there anyone who is unaware that the class struggle in West European society is daily becoming more and more acute? Is there anyone who does not understand that the defence of the existing social order must, for this reason, be of ever growing importance in the eyes of the ruling classes?

Windelband reproaches Bolingbroke with being a *"conscious hypocrite"* and says that it is easy to notice the "short-sightedness of his argumentation". He is right here too. When the leading ideologists of the upper classes recommend to the "masses" "truths" which they themselves deride in their own circle, the danger arises of their own real mode of thought becoming known to the people and spreading among them. And then the "obedience of the masses", this "foundation of the state", may really be shaken. From the point of view of the social order, the prevalence of the "esoter-

---

* W. Windelband. *History of Modern Philosophy* (Russian translation, edited by Mr. A. Vvedensky). Vol. I, St. Petersburg. 1908, pp. 238-39.

ric view" among the upper class ideologists is very inexpedient. The maintenance of the social order is more likely to be assured if these ideologists renounce that view and conclude an honest peace with "positive religion". But can we make such a demand of them? No matter how great their store of "conscious hypocrisy", we cannot coerce them into sharing beliefs they do not possess. And this means that they must be inoculated afresh with these beliefs, and for this their concepts will have to be refashioned and, most important, an attempt must be made to demolish the main theoretical basis of their "esoteric view" which is so dangerous to social peace.

What was the essence of that British free-thinking which even its own supporters among the privileged had begun to regard as dangerous? In the final analysis, it amounted to the conviction that all phenomena of nature are invariably subordinated to her own laws. In other words, it consisted in the materialist view of nature. It is easy to verify this by acquainting oneself with the works of such a prominent free-thinker as John Toland (1670-1722); his teaching is thoroughly permeated with the spirit of materialism.* Therefore it was against materialism that war had first to be declared by those English guardians of order who found that the dissemination of the "esoteric view", even if confined to the upper strata of society, was harmful from the standpoint both of the Church of England and of social peace.

When a particular need arises which is of great significance to society as a whole or to a particular social class, people will almost always be found who are sincerely prepared to accept the responsibility of satisfying this need. In England, George Berkeley (1684-1753) stepped into the breach against free-thinking. But his main concern in this struggle was precisely to destroy the materialist basis of free-thinking.

Berkeley subsequently became a Bishop. But from notes dating back to the years of his studies, it may be seen that already in his youth he had set himself the task of forging a good "spiritual weapon" for the defence of traditional beliefs. While still a student, he worked out his famous principle of esse est percipi (to be is to be in perception). It is not hard to see what induced him to elaborate and defend this principle. He says in his Commonplace Book: "Opinion that existence is distinct from perception is of horrible consequence: it is the foundation of Hobbes's doctrine, etc." (i.e. of materialism —G.P.)** Elsewhere in the same Commonplace

---

* Toland wrote of himself and his like-minded associates: "We, free-thinkers." It is even said that he was the first to whom the appellation "free-thinker" was given.

** Le Journal philosophique de Berkeley, étude et traduction par Raymond Gourg, Paris, 1908, pp. 107-08.

Book, the young student says: "Matter once allowed, I defy any man to prove that God is not Matter."* There was only one way of avoiding such a "horrible consequence", and that was *not to admit the existence of matter.*** This was achieved through the principle that *being is equal to being in perception* (esse est percipi). From this followed the soothing conclusion that matter itself is but one of our perceptions, and that we have no right to say: this is God's doineg and that is Nature's. "The cause of all natural things is only God,"said the future Bishop.*** And we have to admit that he was not mistaken when he wrote: "My doctrines rightly understood, all that philosophy of Epicurus, Hobbes, Spinoza, etc., which has been a declared enemy of religion comes to the ground."**** I should think so! If there is no matter, there is no materialism.

VI

But there was one thing that did not turn out so well. It seemed to Berkeley that to have a good understanding of his doctrine was to be convinced of its indisputable correctness. In point of fact, it simply meant exposing its inconsistency.

If esse est percipi—and this principle of Berkeley remained with him till the end of his days—then God shares the same fate as matter: like matter, God exists only in our perceptions. Thus, not only does materialism come to the ground, but religion as well. Berkeley's doctrine, therefore, brings us by a new route to that same "horrible consequence" which our well-intentioned author wished to avoid. Berkeley did not notice this contradiction, or did not wish to notice it. He was blinded by the desire to defend his traditional beliefs at all cost.

Kant, too, was blinded by the same desire. His "critical" system was, indeed, an attempt to reconcile certain views inherited from his Protestant predecessors with the conclusions of the really critical thought of the eighteenth century. Kant thought they could be reconciled by separating the domain of *belief* from the domain of *knowledge*: *belief* to be related to *noumena*, and the rights of science to be restricted to *phenomena*.***** And he, too, did not hide from his readers why it was necessary for him to limit

---

* Ibid., p. 123.

** For Berkeley, according to Stephen, "to destroy matter was to free the soul" *(History of English Thought in the Eighteenth Century*, London, 1881, Vol. I, p. 39).

*** Ibid., p. 89.

**** Ibid., p. 125.

***** This is extremely well explained in *Philosophical Essays*, by *Orthodox* (L. I. Axelrod), St. Petersburg, 1906 (in Russian), which I urgently recommend to the attention of readers.

the rights of science. In the preface to the second edition of his
Kritik der reinen Vernunft, he says outright that he was induced
to do this by a desire *to make room for belief.* *

Voltaire was an irreconcilable enemy of the *Catholic Church*:
remember his motto: "écrasons l'infâme!" But Voltaire, too, like
Kant, was convinced that room had to be left for *belief*. While
waging a bitter war against Catholicism, he was a deist, and
preached *theism*, that is to say, belief in a god who rewarded people
for good conduct and punished them for bad. It is sufficient to
acquaint oneself even a little with his arguments in favour of such
a faith, to grasp why he thought it was necessary. Mallet du Pan
tells us in his *Reminiscences* that once at supper d'Alembert and
Condorcet began to defend atheism in the presence of Voltaire.
The "old man of Ferney" hurriedly sent his servants out of the
room and exclaimed: "Now, gentlemen, continue your speeches
against God; but as I don't want to be murdered and robbed to-
night by my servants, I prefer them not to hear you." This reminds
us of the remark made by the same Voltaire about Bayle, whom he
regarded as the apostle of atheism: "If he had had to manage
five or six hundred peasants, he would not have failed to proclaim
to them that there is a god who rewards and punishes." In
this respect the celebrated French Enlightener is reminiscent of
the Englishman Bolingbroke who, in general, greatly influenced
Voltaire's ideas. In making room for belief in God in the
interests of public order, Voltaire was probably not averse to
"conscious hypocrisy".

Voltaire was an ideologist of the French third estate, which was
fighting for its emancipation against the spiritual and temporal
aristocracy. From the point of view of sociology, it is a highly
important fact that class antagonism, the germ of which lay
hidden within the third estate, found expression even before the
Revolution, in the concern of the French Enlighteners to elaborate a world-outlook which, on the one hand, would be free of obsolete religious and all other prejudices and, on the other, would
command the obedience of the economically destitute mass of the
population. Only an insignificant section of the eighteenth-century French Enlighteners were not affected by this circumspection,
and, indeed, ridiculed it. Where the "patriarch" stopped to glance
uneasily over his shoulder at his servants and his Ferney peasants,
the materialists went right on to the end. Even before the Revolution, materialism was far from being the dominant trend in the
philosophical thought of the enlightened French bourgeoisie. And

---

* "Ich musste also das *Wissen* aufheben, um zum *Glauben* Platz zu bekom-
men", *Kritik der reinen Vernunft*, herausgegeben von Dr. K. Kehrbach,
Verlag von Reclam, Vorrede zur zweiten Ausgabe, S. 25-26. [I therefore had
to restrict the domain of *knowledge* to make room for *belief*.)

after the Revolution the latter would have nothing to do with materialism. Phlegmatic, prudent and ¡mealy-mouthed *eclecticism* was much more congenial to it.

When I say that the history of philosophy, like the history of all ideologies, fully confirms the materialist proposition that it is not consciousness which determines being, but being which determines consciousness, I have no wish to infer that philosophers have always striven *consciously* to turn their systems into a "spiritual weapon" to further the interests of their class. That would be an unwarranted assertion. True, Windelband has already told us that there are periods when "*conscious hypocrisy*" plays a very great part in the destiny of philosophical ideas. But we shall be more prudent if we regard such periods as *exceptional*. The individual does not necessarily have to be a "conscious hypocrite" when striving to co-ordinate his views with the interests of his class. All that he needs is the sincere conviction that the given class interest coincides with the interests of society as a whole. When there is this conviction—and it comes naturally to individual persons under the influence of their environment—then the best instincts of man: allegiance to the whole, selflessness, etc., dispose him to think those ideas *mistaken* which threaten to bring a "*horrible consequence*" to his class (remember the young Berkeley), and, on the other hand, to recognise as *true* those ideas which promise *to be useful* to this class. What is useful to a particular social class is *true* in the eyes of the individuals who compose it. Of course, so long as the class in question lives by exploiting another class or classes, this psychological process of identifying the useful with the *true* will always presuppose a certain measure of *unconscious hypocrisy*, which obliges it to turn away from everything likely to hinder this process. And as a given ruling class approaches its decline, this measure increases more and more, with *unconscious* hypocrisy being joined by conscious hypocrisy. What has been said here is thoroughly borne out by the example of contemporary *pragmatical* philosophy, to which Deborin devotes some instructive pages.

But whatever the role of conscious or unconscious hypocrisy in the psychological process of identifying what is useful with what is true, this process is inevitable in the course of social development, and we shall understand nothing in the history of ideas in general and the history of philosophical ideas in particular if we lose sight of it.*

---

* Even the neo-Kantian Lange admits that "there is no philosophy that develops out of itself", but "there are only philosophising people who together with their teachings are essentially children of their time" (*History of Materialism*, translateed by N. N. Strakhov, second Russian edition, p. 39). This, by the way, is simply a repetition of Hegel's well-known idea that the phi-

VII

Kant's "critical" philosophy is guilty of *dualism*. This was already clear to Fichte. But if the dualism of the Königsberg thinker is a *defect* from the standpoint of *theory*, from the *practical* point of view it was very *convenient* for the ideologists of the present-day bourgeoisie in the West European countries. While representing the latest edition of the fairly old *doctrine of two truths*, it enabled the ideologists of the ruling class to be *materialists in science* and simultaneously to cling to *idealism* in the sphere of those concepts which are said to be outside the bounds of scientific cognition. The Kantian variety of the doctrine of two truths is very widespread in *Germany*. British scientists, who are not too well acquainted with Kant, more readily associate the doctrine of two truths *with the philosophy of Hume*. I have often used the example of Huxley in my articles; I did so because it is a very instructive one.

On the one hand, the celebrated naturalist stated: "Surely no one who is cognisant of the facts of the case, nowadays, doubts that the roots of psychology lie in the physiology of the nervous system. What we call the operations of the mind are functions of the brain, and the materials of consciousness are products of cerebral activity."* The most "extreme" materialists never went beyond this. Besides this, we find Huxley admitting that contemporary physiology leads by the most direct route to materialism, in so far as one may apply this designation to a theory which declares that apart from substance possessing extension there is no other thinking substance. This is avowed materialism, and, moreover, in its most correct expression, that is to say, Spinozism stripped of its theological garb.

But this same naturalist, as though in alarm at his own boldness, tries to emasculate his purely materialist view with this qualification: "But it is, nevertheless, true that the doctrine contains nothing inconsistent with the purest idealism."**

Huxley tries to prove this by arguing that in essence we know only our sensations.

"A brain may be the machinery by which the material universe becomes conscious of itself. But it is important to notice that, even if this conception of the universe and of the relation of consciousness to its other components should be true, we should,

---

losophy of a particular age is its expression in ideas. Only this need be added: in human history the character of each particular age, in the last analysis, is determined by the character of its social relations.

* *Hume, sa vie, sa philosophie*, par Th. Huxley, trad. par Compayré, Paris, 1880, p. 108. [See: *Hume* by Thomas Huxley, London, 1879, p. 80.]
** *Hume*, pp. 108-09. [80.]

nevertheless, be still bound by the limits of thought, still unable to refute the arguments of pure idealism. The more completely the materialistic position is admitted, the easier is it to show that the idealistic position is unassailable, if the idealist confines himself within the limits of positive knowledge."*

Such ideas would help to reconcile the "respectable" British public to Huxley's theories on natural science.** They may have set his own mind at rest, to the extent that he still preserved traces of animist views—and he apparently held them pretty firmly, as did almost all Britons of the nineteenth century who in their own fashion were very free-thinking; but it is incomprehensible that he should think of them as being "unassailable".

The reader will remember that in denying the existence of matter independently of perception, Berkeley would have had, *if he had wished to think logically,* to arrive at denial of the existence of God. Huxley, in trying to make his materialist conclusions less frightening by adopting the main principle of idealism, found himself in a similar situation: to be logical, our biologist would have had to negate the existence of organic life and nature in general independently of perception.

Organic life is unthinkable without the exchange of substances between the organism and its environment. If Descartes said: "I think, therefore I am", the naturalist can and is bound to say: "I exist, consequently, nature, too, exists apart from my perception of it." Of course, I can declare that in the final analysis I am not an organism but only a sum of certain sensations and conceptions. This was the "positive knowledge" that Huxley had in mind.... But it probably did not occur to him how easy it was to reduce this type of "positive knowledge" to absurdity.

Let us take for granted that Berkeley was right, i.e., that in fact being is equal to being in perception (esse est percipi). But if this is true, not only matter, not only nature, and not only God have no existence outside my perception. All my fellow-men, too, have no existence; their being is also equal to being in my perception. Nothing and nobody exists except myself and various states of my cosciousness—such is the only correct conclusion to be drawn from the basic idealist principle which proclaims that being is equal to being in perception.

Nothing and nobody! Do you understand what that means, reader? It means that you are not the offspring of your parents, but they are your offspring, since their being reduces itself to being in your perception. If the idealists are capable of waving

---

* Ibid., p. 111 [81-82].
** See how his biographer, P. Chalmers Mitchell, in *Life of Thomas Henry Huxley* approves of this point (Chapter XIII, pp. 210-22).

materialism aside only by conjuring up such stupidities, which can be taken seriously only, say, by the inmates of Chekhov's *Ward No. 6*, then in *theory* the cause of idealism is hopelessly lost.

The doctrine that nothing and nobody exists except myself and my perceptions is called *solipsism*. It can be seen that solipsism is unavoidable where the starting point is *individual consciousness*, that is to say, where the thinker adheres to *subjective* idealism.

VIII

Since solipsism is so obviously absurd, let us leave the domain of *subjective* idealism, and have a look at the form which the dispute between idealism and materialism takes when being in perception is regarded from the standpoint of that *super-individual consciousness* to which the idealists appeal when they lack the courage to admit to solipsism.

And first of all, what is super-individual consciousness? Where does it spring from? If being is equal to being in perception, then I have decidedly no (NB *logical*) right to talk of some kind of *super-individual consciousness* that allegedly exists *outside* my *individual* consciousness. Here is a repetition of Berkeley's error, when he first said that there is no being of any kind independent of perception, and then declared that God has being independently of perception.

The idealist who recognises the existence of super-individual consciousness will remain a dogmatist, no matter how much he reiterates the need for criticism. However, we shall be complaisant here too. Let us acknowledge this *dogma*, and see what follows.

The dogmatic teaching of super-individual consciousness had its most systematic exposition in the works of Schelling and Hegel. Their absolute spirit is nothing else than super-individual consciousness which is supposed to embrace both the object and the subject, both nature and (subjective) spirit. But to Schelling this meant that *the universe is only the self-contemplation of this spirit*. According to Hegel's teaching, in which so much space is allotted to the (impersonal, "absolute") *logical process*, the universe is the self-thought of the *absolute spirit*. Essentially, this is one and the same thing. And if Huxley, in waving the materialists aside, had thought to seek salvation on the basis of absolute idealism, he would have been forced to tell us: "As a *biologist*, I admit, of course, the existence both of living organisms and their material environment. But as a *philosopher*, I think that the material environment surrounding the organisms, the organisms themselves, as well as myself, the biologist, who with great endeavour and success is studying their comparative anatomy and elaborating the theory of their development—in short, all that was, is or will be—was, is or will be only in the self-contemplation or self-thought of the absolute spirit."

Seriously to accept such an "apparition" (recall Kant's opinion of Fichte's system) is again out of the question. Schelling's and Hegel's systems had their own great merits. They contributed very much indeed to thinking mankind. But they made that great contribution not because they proclaimed the universe to be a process taking place in the absolute spirit. On the contrary, that was their weakest side, which to a very large extent depreciated the brilliant discoveries made by these outstanding authors when they addressed their attention to the real world.

Once more: in a theoretical sense, all attempts to talk one's way out of materialism by appealing to the basic principle of idealism (esse est percipi, without the subject there is no object, etc.) are foredoomed to abject failure. If, in spite of this, these attempts were stubbornly repeated, are still being repeated, and will for long go on being repeated, it is not a matter of theory at all. The stubborn repetition of these theoretically hopeless attempts is to be explained by the *socio-psychological cause* given above.

But how can the basic question of philosophy be resolved by thinkers who for one reason or another have not themselves experienced the influence of this cause? That is what we shall now see.

IX

The idealists and neo-Kantians reproach the materialists with *"reducing" psychical* phenomena to material phenomena. F. A. Lange says that "materialism is constantly faced with the insurmountable obstacle of explaining how conscious sensation can arise from material motion".* Lange as a historian of materialism should, however, have known that the materialists have never promised to answer this question. They assert only—to use Huxley's above-mentioned and extremely apt expression—that apart from substance possessing extension there is no other thinking substance and that, like motion, consciousness is a function of matter. *This* materialist idea was already expressed—true, extremely naively—in the teaching of Diogenes of Apollonia, who maintained that the primary matter—air, according to his teaching—was endowed with consciousness and "knew much". La Mettrie, who is looked on as a "most crude materialist", declined to explain *whence* came the capacity of matter to have sensation. He accepted this capacity as a fact, he believed it was as much an attribute of matter as its capacity for motion. La Mettrie's

---

* *History of Materialism*, p. 653.

38—01230

views on this subject were very close to Spinoza's, which is not surprising, since he was influenced by Descartes in elaborating his theory; but, *like Spinoza*, he rejected the *dualism* of the great Frenchman. In his work *L'Homme-plante*, he says that of all living creatures, man is the one which has the most soul and the plant is the one which has the least. But he gives us to understand at the very same time that the "soul" of the plant does not at all resemble the soul of man. "The beautiful soul, which concerns itself with no objects, no desires, has no passions, no vices, no virtues, and above all, no needs, would not be burdened even with the care of providing food for its body!" By this he meant that to the various forms of material organisation correspond various degrees of "animation".***

In my controversy with Bernstein,[282] I gave documentary proof that the most brilliant representative of another trend in eighteenth-century French materialism, Diderot, held the point of view of "modern Spinozists" (his own expression), who "proceed from the basic principle that matter is capable of sensation", and are convinced that only matter "exists" and that its existence is an adequate explanation of all phenomena.** To avoid unnecessary repetition, I shall add just this: the materialist Moleschott, who at one time was also very well known in Russia, tried to incorporate the same view in his own works, giving it, by the way, the characteristic title of *material-spiritual* view (stoffgeistige Anschauung).***

With the present universal domination of idealism, it is quite natural that the history of philosophy should be expounded from the idealist standpoint. As a consequence, Spinoza has long since been listed among the idealists; so that some reader will probably be very surprised that I understand Spinozism in the materialist sense. But this is the only correct way to understand it.

Already in 1843 Feuerbach expressed the quite justified conviction that Spinoza's teaching was an "expression of the materialist trend of the recent epoch". Of course, Spinoza too did not escape the influence of his time. As Feuerbach remarked, his

---

* It is worth noting that Du Bois-Raymond, in his speech on La Mettrie (Berlin, 1875), not only correctly presented this view of La Mettrie's, but acknowledged it as the *monist* view which is now held by very many naturalists. This speech could serve as the reply to the same Du Bois-Raymond's much-talked-of speech on the limits to cognisance of nature.

** "Il ne faut pas confondre les spinosistes anciens avec les spinosistes modernes. Le principe général de ceux-ci, c'est que la matière est sensible," and so on (*Encyclopedie*, t. XV. p. 474). ["One should not confuse the old Spinozists with the modern Spinozists. The main principle of the latter is that matter is sensible."] Then follows a brief exposition of Diderot's own views.

*** *Für meine Freunde. Lebenserinnerungen von Jacques Moleschott*, Giessen, 1901, pp. 222, 230, 239.

materialism was clad in *theological costume.** The important point was, however, that he eliminated the dualism of spirit and nature. If Spinoza does refer to nature as God, one of the attributes of his God is *extension*. Therein lies the cardinal distinction between Spinozism and idealism.**

The dualism of spirit and nature is also eliminated in idealism. Absolute idealism preached the *identity of subject and object in the womb of the absolute.* But this identity was achieved by declaring that the existence of the object was nothing more than its existence in the *"self-contemplation"* (or self-thought) of the absolute spirit. Here too, in the final analysis, *to be* meant *"to be in perception"* (esse est percipi). It was on this basis that the idealists could speak of the *identity of subject and object.*

Materialists assert, not the identity of subject and object, but their unity. "I" am not only a subject, but also an object: each given "I" is a *subject* for itself and an *object* for another. That, "which for me, or subjectively, is a purely spiritual, immaterial, insensible act, in itself, or objectively, is a material, sensible act" (Feuerbach).

If this is the case, *we have no right to speak of the unknowability of the object.*

<h1 style="text-align:center">X</h1>

The "critical" doctrine of the unknowability of the object (the thing-in-itself), which is closely associated with the name of Kant, is in fact a very old theory. It came to modern philosophy from Plato's idealism which, in turn, took it from primitive animism, as we have seen above.

In Plato's *Phaedo*, Socrates asserts that the soul contemplates existence through the body "as through prison bars but not with its own unhindered vision", and is therefore "wallowing in utter ignorance".*** In another part of the same conversation, he expresses himself even more definitely: "So long as we have the body, and the soul is contaminated by such an evil, we shall never attain completely what we desire, which I take to be the truth."**** Truth is inaccessible to cognition "through the body", that is to say, through our external senses, through this prison of the soul — all Plato's doctrine of cognition is constructed on this. And this

---

* The brilliant Diderot understood this; hence the reason why as we have seen, he did not wish to confuse the "modern Spinozists" with the "old".

** Berkeley said (see above) that recognition of the existence of matter independently of consciousness leads inevitably to recognition of extension in God, and this, in his opinion, was the essence of materialism.

*** *Phaedo*, translated by Dmitri Lebedev, Moscow, 1896, pp. 60-61. [H. N. Fowler's translation. Look Classical Library, London, 1914, pp. 289, 229-231.]

**** Page 23 of the same [Russian] translation.

same proposition was—*without criticism*—assimilated by the father of "critical" philosophy, as it was even earlier assimilated by the idealists of modern times and even of the Middle Ages (the "Realists").

The doctrine of the unknowability of things-in-themselves makes sense only if seen in the light of this—*absolutely primitive*—theory of cognition. Deprived of its decrepit basis, the doctrine of unknowability inevitably leads into insoluble contradictions, in struggling with which the thoughtful Kant earned Fichte's description of a "Dreiviertelskopf".

Cognition presupposes the presence of two things: first, that which is *cognised*, and second, that which *cognises*. *That which cognises* is known as the *subject*. In order that an object be known to a larger or lesser measure to the subject, it must exert some action upon the subject. "In so far as the human body is affected in any way by a given external body, thus far it perceives the external body," says Spinoza.*

For the human body, the *result* of the action of an external body upon it will be *objectively* purely *material* (change in the state of certain tissues) and *subjectively* it will be *psychical* (a certain perception). But in both cases, it will be a state of *that which cognises*, that is to say, *the subject. In this sense, all knowledge is subjective. To be cognised means to be for another.* But it does not at all follow from this that true cognition of the object is inaccessible to the subject, or, in other words, that *being for another does not* correspond to *being -in-itself.* It was possible to assume this only as long as the cognitive *ego* was regarded as something immaterial, standing *outside nature.* This, however, is entirely wrong. "My body as a whole," said Feuerbach rightly, "is my *Ego*, my true essence. It is not an abstract being that thinks" (and, consequently, knows the external world—*G. P.*) "but this real being, this body." This body is part of the cosmos. If it is acted upon by external objects in such a manner and not otherwise, then—*both from the objective and subjective aspects*—this is conditioned by the *nature of the whole.* As Huxley aptly put it, the human brain is the organ

---

* *Ethics*, translated by V. I. Modestov, fourth Russian edition, p. 86. As this part of *Ethics* is extremely important, I give it here in the original: "At quatenus corpus humanum a corpore aliquo externo aliquo modo afficitur, eatenus corpus externum percipit." (Benedicti de Spinoza, *Opera quae supersunt omnia*, Vol. II, Jena, 1803, p. 104). It would be useful to compare this with the following words of Engels: "Von Körpern, ausser der Bewegung, ausser allem Verhältnis zu den anderen Körpern ist nichts zu sagen." (*Briefwechsel zwischen Friedrich Engels und Karl Marx*, herausgegeben von A. Bebel und Ed. Bernstein, Stuttgart, 1913, IV. Band, S. 344)[283] ["...of bodies out of motion, out of all relation to other bodies, nothing can be asserted."]

of the self-consciousness of the cosmos. But the body that possesses this organ lives in a definite material environment, and if the brain could not know at least some of the properties of that environment, it would be impossible for the human organism to exist. In order *to exist*, people must be able *to foresee* at least some phenomena. *This foresight presumes true knowledge at least of some properties of that whole of which the cognitive subject constitutes a small part.**

Finally, those eclectically-minded "thinkers" who strive to combine the *materialist* explanation of history *with an idealist* theory of cognition overlook the fact that if the *object* were unknowable to the *subject*, neither the development of society nor its very existence would be possible: both one and the other presuppose the existence of a certain number of *objects-subjects*, capable of co-ordinating their actions in one way or another, that is to say, of *knowing one another.*

The material by which we get to know nature and one another is provided to us by our external senses. Our reason introduces a certain order into the material provided: it combines some phenomena and separates others. It was on this basis that Kant spoke of reason dictating its laws to nature. In fact, reason only adduces, "develops", what is dictated to it by nature. "We separate that which is separate in nature," said Feuerbach, "and connect that which is connected in nature. We subordinate the phenomena and things of nature to one another, in the relationship of basis and consequence, cause and effect, because this is their factual, sensuous, objective, real interrelationship."**

The scientific theory of evolution teaches us that matter existed not only before people and their ideas, or living creatures general-

---

* "Pour établir la valeur de nos sensations," as Pierre Delbet says very well, "...il suffit, que pour une même excitation la réaction céllulaire soit la même, et aucun esprit scientifique ne saurait douter un instant qu'elle le soit. Si elle est la même pour une même excitation ... la répétition du phénomène entraîne nécessairement à établir une concordance entre l'excitation et la réaction, de telle sorte que cette réaction devient révélatrice de l'excitation. Ainsi s'établit une connaissance du monde extérieur qui ne peut pas être trompeuse"(*La Science et la Réalité*,Paris,1913,p.90.)[In order to establish the significance of our sensations ... it suffices that one and the same irritation should produce one and the same cellular reaction, and not one scientific mind could doubt for a minute that it is so. If the sensation is one and the same with one and the same irritation ... the repetition of this phenomenon necessarily leads to the establ ishment of such concord between irritation and reaction that from the reaction we may judge the irritation that produced it. Thus there is established a knowledge of the external world which cannot be deceptive.]

** "Kritische Bemerkungen zu den Grundsätzen der Philosophie" (aus dem handschriftlichen Nachlass), *Feuerbach's Werke*, II. Band, Stuttgart. 1904. S.S. 322-23.

ly existed, but even before the earth itself and the solar system were formed.

We are told also that many naturalists are nowadays inclined to *a conception of the world based on energy.* More than that. The German chemist Ostwald, a well-known exponent of energetics, has for long been applying himself to the "overcoming of scientific materialism" (Überwindung des wissenschaftlichen Materialismus). But this is a mere misunderstanding. The good chemist Ostwald hopes to "overcome" materialism by means of energetics only because he is too *poorly versed in philosophy.*

I do not consider this conception of the world based on energy a satisfactory one. I think it is weak in *many* respects. The theory of cognition based on energy, in my opinion, entangles itself in insoluble and, one might say, disgraceful contradictions.* But when someone opposes this conception of the world based on *energy* to the *materialist,* I can only shrug my shoulders.

Joseph Priestley, who was not only a remarkable chemist but, as distinct from Ostwald, also a subtle thinker, refused to attribute to matter the property of impenetrability or solidity. His theory was that matter has only two properties: attraction and repulsion.** By his own admission, his view on matter was taken from Boscowic.*** In other words, the material particle, as Priestley saw it, was but the centre of certain forces. But this point of view, which was *essentially* very close to the conception based on energy, did not hinder Priestley from persistently defending materialism. And we shall agree that he was fully entitled to do so if we recall the definition the materialists have given and still give to matter: it is that which in one way or another, directly or indirectly, acts on our external senses.****

Instead of the words "our senses" it would be better to say: "on the senses of living organisms". Be that as it may, *"energy",* too, will come under this definition, as long as it is not thought of as something that does not act upon the senses of living beings.

This means that *the conception of the world based on energy may be opposed to the mechanical,***** but not in the least to the materialist.*

---

* It would be very desirable that Deborin in the second edition of his *Introduction* devote a special chapter to a criticism of this conception of the world based on energy, and to gnosiology based on it.

** "...matter is a substance possessed of the properties of attraction and repulsion only." (*Disquisitions Relating to Matter and Spirit,* second edition, Birmingham, MDCCLXXXII, p. 32.)

*** Ibid., pp. 23-24.

**** It is easy to understand the origin of this definition: the spiritualists considered, as is generally known, that the "spirit" did not act upon the senses.

***** See the interesting book by Abel Rey, *L'Energétique et le Méchanisme,* Paris. 1908.

Some German idealists, and with them all others of all kinds and sorts, as Herzen used to say, also grab at the latest discoveries in chemistry as an argument against materialism. Deborin does very well to expose the bankruptcy of this type of spurious argument. I should like to add a few words of my own to what he has said about this (see pages 244-45).

Professor N. A. Shilov put it very well when he said that, in accepting in principle the possibility of the motion and fluctuation of electrons "more or less closely connected with atoms and molecules, the electronic theory thereby, obviously, already acknowledges the electron as a component part of matter". The same naturalist rightly thinks that modern chemical discoveries suggest the idea of the existence of some materia prima, "more subtle than the atoms themselves".* It should be noted, however, that the phenomena taking place "within the atom" are the best possible confirmation of the *dialectical view of nature*.

Hegel once reproached "ultimate physics" (die endliche Physik) that it held too firmly to definitions based on abstract reasoning. One of the main errors resulting from this was, he said, that "ultimate physics" negated the possibility of the transformation of elements.** Later, at the end of the 1850s, Engels, who was then studying comparative anatomy and physiology, remarked that if "the old man" (der Alte) had been writing his *Philosophy of Nature* "today" (1858), the facts would come flowing to him from every side, to confirm the correctness of his dialectical conception of the processes of nature.*** What would Engels say nowadays, when there have been such astonishing discoveries of the transformation of matter, going on "within the atom", which not so long ago was considered to be quite immutable?

Everything is fluid; everything changes. One cannot enter the same stream twice. Now we see the truth of this more clearly than ever before!

---

* "Within the Atom", *Priroda*, February 1915, pp. 182 and 179.
** *Naturphilosophie*, § 286 and Zusatz, Hegel's *Werke*, VII. Band. pp. 172-73.
*** See his letter to Marx of July 14, 1858 (the above-cited *Briefwechsel*, II. Band, S. 278-79.)[284]

FROM IDEALISM TO MATERIALISM

(Hegel and Left Hegelians—David Friedrich Strauss.—
The Brothers Bruno and Edgar Bauer.—Feuerbach.)

German idealist philosophy played an extremely important role in the history of the development of science in the nineteenth century. It had an impressive impact even on natural science. But incomparably more powerful was its influence on those "disciplines" which in France are called the moral and political sciences. Here the influence of German idealist philosophy must be recognised as decisive in the full meaning of the word. It raised, and to some extent solved, problems of which the solution was absolutely imperative if scientific investigation of the process of social development was to be possible. As an example, it is sufficient to refer to Schelling's solution of the problem of the relationship of freedom to necessity (in his *System des transzendentalen Idealismus*, Tübingen, 1800). But Schelling was only a forerunner; German idealism found its most complete exponent in the person of Georg Wilhelm Friedrich Hegel.

It was quite natural that his influence should be felt most of all in his native land, Germany. But after Germany, there was no country where Hegel's teaching had such an influence as it had in Russia.*

It is impossible to understand the history of West European philosophy and West European social science in the nineteenth century unless one is acquainted with the main features of the philosophies of Hegel and Feuerbach. That is self-evident. But at first glance it is much less easy to grasp the incontestable fact that it was precisely to these two non-Russian thinkers that those Russian writers had to refer who were attempting to solve what might appear to be purely Russian problems. Further consideration will show, I hope, that there was in fact nothing at all strange about that. For the moment I will confine myself to saying that the whole point is the *scientific character of the philosophical systems of Hegel and Feuerbach*. It is this character in particular we have to note above all, beginning, of course, with Hegel.

---

* The consistent influence of Hegel and Feuerbach on Belinsky and of Feuerbach on Chernyshevsky, who said that as a youth he could recite whole pages of Feuerbach by heart, is generally known.

I

After the forcible removal of Chernyshevsky from the literary scene,[285] a disregard for German "metaphysics" began to spread in our advanced circles, where Hegel came to be regarded as predominantly a conservative, if not reactionary thinker. This was a grave error. It is indisputable that towards the end of his life, Hegel was very far from being what he had been earlier. As young men, he and Schelling had planted a tree of liberty in a meadow near Tübingen, and he had filled pages of his album with exclamations such as "Vive la liberté", "Vive Jean-Jacques!", etc. And in the sunset of his day, as he worked on his *Philosophie des Rechts*, he was indeed ready to preach philosophical "reconciliation with reality" (Belinsky well understood Hegel as he was then). But the chief distinguishing feature of the Hegelian system is by no means that in his old age its creator drew conservative practical conclusions from his theoretical premises. That system occupies one of the first places—if not the very first—in the history of philosophical thought, not because it came to any specially valuable practical conclusions, but because it established certain theoretical principles of such outstanding importance that they must be mastered, not only by the thinker who wishes to work out for himself a correct theoretical conception of the world, but also by every practical worker consciously striving to reconstruct the social order around him. Hegel himself used to say that in philosophy the important thing is *method* and not results, that is to say, not some particular conclusions or others. So it is from the point of view of method that we should look first of all at his philosophy.

We know that Hegel called his method *dialectical*; why did he do so?

In his *Phänomenologie des Geistes* he compares human life with dialogue, in the sense that under the pressure of experience our views gradually change, as happens to the opinions of disputants participating in a discussion of a profound intellectual nature. Comparing the course of development of consciousness with the progress of such a discussion, Hegel designated it by the word *dialectics*, or dialectical motion. This word had already been used by Plato, but it was Hegel who gave it its especially profound and important meaning. To Hegel, dialectics is the soul of all scientific knowledge. It is of extraordinary importance to comprehend its nature. It is the principle of all motion, of all life, of all that occurs in reality. According to Hegel, the finite is not only limited from without, but by virtue of its own nature it negates itself and passes into its own opposite. All that exists can be taken as an example to explain the nature of dialectics.

Everything is fluid, everything changes, everything passes away. Hegel compares the power of dialectics with divine omnipotence. Dialectics is that universal irresistible force which nothing can withstand. At the same time dialectics makes itself felt in each separate phenomenon of each separate sphere of life. Take motion. At a given moment, a body in motion is at a given point, but at the very same moment it is also beyond that point too, since if it remained *only* at the given point it would be *motionless*. All motion is a living contradiction; all motion is a dialectical process. But the whole life of nature is motion; so that in the study of nature it is absolutely essential to adopt the dialectical viewpoint. Hegel sharply condemns those naturalists who forget this.*
But the main reproach he addresses to them is that in their classifications they put a wide and impassable gulf between things which in fact pass into one another in obedience to the irresistible force of the law of dialectical motion. The subsequent triumph of transformism in biology clearly demonstrated that this reproach had a quite sound theoretical basis. Exactly the same is being demonstrated by the remarkable discoveries in chemistry which are proceeding before our very eyes. However, there is no doubt that the philosophy of nature is the weakest part of Hegel's system. He is incomparably stronger in his "logic", in the "philosophy of history", and in the philosophy of social life in general, as well as in the "philosophy of mind". It was here especially that his influence upon the development of social thought in the nineteenth century was most fruitful.

The following, however, should be noted. Hegel's viewpoint was that of development. But development may be understood variously. Even now there are naturalists who reiterate with an air of importance: "Nature does not make leaps." Sociologists, too, frequently say: "Social development is accomplished through slow, gradual changes." Hegel, on the contrary, affirmed that just as in nature so also in history, *leaps are inevitable*. "The changes of Being," he says, "are in general not only a transition of one quantity into another, but also a transition from the qualitative into the quantitative, and conversely; a process of becoming other which breaks off graduality (ein Abbrechen des Allmählichen) and is qualitatively other as against the preceding determinate being. Water on being cooled does not little by little become solid ... but is suddenly solid; when it has already attained freezing point it may (if it stands still) be wholly liquid, and a slight shake brings it into the state of solidity." Development becomes comprehensible only when we regard *gradual changes* as a process through which a leap (or leaps) is prepared and evoked. Whoever

---

* Actually in Hegel's time almost all of them forgot this.

wishes to explain the origin of a given phenomenon by slow changes alone is in fact unconsciously assuming that it *is already actually there and is imperceptible only on account of its smallness.* Such a supposed explanation substitutes for the concept of *origin* the concept of *growth*, of a simple change in magnitude, that is to say, it arbitrarily eliminates precisely that which required explanation.* We know that modern biology fully recognises the importance of "breaks of graduality in the process of development of animal and vegetable species".

Hegel was an absolute idealist. He taught that the motive force of world development is, in the final analysis, the power of the absolute idea. That, of course, is quite an arbitrary and, one might say, fantastic assumption. Trendelenburg had no difficulty later in demonstrating in his *Logische Untersuchungen* that reference to the idea in reality has never explained anything. However, as I remarked in another place, Trendelenburg, in aiming his blows against dialectics, actually hit only its *idealist basis.*** Trendelenburg was quite right when he blamed *Hegel's dialectics* for "asserting the spontaneous motion of pure thought constituting at the same time the self-generation of being". But in this assertion lies not the nature of all dialectics in general, but the shortcoming of *idealist* dialectics. This shortcoming was eliminated by the materialist Marx, so that Trendelenburg's objection to dialectics has now lost all importance. But Marx himself, before he became a materialist, was a follower of Hegel.

II

Hegel erred *as an idealist,* that is to say, in so far as he believed the power of the idea to be the motive force of world development. But he was right *as a dialectician,* that is to say, in so far as he observed all phenomena from the standpoint of their development. Whoever regards phenomena from the standpoint of their development refuses to apply to them the yardstick of this or that abstract principle. This was explained excellently by Chernyshevsky. "Everything depends on circumstances, on conditions of place and time," he wrote in his *Essays on the Gogol Period in Russian Literature,* describing the chief distinguishing feature of the dialectical view of phenomena. This view was especially fertile in the field of journalism and in the social sciences, in which it had become the custom to pronounce judgment on phenomena proceeding from this or that abstract principle, accepted once and for all. It was no accident that the French called these sciences "sciences morales

---

* *Wissenschaft der Logik,* Nürnberg, pp. 313, 314.
** See the preface to my translation of Engels' *Ludwig Feuerbach.*[286]

et politiques". In the same *Essays*, Chernyshevsky wrote: "There is no abstract truth; truth is always concrete." He pointed to war, among other things, as an example. "Is war disastrous or beneficial? This cannot be answered definitely, as a general rule. One must know what kind of war is meant.... For civilised peoples, war usually does more harm than good. But ... the war of 1812 was a war of salvation for the Russian people. The Battle of Marathon was a most beneficial event in the history of mankind." That is so. And if that is so, there is no point in asking which particular social and political structure must be regarded as the best; surely here, too, everything depends upon the circumstances, upon the conditions of place and time. Thus Hegel's philosophy mercilessly condemned Utopianism. A pupil of Hegel, if he remained true to his teacher's method, could become a Socialist only if scientific investigation of the modern economic system led him to conclude that the internal laws of development of that system would bring about the formation of a socialist system. Socialism had to become a science or cease to exist. This makes it understandable why Marx and Engels, the founders of scientific socialism, came precisely from Hegel's school.

Take another example, J. B. Say considered it a waste of time to study the history of political economy, on the ground that before Adam Smith, whose follower he mistakenly thought himself to be, all economists had held erroneous views. Hegel, his contemporary, viewed the history of philosophy quite differently. To Hegel, philosophy was the self-knowledge of the spirit. Since the spirit progresses, since it develops with the development of mankind, philosophy, too, does not stand still. Each, now "surpassed" philosophical system was the intellectual expression of its time (seine Zeit in Gedanken erfasst), and this constitutes its relative justification. Besides, "the latest philosophy in point of time is the result of all preceding philosophies and consequently must embrace the principles of all of them."*

Only being viewed in this way could the history of philosophy become a subject of close, *scientific* study. And although Hegel was accused, not without reason, of treating historical data at times with a fair amount of disrespect, arranging them to suit the needs of his philosophical system,** nevertheless there is no doubt at all that his *Vorlesungen über die Geschichte der Philosophie* is still the best history of philosophy, i.e., the most instructive, shedding the clearest light on the theoretical content of the various philosophical doctrines.

---

* *Encyclopädie der philosophischen Wissenschaften*, § 13.
** We shall see later what led him to commit this sin.

Hegel considered the problems of law, morality, art, and religion from the selfsame dialectical viewpoint. All these "disciplines" were studied by him in their mutual relationships. He taught that "only in connection with this particular religion, can this particular form of state exist; just as only this philosophy and this art can exist in this state".* This view is interpreted sometimes very superficially; it is said that each of the myriad aspects of social life influences all the rest, and, in turn, experiences the influence of all other aspects on itself. This is the well-known theory of the interaction of social phenomena. But though Hegel accepted this theory, he maintained that we could not stop at it.

"The inadequacy of the method of examining phenomena from the point of view of reciprocal action," he says, "consists of this, that the relation of reciprocal action, instead of serving as the equivalent of concept, must itself be understood." The meaning of this is: if I succeed in discovering that the state structure of a particular country influences its religion and its religion influences its state structure, my discovery will, naturally, be of a certain amount of use to me. However, it will not explain to me the origin of these interacting phenomena—the particular state structure and the particular religion. To solve *this* problem, I must dig deeper and, not content with the *interaction* of religion and state structure, try *to discover the common basis upon which both religion and state structure rest*. Hegel expressed this very well when he said that "cause not only has an effect, but in the effect, as cause, it stands related to itself",** and that the interacting sides cannot be accepted just as they stand, but must be conceived as elements of a third, "higher", something.

In respect of methodology, this demand was extremely important, because it impelled a search for the *root cause* which, in *the last analysis*, brings about the historical motion of mankind. Hegel as an idealist considered the root cause of this motion to be the universal spirit. History is nothing more than its "exposition and realisation", i.e., to put it simply, motion. This motion takes place in stages. Each separate stage has its own special principle, whose bearer in a particular epoch is a particular nation, constituting then something in the nature of a chosen people. This special principle determines the whole spirit of the epoch. The specific spirit of a nation, says Hegel, "expresses in concrete form all aspects of the consciousness and will of that people, its entire reality; this specific spirit is a common hallmark of the nation's religion, system of government, ethics, legislation, customs, and also science,

---

* *Philosophie der Geschichte*, Dritte Auflage, Einleitung, p. 66.
** *Wissenschaft der Logik*, Zweites Buch, dritter Abschnitt: "Die Wechselwirkung".

art and, technical' skill. These special peculiarities are to be understood from the common peculiarity, a particular principle of a nation, in the same way as, on the contrary, the common in the special should be detected in the factual detail of history."*

References to the specific spirit of the nation are much misused in social science and by journalists. But every particular theory is subject to misuse, *especially when it is already outliving its time*. In itself, the doctrine that the "spirit" of a particular nation is distinguished by special features at a particular stage of the nation's development is not so mistaken as might be thought, when reading the opinions of some nationalists. There is not the slightest doubt that "social man" has a particular psychology, the qualities of which determine all the ideologies he creates. This *psychology* of his might, if you like, be called his *spirit*. Of course it must always be remembered that the psychology of social man *develops*, i.e., *changes*. But Hegel was well aware of this. It is also necessary to bear in mind that the *psychology* of social man *does not explain his historical progress: it is itself explained by it*. Hegel, however, put this the other way round: the "spirit" of every particular nation explained its *historical destiny*, and indeed all its *reality*, that is to say, all its social *life*. That is a mistake, the origin of which is quite comprehensible. As an idealist, Hegel was convinced that *being* is conditioned by *consciousness* and not the other way round. Apply this general idealist view to history, and you will have social being determined by social consciousness, or, if you prefer the expression, by the national spirit. That is why Hegel contended that the spirit of each particular nation determines—note, however, *only in the final analysis*—not only its art, its religion, and its philosophy, i.e., not only the totality of its ideologies, but also its political system and even its technology and the sum-total of its social relationships. His error was brought to light only with the discovery of the unsoundness of the general (*idealist*) basis of his philosophy and then by no means at once. Every stage of the development of the world spirit is represented on the historical scene by a separate nation. *The present historical epoch is the epoch of German culture*. According to Hegel, the nation representing the highest stage of development of the world spirit is entitled to regard other nations as mere instruments for the realisation of its historical aims. This is worth noting. If today the Germans do not stand on ceremony with the vanquished, there is in this, unfortunately, a drop of Hegelian honey.

But the Slav peoples could not willingly accept the hegemony

---

* *Philosophie der Geschichte*, Einleitung, p. 79. See also *Grundlinien der Philosophie des Rechts*, paragraphs 344 and 352.

of the Germans. Since Schelling's time part of the intelligentsia in the Slav countries have been busily occupied with the question of which exact stage of development of the world spirit these peoples are fated to represent.

Earlier I said that Hegel had often been accused of arbitrarily arranging *facts*, historical and others, in the interests of *his system*. Now I will add that, as an idealist, he could not entirely deny himself some arbitrariness in the treatment of factual data. But he was much less guilty in this respect than other founders of idealist systems. Those who, through ignorance of Hegel's philosophy of history, naively believe that in it Hegel never descended to concrete historical ground* are very much mistaken. On the contrary, he did so often, and when he did, his *philosophical-historical* considerations vividly illuminated many important problems of mankind's historical development. Speaking, for instance, of the fall of Sparta, he was not content with what could be said of it from the standpoint of the "world spirit", and sought its cause in the inequality of property (Ungleichheit des Besitzes). He explains the origin of the *state*, too, by the growth of property inequality, and this absolute "idealist" believed that *agriculture* was the historical basis of marriage. Hegel was fond of repeating that on closer examination idealism proves to be the truth of *materialism*. The examples I have just mentioned—and I could easily advance many more—convincingly demonstrate that, in fact, in his own philosophy of history it turned out that on closer examination the opposite was the case: *materialism proved to be the truth of idealism.*** This circumstance will become of no small importance to us when we recall that Marx and Engels, who subsequently founded the theory of *historical materialism*, were *Hegelians* to start with.

III

Whoever regards social relationships from the standpoint of their *development* cannot be a supporter of *stagnation*.

When Herzen became acquainted with Hegel's philosophy, he called it the *algebra of revolution*.[286] Even though this assessment was not without a certain element of exaggeration, it is nevertheless incontestable that so long as Hegel remained true to his powerful dialectical method he was an advocate of progress. In concluding his lectures on the history of philosophy, he said that the world spirit never stands still, since forward motion is its intimate na-

---

* His own words.
** For more details concerning this, see my brochure: *A Critique of Our Critics* (St. Petersburg, 1906) and the article: "For the Sixtieth Anniversary of Hegel's Death".[287]

ture. "Frequently it seems that the world spirit has forgotten and lost itself. But inside it resists. Internally it continues to labour—as Hamlet said of his father's ghost: 'Well said, old mole! canst work i' the ground so fast?'—until it gathers strength, and breaks through the earth's crust separating it from its sun, from its reason. And then the world spirit forges ahead rejuvenated with giant strides."* The same can be said of the world spirit:"it works fast!"

Call this what you will, but it is not the philosophy of a guardian of the existing order of things!

As we know, Hegel was accused of conservatism on the grounds that he proclaimed the identity of the *rational* and the *real*. But *in themselves*, the words: "what is real is rational; what is rational is real" (was wirklich ist, das ist vernünftig; was vernünftig ist, das ist wirklich) are not an indication of Hegel's readiness to accept every given social order, or, for that matter, every given social institution. To be convinced of this, it will be sufficient to remember his attitude to the excessive power of the father in the Roman family. To Hegel, not everything by far that existed was real. He actually said: "Reality is *higher than existence*" (die Wirklichkeit steht höher als die Existenz). The real is necessary, while not all that exists is necessary. As we have seen, the world spirit does not stand still. Its eternal motion, its tireless work, little by little deprives the given social order of its essential content, transforms it into an empty form that has outlived its time and therefore makes necessary its replacement by a new order. If the real is rational, it must be remembered that the rational is real. But if the *rational is real*, it follows that there is not, and cannot be any authority capable of halting its progressive dialectical motion. It was not for nothing that Hegel defined dialectics as a universal irresistible force which must destroy even that which is most stable.

IV

"Everything is fluid, everything changes; one cannot enter the same stream twice and no one touches the fatal essence twice." So spoke the profound (the "dark") thinker of Ephesus.[289] This same thought, but tempered in the crucible of an incomparably stricter logic, underlies Hegel's philosophy. But if everything is fluid, if everything changes, and if the mighty force of dialectical motion does not spare even the most stable phenomena, we have no right to regard any of the latter *from the viewpoint of mysticism*. On the contrary, they can and must be examined only *from the standpoint of science*.

---

* *Vorlesungen über die Geschichte der Philosophie*, Vo. III, p. 685.

The reader must be aware of the celebrated contrast of the infiniteness of the Universe to moral law made by Kant in his *Critique of Practical Reason*. "The very first view of the infiniteness of the Universe annihilates as it were my importance as an animal creature.... Moral law, on the contrary, infinitely raises my value as an intelligent being owing to my personality in which the moral law reveals to me a life independent of the world of beasts, and even of the entire sensible world." Thus for Kant, as well as for Fichte, moral law was a kind of key which opened the door to the world beyond. Hegel saw it quite differently. According to his teaching morality is the inevitable product and necessary condition of social life. Hegel recalls Aristotle's saying that the people existed before the individual man. The individual person is something dependent, and therefore must exist in unity with the whole. *To be moral is to live according to the morals of one's country.* For man to be given a good upbringing, he had to be made a citizen of a well-ordered state.*

It would appear from this that ethics is rooted in politics. There is a strong resemblance here to the revolutionary doctrine on morality elaborated by the eighteenth-century French Enlighteners. This resemblance could, however, give rise to misunderstanding. If to be moral means to live in accordance with the morals of one's own country, this would appear to condemn beforehand *innovators*, whose activity always and unavoidably places them *in opposition to some of their country's morals*, that is to say, it makes them *immoral*, in a certain sense of the word. Aristophanes charged Socrates with immorality. And the death of Socrates demonstrates that the people of Athens found this charge grounded.

However, the contradiction may be solved easily with the aid of the dialectical method. In the Introduction to his *Philosophy of History*, Hegel notes: "Generally, as regards the withering, the injury and decline of religious, ethical and moral aims and conditions it must be said that, although by their inner essence these aims and conditions are infinite and eternal, their manifestation, however, may be of a limited character, they have a natural bond with each other and are subject to the command of chance. Therefore they are transient, subject to withering and injury." There, too, Hegel expresses a thought which was developed in detail later by Lassalle in his *Systeme der erworbenen Rechte*: "The right of the world spirit is higher than all particular rights" (Das Recht des Weltgeistes geht über alle besonderen Berechtigungen).

Great personalities, appearing in history as the bearers and defenders of "the right of the world spirit", found their complete justification in Hegel's philosophy of history, notwithstanding

---

* *Rechtsphilosophie*, § 153, Anmerkung.

the fact that their actions constituted a violation of particular
rights and threatened the prevailing social order. Hegel called
these personalities *heroes* who by their activity created a new world.
He says that "they come into collision with the old order and
destroy it, they are the violators of the existing laws. Therefore
they perish, but perish as individual personalities. Their punishment does not destroy the principle they represent ... the principle
triumphs later although in another form." Aristophanes was not
mistaken; Socrates was, in fact, destroying the old morality of
his people, who could not be blamed for condemning him to
death when they sensed he was a danger to their cherished social
system. The Athenians were right in their own way; however,
Socrates too was right, and even more than his judges, since he
was the conscious spokesman of a new and higher principle.

Hegel had a positive weakness for these "violators of existing
laws" and poured scorn on those erudite psychologists who tried
to explain the actions of great historical figures by self-interest and
personal motives. He thought it was perfectly natural that, if a
man is devoted to a cause, his work for this cause will bring him,
among other things, personal satisfaction which may, perhaps, be
decomposed into all the forms of self-love. But to think on these
grounds that great historical figures were guided solely by personal
motives is possible only for "psychological valets" to whom no man
is a hero, not because there actually are no heroes, but because
these judges are *only valets*.

V

Hegel's *ethics* was a great step forward by philosophy in the
scientific explanation of the moral development of mankind.
His *aesthetics* is just as great a step forward in comprehending the
essence and history of art. Through Belinsky, it exerted an enormous influence on Russian criticism, and even for this reason alone
its fundamental propositions deserve the greatest attention of
the Russian   reader.

Hegel's aesthetics is akin to the views of his nearest philosophical predecessor, Schelling, on this question. Schelling said that
beauty is the *infinite* expressed in a *finite form*. And since the
poetically creative fantasy is conditioned by the epochs of world
development, art is subject to law-governed and necessary development, the portrayal (Schelling called it the *designing*) of which is
the task of aesthetics. To place such a task before aesthetics was
to proclaim the necessity for scientific study of the history of art.
Of course, there's many a slip twixt the cup and the lip. It is
one thing to *pose* a certain problem; it is quite another matter to
solve it. Moreover, scientific problems are not solved by "designing",

and without it it was very difficult for the idealist philosophers
to get along. However, Schelling did an unforgettable service in
correctly posing the problem.

Besides, to define beauty as the expression of the infinite in a
finite form is to show that content is not something of no consequence in a work of art, but is, on the contrary, of the greatest
importance. In any case, from Schelling's point of view, the contraposing of *form to content* was void of all meaning. Schelling
insisted that *form cannot exist without content, since form is determined by content.* A work of art exists only for its own sake. In
this lies the sanctity of art, that its creations arise, not for the
sake of any aims alien to it—for example, sensuous enjoyment, or
economic advantage, or the moral improvement of man, or his
enlightenment. *Art exists for art's sake.* This idea of Schelling's was
repeated with enthusiasm by all Schelling's followers in general
and our Russian ones in particular. In a certain sense they were
absolutely right. However, if *works* of art are the finite expression
of the *infinite,* while *its evolution* is determined by the *evolution of
the world,* it is clear that the art of each particular historical epoch
has as its content that which is most important to the people of
that epoch.

Schelling's basic ideas on aesthetics were still more deeply propounded and much more systematically elaborated by Hegel.

We already know that the *spirit,* to which Hegel is always appealing as the final authority, is not an unchangeable, immobile *substance.* It moves; it develops; it differs in itself; it reveals itself in
nature, in the state, in universal history. The *aim*—it would be
more exact to say the *fruit*—of its eternal motion is *self-cognition.*
It is for the spirit precisely to cognise itself. This striving towards
self-cognition is realised in the process of the spiritual development of humanity, expressed in art, in religion and in
philosophy. The spirit freely *contemplating* its own essence is
fine, or aesthetic, art; the spirit reverently *representing* this essence
to itself is *religion;* lastly, the spirit, *cognising* this essence is
philosophy.

The definition of art as the *free contemplation by the spirit of
its own essence* is important because it brings out the complete
independence of the domain of artistic creation and enjoyment.
According to Hegel, as well as Schelling and Kant, works of art
exist and must exist not for the sake of any outside aims. "Contemplation of the beautiful," says Hegel, "is liberal (liberaler Art);
it treats the objects as free and infinite in themselves, without
wishing to possess and utilise them as useful for finite needs
and designs." At the same time, the definition of art as the
domain in which the spirit contemplates its own essence
signifies that the *subject* of art is identical with the subject of

philosophy (and religion). This brings out the enormous value
of the *content* of artistic productions. Philosophy has to do with
truth. Art, too, has to do with truth. But whereas the *philosopher*
cognises the truth in the *concept*, the *artist* contemplates it
in the *image*.* Since we already know that the *true* (the *"rational"*) is *real*, we may say that it is precisely *reality* that serves
as the content of art. In saying this, however, we must remember that by far not all that exists is real. Hegel remarks that
it would be a mistake to think that artistic creation is the
simple reproduction of a thing seen by the artist, only in an em-
bellished form, that the artist's ideal is related to the existing
as a portrait in which the painter has flattered the original.
The artistic ideal is reality freed from those elements of chance
which are unavoidable in every finite existence. Art brings things—
blemished, in Hegel's expression, by the fortuities and externals
of everyday existence—into harmony with their concept, casting
aside all that is irrelevant.

It is by such casting aside that the artistic ideal is created.
That is why Hegel says that the artistic ideal is reality in all
the fulness of its power.

There were three main stages in the historical development of
mankind: the eastern world, the world of antiquity and the
Christian or German world. And since to the stages of historical
development there correspond stages in the development of the
artistic ideal, Hegel counted three of these too.

The art of the eastern world has a symbolic character; in it
the idea is connected with the material object, but has not yet
penetrated it. Besides, the idea itself remains undefined. The
definiteness of the idea and its penetration of the object are
achieved only in the art of the antique world, in other words, in
classical art. Here the artistic ideal appears in human form. Such
humanising of the ideal was subjected to condemnation, but Hegel
says that, inasmuch as art has the aim of expressing spiritual content in a sensuous form, it had to resort to such humanising, since
only the human body can serve as the sensuous form corresponding
to the spirit. That is why classical art is the realm of beauty.
'There is not and cannot be greater beauty," says Hegel raptu-
rously. But when the world of antiquity had outlived its time, a
new world-outlook came to be, and with it a new artistic ideal—
the romantic. The new world-outlook consisted in the spirit seeking its purpose not outside itself, but only within itself. In Romantic art, the idea began to take precedence over sensuous form.
Consequently, external beauty began to play a subordinate part

---

* Accordingly, Hegel calls *the beautiful the sensuous manifestation of the
idea*.

in it, with the main role now being played by spiritual beauty. However, because of this, *art* displayed a tendency to overstep its limits and enter the domain of religion.

In Hegel's view architecture is a predominantly symbolic art, whereas *sculpture* is a classical art and *painting, music, and poetry* are essentially romantic.

We can see what a close theoretical connection exists between Hegel's aesthetics and his philosophy of history. In both there is the same method and the same point of departure: *the motion of the spirit* is proclaimed the basic cause of development. Hence in both domains there is one and the same defect: in order to depict the course of development as the result of the motion of the spirit, one sometimes has to resort to an arbitrary treatment of facts. But both in aesthetics and in the philosophy of history Hegel reveals a striking depth of thought. Apart from this, in aesthetics he readily descends to "concrete historical ground",* and then his observations on the evolution of art become truly enlightening. Unfortunately, lack of space prevents me from confirming this by examples. I shall, however, mention the superb pages he devotes to the history of Dutch painting in the seventeenth century.**

VI

Fine art arises because the spirit freely *contemplates* its own essence. Religion owes its origin to the circumstance that the spirit *conceives* of this essence. So taught Hegel. But can the domain of conception be separated from the domain of contemplation? If so, it is not without difficulty, since when we *conceive* of a particular object we at the same time *contemplate* it. Not without reason did Hegel himself point out that Romantic art oversteps the limits of aesthetic creation and enters the domain of religion. To understand the subsequent course of development of philosophical thought in Germany it is essential to know Hegel's views on religion as thoroughly as possible. Therefore I invite the reader to look at the question from another angle.

According to Hegel the spirit is in a process of constant motion. The process of its *motion* is the process of its *self-revelation*. The spirit reveals itself in nature, in social life, in world history. Its self-revelation is realised *in time and in space*. The *infinite*

---

* His own expression.
** See his *Vorlesungen über die Aesthetik*, Part I, pp. 217-18 and Part II, pp. 217-33. It would be instructive to compare what Hegel says there with what Fromentin says of the character and origin of the Dutch school in his famous book: *Les maîtres d'autrefois*. Fromentin's basic idea is that Dutch painting was a portrayal of the Dutch bourgeoisie at a certain stage of its development, and this fully coincides with Hegel's view.

power of the spirit is thus *manifested* in *finite* form. Do away with
this finite form and you have the *religious point of view*. Hegel
says that the person holding this view conceives of God as an absolute force and absolute substance, into which all the wealth of
the natural and spiritual world returns. The spirit is revealed to
the imagination as something supernatural, quite independent of
the finite subject, but for all that closely bound to it. But here too
it is not always revealed in the same way. The conception of the
spirit as a supernatural being changes—*develops*—together with
the historical development of man. In the East, God is conceived
of as an absolute force of nature, or as substance before which man
admits himself to be insignificant and unfree. At the next stage,
God is conceived of as a *subject*. Finally, there is Christianity,
which Hegel sees as the *absolute religion*, proclaiming the absolute
unity and reconciliation of the infinite and the finite. In the
centre of this religion is Christ as the redeemer of the world, as
the son of God, and above all as God the Man.

That is what is meant by the phrase: religion is true content
in a conceptual form. But this form is not yet an adequate expression of absolute truth. This adequate expression of truth is to
be found only in philosophy. The concept preserves figurative
forms and considers them essential. Religion speaks of divine
wrath, of the birth of the Son of God, and so on. Hegel defended
energetically the "inner truth" of Christianity, but he did not
find it possible to believe in the authenticity of the Bible stories
presenting divine actions as historical events. He said they had
to be regarded as allegorical portrayals of the truth, like the myths
of Plato.* Hegel's philosophy was inimical to *subjective arbitrariness*. From the point of view of this philosophy, the ideal of a
particular personality has value only when it expresses the objective course of social development, conditioned by the motion of
the world spirit. The heroes about whom Hegel speaks with such
sympathy were instruments of this development. For this reason
alone his philosophy left no place for *Utopianism*. Apart from
this, his philosophy could not find common ground with Uttopia
nism for another reason, that the firm belief in the possibility of
devising a plan for the best social order, which is characteristic
of Utopianism, is devoid of all meaning in the light of dialectics.
If everything depends on the circumstances of time and place, if
everything is relative, if everything is fluid and everything changes,
then there is no doubt about one thing: the social order changes
in conformity with the social relations formed in the particular

---

* The view of the Bible stories as myths had been expressed already
by Schelling: "Christ," he said, "is an historical personality whose biography
had already been written before he was born" (Cuno Fischer, *Schelling*,
St. Petersburg, p. 768).

country at the particular time. It is no wonder that Hegel was disliked both by the *Romanticists*, who were so strongly attached to subjective arbitrariness, and by the *Utopians*, who had no conception of the dialectical method and, as is known, had the closest affinity with the Romanticists. At first only very few representatives of the opposition in Germany understood that Hegel's philosophy could provide the most lasting theoretical foundation for the aspirations to freedom of its age. Among these very few was Heinrich Heine. In the forties of last century, humorously describing a conversation supposedly going on between himself and Hegel, he warned the reader that the words: "Everything existing is rational" mean also that everything rational must exist. It is worthy of note that Heine substituted the word *"existing"* for the word *"real"* in Hegel's famous formula, probably hoping to demonstrate that, even in a vulgar conception of this formula, its progressive meaning was preserved.

After all that has been said, it is hardly necessary to add that Heine was right, in so far as he was speaking of the *dialectical character of Hegel's* philosophy. It should not be forgotten, however, that with the aid of the dialectical method Hegel attempted to construct a *system of absolute idealism.*

A system of absolute idealism is a system of absolute truth. If Hegel had constructed such a system—and he believed he had succeeded in doing so—then, reasoning from the standpoint of idealism, we have to recognise that the aim of the uninterrupted motion of the spirit had already been achieved: in the person of Hegel, the spirit had arrived at self-knowledge in its true, "adequate" form, i.e., in the *form of concept.* And once the aim of motion has been achieved, motion must cease. Thus, if *prior to Hegel*, philosophical thought *constantly moved forward*, the appearance of Hegel heralds the *beginning of its stagnation.* Hegel's *absolute idealism* came into irreconcilable contradiction with his own dialectical method and—please note—not only in the domain of philosophical thought. If every philosophy is the intellectual expression of its time, the philosophy that represents a system of absolute truth is the intellectual expression of that historical period to which corresponds an absolute social order, i.e., an order serving as the objective realisation of absolute truth. And since absolute truth is *eternal* truth, the social order which serves as its objective expression acquires permanent significance. Certain details may be modified in it, but it cannot be subjected to essential changes. That is why, in those very lectures on the history of philosophy in which Hegel speaks enthusiastically of the heroes of antiquity who rebelled against the established order, we come upon an edifying discourse on how, in modern society, in contras to antiquity, philosophical activity can and must be restricted to

the *internal world*, since the *external world*, the social system, has
arrived at a certain rational order, has become *"reconciled with
itself"*. *Thus, where previously there had been motion in the sphere
of social relations, too, now it must come to an end.* This means that,
in its teaching on the question of social relations also, Hegel's
absolute idealism came into conflict with his dialectical method.

And so Hegel's philosophy has two sides: a *progressive* side (closely bound up with his method) and a *conservative* one (no less
closely linked with his claim to possession of absolute truth).
With the passing years, the conservative side increased very significantly at the expense of the progressive. This is most vividly
revealed in his *Philosophie des Rechts*. This celebrated work is
a veritable storehouse of profound thought. But at the same time,
on almost every page, there stands out Hegel's desire to remain
at peace with the existing order. It is remarkable that we even
meet here the expression: *"peace with reality"*, so often used by
Belinsky in the period of his articles on the Borodino Anniversary.* It follows from this that if Hegel's idea regarding the rationality of all reality gave occasion for misunderstandings, he
himself more than anyone was responsible for this, in depriving
the idea of its former dialectical content and recognising dismal
Russian reality as the very accomplishment of reason.

Those of Hegel's followers who were more influenced by the
dialectical element in his philosophy understood it, as Herzen did,
as the *algebra of revolution*; those who were mostly influenced by
the element of absolute idealism were inclined to perceive this
philosophy as the *arithmetic of stagnation*. In 1838 there appeared
in Leipzig a book by the Hegelian Karl Bayrhoffer (in its way a
very interesting book), *Die Ideen und Geschichte der Philosophie.*
Bayrhoffer asserted that Hegel was the peak of the world spirit,
and that in him the idea of philosophy existing in-itself-and-
for-itself had found its double. (Hegel ist diese Spitze des Weltgeistes.... Die an-und-für-sich-seiende Idee der Philosophie hat sich
in Hegel verdoppelt.)** It was impossible to go further than this
in recognising the absolute character of Hegel's philosophy. Immediately following this pronouncement, Bayrhoffer draws in
this case inevitable and logical conclusion that now the absolute
idea itself has become reality (selbst Wirklichkeit geworden)***
and that the world has now reached its aim (die Welt hat ihr
Ziel erreicht).**** It is hardly necessary to enlarge upon the fact

---

* It was Hege who said that man, having discovered the intellect
hidden in reality, does not rebel against reality, but makes peace with it and
rejoices in it.
  ** Op. cit., pp. 423-24.
  *** Ibid., p. 424.
  **** Ibid.. n. 425.

that such a conclusion favoured every kind of conservative tendency both in Germany itself and in all the other countries where the influence of German philosophy had penetrated.

VII

Hegel's system had its own destiny, which confirmed for the thousand-and-first time the truth that the course of development of philosophy, as of every other ideology, is determined by the course of historical development. So long as the pulse of public life in Germany was beating sluggishly, conservative conclusions, in the main, were being drawn from Hegel's philosophical teaching. That was when it became the officially recognised Royal-Prussian philosophy. But as the pulse of public life quickened, the conservative element in Hegel's philosophy was pushed more and more into the background by its *dialectical* progressive element. In the second half of the 1830s, one could speak with complete justification of a split in the Hegelian camp.

In 1838, A. Ruge and T. Echtermeyer founded the *Hallische Jahrbücher für deutsche Wissenschaft und Kunst*, which, in 1841, was transferred from Halle to Leipzig, its title being changed to *Deutsche Jahrbücher*.[290] The journal was of a radical trend. In consequence it was not destined to have a long life in Saxony. It was banned in 1843, and Ruge then made an attempt to publish it in Paris under the title of *Deutsch-französische Jahrbücher*. In its new form it proved to be quite short-lived: only one issue (a double one) appeared. But it is very remarkable in this respect that its publisher, in addition to Ruge, was Karl Marx, while one of its active collaborators was Frederick Engels. Left Hegelianism was gradually abandoning its own philosophical basis, and more and more acquiring a political and socialist colouring.

But prior to its appearance in *politics* and in *socialism*, the onward movement of philosophical thought inherited by the Hegelians from their teacher revealed itself in *theology*.

As we already know, Hegel did not admit the historical authenticity of the Bible stories and, like Schelling, regarded them as allegorical myths similar to those of Plato (see above). On the other hand, Hegel held that the task of philosophy of religion was the cognition of positive religion. In this way, religion became for the philosopher a subject of scientific cognition. But what does the cognition of religion mean? It means, *among other things*, to submit to scientific, critical examination the question of the origin of those narratives, those allegorical myths, through which religion *conceives* of truth. *David Friedrich Strauss* (1808-1874), a pupil of Hegel's, took this task upon himself.

His book *Das Leben Jesu, kritisch bearbeitet* was published in
1835. It was the first great theoretical event in the process of disintegration of the Hegelian school. Strauss was at no time disposed
to political radicalism. In the revolutionary period of 1848-49, he
showed himself to be an out-and-out opportunist. However, in
the theological literature of Germany, the appearance of his book
was a truly revolutionary epoch-making event. T. Ziegler thinks
that hardly any other book had so much influence in the nineteenth
century as Strauss' *Life of Jesus.*

Strauss considered the miracles as the strongest proof of the
very meagre historical authenticity of the Gospel stories.

In the theological literature of Germany at that time there was
a twofold attitude to miracles. The "*Supernaturalists*" acknowledged them as real, whereas the rationalists denied them and strove
to find a natural explanation of the alleged miracles. Strauss disagreed with both these viewpoints. He not only refused to believe
in the *miracles*, but said that the *very events* which were presented
by the Evangelists as miracles, and which the resourceful rationalists were explaining by natural causes, were themselves un-
authentic. He declared that the time was ripe to put an end to
unscientific attempts to "make the improbable probable, to make
historically conceivable that which had not occurred in history".
Following Schelling and Hegel, he expressed the opinion that
the Gospel stories had to be taken not as accounts of real
happenings, but only as *myths* that had sprung up within the
Christian communities and reflected the Messianic ideas of the
time. Here is how he himself subsequently expounded his views
on the origin of these myths.

"It would be of no avail, I said, to want to make intelligible
as natural processes, for example, the tales about the star appearing
to the wise men, about the transfiguration, the miraculous feeding,
etc. But since it is equally impossible to imagine unnatural things
as having actually occurred, all such tales are to be regarded as
inventions. If it was asked how, at the time when the Gospels
came into being, such tales about Jesus came to be invented I
replied, first of all, by pointing to the then prevailing expectation
of the Messiah. I said that after first a few, and then an ever growing number of people came to recognise Jesus as the Messiah;
they believed that everything must have been fulfilled in him
which they expected of the Messiah, in accordance with the Old
Testament prophecies and prefigures and their widespread interpretations. No matter how well known it was that Jesus was born
in Nazareth, as the Messiah and the Son of David he had none the
less to be born in Bethlehem, because this had been prophesied by
Micah. The so severe reproaches addressed by Jesus to his fellow-
countrymen for their passion for miracles, could be preserved in

tradition, but since the first liberator of the people, Moses, had performed miracles, so also had the last liberator, the Messiah, i.e., Jesus, to perform them. Isaiah had prophesied that when the Messiah appeared, the eyes of the blind would be opened, the deaf would hear, the lame would run like deer and the tongue-tied would speak fluently. Thus, it was known exactly even in detail which particular miracles must have been performed by Jesus, since he was the Messiah. So it was that the first Christian communities not only could but had to invent tales about Jesus, without realising, however, that they were inventing them.... This view puts the origin of the early Christian myths on the same footing with the origin of those we meet in the history of the appearance of other religions. This is just what constitutes the latest successes of science in the sphere of mythology—its understanding of how myths arise, in their original shape representing, not the conscious and deliberate invention of a single person, but the product of the collective consciousness of a whole people or a religious group, expressed, perhaps originally by a single individual, but believed precisely because thereby he is but the mouthpiece of the general conviction. It was not the shell into which a wise man put an idea conceived by him for the pious use of the ignorant crowd, but in the tale, and in the form of the tale which he related he became conscious of the idea which purely as such he himself could not yet have grasped."*

VIII

There is no doubt that only such a way of posing the question may be considered scientific. In the person of Strauss, the school of Hegel did in fact approach religion—or, at least, some fruits of religious creation—wielding the surgical knife of scientific research. However, the correct *posing* of a problem is not equivalent to its correct *solution*. Strauss' book excited much comment and objection. Thus, for example, Weisse (*Die evangelische Geschichte kritisch und philosophisch bearbeitet*, 1838) asserted that at the time when our first three Gospels were written, no tradition "of a definite type" had yet taken shape in the Christian communities. Consequently, the content of these Gospels could not be explained by tradition. Weisse, who considered that the Gospel according to St. Mark was the first in point of time of our Gospels, sought to prove that this first Gospel had provided the basis for the narrations of St. Matthew and St. Luke. But if one

* See *Das Leben Jesu, für das deutsche Volk bearbeitet von David-Friedrich Strauss*, Dritte Auflage, pp. 150-54. There is a Russian translation by M. Sinyavsky, edited by N. M. Nikolsky, in two volumes, Moscow, 1907.

Evangelist borrowed his material from another, there was nothing
to stop him from rewriting it. This shows that in the Gospels we
are probably dealing not only with myths, but also with the products of the Evangelists' personal creation. Finally, the opinion
was expressed that, in the period preceding the appearance of
Christ and the formation of the Christian communities, the notion
of the Messiah was not so widespread in the Jewish world as
Strauss thought.

The most resolute of all Strauss' critics was *Bruno Bauer* (1809-
1882).

In replying to his critics, Strauss noted that there were now
three shades of opinion in the Hegelian school: the centre had two
wings, a right and a left.* Bruno Bauer, also a former pupil of
Hegel's, belonged at the start to the right wing. But at the end
of the thirties, he became one of the most extreme on the left
wing. In 1840, he published his *Kritik der evangelischen Geschichte
des Johannes*, and in 1841-42, *Kritik der evangelischen Geschichte
der Synoptiker und des Johannes*. These works, especially the latter,
created a great stir. The orthodox were so irritated with Bauer
that they succeeded in having him deprived of his post as university lecturer.**

According to Bauer, Strauss' lasting merit lay in the fact that
he had made a final break with orthodoxy. But in doing so, he
had taken only the first step towards a proper understanding of
the Gospel story. His theory of myths would not stand up to criticism; it itself suffered from mysticism. In saying that the Gospel story had its source in tradition Strauss explained very little,
since the task is precisely to investigate the process which gives
rise to tradition.*** The Gospel story was not the mysterious and
unconscious creation of the Christian community, it was the
quite conscious creation of individual persons pursuing definite
religious aims. This is most obvious from a reading of the fourth
Gospel, but is noticeable also in the others. The so-called St.
Luke refashioned in his own way the Gospel of the so-called St.
Mark, and the so-called St. Matthew recarved both of these, endeavouring to adapt their stories to the ideas and spiritual needs
of his own time. He tried to get them to agree with one another,
but himself became entangled in many contradictions.

---

* See his interesting article: "Verschiedene Richtungen innerhalb der
Hegel'schen Schule in Betreff der Christologie", in the collection: *Streitschrif-
ten zur Verteidigung meiner Schrift über das Leben Jesu und zur Charakteristik
der gegenwärtigen Theologie.* [The Various Trends in the Hegelian School in
Relation to Christ int he collection: Polemical Works dedicated to the defence
of my Life of Jesus and the characterisation of contemporary theology.]
** He was then an assistant professor at Bonn.
*** *Kritik der evangelischen Geschichte der Synoptiker*, Zweite Auflage,
Leipzig, 1846, T. I, Vorrede, p. VII.

Strauss had already come to the conclusion that there were insufficient data at our disposal to permit us to form a definite impression of the personality of Jesus. Bruno Bauer utterly rejected Jesus' existence in history. It is understandable what indignation he must have aroused among the immense majority of his readers. And, of course, it should not be forgotten that Bauer had nevertheless posed the question much more correctly than Strauss had done. The investigators who supported Bauer's views had in any case to regard Christianity, not as the fruit that had finally ripened in the soil of Jewish Messianic expectations, but as the spiritual outcome of the development of Greco-Roman culture. Bauer insisted that Christianity was the product of specific social relations. True, he began to talk in this way only much later, in the seventies of last century. At the time of his controversy with Strauss, he himself in his comprehension of Christianity was a thorough-going idealist, and this brought him some years later the reproach from Marx that, according to Bauer, the Gospels were dictated not by the Holy Ghost but by infinite self-consciousness.[291]

To grasp the philosophical meaning of this reproach and thus elucidate the role of Bauer in the history of German Hegelianism after Hegel, it is necessary to take into account the significance Bauer himself attached to his dispute with Strauss.

IX

In his view, this dispute was one about *substance* on the one hand and *self-consciousness* on the other. Strauss, in his explanation that the Gospels were the unconscious creation of the Christian community, adhered to the point of view of *substance*. Rejecting this viewpoint and proving that the evangelical narratives had been consciously invented by the Evangelists, B. Bauer proclaimed himself a representative of *self-consciousness*.

The question upon which he had entered into controversy with Strauss was in fact much wider than that of the origin of the Gospel stories. It was the great philosophical and historical question of how the law-governed course of history in general, and the history of thought in particular, is related to the conscious activity of individual persons. This question finds its complete answer in the proposition that the law-governed course of history is determined by the aggregate of the actions of individuals and that, in consequence, it must in no case be considered in contrast to law-governed historical motion. True, the concept of *conformity to law* coincides with the *concept of necessity*, whereas the conscious activity of individual persons seems to them not to be governed by necessity, or, to use an expression more common in such cases, to

be free. But it seems so to them because, being conscious of themselves as the *cause* of certain social happenings, they are not conscious of themselves as the consequence of that social situation in
which their desire to act in a particular way and not in some other
way was born. To act freely means to realise one's aims, and not
to be the instrument for the achievement of the aims of others—
that and no more. *Freedom* is the opposite of *compulsion*, and not at
all of *necessity*. The conscious activity of great men in every particular historical period was *free* in the sense that they were achieving their own and not somebody else's ideals, and at the same
time it was *necessary*, because their decision to serve these ideals
was conditioned by all the previous course of social development.
Furthermore, even the most free and fruitful activity of individuals always arouses, by the way, consequences which they themselves had not foreseen at all. It is clear from even the first, superficial glance that these consequences can find their explanation
only in a certain necessary law-governed connection between social
phenomena. But no matter how clear all this may be, the free
activity of individual persons all the same very often and—for
certain psychological motives—very willingly is contrasted to
the law-governed general course of development. Although Hegel's philosophy explained all the futility of such an antinomy,
even the most gifted Hegelians, which Strauss and B. Bauer were
without any doubt, could not always cope with it. Strauss, in
asserting that the Gospel story arose from tradition, and in not
admitting, at least at the beginning, that there was any room for
the elaboration of tradition by the creative effort of individual
persons, leaned to one side of the antinomy. In his own Hegelian
language Bauer expressed this by saying that Strauss adhered to
the point of view of substance. Citing Hegel, Bauer averred that
such an attitude on Strauss' part was a great sin against philosophy—of course, Hegelian philosophy—which required progress from
substance to self-consciousness. He was prepared, perhaps, to admit
the right of substance, but demanded that self-consciousness, too,
be accorded its right. "Strauss' error," he said, "consists not in
having brought into motion that common force, but in compelling
it to act directly from its community."* This was said truly su-
perbly. However, Bauer showed too much zeal in his defence of the
right of "self-consciousness". He defended it with such enthusiasm
that the "common force" proved to be completely outside his view
as well. In other words, he leaned to the other side of the antinomy: he so reconciled "substance" with "self-consciousness",
that self-consciousness became *all* to him, and substance *nothing*.

---

* *Die gute Sache der Freiheit und meine eigene Angelegenheit*, Zürich.

It was this that led Marx to make the mocking remark we quoted above, one that was equivalent to reproaching him with extreme *historical idealism.*

The differences between Strauss and Bauer were differences based on Hegelian speculation. But as we have seen, each of them leaned to one of the opposing sides of the antinomy between the law-governed course of history and the free activity of invididuals. To the same extent that they were guilty of this one-sidedness, they differed from their teacher. Bauer's difference with Hegel involved rejection of the Hegelian philosophy of history and a return to the views of the French eighteenth-century Enlighteners, according to whom the "world is governed by opinion" (c'est l'opinion qui gouverne le monde).

But this return was a *step back,* a retrograde movement in the understanding of the historical process. No one denies that "opinion" influences the course of social development. The question is, however, must we not recognise that the process of the formation and development of "opinion" has its own conformity to law, that is to say, necessity? Helvétius, one of the most brilliant and courageous representatives of French Enlightenment philosophy of the eighteenth century, already suspected that such necessity exists. He said that the development of knowledge (and consequently of "opinion" generally) is subject to certain laws and that there are unknown causes by which that development is determined. In saying this, he put before the philosophy of history—or, if you like, before social science—the new and extremely important task of discovering the unknown causes determining the course of development of "opinion". The great Hegel grasped the vast importance of this task, although maybe he was not aware of who had formulated it. He touched upon it in his lectures on the history of philosophy while making an assessment of Anaxagoras. The latter said that the world is moved by reason. Hegel fully approved of this idea. But in applying it to the explanation of the historical process, he remarked that reason guides history only in the sense in which it guides the motion of the celestial bodies, that is to say, in the sense of conformity to law. The historical progress of humanity is subject to certain laws. This does not mean, however, that its course is guided by men's opinions. Minerva's owl flies only by night. Men start to ponder over their own social relations only when these are tending to decay and are preparing to give way to a new system. But how do social relations arise? We already know that, in Hegel's view, the ultimate cause of historical development is the motion of the world spirit. We know too that at times Hegel himself seemed to feel the futility of referring to the world spirit, and then this "absolute idealist" made unexpected excursions into the domain of the materialist

explanation of history. B. Bauer and those who held similar views
to his, among whom a prominent role was played by his brother
Edgar, were even less satisfied than Hegel with references to
the world spirit, absolute reason and so forth. Edgar Bauer wrote
that contemplative (i.e., Hegel's) philosophy was much in error
in speaking of reason as of an abstract absolute force. There is no
absolute reason,* he argued; and, of course, he was right. But
although the Hegelian reference to the world spirit or, what is the
same thing, to absolute reason, was unsound, nevertheless it
signified acknowledgement of that incontestable truth that the
progressive development of "opinion" is not the ultimate cause
of historical development, since it itself depends upon some unknown and hidden causes. In rejecting reference to absolute reason,
it was necessary either to forget altogether the existence of
these causes—and thus overlook the most important task of the
scientific explanation of the historical process—or to continue
to search for them in the same direction in which Hegel at times
sought them, that is to say, in the direction of historical materialism. There could be no third road. However, B. Bauer and his
associates attached absolutely no value to Hegel's excursions into
the domain of the materialist explanation of history: they simply
did not notice them. Therefore they could only go back, return
to the superficial historical idealism of the eighteenth century.
This they did, when they recognised "opinion" as the motive force
of world history.**

The historical idealism of the French Enlighteners did not prevent their doing great revolutionary work. Although their own
"opinion", like all others, was the natural outcome of social development, yet once formed, it became a mighty lever of the
further development of society. B. Bauer and his associates also
considered themselves to be great revolutionaries. Edgar Bauer
believed that our times are above all distinguished by their revolutionary character.*** Neither he nor anyone else among the
extreme representatives of "criticism" ever suspected that, at the
stage of development reached by West European society in the
forties of last century, the idealist viewpoint was incompatible
with a revolutionary mode of thought in the field of social and
political theory. Here I have in mind, of course, a *consistently*
revolutionary mode of thought, since the *inconsistent adapts itself* with great facility *to every point of departure.*

---

* *Der Streit der Kritik mit Kirche und Staat*, Berne, 1844, p. 184.
** See Edgar Bauer, op. cit., p. 185; also his work *Bruno Bauer und seine
Gegner*, Berlin, 1842, pp. 89-90.
*** "Der Charakter unserer Zeit ist die Revolution", see op. cit., *Bruno
Bauer und seine Gegner*, p. 5.

X

The mode of thought of the Bauer brothers was very radical in the field of *theology*. This need not be surprising. According to the theory of their teacher Hegel, in religion the spirit conceives of its own essence. However, the Bauer brothers had come to the conclusion that the spirit generally did not exist as something independent of human consciousness. It is clear that they could no longer look at religion through Hegel's eyes. They argued that not *spirit* but *man* conceives of his essence in religion. But the religious conception of the essence of man is a *mistaken* one, and as such should be eliminated. The Bauers took this viewpoint of religion from Ludwig Feuerbach, and we shall deal with it when we come to speak of Feuerbach. Here it is only necessary to note that in their view of religion—although it was not an independent one—the Bauers were significantly in advance of Strauss, who for a fairly long time stuck fast in the space separating Feuerbach from Hegel. With the Bauers there was no question of peace between religion and philosophy. When one of the supporters of such a peace said that the thinker who rebelled against one religion was duty bound to put another religion in its place, Bruno Bauer objected sharply, saying that when we try to pull someone out of one blunder we are not obliged to push him into another: and if we wish to expiate one crime it does not follow that we must commit a new one.*

The "critics" desired to put philosophy in the place of religion. However, in their eyes philosophy too was not an aim in itself. The triumph of philosophy was to clear the path for the reconstruction of society on rational foundations and for the further forward movement of humanity. This would seem to be a fully progressive programme. But it was here that it was revealed how difficult it was, in the middle of the nineteenth century, to get agreement between consistent revolutionary thinking and idealism.

The programme of B. Bauer and his associates remained progressive only so long as it kept the form of an algebraic formula. But when it became necessary to replace the *algebraic symbols with definite arithmetical figures*, it acquired a dubious and even a directly conservative character. The Bauer brothers were unable to link up the abstract radicalism of their thinking with the social aspirations of their time. Proud of their *"critical spirit"*, they looked scornfully on the *"mass"*, alien, as they thought, to all criticism, and considered harmful any contact with it. They uttered the strange view that all previous great historical actions

---

* *Die gute Sache...* etc., p. 201.

40—01230

had had no decisive success because they had interested and attracted the masses, or, in other words, because the idea in the name
of which they were being accomplished had to appeal to the
masses. In this regard, Marx made the very valid point that
the "idea" suffered shameful defeat every time it separated itself
from "interest", that is to say, did not express the needs of society
as a whole or of a particular class.* The sublime contempt
of idealist "criticism" for the material interests of the mass
prevented it from understanding the meaning of the proletarian
emancipation movement, and even brought it into opposition
to this movement. In this respect, Feuerbach showed much
greater understanding of the movement; but the remarkable
thing is that in his person German philosophy was breaking with
idealism and becoming materialist.

XI

In order to grasp *how this happened* and why it *had to happen,*
we have to recall in broad outline the progress of thought that
brought German philosophy to the absolute idealism of Hegel.

It was correctly said that the fundamental question of philosophy, especially the philosophy of modern times, is the question
of the relationship of consciousness to nature, of the subject to the
object. Around this question, German philosophical thought of
the nineteenth century revolved as around its axis.

In the philosophy of Kant, the world of phenomena was sharply
contrasted to the world of noumena, man to nature, the subject to
the object. This is dualism; but philosophy, if it is not to mark
time, cannot be content with dualism. It strives towards *monism.*
It is easy to understand why: because *only* monism, explaining the
world by means of *one* principle, has the right to claim a (more or
less correct) solution of the question of the relationship of subject
to object. Dualism does not solve this question; it either declares
it to be insoluble or appeals to a miracle, that is to say, to the
intervention of an omnipotent being standing *above both subject
and object.* But the supreme being is *one*: so that the appeal to it
is itself an attempt to solve—true, by means of a phantom—the
fundamental question of philosophy in a monistic sense.**

Fichte wished to eliminate Kant's dualism by declaring it
a mistake to see in the non-*ego* (in the object, in nature) something independent of the *ego* (of the subject, of self-consciousness)
and separated from it by an impassable gulf. In reality the "ego"

---

* See *Die heilige Familie, oder Kritik der kritischen Kritik. Gegen Bruno
Bauer und Konsorten.*[292]
** Science also strives towards monism. One of the most brilliant repre-
sentatives of science in modern times, Newton, was attracted to it.

contrasts itself to itself, and thereby posits the non-"ego". Thus all that exists does so in the "ego" and *through* the "ego". In other words, nature owes its existence to the creative activity of consciousness, and exists only in it. This solution of the problem of the relationship of subject to object had two advantages in the eyes of his contemporaries; it was, first of all, *monistic*, and, secondly, monistic in an idealist sense. The celebrated Romanticist, Novalis, called Fichte the new Newton who had discovered the law of the inner system of the worlds.* Schelling at first also came out as Fichte's pupil. However, the Romanticists soon found that they were able to "Fichticise" better than Fichte (besser fichtisieren als Fichte). They proclaimed that the world was a dream, and the dream was the world, becoming addicts of "magical" idealism. The same Novalis asserted that nature was a fantasy which had been transformed into a machine, and that physics was the doctrine of fantasy.** It was probably such extravagances of the Romanticists that obliged Schelling to review critically the question of what in Fichte's teaching is the "ego" which "*posits*" *nature*. He came to the conclusion that, in Fichte's opinion, nature is created by the finite human *ego*, the subject, possessing consciousness and will. To proclaim such an *ego* the creator of nature was an absurdity to which no serious thinker could reconcile himself. Schelling hastened to finish with it, and to see nature as the fruit of the activity, not of a finite human *ego*, but of an infinite subject, the absolute *ego*. It must be added here that the activity of the absolute *ego* creating nature was, in Schelling's view, *unconscious activity*. Schelling's philosophy of nature was engendered by the effort to penetrate into the meaning of this unconscious activity of the absolute *ego*. Some historians of philosophy contend that in elaborating his philosophy of nature, Schelling indeed went further than Fichte, but in the same direction. There is much truth in this; of course, Fichte could not consider that nature is created by the finite human *ego*. But, on the other hand, he never managed to cope with the question of the relationship of the *finite* "ego" to the *infinite*, or, in other words, of *human self-consciousness to that infinite subject whose unconscious activity creates nature*. Schelling analysed the problem much more deeply.

To him the finite *ego* is also created by the activity of the infinite *ego*, just as is nature. Nature is the necessary product of the *infinite* "ego" or—because, strictly speaking, it *is* not, but *originates* thanks to the activity of the absolute *ego*—nature has to

---

* Haym, *The Romantic School*, Russian translation by I. Nevedomsky, Moscow, 1891, p. 317.
** Novalis' phrase; see E. Spenlé, *Novalis*, Paris, 1904, p. 133, also Haym, op. cit., p. 324.

be understood as the unconscious development of this *ego*. But the activity of this *ego* is not confined to the unconscious creation of nature. Among natural phenomena there is also *man*—the *finite* subject in whom the *infinite* "ego" comes to self-consciousness. Thus the *subject* has its beginning at the same point as the object: in the *infinite subject, in the absolute* "ego".

And precisely because both subject and object have their beginning in the *absolute* "ego", the latter is *neither subject nor object*, neither consciousness nor being; it is subject-object, that is to say, *the unity, the identity* of thinking and being.

Hegel's system was but the further elaboration of Schelling's philosophy of identity. Justice demands an unqualified acknowledgement of the fact that Hegel gave this philosophy an incomparably more systematic form. Thus, for instance, for the history of philosophical theory it is of great significance that Hegel noted and eliminated the element of dualism which had crept unnoticed into the system of identity and which consisted *in the absolute* "ego", *the spirit*, or simply *the absolute*, being placed by Schelling *outside nature and outside human consciousness.* According to Hegel, the world *is not only rooted* in the absolute, *but is within it.* The world is the totality of nature and spirit. The development of the world is the development of the absolute, its revelation. Such a conception of the world process saved the philosophy of identity from the risk of coming into contradiction with itself and ending in dualism. You will agree, though, that it put a barrier in the way of the reconciliation of philosophy with religion, to which Hegel was sincerely striving. The conception of God as a power beyond the world proved to be incompatible with the true character of the world process. The Hegelians who wished to defend this conception—the right wing of the Hegelian school: Göschel, Marheineke—were moving away from their teacher. Even the left Hegelians were closer to him—Bruno Bauer, Feuerbach, both of whom had broken with religion; and still closer to Hegel were those who composed the centre of the school: Rosenkranz, Michelet and Strauss who inclined towards pantheism.* That is why there came from the Hegelian school the criticism of the Gospel story in particular and criticism of religion in general, whereas Schelling's philosophical thought inclined subsequently to *theosophy*.

The most remarkable and most important circumstance for the further history of philosophy was that idealist monism, which had received its most orderly expression in Hegel's system,

---

* Later Strauss became a materialist, and did not hesitate to express his new views in the work: *Der alte und der neue Glaube. Ein Bekenntnis.* It had an immense success. But this occurred much later: the book just mentioned appeared in October 1872.

disclosed in the latter more clearly than in any other, its extremely *one-sided nature.*

The absolute is the subject-object, the identity of thinking and being. So taught Schelling; so taught Hegel. But at the same time, the absolute is the *ego*, the infinite *subject of the spirit.* Schelling and Hegel both insisted strongly on this conception. Both condemned Spinoza who, in their words, could not rise from the concept of *substance* to the concept of *self-consciousness.* However, Spinoza's substance, which had two attributes—thinking and extension—had the advantage, that it was in fact the subject-object, the unity of thinking and being. To "rise" from substance to self-consciousness, that is to say, to conceive of substance in the manner demanded by Schelling and Hegel, as the absolute *ego*, as spirit, would have meant reducing it to one of its attributes, namely to *thinking.* He who reduces everything to thinking is, of course, a monist. But his monism does not solve the problem of the relation of subject to object, of thinking to being: it *evades its solution*, quite arbitrarily deleting one of the conditions of the problem. Feuerbach, at the beginning an enthusiastic pupil of Hegel's, later on noticed this weak side of *idealist* monism, and then he became a materialist.

XII

The idealist theory that nature owes its existence to the creative activity of the infinite subject, or, as Hegel described it, is but the other being of spirit, was conceived by Feuerbach simply as the translation into the language of philosophy of the theological doctrine of God having created the world. "Our philosophers," he said, "till now have been nothing more than mediatised theologians."* Hegel's philosophy—that last stage in the development of German idealism—is the last refuge, the last rational basis of theology. He who does not reject Hegelian philosophy, does not reject theology.**

Idealism commits a grave error in taking the doctrine of *ego* as its starting point. Philosophy has to find a new point of departure—the doctrine of *ego* and *tu.**** I do not only *see*, but I am also

---

* Feuerbach's *Werke*, neue Ausgabe. *Nachgelassene Aphorismen*, Stuttgart, 1911, Vol. X, p. 318.

** "Vorläufige Thesen zur Reform der Philosophie", *Werke*, the same edition, Vol. II, p. 239.

*** Nicht Ich, nein! Ich und Du, Subjekt und Objekt, unterschieden und doch unzertrennlich verbunden, ist das wahre Princip des Denkens und Lebens, der Philosophie und der Physiologie (*Über Spiritualismus und Materialismus*, Feuerbach's *Werke*, B.X., neue Ausgabe). [Not I, no! I and Thou, subject and object, distinct yet indissolubly connected—this is the true principle of thinking and life, of philosophy and physiology."]

seen by others. The real *ego* is only that *ego* to which is opposed *tu*
and which, in turn, becomes *tu*, i.e., an object for another *ego*.
I am a *subject* for myself and an *object* for others. Therefore, *I* am
simultaneously both *subject* and *object*, or, briefly, a *subject-
object*. Whoever regards consciousness as being independent of men
—or, as Fichte would have said, independent of the plurality
of individuals—severs all connection between consciousness and
the world. Yet the world is the necessary prerequisite of consciousness. Our *ego* is by no means that abstract being which is the
plaything of the idealist philosophers. *I* am a real being. To my
essence belongs also my body. More than that, my body, seen
in its totality, is my true essence; it is what composes my *ego*.
The process of thinking takes place not in some abstract being,
but precisely in my, thy, his body. Thinking, consciousness, is
but a predicate of the real being, a property of being. Being precedes thinking (das Sein geht dem Denken vorher). And it is not
thinking that determines being; it is being that determines thinking.

In conformity with all this, Feuerbach establishes *his* categorical imperative: "Think not as a thinker, but as a living, real
being, in which capacity you breast the waves of the world sea."

Feuerbach affirmed that only his theory of *ego* and *tu* resolves
that antinomy of spirit and matter with which neither Schelling
nor Hegel could cope. "What for me, or subjectively, is a purely
spiritual, non-material, non-sensuous act, is in itself, objectively, a
material, sensuous act." Neither side of the antinomy is eliminated
here; and here is revealed the true unity of these sides.*

Unity, but not by any means identity. Identity was proclaimed
by idealist philosophy, which reduced everything to spirit.

The *idealist* monism of Fichte, Schelling and Hegel arose out
of opposition to Spinoza, who with his doctrine of the substance
allegedly "abolished" the freedom of man. Feuerbach, with his
materialist monism, returned to the viewpoint of Spinoza. In general he valued Spinoza very highly, and called him the "Moses of
modern freethinkers and materialists".

This may appear strange, since Spinozism is usually interpreted nowadays in an idealist sense. But Feuerbach looked at Spinoza's teaching through quite different spectacles. To a question
put by himself: "What actually is, on close examination, that

---

* Das Objekt ist ... für uns nicht nur Gegenstand der Empfindung. es
ist auch die Grundlage, die Bedingung, die Voraussetzung der Empfindung;
wir haben in [nerhalb] der Haut eine objektive Welt, und nur diese ist der
Grund, dass wir eine ihr entsprechende ausser unsere Haut hinaussetzen"
(Feuerbach's *Werke*, X, 220). ["The object for us is not only an object of sensation; it is also the basis, the condition, the prerequisite of sensation; we
have an objective world inside our skin and that alone is the reason why we
presuppose one corresponding to it outside our skin."]

which Spinoza *logically* or *metaphysically* calls *substance*, and *theologically God?*" he replied: "Nothing else but *Nature.*" In Spinoza's teaching there was, however, the shortcoming that nature in it appeared as an abstract, metaphysical being. The actions of nature are presented as the actions of God. Spinozism is materialism clad in theological garb. And this garb has to be stripped from the essentially correct philosophical theory of Spinoza. "Not *Deus sive Natura* but *aut Deus, aut Natura** is the watchword of truth," exclaims Feuerbach.

Since Lange's time, Feuerbach's philosophy has often been referred to as "humanism". To justify this, Feuerbach has been quoted—again following Lange's example—in his famous sentence: "God was my first thought, Reason my second, Man my third and last thought." Unfortunately, Feuerbach's "third and last thought" was understood very badly at that. Actually, this sentence, characterising in abridged form the course of his philosophical development, means only that in the end he changed from a theologian into a materialist. We are already aware that to him "man" as a *real, material being* was contrasted to the abstract *ego* of the idealists. Anyone who is not clear about the philosophical meaning of this contrast should recall the following observation of Feuerbach: "In the dispute between materialism and spiritualism ... the question at issue is the human mind.... Once we know the matter of which the brain is composed, we shall quickly reach a clear understanding concerning all other matter, concerning matter in general."** Now it is quite easy to grasp the sense in which man was Feuerbach's last thought: the study of man had to help fashion a correct conception of matter and its relation to "spirit", to consciousness.

Developing his "third and last thought", Feuerbach asserted that man is part of nature, part of being, and this assures him the possibility of knowing the world. As the object is, so also is the subject (wie Objekt, so Subjekt).There can be no contradiction between being and thinking. Space and time are forms of my contemplation, as Kant taught. But they are also forms of being. And they can be forms of my contemplation only because I myself am part of being, am a being living in time and space. Generally, the laws of being are at the same time the laws of thinking. This proposition of Feuerbach's is reminiscent of Spinoza's well-known dictum: *ordo et connexio idearum idem est ac ordo et connexio rerum* (the order and connection of ideas are the same as the order and connection of things).

---

* [Not *God or nature*, but *either God or nature*.]

** It is interesting to note that Feuerbach's contemporaries had no hesitation in listing him among the materialists. This was the case with A. S. Khomyakov in our philosophical literature (see his article: "Contemporary Phenomena in the Domain of Philosophy", letter to Y. F. Samarin).

The opponents of materialism object that consciousness cannot be explained by material phenomena. The preceding exposition of Feuerbach's views has shown the reader, I trust, that this objection does not in any way affect the basis of Feuerbach's materialist doctrine, which consists in the proposition that the world of *subjective* phenomena is but the other side of the world of objective phenomena. Anyone who would wish to *explain* the subjective world *by means of* the objective world, to *deduce* the first from the second, would thereby demonstrate that he has understood nothing whatsoever of Feuerbach's materialism. This doctrine, like that of Spinoza, does not *deduce* one side from the other, but simply establishes that they are two sides of the one whole. By the way, in this respect other major varieties of materialism, at least of present-day materialism, do not differ in any way from Feuerbach's.

Efforts are sometimes made at present to bring Feuerbach's teaching closer to monistic doctrines of the *Machian* type, according to which matter is "a complex of sensations". But Feuerbach would have described such monism as the restoration of idealism, solving the antinomy of being and thinking by abstracting one side to the benefit of the other; *being* to the benefit of *thinking*, or (in the present case) of *sensation*. Feuerbach did not take to be as meaning *to exist only in thinking or in sensation*. "To prove that something exists is to prove that it exists not only in thought," he said, having the idealists of his time in mind. If he could only have foreseen the coming of the idealist, or, if you will, the sensualist, monism of Mach, he would have said that to exist means to exist *not only in sensation*.

XIII

We are now well enough acquainted with Feuerbach's philosophy to understand the conclusions drawn from it by him in application to *religion, ethics,* and *social life,* and by some of his pupils in application to aesthetics.

As has been said above, the Bauer brothers, by affirming that in religion it is not spirit but man that contemplates his own essence, were following Feuerbach. No other view of religion could be held by any thinker who, before returning to the Anglo-French materialism of the seventeenth and eighteenth centuries, had passed through that school of idealism which, in the person of Hegel, made it obligatory for philosophers to study phenomena in their process of development. The French Enlighteners in general and in particular the French materialists, who were the advance guard of the army of the Enlighteners, regarded religion as the product of priests or legislators, who had devised certain beliefs as a means of influencing the simple-minded mass of the people, for the purpose of exploiting or educating them. Remember Voltaire's tragedy: *Le fanatisme, ou Mahomet le prophète*. In the nineteenth century, it became obvious to Hegel's followers that this conception of religion was untenable, being reduced to the belief that "opinion" not only rules the world, but also *creates and refashions itself to suit the practical aims of its chief representatives*. Hegel's dialectical method paved the way for a view of religion, and indeed of every other ideology, as being the natural outcome of the law-governed development of social consciousness. The main distinguishing feature of this process is that its participants, conscious of themselves as the *cause of subsequent events*, very rarely rise to the height of seeing themselves as the consequence of *foregoing* events. To put it differently, the process of the development of social *consciousness* is itself, in a certain sense, an *unconscious* process. According to Feuerbach, religion is the result of this process in its unconscious aspect. Religion is the unconscious deifying of essence—not of spirit, of course, because spirit itself exists only thanks to the abstract activity of philosophical thought—but of *man*. Therefore, Feuerbach says religion is the unconscious consciousness of man. The essence of God is the essence of man, but an essence freed from the limitedness of the individual, i.e., the essence of the given social whole, or, as Feuerbach expresses it, of the *species*.

Thinking in this fashion, Feuerbach laid the theoretical foundations for the conception of religion as a product of social development. He himself said that the properties of God change in accordance with changes in the essence of (*social*) man.

In religion, man is not conscious that he is deifying himself. He is giving his own essence *objectivity*, conceiving of and revering it as another being distinct from himself and stronger than himself. He is *dividing* and *devastating* himself, attributing to a higher being his own (social man's) best properties. This gives rise to a series of contradictions.

When man says "God is Love", he means that love transcends everything on this earth. But in his consciousness, love is degraded to the level of the property of a being independent of man. Consequently, belief in God becomes for him a necessary condition of love for his neighbours. He hates the atheist in the name of the selfsame love he preaches. Religion damns in the name of salvation, commits cruelties in the name of felicity. Reason which *has grown to self-consciousness* rejects religion. It turns inside out the relations which religion has created. Since these relations are themselves the result of the turning inside out of true relationships, reason restores the latter, realising its aim by turning inside out that which had been turned inside out. Virtue, which has a great social significance, but which in religion has become *a means of acquiring happiness beyond the grave*, must become an aim. "Justice, truth, good, have their sacred justification in themselves, in their own quality. For man there is no being higher than man." This is why Feuerbach proclaims, using the old terminology, that man to man is God.

Terminology of this kind had its great inconveniences. To pronounce God to be an illusion, and then to say that man is God is really tantamount to transforming man himself into an illusion. At this point Feuerbach himself got involved in a contradiction. In declaring "Meine Religion—keine Religion"[293] (My religion is no religion), he recollected that the word "religion" is derived from the verb "religare", and at first meant "bond". From this he deduced that every bond between people is a religion. Engels remarked that "such etymological tricks are the last resort of idealist philosophy".[294] That is certainly right.* However, the historical significance of the book *Das Wesen des Christentums* which was published in 1841 and was the first printed exposition of the Feuerbachian philosophy of religion, is shown by the testimony of the same Engels.

In relating the difficulties experienced by the extreme Left-wing Hegelians in reconciling their attraction to Anglo-French materialism with Hegel's idealist teaching that nature is but the other being of spirit, he went on:

"Then came Feuerbach's *Essence of Christianity*. With one blow it pulverised the contradiction, in that without circumlocutions it placed materialism on the throne again.... Nothing exists outside nature and man, and the higher beings our religious fantasies have created are only the fantastic reflection of our own essence.... One must himself have experienced the liberating effect of this book to get an idea of it. Enthusiasm was general; we all became at once Feuerbachians."**

XIV

Having defined the essence of religion in the manner just expounded, Feuerbach naturally could not agree with those who said:

---

* As confirmation of this, one may quote Feuerbach's own truly excellent remark: "Every religious or theological sanctification is simply a phantom. That which has foundation and truth can stand by itself, without being proclaimed holy." (Was Grund und Wahrheit hat, behauptet sich durch sich selbst, ohne heilig gesprochen zu werden.)

** Engels, *Ludwig Feuerbach*, p. 10 of the foreign edition of my Russian translation of this pamphlet.[295] In Germany, many of Feuerbach's admirers shared his views on religion, but did not follow him into accepting the materialist basis of these views. This was the case originally with Herzen too (see my article "The Philosophical Views of A. I. Herzen" in *Contemporary World*, 1912, Books 3 and 4).

"There is no morality without faith." To him, this was just the same as if we had said: there is no education without barbarism, or there is no love without hatred. The morality that results from religion is only the alms which the church or theology throw from their treasuries to poor, destitute humanity. Morality must have a totally different basis. Materialism alone can be its solid basis (Der Materialismus ist die einzige solide Grundlage der Moral).*

By this, Feuerbach means that moral precepts must be based on *interest*. In contrast to the Bauer brothers, he did not consider it possible to disregard interest. A note has been preserved among his papers containing the following excerpt from a speech by Emilio Castelar, the renowned Spanish Republican:

"The history of mankind is a constant struggle between ideas and interests. For a time the latter win, in the long run, ideas are victorious."

In the same note, Feuerbach objects:

"What a contradiction! Are ideas then not also interests? Are they not general interests of humanity, though for a time misunderstood, despised, persecuted, not yet come into reality, unrecognised by law, contradicting the particular interests of individual, now dominant estates or classes, and as yet existing only in the idea? Is not justice a general *interest*,** an interest of those who are treated unjustly though naturally not of those who practise this injustice, the interests of the estates and classes who find their interests only in privileges? In short, the struggle between *ideas and interests* is only the struggle between *the old* and *the new*."***

It must be admitted that here the true essence of the matter is brought out astonishingly well, even better than in the remark we quoted above, which Marx addressed to "the Holy family" of the Bauers, that the idea suffered shameful defeat wherever it diverged from interest.

What the moral rules of this terrible man were, who from his earliest years did not believe in the immortality of the soul and based his morality upon a materialist foundation, may be seen, incidentally, from the following moral rule of his:

"*In relation to oneself*, one cannot be *idealist* enough making idealist demands of the will, 'categorical imperatives', but *in relation to others*, with the exception of certain cases which are extremely difficult to define, one cannot be *materialist* enough; in relation to oneself, one cannot be a stoic enough, in relation to others—Epicurean enough."****

---

* *Werke*, Vol. X. p. 151.
** Italics in the original.
*** *Werke*, X. pp. 315-16. Again the italics are in the original.
**** *Werke*, X, p. 291.

These golden words embody the whole secret of the morality upheld by our "people of the sixties",* who firmly kept to Feuerbach's rules: read through Chernyshevsky's letters from Siberia, and you will see that he was, indeed, harsh—I almost wrote cruel—in relation to himself, and a mild Epicurean in relation to others. On the soil of Feuerbach's materialist morality grew the luxuriant blooms of moral selflessness (an idealist would say by force of habit: *idealism*).

How could this be? Is there not some contradiction here? Not the slightest! The seeming contradiction disappears as soon as we take into consideration Feuerbach's teaching on *ego* and *tu*, which is at the root of his theory of cognition.

In accordance with this theory, the *ego* from which idealist philosophy starts off in its attempt to understand the world, is an "idealist chimera", a mere fiction. Feuerbach held that his *ego* is just as much a chimera, a mere fiction in the doctrine of morality. "Where outside *ego* there is no *tu*, no other person, there can be no talk of morality," he said. "Only social man is man. *I* am *I* only through Thee and with Thee. I am conscious of myself only because *Thou* art contrasted to my consciousness as a visible and tangible *ego*, as another person.... One may speak of morality only where there is relationship of man to man, one to the other, *ego* to *tu*."

People talk of duties towards oneself. But for these duties to have meaning one condition is essential: indirectly they must also be duties towards others. I have duties towards myself only because I have duties towards the family, the community, the people, the country. The good and morality are one and the same thing. *But the good can be acknowledged as such only if it is good in respect to others.***

The moral upbringing of people consists precisely in inculcating into each one the consciousness of his duties towards all the others. Nature herself assures us of the possibility of such upbringing, for it has provided man with a twofold striving for happiness: the first, that which is satisfied by assuring the exclusive interests of the given person; the second, that which requires for its satisfaction at least two persons (man and woman, mother and child, etc.). Already from his earliest years man is taught to use the good things of life in common with other people. He who assimilates this lesson badly is punished by the dissatisfaction of his neighbours, which finds the most varied expressions—from verbal

---

* [The self-sacrificing young men and women of the Russian educated classes who in those years, seeing the misery of the peasantry following the end of serfdom in 1861, began the movement known as "going to the people".— *Ed.*]
** *Werke.* X, pp. 269-70.

reproach to blows. Conscience is not something inborn in man; he has to acquire it by education, in which example has its part to play. "A man does with an easy conscience that which he sees others do and approve," said Feuerbach, "his parents, those of his age and estate, his countrymen."* In some the motion of conscience is confined to fear of what others will say. But a deeper education leads to the creation in man of an imperative need to conduct himself thus, and not otherwise.

Law, like morality, must not be opposed to interest. It is founded upon interest: of course, not personal interest, but social interest.**

This is exactly that very doctrine of morality and law which was preached by the French materialists of the eighteenth century. Feuerbach however made a better analysis of the process of the development of *altruistic* aspirations out of the *egotistical*. This is not surprising, since Feuerbach learned dialectics from Hegel; but the following is of particular interest.

In Hegel's system, morality and law already had a purely social origin. Feuerbach, as we have seen, also deduces them from social relations. In this, he is true to his teacher. But living in a different historical period, he is in a different frame of mind. In his ethics one feels the approach of 1848. The social origin of morality and law provides him in the first place with a reason to link his theory concerning them with the materialist basis of his theory of cognition. Besides, and this is the main point, the materialist philosophy of morality and law leads him to the very same revolutionary conclusions at which the French materialists of the eighteenth century had arrived earlier.

Man aspires to happiness. This aspiration cannot and should not be taken from him. It becomes harmful only when it becomes "exclusive", egotistical, that is to say, when the happiness of some is achieved by the unhappiness of others. When the whole people, and not only a part of it, aspires to happiness, this aspiration will coincide with the aspiration to *justice*. That is why Feuerbach says: "Happiness? No, justice." (Glückseligkeit? Nein, Gerechtigkeit, la justice). In his doctrine, justice is nothing else but reciprocal, mutual happiness as opposed to the exclusive, egotistical happiness of the old world (der einseitigen, egoistischen oder parteiischen Glückseligkeit der alten Welt).

When society is so organised that its members cannot satisfy their natural aspirations to happiness except by encroaching upon the interests of other members, they will certainly do so. "People are people only where this conforms to their interests, or where

---

* "Theogonie", *Feuerbach's Werke*, B. IX, p. 169 (I have only the 1857 edition of this volume by me at the moment).

** *Werke*, X, pp. 269-70.

their interests do not prevent them from being people," Feuerbach affirmed. "But where they can become people only by sacrificing their interests, they prefer to become beasts (Bestien).* Therefore, in order that they should become people, a social structure corresponding to justice, that is to say, to the interests of the whole people, is essential."** Accordingly, Feuerbach was strongly radical in politics and sympathised warmly with the emancipation movement of his time. Just a few years before his death, in a letter to L. Kapp, he said that the terrorism practised during the Great French Revolution was still necessary for Germany. He is known to have become a Social-Democrat towards the end of his life.

In this respect there was an immeasurable difference between him and Bruno Bauer, who ended his life in the ranks of reaction.

XV

As in morals, so also in politics, as well as in the social field, Feuerbach quite consciously linked his *radicalism* with his *materialism*. He wrote: "I do not understand how the idealist or the spiritualist, at least one who is consistent, can make external political freedom the aim of his practical activity. Spiritual freedom is enough for the spiritualist.... From the spiritualist point of view, political freedom is materialism in the field of politics.... For the spiritualist, freedom in thought is sufficient" (Dem Spiritualisten genügt die gedachte Freiheit).***

In his *Letters on Dogmatism and Criticism*, Schelling accepted as proved the proposition that the concept of freedom is incompatible with Spinozism, that is to say, in effect, with materialism. The further course of development of philosophical thought in Germany demonstrated the utter groundlessness of this proposition, which, incidentally, Schelling assimilated quite "*dogmatically*".

If the idealist Fichte in his sympathy with the Great French Revolution even went as far as to justify extreme revolutionary actions, German idealism in its development moved gradually but very far away from such views: while in the person of Schelling (in his latest style) it completely hid the concept of freedom under its night-cap. It was only in Feuerbach's materialist philosophy that the freedom-loving aspirations of the noble Fichte were revived and further developed, on an incomparably more reliable theoretical basis.

Feuerbach did not want to be a philosopher in the sense in

---

* L. Feuerbach's *Briefwechsel und Nachlass*, Vol. II, p. 317.
** This argument of Feuerbach's is almost word for word repeated in Chernyshevsky's article: "The Anthropological Principle" mentioned above and in his novel: *What Is to Be Done?*
*** *Briefwechsel und Nachlass*, B. II, S. 328.

which this word had always been understood in Germany. Hence his remark: "Meine Philosophie— keine Philosophie."[296] Philosophy must not move away from life. On the contrary, it must approach closer to life. This is essential even for theory.

Marx wrote: "The question whether objective truth can be attributed to human thinking is not a question of theory but is a *practical* question. Man must prove the truth, i.e. the reality and power, the this-worldliness of his thinking in practice."[297] We find the same idea in the writings of Feuerbach, who said that the cardinal defect of idealism was that "it examined the problem of objectivity or subjectivity, the reality or the unreality of the world, exclusively from the point of view of theory, whereas the world became a subject of debate only because first of all it became a subject of desire."* True, Feuerbach wrote this some twenty years *after* Marx had penned the above lines. But chronology hardly counts for anything in this case, since the idea of the destructive influence on philosophical theory of its rupture with practical activity corresponds fully with the spirit of Feuerbachian philosophy.** Not without reason did he write that philosophy in comparison with practice is but a "necessary evil" (ein notwendiges Uebel).

Marx was wrong when he reproached Feuerbach for not comprehending "'practical-critical' activity".[298] Feuerbach did understand it. But Marx was right in saying that Feuerbach's concept of the "essence of man", which he used in his explanation of the "essence of religion", suffered from abstractness. This was inevitable. Feuerbach could have eliminated *this* defect in his teaching only by attaining the materialist explanation of history. But that he did not manage to reach, although he did feel a vague but fairly strong theoretical need for it.

In his *Nachgelassene Aphorismen* there is a passage which has been a source of error to many historians. Here it is: "To me materialism is the foundation of the edifice of the human essence and knowledge; but for me it is not what it is for the physiologists, the natural scientists in the narrower sense, for example, Moleschott. For them it is not the foundation of the edifice, but the edifice itself. Going backwards from this point, I fully agree with the materialists, but going forwards, I disagree with them."***

---

* See the chapter: "Kritik des Idealismus" in the work *Spiritualismus und Materialismus.*

** I think it my duty to say that in my pamphlet: *Fundamental Problems of Marxism* the relationship between Marx and Feuerbach is presented not quite like this as far as the question of method is concerned. I think I have now explained this relationship more correctly.

*** L. Feuerbach's *Briefwechsel und Nachlass,* B. II, p. 308. [Compare the passage in Marx and Engels, *Selected Works,* Moscow, 1958, Vol. II, p. 376.]

In referring to this passage, it is frequently said: "There you are, you can see for yourself that Feuerbach admits to being only half a materialist." However, those who say this forget to ask themselves precisely what materialism is meant here? It will do no harm to clear this up.

In his *Theogony*, Feuerbach denounces those who want "to draw from one and the same source both natural laws and human laws". Of course, indirectly—inasmuch as man himself is a part of nature—human laws are also rooted in nature. But it does not follow from this that (to use a picturesque phrase of Feuerbach's) the Ten Commandments are written by the same hand that sends the peals of thunder. In the final analysis, paper is a product of the vegetable world. However, it would be highly ridiculous for anyone to claim that nature was a paper manufacturer.*

It was precisely with those materialists who did not see anything ridiculous in this that Feuerbach found it impossible to go forward. It was quite clear to Feuerbach that to regard nature as a manufacturer of paper was the surest way to commit numerous gross errors both in economic theory and in economic practice (politics). To accept this proposition would be equal to reducing *sociology* to *natural science*. Later, Marx described short-sighted materialism of this type as *natural-scientific* materialism. Feuerbach was not satisfied with a materialism that was incapable of distinguishing between man as the object of biology and the man of social *science*. It is obvious from this, however, not that he was *only partly* a materialist; on the contrary, it is perfectly plain that he felt the need for a *consistent* materialist world-outlook. For in fact, natural-scientific materialism is *inconsistent*. When those who uphold this view discuss the phenomena of social life, they show themselves to be *idealists*. It would be hard to find more persistent adherents of the idealist interpretation of history than these *materialists*.** None the less, Feuerbach did not succeed in correcting the defect of the "physiologists'" materialism by working out a materialist conception of history. He, who felt so strongly the limitations of Moleschott's materialist view, nevertheless made great and quite impermissible concessions to

---

* *Theogonie*, pp. 280-81. Feuerbach makes there the striking remark that as distinct from man, nature does not know the difference between "können und müssen" [can and must].

** Perhaps an even more vivid expression of Feuerbach's true attitude to the natural-scientific materialism is his letter to G. Bäuerle of May 31, 1867 (*Nachlass*, II, pp. 187-88). Feuerbach says there: "For me, as for you, man is a being of nature, originating in nature; but the main subject of my investigations are those ideas and fantastic beings originating in man which in the opinions and traditions of mankind are accepted as real beings." It goes without saying that Feuerbach could not have studied *this* subject while confining himself to the point of view of *biology*.

Moleschott from the standpoint of correct theory.* It is quite obvious that in making these concessions, he himself voiced idealist views on social life. The materialist explanation of history must be acknowledged as one of the most important theoretical services rendered by Marx and Engels. But we already know that for some time Marx and Engels themselves were followers of Feuerbach. Moreover, until the end of their days they remained such followers as regards the general philosophical view of the relation of subject to object.**

The *dialectical* view of phenomena presupposes the conviction that they *conform to law*, i.e., are *necessary. Historical idealism* does not concur with this conviction, since it sees the *conscious* (free) *activity* of man as the mainspring of historical progress. Feuerbach, who had not reached a complete understanding of historical materialism, could not work out either *a dialectical view of social life*. Dialectics again came into its own only with Marx and Engels, *who first placed it on a materialist foundation.*

We are entitled to say that Feuerbach's starting point in his theory of cognition—not *ego*, but *ego* and *tu*—was also the starting point of some (in their own way interesting) trends of German social thought. On the basis of the Utopian application of this doctrine to questions of the social system there arose, in the person of Karl Grün and others, "*German*" or "*true*" *socialism.*[299] The *individualist* rejection of the doctrine in the domain of morals— i.e., once again *ego*, not *tu* and *ego*—led to the appearance of an original German *anarchism*, as represented by Max Stirner (pseudonym of Kaspar Schmidt) who in 1845 published a work, fairly well known at one time, entitled: *Der Einzige und sein Eigenthum.****

However, it should not be thought that Feuerbach's influence was confined to the extreme trends of social thinking. It extended partly even to natural science. Moleschott, sincerely though one-sidedly attracted by Feuerbach, was a prominent naturalist. Feuerbach's influence was at its strongest, as could be expected, in philosophy. But here his influence was more *negative* than *positive.* True, that was not his fault.

---

* For example, in the article: "Naturwissenschaft und die Revolution" written in connection with the publication of Moleschott's book *Die Lehre der Nahrungsmittel. Für das Volk*, Erlangen. 1850.

** It is interesting that Chernyshevsky, the Russian student of Feuerbach, also declared his disagreement with Moleschott; but neither did he reach historical materialism.

*** There is a Russian translation. Marx and Engels sharply criticised Stirner's teaching in the article: "Sankt Max",[300] which appeared recently in *Dokumente des Sozialismus*, published by Ed. Bernstein, 1903, July and August, and 1904, May, June, July, August and September. I should like also to point out that there is a chapter on Max Stirner in my pamphlet on anarchism and socialism (a Russian translation has been published by Mme. Malykh).

If Marx and Engels always remained, generally speaking, of
the same mind as Feuerbach on question of philosophy, strictly
so called, the majority of those Germans who were interested in
philosophy did not find it possible to accept his philosophical
views. They were frightened both of Feuerbach's *materialism* and
his *socialism* which was closely associated with his philosophical views.* The reaction which followed the failure of the revolutionary movement of 1848-49 gradually brought German philosophy back into the fold of idealism. And it is self-evident that
the imperialist Germany of modern times could not recognise
Feuerbach as its ideologist. It required philosophers of quite
another brand....

XVI

Feuerbach himself rarely and only in passing touched upon art.
But his philosophy did not remain without a very considerable
impact on literature and aesthetics.

In the first place, his sober world-outlook, alien to all mysticism, linked with his radicalism, facilitated the liberation of the
advanced German artists of the "pre-March", i.e., the pre-revolutionary period, from some of their Romanticist conceptions. It is
probable that Heine wrote his "New Song" under the influence
of Feuerbach:

> *Ein neues Lied, ein besseres Lied,*
> *O Freunde, will ich euch dichten:*
> *Wir wollen hier auf Erden schon*
> *Das Himmelreich errichten, etc.***

That is the real echo of Feuerbach! Herwegh, and for some time
too Richard Wagner, were conscious followers of Feuerbach.*** In
German Switzerland, the now famous Gottfried Keller was his
pupil.

From the standpoint of the new philosophy, the "philosophy
of the future" (Philosophie der Zukunft), art could not be regarded
as a domain where the infinite spirit creates its own essence. The
new philosophy broke with Hegel's infinite spirit. Art, like religion, was looked upon as expressing the essence of *man*. But reli-

---

    * Granted, not all "true" German socialists, though accepting Feuer-
bach's teaching, were reconciled to his materialism. But more of this in
another article.

    ** [A song, friends, that's new, and a better one, too,
      Shall be now for your benefit given!
      Our object is, that here on earth
      We may mount to the realms of heaven.]

    *** Regarding Feuerbach's influence upon Herwegh and R. Wagner see
the work of Albert Levy: *La philosophie de Feuerbach*, Paris, 1904, Part II,
Chapter VIII (Herwegh) and Chapter IX (R. Wagner).

gion proved to be the sphere in which man could not express his own essence *otherwise* than *by self-deception*. Consequently, only in art does this essence find an expression in images free from self-deception. All the more reason why it should be valued.

Furthermore, for the artist who holds the viewpoint of the new philosophy, there is no being higher than man. But in man nature recognises itself. *The human spirit is the self-consciousness of nature.* Therefore the idealist opposing of nature to spirit is utterly unfounded, and must cease in art no less than in philosophy.

Feuerbach's pupils were ready to reproach "speculative aesthetics" for not triumphantly enough proclaiming the independence of art. So highly did they value that independence! However, they themselves gave a more vivid and exact formulation of the idea they had inherited from speculative aesthetics, that form is determined by content. In the article: "Gegen die spekulative Aesthetik", Hermann Hettner—subsequently the author of a well-known history of literature in the eighteenth century—strove to demonstrate that no matter how important *form* may be in works of art, it lives only *because of its content* and without this it dies, becomes formal and abstract.*

In addition to Hettner I shall mention Ludwig Pfau, poet and literary critic, who like Hettner was a personal friend of Feuerbach's. He took part in the Baden rebellion, and up to 1865 lived in emigration, chiefly in Belgium and France, where he wrote his critical articles. In 1865-66 a collection of his articles was published in German, evoking a warm response from Feuerbach. This collection can now too be recommended to readers who have not as yet relinquished the completely erroneous idea that art owes its existence to religion, and cannot flourish without it.**

---

* See his *Kleine Schriften*, Braunschweig, 1884, p. 205. The article: "Gegen die spekulative Aesthetik" appeared first in 1845 in *Wigand's Quarterly* (Wigand's "Vierteljahrschrift").
** See *Freie Studien: Die Kunst im Staat*, 3rd edition, Stuttgart, 1888. See also another article by Pfau: "Proudhon und die Franzosen" in the sixth volume of his *Aesthetischen Schriften*, Stuttgart, 1888.

NOTES

PREFACE TO THE THIRD RUSSIAN EDITION
OF ENGELS' *SOCIALISM:*
UTOPIAN AND SCIENTIFIC

The preface was published in Geneva in 1902. In 1906 it was published in Russia in the Odessa Burevestnik edition, together with E. Bernstein's article "Wie ist wissenschaftlicher Sozialismus möglich?" (Is Scientific Socialism Possible?) to which it was in fact an answer. It was headed "G. Plekhanov's Answer".

1 The first Russian edition of Engels' pamphlet: *Socialism: Utopian and Scientific* appeared in Geneva in 1884.   p. 31

2 These are the words of Skalozub, a character from Griboyedov's *Wit Works Woe.*   p. 33

3 K. Marx and F. Engels, *Selected Works* in three volumes, Vol. 3, Moscow, 1973, p. 126.   p. 36

4 See present edition, Vol. II, pp. 427-73.   p. 41

5 See present edition, Vol. I, p. 565 et seq.   p. 41

6 See present edition, Vol. I, p. 566.   p. 42

7 See present edition, Vol. I, p. 562.   p. 43

8 See present edition, Vol. I, pp. 401-26.   p. 43

9 K. Marx and F. Engels, *Selected Works* in three volumes, Vol. 3, Moscow, 1973, pp. 133-34.   p. 44

10 F. Engels, *Anti-Dühring*, Moscow 1975, pp. 180-81.   p. 48

11 Plekhanov is here referring to his second article against Struve (see present edition, Vol. II, pp. 513-66).
   Zarya (Dawn)—a Marxist scientific and political journal published legally in Stuttgart in 1901-02 with Lenin, Plekhanov and Zasulich as its contributors. The journal criticised international and Russian revisionism and came out in defence of the theoretical principles of Marxism.
                                                                             p. 52

12 The *theory of "marginal utility"* was a vulgar economic theory which came to the fore in the 1870s in opposition to Marx's labour theory of value. According to the theory of "marginal utility", the source of value is not socially-necessary labour, but the so-called marginal utility of a commodity, reflecting the subjective estimation of the utility of a commodity which satisfies the least pressing demand.   p. 53

13 *Physiocrats*—representatives of a trend in bourgeois classical political economy which arose in France in 1750s. They proclaimed unrestricted rule of private ownership, rejected protectionism and demanded freedom of trade and competition. They advocated a "Laissez faire, laissez passer" economic policy.   p. 53

14 This reference is to Volume IV of *Capital (Theories of Surplus-Value)*, published by Karl Kautsky from 1905 to 1910.   p. 53

SCIENTIFIC SOCIALISM AND RELIGION

The lecture "Scientific Socialism and Religion" was delivered by Plekhanov in Zurich in 1904. Only the synopsis, some points of which were developed by Plekhanov in his later articles on religion, is extant.

[15] In 1904, on the eve of the first Russian revolution a sharp struggle was going on within the R.S.D.L.P. on the attitude of the proletariat towards the peasantry and against the nationalism of the Bund and others.

Bund (The General Jewish Workers' Union of Lithuania, Poland and Russia) was organised in 1897; in 1898 it joined the R.S.D.L.P. "as an autonomous organisation, independent only in respect to issues specifically concerning the Jewish proletariat".

After the Second Congress of the R.S.D.L.P. (1903) which rejected a demand to recognise the Bund as the sole representative of the Jewish proletariat, the latter left the Party. Bundists had continuously supported the opportunists within the R.S.D.L.P. (Mensheviks, "economists" etc.)   p. 56

[16] Plekhanov is here referring to the "Yakutsk protest" of February 18, 1904 against the arduous conditions of life in exile and arbitrariness of the authorities, when fifty-seven exiles barricaded themselves in the house of Romanov, a local inhabitant. During the firing the exile Matlakhov was killed. On March 7 the "Romanovists" surrendered.   p. 56

[17] This questionnaire was circulated by the socialist journal *Le Mouvement socialiste* (published from 1899 and edited by Lagardelle) in connection with the bitter struggle between the French republican government and the Catholic church which ended in separation of the church from the state. Replies to the questionnaire were received from socialists in various countries and printed in Nos. 107-110 of the journal for 1902.

     p. 56

[18] The reference is to a statement by Rudolf Stammler in his work *Wirtschaft und Recht nach der materialistischen Geschichtsauffassung* (Economy and Law from the Standpoint of the Materialist Understanding of History) concerning the contradiction into which the Social-Democrats allegedly fall, on the one hand, by considering the proletarian revolution to be inevitable and, on the other, by calling for action to bring it about. To Stammler this seemed just as strange as organising a group to assist lunar eclipses.   p. 57

[19] Karl Marx and Frederick Engels, *Collected Works*, Vol. 3, Moscow, 1975, p. 175.   p. 57

[20] Below in the text there are two excerpts from Engels' article "The Condition of England. *Past and Present* by Thomas Carlyle, London, 1843", used by Plekhanov in his lecture.   p. 59

[21] Karl Marx and Frederick Engels, *Collected Works*, Vol. 3, Moscow, 1975, p. 463.   p. 59

[22] Karl Marx and Frederick Engels, *Collected Works*, Vol. 3, p. 464.

     p. 59

[23] The Russian philosopher and economist Bulgakov considered socialism not as a necessary phase in social development, nor as a result of the class struggle, but merely as the moral ideal of human free will.

     p. 60

[24] *Smerdyakov*—a character from Dostoyevsky's novel *The Karamazov Brothers*, who commits murder under the influence of ideas suggested to him by Ivan Karamazov. Bulgakov writes about Ivan Karamazov: "Ivan speaks indecisively and conditionally about morality: he says: 'If there is no God and no immortality of the soul, then all is permissible'."

p. 60

[25] Plekhanov rephrases a line from Hauptmann's play *Die Versunkene Glocke* (The Sunken Bell).   p. 60

[26] "Sonate, que me veux-tu?" (Sonata, what do you want of me?)—an expression used by the French writer and scientist Fontenelle. The meaning of Plekhanov's comparison is apparently as follows: Fontenelle, who had no musical ear, demands that the sonata prove its value to him, so Bulgakov, who is hostile to the working-class movement and socialism, demands that the workers prove to him something that cannot be proved.

p. 60

[27] *Ni dieu, ni maître!* (Neither God, nor Master)—the revolutionary slogan that the French revolutionary Blanqui used as the heading for his newspaper.   p. 60

[28] Karl Marx and Frederick Engels, *Collected Works*, Vol. 3, Moscow, 1975, p. 461.   p. 60

[29] Karl Marx and Frederick Engels, *Collected Works*, Vol. 3, Moscow, 1975, p. 465.   p. 61

[30] The two quotations cited below are taken from Marx's article: "Contribution to the Critique of Hegel's Philosophy of Law, Introduction." (Karl Marx and Frederick Engels, *Collected Works*, Vol. 3, Moscow, 1975, p. 176.)   p. 61

[31] The reference is to Kant's books *Kritik der reinen Vernunft* (Critique of Pure Reason) and *Kritik der praktischen Vernunft* (Critique of Practical Reason).   p. 62

[32] In the notes on the discussion with Volsky (Makhaisky) the latter's points are intermingled with Plekhanov's objections.
A. Volsky—an ideologist of Makhayevism—a petty-bourgeois anarchist trend which was hostile to the intelligentsia.   p. 62

TRANSLATOR'S PREFACE TO THE SECOND EDITION
OF F. ENGELS' *LUDWIG FEUERBACH*
AND THE END OF CLASSICAL
GERMAN PHILOSOPHY

The second edition of F. Engels' *Ludwig Feuerbach and the End of Classical German Philosophy* translated into Russian by Plekhanov, was issued in Geneva in 1905. The first Russian edition was published in 1892.

[33] The reference is to the "legal Marxists"—liberal bourgeois, who in the 1890s came out in the Russian legal press under the banner of Marxism. "Legal Marxism" by its character was akin to Bernsteinianism.

p. 65

[34] See present edition, Vol. I, pp. 449-61.   p. 66

[35] *Poprishchin*—a character from Gogol's story *Notes of a Madman*.

p. 69

[36] The supplement mentioned is an excerpt from Marx and Engels' *The Holy Family*, Chapter VI, item "Critical Battle Against French Materialism". p. 69

[37] Karl Marx and Frederick Engels, *Collected Works*, Vol. 4, Moscow, 1975, pp. 130-31. p. 70

[38] K. Marx and F. Engels, *Selected Works* in three volumes, Vol. 3, Moscow, 1975, p. 346. p. 70

[39] *Russkoye Bogatstvo* (Russian Wealth)—a monthly magazine published in St. Petersburg from 1876 to 1918. From the early 1890s it became an organ of the liberal Narodniks under the editorship of N. K. Mikhailovsky. The journal distorted and falsified Marxism and came out against the Social-Democrats and in defence of revisionism. p. 75

[40] Karl Marx, *Capital*, Vol. I, Moscow, 1974, p. 29. p. 80

[41] F. Engels, *Anti-Dühring*, Moscow, 1975, pp. 29, 30. p. 81

[42] Karl Marx and Frederick Engels, *Collected Works*, Vol. 6, Moscow, 1976, p. 192. p. 81

[43] Karl Marx, *Capital*, Vol. I, Moscow, 1974, p. 173. p. 82

[44] Goethe, *Faust*, Part One, Scene Four. p. 82

[45] Plekhanov is referring here to Hegel's *Encyklopädie d. philos. Wissenschaften in Grundrisse* (Encyclopaedia of Philosophical Sciences). p. 83

[46] See N. Berdayev, *A Diary of A Publicist. Catechism of Marxism* (*Voprosy Zhizni* [Life's Problems], No. 2, 1915). p. 83

PATRIOTISM AND SOCIALISM

The article is Plekhanov's answer to the questionnaire by the journal *La vie socialiste*, which was published in its No. 18 of July 20, 1905. In Russian it appeared in *Dnevnik Sotsial-Demokrata* (Diary of Social-Democrat) No. 2, published in Geneva in August 1905.

Dnevnik Sotsial-Demokrata (Diary of a Social-Democrat) was a non-periodical organ published by Plekhanov in Geneva from March 1905 to April 1912 (with long intervals). In all, sixteen numbers were published. In the first eight numbers (1905-06) Plekhanov came out in defence of the bloc of Social-Democracy with the liberal bourgeoisie, and rejected an alliance of the proletariat and the peasantry. Between 1909 and 1912 Plekhanov was against the Menshevik liquidators who wanted the illegal Party liquidated, but on the major tactical issues he held his former stand. p. 84

[47] Gustav Hervé maintained that, as the proletariat has no country, all wars serve only the interests of capitalists, and therefore the proletariat must answer any declaration of war with a general strike and an uprising, even if the conditions in the country were not yet ripe. p. 84

[48] Bernstein expressed this opinion in his reply to the *La vie socialiste* questionnaire. He concluded that the proposition in the *Manifesto of the Communist Party* that "the working men have no country" had lost its meaning. (See *La vie socialiste*, No. 15, 1905, p. 897.) p. 85

[49] The reference is to the French armed intervention in Spain from 1820 to 1823, which was aimed at crushing the Spanish bourgeois revolution. The Frenchman Armand Carrel took part in this war in 1823 as a volunteer on the Spanish side. p. 87

[50] The reference is to I. S. Turgenev's novel *On the Eve*.   p. 88

[51] In 1669 Crete was seized by Turkey, but the Greek population continued their armed struggle against the invaders. In 1897, after the end of the Greco-Turkish war, Crete became an administratively autonomous unit, although it remained within the Turkish empire. Only in 1913 did it become part of Greece.   p. 88

[52] *The Young Turks*—the European name for members of the Turkish nationalist Unity and Progress party of bourgeoisie and landowners which was founded in 1889. The Young Turks strove to restrict the absolute power of the sultan, to turn the feudal empire into a bourgeois constitutional monarchy and to enhance the role of the Turkish bourgeoisie in the economic and political life of the country.   p. 88

[53] Here Plekhanov, like other Marxists of the period, proceeded from the well-known theses of Marx and Engels which were true for pre-monopoly capitalism, that the socialist revolution would triumph simultaneously in a number of countries. The possibility of a socialist revolution taking place first in a single country was an idea expressed originally by Lenin in his article "On the United States of Europe". (V. I. Lenin, *Collected Works*, Vol. 21.)   p. 89

[54] The reference is to the decisions of the Brussels (1891) and Zurich (1893) congresses of the Second International on militarism.   p. 90

[55] The resolution of the Brussels Congress on the working-class attitude towards militarism stated that militarism was inevitably engendered by the capitalist system and that only the establishment of a socialist society could do away with militarism and bring peace among nations. The resolution ended with an appeal to the workers of all countries to protest actively against preparations for war and military alliances and to further the victory of socialism by improving the international organisation of the proletariat.   p. 92

ON A. PANNEKOEK'S PAMPHLET

Plekhanov's review of Pannekoek's pamphlet was published in the journal *Sovremennaya Zhizn* (Modern Life) No. 1, 1907. This was a Menshevik journal published in Moscow in 1906-07.

[56] *Die Neue Zeit* (New Times)—a theoretical journal of German Social-Democracy published in Stuttgart from 1883 to 1923. In 1885-94 Engels published a series of his works in it and gave constant advice to its editorial board, often criticising it for deviations from Marxism. From the late 1890s the journal began systematic publication of revisionist articles.

Plekhanov has in mind two articles by Pannekoek: "Historischer Materialismus und Religion" (Historical Materialism and Religion) published in Nos. 31 and 32, 1904 (Jahrg. XXII, II. Bd. S. 133 und 180) and "Klassenwissenschaft und Philosophie" (Class Sciences and Philosophy) published in No. 19, 1905 (Jahrg. XXIII, Bd. I, S. 604).   p. 93

REPLY TO QUESTIONNAIRE FROM THE JOURNAL
MERCURE DE FRANCE
ON THE FUTURE OF RELIGION

In 1907 the journal *Mercure de France* sponsored a questionnaire consisting of a single question: "Assistons-nous à une dissolution ou à une évolution de l'idée religieuse et du sentiment religieux?" (Are we witnessing the dissolution or the evolution of the religious idea and religious sentiment?) Thirty-three replies were published in No. 236 of the journal for April 15, 1907, from political and social figures and writers in various countries, including Maxim Gorky, Strindberg, Vandervelde and Verhaeren.

p. 98

JOSEPH DIETZGEN

The article was published in the journal *Sovremenny Mir*, Nos. 7-8, 1907.

Sovremenny Mir (Contemporary World)—a literary, scientific and political monthly published in St. Petersburg from 1906 to 1918.

[57] The reference is apparently to *The German Ideology*.   p. 100

[58] Karl Marx, *Capital*, Vol. I, Moscow, 1974, p. 29.   p. 101

[59] The reference is to F. Engels' statement in his article "Programme of the Blanquist Commune Emigrants" from the series *Flüchtlingsliteratur* (Emigrant Literature). See K. Marx and F. Engels, *Selected Works*, in three volumes, Vol. 2, Moscow, 1973, p. 383.   p. 102

[60] F. Engels, *Anti-Dühring*, Moscow, 1975, p. 15.   p. 103

[61] Plekhanov reminds the reader that Eduard Bernstein's revision of Marxism had not been decisively rebuffed by German Social-Democracy.

p. 104

[62] See this volume, p. 125 et seq.   p. 105

[63] See Plekhanov's article "Bernstein and Materialism" in volume II of the present edition, pp. 326-39.   p. 113

[64] F. Engels, *Anti-Dühring*, Moscow, 1975, p. 52.   p. 114

[65] *Rus* (Russia)—a liberal bourgeois daily, published in St. Petersburg in 1903-05.   p. 115

FUNDAMENTAL PROBLEMS OF MARXISM

This work was written in November and December 1907 for the collection of articles which was being prepared for the twenty-fifth anniversary of Marx's death. For a number of reasons this collection never came out, but the article was published in pamphlet form in 1908.

[66] F. Engels, *Anti-Dühring*, Moscow, 1975, p. 15.   p. 118

[67] *Deutsch-Französische Jahrbücher* was published in Paris and edited by Karl Marx and Arnold Ruge. Only one double number, containing a number of works by Marx and Engels, was issued, in February 1844.

p. 119

[68] Karl Marx and Frederick Engels, *Collected Works*, Vol. 3, Moscow, 1975, pp. 350-51 (Letter of October 3, 1843).   p. 120

[69] K. Marx and F. Engels, *Selected Works* in three volumes, Vol. 3, Moscow, 1973, p. 348.   p. 123

[70] Karl Marx and Frederick Engels, *Collected Works*, Vol. 4, Moscow, 1975, p. 131.   p. 124

[71] Karl Marx and Frederick Engels, *Collected Works*, Vol. 4, Moscow, 1975, pp. 125 and 105.   p. 124

[72] Karl Marx and Frederick Engels, *Collected Works*, Vol. 4, Moscow, 1975, p. 131.   **p. 127**

[73] F. Engels, *Anti-Dühring*, Moscow, 1975, p. 132.   **p. 127**

[74] Karl Marx and Frederick Engels, *Collected Works*, Vol. 5, Moscow, 1975, p. 3.   **p. 128**

[75] Karl Marx, *Capital*, Vol. I, Moscow, 1974, p. 173.   **p. 129**

[76] See present edition, Vol. II, Moscow, 1976, pp. 326-39.   **p. 129**

[77] K. Marx and F. Engels, *Selected Works*, in three volumes, Vol. 3, Moscow, 1973, p. 335.   **p. 132**

[78] Karl Marx and Frederick Engels, *Collected Works*, Vol. 5, Moscow, 1975, p. 4.   **p. 135**

[79] See present edition, Vol. I, Moscow, 1974, pp. 401-26.
    p. 136

[80] Karl Marx, *A Contribution to the Critique of Political Economy*, Moscow, 1971, p. 20.
The manuscript of the earlier version shows that, having written the words "In his 'Contribution to the Critique of Hegel's Philosophy of Law', he has shown that relations of people in society...." Plekhanov intended to continue his thought. Then he crossed out this sentence and instead cited a passage from the preface to Marx's "Contribution to the Critique of Political Economy", which began with the words: "Legal relations" and added: "he wrote there". So it strongly appeared as if the cited passage had been taken from the "Contribution to the Critique of Hegel's Philosophy of Law".
    p. 137

[81] Karl Marx and Frederick Engels, *Collected Works*, Vol. 3, Moscow, 1975, p. 457.   **p. 137**

[82] Karl Marx and Frederick Engels, *Collected Works*, Vol. 6, Moscow, 1976, pp. 165-66.   **p. 138**

[83] Karl Marx, *Capital*, Vol. I, Moscow, 1974, p. 29.   **p. 138**

[84] See present edition, Vol. I, Moscow, 1974, pp. 365-72.   **p. 139**

[85] F. Engels, *Anti-Dühring*, Moscow, 1975, p. 80.   **p. 140**

[86] K. Marx and F. Engels, *Selected Works*, in three volumes, Vol. 3, Moscow, 1973, pp. 337-42.   **p. 141**

[87] Karl Marx, *Capital*, Vol. I, Moscow, 1974, p. 29.   **p. 141**

[88] Karl Marx. *A Contribution to the Critique of Political Economy*, Moscow, 1971, p. 20.   **p. 142**

[89] Karl Marx, *Capital*, Vol. I, Moscow, 1974, p. 481.   **p. 143**

[90] K. Marx and F. Engels, *Selected Works* in three volumes, Vol. 1, Moscow, 1973, p. 159.   **p. 144**

[91] Karl Marx, *Capital*, Vol. I, Moscow, 1974, p. 481.   **p. 147**

[92] K. Marx and F. Engels, *Selected Works*, in three volumes, Vol. 1. Moscow, 1973, p. 421.   **p. 149**

[93] This passage is characteristic of Plekhanov's Menshevik stand concerning the character of and the driving forces behind the Russian revolution. Convinced that the revolution in Russia was to follow the bourgeois revolutions

in the West, Plekhanov held the erroneous view that a whole historical epoch must separate the socialist from the bourgeois revolution. Plekhanov thought that in Russia, where industrial development began later than in the West, and where peasant population predominated, no conflict had as yet matured between the productive forces and capitalist relations of production, and so the objective conditions for a socialist revolution in Russia were lacking.   p. 153

[94] Karl Marx, *A Contribution to the Critique of Political Economy*, Moscow, 1971, p. 21.   p. 153

[95] Karl Marx, *A Contribution to the Critique of Political Economy*, Moscow, 1971, p. 21.   p. 153

[96] Karl Marx and Frederick Engels, *Collected Works*, Vol. 6, Moscow, 1976, p. 486.   p. 155

[97] Karl Marx and Frederick Engels, *Collected Works*, Vol. 6, Moscow, 1976, p. 503.   p. 156

[98] Letter to Joseph Bloch, September 21 [-22], 1890. See Marx and Engels, *Selected Correspondence*, Moscow, 1975, p. 395.   p. 157

[99] Letter to W. Borgius, January 25, 1894. See Marx and Engels, *Selected Correspondence*, Moscow, 1975, pp. 441-42.   p. 157

[100] Karl Marx and Frederick Engels, *Selected Correspondence*, Moscow, 1975, p. 442.   p. 157

[101] See Karl Marx and Frederick Engels, *Collected Works*, Vol. 5, Moscow, 1976. p. 4.   p. 158

[102] Karl Marx and Frederick Engels, *Selected Correspondence*, Moscow, 1975, p. 442.   p. 159

[103] Karl Marx and Frederick Engels, *Selected Correspondence*, Moscow, 1975, pp. 442-43.   p. 166

[104] See present edition, Vol. II, Moscow, 1976, pp. 283-315.   p. 166

[105] See present edition, Vol. II, Moscow, 1976, pp. 427-73.   p. 166

[106] Karl Marx and Frederick Engels, *Collected Works*, Vol. 4, Moscow, 1975. pp. 124-25 (*The Holy Family*).   p. 171

[107] K. Marx and F. Engels, *Selected Works* in three volumes, Vol. 3, Moscow, 1973, p. 101.   p. 172

[108] Karl Marx, *Capital*, Vol. I, Moscow, 1974, p. 29.   p. 173

[109] "Saint Max" —a chapter from K. Marx and F. Engels, *The German Ideology*.
    Plekhanov quotes from the journal *Documents of Socialism* (see Karl Marx and Frederick Engels, *Collected Works*, Vol. 5, Moscow, 1976, pp. 292-94).   p. 174

[110] Karl Marx and Frederick Engels, *Collected Works*, Vol. 6, Moscow, 1976, p. 165.   p. 175

[111] K. Marx and F. Engels, *Selected Works*, in three volumes, Vol. 3, Moscow, 1973, p. 150.   p. 176

[112] F. Engels, *Anti-Dühring*, Moscow, 1975, pp. 136-37.   p. 176

[113] *Cadets*—members of the Constitutional-Democratic Party which was the party of the liberal monarchical bourgeoisie, founded in October 1905. In an attempt to win over the peasantry, the Cadets included in their

agrarian programme a clause on the possibility of extending peasant-owned lands through purchasing of lands at a "fair" price from the state, monasteries and private owners. The programme also mentioned "compulsory alienation" of landowners' estates for this purpose. "The Cadets," wrote Lenin, "want to preserve the landlord system of agriculture by means of concessions. They propose redemption payments by the peasants which already once before in 1861 ruined the peasants" (V. I. Lenin. *Collected Works*, Vol. 11, p. 328).   p. 177

[114] Karl Marx, *A Contribution to the Critique of Political Economy*, Moscow, 1971, p. 20.   p. 178

[115] See present edition, Vol. I, Moscow, 1974, pp. 480-697.   p. 180

[116] K. Marx and F. Engels, *Selected Works*, in three volumes, Vol. 3, Moscow, 1973, p. 133.   p. 181

[117] Karl Marx, *A Contribution to the Critique of Political Economy*, Moscow, 1971, p. 21.   p. 182

[118] *Revolutionary syndicalism*—a petty-bourgeois semi-anarchist trend in the working-class movement in Western Europe at the turn of the century. Syndicalists denied the necessity of the political struggle of the working class, considering the trade unions capable of overthrowing capitalism and taking management of production into their own hands without a revolution, simply by organising a general strike.   p. 182

[119] Karl Marx and Frederick Engels, *Collected Works*, Vol. 4, Moscow, 1975, (*The Holy Family*), p. 82.   p. 183

TWENTY-FIFTH ANNIVERSARY OF THE DEATH OF KARL MARX

This article was written at the beginning of 1908 and was apparently intended for the Italian press. It is not known whether it was published at that time or not; in Russian it was first published in the journal *Vestnik Kommunisticheskoi akademii* (The Proceedings of the Communist Academy), Nos. 2-3, 1933.

[120] Plekhanov is referring to A. Bonomi's book: *Le vie nuove del socialismo* (The New Ways of Socialism), Milano-Palermo-Napoli, Remo Sandron, 1907.   p. 185

[121] Karl Marx and Frederick Engels, *Collected Works*, Vol. 6, Moscow, 1976, p. 160.   p. 187

[122] Plekhanov was misled in denying the absolute impoverishment of the working class under capitalism. Numerous facts testify that absolute impoverishment of the proletariat is taking place in capitalist society. His reference to Marx is also unfounded as Marx proved that accumulation of capital is accompanied by absolute and relative impoverishment of the proletariat.   p. 187

MATERIALISMUS MILITANS

The three letters *Materialismus militans* were written between 1908 and 1910. They were prompted by an "Open Letter to Plekhanov" printed by A. Bogdanov in the monthly *Vestnik Zhizni* (The Herald of Life) No. 7, 1907. The First and Second letters were published in the *Golos Sotsial-Demokrata* (The Voice of a Social-Democrat) Nos. 6-7, 8-9, 1908. The Third letter did not appear in the journal because Plekhanov broke off relations with its editors at the end of 1908. It was written specially for the collection of his articles against revisionists entitled *From Defence to Attack* (1910). In the introduction to the collection, which included all the three articles against A. Bogdanov, Plekhanov wrote the following with regard to the empirio-critics: "Some of these industrious people even call themselves and sincerely believe themselves to be enemies of the bourgeoisie. Such are A. Bogdanov and A. Lunacharsky. But all that one can say about such people is that there is a bitter discord between their hearts and their heads: their heads are working for the benefit of the particular class against which their hearts rebel."

[123] As an epigraph to each letter Plekhanov used the exclamation of the ill-starred peasant Georges Dandin, the title character of Molière's play. The choice of the epigraph is explained by the fact that by his "Open Letter to Plekhanov" A. Bogdanov provoked Plekhanov to criticise empirio-monism.   p. 188

[124] *Vestnik Zhizni* (Herald of Life)—a scientific, literary and political journal, the legal organ of the R.S.D.L.P. (Bolsheviks) which was published in St. Petersburg from March 1906 to September 1907. Besides articles devoted to current political problems, the journal printed many items on literary criticism, art and philosophy.   p. 188

[125] *Pompadour*—a collective satirical character created by M. Y. Saltykov-Shchedrin in his *Messieurs et Mesdames Pompadours*, in which the great Russian satirist branded high tsarist officials, ministers and governors. The word became synonymous with petty tyranny and arbitrary administration.   p. 189

[126] Quotation from Pushkin's poem *Poltava*.   p. 193

[127] The reference is to A. Labriola's book, *Reformism and Syndicalism*.
                                                                            p. 195

[128] The reference is to *god-building*—a religious philosophical trend which arose in Russia during the years of reaction (1907-10) among a group of Party intellectuals who deserted Marxism after the defeat of the 1905-07 revolution. The god-builders (A. Lunacharsky, V. Bazarov and others) advocated the establishment of a new, "socialist" religion, trying to blend Marxism with religion.   p. 195

[129] Karl Marx and Frederick Engels, *Collected Works*, Vol. 3, Moscow, 1975, p. 462.   p. 196

[130] P. B. Struve, *Critical Notes on Russia's Economic Development*, Russ. ed., Issue I, St. Petersburg, 1894.   p. 196

[131] *Molchalin*—a character from A. Griboyedov's *Wit Works Woe*, synonymous with servility and toadyism.   p. 198

[132] K. Marx and F. Engels, *Selected Works*, in three volumes, Vol. 3, Moscow, 1973, p. 337.   p. 203

[133] Karl Marx and Frederick Engels, *Collected Works*, Vol. 4, Moscow, 1975, p. 130.   p. 204

[134] Karl Marx and Frederick Engels, *Collected Works*, Vol. 4, Moscow, 1975, p. 131.   p. 204

[135] *Blessed Anatoly*—A. V. Lunacharsky.   p. 205

[136] K. Marx and F. Engels, *Selected Works*, in three volumes, Vol. 2, Moscow, 1973, p. 383.   p. 205

[137] K. Marx and F. Engels, *Selected Works*, in three volumes, Vol. 3, Moscow, 1973, p. 335.   p. 205

[138] K. Marx and F. Engels, *Selected Works* in three volumes, Vol. 3, Moscow, 1973, pp. 107, 108-09.   p. 207

[139] K. Marx and F. Engels, *Selected Works* in three volumes, Vol. 3, Moscow, 1973, p. 113.   p. 208

[140] K. Marx and F. Engels, *Selected Works* in three volumes, Vol. 3, Moscow, 1973, p. 347.   p. 210

[141] K. Marx and F. Engels, *Selected Works* in three volumes. Vol. 3, Moscow, 1973, p. 346.   p. 211

[142] See present edition, Vol. II, Moscow, 1976, pp. 379-97, 398-414.
                                                                       p. 213

[143] Frederick Engels, *Anti-Dühring*, Moscow, 1975, p. 55.   p. 214

[144] See present edition, Vol. I, Moscow, 1974, p. 459.   p. 218

[145] See present edition, Vol. II, Moscow, 1976, p. 379 et seq.   p. 219

[146] See present edition, Vol. II, Moscow, 1976, pp. 398-414.   p. 222

[147] Plekhanov makes a concession to agnosticism when he asserts that the first distinctive feature of space and time is subjectivity. In actual fact, space and time are objective, real forms of matter reflected by the human mind.   p. 223

[148] See this volume, p. 125 et seq.   p. 223

[149] See present edition, Vol. II, Moscow, 1976, p. 419.   p. 224

[150] See present edition, Vol. I, Moscow, 1974, p. 454.   p. 226

[151] See present edition, Vol. I, Moscow, 1974, pp. 454-55.   p. 227

[152] See present edition, Vol. I, Moscow, 1974, p. 455.   p. 227

[153] In expounding and defending the Marxist theory of knowledge, Plekhanov made a mistake when he asserted that man's perceptions are not copies of real things and processes of nature, but conventional signs, hieroglyphs. Lenin remarked in his *Materialism and Empirio-Criticism* that "Plekhanov was guilty of an obvious mistake in his exposition of materialism", that "Machists fastened with glee on Plekhanov's 'hieroglyphs' palming off their renunciation of materialism as a criticism of 'hieroglyphism'" (V. I. Lenin, *Collected Works*, Vol. 14, pp. 238 and 232). p. 228

[154] See present edition, Vol. I, Moscow, 1974, p. 455.   p. 230

[155] See this volume, p. 125 et seq.   p. 232

[156] K. Marx and F. Engels, *Selected Works* in three volumes, Vol. 3, Moscow, 1973, p. 101.   p. 234

[157] K. Marx and F. Engels, *Selected Works* in three volumes, Vol. 3. Moscow, 1973, p. 101.   p. 234

[158] K. Marx and F. Engels, *Selected Works* in three volumes, Vol. 3, Moscow, 1973, p. 102.   p. 234

[159] Plekhanov put in inverted commas the expression from Heine's poem *To Lazarus*.   p. 235

[160] See present edition, Vol. II, Moscow, 1976, pp. 379-414.   p. 235

[161] *Sovremennik* (The Contemporary)—a scientific, political and literary monthly published in St. Petersburg from 1836 to 1866. Among its contributors were N. G. Chernyshevsky, V. G. Belinsky, and M. Y. Saltykov-Shchedrin. It was the best journal of the time expressing the aspi-

rations of the revolutionary democrats and exerting a considerable influence on progressive elements in Russia.   p. 247

[162] F. Engels, *Anti-Dühring*, Moscow, 1975, p. 15.   p. 249

[163] F. Engels, *Anti-Dühring*, Moscow, 1975, p. 63.   p. 259

[164] The expression is taken from a Russian chronicle, according to which the
Slav tribes appealed to the Varangians saying: "Our land is great and
fertile, but there is no order in it. Come and rule us." Modern historical
science has proved the untenability of this allegation.   p. 260

[165] F. Engels, *Anti-Dühring*, Moscow, 1975, p. 64.   p. 263

[166] From Ivan Krylov's fable "The Mirror and the Monkey".   p. 266

[167] Plekhanov is mistaken. This thesis, as well as two others cited below,
are actually from Feuerbach's *Grundsätze der Philosophie der Zukunft*
(Fundamental Principles of the Philosophy of the Future), *Werke*, Bd. II,
Leipzig, 1846, S. 322.   p. 271

[168] *Chichikov, Korobochka*—characters from Nikolai Gogol's *Dead Souls*. p. 281

ON F. LÜTGENAU'S BOOK

Plekhanov's review of F. Lütgenau's book was published in the
journal *Sovremenny Mir*, No. 5, 1908.

[169] Karl Marx and Frederick Engels, *Collected Works*, Vol. 3, Moscow, 1975,
p. 175. ("Contribution to the Critique of Hegel's Philosophy of Law. Introduction").   p. 293

HENRI BERGSON

Plekhanov's review of Henri Bergson's book *L'Evolution créatrice* (Creative Evolution) was published in the journal *Sovremenny Mir*, No. 3,
1909.

[170] Plekhanov has in mind his article "Something About History", included
in Volume II of the present edition.   p. 295

[171] See present edition, Vol. II, Moscow, 1976, pp. 379-97.   p. 296

ON MR. V. SHULYATIKOV'S BOOK

Plekhanov's review of V. Shulyatikov's book was published in the
journal *Sovremenny Mir*, No. 5, 1909.

[172] *Suzdal*—here rough work. Prior to the Revolution cheap icons were produced in the Suzdal uyezd, hence the term.   p. 302

ON THE SO-CALLED RELIGIOUS
SEEKINGS IN RUSSIA

The articles under this title were published in the journal *Sovremenny
Mir*, Nos. 9, 10, 12, 1909. Plekhanov wrote these articles because the
religious seekings among the intelligensia in Russia acquired considerable
scope after the defeat of the 1905-07 Revolution.

173 *Vekhi*—a collection of articles by prominent Cadet publicists, representatives of the counter-revolutionary liberal bourgeoisie—S. N. Bulgakov, N. A. Berdayev, P. B. Struve and others—was published in Moscow in the spring of 1909. The contributors to *Vekhi* tried to discredit the democratic revolutionary traditions of the liberation movement in Russia, and also the views and activities of V. G. Belinsky, N. A. Dobrolyubov, and N. G. Chernyshevsky. They derided the revolution of 1905-07 and thanked the tsarist government for using "its bayonets and prisons" to save the bourgeoisie from the "wrath of the people".   p. 306

174 *Novoye Vremya* (New Times)—a daily newspaper published in St. Petersburg from 1868 to 1917, an organ of reactionary landowner circles and bureaucratic officialdom.   p. 310

175 K. Marx and F. Engels, *Selected Works*, in three volumes, Vol. 3, Moscow, 1973, p. 345.   p. 317

176 K. Marx and F. Engels, *Selected Works*, in three volumes, Vol. 3, Moscow, 1973, p. 345.   p. 317

177 K. Marx and F. Engels, *Selected Works*, in three volumes, Vol. 3, Moscow, 1973, p. 206.   p. 318

178 Plekhanov refers to his first letter about the arts in the primitive society, which was included in the collection of articles *Unaddressed Letters*.
                                                                       p. 318

179 Karl Marx, *Capital*, Vol. I, Moscow, 1974, p. 173.   p. 331

180 See present edition, Vol. II, Moscow, 1976, pp. 459-61.   p. 334

181 Karl Marx and Frederick Engels, *Collected Works*, Vol. 4, p. 108 (*The Holy Family*).   p. 342

182 Plekhanov's reply to *Mercure de France* questionnaire. See this volume, pp. 98-99.   p. 348

183 Lunacharsky gives a number of quotations from Vandervelde's book *Le Socialisme et la religion* (Socialism and Religion). According to Vandervelde, science was powerless to explain the essence of things, and only if this was not understood was it possible to "cherish the illusion that the progress of scientific knowledge will put an end to philosophical ignorance". Lunacharsky adds: "Vandervelde calls invasion of this field of ignorance religion."   p. 349

184 See this volume, pp. 117-18.   p. 350

185 The reference is to K. Marx's article "On Proudhon (A letter to I. B. Schweitzer)". (K. Marx and F. Engels, *Selected Works*, in three volumes, Vol. 2, Moscow, 1973, p. 29.)   p. 351

186 Karl Marx and Frederick Engels, *Collected Works*, Vol. 3, Moscow, 1975, pp. 175-76.   p. 352

187 Karl Marx and Frederick Engels, *Collected Works*, Vol. 3, Moscow, 1975, p. 461.   p. 352

188 Karl Marx and Frederick Engels, *Collected Works*, Vol. 3, Moscow, 1975, p. 463.   p. 353

189 K. Marx and F. Engels, *Selected Works* in three volumes, Vol. 3, Moscow, 1973, pp. 353, 354.   p. 353

190 K. Marx and F. Engels, *Selected Works* in three volumes, Vol. 3, Moscow, 1973, p. 354.   p. 354

[191] K. Marx and F. Engels, *Selected Works* in three volumes, Vol. 3, Moscow, 1973, p. 355   p. 354

[192] "I'm happy, I'm happy"—these words are often uttered by the narrow-minded and self-conceited teacher Kulygin, a character from Anton Chekhov's *Three Sisters.*   p. 356

[193] *Essays on the Philosophy of Marxism*—a collection of philosophical works published in St. Petersburg in 1908 containing contributions by Machists, empirio-monists and other "critics" of Marxism: Bazarov, Bogdanov, Lunacharsky and others.   p. 358

[194] The 1880s—were the years of political reaction in Russia following the assassination of Alexander II (1881). These years, like the period of reaction after the 1905-07 revolution, were characterised by a mood of decadence among the intelligentsia, extreme individualism, infatuation with "pure art", mysticism and religion.   p. 362

[195] *Encyclopaedists*—a group of French Enlighteners of the eighteenth century—philosophers, naturalists, publicists, who published the *Encyclopédie ou Dictionnaire raisonne des sciences, des arts et des métiers* (1751-80) (An Encyclopaedia or Dictionary of Sciences, Arts and Crafts). They included Diderot, D'Alembert, Holbach, Helvétius, Voltaire and others.   p. 365

[196] From Mikhail Lermontov's poem "Borodino".   p. 364

[197] K. Marx and F. Engels, *Selected Works* in three volumes, Vol. 2, Moscow, 1973, p. 26.   p. 366

[198] From Ivan Krylov's "The Pike and the Cat".   p. 367

[199] *S.R.s* (Socialist-Revolutionaries)—a petty-bourgeois party founded in Russia at the end of 1901. They did considerable harm to the revolutionary movement by their tactics of individual terror.   p. 369

[200] *Lourdes*—town in the southwest of France, a centre of Catholic pilgrimage, described by Emile Zola in his novel *Lourdes.*   p. 371

[201] Karl Marx and Frederick Engels, *Collected Works*, Vol. 3, Moscow, 1975, p. 464.   p. 372

[202] Karl Marx and Frederick Engels, *Collected Works*, Vol. 3, Moscow, 1975, p. 465.   p. 372

[203] F. Engels, *Anti-Dühring*, Moscow, 1975, pp. 126-37.   p. 375

[204] See present edition, Vol. I, Moscow, 1974, pp. 563-68.   p. 375

[205] Karl Marx and Frederick Engels, *Collected Works*, Vol. 6, Moscow, 1976, pp. 35-51 ("Circular Against Kriege").   p. 378

[206] K. Marx and F. Engels, *Selected Works*, in three volumes, Moscow, 1973, Vol. 3, p. 353.   p. 385

[207] The words of Ivan Karamazov in Dostoyevsky's novel *The Karamazov Brothers.*   p. 385

[208] *Il Principe*—the famous book by Machiavelli justifying any means of ruling a state in order to establish a strong government. *Anti-Machiavel, ou essai critique sur "Le prince" de Machiavel* (Anti-Machiavelli, or a Critical Essay on *The Prince* by Machiavelli) was written by Frederick II.   p. 386

[209] Karl Marx and Frederick Engels, *Collected Works*, Vol. 3, Moscow, 1975, p. 461.   p. 387

[210] *Kashchei*—a principal character of A. Sumarokov's comedy *The Usurer.*
p. 390

[211] From Heinrich Heine's poem *Deutschland. Ein Wintermärchen* (Germany. A Winter's Tale).
p. 392

[212] *Caliban* and *Prospero*—characters from Shakespeare's *The Tempest.*
p. 394

[213] *Parnassians*—a group of French poets of the second half of the nineteenth century (Théophile Gautier, Charles Leconte de Lisle, Charles Baudelaire, Paul Verlaine and others) who published their verses in the almanac *Contemporary Parnass* (issues of 1866, 1871, 1876); they were advocates of the theory of "art for art's sake").
p. 394

[214] From Pushkin's poem, *The Poet and the Crowd.*
p. 394

[215] The title of the book by Minsky was *Religion of the Future.*
p. 397

[216] For a short period in 1905 Minsky was formally editor of the Bolshevik newspaper *Novaya Zhizn.*
p. 397

[217] The World of Art (*Mir iskusstva*)—an association of artists which published a magazine of the same name. It was founded in Russia in the nineties of the last century and lasted till 1924. Its programme was mainly one of refined aesthetic art directed to the past. The association included various artists, aesthetes and stylists as well as prominent realists (N. Rerich, V. Serov, B. Kustodiyev, A. Benois and others).
p. 398

[218] The reference is to the satirical magazines *Zhupel* (Bugbear) and *Adskaya Pochta* (Devil's Post).
p. 398

[219] This stanza is taken from Zinaida Hippius' poem "Thirteen".
p. 401

[220] From Alexander Griboyedov's *Wit Works Woe.*
p. 401

[221] *Sovremennik* (The Contemporary)—See Note 161.
Dyelo (Cause)—science-literary monthly of democratic orientation published in St. Petersburg from 1866 to 1888.
Otechestvenniye Zapiski (Fatherland Notes)—literary and political journal published in St. Petersburg from 1820 to 1884. In the period between 1839 and 1846 it became one of the best progressive magazines of its time. Vissarion Belinsky and Alexander Herzen were among its editors. From 1863 Nikolai Nekrasov and Mikhail Saltykov-Shchedrin were its editors, and it became a revolutionary-democratic journal.
p. 402

[222] An old Russian saying meaning: come out of the water, rise, stand up. According to the legend, when being baptised in the Dnieper (988) people shouted these words to the idol Perun thrown into the water, asking it to rise to the surface.
p. 409

ON MR. GUYAU'S BOOK

The review of Guyau's book was published in *Sovremenny Mir* (The Contemporary World) No. 9, 1909.
p. 414

ON W. WINDELBAND'S BOOK

Plekhanov's review was published in *Sovremenny Mir* No. 1, 1910.

[223] The first line of A. D. Kantemir's (1708-1744) satirical poem *To My Intellect* (on those who disparage learning).
p. 420

COWARDLY IDEALISM

The article on Joseph Petzoldt's book *Das Weltproblem von politischen Standpunkte aus* (*The Problem of the World from the Standpoint of Positivism*) was written by Plekhanov for the collection of articles *From Defence to Attack*, which appeared in 1910.

[224] *Poprishchin*—a character from Gogol's *Notes of a Madman.*   p. 437

[225] Plekhanov apparently has in mind the French sensualist Cabanis (1757-1808) who reduced all mental phenomena to physiological ones and maintained that the brain secretes thought as the liver does bile. This proposition was repeatedly criticised and in fact became a "celebrated phrase". Cabanis was a precursor of the vulgar materialists in Germany of the 1850s, Büchner, Vogt and Moleschott, who repeated in particular this proposition of his.   p. 442

ON THE STUDY OF PHILOSOPHY

This article appeared in June 1910 in *Dnevnik Sotsial Demokrata* (Diary of a Social-Democrat), No. 12.

[226] Plekhanov refers to A. M. Deborin's book *Introduction to the Philosophy of Dialectical Materialism* which was published by Zhizn i Znaniye (Life and Knowledge) Publishers in Petrograd in 1916, with a preface by Plekhanov.   p. 456

SCEPTICISM IN PHILOSOPHY

This article was published in *Sovremenny Mir* No. 7, 1911.

[227] The philosopher *Khoma Brut*, the theologian *Khalyava* and the rhetorician *Tibery Gorobets*, mentioned below—all seminarists—are characters from Gogol's story *Viy.*   p. 461

[228] *Slavophiles*—a trend in Russian social thought of the mid-nineteenth century.
The Slavophiles put forward the "theory" of a special and exceptional road for Russia's historical development, based on the communal system and Orthodoxy as inherent only in the Slavs. Maintaining that Russia's historical development precluded any possibility of revolutionary upheavals, they strongly opposed to the revolutionary movement in Russia and in the West.   p. 476

[229] Plekhanov's idea that the bourgeoisie in Russia, a country of not "fully developed capitalist economy", was allegedly not a "declining class" testifies to his Menshevik conception that Russia still lacked the conditions for the socialist revolution.   p. 476

[230] The German humanist, opponent of scholasticism and theology Ulrich von Gutten (1488-1523) finished his "Address to Nuremberg Patrician and Humanist Pirkheimer" with the words: "O seculum! O literae! Juvat vivere, et si quiescere nondum juvat" (O age! O science! How good to be alive, although it is no time to give up to peace!)   p. 476

ON MR. H. RICKERT'S BOOK

The review of Rickert's book *Sciences of Nature and Sciences of Culture* was published in *Sovremenny Mir*, No. 9, 1911.   p. 481

ON E. BOUTROUX'S BOOK

The review of Boutroux's book *Science et Religion dans la philosophie contemporaine* (Science and Religion in Modern Philosophy) was published in *Sovremenny Mir*, No. 12, 1911.

[231] The founder of the theory of the "dual truth" was Averroes. Later this theory was widespread in other countries including England, where Bacon became Averroes' follower.   **p. 488**

FRENCH UTOPIAN SOCIALISM
OF THE NINETEENTH CENTURY

At the end of June 1911 Plekhanov was asked by Mir Publishers to write an essay on "development of social utopian theories in France and Hegelianism with its variants in Germany". The essay was to be included in one of the volumes of *The History of Western Literature in the Nineteenth Century* which was being issued by these publishers.

Early in 1912 the essay was ready and sent to the Publishers, but they returned it back with a request to shorten it. Plekhanov published his article in *Sovremenny Mir* Nos. 6-7, 1913. For *The History of Western Literature in the Nineteenth Century* he wrote two new articles: "Utopian Socialism of the Nineteenth Century" and "From Idealism to Materialism".

[232] Karl Marx and Frederick Engels, *Collected Works*, Vol. 4, Moscow, 1975, p. 30 (*The Holy Family*).   **p. 493**

[233] Karl Marx and Frederick Engels, *Collected Works*, Vol. 4, Moscow, 1975, p. 131 (*The Holy Family*).   **p. 493**

[234] By the *catastrophe of 1793* Fourier meant the Jacobin dictatorship during the French Revolution.   **p. 494**

[235] In December 1828 the Saint-Simonists Enfantin, Bazard and others organised a series of public lectures in Paris which are known as the "Lectures at the Street-Taranne". A narrow circle of the leaders of the Saint-Simonist school discussed the subject-matter of each lecture.

The first edition of the *Exposition of Saint-Simon's Theory* included a series of lectures delivered during the period from December 17, 1828 to August 12, 1829 and was issued in Paris in 1830.   **p. 502**

[236] At the end of 1829 the Saint-Simonist school was turned into a religious community, and Bazard and Enfantin were proclaimed its "fathers". At the end of 1830, the most zealous adherents to Saint-Simon's ideas constituted a "family" residing in a separate building. Subsequently Enfantin and Bazard parted and the Saint-Simonist community dissolved.

    p. 502

[237] *Le Globe*—the Saint-Simonist organ founded in Paris in 1824. In 1832 its publication was discontinued.   **p. 504**

[238] During the first days of the French Republic in 1848 the question of the state flag was raised. The workers were for the red flag, the bourgeoisie for the Tricolour which had been the flag of the French Revolution and of Napoleon's empire. Workers' representatives were forced to accept the Tricolour as the state flag of the French Republic.   **p. 504**

[239] *La Voix du Peuple* (The Voice of the People)—a daily newspaper published by Proudhon in Paris from October 1, 1849 to May 14, 1850.

    p. 505

240 The first edition of Cabet's book published in Paris in 1840 was entitled *Voyage et aventures de lord William Carisdall en Icarie*. In 1842 a second edition appeared under the title: *Voyage en Icarie. Roman philosophique et sociale.* p. 506

241 *The Holy Alliance*—a reactionary alliance of European monarchies founded in 1815 by tsarist Russia, Austria and Prussia to suppress revolutionary movements in various countries and preserve the monarchical regimes there. p. 508

242 The reference is to the counter-revolutionary coup of December 2, 1851 by Louis Bonaparte, who was proclaimed Emperor of France under the name of Napoleon III. p. 509

243 Criticising the Narodnik views on the development of capitalism in Russia, the "legal Marxist" Struve wrote the following in his book *Critical Remarks on Russia's Economic Development* (St. Petersburg, 1894): "Let us recognise our lack of culture and go for training to capitalism". p. 519

244 On June 13, 1849 the petty-bourgeois Mountain party organised a peaceful protest demonstration against the dispatch of the French troops to suppress the revolution in Italy. The demonstration was dispersed by the troops and many leaders of the Mountain were arrested and banished, or were compelled to leave France. p. 525

245 See this volume, pp. 36-40. p. 527

246 *La Phalange*—(full title: *La Phalange. Revue de la science sociale. Politique, industrie, sciences, arts et littérature*)—the organ of the Fourierists published between 1832 and 1849. p. 528

247 Plekhanov is mistaken; the name of the author he is referring to was Felicité-Robert Lamennais. p. 530

248 See present edition, Vol. II, pp. 427-73. p. 531

249 See Note 27. p. 531

250 *Conspiracy of Equals* — a Utopian communist movement in France in 1795-96. guided by the conspiratorial society of "equals" with Babeuf at its head. The aim of the society was to prepare and carry out the revolution, to attain complete equality of men through a communist reorganisation of society. The society of "equals" attached to communism roughly egalitarian features. The conspiracy was disclosed, Babeuf and Darthé were sentenced to death, the rest of the members exiled. p. 532

251 Bounarroti's book was entitled *Conspiration pour l'égalité dite de Babeuf, suivie du Procès auquel elle donna lieu et des pièces justificatives...* and was published in 1828. p. 532

UTOPIAN SOCIALISM
IN THE NINETEETH CENTURY

This article was written by Plekhanov for Mir Publishers in August and September 1913 and published in Volume II of *The History of Western Literature in the Nineteenth Century*, in the section "The Epoch of Romanticism" (Moscow, 1913).

252 *Natural law*—doctrine that law supposedly emerged from the reason and conception of man and independently of the state. p. 534

[253] The *London Corresponding Society* formed in 1792, was the first working class political organisation in England. The members of the Society corresponded with each other, hence the name. Officially it merely presented a programme of universal suffrage and annual parliamentary elections; most of its members were in favour of a republic.   p. 536

[254] The reference is to Malthus' work *An Essay on the Principle of Population*, published in 1798.   p. 536

[255] Charles Hall's work was entitled *Effects of Civilisation on the People in European States*.   p. 537

[256] In Britain in the 1830s-40s the working day in many enterprises still lasted fourteen to sixteen hours. The shorter working hours introduced by Parliament in 1833 applied only to juveniles of between thirteen and eighteen years of age; their working day was reduced to twelve hours.
                                                           p. 539

[257] Child labour under nine years of age was prohibited at cotton mills by the Act of 1819; the working day for children and juveniles from nine to sixteen years of age was thirteen and a half hours.   p. 542

[258] Karl Marx, *Capital*, 1974, Vol. I, p. 264.   p. 542

[259] *Chartism*—a mass revolutionary movement of British workers in 1830-40s. The movement started with huge meetings and demonstrations and was carried under the slogan of the People's Charter, which demanded changes in the electoral law. The three petitions submitted to Parliament were rejected and after 1848 the movement declined.   p. 546

[260] Karl Marx, *Theories of Surplus Value*, Vol. III, Moscow, 1975, pp. 238-57.
                                                           p. 550

[261] Karl Marx, *Theories of Surplus Value*, Vol. III, Moscow, 1975, pp. 257-319.
                                                           p. 550

[262] Karl Marx, *Theories of Surplus Value*, Vol. III, Moscow, 1975, p. 238.
                                                           p. 551

[263] See Note 13.   p. 552

[264] Karl Marx and Frederick Engels, *Collected Works*, Vol. 6, Moscow, 1976, p. 514.   p. 553

[265] *Trudoviks*—a group of petty-bourgeois democrats in the State dumas in Russia composed of peasants and intellectuals of Narodnik leanings. The Trudoviks demanded abolition of all estate and national restrictions. and democratisation of local self-government. The Trudovik agrarian programme was based on Narodnik principles of egalitarian land tenure and alienation of privately-owned land with compensation.
                                                           p. 556

[266] *Convention*—the third National Assembly during the French Revolution. It was established as a higher representative institution in France and lasted from September 1792 till October 26, 1795. It proclaimed the First French Republic, completed the abolition of feudalism and ruthlessly disposed of all counter-revolutionary and conciliatory elements.
                                                           p. 559

[267] Karl Marx and Frederick Engels, *Collected Works*, Vol. 4, Moscow, 1975, p. 131 (*The Holy Family*).   p. 560

[268] "The Golden Age, which a blind tradition has hitherto placed in the past, is before us,"—this is one of the principal theses of Saint-Simon's philosophical historical system, which he used as an epigraph to his work

Opinions littéraires, philosophiques et industrielles. The same words were used as an epigraph to the Saint-Simonist journal *Le Producteur.*

In his series of essays *Abroad,* Saltykov-Shchedrin wrote: "...from there (from... France of Saint-Simon, Cabet, Fourier...) faith in humanity poured into us, from there the conviction came that 'the golden age' is not behind us but in front of us.... In short, everything good, everything desirable and everything that is full of love—all this came from there."

p. 561

[269] From Heinrich Heine's poem *Deutschland. Ein Wintermärchen* (Germany. Winter's Tale). p. 562

[270] *Westerners*—a trend in Russian social thought in the mid-nineteenth century that admitted that Russia would follow the same path of development as Western Europe (hence the name) and pass through the capitalist stage. The Westerners stressed the progressive nature of the bourgeois system (in comparison with serf-owning Russia), had a negative attitude towards serfdom, their political ideals being the constitutional monarchies and bourgeois parliamentary states in Western Europe, Britain and France, in particular. p. 565

[271] See article "From Idealism to Materialism" in this volume. Plekhanov did not write the article about "true socialists". p. 566

[272] K. Marx and F. Engels, *Selected Works,* Vol. 3, Moscow, 1973, p. 178. p. 572

[273] Karl Marx. *The Poverty of Philosophy,* Moscow, 1975, pp. 9-24 ("Marx and Rodbertus". Preface to the First German edition of Marx's *Poverty of Philosophy).* p. 576

[274] Karl Marx, *Theories of Surplus-Value.* Vol. II, Moscow, 1975. pp. 15-113. p. 576

[275] *Yuridichesky Vestnik* (Juridical Herald)—a liberal bourgeois monthly published in Moscow from 1867 to 1892.

On *Otechestvenniye Zapiski* see Note 221. p. 576

PREFACE TO A. DEBORIN'S BOOK
AN INTRODUCTION TO PHILOSOPHY
OF DIALECTICAL MATERIALISM

The Preface was written at the end of 1915 and published in the book: A. Deborin, *An Introduction to Philosophy of Dialectical Materialism.* With a Preface by G. V. Plekhanov, Zhizn i Znaniye Publishers, Petrograd, 1916.

[276] See E. Zeller, *An Outline of the History of Greek Philosophy,* Moscow, 1913, p. 1. p. 577

[277] See present edition, Vol. II, Moscow, 1976, pp. 398-414. p. 578

[278] See this volume, pp. 306-413 p. 580

[279] K. Marx and F. Engels, *Selected Works,* in three volumes, Vol. 3, Moscow, 1973, p. 346. p. 580

[280] The *Ionian school* was the earliest materialist trend in Greek philosophy which arose in the VI-IV centuries B. C. in the cities along the Ionian coast of Asia Minor; its main representatives were Thales, Anaximander, Anaxagoras and Heraclitus. p. 581

[281] See W. Windelband, *History of Modern Philosophy and Its Relation to General Culture and the Individual Sciences*, Vol. I, St. Petersburg, 1908, pp. 238-39.   p. 584

[282] See present edition, Vol. II, Moscow, 1976, pp. 335.   p. 594

[283] Karl Marx and Frederick Engels, *Selected Correspondence*, Moscow, 1975, p. 264.   p. 596

[284] Karl Marx and Frederick Engels, *Selected Correspondence*, Moscow, 1975. p. 101.   p. 599

FROM IDEALISM TO MATERIALISM

This article was written for *The History of Western Literature in the Nineteenth Century* which was being prepared by Mir Publishers. The article was completed by Plekhanov at the beginning of 1915 and was published in Moscow in 1917 as the first chapter of Volume Four of *The History of Western Literature in the Nineteenth Century*.

[285] The reference is to Chernyshevsky's arrest by the tsarist government in 1862 after which he was sentenced to penal servitude and exile to Siberia for life.   p. 601

[286] See this volume, pp. 64-83.   p. 603

[287] See present edition, Vol. I, Moscow, 1974, pp. 401-26.   p. 607

[288] A. Herzen, *My Life and Thoughts* (See Herzen's *Collected Works*, Vol. IX, Russ. ed., 1956, p. 23).   p. 607

[289] The reference is to Heraclitus.   p. 608

[290] The full title of this journal was *Deutsche Jahrbücher für Wissenschaft und Kunst*.   p. 617

[291] Plekhanov refers here to Marx's criticism of Bruno Bauer in *The Holy Family*. (See Karl Marx and Frederick Engels, *Collected Works*, Vol. 4, Moscow, 1975, pp. 39, 40, et seq.)   p. 621

[292] Karl Marx and Frederick Engels, *Collected Works*, Vol. 4, Moscow, 1975, p. 81.   p. 626

[293] Feuerbach's actual words are: "Keine Religion—ist meine Religion". (*Sämmtliche Werke*, Bd. 2, 1846, S. 414.)   p. 634

[294] K. Marx and F. Engels, *Selected Works* in three volumes, Vol. 3, Moscow, 1973, p. 354.   p. 634

[295] K. Marx and F. Engels, *Selected Works* in three volumes, Vol. 3, Moscow, 1973, p. 344.   p. 634

[296] Feuerbach's actual words are: "Keine Philosophie!—meine Philosophie". (*Sämmtliche Werke*, Bd. 2, 1846, S. 414).   p. 638

[297] Karl Marx and Frederick Engels, *Collected Works*, Vol. 5, Moscow, 1976, p. 3.   p. 639

[298] Karl Marx and Frederick Engels, *Collected Works*, Vol. 5, Moscow, 1976, p. 3.   p. 639

[299] *"True socialism"*—a trend which existed among the German petty bourgeoisie in the 1840s. They called for a rejection of political activity and

of the struggle for democracy and proclaimed the cult of love for next-of-kin and abstract "humaneness". For criticism of this trend see Karl Marx and Frederick Engels, *The German Ideology* (Karl Marx and Frederick Engels, *Collected Works*, Vol. 5).   p. 641

[300] See Karl Marx and Frederick Engels, *Collected Works*, Vol. 5, Moscow, 1976, pp. 117-450. (*The German Ideology*).   p. 641

NAME INDEX

A

Achelis, Thomas (1850-1909)—German philosopher and ethnographer.—149

Adler, Friedrich (1879-1960)—a leader of the Austrian right-wing Social Democrats; theoretician of Austro-Marxism.—243

Adler, Georg (1863-1908)—German bourgeois economist.—537, 571, 576

Adler, Victor (1852-1918)—a reformist leader of the Austrian Social-Democratic party and the Second International.—117-18

Akimov, Vladimir Petrovich (*Makhnovets*) (1872-1921)—Russian Social Democrat, one of the most extreme opportunists.—63

Albrecht, Karl (1788-1844)—preacher of Christian Socialism in Switzerland; follower of Weitling.—366

Alcibiades (c. 451-404 B.C.)—Athenian politician.—62

Anaxagoras (c. 500-428 B.C.)—Greek materialist philosopher.—623

Anaximenes (585-525 B.C.)—Greek spontaneous materialist philosopher.—577

Andree, Richard (1835-1912)—German ethnographer, author of works on comparative ethnography.—150

Aquinas, Thomas (1225-1274)—Italian philosopher, objective idealist.—118

Aristotle (384-322 B.C.)—Greek philosopher and scientist. In philosophy, wavered between materialism and idealism.—75, 82, 176-77, 295, 360, 609

Aristophanes (c. 446-385 B.C.)—Greek dramatist.—609-10

Artsybashev, Mikhail Petrovich (1878-1927)—Russian novelist; his works reflected the decadent trends during the period of reaction (1907-1910).—197

Augustus (63 B.C.-A.D. 14)—Roman Emperor (27 B.C.-A.D. 14).—165

Avenarius, Richard (1843-1896)—German idealist philosopher, formulated the basic principles of empirio-criticism.—66, 118, 197, 209, 220, 231, 250-51, 258, 264, 266, 274, 278, 280, 305, 357, 384, 428, 431, 442, 457

Axelrod, Lyubov Isaakovna (pseudonym "Orthodox") (1868-1946)—philosopher and literary critic, Social Democrat. After the Second Congress of the RSDLP (1903), joined the Mensheviks and opposed Lenin's philosophical views.—264, 345, 457, 587

B

Babeuf, Gracchus (real name *François Noel*) (1760-1797)—French revolutionary, utopian communist; led the "Conspiracy of Equals" (1796).—531-33, 552-53, 559

Bacon, Francis (1561-1626)—English philosopher, naturalist, historian and statesman, founder of materialism in England.—37, 83, 383

Bain, Alexander (1813-1903)—Scottish psychologist, professor of logic.—73

classical mechanics.—35, 37, 173,
257, 527, 627
Noiré, Ludwig (1829-1889)—German philosopher.—149
Novalis (Friedrich von Hardenberg)
(1772-1801)—German romanticist writer; idealised the Middle
Ages.—627

O

Ogilvie, William (1736-1819)—British utopian socialist.—537
Oltramare, Paul Jean (b. 1854)—
French historian of religion.—
343
Orcagna, Andrea (c. 1308-c. 1368)—
Italian sculptor, painter, and
architect.—315
Ostwald, Wilhelm Friedrich (1853-
1932)—German chemist and
idealist philosopher; exponent
of energism, a variety of Machism.
—118, 446, 598
Ovsyaniko-Kulikovsky, Dmitri Nikolayevich (1853-1920)—Russian literary critic and linguist.—414-
16
Owen, Robert (1771-1858)—British utopian socialist.—34-36,
38-40, 534, 539-50, 562

P

Paine, Thomas (1737-1809)—American political figure and publicist.—537
Paget—disciple of Fourier.—502
Pannekoek, Anthony (1873-1960)—
Dutch left-wing socialist; actively opposed reformism. After
1921 withdrew from political
activity.—93-97, 106
Parmenides (late 6th century-early
5th century B.C.)—Greek philosopher; chief representative of
the Eleatic school.—80, 426,
440-41
Paulsen, Friedrich (1846-1908)—
German educationist and neo-Kantian philosopher.—454
Pereire, Isaac (1806-1880)—French
financier, follower of Saint-Simon.—514
Pericles, (c. 490-429 B. C.)—leader of the Athenian slave-holding democracy.—464

Peshekhonov, Alexei Vasilyevich
(1867-1933) Russian publicist
and statistician; a right-wing
Narodnik.—523
Peter I (1672-1725)—Russian tsar
(1682-1721)—and emperor (1721-
1725).—351
Petzoldt, Joseph (1862-1929)—German idealist philosopher, pupil
of Mach and Avenarius.—222,
231, 384, 424-37, 439-54
Pfau, Ludwig (1821-1894)—German lyrical poet and literary
critic.—643
Picavet, François Joseph (1851-
1921)—French historian of philosophy.—163
Pisarev, Dmitri Ivanovich (1840-
1868)—Russian literary critic,
materialist philosopher, and revolutionary democrat.—402
Plato (427-347 B.C.)—Greek philosopher, objective idealist.—
76-77, 82, 217, 221, 339, 440,
595, 601, 614
Plotinus (204-270)—Greek mystic
philosopher.—298
Poincaré, Henri (1854-1912)—
French mathematician and physicist; in his philosophical views
was close to Machism.—197
Polenz, Wilhelm von (1861-1903)—
German writer.—285
Powell, John Wesley (1834-1902)—
American ethnographer.—336
Price, Richard (1723-1791)—Welsh
radical publicist, economist and
moral philosopher.—200
Priestley, Joseph (1733-1804)—
English chemist and materialist
philosopher.—71-72, 107, 200,
217, 534, 582, 598
Protagoras of Abdera (481-411 B.C.)
—Greek sophist philosopher,
ideologist of slave-holding democracy.—428-29, 431, 440, 451-52
Protopopov, Mikhail Alexeyevich
(1848-1915)—Russian literary
critic, liberal Narodnik.—397
Proudhon, Pierre-Joseph (1809-
1865)—French publicist, economist and sociologist, ideologist
of the petty bourgeoisie, one
of the founders of anarchism.—
81, 138, 351, 366, 504-05, 509,
512, 517, 525, 550, 554-55,
575

philosophy, especially his dialectics.—74, 77-78, 80, 603

Tsertelev, Dmitri Nikolayevich (1852-1911)—Russian writer.—398

Tucker, Benjamin (1854-1939)—American anarchist, journalist, founder and editor of a number of anarchist publications.—410

Turati, Filippo (1857-1932)—prominent figure in the Italian labour movement, one of the leaders of the reformist wing of the Italian Socialist Party.—118

Turgenev, Ivan Sergeyevich (1818-1883)—Russian writer.—88, 403

Tylor, Edward Burnett (1832-1917)—English anthropologist, student of primitive culture.—96, 98, 132, 151, 290, 302, 312, 316, 319-20, 337, 350-51, 579

U

Überweg, Friedrich (1826-1871)—German historian of philosophy and psychologist.—74, 76, 78, 80, 471

Untermann Ernest—American socialist, revisionist.—100-03, 115

Uspensky, Gleb Ivanovich (1843-1902)—Russian novelist and publicist; revolutionary democrat.—194, 305, 333

V

Vaccaro, Michel Angelo (1854-1937)—Italian sociologist.—149

Valentinov, N. (pseudonym of Volsky, Nikolai Vladislavovich) (b. 1879)—Social-Democrat, Menshevik and Machist philosopher.—266, 287

Vandervelde, Emile (1866-1938)—leader of the Belgian Labour Party, extreme opportunist.—63, 349

Velichkina, Vera Mikhailovna (1868-1918)—Russian Social-Democrat, contributed to Bolshevik publications, translated K. Marx and F. Engels into Russian.—284

Venevitinov, Dmitri Vladimirovich (1805-1827)—Russian poet, active member of a study group in

philosophy known as "Lovers of Wisdom".—225

Verhaeren, Emile (1855-1916)—Belgian poet.—398, 400

Verworn, Max (1863-1921)—German physiologist.—231, 458

Vidal, François (1814-1872)—French utopian socialist, took part in the 1848 revolution.—525

Violand—567

Virgil (70-19 B.C.)—Roman poet.—168

Vogt, Karl (1817-1895)—German naturalist, vulgar materialist.—442

Volsky, A. (Makhaisky, Yan Vaclav Konstantinovich) (1867-1926)—devised a petty-bourgeois anarchist theory known as "Makhayevism".—63

Voltaire, François Marie Arouet de (1694-1778)—French deist philosopher, satirist, opposed absolutism and Catholicism.—278, 404, 588, 633

Vvedensky, Alexander Ivanovich (1856-1925)—Russian neo-Kantian philosopher, author of works on logic and psychology.—585

W

Wagner, Richard (1813-1883)—German composer.—115, 642

Waitz, Theodor (1821-1864)—German anthropologist, philosopher, and educationalist.—143, 148

Wallaschek, Richard (1860-1917)—Austrian scholar in the fields of linguistics and musical ethnology, specialist in primitive art.—151-52

Watson, James (1799-1874)—British worker, follower of Owen.—548

Watteau, Antoine (1684-1721)—French painter.—399

Webb, Sidney (1859-1947) and Beatrice (1858-1943)—British reformists, authors of a number of works on the history and theory of the British labour movement.—550

Weisse, Christian Hermann (1808-1871)—German professor of philosophy.—649

SUBJECT INDEX